Communications in Computer and Information Science **1582**

More information about this series at https://link.springer.com/bookseries/7899

Constantine Stephanidis · Margherita Antona ·
Stavroula Ntoa (Eds.)

HCI International 2022 Posters

24th International Conference
on Human-Computer Interaction, HCII 2022
Virtual Event, June 26 – July 1, 2022
Proceedings, Part III

 Springer

Editors
Constantine Stephanidis
University of Crete and Foundation for
Research and Technology – Hellas (FORTH)
Heraklion, Crete, Greece

Margherita Antona
Foundation for Research and Technology –
Hellas (FORTH)
Heraklion, Crete, Greece

Stavroula Ntoa
Foundation for Research and Technology –
Hellas (FORTH)
Heraklion, Crete, Greece

ISSN 1865-0929   ISSN 1865-0937 (electronic)
Communications in Computer and Information Science
ISBN 978-3-031-06390-9   ISBN 978-3-031-06391-6 (eBook)
https://doi.org/10.1007/978-3-031-06391-6

Foreword

Human-computer interaction (HCI) is acquiring an ever-increasing scientific and industrial importance, as well as having more impact on people's everyday life, as an ever-growing number of human activities are progressively moving from the physical to the digital world. This process, which has been ongoing for some time now, has been dramatically accelerated by the COVID-19 pandemic. The HCI International (HCII) conference series, held yearly, aims to respond to the compelling need to advance the exchange of knowledge and research and development efforts on the human aspects of design and use of computing systems.

The 24th International Conference on Human-Computer Interaction, HCI International 2022 (HCII 2022), was planned to be held at the Gothia Towers Hotel and Swedish Exhibition & Congress Centre, Göteborg, Sweden, during June 26 to July 1, 2022. Due to the COVID-19 pandemic and with everyone's health and safety in mind, HCII 2022 was organized and run as a virtual conference. It incorporated the 21 thematic areas and affiliated conferences listed on the following page.

A total of 5583 individuals from academia, research institutes, industry, and governmental agencies from 88 countries submitted contributions, and 1276 papers and 275 posters were included in the proceedings to appear just before the start of the conference. The contributions thoroughly cover the entire field of human-computer interaction, addressing major advances in knowledge and effective use of computers in a variety of application areas. These papers provide academics, researchers, engineers, scientists, practitioners, and students with state-of-the-art information on the most recent advances in HCI. The volumes constituting the set of proceedings to appear before the start of the conference are listed in the following pages.

The HCI International (HCII) conference also offers the option of 'Late Breaking Work' which applies both for papers and posters, and the corresponding volume(s) of the proceedings will appear after the conference. Full papers will be included in the 'HCII 2022 - Late Breaking Papers' volumes of the proceedings to be published in the Springer LNCS series, while 'Poster Extended Abstracts' will be included as short research papers in the 'HCII 2022 - Late Breaking Posters' volumes to be published in the Springer CCIS series.

I would like to thank the Program Board Chairs and the members of the Program Boards of all thematic areas and affiliated conferences for their contribution and support towards the highest scientific quality and overall success of the HCI International 2022 conference; they have helped in so many ways, including session organization, paper reviewing (single-blind review process, with a minimum of two reviews per submission) and, more generally, acting as goodwill ambassadors for the HCII conference.

This conference would not have been possible without the continuous and unwavering support and advice of Gavriel Salvendy, founder, General Chair Emeritus, and Scientific Advisor. For his outstanding efforts, I would like to express my appreciation to Abbas Moallem, Communications Chair and Editor of HCI International News.

June 2022   Constantine Stephanidis

HCI International 2022 Thematic Areas and Affiliated Conferences

Thematic Areas

- HCI: Human-Computer Interaction
- HIMI: Human Interface and the Management of Information

Affiliated Conferences

- EPCE: 19th International Conference on Engineering Psychology and Cognitive Ergonomics
- AC: 16th International Conference on Augmented Cognition
- UAHCI: 16th International Conference on Universal Access in Human-Computer Interaction
- CCD: 14th International Conference on Cross-Cultural Design
- SCSM: 14th International Conference on Social Computing and Social Media
- VAMR: 14th International Conference on Virtual, Augmented and Mixed Reality
- DHM: 13th International Conference on Digital Human Modeling and Applications in Health, Safety, Ergonomics and Risk Management
- DUXU: 11th International Conference on Design, User Experience and Usability
- C&C: 10th International Conference on Culture and Computing
- DAPI: 10th International Conference on Distributed, Ambient and Pervasive Interactions
- HCIBGO: 9th International Conference on HCI in Business, Government and Organizations
- LCT: 9th International Conference on Learning and Collaboration Technologies
- ITAP: 8th International Conference on Human Aspects of IT for the Aged Population
- AIS: 4th International Conference on Adaptive Instructional Systems
- HCI-CPT: 4th International Conference on HCI for Cybersecurity, Privacy and Trust
- HCI-Games: 4th International Conference on HCI in Games
- MobiTAS: 4th International Conference on HCI in Mobility, Transport and Automotive Systems
- AI-HCI: 3rd International Conference on Artificial Intelligence in HCI
- MOBILE: 3rd International Conference on Design, Operation and Evaluation of Mobile Communications

List of Conference Proceedings Volumes Appearing Before the Conference

1. LNCS 13302, Human-Computer Interaction: Theoretical Approaches and Design Methods (Part I), edited by Masaaki Kurosu
2. LNCS 13303, Human-Computer Interaction: Technological Innovation (Part II), edited by Masaaki Kurosu
3. LNCS 13304, Human-Computer Interaction: User Experience and Behavior (Part III), edited by Masaaki Kurosu
4. LNCS 13305, Human Interface and the Management of Information: Visual and Information Design (Part I), edited by Sakae Yamamoto and Hirohiko Mori
5. LNCS 13306, Human Interface and the Management of Information: Applications in Complex Technological Environments (Part II), edited by Sakae Yamamoto and Hirohiko Mori
6. LNAI 13307, Engineering Psychology and Cognitive Ergonomics, edited by Don Harris and Wen-Chin Li
7. LNCS 13308, Universal Access in Human-Computer Interaction: Novel Design Approaches and Technologies (Part I), edited by Margherita Antona and Constantine Stephanidis
8. LNCS 13309, Universal Access in Human-Computer Interaction: User and Context Diversity (Part II), edited by Margherita Antona and Constantine Stephanidis
9. LNAI 13310, Augmented Cognition, edited by Dylan D. Schmorrow and Cali M. Fidopiastis
10. LNCS 13311, Cross-Cultural Design: Interaction Design Across Cultures (Part I), edited by Pei-Luen Patrick Rau
11. LNCS 13312, Cross-Cultural Design: Applications in Learning, Arts, Cultural Heritage, Creative Industries, and Virtual Reality (Part II), edited by Pei-Luen Patrick Rau
12. LNCS 13313, Cross-Cultural Design: Applications in Business, Communication, Health, Well-being, and Inclusiveness (Part III), edited by Pei-Luen Patrick Rau
13. LNCS 13314, Cross-Cultural Design: Product and Service Design, Mobility and Automotive Design, Cities, Urban Areas, and Intelligent Environments Design (Part IV), edited by Pei-Luen Patrick Rau
14. LNCS 13315, Social Computing and Social Media: Design, User Experience and Impact (Part I), edited by Gabriele Meiselwitz
15. LNCS 13316, Social Computing and Social Media: Applications in Education and Commerce (Part II), edited by Gabriele Meiselwitz
16. LNCS 13317, Virtual, Augmented and Mixed Reality: Design and Development (Part I), edited by Jessie Y. C. Chen and Gino Fragomeni
17. LNCS 13318, Virtual, Augmented and Mixed Reality: Applications in Education, Aviation and Industry (Part II), edited by Jessie Y. C. Chen and Gino Fragomeni

http://2022.hci.international/proceedings

Preface

Preliminary scientific results, professional news, or work in progress, described in the form of short research papers (4–8 pages long), constitute a popular submission type among the International Conference on Human-Computer Interaction (HCII) participants. Extended abstracts are particularly suited for reporting ongoing work, which can benefit from a visual presentation, and are presented during the conference in the form of posters. The latter allow a focus on novel ideas and are appropriate for presenting project results in a simple, concise, and visually appealing manner. At the same time, they are also suitable for attracting feedback from an international community of HCI academics, researchers, and practitioners. Poster submissions span the wide range of topics of all HCII thematic areas and affiliated conferences.

Four volumes of the HCII 2022 proceedings are dedicated to this year's poster extended abstracts, in the form of short research papers, focusing on the following topics:

- Volume I: User Experience Design and Evaluation; Visual Design and Visualization; Data, Information, and Knowledge; Interacting with AI; Universal Access, Accessibility, and Design for Aging.
- Volume II: Multimodal and Natural Interaction; Perception, Cognition, Emotion, and Psychophysiological Monitoring; Human Motion Modelling and Monitoring; IoT and Intelligent Living Environments.
- Volume III: Learning Technologies; HCI, Cultural Heritage and Art; eGovernment and eBusiness; Digital Commerce and the Customer Experience; Social Media and the Metaverse.
- Volume IV: Virtual and Augmented Reality; Autonomous Vehicles and Urban Mobility; Product and Robot Design; HCI and Wellbeing; HCI and Cybersecurity.

Poster extended abstracts are included for publication in these volumes following a minimum of two single-blind reviews from the members of the HCII 2022 international Program Boards. We would like to thank all of them for their invaluable contribution, support, and efforts.

June 2022

Constantine Stephanidis
Margherita Antona
Stavroula Ntoa

24th International Conference on Human-Computer Interaction (HCII 2022)

The full list with the Program Board Chairs and the members of the Program Boards of all thematic areas and affiliated conferences is available online at

http://www.hci.international/board-members-2022.php

HCI International 2023

The 25th International Conference on Human-Computer Interaction, HCI International 2023, will be held jointly with the affiliated conferences at the AC Bella Sky Hotel and Bella Center, Copenhagen, Denmark, 23–28 July 2023. It will cover a broad spectrum of themes related to human-computer interaction, including theoretical issues, methods, tools, processes, and case studies in HCI design, as well as novel interaction techniques, interfaces, and applications. The proceedings will be published by Springer. More information will be available on the conference website: http://2023.hci.international/.

General Chair
Constantine Stephanidis
University of Crete and ICS-FORTH
Heraklion, Crete, Greece
Email: general_chair@hcii2023.org

http://2023.hci.international/

Contents – Part III

HCI, Cultural Heritage and Art

eGovernment and eBusiness

Digital Commerce and the Customer Experience

Social Media and the Metaverse

Learning Technologies

Students' Adoption of Online Platforms for Learning Purposes in Bangladesh

Rudaiba Adnin$^{(\boxtimes)}$ ⓘ, Sadia Afroz ⓘ, Montaser Majid Taseen ⓘ,
and Sadia Sharmin ⓘ

Bangladesh University of Engineering and Technology, Dhaka, Bangladesh
{1505032.ra,1505030.sa}@ugrad.cse.buet.ac.bd, sadiasharmin@cse.buet.ac.bd

Abstract. Online learning plays a significant role for students. However, with the increasing number of online platforms such as MOOCs, YouTube, etc. students can find it challenging to conveniently use them for learning purposes. Here, technological solutions are yet to achieve proper utilization of those platforms. Therefore, in this paper, we perform a mixed-method study through semi-structured interviews with 18 university students and an online survey of 239 university students from an engineering university situated in Bangladesh. Our findings reveal several influential factors, experiences, challenges of the conventional usage of online platforms for learning. One of the noteworthy findings of our study is that most students use multiple online platforms for an effective learning experience. These findings point to opportunities for design interventions in existing platforms and a need for personalized online platforms for learning purposes.

Keywords: Online learning · Platforms · Students · Survey · Interview

1 Introduction

Online Learning has many benefits, perhaps the most significant is widening access to education to the reach of many in a flexible manner, thus allowing learning to take place anywhere at any time. Like many other countries in the Global South [10], the availability of the mobile Internet has made online learning easily available to the students of Bangladesh [1]. Massive Open Online Courses (MOOCs), YouTube, discrete websites (Google, Bing, etc.) are some of the online platforms which play essential roles in learning [3,7]. However, one of the challenges of online learning is how to choose an effective platform for learning that meets learners' expectations and requirements [6,9]. However, limited research on the challenges faced while using those platforms and the increasing potential of online learning in the Global South [10] have motivated us to explore the online learning experiences of students in Bangladesh.

In this study, we perform a mixed-method study by conducting semi-structured interviews and an online survey of students. Based on our interviews,

C. Stephanidis et al. (Eds.): HCII 2022, CCIS 1582, pp. 3–11, 2022.
https://doi.org/10.1007/978-3-031-06391-6_1

we have taken the early steps to understand the influential factors, experiences, challenges faced by students while using online platforms for learning and identified the design issues of the online learning resources, which cause limited interaction. These will help HCI to better understand these issues. We have also identified how current online platforms often fail to address these challenges of the students and proposed some socio-culturally appropriate insights to increase the convenience of students in getting the preferred type of learning resources, which shows novel ways for HCI to address these issues.

2   Related Work

One of the main characteristics of online learning is that it requires learners' ability to self-regulate their learning process to achieve a positive learning outcome. Learners tend to adopt online learning that can fulfill their functional motive, social motive, and emotional motive [11]. A study [6] examines the principal factors for the use of online learning among university students where it is found that perceived usefulness and perceived ease of use influence inclination for online learning. Accordingly, researchers worked on showing the engagement, motivation, flexibilities, and impact on academics of different types of online platforms such as MOOCs, YouTube, discrete websites [3,7,9]. These online platforms enable learners of all ages, competencies, and preferences to look for information or knowledge anywhere and anytime [8]. Studies on YouTube show that students can understand and remember complex concepts much better when they are exposed to a visual explanation video [7]. Websites offering learning resources found to have diverse quality content and usability criteria for learning purposes [3]. The impact of integrating MOOCs with traditional in-class learning was discovered in a research [9], where researchers find that learning objectives were in most parts better satisfied in this integrated way because students were more involved and eager to learn. However, most of these researches focused on specific types of online platforms or particular learning materials. They face several challenges while trying to get an effective learning experience from these platforms which varies with the social-cultural differences of the learners [12]. In a work [12], socioeconomic, sociocultural, and IT infrastructural factors are categorized as challenges hindering the adoption of online learning. However, most of these researches investigate the challenges of online learning in general, not while they are using online platforms for learning. Moreover, it can be seen that providing learners with the same learning resources may not create similar learning experiences. Instead, it may reduce learners' learning performances [5]. Additionally, learners' motivations and influential factors vary because of socio-cultural differences in different communities. This requires effective design interventions considering learners' motivations, expectations, experiences within online learning environments, and socio-cultural differences [12].

Despite numerous benefits and usefulness of online learning highlighted in literature [8], the majority are hesitant and reluctant to use online platforms for learning in Bangladesh [4]. In a study [4], researchers find most of the students of

Bangladesh at the university level have a positive perception of online learning. However, there are constraints as well, for example, poorly designed learning materials allow limited interaction. Therefore, it is imperative to investigate the hardships learners face in Bangladesh with the conventional usage of online platforms for learning.

3 Methodology

We framed our research from the perspective of students to understand the usage of existing online platforms by surfacing the current usage challenges. Therefore, we performed a mixed-method study which included semi-structured interviews and an online survey. The target participants are undergraduate students of an engineering university of department computer science and engineering in Bangladesh. The research study was approved by the Ethics Committee, a part of the Integrity Strategy and Innovation, of the institution of the authors. Firstly, we interviewed 18 engineering students. We maintained diversity in the class standings (first, second, third, fourth), and gender during recruitment. 18 interviewees participated in 20 min to 40 min long semi-structured interviews in the local language, i.e., Bengali. over phone calls or Zoom meetings. The interviews were audio-recorded with the permission of the interviewees. Out of 18 participants aged between 20 to 25 years, 10 participants reported being male and 8 participants reported being female. Accordingly, the audio data of the interviews were transcribed, anonymized, and translated into English. We used thematic analysis and the open coding procedure [2] to discover various themes from the transcripted audio data. Subsequently, we surveyed 239 students aged between 20 to 25 following non-probabilistic sampling and snowball sampling. Among our 239 participants, 156 reported as males, and 83 reported as females. Among the survey participants, 15.48% were the first year, 20.92% were the second year, 20.5% were the third year, 43.1% were the fourth year undergrad students. The questionnaire of the survey was distributed using Google form and it includes both open-ended and closed-ended questions. The options for close-ended questions in the survey were placed with the help of responses of the interviews since we surveyed after taking the interviews. Accordingly, the survey questions were categorized into themes that were derived from the interviews. From the interviews and survey, we discover the influential factors that motivate them to take help from online platforms for learning, their preferred platforms, challenges they face while using those online platforms.

4 Results

Here, we discuss our findings associated with the themes (Table 1) developed from the interview study and the survey of participant students.

Table 1. List of themes and descriptions associated with the interviews and the survey.

Theme	Description
Influential factors	The influential factors behind taking help from online platforms for learning purposes
Usage Pattern	The online platforms that are more preferable than others for learning purpose and the reasons for this usage
Challenges	The issues students face while they use online platforms with learning
Expectations	The expectations from online platforms with to meet requirements

Table 2. Shows (a) influential factors to take help from online platforms for learning, (b) challenges faced while using learning resources, and (c) challenges faced while using online platforms by the students of the survey (n = 239)

Influential factors to take help from online learning platforms	Survey (%)
Easier to understand	71.5
International standard	29.3
Availability of resources	56.1
Readily accessible	70
Numerous types of resources	51.5
Outcome of the learning resources	33.1
Less self-consciousness	11.7

(a)

Challenges faced while using online learning resources	Survey (%)
Lengthy course-outline	62.3
Lack of proper evaluation	33.5
Hard to navigate to previous sessions	19.7
Non-updated help page	26.4
Less interaction	32.6
Lack of consistent monitoring	13.4
Paid resource	38.9
Trust issues with less familiar resources	22.6
Instructors' accent	8.8

(b)

Challenges faced while using online platforms	Survey (%)
Delay to find suitable learning resource	77.4
Inconsistent ranking of the links of preferred resources	38.89
Not showing important links if the entered keyword is slightly inaccurate	50.2

(c)

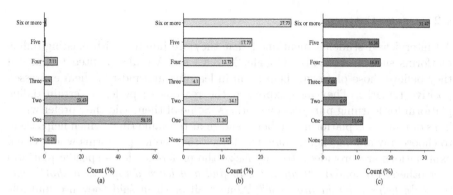

Fig. 1. Shows (a) the number of MOOC platforms, (b) the number of YouTube educational channel, (c) the number of learning websites, students (n = 239) follow

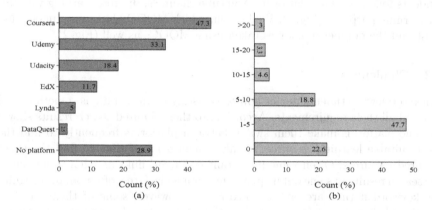

Fig. 2. Shows (a) the most used MOOC platforms by the students (n = 239), (b) the number of online courses taken by the students (n = 239) through MOOC platforms

4.1   Influential Factors

All interviewed students expressed they take help from online platforms for their learning purposes. From the interviews, it was revealed that several factors influence them to take online help which includes easier understandability than the physical resources, numerous types of resources with the flexibility to choose from them, the standard of the learning resources without any bias, availability of the resources which gives them the flexibility to learn any time, the outcome of the learning resources such as certificate after completion of a course, and less self-consciousness while taking help online. Some participants mentioned they feel comfortable interacting with others virtually rather than physically. Table 2 (a) informs the influencing factors related to the usage of online platforms for learning from our survey results.

4.2 Usage Pattern

All interviewed students mentioned that they are familiar with existing online platforms such as YouTube, Google, MOOC, etc. We also wanted to know if they believe those platforms help them in learning and most of them expressed positive remarks. They also expressed the reasons to prefer a certain online platform for learning purposes over others. Some of them said they prefer where links of numerous platforms are being shown at the same time, which helps them to choose any among them. Some mentioned they prefer platforms where visual explanations are provided. To emphasize the preference for a specific platform over others, P6 shared, *"I often try to find and learn a topic in a short time. YouTube helps a lot in this case"*. Almost all of them said they use multiple online platforms while learning a topic because sometimes only one platform does not provide them with their required resources. Accordingly, our surveyed students follow MOOC platforms, YouTube channels, discrete learning websites for learning purposes (Fig. 1). We find out which MOOC platforms students use most and the number of courses taken using MOOCs as well (Fig. 2).

4.3 Challenges

Our interviewed students depict how the existing online solutions sometimes fail to fulfill all their requirements. According to them, limited search results shown in some platforms make them switch between platforms frequently to find the most suitable learning resource. It takes them a lot of time to find the exact required resources. Often some important resources' links are shown bottom in the search results in some online platforms. Some platforms often fail to recognize the keyword if they are entered incorrectly. However, some of them (n = 6) mentioned they do not feel any lack in the existing learning resource platforms. Interestingly, the participants who mentioned they do not face any issues with the existing platforms are the first year (n = 3) and second-year (n = 2) students except one. We discover the challenges our surveyed students come across while using online learning resources and platforms (Table 2 (b) and (c)). Further, our interviewees mention the disadvantages of taking this online help for learning purposes. Some feel since many resources can be found, online plagiarism while doing academic tasks has become common. Many lose interest to dive deep into a certain topic since there are various types of resources available online which make them confused and distracted.

4.4 Expectations

Interviewed students' mentioned their expected characteristics in an online platform, which will assist them to access their required learning resources without any delay. They wanted their required resources' links to be shown above the search results, multiple types of resources being provided at the same time, accessing their required resources without being familiar with so many online platforms, etc. Mainly they wanted to mitigate the challenges they face while using online platforms. The interviewed students also came up with their expected characteristics in learning resources, which include a short but in-depth explanation, updated help page, easy navigation, communication among the learners, availability of practice module, proper evaluation of the learners, the international standard, updated frequently asked question, free of cost, etc.

5   Discussion

This study provided insights on the role of online platforms for learning purposes by surfacing the challenges of students.

5.1   Influential Factors for Online Learning

We investigated the influential factors related to students' using online platforms for learning which contribute to prior research [6,11] on the adoption of online learning. Our discovered influential factors can categorize into four categories- a) social factors b) human factors c) system quality d) information quality. Students look for trusted, credible, and familiar online platforms to search for resources. They feel self-conscious while interacting with instructors, peers for learning purposes physically, which is not in the case with virtual interaction. These are social factors. Human factors such as easier understandability, ready accessibility, gaining a certificate affect them as well. System quality factors include showing preferred resources at the beginning of the search results, having an evaluation system, etc. as well. Information quality factors such as high standards, more structured resources with effective information motivate students to take help from online platforms for learning purposes.

5.2   Managing Online Platforms Multiplexity for Effective Learning

Students use online platforms and communication media for learning purposes. However, they are not satisfied as per expectation in terms of their required needs. They feel there is less opportunity to customize a platform. They face delays in finding suitable learning resources using existing online platforms. However, the challenges of engaging with online platforms for learners involve not just one single platform, but a complex online learning ecosystem. Accordingly, we provide evidence of how students perceive the effectiveness of different online platforms for learning: Google was seen effective at showing numerous types of resources at the same time, YouTube was seen as particularly useful for providing learners opportunity to learn in a short time and MOOCs were seen effective at aggregating detailed information about a learning topic. However, using multiple online learning platforms requires time, a relatively stable motivation, collaborations among peers for effective learning. Most learners are constrained in their capacities to be able to manage and fully maximize the power of multiple online learning platforms. These insights extend prior work [3,7,9] examining learners' practices in specific types of online platforms for learning.

5.3 Design Implications

Students' expectations suggest that they need interlinking between platforms to reduce delay to find their suitable learning resources and their required learning resources' links should be shown at the beginning in the search results. From these, we can propose a platform where learners can select which type of resources they wish to get so that they do not need to search for a long time to find the perfect resource. We can also propose a personalized search engine for learning resources, where search results links will be shown with appropriate ranking based on students' preferences. These preferences will be derived from students' profiles, preferred resource types, students' most used platforms. Thus, this study extends our thinking of enabling interactions beyond the traditional online platforms and yet to build a specific platform for learning with specific needs that can make learners' searching and navigation easier along with personalization. We find that most students do not prefer native resources and the reasons specified are a scarcity of resources and low standards. Additionally, challenges and design issues specified by the students can help to create future design interventions. The content creators should keep in mind the design issues while creating content for the learners.

6 Conclusion

Online platforms have become important for students to gain knowledge. We conduct an interview study and an online survey to find out the usage pattern, motivating factors behind their interaction with different types of online platforms for learning purposes, and issues they identify while using those. We present several insightful findings from our rigorous user studies. We find that learners use multiple online platforms simultaneously for the effective learning experience. We also discuss design implications to address the concerns of students.

References

1. ICT Use and Access by Individuals and Households Bangladesh 2013, ICT Use and Access by Individuals and Households Bangladesh 2013 (2015)
2. Lune, H., Berg, B.L.: Qualitative research methods for the social sciences, Pearson Higher Ed (2016)
3. Santos, A.M., García, J.A.C., Díaz, R.: Websites of learning support in primary and high school in Portugal: A performance and usability study. In: Proceedings of the Fourth International Conference on Technological Ecosystems for Enhancing Multiculturality, pp. 1121–1125 (2016)
4. Amin, Md., Akter, A., Azhar, A., et al.: Factors affecting private university students' intention to adopt e-learning system in Bangladesh, Daffodil International University (2016)
5. Premlatha, K.R., Dharani, B., Geetha, T.V.: Dynamic learner profiling and automatic learner classification for adaptive e-learning environment. Interact. Learn. Environ. 24(6), 1054–1075 (2016)

6. Ngemba, H.R., Hendra, S.: Factors affecting student adoption of e-learning systems in Indonesia. In: Proceedings of the 2017 International Conference on Education and Multimedia Technology, pp. 43–47 (2017)
7. Godwin, H.T., Khan, M., Yellowlees, P.: The educational potential of YouTube. Acad. Psychiatry **41**(6), 823–827 (2017)
8. Rajab, K.D.: The effectiveness and potential of E-learning in war zones: an empirical comparison of face-to-face and online education in Saudi Arabia. IEEE Access **6**(4), 6783–6794 (2018)
9. Andone, D., Mihaescu, V.: Blending MOOCs into higher education courses-a case study (2018)
10. King, M., Pegrum, M., Forsey, M.: MOOCs and OER in the global south: problems and potential. Int. Rev. Res. Open Distrib. Learn. **19**(5), 1–20 (2018)
11. Watjatrakul, B.: Online learning adoption: effects of perceived value and the moderating role of neuroticism. In: Proceedings of the 2019 4th International Conference on Distance Education and Learning, pp. 40–44 (2019)
12. Abdulmajeed, K., Joyner, D.A., McManus, C.: Challenges of online learning in Nigeria. In: Proceedings of the Seventh ACM Conference on Learning@ Scale, pp. 417–420 (2020)

Towards Emotionally Expressive Virtual Agent to Foster Independent Speaking Tasks: A Preliminary Study

Emmanuel Ayedoun[(✉)] [iD] and Masataka Tokumaru

Faculty of Engineering Science, Kansai University, Osaka 564-8680, Japan
emay@kansai-u.ac.jp

Abstract. When communicating with second language learners, empathetic conversational partners that can convey a suitable amount of emotional feedbacks may play a facilitative role in instilling positive emotions and thus catalyze learner's production of the target language. On the other hand, facial expressions play a preponderant role in communicating emotion, intent, and even desired actions in a readily interpretable fashion. Moreover, the facial feedback hypothesis, an important part of several contemporary theories of emotion, suggests that facial expressions play a causal role in regulating emotional experience and behavior. In this study, we aim to investigate whether and how emotionally expressive computer-based agents that emulate non-verbal facial expressions may convey empathetic support to second language learners during communication tasks. To such extent, we leveraged the Facial Coding Action System and implemented a prototype virtual agent that can display a set of nonverbal feedbacks including Ekman' six basic universal emotions in addition to gazing and nodding behaviors. Then, we designed a Wizard of Oz experiment in which second language learners are assigned independent speaking tasks with a virtual agent whose feedbacks are indirectly driven by the wizard's facial expressions. In this paper, we present the outlines of our proposed method and our experimental settings towards validating the meaningfulness of our approach. We also present our next steps towards improving the system and validate its meaningfulness through large scale experiments.

Keywords: Virtual agents · Attentive listening · Facial feedbacks · Second language acquisition

1 Introduction

In communication settings, nonverbal behaviors such as facial expressions, nodding or eye gazing play a preponderant role in complementing and regulating interaction among participants [1]. For instance, the facial feedback hypothesis [2], an important part of several contemporary theories of emotion, suggests that facial expressions play a causal role in regulating emotional experience and behavior. On the other hand, when communicating with second language learners, empathetic conversational partners that can convey a suitable amount of emotional feedbacks may play a facilitative role in

C. Stephanidis et al. (Eds.): HCII 2022, CCIS 1582, pp. 12–18, 2022.
https://doi.org/10.1007/978-3-031-06391-6_2

instilling positive emotions and thus catalyze learner's production of the target language [3].

Moreover, the literature suggests that a conversational agent which has the ability to effectively convey appropriate emotional responses greatly augment the illusion of life because emotions are something that we find at the heart of what it means to be human [4].

In this study, we aim to investigate whether and how emotionally expressive computer-based conversational agents that emulate non-verbal facial expressions may convey empathetic support to second language learners when carrying out independent speaking tasks. To such extent, we propose a facial expressions generation method which is based on the Facial Coding Action System [5]. Then, we implement a prototype virtual agent that can display a set of non-verbal feedbacks including Ekman' six basic universal emotions [6] in addition of gazing and nodding behaviors. Here, we report on initial insights regarding the meaningfulness of our approach towards eliciting second language communication.

The rest of this paper is organized as follows. We begin an outline of the novelty and main objectives of our work. Then, we provide an overview of the proposed facial expression modeling and generation method. Later, we describe the pilot study and its preliminary results. Finally, we present some concluding remarks and discuss directions for future work.

2 Novelty and Research Goal

Nonverbal signals such as facial expressions, body language, eye-contact, etc. play a central role in human communication, sending strong messages about one's cognitive and emotional state. Depending on their nature, these cues may put people at ease, build trust, or they can offend, confuse, and undermine what the speaker is trying to convey [7]. For instance, the use of facial expression enables virtual agents to engage with users on an affective level, making them more capable social actors [8]. Hence, developing an embodied conversational agent that is able to exhibit a humanlike behavior when communicating with humans requires enriching the dialogue of the agent with well-designed non-verbal communication signals. In addition, while several approaches have been adopted to achieve such multimodal computer supported conversational agents, it seems important to bear in mind that less effort has been expanded on devising conversational agents that could display empathetic non-verbal listening behaviors. Furthermore, the potential of such nonverbal cues for fostering second language communication is not clearly established.

For instance, independent speaking task is a storytelling like communication task where second language learners are required to clearly express their opinion or thoughts on a topic within a limited amount of time. However, some learners despite their linguistic abilities may fail to perform at the best of their capabilities due to the amount of stress associated with such resource demanding activity. As a promising approach towards solving such issue, we are interested in investigating whether and how a virtual human agent that can display empathetic listening behavior could help such learners overcome their fear of failing, gain confidence, and communicate at the best of their linguistic resources. On the lights of the above, the goal of this study is two-fold:

- propose a method for achieving emotionally expressive computer-based agents that could display attentive nonverbal signals while listening to human conversation partners
- investigate whether such agents can convey enough empathetic support to the extent of regulating second language learners emotional experience and fostering communication task.

3   Proposed Method

To the extent of achieving the above-mentioned research goal, we propose a method that enables a virtual human agent to display believable nonverbal listening behavior using the following three types of nonverbal signals: facial expressions, nodding, and finally gazing. We employed a digital human agent developed by Trulience [9], which offers super realistic, interactive video avatars suitable for the high level of expressivity needed in the context of this work.

3.1   FACS Based Empathic Listening Behavior Modelling

To achieve an attentive listening behavior, it is necessary for the virtual human agent to display believable nonverbal feedbacks that are aligned with the status of the inter-action. In our work, such attentive listening behavior is realized by endowing a virtual human with the ability to convey specific emotions through facial expressions, nodding and gazing behavior. To this end, we adopt the Facial Action Coding System (FACS) [5] to design and code in a reliable fashion the virtual agent's facial expressions and movements.

FACS is an anatomically based system for describing all visually discernible facial movements. It breaks down facial expressions into individual components of muscle movement, called Action Units (AUs). Moreover, targeting such AUs is especially quite interesting since it is believed that facial expressions for displaying basic emotions such as *happiness, sadness, anger, surprise, fear*, and *disgust* are universal and can be coded as combination of multiple AUs. For this reason, in this work, we adopted the method described in [10] and carefully categorized our virtual agent's face blendshapes so as to target each of the 64 AUs identified in Ekman's work. By combining some specific AUs, we are able to enable the virtual agent to display each the Ekman's six basic universal emotions in addition to nodding and gazing behavior, as illustrated in Table 1. For example, *surprise* is generated from the combination of Action Unit 1 (Inner Brow Raiser), Action Unit 2 (Outer Brow Raiser), Action Unit 5 (Upper Lid Raiser), and Action Unit 26 (Jaw Drop). On the other hand, gazing and nodding behaviord are generated either from a single or combination of corresponding AUs. Figure 1 shows an illustration of the different facial expressions implemented in the virtual human agent, in addition to *nodding* and *gazing*.

Table 1. Combining multiple AUs to achieve various nonverbal feedbacks signals, adapted from [9].

Emotion/Feedback	Action unit combination	Description
Happiness	6 + 12	Cheek Raiser + Lip Corner Puller
Sadness	1 + 4 + 15	Inner Brow Raiser + Brow Lowerer + Lip Corner Depressor
Anger	4 + 5 + 7 + 23	Brow Lowerer + Upper Lid Raiser + Lid Tightener + Lip Tightener
Surprise	1 + 2 + 5 + 26	Inner Brow Raiser + Outer Brow Raiser + Upper Lid Raiser + Jaw Drop
Fear	1 + 2 + 4 + 5 + 7 + 20 + 26	Inner Brow Raiser + Outer Brow Raiser + Brow Lowerer + Upper Lid Raiser + Lid Tightener + Lip Stretcher + Jaw Drop
Disgust	9 + 15 + 16	Nose Wrinkler + Lip Corner Depressor + Lower Lip Depressor
Gazing	61/62/63/64	Eyes Turn Left/Eyes Turn Right/Eyes Up/Eyes Down
Nodding	51/52/53/54	Head Turn Left/Head Turn Right/Head Up/Head Down

Fig. 1. Virtual agent displaying different facial expressions including Ekman's six basic emotions in addition to gazing and nodding.

3.2 Triggering Specific Facial Expressions with a Wizard

In order to display a particular attentive listening behavior at a particular time of the interaction in a natural fashion, it is necessary for the virtual agent to be endowed with the ability of displaying facial expressions that are aligned with the content of the ongoing conversation. This is not easy to achieve as it requires real-time processing and understanding of the current state of the interaction. In other terms, it would be desirable that the virtual agent aligns its facial expression with the contents of the interlocutor's speech at any time of the interaction in order in convey an empathetic and natural listening behavior. For example, when the agent's interlocutor is talking about a happy or fun story, the virtual agent would be expected to display some facial feedbacks that convey some happiness.

To achieve such challenging task and evaluate the meaningfulness of the proposed system in a cost-effective fashion, we adopted a Wizard of Oz (Woz) [11] experiment style and implemented a prototype version of the system where ideal timing and type of displayed feedbacks are indirectly triggered by a wizard (i.e., an human being that partially operates the agent behind the scenes), as shown in Fig. 2. The wizard's face expressions were detected in real time using a third-party face recognition API [12], and based on the detected face expression, the virtual agent's nonverbal signals were generated. With such a setting, we designed an experimental environment in which subjects (second language learners) interact with the virtual agent without being aware that the virtual agent is actually being operated by the wizard.

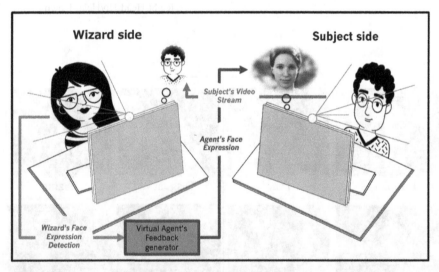

Fig. 2. Overview of system implementation for Wizard of Oz experiment

4   Preliminary Evaluation

We conducted a preliminary evaluation of the proposed system in which the virtual agent engages in a conversation with a human subject. Within this scenario, the human subject, a second language learner is presented with an independent speaking task such as "*Describe any one of the best moments of your life*". While the learner is speaking, the virtual agent displays some nonverbal feedbacks to the extent of achieving some attentive listening behavior toward the subject. We prepared three versions of the system, a first one where non-verbal feedbacks were indirectly triggered by the wizard, as described in the previous sections, a second one where non-verbal feedbacks were randomly triggered, and a third one where the virtual agent was just in an idle state and did not provide any facial feedbacks. Two undergraduate university students were recruited to evaluate the usability of the system. After interacting with each of the three system versions, they were asked to fill in a questionnaire survey about the naturalness of the virtual agent's listening attitude and their preference. Although, we do not have enough evidence to confirm the effectiveness of the proposed system at the current stage of our study, still we could observe that in general learners tend to prefer the system version involving the wizard.

5 Conclusion and Future Works

It is well known that emotional expression transcends the barriers of race, ethnicity, culture, gender, religion, and age. However, whether an emotionally expressive computer agent could have a beneficial impact for human communication is still to be demonstrated. In this study, we proposed an approach that could help evaluate to which extent nonverbal emotional signals displayed by a virtual agent could play a facilitative role in instilling positive emotions and thus catalyze learner's production of the target language. Tendencies observed from a preliminary pilot study of the proposed system hinted at the meaningfulness of our approach.

Future works will be dedicated to conduct large scale and more in-depth evaluation of the proposed system. We will also work towards leveraging both the learner's verbal input as well as their facial expressions to enable the virtual agent to autonomously respond in an emotionally meaningful way. In addition, although providing virtual humans with features like affect, personality, and the ability to build social relationships is the subject of increasing interest, little attention has been devoted to the role of such features as factors modulating their empathetic behavior. Thus, we believe that a modulation of a virtual agent's empathic behavior through factors like its mood, personality, and relationship to its interaction partner will lead to the generation of more appropriate listening behavior.

References

1. Horstmann, G.: What do facial expressions convey: feeling states, behavioral intentions, or actions requests? Emotion **3**(2), 150–166 (2003)
2. Buck, R.: Nonverbal behavior and the theory of emotion: the facial feedback hypothesis. J. Pers. Soc. Psychol. **38**(5), 811–824 (1980)
3. Krashen, S.: Principles and Practice in Second Language Acquisition. Prentice-Hall, London (1982)

4. Heckman, C.E., Wobbrock, J.O.: Put your best face forward: anthropomorphic agents, e-commerce consumers, and the law. In: Proceedings of the Fourth International Conference on Autonomous agents, pp. 435–442 (2000)
5. Ekman, P., Friesen, W.V., Hager, J.C.: The Facial Action Coding System: A Technique for the Measurement of Facial Movement. Consulting Psychologists Press, San Francisco (2002)
6. Ekman, P., Keltner, D.: Universal facial expressions of emotion. In: Segerstrale, U., Molnar, P. (eds.) Nonverbal communication: Where Nature Meets Culture, pp. 27–46 (1997)
7. Carolis, B.D., Pelachaud, C., Poggi, I., Steedman, M.: APML, a markup language for believable behavior generation. In: Life-Like Characters, pp. 65–85 (2004)
8. Wang, I., Ruiz, J.: Examining the use of nonverbal communication in virtual agents. Int. J. Hum.-Comput. Interact. **37**(17), 1648–1673 (2021)
9. https://www.trulience.com/. Accessed 15 Mar 2022
10. https://imotions.com/blog/facial-action-coding-system/#emotions-action-units. Accessed 15 Mar 2022
11. Kelley, J.F.: An empirical methodology for writing user-friendly natural language computer applications. In: Proceedings of the CHI 1983 Conference on Human Factors in Computing Systems, pp. 193–196 (1983)
12. https://github.com/justadudewhohacks/face-api.js/. Accessed 15 Mar 2022

A Guitar Training System for Beginners Using a Mixed Reality Device and a MIDI Guitar

Yoshiki Azuma, Hidetoshi Miyao[✉], and Minoru Maruyama

Faculty of Engineering, Shinshu University, Nagano, Japan
{miyao,maruyama}@cs.shinshu-u.ac.jp

Abstract. To represent how to play a guitar chord for beginners, our system displays the following two 3D objects in virtual space using a mixed reality device and a 3D game engine (Unity): (1) 3D guitar object displays a sphere at the position of the string to be pressed where each color of the spheres represents the finger to be used. (2) 3D hand object expresses an ideal finger shape when playing the chord. Moreover, to visualize the goodness of pressing the strings, we used a MIDI guitar controller which can acquire information on which string was pressed during performance. After a performance, using the acquired information, the system displays figures showing the correct way to press the strings and the state of the strings pressed during the performance. Moreover, our system can show how to correct mistakes using animation. A comparative experiment was performed between our system and a general system by 14 test users. As a result, it was shown that our system is superior in terms of clarity and users can learn guitar chords by themselves.

Keywords: Guitar training · HoloLens · Mixed reality

1 Introduction

For guitar beginners, when playing a guitar chord, it is difficult to know which string to press down, which finger to use, and what hand shape to use. Furthermore, even if a user intends to press down the strings correctly by himself/herself, he/she is not sure if he/she is pressing the strings well. Therefore, many guitar training systems using a mixed reality (MR) or an augmented reality (AR) have been proposed.

Löchtefeld et al. [1] have proposed a training system with a mobile projector attached to a guitar headstock. It can project colored light at the position of the string to be pressed where the color is different depending on the finger to be used. In addition, it can display information such as playing techniques on the fretboard. Rio-Guerra et al. [2] have developed an AR-based app designed for guitar beginners to learn basic music chords using a camera and a computer display connected to a PC. In the app, the fretboard is shot with the camera, the mirror image is displayed on the display, the position of the fretboard is recognized, and a colored virtual object is also displayed at the position of the string to be pressed. As a result, it can realize a practice environment where a user can play guitar while watching the instructional guitar in the mirror. When playing a

C. Stephanidis et al. (Eds.): HCII 2022, CCIS 1582, pp. 19–26, 2022.
https://doi.org/10.1007/978-3-031-06391-6_3

music chord, these systems can provide information on which part of the string should be pressed with which finger, but not on what hand shape to use.

Motokawa et al. [3] have developed an AR-based system which displays virtual 3D hand objects on a guitar fretboard as a mirror image like the app [2] using an AR marker attached to the guitar fretboard so that a user can know what hand shape to use when playing a music chord. Moreover, if the AR marker cannot be detected, to obtain the position of the guitar, the boundary of the guitar image is detected by image processing technique and used. Since these systems ([2] and [3]) require a guitar fretboard to face the camera to some extent, even if the user wants to know the shape of the hand on the back of the fretboard, he/she cannot see it. In addition, when playing guitar, the user wants to check the hand holding the guitar, so it is necessary to look at the PC display and his/her hand alternately in these systems. In this respect, the system [1] is excellent in that performance information is displayed directly on the fretboard and the position of the guitar is not restricted. On the other hand, in our preliminary experiment, it has been found that when a virtual object is superimposed on an actual fretboard, the user's hand and the virtual object overlap, making it difficult to see the virtual object. From this point of view, it seems that the representation method of these systems ([1, 2], and [3]) is difficult for the user to understand.

When learning to play the guitar on your own, it is important for the user to know if the strings are pressed with the correct fingering and the correct sound is being played. Kerdvibulvech et al. [4] have proposed a system that can acquire the position of the fingertips with colored markers on real time by integrating a Bayesian classifier into particle filters. This system can check the correctness of the finger position in real time, but it cannot check whether the correct sound is output. On the other hand, in the system [2], it is also check whether the correct chord is played based on the frequency analysis of the sound picked up by a microphone attached to the guitar. However, it is not easy to identify the frequencies when multiple strings are ringing at the same time, and it is considered difficult to accurately extract which string each finger is pressing.

Considering the shortcomings to the above-mentioned methods, we develop a system with the following features as a learning support system for learning basic music chord performance for guitar beginners:

- Using an MR device and an AR marker attached to a guitar, our system displays 3D virtual objects around the real guitar, instead of displaying the objects on the real fretboard. Moreover, a mode for fixing 3D hand model in virtual space is provided so that a user can see the hand model from various directions.
- Using a MIDI guitar controller, our system can acquire accurate information about which position of the guitar a user pressing. After a performance, using the acquired information, the system displays figures showing the correct way to press the strings and the state of the strings pressed during the performance.

2   Guitar Training System

Our system consists of the following two systems:

- **Performance support system:** This system displays 3D virtual objects expressing fingering around a guitar by using an MR device.
- **Performance evaluation system:** After a MIDI guitar is played, this system visualizes whether the strings was pressed correctly.

We explain the details of these two systems in the following sections.

2.1 Performance Support System

To display computer-generated virtual objects around a guitar, we use Microsoft HoloLens2 as an MR device. This device is equipped with an optical see-through head-mounted display, and it can superimpose and display a virtual object on objects in real world space. In our system, to align virtual and real coordinate spaces, we use Vuforia SDK [5] in Unity game engine [6] and an AR marker taken with the HoloLens camera. The marker is attached to the headstock of a MIDI guitar controller (Artiphon INSTRU-MENT 1). As a result, virtual objects can be displayed moving on with the marker. Here, virtual objects are also generated using Unity.

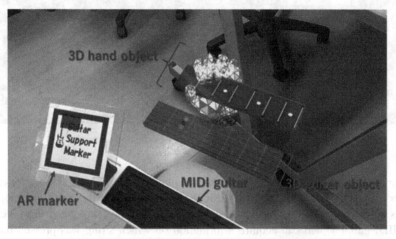

Fig. 1. Overview of performance support system

To help guitar beginners play music chords, the system displays two virtual objects (3D hand object and 3D guitar object) around the guitar headstock as shown in Fig. 1. 3D hand object expresses an ideal finger shape when playing the chord. This 3D model is generated by using the hand tracking function of MRTK (Mixed Reality Toolkit) provided by Microsoft. However, it is difficult to generate a precise hand model with this function, and the system cannot accurately visualize where each finger is pressing the string. Therefore, to accurately represent the position of the string to be pressed, the 3D guitar object is also displayed. This 3D object consists of a neck, frets, strings, and colored spheres. Each sphere expresses the position of the string to be pressed and its color expresses the finger to be used: blue is the index finger, red is the middle finger, green is the ring finger, and yellow is the little finger. These spheres are also displays at the fingertips of 3D hand object so that a user can associate them. By using the performance support system, a user can grasp the overall shape of the hand by looking at the 3D hand object and he/she can check the exact positions of the strings to be pressed by looking at the 3D guitar object.

Moreover, the virtual objects can be fixed in virtual space by hiding the AR marker. It can be realized by using the spatial awareness function of MRTK. This makes it possible to observe the 3D hand object from various angles, such as checking the position of the thumb on the back side of the fretboard.

2.2   Performance Evaluation System

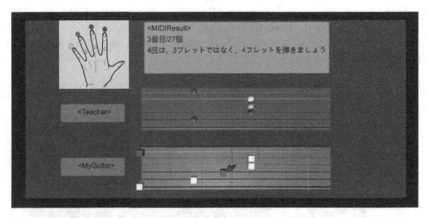

Fig. 2. Overview of performance evaluation system

For a guitar beginner, even if he/she tries to play by imitating the appearance using the performance support system, it is difficult to judge whether it is really pressing the strings correctly. Therefore, to visualize the goodness of pressing the strings, we use the MIDI guitar which can acquire information on which string was pressed during performance. After a performance, using the acquired information, the system displays figures as shown in Fig. 2 on a PC display. Here, the "Teacher" part shows the correct way to press the strings, and the "MyGuitar" part shows the state of the strings pressed during the performance. Here, white cubes mean their strings are pressed correctly and reds incorrectly. If there is an incorrect part (red cube), the user can select it with up and down arrow keys on the PC keyboard, the selected red cube is indicated by the gray arrow, and the correction advice for it is displayed in text in the upper part of the display. Moreover, the "Teacher" part can show how to correct mistakes using animation.

In addition, by playing the MIDI guitar connected to the PC, if the displayed chord is played correctly, a sound indicating the correct answer will be generated. This allows a learner to try to correct mistakes on the fly.

3 Experimental Results and Discussion

Our system was developed by using the game engine Unity 2018.4.23f1 (Libraries: Vuforia Ver.9.2.7 and Microsoft Mixed Reality Toolkit, Plug-in: MidiJack).

To verify the effectiveness of our system, we conducted an experiment on 14 guitar beginners. As a comparative experiment with our system, we used a system that displays a chord diagram and a photo expressing an ideal hand shape as virtual plane object (See Fig. 3). In the experiment, the participants learned how to play the seven basic major chords (C major, D major, E major, F major, G major, A major, and B major chords) using both systems. Here, music chords are randomly selected and displayed in turn for 15 s for each. The experimental procedure is as follows:

1. Participants learn how to play the music chords for 5 min using the comparison system.
2. Participants learn how to play the music chords for 5 min using our performance support system.
3. Participants review how to play the music chords using the performance evaluation system based on the information acquired by the above item (2).
4. Participants relearn how to play the music chords for 5 min using our performance support system. In this experiment, the participants are asked to use two modes: one is that the virtual objects move on with the guitar headstock, and the other is that they are fixed in their favorite position in the virtual space. The participants are also asked to play not only the MIDI guitar but also an actual acoustic guitar.

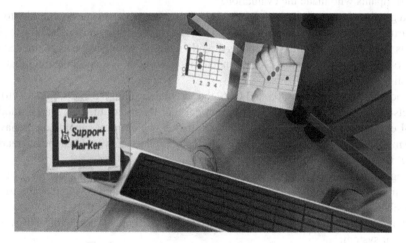

Fig. 3. Comparison system using a chord diagram

After the experiment, we asked the participants to answer the following 11 questions:

- Q01: Were the displayed chord diagram and photo easy to see for the comparison system?

- Q02: Were the 3D hand object and the 3D guitar object easy to see for our system?
- Q03: Did you understand how to play chords by using the comparison system?
- Q04: Did you understand how to play chords by using our performance support system?
- Q05: Didn't the virtual objects disappear or unexpectedly appear in an unusual position for the use of the 'AR marker mode'? (In this mode, the virtual objects move on with the guitar headstock.)
- Q06: Didn't the virtual objects disappear or unexpectedly appear in an unusual position for the use of the 'no marker mode'? (In this mode, the virtual objects are fixed in the virtual space.)
- Q07: Was the interface easy to see and understand for the performance evaluation system?
- Q08: Were the error correction animation and the text of advice easy to understand for the performance evaluation system?
- Q09: Were you able to learn how to play chords by using the performance evaluation system?
- Q10: For the experiment (4), were you able to play chords correctly compared to before using the performance evaluation system?
- Q11: Were you able to play chords correctly using an acoustic guitar after the training?

As a choice of answers, a Five-grade evaluation of Rickert standards was used: 1: Disagree, 2: Moderately disagree, 3: Neutral, 4: Moderately agree, and 5: Agree. Therefore, for all questions, the larger the value, the better the result. Table 1 shows the evaluation distribution for questions where the value in each cell indicates the number of participants who made the evaluation.

Regarding the questions from Q01 to Q04, it is shown that our system is easier to see the virtual objects than the comparison system, and it is easier to understand how to play chords. When we asked the participants directly which system was easier to understand how to play chords, 12 out of 14 responded that it was our system, indicating that our system is superior.

Looking the results for Q05 and Q06, the 'no marker mode' can display the virtual objects more stably than the 'AR marker mode'. For the use of the 'AR marker mode', HoloLens2 must always track the moving AR marker, which causes anomalous behavior if the marker cannot be detected. As a result, 10 participants answered that the 'no marker mode' is easier to use.

Regarding the questions from Q07 to Q11, it is considered that the GUI of the performance evaluation system is appropriate and users can learn how to play chords by themselves.

Here are some of the comments received from the participants during the experiment using our system:

- It was nice to be able to adjust the display position and angle of the virtual objects by myself.
- Information that is not expressed in the music score is also presented, and I think that users can learn efficiently.

- It's hard to get bored because users can practice like a game rather than practicing while looking at the music score.
- The shape of some 3D hand objects was not accurate.
- It would be nice if the system could evaluate the performance in real time.
- The thick fretboard of the MIDI guitar makes it difficult to press the strings.

Table 1. Evaluation distribution for questions

Questions	Evaluation(1:Disagree,5:Agree)				
	1	2	3	4	5
Q01	0	1	3	6	4
Q02	0	0	0	7	7
Q03	0	2	4	4	4
Q04	0	0	0	4	10
Q05	2	2	2	7	1
Q06	0	1	0	6	7
Q07	0	0	2	4	8
Q08	0	0	1	8	5
Q09	0	0	0	3	11
Q10	0	0	1	3	10
Q11	0	0	0	10	4

4 Conclusion

To help guitar beginners learn how to play music chords efficiently, we have proposed the following system: (1) The performance support system can display the virtual objects (3D hand object and 3D guitar object) around the guitar headstock using HoloLens2, and (2) the performance evaluation system by using a MIDI guitar can visualize whether the strings were pressed correctly during the performance. The comparative experiment was performed between our system and the comparison system displaying a chord diagram, it was shown that our system is easier to understand how to play chords than the comparison system. Moreover, it was shown that users can learn how to play chords by themselves using the performance evaluation system.

The future works are as follows:

- We need to generate more accurate 3D hand objects.
- In our system, the performance is evaluated after all the performance is done, and it cannot judge the goodness of the performance in real time while playing. In this regard, improvements should be made so that judgment can be made in real time.
- Since the handling of MIDI guitars is different from that of acoustic ones, it is necessary to propose a method that can judge whether the performance is correct or incorrect even if an acoustic guitar is used.

Acknowledgments. This work was supported by JSPS KAKENHI Grant Number JP18K11564.

References

1. Löchtefeld, M., Gehring, S., Jung, R., Krüger, A.: guitAR: supporting guitar learning through mobile projection. In: CHI 2011 Extended Abstracts on Human Factors in Computing System, pp. 1447–1452 (2011)
2. Rio-Guerra, M.S.D., Martin-Gutierrez, J., Lopez-Chao, V.A., Parra, R.F., Sosa, M.A.R.: AR graphic representation of musical notes for self-learning on guitar. Applied Sciences **9**, 4527 (2019)
3. Motokawa, Y., Saito, H.: Support system for guitar playing using augmented reality display. In: 2006 IEEE/ACM International Symposium on Mixed and Augmented Reality, pp. 243–244 (2006)
4. Kerdvibulvech, C., Saito, H.: Guitarist fingertip tracking by integrating a Bayesian classifier into particle filters. In: Advances in Human-Computer Interaction (2008)
5. Vuforia Engine Developer Portal. https://developer.vuforia.com/. Accessed 9 Mar 2022
6. Unity. https://unity.com/. Accessed 9 Mar 2022

Designing a Digital Reading Tool for Middle School Students and Teachers: A Grounded, User-Centered Design Approach

John P. Hutson[(✉)], Kinta D. Montilus, Kristen S. Herrick, and Michelle R. Lamond

Educational Testing Service, Princeton, NJ 08541, USA
jhutson@ets.org

Abstract. Across English Language Arts classrooms in the United States many students experience low reading comprehension and struggle to stay engaged with their learning while working independently [1]. Our cross-functional team partnered with middle school teachers and students to develop an educational tool that provides reading skills support. Through three design thinking stages, we present our method, experiences, and initial outcomes developing a reading tool for middle school English Language Arts classrooms. In Stage One, we empathized with users to understand their needs and pain points and identified the problem statement: students often do not work well independently and struggle to stay engaged with reading. In Stage Two, we explored design solutions to address the problem statement and engaged in iterative prototyping. At the end of this stage, we developed an alpha version of our reading tool that included both annotation and reading comprehension check features. In Stage Three, we conducted initial user testing and evaluation of the tool in middle school classrooms (Teacher N = 3; Student N = 171). Teachers found they were able to implement the tool flexibly to fit their planned lessons and instruct students at different reading levels. Students worked independently with the tool, reported that it was usable, and perceived it would improve their reading comprehension. Overall, this study shows how a tool with annotation and metacognitive-check features can support students in the classroom, and offers next steps for the development of effective reading tools.

Keywords: User studies · Education technology · Reading literacy

1 Introduction

Low reading literacy among middle school students is a problem across the United States. In 2019, 66% of 8th grade students read below a proficient level [2], and 27% of those were below the basic level. Given the breadth of the reading skills needed to be a proficient reader and the abundance of work in this area, there are many competing theories, practices, and technologies. We engaged in a grounded, user-centered design approach, and present work leading up to and including an initial implementation of our tool in classrooms.

© The Author(s), under exclusive license to Springer Nature Switzerland AG 2022
C. Stephanidis et al. (Eds.): HCII 2022, CCIS 1582, pp. 27–34, 2022.
https://doi.org/10.1007/978-3-031-06391-6_4

1.1 Method Overview

Our interdisciplinary team implemented two key approaches to develop a solution to support reading comprehension skills of struggling middle school readers: (1) user-centered design [3] and (2) grounding in science and practice [4]. While both approaches have been used widely, their combination to address reading literacy in the middle school classroom created unique opportunities, challenges, and methodological choices that our team learned from, and we expect others could incorporate into their work.

In Stage One of the design thinking process we engaged in a discovery process by conducting interviews with teachers and students to identify pain points and needs. In Stage Two we explored potential design solutions rooted in learning science and instructional design principles, and conducted frequent user tests to develop an alpha version of the reading tool. Finally, in Stage Three, we conducted an alpha study of the tool in classrooms with teachers and students to evaluate perceptions of usability and preliminary evidence of effectiveness. All studies were approved by IRB and participants completed informed consent (see Stage Three for full study ethics).

2 Stage One: Empathize with Users and Define Problem

The work in stage one aligned with the first step in the HCI Design Process: research and requirements gathering. We conducted surveys ($n = 31$), focus groups ($n = 27$), and journey map interviews ($n = 4$) with middle school English Language Arts (ELA) teachers. We also conducted surveys with students ($n = 47$). The two main outcomes of Stage One were developing an empathy map to understand teacher and student needs and pain points, and using those to develop a problem statement to guide the development of the learning solution.

Through empathy mapping, we established that middle school teachers would benefit from support meeting the needs of learners at different levels, helping learners to get started with their work, helping learners to feel empowered and encouraged to complete work independently, helping learners feel engaged/excited to read, and providing adequate and appropriate resources.

After summarizing the major pain points of middle school ELA teachers and students, we curated six problem statements and tested them with teachers ($n = 3$). Teachers rated how much they identify with the problem statements and edited the problem statements to align it with their actual needs. After this feedback, the team selected the problem statement: *As a general education 7th-grade ELA teacher, I am discouraged when my low reading comprehension students do not work well independently because they struggle to stay engaged with their learning.*

3 Stage Two: Explore Design Solutions and Engage Users in Iterative Prototyping

Equipped with a better understanding of our users' needs and experiences, in Stage Two, we explored and collaboratively ideated on potential solutions. The problem statement served as our guide throughout this stage. The work in stage two aligned with the second step in the HCI Design Process: Design and Prototyping.

First, we identified and considered applicable learning science research concerning reading comprehension, motivation to read, metacognition, and self-regulated learning. Given that teaching and learning related to middle school literacy is a well-researched area, we wanted to ensure we incorporated insights from applicable learning science research into our brainstorming, design thinking, and ideation work. We also reviewed and incorporated applicable learning design principles (LDPs) and instructional best practices while exploring design solutions.

To ground our work, we adopted the comprehensive Cognitive Based Assessment of, for, and as Learning (CBAL) reading framework [5] as our primary learning framework underpinning design solution exploration. Drawing from the framework, we divided the reading process into the following dimensions: 1) preparing to read, 2) understanding the text, 3) digging deeper or going beyond the text, 4) re-representing text information, and 5) applying and reflecting.

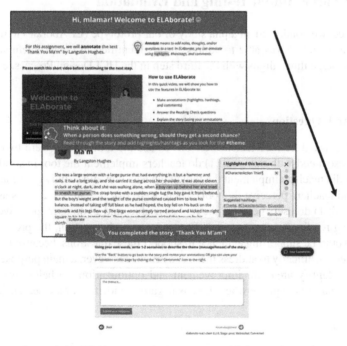

Fig. 1. Screenshots of the ELAborate welcome screen with instructions, the text view with annotation modal window, and the final theme response box.

Having established a strong learning science and instructional design foundation on which to build, we ideated and created rapid prototypes. In Stage Two we regularly conducted studies with students and teachers on our rapid prototypes to evaluate the extent to which design decisions met their needs. The two key features we decided to focus on in the initial prototype were 1) annotation and 2) reading comprehension self-check questions. Annotating text has positive impacts on student reading comprehension through reading skill, metacognition, and socio-emotional learning [6]. Reading comprehension checks presented with the text have positive impacts on reading comprehension, metacognition, and socio-emotional mechanisms [5].

Through exploration of design solutions and iterative, rapid prototyping, we integrated insights from learning sciences research and instructional design principles with the expertise of our users to create a functional prototype – ELAborate. In ELAborate (Fig. 1), students: 1) view a demo video to help them understand how to use the tool as well as the assignment instructions [7], 2) answer a guiding question [8], 3) read the text while annotating via hashtags, highlights, and comments and review their annotations as needed [9], 4) answer reading comprehension check questions [10], and 5) write a brief summary about the story's theme [11]. ELAborate had a single text, Thank you M'am by Langston Hughes.

4 Stage Three: Initial Testing and Evaluation

In stage three, we conducted an alpha study of our prototype (ELAborate) to determine the extent to which it was able to address needs identified in our problem statement. The work in stage three aligns with the third step in the HCI Design Process: evaluating designs.

4.1 Research Questions

Study goal 1 asked how do teachers choose to use the tool? There were two research questions associated with this goal: 1) do teachers implement the tool in similar ways, and 2) why did teachers implement the tool in the way they did? Study goal 2 asked how students and teachers perceive the tool? There were two research questions associated with this goal: 1) do users perceive the tool as usable, and 2) do users perceive the tool as improving reading comprehension? For each research question, the prediction was that there would be supporting evidence to support these questions, because ELAborate was designed specifically to address these constructs. However, a main purpose of Stage Three is to identify areas for improvement and optimization, so below we also use exploratory analyses to probe when there is negative evidence for a research question.

4.2 Method

The study was conducted in middle school (7th & 8th grade) ELA classrooms. ELAborate was implemented as a regular classroom activity. There were three teachers in the study, with a total of 9 classes. A total of 171 students participated in at least a portion of the classroom activities. Data collection was remote, and we only had contact with teachers. Teachers chose how to implement the tool into their classroom instructions and additional activities for their class around the reading. Teachers were paid $100 per hour for participation outside of classroom (e.g., training and interviews). Schools were compensated $20 per student who completed the study. The full study design was approved by IRB, and approval was received for each school using their district protocols. All participation was voluntary, and participants consented to participate. Students used anonymous participant IDs assigned by teachers throughout the study, so all student data was deidentified throughout the study. Teacher data was deidentified upon completion of the study.

Students completed multiple surveys in addition to their engagement with the ELAborate prototype. Before using ELAborate, students were asked five questions to gauge their motivation, reading habits, and comfort with technology. While reading, students were given the goal of identifying the theme of the story. Use of the annotation feature was optional, but all reading check questions had to be answered correctly before moving on. After using the tool, students completed usability items (System Usability Scale [SUS; 12], and perception of impact items. The perception of impact questions gathered students' agreement (1 = Strongly disagree, 5 = Strongly agree) that ELAborate supported six outcomes the tool was designed to address: Overall text comprehension, vocabulary, ability to annotate, motivation, engagement, and independent reading. Students also rated agreement (1 = Strongly disagree, 4 = Strongly agree) with two reading assignment specific items: needed support from teacher to understand 1) plot and 2) theme. Teachers participated in follow-up interviews to discuss the implementation of the tool.

For teacher interviews, we conducted a thematic analysis. The implementation themes were flexibility of implementation and logistics of implementation. We present descriptive statistics for the survey items to illustrate the trends in the data. Additionally, we use correlations and Bayes factors as exploratory analyses to probe the data. Finally, where applicable, we present the interview and survey data together to put the survey results in context.

4.3 Results

Study Goal 1: Teacher Implementation. (1) Do teachers implement the tool in similar ways, and (2) why did teachers implement the tool in the way they did? All teachers in this study implemented the tool differently. There were some similarities, such as completing most of the reading independently. Notably, all teachers provided different levels of support and structure during the reading component. As such, the key outcome here is that teachers found the tool flexible to different implementations, and the tool did not create limitations on their implementation plans.

Teachers who gave their students the most freedom to complete the reading independently stated that they wanted to understand how students would naturally use the tool. However, one of these teachers changed their implementation based on the reading level of their students. For example, they varied how much annotation demonstration they did. Another teacher chose to scaffold their students through the first use of the tool in order to increase the likelihood they would understand how to use all the tool features. They also indicated that with future uses they would increase the amount of independent work in ELAborate.

Study goal 2: Perception of Usability and Impact of Reading Comprehension. (1) Do users perceive the tool as usable? Overall, students gave the tool high usability ratings. This aligned with teachers' perceptions that the tool was easy for students to use. The System Usability Scale (SUS) score for ELAborate was in the "Good" range ($M = 74.14$; $SD = 15.23$), which is especially high for the first classroom release of ELAborate. SUS scores did not vary between teachers ($BF = .10$). ELAborate usability can still increase, and one feature identified for improvement was that the process to save annotations was cumbersome for certain students ("I believe it would be easier if the quotations automatically save as you type them.").

(2) Do users perceive the tool as improving reading comprehension? Overall, on the six reading comprehension outcomes completed after using the tool, students perceived that using ELAborate supported their reading comprehension (Fig. 2A), with each measure above the neutral point on the scale (p's $< .001$). Importantly, these measures were the same across teachers (BF range $.47–.11$) with one exception. For working independently, one teacher's students perceived the tool as not having a positive or negative impact on working independently ($BF = 1.53$; working independent $M = 3.2$, $SE = .21$). There was not clear evidence to explain this result in the implementation data, but future work should explore this key outcome from the problem statement.

We ran correlations on the six reading comprehension outcomes, and all were positive (p's $< .05$; min $r = .21$; max $r = .75$). However, annotation is one of the key features of ELAborate, and critically most of the lower correlations include the item that ELAborate would support students in "annotating more." For example, the lowest correlation ($r = .21$) is between annotating more and "understood text more," which using Fisher's Z transformation is significantly weaker than the relationship between both vocabulary and motivation with understanding (p's $< .05$). In other words, students perceived that reading the story in ELAborate supported their comprehension of the story, but that annotation may have had less of a relationship with comprehension improvements than other features in the tool. This appears to be driven by students who indicated the tool allowed for a good understanding of the text (Fig. 2B), such that students who gave high understanding ratings were more likely to give lower annotation ratings. Future research with the tool should explore when annotations support comprehension.

Most students indicated they did not need help to understand the plot ($M = 1.59$) or theme ($M = 1.81$) of the story (p's $< .001$). However, there was one teacher for whom students perceived they needed more help compared to the other two classes for both theme and plot (BF's > 1084). Importantly, their means were above the midpoint of the

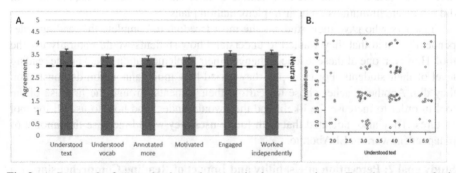

Fig. 2. A. Bar graph of means for the student perceived outcomes items. Error bars are standard error. B. Scatter plot of the outcomes understood text (x-axis) and annotated more (y-axis).

scale (Plot $M = 2.29$; Theme $M = 2.79$) and were a full point higher than the next score on the four-point scale used. One potential reason for this is that this teacher discussed each page of the story with their students before moving on to the next page, which suggests implementation can impact perceptions of the impact of the tool.

5 Discussion

How can we help teachers in middle school ELA classrooms support students who are struggling to read, work independently, and engage in their learning? We developed a prototype reading tool (ELAborate) for use in classrooms through a three-stage research and design process of 1) defining a problem statement, 2) designing a prototype, and 3) testing the solution. In this report, we presented the method and key results/outcomes from an interdisciplinary approach of frequent user testing and grounding solution features in science and practice.

5.1 Implications

This study has implications both specific to ELAborate and learning tools, and to reading broadly. For both teachers and students, it was important that the tool gave them flexibility in implementation to fit their needs. However, the way the tool is implemented is likely to impact its effectiveness, which means it is important for the development team to understand this relationship and communicate it to teachers to support their implementation and/or create features in the system to support students while working independently. Also, students perceived that ELAborate's features of annotation and comprehension check questions supported their comprehension overall. However, the perceived impact of annotation was weaker than some other components. As such, future work will need to identify the unique impact of annotation features above and beyond other potential areas for development.

5.2 Conclusion

Our team developed a unique solution to a highly complex problem (low reading literacy) in a context with multiple users (students & teachers). Through the discovery phase we identified annotation and reading comprehension checks as key features to support student literacy. Initial testing of these features in ELAborate was positive, and identified future development and research needed to create an effective reading solution. Our approach to this work had aspects that were unique to the classroom context that we hope other researchers focusing on classroom challenges can learn from.

References

1. Sabatini, J., O'Reilly, T., Doorey, N.A.: Retooling Literacy Education for the 21st Century: Key Findings of the Reading for Understanding Initiative and Their Implications. Educational Testing Service, 2018. Center for Research on Human Capital and Education

2. Institute of Education Sciences, National Center for Education Statistics, U.S. Department of Education (ed.), National Assessment of Educational Progress (2019)
3. McWilliams, K., et al.: Unpacking the black box of efficacy: a framework for evaluating the effectiveness and researching the impact of digital learning tools [White Paper]. In: MacMillan Learning (2017)
4. Graesser, A.C., et al.: Educational technologies that support reading comprehension for adults who have low literacy skills. In: The Wiley Handbook of Adult Literacy, pp. 471–493 (2019)
5. O'Reilly, T., Sheehan, K.M.: Cognitively based assessment of, for, and as learning: a framework for assessing reading competency. ETS Res. Rep. Ser. **2009**(2), i–43 (2009)
6. Johnson, T.E., Archibald, T.N., Tenenbaum, G.: Individual and team annotation effects on students' reading comprehension, critical thinking, and meta-cognitive skills. Comput. Hum. Behav. **26**(6), 1496–1507 (2010)
7. Collins, A., Kapur, M.: Cognitive apprenticeship. In: Sawyer, R.K. (ed.) The Cambridge Handbook of the Learning Sciences, pp. 109–127. Cambridge University Press, Cambridge (2014)
8. Rosenshine, B., Meister, C., Chapman, S.: Teaching students to generate questions: a review of the intervention studies. Rev. Educ. Res. **66**(2), 181–221 (1996)
9. AbuSeileek, A.F.: Hypermedia annotation presentation: the effect of location and type on the EFL learners' achievement in reading comprehension and vocabulary acquisition. Comput. Educ. **57**(1), 1281–1291 (2011)
10. Agarwal, P.K., Nunes, L.D., Blunt, J.R.: Retrieval practice consistently benefits student learning: a systematic review of applied research in schools and classrooms. Educ. Psychol. Rev. **33**(4), 1409–1453 (2021)
11. Graham, S., Hebert, M.: Writing to read: evidence for how writing can improve reading. In: A report from Carnegie Corporation of New York. 2010, Alliance for Excellent Education: Washington, DC
12. Sauro, J., Lewis, J.R.: When designing usability questionnaires, does it hurt to be positive? In: Proceedings of the SIGCHI Conference on Human Factors in Computing Systems (2011)

Monitoring and Regulating Sonic Activity Through Feedback in Learning Environments

Per-Arne Jørgensen[✉], Tommy Stefanac, Bipashna Kshetree,
and Georgios Marentakis

Østfold University College, 1751 Halden, Norway
per.a.jorgensen@hiof.no

Abstract. Learning environments and the classroom setting abound with sonic activity which may be desired or not depending on the listener context. Undesired sonic activity is often perceived as noise and can result to loss of concentration, disturbances to learning, and hearing issues related to health. Technology could potentially be used to design tools that help regulate sonic activity in the classroom. In this paper, we embark on a user-centred-design process to explore sonic activity in the classroom and design and evaluate tangible prototypes that monitors sound level in the classroom and gives ambient feedback to students and teachers. We started by interviewing teachers from three schools and obtained requirements. Regulating sonic activity turned out to be a complex process that requires the participation and negotiation from both teachers and students due to the subjective nature of sound perception. Furthermore, solutions based on smartphones are not practical because they divert student attention. A tangible device coupled with an ambient display may provide a viable solution. We sketched and evaluated several possibilities which addressed the requirements as well as possible. Based on feedback from teachers, we developed 3D printed tangible prototypes with input controls that provide visual and sonic feedback and can be coupled to an ambient display. These were further developed based on two iterations which included evaluation in a controlled environment. The solution monitors sound level and reports violations but also allows both students and teachers to report annoyance due to noise to the rest of the classroom. Furthermore, it can be coupled to an ambient display of sonic activity. The result from the iterations indicates that monitoring and negotiation sonic activity in classrooms with an IoT device can help teachers regulate the unwanted "noise" through enabling feedback from students.

Keywords: Noise · Ambient feedback · Interaction design · Human-computer interaction · Tangible device · Sonification · Sound monitoring · Sonic activity

1 Introduction

A common factor in classrooms around the world is sonic activity which can be wanted or unwanted and originate in external and internal sound sources, as well as technological devices: sounds emitting from laptops, screens, iPads, phones, smart watches, etc.

© The Author(s), under exclusive license to Springer Nature Switzerland AG 2022
C. Stephanidis et al. (Eds.): HCII 2022, CCIS 1582, pp. 35–42, 2022.
https://doi.org/10.1007/978-3-031-06391-6_5

Several research studies have shown that unwanted sonic activity has detrimental effects upon children's and teacher's performance at school which include reduced memory, motivation, and reading ability and degrades the learning experience [1, 2].

Smart classroom technologies are becoming ubiquitous nowadays. Interactive flat screens, smart boards, laptops and tablets, assistive and video conferencing technologies, and other audio/visual elements are incorporated into the classroom to make lessons simpler, more interesting, and participatory. Research in smart systems for regulating sonic activity seems limited. A system for regulating sonic activity may also find its place in the smart classroom [3] and improve student-teacher interaction and learning [3].

The rest of this paper is organised as follows. Section 2 presents the background on the paper where we look at recent literature and how sonic activity can become a problem and an overview of the research questions (RQs). Section 3 describes the methods we used in this paper and the results including the informing, designing, prototyping, and evaluating phases. In Sect. 4 we discuss the findings in relation to the RQs and Sect. 5 the conclusion.

2 Background

Sonic activity in the classroom may originate in several sources. Some are external such as construction work, nearby roads and highways, or ventilations [1]. According to the World Health Organization (WHO) in order "to hear and understand spoken messages in a classroom" the background sonic activity level should not exceed 35 dB in schools and preschools [4]. Long-term sonic activity above the recommended levels will affect the learning environment in a negative way [5, 6]. In particular, noise in schools results in speech interference, disturbance of information extraction (e.g. comprehension and reading acquisition), message communication and annoyance. Noise also increases learners listening effort [7] and can also result in long term hearing loss. External noise needs to be handled by room acoustics. Our focus is on sonic activity from the class members in particular the students. Learners often generate their own sonic activity based on their behaviour [8]. This may originate in sounds created while engaging in different activities or interacting with each other or with computing devices. In a classroom setting, such unwanted sonic activity may become an unpleasant disturbance with a negative impact on students' performance, focus and concentration. It also requires intervention by teachers and may also put strain on their voice as they try to be heard in the classroom [2]. It is this kind of sonic activity that we target in this work.

Among several interventions for enhancing learning in the classroom a few have targeted regulating sonic activity. Lyk and Lyk [9] designed the robot Nao which functions as an authority figure to help the teacher moderate the noise level in the classroom by asking children if they could be quieter once the noise level reached a certain value. The robot did not only have an immediate effect on the noise level, but also raised the general awareness on the level of noise. Van Tonder et al. [10] used a SoundEar II device and provided visual feedback on noise levels in real time using a LED based lighting system with colours green, yellow, and red. Evaluation in three primary school classrooms showed a 1.4 dB reduction in the average noise levels. Prakash [11] used a similar three-color feedback approach and advised teachers to take action based on the indication and also registered positive changes in the learning environment. Reis and Correia [2] created a serious game featuring characters presented on ambient displays that changed their appearance depending on the level of noise. Student groups received points for being quiet. They reported a significant reduction in noise level due to the intervention in 3 out of 4 classes. However, the game did not have an impact in increasing students' concentration. Finally, Tabuenca [12] presented a system for regulating sonic activity that consists of a feedback cube [13] built on an Arduino microcontroller that provides visual and audio feedback. Visual feedback is provided using a ring of LEDs that can be controlled individually and a mini speaker plays sound. The color corresponds to the sound level (green, yellow, red). Furthermore, their system includes a mobile app that can calculate the noise level in dB. In an evaluation study, they found that their system was able to help moderate noise levels, however the system was not equally effective for all groups as some groups deliberately made noise to explore how the system works and thus overall level increased.

2.1 Summary and Research Questions

We see that despite that unwanted sonic activity from class members is an issue in the classroom relatively few interventions have been designed to help with its regulation. Furthermore, the majority of the interventions focus on a simplified model in which annoyance is associated directly with sound pressure level and a visual indication of sound level is provided. Even systems that use gamification or tangible displays do not cater for feedback from class members. This is not necessarily a valid approach as the extent to which sonic activity becomes noise depends on several subjective factors. Several activities in the classroom result in increased sonic activity which may also be desired. Classifying whether sonic activity as unwanted is quite difficult to achieve without input from teachers and learners as this is quite context dependent. Unfortunately, existing monitoring systems[1,2] do not have an option for receiving feedback from learners to help with such disambiguation and were designed with limited input from stakeholders in the design process. More input from stakeholders could lead to further ideas about how to best design such systems.

The following research questions were defined which address designing the system and negotiating sonic activity: (RQ1): *"How to design a system for interactively regulate sonic activity in classrooms?"*, *(RQ2): "What type of techniques can be used to "silence" a loud room when it is too loud?"*, *(RQ3): "How can the negotiation of the sonic activity between teacher and students be regulated?"*. RQs were examined by involving teachers in the design process and obtain requirements based on their input. We have applied an interaction design process (lifecycle model) consisting of the following phases: (1) informing, (2) designing, (3) prototyping and (4) evaluating [14]. We want to see if this approach can lead to new understanding and ideas for systems assisting with the management of sonic activity in classrooms.

---

[1] https://pulsarinstruments.com/en/product/pulsar-nova-decibel-meters-models-43-44.

[2] https://soundear.com/soundear3-300/.

3 Designing Our Intervention

Informing: Two semi-structured interviews and a focus group were performed with professional teachers with the goal to understand better how learners and teachers behave in a classroom setting when sonic activity is high. The interviews were conducted using a videoconference system and the focus group onsite at the school. Four teachers from three different schools participated in the interviews. Two were from primary schools in Norway and one from Nepal. Teachers were introduced to the problem statement, answered questions, and participated in an informal discussion. Key aspects that were mentioned by the teachers during the interviews were that: *teachers wanted to decide when sonic activity is an issue; using app as a tool was not a good idea; teachers wanted something visual to show sonic activity; be careful with lights and sound feedback due to some learners´ sensitivity; the solution could be both an automated and a semi-automated system; and the teachers wanted to decide when to use the system and also have control over the system.* Based on this, we iterated ideas for a system with the following requirements: (1) it should not attract too much attention, (2) it should be possible to deactivate and operate in the background, (3) it should be controllable by the teachers, (4) it should be able to visualise (ambient display) the sonic activity, (5) possibly combine both sound and light to notify the activity, and (6) consider the sensitivity and views of students.

Designing: Based on the results of the informing phase several ideas of a product design were explored based on scenarios of learners disturbing each other during lecture hours and group work. The conceptual design of the system and its components is shown in Fig. 1.

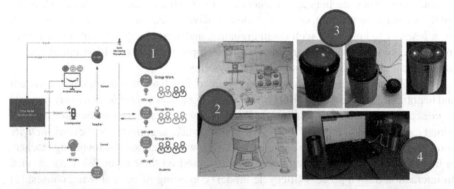

Fig. 1. Design (1) concept, (2) sketches, (3) first prototype, and (4) second prototype.

The results of the informing phase led us to the conclusion that it is best to create a system which can monitor sonic activity level based on objective measurement but can also give students and teachers the opportunity to express whether they are getting annoyed by sonic activity. Concerning interaction, it appeared that incorporating components from tangible interaction design had the advantage of allowing for implementing a distributed system, supporting "active" engagement, without involving interaction with a screen-based interface during lecture hours (2). We then created several sketches which converged in what is presented in Fig. 1 (part 2). The system consists of one central device that monitors sound level and received input from the teacher and one or more distributed devices that provide feedback to students and receive input from them. The teacher and the students indicate that sonic activity reaches an unacceptable level using a simple button on the device for ease of usability and less distraction. Light and sound are used to show the objectively measured sound level and input from the teacher or the students.

We have also brainstormed ideas about an ambient display. These ranged from simple ideas using emoji's to more complex displays using gamification. The latter involved a visualization of different class groups to students in a game involving ascending a mountain. The intention with the ambient display is to help students self-regulate their behaviour to a lower level in addition to visual light effects and sound. Players advance as long as others do not complain about their sonic activity otherwise, they retreat on their ascent. An ambient display was desired by the teachers and was also found to help reduce average sonic activity levels [8].

Designs were communicated to the teachers. There were some concerns from the teachers that certain elements of the sketches could become a source of distraction for the learners. These are related to the ambient display and buttons to be pushed. They were less concerned about the last resort with sound notification.

Prototyping and Evaluation: Through iterative prototyping we experimented with different ideas of sharable and tangible forms from low fidelity to high-fidelity digital models and refined our designs [9]. Prototyping was based on the scenario of *group work* in an "Arts & Craft" lecture and involved two iterations. We prototyped two IoT devices as shown in Fig. 1 (parts 3 and 4), one central sonic monitoring device equipped with a microphone to monitor the sonic activity in the classroom and receive input from the teacher and one distributed tangible device for obtaining and providing feedback on sonic activity to students.

The central device was equipped with a red led diode and a loudspeaker to visualise the current sonic activity and play an alarm if sonic activity exceeded accepted norms. When the central device registers sonic activity above a user-configured threshold or receives input from the teacher, it sends a signal to the student devices and activates the red led light. The distributed feedback devices were equipped with a push button and led diode light. If the students press the button on a distributed device, a signal is sent to the central device which plays back a loud high-pitched tone into the classroom indicating that sonic activity is too high. The learners are notified by the light if sonic activity level exceeds threshold, or the teacher decides the sonic activity is unacceptable and if another student presses the button audio feedback is generated. The auditory feedback plays for a fixed duration and stops.

The prototype was put together in two prototyping rounds using BBC micro:bit[3] controllers, a small sized computer with easy input and output interfaces to make software

---

[3] Introduction | micro:bit (microbit.org).

and hardware work together wirelessly. In the first prototyping round, we tested basic functionality in the lab with respect to sound level monitoring, light activation, and signal reception and transmission. The second round focused on hiding the electronics and finalizing the distributed device. We made a new design and 3D printed a larger casing to hide wires and the micro:bit IoT device in the learners' feedback device.

An early version of an ambient display that present information thought emoji icons based on sonic activity was also implemented. Different ambient display visualisation is developed as a green smiley emoji, red upset emoji, and a smiley. Another version we tested was a "talking" smiley emoji mimicking the lips movement according to the noise level. The second prototype was tested in a controlled environment while playing an engaging card game called War[4] using the designed solution to demonstrate how learners can regulate their sonic activity behaviour level. The system responded as intended activating the red light when the students behaved loud (shouting etc.). The teacher also responded by pushing the button to activate the sound feedback with a high tone. The students were notified and regulated their activity and behaviour.

4 Discussion

To answer RQ1, we have investigated the design of a smart classroom solution to help students and teachers regulate sonic activity in classrooms based on a user-centred design process involving teachers. We found that it is important that students and teachers can express their opinion on whether sonic activity is disturbing or not, and also be able to interact with the system. In total, based on input from the teachers we ended up with six requirements to implement the system. The system we designed allows students and teachers to indicate whether sonic activity is exceeding acceptable levels but can also monitor sonic activity level in the background and provide feedback as needed. The system provides both visual and auditory feedback based on the level of asonic activity and input by the students and the teachers. Furthermore, we have experimented with designing an ambient display that gives the system a chance to monitor long-term behaviour using principles of gamification.

Concerning *RQ2* addressing *type of techniques that can be used to "silence" a loud room,* we have found out that visual and auditory feedback may be used to indicate the level of sonic activity locally at the devices used by the students and in an ambient way using an ambient display which shows the behaviour emoji icons. We informally observed a positive impact on the situation from our second test and evaluation.

Concerning *RQ3,* the two-way interaction between students and teacher using IoT devices allows a simple but effective way to negotiate the perception of sonic activity and communicate student and teacher perceptions using lights, buttons, emojis, and sound in a classroom setting. We observed informally that allowing for negotiation appears to increase the awareness of class members to sonic activity aspects during *group work* and hope that this will have a positive impact on the learning experience.

Our project provided early prototypes and future work aims to come up with a mature prototype. As a first step, we want to attempt a more systematic evaluation over a longer

---

[4] War – Card Game Rules I Bicycle Playing Cards (bicyclecards.com).

period in a classroom environment. We want to fine tune system parameters, evaluate the usability and appropriateness of the solution, how well it is used by students and teachers, and how well it can merge with the learning process. Furthermore, we want to establish the relevance and importance of different ambient display designs.

5 Conclusion

We have designed and demonstrated early prototypes of IoT devices for helping students and teachers regulated sonic activity. Our system recognizes the subjective nature of sonic activity and in addition to providing objective measurements is also designed to allow students and teachers to indicate whether they are using the design process method, we can conclude that using such a system can be a positive contribution in helping teacher to control and reduce the classroom sonic activity generated by the learners. Using a sonic monitoring system with feedback mechanism and ambient displays can be a positive supplement in classrooms to address sonic activity such as negative noise. Furthermore, the health of both teachers and learners in their long-term exposure of sonic activity can help reducing future health issues and hearing reductions.

References

1. Shield, B.M., Dockrell, J.E.: The effects of environmental and classroom noise on the academic attainments of primary school children. J. Acoust. Soc. Am. **123**(1), 133–144 (2008)
2. Reis, S., Correia, N.: The Perception of Sound and its Influence in the Classroom. In: Campos, Pedro, Graham, Nicholas, Jorge, Joaquim, Nunes, Nuno, Palanque, Philippe, Winckler, Marco (eds.) INTERACT 2011. LNCS, vol. 6946, pp. 609–626. Springer, Heidelberg (2011). https://doi.org/10.1007/978-3-642-23774-4_48
3. Saini, M.K., Goel, N.: How smart are smart classrooms? A review of smart classroom technologies. ACM Comput. Surv. (CSUR) **52**(6), 1–28 (2019)
4. Berglund, B., Lindvall, T., Schwela, D.: Guidelines for community noise: World Health Organization 1999 (2020)
5. Seetha, P., et al.: Effects to teaching environment of noise level in school classrooms (2008)
6. Leo-Ramrez, A., et al.: Solutions to ventilate learning spaces: a review of current CO2 sensors for IoT systems, pp. 1544–1551 (2021)
7. Howard, C.S., Munro, K.J., Plack, C.J.: Listening effort at signal-to-noise ratios that are typical of the school classroom. Int. J. Audiol. **49**(12), 928–932 (2010)
8. Fidncio, V.L.D., Moret, A.L.M., Jacob, R.T.D.S.: Measuring noise in classrooms: a systematic review, pp. 155–158
9. Lyk, P.B., Lyk, M.: Nao as an authority in the classroom: can Nao help the teacher to keep an acceptable noise level? In: Proceedings of the Tenth Annual ACM/IEEE International Conference on Human-Robot Interaction Extended Abstracts (2015)
10. Van Tonder, J., et al.: Effect of visual feedback on classroom noise levels. South Afr. J. Childhood Educ. **5**(3), 1–6 (2015)
11. Prakash, S., Rangasayee, R., Jeethendra, P.: Low cost assistive noise level indicator for facilitating the learning environment of school going children with hearing disability in inclusive educational setup. Indian J. Sci. Technol. **4**(11), 1495–1504 (2011)
12. Tabuenca, B., Borner, D., Kalz, M.: Effects of an ambient learning display on noise levels and perceived learning in a secondary school. IEEE Trans. Learn. Technol. **14**(1), 69–80 (2021)

13. Börner, D., et al.: Tangible interactive ambient display prototypes to support learning scenarios. In: Proceedings of the Ninth International Conference on Tangible, Embedded, and Embodied Interaction (2015)
14. Sharp, H.: Interaction Design. Wiley, Chichester (2003)

Exploring the Effect of Study with Me on Parasocial Interaction and Learning Productivity: Lessons Learned in a Field Study

Yi-Ci Jhuang[1], Yu Hsien Chiu[2], Hsuan-Jen Lee[2], Yen Ting Lee[2], Guan-You Lin[3], Nien-Hsin Wu[2], and Pei-Yi Patricia Kuo[2(✉)] ⓘ

[1] Institute of Systems Neuroscience, National Tsing Hua University, Hsinchu, Taiwan
[2] Institute of Service Science, National Tsing Hua University, Hsinchu, Taiwan
pykuo@iss.nthu.edu.tw
[3] Undergraduate Honors Program for Nano Science and Engineering of Science, National Yang Ming Chiao Tung University, Hsinchu, Taiwan

Abstract. *Study with Me (SWM)* is a popular type of in-real-life (IRL) streaming among students nowadays. Existing research suggests that parasocial interaction could potentially increase viewers' learning productivity. However, limited research examines how watching *SWM* streaming and parasocial interaction help increase one's learning productivity. This paper takes the initiative to investigate how two types of *SWM* content influence participants' learning productivity through a two-week field study. Our data suggested three ways that parasocial interaction with streamers influenced participants' learning productivity – encouragement/ companionship, sense of guilt, and sense of ritual. Moreover, participants' distraction time decreased after watching *SWM* content showing only body parts and environmental sounds, and that female participants' completion rates of study plans increased after watching such *SWM* content. We discuss how *SWM* streaming influenced participants' learning productivity and perceived parasocial interaction, and provide suggestions for further investigation on this topic.

Keywords: Parasocial interaction · Learning productivity · Study with me

1 Introduction

Recently, in-real-life (IRL) streaming is popular among the younger generation. *Study with Me (SWM)*, one kind of IRL content, is becoming a popular tool for students to keep motivated while studying [21]. In *SWM*, the streamers livestream themselves while studying, and this type of streaming content is prevalent worldwide. Research has found that viewers of IRL streams would have parasocial interactions with the streamers [8]. This kind of relationship could provide support to the viewers and has the potential to improve their productivity [1, 16]. However, research is limited regarding how IRL streaming and its content components help people in the context of learning. This study aims to conduct a field study to examine how *SWM* content and streamers influence people's learning productivity through parasocial interaction.

C. Stephanidis et al. (Eds.): HCII 2022, CCIS 1582, pp. 43–49, 2022.
https://doi.org/10.1007/978-3-031-06391-6_6

2 Related Work

2.1 Effect of In-Real-Life (IRL) Streaming Content Components on Parasocial Interaction

In-real-life (IRL) streaming is a popular way for the younger generation to build parasocial relationships with streamers and other viewers [4, 8, 17, 22]. There are many categories of IRL content, including E-sports games, makeup tutorials, and studying. In *SWM* [21], streamers would livestream themselves while studying at the library or home. Most *SWM* streamers are students, and some of them would share their study plans with the viewers on the screen (e.g., preparing for an upcoming exam). Studies have shown that the media performer's bodily addressing style impacts the level of parasocial interaction, and viewers perceive stronger parasocial interaction when performer's face directly looks at them [5, 7]. In the context of *SWM* streaming, streamers would show their faces, parts of their body (e.g., hands), or only virtual figures to represent themselves. Physical attractiveness has also been reported to be a statistically significant predictor of parasocial interaction [7, 12]. Additionally, research has shown that each component in the video has the potential to influence the viewers' experience [19]. For instance, Lo-Fi music in the video makes it easier for viewers to concentrate on their work and helps reduce their anxiety. Timer on the screen provides synchronicity, which stimulates users' perception of co-presence, and leads to the positive result of task impression in the CMC context [15]. Additionally, sharing the study plan information helps learning become more effective [20].

2.2 Effect of Parasocial Interaction on Productivity

Existing research has shown that parasocial interaction could potentially increase one's learning productivity, as it can enhance one's intrinsic motivation while attaining a goal [6, 14]. Although parasocial interaction was originally defined to describe the one-sided relationship people form with television personas, new media such as in-real-life (IRL) streaming videos on YouTube and Twitch have blurred the line between a real person and a media personality [19]. Building on these empirical findings, the study aims to examine how parasocial interaction with *SWM* streamers and *SWM* content components help increase one's learning productivity.

3 Methods

3.1 Study Design and Procedure

To examine how different *SWM* content influence people's parasocial interaction and learning productivity, two types of *SWM* videos were created by adapting existing videos and obtaining permissions from owners of two popular YouTube channels [13, 18]. These two types of *SWM* videos contain different content components according to prior work [5, 7, 15, 19, 20] (Fig. 1). Content A (for condition 2) features the streamer's face, environmental sounds, and the additional contextual information components (clock, study plans, Lo-Fi music) which were added to the original video during our post-production editing. Content B (for condition 3) features only the hands of the streamer and environmental sounds. To work with the *SWM* content available on the Internet and for this study's purpose, we focus on assessing how showing a streamer's face versus his/her body part (hands) and the additional contextual information components influence users differently. We assume that content A with all components would yield higher level of parasocial interaction and learning productivity based on prior studies [5, 7, 15, 19, 20].

Table 1. Overview of study design (three study conditions).

Condition	Number of participants	Week 1	Week 2
1	7 (P1 - P7)	Make study plan	Make study plan
2	8 (P8 - P15)	Make study plan	Make study plan + *SWM* (A)
3	8 (P16 - P23)	Make study plan	Make study plan + *SWM* (B)

Fig. 1. Screenshots of the two types of *SWM* content (Content A and B).

We conducted a 2-week field study to examine how watching *SWM* streaming influences participants' learning productivity by randomly assigning participants into three conditions – the control condition (condition 1) and two experimental conditions (conditions 2 and 3) (Table 1). Twenty-four participants were recruited and consented to participate in this study (12 males and 12 females, aged between 22 and 25). We recruited people who: (1) are graduate students, (2) did not have prior experience of watching *SWM* videos, and (3) are willing to spend 1.5 h studying every day. One participant from condition 1 was excluded from data analysis due to data incompleteness.

In terms of study procedure, for the first week all participants across three study conditions were instructed to set their daily study plan(s) that can be achieved in 1.5 h every day. At the end of each day, they were asked to self- evaluate the percentage of completion of their daily plan(s) (out of 100%), and provide a brief written response to describe their progress. For the second week, participants in conditions 2 and 3 were instructed to join a *SWM* streaming for 1.5 h every day via an invite link while fulfilling their daily study plan(s). The procedure of setting daily study plans was the same as the first week, and the daily plans should be accomplished during the livestream. Participants in condition 1 performed the same procedure as the first week.

3.2 Measurements and Post-study Interview

We collected both objective and subject data from participants regarding their learning productivity to minimize bias [9]: (1) Objective data - participants' daily smartphone screen usage data during the 1.5-h study periods, as mobile phone distraction occurs most frequently during studying [2]. Distraction time in minutes was then calculated based on the total length of time when participants used applications not related to their study plans. (2) Subjective data - participants' daily self-reported completion rate of their daily study plan(s) out of 100%. (3) Participants' parasocial interaction scores using the PSI scale on a 5-point Likert scale [3, 5]. We also conducted post-study interviews with 8 participants from groups 2 and 3. Questions mainly focus on their feelings and reactions toward the *SWM* content and streamers, as well as their study participation experience.

4 Results

4.1 Qualitative Results

Effects of *SWM* on Parasocial Interaction and Learning Productivity. Our interview data revealed three ways the parasocial interaction with streamers influenced participants' learning productivity –encouragement/companionship, sense of guilt, and sense of ritual. First, some participants felt encouraged by the streamer, increasing their intrinsic motivation to study ("...... *if he could make it, why could I not?*"-P14). The feeling of encouragement was also accompanied by the feeling of companionship ("*I felt that he was with me, so I was not alone.*"-P22). Second, almost all of our interviewees mentioned that they were tempted to check whether live streamers focused on finishing their plans when feeling distracted. By doing so, a sense of guilt occurred when participants found the live streamers still strived to work hard ("*Somewhat it became a pressure because other people were still learning, and I felt bad for giving up.*"- P19). Third, P9 and P19 mentioned that joining *SWM* was like a ritual to begin studying, and helped them concentrate on finishing their daily plans ("*Watching SWM streaming was similar to pressing the 'start' button on my Pomodoro clock to switch myself into study mode.*"-P9).

Reactions Toward the SWM Content and Streamer. Some participants viewed the streamers as their study partners, and paid attention to what the streamers were studying. They would be more engaged if streamers were studying what was similar to them. As for the audio component, most participants in condition 2 reported that the Lo-Fi music helped them feel relaxed and focused (P12, P13, P14). However, the acceptance of pure environmental sounds (e.g., sound of turning pages) in condition 3 varied by participants' personal preference and prior study habit. We received positive feedback from our participants regarding the clock component. Paying attention to the clock made it easier for participants to assess their time management and helped them conceptualize their study efforts. Moreover, all participants found the streamers were hardworking, yet several participants in both condition 2 and 3 held subjective comments on streamers' appearance (P9, P12, P15, P16). It appears that participants reacted positively to all contextual information components (clock, study plan, Lo-Fi music), while streamers' appearance is the only component involving mixed opinions.

4.2 Quantitative Results: Effect of *SWM* on Distraction Time, Study Plan Completion Rate, PSI Score

The mean distraction time of those in condition 3 during week 2 was significantly lower than week 1 ($t(7) = 3.95, p = 0.01$) according to the paired sample t-test. Watching *SWM* in content B (streamer showing hands instead of face, no additional component added) significantly decreased their distraction time. We also found that whether watching *SWM* streaming or not did not influence participants' self-reported mean completion rates of the daily plans in general. However, we found that female participants in condition 3 had significantly increased their study plan completion rates during week 2 ($t(7) = 3.18$, $p = 0.03$). Furthermore, our results suggested that the average PSI score of those in condition 3 (2.45) was higher than those in condition 2 (2.13), though this did not reach a statistically significant level.

5 Discussion

5.1 Effect of *SWM* on Completion Rate, Distraction Time and PSI Score

The mean completion rates of study plans did not increase after participants watched *SWM* in conditions 2 and 3. Our qualitative and quantitative data suggested that this was possibly driven by participants' preferences toward the *SWM* streamers and content (opinion toward streamers' appearance influenced their engagement and thus learning productivity). However, contrary to our original assumption, we found that *SWM* content containing body parts (content B) instead of face helped increase the completion rates of female participants in condition 3. Positive outcome was also observed in terms of the reduction in distraction time during week two from participants in condition 3, regardless of gender. To our surprise, participants' PSI scores did not influence their completion rate nor distraction time in conditions 2 and 3, contrary to prior studies [5, 7]. Our interview data suggested this may be attributed to a lack of freedom to choose their preferred streamer's video (gender, appearance, content), or understanding of streamers' background. Importantly, although we found that certain *SWM* content (e.g., streamer's face/ body parts, clock, study plan) influenced participants' perceived parasocial interaction, the questions in the PSI scale used in this study did not capture these effects. For instance, one question item asks about participants' impression toward the streamer's appearance, yet it does not specify whether appearance refers to the face or certain body part of the streamer. We believe this information is important to tease out the factors influencing participants' PSI scores in the context of *SWM* streaming.

5.2 Participants' Reactions Toward the *SWM* Streamer and Content

Our data suggested that showing streamer's face or his/her body part positively influenced participants' parasocial interaction and their learning productivity. As prior studies did not touch base on how one's parasocial interaction can be influenced by streamer's face versus his/her body part(s) in terms of appearance [5, 7, 12], more research with larger sample size is needed to see how our findings can be generalized. In addition, participants in both conditions 2 and 3 showed their curiosity about the streamers' study content. They indicated sharing similar study content is an important driver to build parasocial interaction with the streamers, which is in line with prior studies about sharing similar activities to perceive social support [10, 11]. Furthermore, although one's reactions to environmental sounds was primarily driven by his/her prior learning habits, all participants in condition 2 indicated the Lo-Fi music helped them stay focused, consistent with [19], but they hope the variety of music can be increased. As for those in condition 3, one's prior familiarity with environmental sounds such as white noise or book flipping tend to influence one's acceptance of these sounds.

6 Limitations, Conclusion, and Future Work

This study explores how *SWM* video content influences people's parasocial interaction and learning productivity via a two-week field study. There are two primary limitations. First, a field study with a larger sample size is needed to help generalize our findings. Second, the way we collected participants' distraction time could extend from phone usage data to other technology devices. We also plan to develop more diverse ways to measure learning productivity. As part of the future work, we will further examine how the gender of streamers influences people's engagement and reactions, as well as to what extent the effect of parasocial interaction on learning productivity can sustain over time.

Acknowledgement. We thank our study participants for their useful feedback and participation, and owners of the two YouTube channels for sharing the *SWM* content with us. This work was supported by the Ministry of Science and Technology in Taiwan (MOST grant 109–2221-E-007–063-MY3).

References

1. Baruch-Feldman, C., Brondolo, E., Ben-Dayan, D., Schwartz, J.: Sources of social support and burnout, job satisfaction, and productivity. J. Occup. Health Psychol. **7**, 84–93 (2002). https://doi.org/10.1037//1076-8998.7.1.84
2. David, P., Kim, J.-H., Brickman, J., Ran, W., Curtis, C.: Mobile phone distraction while studying. New Media Soc. **17** (2014). https://doi.org/10.1177/1461444814531692
3. de Bérail, P., Guillon, M., Bungener, C.: The relations between YouTube addiction, social anxiety and parasocial relationships with YouTubers: a moderated-mediation model based on a cognitive-behavioral framework. Comput. Hum. Behav. **99**, 190–204 (2019). https://doi.org/10.1016/j.chb.2019.05.007

4. Derrick, J.L., Gabriel, S., Hugenberg, K.: Social surrogacy: how favored television programs provide the experience of belonging. J. Exp. Soc. Psychol. **45**(2), 352–362 (2009). https://doi.org/10.1016/j.jesp.2008.12.003

5. Dibble, J., Hartmann, T., Rosaen, S.: Parasocial interaction and parasocial relationship: conceptual clarification and a critical assessment of measures. Hum. Commun. Res. **42** (2015), https://doi.org/10.1111/hcre.12063

6. Frost, J., Boukris, N., Roelofsma, P.: We like to move it move it! motivation and parasocial interaction. In: CHI 2012 Extended Abstracts on Human Factors in Computing Systems, pp. 2465–2470 (2012)

7. Hartmann, T., Goldhoorn, C.: Horton and wohl revisited: exploring viewers' experience of parasocial interaction. J. Commun. **61**, 1104–1121 (2011). https://doi.org/10.1111/j.1460-2466.2011.01595.x

8. Horton, D., Wohl, R.R.: Mass communication and para-social interaction: observations on intimacy at a distance. Psychiatry **19**(3), 215–229 (1956). https://doi.org/10.1080/00332747.1956.11023049

9. Kim, K.R., Seo, E.H.: The relationship between procrastination and academic performance: a meta-analysis. Person. Indiv. Diff. **82**, 26–33 (2015). https://doi.org/10.1016/j.paid.2015.02.038

10. Lakey, B., Cooper, C., Cronin, A., Whitaker, T.: Symbolic providers help people regulate affect relationally: implications for perceived support. Pers. Relat. **21**(3), 404–419 (2014). https://doi.org/10.1111/pere.12038

11. Lakey, B., Orehek, E.: Relational regulation theory: a new approach to explain the link between perceived social support and mental health. Psychol. Rev. **118**(3), 482 (2011). https://doi.org/10.1037/a0023477

12. Lee, J.E., Watkins, B.: YouTube vloggers' influence on consumer luxury brand perceptions and intentions. J. Bus. Res. **69**(12), 5753–5760 (2016). https://doi.org/10.1016/j.jbusres.2016.04.171

13. Merve. https://www.youtube.com/channel/UCkPgEucgqedbckpzC2EUwIA

14. Ng, J.Y.Y., et al.: Self-determination theory applied to health contexts: a meta-analysis. Perspect. Psychol. Sci. **7**(4), 325–340 (2012). https://doi.org/10.1177/1745691612447309

15. Park, E., Shyam Sundar, S.: Can synchronicity and visual modality enhance social presence in mobile messaging? Comput. Hum. Behav. **45** (2015). https://doi.org/10.1016/j.chb.2014.12.001

16. Park, K.-O., Wilson, M., Lee, M.: Effects of social support at work on depression and organizational productivity. Am. J. Health Behav. **28**, 444–455 (2004). https://doi.org/10.5993/AJHB.28.5.7

17. Rubin, A.M., Step, M.M.: Impact of motivation, attraction, and parasocial interaction on talk radio listening. J. Broadcast. Electron. Media **44**(4), 635–654 (2000). https://doi.org/10.1207/s15506878jobem4404_7

18. Kin Thong Life Space. https://www.youtube.com/channel/UC8_o9aFpknEMck7D43E5Zww

19. Taber, L., Baltaxe-Admony, L.B., Weatherwax, K.: What makes a live stream companion? Animation, beats, and parasocial relationships. Interactions **27**(1), 52–57 (2019). https://doi.org/10.1145/3372042

20. Vonderwell, S., Zachariah, S.: Factors that influence participation in online learning. J. Res. Technol. Educ. **38**(2), 213–230 (2005). https://doi.org/10.1080/15391523.2005.10782457

21. Welsh. R.: Study with me: YouTube trend gives students new study tools (2017). https://digitalalberta.com/. Accessed 16 Dec 2020

22. Wohn, D.Y., Freeman, G., McLaughlin, C.: Explaining viewers' emotional, instrumental, and financial support provision for live streamers. City (2018)

Development of Fingering Learning Support System Using Fingertip Tracking from Monocular Camera

Takuya Kishimoto and Masataka Imura$^{(\boxtimes)}$

Kwansei Gakuin University, 2-1 Gakuen, Sanda, Hyogo 669-1337, Japan
imu15563@kwansei.ac.jp

Abstract. In recent years, as smartphones have become a part of life of young generation, opportunities to enter text using keyboards have decreased, and the speed of keyboard text entry has declined. However, it is still necessary for young children to use keyboards. In typing using a keyboard, the correspondence between keys and fingers is defined; however, there is no practical system for learning fingering to press keys with the correct fingers. A general typing learning software can only judge whether the correct input has been given or not and does not consider the correct fingering of the keys. If the system can evaluate fingering when learning typing, the user can concentrate on typing without having to judge the correctness of their own fingering. In previous research, there have been methods to acquire fingertip coordinates by attaching color stickers to fingers as markers or by using a distance camera, but these methods lack versatility. In this study, we used a monocular camera to acquire fingertip images on a keyboard. After obtaining images, we used MediaPipe to perform hand tracking and obtain the position of the fingertip. For each frame, the system calculates the distance between each key coordinate and each fingertip coordinate, determines that the closest finger hits the key, and feeds back the fingering information.

Keywords: Touch typing · Hand tracking · Image processing

1 Introduction

In recent years, smartphones and tablet devices have facilitated several tasks such as e-mail, searching, and writing. As smartphones have become a part of young people's lives, opportunities to use keyboards to input text have decreased, and the keyboard input speed of young people has declined [1]. However, keyboarding remains a necessary skill in productive work. Keyboarding is also becoming increasingly important at younger ages, as the Courses of Study were revised in 2017 and 2018 and programming education was introduced into elementary schools in Japan.

Keyboard typing practice software is already in use. However, existing typing practice software can only determine whether the correct input was made and

© The Author(s), under exclusive license to Springer Nature Switzerland AG 2022
C. Stephanidis et al. (Eds.): HCII 2022, CCIS 1582, pp. 50–56, 2022.
https://doi.org/10.1007/978-3-031-06391-6_7

does not consider the correct fingering of the keystrokes, that is, whether or not the keys were struck with the proper fingers. Because fingering decisions are made by the user and not by the system, the learning of fingering is not supported. If the system could automatically evaluate fingering when practicing typing, it would be ideal for learning, allowing the user to concentrate on typing without having to judge the fingerings themselves.

2   Related Research

To support the learning of fingering in typing, it is necessary to determine which fingers hit the keys. Masson et al. have proposed a method of attaching vibration sensors to fingers [2]. Although the accuracy of recognizing the finger that struck the key is high, the device has the disadvantage of being highly constrained because of its glove-like shape. In addition to finger sensors, there are other methods that measure the position of the fingertip during keystrokes and use fingertip position information to estimate the finger to be used for keystrokes. Soga et al. constructed a system that recognizes typed fingers by attaching colored stickers as markers to the fingertips of typing learners and using a webcam to capture their hands as they type [3]. The authors have proposed a method to obtain fingertip coordinates without markers using a distance sensor [4]; however, the distance sensor is not widely used and the system lacks versatility.

In this study, we aim to maintain the simplicity of the system and estimate the keystroke finger by acquiring fingertip coordinates without using a marker.

3   Proposed Method

3.1   System Overview

In this study, to learn proper fingering when typing, we construct a system that supports learning by feeding back correct fingering information when typing with incorrect fingering and prompting the user to type again. The configuration of the system is shown in Fig. 1. A monocular camera is placed on the display to measure the fingertip coordinates while typing, such that the keyboard is visible. The process flow of the proposed method is shown in Fig. 2. First, an RGB image of the hand on the keyboard is acquired using a monocular camera. Because the keyboard and hands are not facing the camera, the acquired image is converted to an image taken from above the keyboard by homographic transformation. From the transformed image, the fingertip coordinates are estimated by machine learning and compared with the previously acquired coordinates of each key to estimate the fingers to be used for keystrokes. The fingers are compared with the correct fingers, and the fingering information is fed back to the learner.

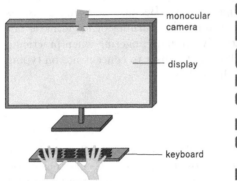

Fig. 1. Configuration of the proposed system

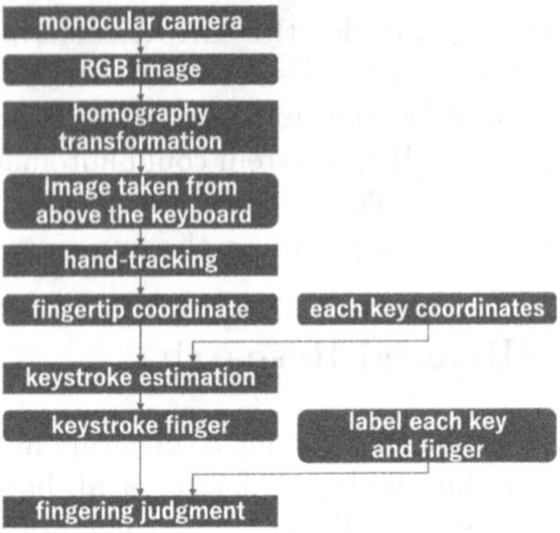

Fig. 2. Process flow of the proposed method

3.2 Method Used to Obtain Key Coordinates

To estimate the fingers that hit the keys, the proposed system acquired the coordinates of each key on the keyboard in advance. First, the displacement vector d_x of the key interval is calculated as

$$d_x = \frac{p_x - q_x}{n}. \tag{1}$$

Because the keys on the keyboard are evenly lined in the horizontal direction, the coordinates p_x and q_x of the keys at both ends of each row were obtained, and the displacement vector d_x of the key spacing was calculated by dividing the difference between the coordinates obtained by n and the number of key spacings in each row. The remaining key coordinates were obtained by summing d_x for the key interval with the leftmost key.

3.3 Method Employed to Determine Fingering

To determine which finger struck a key when it was pressed, the distance between the coordinates of each fingertip at the time the key was pressed and the coordinates of the key that was pressed, ware calculated. The finger closest to the input key is considered to have struck the key. To determine if the finger is the correct finger, the correspondence between each key and finger is stored in advance, and when a key is hit, it is compared with the finger to determine if the input is made with proper fingering.

4   Implementation

In this section, we describe the implementation of the proposed system. The flow-up to obtain the fingertip coordinates is as follows:

 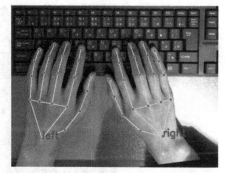

Fig. 3. Image acquired from monocular camera

Fig. 4. Image after hand tracking

1. Acquire an image from the monocular camera (Fig. 3).
2. Obtains the coordinates of the four corners of the keyboard and performs a homographic transformation.
3. Flip the homographically transformed image left and right.
4. Perform hand tracking using the machine learning framework MediaPipe.
5. Flip the image left and right after hand-tracking (Fig. 4).

4.1 Homographic Transformation

We wanted to set up a camera above the keyboard and use the image taken from above the keyboard as the input image for hand tracking; however, physical limitations prevented us from setting up a camera above the keyboard. The keyboard is considered to be a plane, and a homographic transformation[5] is performed to obtain an image captured from above the keyboard. The homography matrix H is a 3×3 matrix, and the points (X, Y) in the transformed image corresponding to the points (x, y) in the pre-transformed image can be found by:

$$\lambda \begin{bmatrix} X \\ Y \\ 1 \end{bmatrix} = H \begin{bmatrix} x \\ y \\ 1 \end{bmatrix}. \tag{2}$$

If the correspondences between the four points are known, the homography matrix H can be found, and the proposed system can determine the correspondence of the points at the four corners of the keyboard. The coordinates of the four corners of the image before homographic transformation were measured manually and set such that the top left corner of the keyboard was at the top left corner of the window. The result of superimposing the acquired key coordinates on the image after homographic transformation is shown in Fig. 5. It can be seen that each key coordinate was obtained correctly.

Fig. 5. Result of superimposing key coordinates

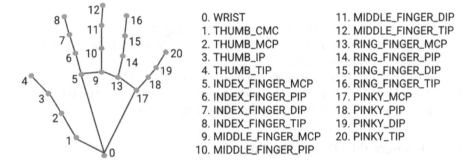

0. WRIST	11. MIDDLE_FINGER_DIP
1. THUMB_CMC	12. MIDDLE_FINGER_TIP
2. THUMB_MCP	13. RING_FINGER_MCP
3. THUMB_IP	14. RING_FINGER_PIP
4. THUMB_TIP	15. RING_FINGER_DIP
5. INDEX_FINGER_MCP	16. RING_FINGER_TIP
6. INDEX_FINGER_PIP	17. PINKY_MCP
7. INDEX_FINGER_DIP	18. PINKY_PIP
8. INDEX_FINGER_TIP	19. PINKY_DIP
9. MIDDLE_FINGER_MCP	20. PINKY_TIP
10. MIDDLE_FINGER_PIP	

Fig. 6. Hand landmarks [7]

4.2 Machine Learning Framework

In this implementation, we used MediaPipe [6] for fingertip detection from camera images, which is an open-source machine learning solution framework provided by Google Inc. We used MediaPipe Hands [7], which is specialized for tracking hands.

MediaPipe Hands assumes that the image is taken from the palm side by the front camera of the smartphone and processes it; however, in the proposed system, the image is taken from the dorsal side of the hand, so the left and right sides are reversed. Therefore, if the camera image is input directly to the MediaPipe, the detected hand orientation will be reversed. The input image for hand tracking is flipped left-to-right and aligned with the image orientation assumed by MediaPipe to compensate for the detected hand orientation.

MediaPipe Hands detects the palm from a single frame captured by a monocular camera and estimates 21 3D hand coordinates (Fig. 6) within the detected hand region. The x and y coordinates are normalized from 0 to 1 according to the width and height of the input image, and the z coordinate represents the relative depth with respect to the wrist, which decreases the closer it is to the camera.

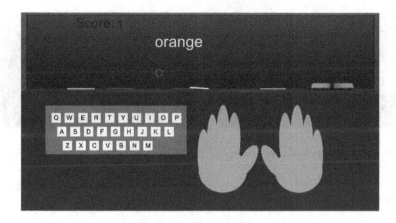

Fig. 7. Typing screen

4.3   Investigation of Device Configuration and Keystroke Finger Estimation Performance

A monocular camera (C270n, Logicool) was used to capture the hands on the keyboard. The frame rate of the camera was up to 30 fps and the size of the acquired image was 640 × 480 pixels. Python was used to acquire images from the camera and estimate the fingers, and Unity 2020.3.25f1 was used to build the typing system. The system determines whether the finger used is the appropriate one for the particular key.

To determine the degree of error between the fingertip coordinates of a keypress and the key coordinates, a test was conducted three times to accurately type 100 letters of the alphabet. The experimental results showed that the average distance between the fingertip coordinates of the typing finger and the key coordinates was approximately 3.9 mm, with a standard deviation of approximately 1.8 mm, a high enough accuracy for the keyboard key pitch of 19 mm. On an average, the finger was estimated to have an accuracy of approximately 99%.

4.4   Implementation of a Typing Learning System

The typing screen of the constructed typing-learning support system is shown in Fig. 7. The white text in the upper center of the screen is the question text and the red text is the user's answer. If the user types with the wrong finger, the character input fails, and the screen displays the correct finger in red, as shown in the lower-right corner of Fig. 8, prompting the user to type the character again with the appropriate finger. If an incorrect key is entered, the correct key is displayed in red, as shown in the lower left of Fig. 9.

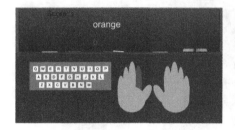
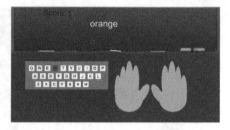

Fig. 8. Feedback on fingering errors   **Fig. 9.** Feedback on typing errors

5   Conclusion

In this paper, we proposed a system to support the learning of typing finger motions by tracking fingertips using a monocular camera. Unlike conventional fingering learning support systems, this system was developed with emphasis on versatility, noncontact, and simplicity. Experiments have shown that the proposed system is highly accurate in estimating keystroke fingers. In the future, we will conduct evaluation experiments using the proposed system and a general typing learning system to prove that learning using the proposed system is more effective in learning fingering. We also aimed to acquire information on eye gaze, which is important for learning typing, and to build a more efficient typing learning system.

References

1. Miyoshi, Y., Kosakai, M.: A study of computer literacy education and keyboard input. Saitama Women's Junior Colle. Res. Bull. **39**, 85–92 (2019)
2. Damien, M., Goguey, A., Malacria, S., Casiez, G.: WhichFingers: identifying fingers on touch surfaces and keyboards using vibration sensors. In: Proceedings of the 30th annual ACM symposium on User Interface Software and Technology, pp. 41–48 (2017). https://doi.org/10.1145/3126594.3126619
3. Soga, S., Tamura, T., Taki, H.: Development of a typing skill learning environment with diagnosis and advice on fingering errors. Procedia Comput. Sci. **22**, 737–744 (2013). https://doi.org/10.1016/j.procs.2013.09.155
4. Kishimoto, T., Imura, M.: Construction of a learning support system for proper fingering in typing practice. In: Proceedings of the 83rd National Convention of Information Processing Society of Japan, No. 1, pp. 713–714 (2021)
5. Hartley, R., Zisserman, A.: Multiple View Geometry in Computer Vision. Cambridge University Press, Cambridge (2003)
6. MediaPipe (2020). https://google.github.io/mediapipe/
7. MediaPipeHands (2020). https://google.github.io/mediapipe/solutions/hands.html

Scaffolding, State-Based Modeling, and Multiple Representation: User Interface Concepts Implemented in an Interactive Online Learning Environment for Synergistic Learning of Physics and Computational Thinking

Midori Kitagawa[1]([✉]), Paul Fishwick[1], Mary Urquhart[1], Michael Kesden[1], Rosanna Guadagno[2], Kieth Gryder[1], Ngoc Tran[3], Alex Najera[1], and Diego Ochoa[1]

[1] University of Texas at Dallas, Dallas, TX 75252, USA
{midori,Paul.Fishwick,Urquhart,kesden,Kieth.Gryder,Alex.Najera,
Diego.Ochoa}@utdallas.edu
[2] University of Oulu, 90014 Oulu, Finland
[3] ActionIQ, New York, NY 10010, USA
mike.tran@actioniq.com

Abstract. With funding from the NSF STEM + Computing Program, an interdisciplinary team of faculty and student researchers collaborated on development of our Scaffolded Training Environment for Physics Programming (STEPP). STEPP is a synergistic learning environment for high school and college students in introductory physics courses to acquire physics concepts and Computational Thinking (CT) through formative experiences modeling and simulating kinematics using modeling tools based on Finite State Machines (FSMs). Three STEPP learning modules have been developed on 1D kinematics, 2D kinematics, and the Newton's Laws of Motion. The modules have been field tested with physics teachers and students at several high schools and a university and are available to the public. The use of FSMs, coupled with the scaffolded approach of STEPP, allows STEPP to provide students with simulations that are physically accurate yet initially described by natural-language states in accord with their intuition. The STEPP architecture is based on scaffolding. Scaffolding in the modules allows the student to understand physics concepts through increasingly detailed module designs. Such concepts include displacement, velocity, and acceleration. In each level of each module, students model physics problems as FSMs and see the resulting simulations displayed in a variety of representation methods: animations, graphs, vectors, free-body diagrams, numbers, and equations, all of which are displayed synchronously. We focus on three user-interface features grounded in educational theories and implemented in STEPP: FSM-based modeling, software-enabled scaffolding, and multiple representations, all of which are applicable to educational applications in many disciplines.

Keywords: Scaffolding · State-based modeling · Multiple representations · Physics · Computational thinking · Simulation · Finite State Machine · STEM

© The Author(s), under exclusive license to Springer Nature Switzerland AG 2022
C. Stephanidis et al. (Eds.): HCII 2022, CCIS 1582, pp. 57–64, 2022.
https://doi.org/10.1007/978-3-031-06391-6_8

1 Introduction: STEPP

The Next Generation Science Standards (NGSS) [1] identify "Developing and using models" and "Use of mathematics and computational thinking (CT)" as two core practices of science and engineering. Although educators, researchers, and policy makers widely recognize the importance of modeling and CT or "the thought processes involved in formulating problems and their solutions so that the solutions are represented in a form that can be effectively carried out by an information-processing agent [2]," the introduction of these concepts into K-12 STEM education is still in an early stage. With funding from the NSF STEM + Computing Program, an interdisciplinary team of faculty and student researchers (graduate and undergraduate students) from Arts & Technology, Computer Science, Physics, Science/Math Education, and Psychology, along with high school physics and computer science teachers are collaborating on development of a Scaffolded Training Environment for Physics Programming (STEPP). STEPP is a synergistic learning environment for high school and college students in introductory physics courses to acquire physics concepts and computational thinking (CT) through formative experiences modeling and simulating kinematics using modeling tools based on Finite State Machines (FSMs).

Scaffolding is an instructional method with two key aspects: (a) providing structure and support for completing the task, and (b) gradually removing supports so that the student can independently solve the problem [3]. **Finite State Machines** (FSMs) [4–6] are a method for state-based modeling and have been used to design algorithms and teach programming and engineering in Computer Science. We have hypothesized that FSMs are extremely effective in teaching CT because FSMs facilitate students to learn all integral elements of CT that include abstraction, structured problem decomposition, iterative/recursive thinking, conditional logic, efficiency, and debugging [3]. Scaffolding and dynamic modeling with FSMs allow students to focus on the aspects of CT that support physics learning, e.g., problem decomposition, abstraction, and algorithms, instead of the aspects that are mainly about programming.

The research team opted for minimal cost and ease of use to promote the adoption of STEPP in physics classes across the United States and looked for portable, affordable, and readily available technology. The Unity game engine was chosen as STEPP's platform because Unity supports a variety of platforms and offers a wide range of ready-to-use functions, components, and plug-ins for animations, simulations, interactions, and user-activity data collection. Moreover, Unity is free for academic use.

Three STEPP learning modules have been developed focusing on 1D kinematics, 2D kinematics, and Newton's Laws of Motion. STEPP is a web application ready to run in a web browser on a laptop or a desktop computer using the Unity game engine. The modules have been field tested with physics teachers and students at high schools and a university and are available to the public at https://stepp.utdallas.edu. The use of FSMs, coupled with a scaffolded approach, allows STEPP to provide students with simulations that are physically accurate yet initially described by natural-language states in accord with their intuition. As physical concepts like displacement, velocity, and acceleration are introduced at increasingly higher levels of each module, students learn how their intuitive states of motion can be more rigorously defined in the language of physics. In each level of each module, students model physics problems as FSMs and see the resulting simulations displayed in a variety of representations: animations, graphs, vectors, free-body diagrams, numbers, and equations, all of which are displayed synchronously. Thus, STEPP is multi-representational. Here we present the following three user-interface features grounded in educational theories and implemented in STEPP: FSM-based modeling, software-enabled scaffolding, and multiple representations, all of which are applicable to educational applications in many disciplines.

2   FSM-Based Modeling and Simulations

There are numerous simulation programs for understanding physics. One early platform called Physlets is now in its 3rd edition [8]. Another major effort is the PhET interactive simulations for physics [9]. Both Physlets and PhET are impressive in terms of scope and ease of use. A main benefit is to supplement classroom instruction with simulations that are interactive in nature. A student can learn about velocity, acceleration, and forces through virtual experimentation on a computer.

The practice of interactive simulations fits within the field of modeling [10, 11]. The simulations use models of physical behavior, in the form of pictures and animations. There are no formal modeling techniques in Physlets or PhET other than equations or equational terms. Equations and mathematical notation are the lingua franca of natural science and physics, so the use of this notation for modeling is standard practice. And yet, can we improve upon the modeling practice through insights gained from decades of modeling and simulation, and the systems approaches therein? We oriented the design of STEPP toward visual programming through the use of FSMs. The parlance of visual programming is similar to system modeling where the system model is diagrammed. The state machine comes from computer science and is found in academic subjects such as digital design (sequential machines), software engineering (e.g. state diagram in the Unified Modeling Language), and automata theory within the Chomsky hierarchy of machines and languages.

An FSM is designed to achieve a task or series of tasks. It consists of a discrete set of states and a set of conditions that trigger transitions between these states. The machine can only be in one of these states at any given time. Figure 1 shows how an FSM built in the first level of STEPP Module 1 with three states. In STEPP, transitions are represented by green triangles and the current state is indicated by a yellow outline.

Fig. 1. FSM in STEPP with three states. (Color figure online)

The main hypothesis behind our grant proposal was that the state machine could be a useful, discrete mathematical method for describing and learning about physical behavior. Since classical physical quantities vary continuously with time, using FSMs to model physical systems by way of sequences of discrete states separated by event transitions is novel in high school physics classes. Since the inception of the project, the research team considered other types of models. For instance, object-oriented design models were originally thought to be a useful way for the student to organize knowledge about physical scenarios. While we have yet to employ this type of design, we have embarked on a scaffolded modeling approach based on conceptual modeling [11, 12]. As described in the next section, the students begin with natural-language constructs about the kinematic system. They gradually turn the natural language (e.g., moving left, speeding up) into physics nomenclature (e.g., velocity, acceleration) and then construct a linear state diagram where the states last for discrete time intervals and the transitional events are based on Boolean conditions involving time, displacement, or velocity.

3   Software-Enabled Scaffolding

In this section, we will illustrate scaffolding using Module 1 (1D kinematics) which is divided into five separate levels in our scaffolded approach. Figure 2 shows Level 1's interface and Fig. 3 shows Level 4's interface. While a soccer ball was used to create the screen capture in Fig. 2 and a chicken in Fig. 3, students can choose different character objects such as a helicopter, a human, a car or a train. In the interfaces of all three STEPP Modules, the upper panel displays the animation (simulation) when the play button is clicked and displays resizable moveable removeable graphs that are dynamically drawn, synchronized with the animation.

Fig. 2. Module 1 Level 1 Interface   **Fig. 3.** Module 1 Level 4 Interface

While no graphs are available in Level 1, position, velocity, and acceleration graphs become available in Levels 2, 3, and 4 respectively (Fig. 3). The middle portion of the lower panel is used to create an FSM. When a state or transition is created or selected, a variable table that is used to input values into the selected state or transition pops up (Fig. 5, 7 and 9). Transitions are introduced in Level 3, and the number of variables increases at higher levels. A yellow border appears around the current state when the simulation (i.e. FSM) is running (Fig. 1), and the trail of the character object in the simulation and graph lines are color-coded with the colors that match the colors of the states (Fig. 2 and 3). While only current time is displayed in the upper right corner in Level 1 (Fig. 2), current time, position, velocity and acceleration are displayed in the upper right corner in Level 4 (Fig. 3). STEPP uses a FSM, simulation, graphs, and numerical data to represent the same physical situation; hence, STEPP is multi-representational. Let us describe each level of Module 1 in more detail.

Level 1 provides students with pre-built states described in natural language (Fig. 4). Students string these states together into an FSM and then run this FSM to produce a simulation of a 1D system (Fig. 1). There is no variable to input at this level.

Level 2 introduces displacement, the vectorial change in the position of an object. The total distance traveled by an object is the sum of the magnitudes of the individual displacements. States in Level 2 are described by their displacements, i.e., students enter a single real number to assign the initial position of the first state and a single real number to assign the displacement of each state (Fig. 5). Transitions between states are implemented automatically after each displacement. The speed is fixed, so the time spent in each state is proportional to the magnitude of the displacement. Students can watch a graph of the position as a function of time (Fig. 6) as the simulation occurs.

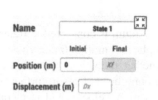

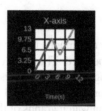

Fig. 4. Pre-built states available from a menu in Level 1

Fig. 5. A variable table for a state of an FSM in Level 2

Fig. 6. A graph of the position as a function of time

Level 3 introduces instantaneous velocity, the time rate of change of displacement. Speed is the magnitude of the instantaneous velocity, while the average velocity is the total displacement over a time interval divided by the length of that interval. States in Level 3 are described by their instantaneous velocity, which is constant within each state but can differ from state to state. Students need to specify the velocity of each state, the initial time and position at the start of the first state of the FSM (Fig. 7), the time or position at which transitions between states occur (Fig. 7 and 8), and the time or position at the end of the final state in variable tables for states. In addition to velocity and speed, this level also teaches important CT skills by introducing the Boolean logic that governs state transitions which are no longer automatic. Students can specify the time or position at which transitions between states occur in variable tables for transitions (Fig. 9). The system transitions between states (a change in instantaneous velocity) if the condition specified for that event is satisfied. These conditions may not be satisfied, such as if a state with negative instantaneous velocity is assigned to end when its final position is larger than its initial position. Students are given helpful hints when transitions fail to be realized, teaching them to "debug" models of nonphysical behavior corresponding to FSMs that fail to reach the final state. Students can watch graphs of the position and instantaneous velocity as functions of time as these simulations occur; the velocity is stepwise constant while the position is a sequence of continuous line segments.

Level 4 introduces acceleration, the rate at which velocity changes with respect to time. States in Level 4 are described by their acceleration, which is constant within each state but can differ from state to state. Students specify the initial time, position, and velocity at the start of the first state of the FSM, the time, position, or velocity at which transitions between states occur, and the time, position, or velocity at the end of the final state. In addition, students have the option to implement impulses or "kicks" that change the velocity at transitions between states. Such kicks were automatic in Level 3, where the states were specified by different velocities, but in level 4, the velocity

Fig. 7. A variable table for a state in Level 3

Fig. 8. A transition between two states of an FSM represented by a green triangle. (Color figure online)

Fig. 9. Time or position is specified as a condition for a transition in a variable table for a transition in Level 3.

is continuous (linear momentum is conserved at transitions) unless kick are explicitly specified. The more complicated motion (nonzero acceleration, kicks) implies that the logic that determines whether transitions are achieved is more advanced in Level 4 compared to Level 3, helping the students to further improve their CT skills. Students can watch graphs of the position, velocity, and acceleration as functions of time as these simulations occur. The acceleration is stepwise constant, the velocity is a sequence of line segments that are discontinuous at transitions with nonzero kicks, and the position is a sequence of continuous parabolic segments. Level 5 is identical to Level 4, except for the object moves vertically along the y-axis.

4 Multiple Representations

In STEPP, students model physics problems as FSMs and see the resulting simulations in a variety of representations: animations, graphs, vectors, free-body diagrams, numbers, and equations, all of which are displayed synchronously and many of them are color-coded. A screen capture of STEPP Module 3 Level 4 on Newton's Second Law in 2D space (Fig. 10) displays the full set of multiple representations: the area under the velocity's x-component graph (at 18.26 s into a 34-s simulation), the readings and slopes of all graphs at this time, a free-body diagram (shown in the light gray square), and the underlying equations powering the simulation. Blue is used to color the portion of the simulation associated with the first state in the FSM, graphs, and animation of a lunar landing module with a trail. Similarly, orange is used to color the portion of the simulation associated with the second state. To avoid showing simulations that are too short or too long for students to observe, STEPP plays back all simulations in 5 s no matter how long the actual simulations are. Students can change the playback if desired. To manage cognitive load, STEPP allows students and instructors to choose which representations are displayed. In addition, STEPP allows users move and resize many of the representations. Figure 10 and Fig. 11 show the same simulation while full selection of optional representations are displayed in Fig. 10 and fewer representations are displayed in Fig. 11.

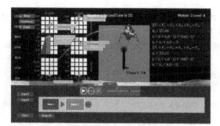

Fig. 10. Full set of multiple representations (Color figure online)

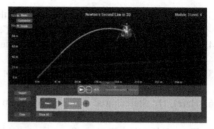

Fig. 11. Fewer representations (Color figure online)

5 Conclusion

The first three STEPP modules aligned with NGSS [1] and Texas' standards [7] have been developed and tested in university and high school classrooms. The topics covered in these modules are commonly taught in introductory physics classes in high schools and universities across the United States and, also, globally. STEPP is a web application which does not require any special software, hardware, or programming knowledge. Thus STEPP can be easily and affordably deployed in other schools, including ones with higher rates of economically disadvantaged students. While useful for refinement of the STEPP modules, field testing in the height of the pandemic complicated data collection. We therefore are unable at this time to draw conclusions on the efficacy of STEPP for simultaneous teaching of physics and CT. We intend to repeat the field test and continue to anticipate that STEPP provides an opportunity to learn physics and CT that might not otherwise be available. STEPP has the potential to transform K-20 education by incorporating the synergistic learning of a STEM subject and computing into classroom education. Moreover, the three features of STEPP's user interface described above – FSM-based modeling, software-enabled scaffolding, and multiple representation -- can be replicated in many educational applications.

Acknowledgements. The authors thank all current and former members of the STEPP team including students serving as Unity and web student developers, student members of the assessment team, student project managers, in-service and pre-service teacher-researchers, focus group teachers, field test partners, and field test participants. The research in this presentation is supported by the National Science Foundation STEM+C award 1741756. Any opinions, findings, conclusions, or recommendations in this material are the findings of the authors and do not necessarily represent those of the National Science Foundation.

References

1. NGSS Lead States. Next Generation Science Standards: For States, By States. http://www.nextgenscience.org. Accessed 27 Jan 2022
2. Wing, J.M.: Research Notebook: Computational Thinking--What and Why? In: The Link. https://www.cs.cmu.edu/link/research-notebook-computational-thinking-what-and-why. Accessed 27 Jan 2022

3. Reiser, J.: Scaffolding complex learning: the mechanisms of structuring and problematizing student work. J. Learn. Sci. **13**, 273–304 (2004)
4. Chow, T.S.: Testing software design modeled by finite-state machines. IEEE Trans. Softw. Eng. **4**, 178–187 (1978)
5. Shannon, C.E.: A mathematical theory of communication. Bell Syst. Tech. J. **27**, 79–423, 623–656 (1948)
6. Harel, D.: Statecharts: a visual formalism for complex systems. Sci. Comput. Program. **8**, 231–274 (1987)
7. Texas Education Agency. Texas Essential Knowledge and Skills. http://tea.texas.gov/index2.aspx?id=6148. Accessed 27 Jan 2022
8. Christian, W., Belloni, M.: Physlet Physics: Interactive Illustrations, Explorations and Problems for Introductory Physics. https://www.compadre.org/physlets/. Accessed 27 Jan 2022
9. Paul, A., Podolefsky, N., Perkins, K.: Guided without feeling guided: implicit scaffolding through interactive simulation design. In: AIP Conference Proceedings, vol. 1513, pp. 302–305 (2013)
10. Fishwick, P.: Simulation Model Design and Execution: Building Digital Worlds. Prentice Hall, Hoboken (1994)
11. Fishwick, P. (ed.): Handbook of Dynamic System Modeling. CRC Computer and Information Science Series. Chapman & Hall, London (2007)
12. Robinson, S.: A tutorial on conceptual modeling for simulation. In: Proceedings of the 2015 Winter Simulation Conference, pp. 1820–1834. IEEE, Piscataway (2015)

Traditional Mural Learning Effectiveness of Using Serious Game Based on Scaffolding Teaching Theory

Qiang Li[✉], Peng Wang, and Zexue Liu

Shenyang Aerospace University, Shenyang, China
qiangli@sau.edu.cn

Abstract. As one of the important components of digital products, serious games have been applied to different learning areas to improve learning efficiency. This paper describes the design of a serious game which reconstructs a traditional Chinese mural Deer king Bensheng map using a mobile platform. The scaffolding teaching theory is referenced and applied in the design of the game learning process. Two future research directions were discussed (1) The evaluation of three variables: learning efficiency, learning ability and learning motivation (2) The comparison of differences in learning effects of scaffolding teaching theory in the serious game and traditional animation.

Keywords: Serious game · Traditional culture learning · Scaffolding teaching theory

1 Introduction

The serious game provides a new medium and method for the spread of traditional culture. The combination of cultural heritage content and digital game technology has formed a new form of dissemination. Ancient murals are one of important part of cultural heritage, and it is the vital carrier of historical culture and ancient art. Ancient Chinese murals have a unique artistic styles and aesthetic properties. In different periods of China, the design of the patterns in the murals can reflect the changes in politics, economy, culture and religion of the dynasties. As a compulsory course of art appreciation in Chinese universities, ancient Chinese murals can meet people's spiritual needs for history and aesthetics. Therefore, it is of great significance to study and spread the ancient Chinese traditional murals in the form of serious games.

Previous studies have confirmed that Digital Game Learning (DGL) can enhance learning motivation [1–3]. DGL is used to improve learning effectiveness and a vivid learning experience in many areas [4]. Many researchers use the DGL approach to study traditional cultural heritage in the area of education. These studies pay a lot of attention to the construction of text-type heritage and architectural-type heritage [5, 6]. Serious games in cultural heritage learning are mostly designed based on immersive digital technology or narrative game process, and the purpose is to create scene reproduction

C. Stephanidis et al. (Eds.): HCII 2022, CCIS 1582, pp. 65–71, 2022.
https://doi.org/10.1007/978-3-031-06391-6_9

experience or vivid storyline experience for players [5, 7]. In 2016, Yuan and Yun used virtual technology to reconstruct traditional Chinese painting [8]. In 2020, Sheng Jin et al. conducted an immersive scene design for the traditional painting Spring Morning in the Han Palace [9]. These studies reconstruct traditional Chinese painting in a virtual space. It can give players an immersive experience. However, this game model may be suitable for museums or architectural sites, but it is inefficient for the heritage that this article focuses on. Previous studies on cultural heritage have paid less attention to the heritage of graphics and patterns, but they have historical and cultural information and educational significance that cannot be ignored [10]. The most prominent feature of Chinese cultural heritage is graphics and patterns [11, 12]. The graphics and patterns of mural art are the most representative of cultural heritage. In addition, improving the entertainment and participation of learners requires a combination of appropriate game modes and learning content [13]. Role-playing games (RPG) are one of the common forms of games, which can be applied to a variety of themes. It can also be used to combine games and content better. Therefore, the RPG game format was used in this study (see Fig. 1).

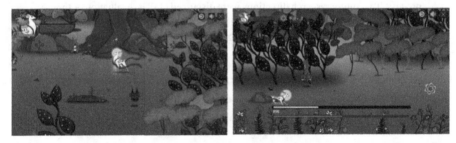

Fig. 1. Game scene and interface.

2   Background

Early digital mural works were generally presented using animation or screen touch (e.g., Nine-Colored Deer and Deer Girl). These early works changed the communication medium of ancient murals. These excellent works are animation creations based on-screen experience and story continuity. The knowledge of ancient murals is reconstructed in the works. The viewer can better understand the Traditional mural. In 2018, the company NetEase launched a digital game, True depiction: Draw thousands of mountains with a wonderful brush adapted from ancient paintings. This digital game is based on A Thousand Miles of Rivers and Mountains by Wang Ximeng, a famous painter in the Northern Song Dynasty of China. The designer reconstructs the 2D picture into a 3D scene in the game. The user moves and draws through a digital device in the scene. However, the purpose is to provide entertainment for players. This game has no clear direction in the process of spreading the knowledge of painting. In addition, the information expressed by the pictures is broken in the game. Fragmented information may affect learning effectiveness.

2.1 Scaffolding Teaching Theory

Scaffolding teaching-assisted (STA) originally came from the area of education. STA is a common method in the learning process. STA is also applied to serious games. STA learning can help players complete learning goals and tasks through appropriate prompts, and this method can provide feedback and task-related supportive learning [13]. Some researchers have found that an appropriate educational strategy in serious games will better achieve learning goals and improve learning outcomes, experience, motivation and even cognitive ability [11]. In digital games, the role of the STA is to give appropriate feedback after the player has chosen an answer [15]. However, STA is rarely used in serious games of traditional cultural heritage learning.

2.2 Purpose

This study is mainly divided into two parts. The first focus is the original painting of creative visual expression. The second focus is the combination of interaction and knowledge learning based on scaffolding teaching theory. The purpose of this study is

(1) Construct a mural scene in the digital game space based on the original painting.
(2) Build a scaffold between the current level of knowledge and the expected level.
(3) The Scaffolding design can assist players in exploring and learning in the game.
(4) Players experience the potential to promote appreciation of traditional art and culture.

3 Serious Game Design

3.1 Research Content

In this work, we mainly focus on traditional Chinese murals. These paintings mainly differ from those from western in form (e.g., long scrolls versus canvases of regular size), colour and composition techniques. Most of the most famous Chinese murals are in Dunhuang Mogao Grottoes. In this study, we took the famous Chinese murals Deer king Bensheng map as our design case. This mural was created during the Northern Wei Dynasty in China. This mural exists in Cave No. 257 of the Mogao Grottoes. This mural is a rectangle with a length of 385 cm and a height of 96 cm. The mural is divided into five parts according to the composition. There are mainly four figures and trees in the mural. The mural uses a composition from both sides to the middle. This mural tells the story of Sakyamuni of past life. His past life was a nine-coloured deer. It saved a man who fell into the water and told him not to tell others about the nine-coloured deer. But the drowning man betrayed the nine-coloured deer. The drowning man was finally met with retribution.

3.2 Content Design

In this study, the digital game prototype was developed through Unity 3D (Fig. 1). The user uses the virtual joystick to control the characters in the scene to complete certain events or freely explore the virtual scene. This study divides the digital game into five stages: save (S), gratitude (G), betrayal (B), crusade (C), and result (R), Based on the story and composition of the murals. Players can enter the next stage when the game needs to achieve the goal in the previous stage. The learning content is gradually increasing the difficulty according to the stage. The game uses the method of rewarding the attributes of the game character to encourage players to learn knowledge and explore the scene.

3.3 Scaffolding Teaching Design

This study divides the knowledge in the murals into three categories: history, shape and colour in the digital game. Knowledge is divided into five levels based on complexity. In the S stage and G stage of the game, the knowledge points are relatively simple. An explanation of knowledge points will appear after the player controls the role of the event. A problem is triggered after the player finishes learning the knowledge points. The player is rewarded for the correct answer. Compared to the S stage, the G stage will demonstrate some knowledge points. In stages B and C, the knowledge points will be more complicated. The way the game will change during these two stages. Enemies will appear in the game from stage B. The enemy will have questions about the knowledge of murals. The player can destroy the enemy only by giving the correct answer. In the R stage, the difficulty of the problem is determined by the performance of the past four stages.

The knowledge points in-game problems are designed based on scaffolding education theory. This study divides existing knowledge and new knowledge into five levels. In the first and second levels, the basic knowledge points of the three types of murals are

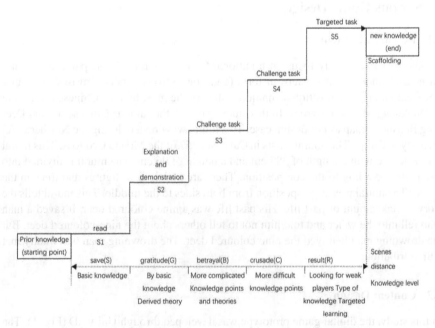

Fig. 2. The relationship between game stages and knowledge levels.

mainly explained. When the player enters the third level, the brackets of the game will use challenging tasks to learn knowledge, and the prompt of the scaffolding will be reduced. In the fourth level, the player needs to find the answer by himself, and the game scaffolding will not help the player. At the fifth level, the game will have random problems recalling past knowledge points to achieve the learning goal (see Fig. 2 and Fig. 3).

Fig. 3. The interface of mural knowledge learning.

3.4 Game Visual Expression

In previous studies, there is an important focus on the visual expression of cultural heritage. This focus is about constructing the authenticity of the visual expression of cultural heritage. In this study, the first challenge in the reality of mural reconstruction is the reorganization of mural elements in space. There are two points to note in this process: (1) The mural becomes incomplete in the long-term impact of the environment. (2) The colours in the murals are made of natural materials (e.g., minerals and plants). The colours in the murals have faded in the long-term effects of the environment. Therefore, this study finds many fresco samples in Dunhuang Research Institute for reference to solve two problems.

The second challenge is character animation design. Interaction is a very important feature in games. Many behavioural animations will be produced during the interaction. A well-made animation has a positive impact on the user experience. The animation design in this study refers to the animation in the video Nine-Colored Deer. This study interviewed related researchers in the design of sound and scene dynamics.

In the study on the reproduction of traditional paintings by Sheng Jin and others, a problem of perception of the artistic style of the original painting was mentioned [9]. It is a perception which includes colour, texture and overall painting style with space. In this study, this perception is also an important concern. Sheng Jin and others tried to restore the characters in the painting with high progress in a 3D space, but they got negative results in the test [9]. This study tried to perform high-quality restoration in 3D space during the G stage of the game. In the end, the following problems appeared in the test: (1) There are many missing details in the murals. It is difficult to construct a mural scene in a 3D scene. (2) The colour reproduction of the murals in the 3D scene is low. (3) 3D scenes are more difficult to express the artistic style of Chinese murals. Therefore, this study chose to build the game in a 2D scene.

4 Conclusion

With the development of digital technology, serious games are increasingly being used in various areas of learning. Therefore, it is very important to design a serious game to achieve "Learning by playing" with high efficiency. This study explores how scaffolding learning theory can be integrated into serious games to enhance users' motivation and effectiveness in learning about cultural heritage through the example of traditional Chinese mural painting cultural heritage. Research has found that using scaffolding theory in serious games can lead to better learning of traditional murals. The study provides a design reference and basis for the design of serious games with cultural heritage as content.

Future plans are to evaluate the cultural learning effects of this seriousness game through empirical studies. Next steps in the study include (1) Compare the teaching effectiveness of traditional teaching models and serious games. (2) Exploring difference between scaffolding teaching theory in digital games and traditional teaching. (3) Testing on the usability of the game teaching framework.

Acknowledgement. The work was supported by Liaoning Province Education Department (JYT2020098), and teaching reform fund of Shenyang Aerospace University (2022).

References

1. Boyle, E.A., et al.: An update to the systematic literature review of empirical evidence of the impacts and outcomes of computer games and serious games. Comput. Educ. **94**, 178–192 (2016)
2. Garris, R., Ahlers, R., Driskell, J.E.: Games, motivation, and learning: a research and practice model. Simul. Gaming **33**(4), 441–467 (2002)
3. Subhash, S., Cudney, E.A.: Gamified learning in higher education: a systematic review of the literature. Comput. Hum. Behav. **87**, 192–206 (2018)
4. Prensky, M.: Digital game-based learning. Comput. Entertain. **1**(1), 21 (2003)
5. Malegiannaki, I., Daradoumis, T: Analyzing the educational design, use and effect of spatial games for cultural heritage: a literature review. Comput. Educ. **108**, 1–10 (2017)
6. Mortara, M., Catalano, C.E., Bellotti, F., Fiucci, G., Houry-Panchetti, M., Petridis, P.: Learning cultural heritage by serious games. J. Cult. Heritage **15**(3), 318–325 (2014)
7. Ibrahim, N., Ali, N.M.: A conceptual framework for designing virtual heritage environment for cultural learning. J. Comput. Cult. Herit. **11**, 2 (2018). Article no. 11, 27 pages
8. Yuan, C., Yun, Z.: Tunable, a VR reconstruction of Listening to a Guqin from emperor Zhao Ji. In: SIGGRAPH ASIA 2016 VR Showcase. ACM (2016). 6
9. Jin, S., Fan, M., Wang, Y., Liu, Q.: Reconstructing traditional Chinese paintings with immersive virtual reality. In: Extended Abstracts of the 2020 CHI Conference on Human Factors in Computing Systems (CHI EA 2020), pp. 1–8. Association for Computing Machinery, New York (2020)
10. Harland, R.G., et al.: Defining urban graphic heritage for economic development in the UK and China. In: Design Revolutions: International Association of Societies of Design Research Conference, pp. 1–14 (2019)
11. Gong, J.: Chinese traditional folk pattern and modern graphic design. Asian Soc. Sci. **4**(2), 65–68 (2008)

12. Sun, L.: Study on the application of Chinese traditional patterns in modern graphic design. In: 2016 2nd International Conference on Arts, Design and Contemporary Education, pp. 404–406 (2016)
13. Melero, J., Hernández-Leo, D.: A model for the design of puzzle-based games including virtual and physical objects. J. Educ. Technol. Soc. **17**(3), 192–207 (2014)
14. Séverine, E., Jamet, E.: Digital game-based learning: impact of instructions and feedback on motivation and learning effectiveness. Comput. Educ. **67**, 156–167 (2013)

Haptic Learning and Technology: Analyses of Digital Use Cases of Haptics Using the Haptic Learning Model

Farzaneh Norouzinia[✉], Bianka Dörr, Mareike Funk, and Dirk Werth

AWS Institut für digitale Produkte und Prozesse gGmbH, Saarbrücken, Germany
{farzaneh.norouzinia,bianka.doerr,mareike.funk,
dirk.werth}@aws-institut.de

Abstract. Learning with involvement of haptic technologies can provide advanced opportunities in digital learning. Especially over the course of the pandemic the value of digital learning solutions became more obvious. There are attempts with various technologies, which can enhance the quality of learning processes and refine the learning results. However, it should be remembered that the sense of touch is not contained in all of them, even though it might be helpful, e.g., in the medical field. To show how haptic technology may improve the digital learning solutions, this paper will briefly define haptic learning and analyze some haptic learning use cases using the Haptic Learning Model of Dörr et al. [2].

We describe haptic learning as the sum of all learning processes which use haptic interactions to enhance the effectiveness and/or efficiency of learning process. In this paper, haptic technology use cases which are not directly related to learning or do not give any haptic feedback to the learners are excluded.

Keywords: Haptic learning · Digital learning · Haptic technology

1 Introduction

In the last decades digital learning increased rapidly, and the value of digital learning solutions became more obvious. Especially learning with involvement of haptic technologies can provide advanced opportunities for many aspects of digital learning. There are attempts with various technologies, which can enhance the quality of learning processes and refine the learning results. Particularly in the medical field, there have been increased approaches to incorporating haptic technologies for learning situations, such as in Kaluschke et al. [3]. They developed a haptic virtual environment for dental students and their teachers in which they can jointly test surgical procedures on patients' teeth. This primarily addresses tactile and kinesthetic senses, which are considered necessary for dental surgery to be able to perform various procedures as a dentist. The haptic feedback is provided by force feedback from a haptic device called the 6-DOF Phantom Omni and a head-mounted display to create a better immersion [3].

As shown in this example, technology can be used to implement haptic learning. In this paper we will give examples of technologies that can be used to realize haptic learning. To achieve this, we draw on the understanding of haptic learning and the Haptic Learning Model developed by Dörr et al. [2]. They define "haptic learning as the sum of all learning processes that are didactically based on the use of haptic interactions to increase or to support learning success. In this context, we make a distinction between the use of haptics as an integral part of learning and the use of haptics to better convey the content. The first case can be described as haptic learning in the narrower sense, whereas the second case describes haptic learning in the broader sense" [2].

At the beginning of the paper, we will briefly describe the Haptic Learning Model which will serve as a theoretical framework to analyze the selected use cases. In the next step, we will analytically select the three use cases which will be further analyzed. The Haptic Learning Model will be applied to analyze the use cases and pursue the aim of the paper to show the variety of technological possibilities that can improve haptic learning. The results of the analyses of the use cases will then be discussed by comparing them with each other and based on the resulting conclusions, we will derive recommendations for action for the technological use of haptic learning. At the end we will give a summary of the paper including the results of the analysis.

2   Haptic Learning Model

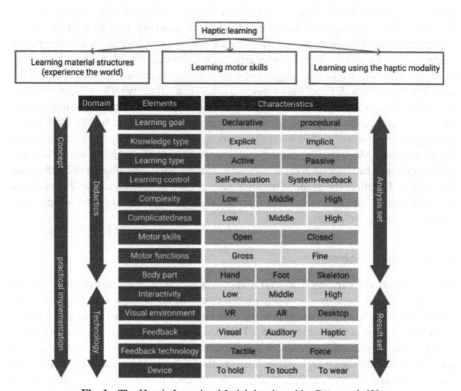

Fig. 1. The Haptic Learning Model developed by Dörr et al. [2]

The model we will focus and base our use case analysis on within this paper is the Haptic Learning Model developed by Dörr et al. [2] which can be seen in Fig. 1. This model describes how haptic learning can be classified in one of three core areas, which means that haptic learning can take place during the learning of material structures, motor skills or generally as an additional support while learning. Furthermore, the model defines fourteen elements that haptic learning may contain, each of them as part of either the didactical or the technology domain. The elements additionally consist each of two or three characteristics. For example, the knowledge type within haptic learning can be implicit or explicit and the device can be holdable, touchable or wearable. The elements can furthermore be divided in the analysis set and the result set. Referring to the previously given examples, the first one would be part of the analysis set and the second one part of the result set. Accordingly, the analysis set creates the basis for how haptic learning should be implemented in the result set.

3   Use Cases

3.1   Selection of Use Cases

As a main part, this paper will analyze three studies taking the Haptic Learning Model [2] into account. However, the question should be answered why these studies were chosen to begin with. The first and most essential aspect was that the studies use any kind of haptic technology within a learning scenario. However, we focused more on the implementation of the learning scenarios e.g., a variety of technologies, and less on the prerequisites of the study like its target group. This allowed us to show the wide variety of possibilities how haptic learning can be used. Another decisive factor was the year the studies were published. Especially regarding e.g., Virtual Reality (VR) a couple of years can make a huge difference, therefore we decided for 2015 as the earliest possible point in time for the use cases. Furthermore, the studies need to be distinguished between haptic learning in real life and digital haptic learning using e.g., wearable devices. Since this Haptic Learning Model focuses on digital haptic learning, only the latter were taken into consideration. A final decision criterion related to the Haptic Learning Model rather than the studies. To reflect the greatest possible range of applications and implementations, each of the three core areas should be represented. Therefore, the use cases which come in next section are selected.

3.2   Use Cases Analyses

First Core Area: Learning Material Structures. To further investigate the first core area of the Haptic Learning Model [2] a use case was chosen that targets people who are missing a leg/foot, with the goal to provide these people with the feeling of walking on different types of floor surfaces [5]. This is done with the help of a head mounted virtual reality display through which participants see the virtual legs of an avatar and through haptic feedback which is transferred to the forearms of the participants via some vibrators. These vibrators transfer different haptic cues to the users depending on the floor on which the avatar is walking. Besides, these haptic cues follow two different patterns which reveal additionally if the avatar's leg is in swing phase, or if the foot is rolling on the floor while walking. During this experiment, the participants hear white noise via their headphones so they are not influenced by the sounds of the vibrators [5].

The goal of this study is to provide the participants with the feeling of walking on different materials. We begin our analyses by considering this point and declare that since this goal is achieved only after repeating a process and is supposed to become automatic after having done some practice, the learning goal of this study is procedural. The knowledge which is supposed to be learned in this study is a sensation, and each person gains this knowledge through experience. Since sensations are not some documented knowledge like facts or principles, we classify the knowledge type of this experiment as implicit. The participants are actively engaged in the process and therefore, the learning type of this study is active. However, they only receive feedback from the system in form of haptic cues coming from the vibrators, but they do not give any feedback back to the system. Therefore, we evaluate the learning control of this experiment as system-feedback.

Moreover, by looking at this haptic system in terms of its usage, we take it as a system with middle complicatedness because although users are not supposed to perform extremely complicated tasks, the devices used in this study are no everyday devices that each person is well familiarized with. Besides, complexity of this learning scenario is also categorized as middle by us. This is because to experience different material is not complex, but the participants are supposed to receive this sensation via additional vibrators, which increases the level of complexity to middle.

Provided that users of this technology receive some haptic feedback from the system and see the avatar via VR, we can confirm that there is an interaction between users and the system, whereas there is not much interaction from the user-side. Therefore, we consider the interactivity level of this design to be low.

Based on the results that Shokur et al. [5] presented within this use case, users got on very well with this system and the combination of virtual leg and vibration (tactile haptic feedback) let them feel as if it was their own leg.

Second Core Area: Learning Motor Skills. Another learning scenario got selected to look into the second core area of Haptic Learning Model [2]. The motor skill the participants should learn within this learning scenario is a proper running style. The motivation of Daiber et al. [1] to design such system was that the way runners land their foot on the ground often causes them knee-related injuries. Therefore, to learn how to land their foot is of high importance.

This learning scenario is designed using a wearable haptic device which is placed under the shoe sole of the participants and transfers force feedback. This device also consists of an electrical muscle stimulation which guides runners to land their foot with an appropriate angle. This guidance is not limited to an assistance but goes further to unconscious motor learning and helps learners to run with the appropriate angle even after deactivating this assistance device [1].

Considering the elements of Haptic Learning Model [1], we start to analyze this use case. The learning goal of this experiment is considered by us as procedural since the participants learn how to perform a skill and to gain this knowledge, they repeat a process which consists of acting, receiving feedback and then adapting their movement based on that feedback. The next element to analyze is the knowledge type which we categorize as implicit. The reason for this categorization is that learning the proper running style requires practicing and comes with experience. This learning process is designed so that the participants are passively engaged in the experiment. Additionally, the learning control element of this experiment follows a system-feedback pattern in which the device used in this study gives feedback to the participants based on their running style. This motor skill can as well be taught by giving verbal explanation, which is a conventional method to teach runners how to run. However, this is less effective than using the technology described in this experiment [1].

Another aspect to be analyzed based on the Haptic Learning Model [2] is the level of complexity of the content as well as the level of complicatedness in this learning scenario. In this regard we believe landing on their mid- or forefoot while running may not be a habit of runners, nevertheless, this is not complicated for them to learn. Moreover, the devices used in this study are not complex to use and learners do not need high level of knowledge to be capable of using these devices. As a result, we consider the level of complexity and the level of complicatedness of this learning scenario as low. To be done with the elements which belong to the didactic domain of the Haptic Learning Model [2], we continue by analyzing the motor skill as open and the motor function as gross. The reason for former is that there are other external factors affecting the learners' performance such as the surface on which they run that makes them to land their foot with different angles. And the reason for categorizing motor function as gross is that large muscles of the body are involved.

With this experiment Daiber et al. [1] indicated a better learning outcome for those who have worked with this approach compared to those who tried to learn the right running style with the help of slow-motion videos or verbal explanations.

Third Core Area: Learning Using the Haptic Modality. In this third use case which corresponds to the third core area of Haptic Learning Model [2], an experiment is designed using the technology of a smartwatch which is not often considered as a learning tool but brought good learning results in this scenario.

Seim et al. [4] designed this study to teach 10 letters of Morse code by using haptic cues transferred via a Smartwatch. Learners hear each letter via headphones while they are busy doing some distracting tasks unrelated to Morse code. The devices that have been used in this study are the Sony Smartwatch 3 to transfer the haptic cues to the learners as well as a headphone to announce each letter.

After receiving a verbal introduction about Morse code and taking a pre-test on that, learners start the learning process in which they have a passive role, since they do not focus on Morse code and haptic cues coming from the Smartwatch, rather on some unrelated tasks. The study consisted of two groups that differed only in the duration of the study (8 vs. 16 min). At the end, it is revealed that those who worked longer with this system learned the Morse code better than the other group [4].

The representation of alphabet letters in Morse code is a knowledge which consists of small components and by learning these components step by step, learners make progress in mastering this knowledge. Having said this, we begin to analyze this use case and based on the mentioned characteristic, we classify the learning goal of this experiment as declarative. Moreover, since one can verbalize the output of this learning process and explain how it works, the knowledge type in this study is analyzed by us as explicit knowledge.

Another characteristic of this learning scenario is that learning is done passively, and learners do not play an active role in it. This characteristic is supported by asking the learners to take care of some unrelated tasks. In this way, their learning is not supported by any means other than the haptic cues provided by the smartwatch and the audio announcement of the letters via the headphones.

Provided that the participants have no previous knowledge regarding Morse code, the complicatedness of the learning scenario can be described as middle. Besides, since there are several elements which should be analyzed and learned simultaneously, this learning scenario is medium complex to go through. The smartwatch interacts with the learners and not vice versa. Because of this one-way communication, we evaluate the interaction level as low. However, the system communicates with the user through two types of feedback namely audio and haptic. Regarding the latter, the system uses tactile feedback.

Although this was a small-scale study, Seim et al. [4] achieved significant results which show that using this system for learning Morse code enhances the learning effi-ciency. Therefore, we believe this is a good example of learning using the haptic modality, whenever it is not about learning a motor skill, but rather having a more efficient learning experience using haptic technology.

4 Discussion

After analyzing the three use cases, each related to one core area of the Haptic Learning Model [2], we now want to take a comparative look at them to point out some similarities and differences of these variations of the aforementioned Haptic Learning Model. In this regard, we focus on the elements which correspond to the technology domain to mention some helpful aspects to consider whenever a learning system using haptic technology should be designed and implemented.

Table 1 summarizes the characteristics of different elements corresponding to each of three use cases that we analyzed in the previous section. As we discussed the elements related to the didactics domain in the analyses section, in this section we focus now on the elements of technology domain. One aspect to consider is the level of interactivity. Although its evaluation as well as categorization in low, middle, or high levels is some-what subjective, it is an important element and should be characterized considering to what extent learners are supposed to interact with the system to be capable of learning the content. Based on our selected use cases it cannot be simply concluded that the interaction level should be high as soon as touch is an essential part of learning. It rather depends on the degree of communication and manipulation between the user and the system. The higher these are for the user, the higher the level of interactivity should be.

Another worth mentioning aspect that goes hand in hand with the level of interactivity is the feedback that should be provided by the system. Of course, as haptic learning is to be integrated in the learning scenario, tactile and/or force haptic feedback need to be included. Depending on the desired learning goal they can be accompanied by auditory and/or visual feedback. However, as the previously described use cases have shown, providing e.g., visual feedback is not an essential feature a learning environment has to have whenever haptics should be included. Therefore, not all learning scenarios with haptic technology include a visual environment. Rather sensors or vibrators can be sufficient to achieve the desired goal. Therefore, the decision for the appropriate feedback should be based on the learning objective of the learning scenario.

Overall, we analyzed three wearable devices which transfer haptic feedback to the user with a wide range of impact on learning. To be more precise, if we put all three core areas of the Haptic Learning Model [2] on a spectrum, we believe by moving towards the first core area which is learning material structures, using haptic technology increases the effectiveness level of learning. Thus, learners are more likely to gain the desired knowledge. And if we move to the other end of this spectrum, using haptic technology makes the learning experience more efficient for the learners.

Table 1. Classification of the use cases in the Haptic Learning Model

	Virtual legs & floor texture	Motor learning in sports	Teaching Morse Code using a smartwatch
Core area	Learning material structures	Learning motor skills	Learning using the haptic modality
Didactics domain			
Learning goal	Procedural	Procedural	Declarative
Knowledge type	Implicit	Implicit	Explicit
Learning type	Active	Passive	Passive
Learning control	System-feedback	System-feedback	System-feedback
Complexity	Middle	Low	Middle
Complicatedness	Middle	Low	Middle
Motor skills	–	Open	–
Motor function	–	Gross	–
Body part	Hand	Foot	Hand
Technology domain			
Interactivity	Low	High	Low
Visual environment	VR	–	–
Feedback	Visual/ Haptic	Haptic	Auditory/Haptic
Feedback technology	Tactile	Force	Tactile
Device	To wear	To wear	To wear

5 Conclusion

In this paper we have shown some possibilities to implement different technologies for haptic learning. Using the Haptic Learning Model by Dörr et al. [2], we systematically analyzed three selected and previously justified use cases. It has been shown that haptic learning can be used in any kind of learning scenario with different complexity, learning objectives or feedback options, just to name a few. In the subsequent comparison of the use cases, we have focused on the technology domain, as the aim of this paper is to show the diverse use of technologies in haptic learning and their enhancing effect on learning outcomes. In doing so, we want to pave the way for further research and promote the use of haptic learning in general, as we think that the use of the Haptic Learning Model [2] can greatly facilitate this process. We would like to encourage both researchers and teachers to give more importance to haptic learning.

References

1. Daiber, F., Kosmalla, F., Hassan, M., Wiehr, F., Krüger, A.: Towards amplified motor learning in sports using EMS. In: Proceedings of the CHI 2017 Workshop on Amplification and Augmentation of Human Perception, Denver, CO (2017). https://www.dfki.de/fileadmin/user_upload/import/9027_amplified-motor-learning-CR-bibcopy.pdf
2. Dörr, B., Funk, M., Norouzinia, F., Werth, D.: Haptic learning and how it can enhance digital learning experiences: an innovative approach. In: INTED 2022 Proceedings, pp. 3909–3917 (2022)
3. Kaluschke, M., Su Yin, M., Haddaway, P., Srimaneekarn, N., Saikaew, P., Zachmann, G.: A shared haptic virtual environment for dental surgical skill training. In: 2021 IEEE Conference on Virtual Reality and 3D User Interfaces Abstracts and Workshops (VRW), Lisabon, pp. 347–52. IEEE (2021). https://doi.org/10.1109/VRW52623.2021.00069
4. Seim, C., Pontes, R., Kadiveti, S., Adamjee, Z., Cochran, A., Aveni, T., et al.: Towards haptic learning on a smartwatch. In: Proceedings of the 2018 ACM International Symposium on Wearable Computers, pp. 228–229. Association for Computing Machinery, New York (2018)
5. Shokur, S., et al.: Assimilation of virtual legs and perception of floor texture by complete paraplegic patients receiving artificial tactile feedback. Sci. Rep. 6(1), 1–14 (2016)

Designing a Shared Workspace for Learning Using Augmented Reality and Social Robots

Christina Pasalidou[1,2](✉) 🆔 and Nikolaos Fachantidis[1,2] 🆔

[1] University of Macedonia, 156 Egnatia Street, 54636 Thessaloniki, Greece
{cpasalidou,nfachantidis}@uom.edu.gr
[2] Laboratory of Informatics and Robotic Applications in Education and Society, University of Macedonia, 156 Egnatia Street, 54636 Thessaloniki, Greece

Abstract. Augmented Reality (AR) is a novel technology utilized for merging real and virtual elements, enhancing the physical world. Developing AR applications in Robotics has been of interest in recent years. The current paper proposes a shared workspace for learning using Augmented Reality. The objective is to implement this approach using robots, not to execute collaborative robotic tasks but to establish a collaborative learning environment among students and social robots. We use an Augmented Reality application to superimpose virtual objects to the users' real world, aiming to achieve joint attention at a common point of interest among humans and social robots. The social robot perceives what occurs in the augmented environment and interacts (e.g., sharing information, making comments and gestures, giving constructive feedback to the users, etc.), intending to support humans to achieve the learning goals of the activities. The virtual objects are approached through AR with the aims and scopes of educational material in a learning process. The environment that this paper describes will be the testbed for exploring and further researching the proposed approach; handling virtual objects as educational material and aiming to joint attention at a common point of interest among humans and robots in this Augmented Reality shared world. In future studies, research and analysis of the characteristics and effectiveness of this approach will be conducted.

Keywords: Augmented Reality · Socially Assistive Robots · Learning environment · Shared workspace

1 Introduction

Developing AR applications in Robotics has been of interest in recent years. Up to date, designing a shared workspace where humans and robots interact and collaborate in Augmented Reality [1, 2] has included mobile robots, robotic arms, and aerial robots [3]. The focus has been on; performing collaborative tasks [4], robot programming [5, 6], manipulation of virtual and/or real objects [7], visualization of the robot's path [8], motion planning and teleoperation [9].

Among other technologies, Augmented Reality has been a widely discussed technology in Industry 4.0 [10]. Augmented Reality can be a valuable and effective approach

C. Stephanidis et al. (Eds.): HCII 2022, CCIS 1582, pp. 80–87, 2022.
https://doi.org/10.1007/978-3-031-06391-6_11

for human-robot collaboration and interaction, providing visual cues through virtual AR elements [4]. Especially for industrial robots, augmented reality technology allows visualization of the robots' motion plan, virtual obstacles, target position and other information that can support Human-Robot Interaction (HRI) [11, 12].

The objective of developing a shared environment with robots is to achieve a high-quality human-robot interaction [1]. According to Galin and Meshcheryakov [13], humans and robots collaborating in a shared workspace is a stimulating characteristic of Industry 4.0.

The aim of this study is to draw a parallel with the Industry sector and implement collaborative augmented reality systems in teaching and learning. To be more specific, the physical manipulation using industrial robots, such as robotic arms will be replaced by cognitive manipulation of the virtual objects with the participation of social robots in a shared workspace, where joint attention activities occur. The role of Augmented Reality will be to enrich the information acquisition of the user's real environment [14]. At the same time, the robot can act as a tutor [15], a companion in the learning process [16], or an educational tool [17].

2 Related Work

2.1 Augmented Reality and Human-Robot Interaction in Shared Workspaces

Human-robot communication enhanced with augmented reality in a shared workspace has already attracted the researchers' interest. In Gao and his colleagues' research [18], visual and spatial information of real objects were fused in a shared workspace through augmented reality technology [18]. Qiu and his fellow researchers [2] proposed a shared augmented reality workspace that establishes active communication between the users and the robots. In their designed AR system, the robot perceives and manipulates the virtual elements, while actively interacting and inferring the utility of the human agent [2]. In the experiment, the physical robot proactively assisted participants to perform a given task successfully in the context of the augmented reality shared environment [2].

Augmented Reality has the potential to show the robots' sensory data, resulting to better understanding the robot's perspective of the world around it [1]. Bolano and his colleagues [19] developed a system utilizing augmented reality to project useful information in the shared workspace, such as the robot's motion intend. Their system was evaluated in various settings. Results indicate that the visualization of information and the display of plan changes achieves a more dynamic and efficient human – robot interaction [19].

An augmented reality-based collaborative workspace was proposed by Materna and fellow researchers [20], using methods such as persona and scenario. In their prototype, users are able to program the robot and perform collaborative tasks effectively. The interaction occurs through an interface projected onto the table [20]. The interface includes various elements to visualize the state of the robot and the task [20].

Effective and substantial human – robot interaction requires bi-directional communication. Chandan and his colleagues [21] introduced a novel Augmented Reality system, called ARROCH, to facilitate collaboration between robots and a human. To be more specific, robots' planned behaviors and state were visualized through Augmented Reality technology for the user to comprehend the robots' intentions. On the other end, robots received feedback from the user, as well [21]. The results from the experiments indicated that humans perform better using the AR system rather than following an approach that does not include augmented reality technology and its potentials [21].

The interaction among humans and robots has been studied not only in the context of industrial robots, such as robotic arms or mobile robots, but also in the field of Social Robotics. Augmented Reality can be utilized to enrich and better study the interaction [22] and support human – robot collaboration [23]. In their study, Bock and his colleagues [24], presented an approach to enable the humanoid robot NAO to play a board game against a human opponent. An AR marker was utilized to help localize the robot and increase the accuracy of the robot behavior [24]. The humanoid NAO robot was also used in Lahemer and Rad's study [14]. The researchers implemented AR technology and vision-based probabilistic landmark-based SLAM for the robot's indoor navigation. The proposed system recognized the location of NAO markers using NAO's camera and displayed the location information to the user's environment through augmented reality technology [14]. Results showed that adaptive augmented ellipsoidal SLAM can improve robot localization and mapping [14].

2.2 Socially Assistive Robots and Augmented Reality in Education

Socially Assistive Robots (SARs), such as the NAO robot, have been widely used in Education, being able to improve the educational experience of the students [25]. Socially Assistive Robots in educational settings aim to supplement the efforts of educators through engaging children in personalized educational activities [26]. Socially Assistive Robots can be utilized so as to assist teachers in the educational settings, promoting social interaction and improving the quality of education [27].

In addition to social robots' positive outcomes in the field of Education, Augmented Reality technology shows potential in making learning processes more interesting and motivating for students [28]. According to Chang and his colleagues [29], integrating robots into Mixed Reality environments improves students' authentic learning experiences.

In the present study, taking into account the literature, we discovered a gap regarding the use of Socially Assistive Robots in an Augmented Reality shared workspace for learning. Our objective is to achieve joint attention at a common point of interest among humans and social robots, such as the NAO robot. Joint attention (JA) is deemed as an important mechanism of social cognition, where "two persons can jointly attend to an object by one person following another person's gaze toward a given object or possibly a third person" [30]. Responsive joint attention mechanisms evoke higher perceived feelings of social presence of the robot in the context of mutual problem-solving tasks [31]. Both the social NAO robot [32] and Augmented Reality technology [33] have been used to assist students in joint attention activities. Thus, studying the integration of augmented reality and social robots in an educational environment seems to be a promising solution for students' learning, interacting and sharing perception with social robots [16].

3   System Design

Based on the review of the literature, we recognized that augmented reality technology is a useful solution for human-robot interaction in an environment where both users and robots share their perception of the world and the events that occur in it. We propose the implementation of an augmented reality system in which a social robot interacts with humans not to execute collaborative robotic tasks, but to facilitate collaborative learning and support the educational process, focusing on the cognitive exploitation of the augmented elements.

The use of augmented reality technology appears to be a solution for human-robot interaction in collaborative workspaces. To achieve that, software and game engines, such as Unity 3D have been utilized for the development of AR applications for smartphone platforms [4]. In our proposed system, an AR application was developed using both Unity 3D and Vuforia software. The designed AR application runs on Android devices.

For the superimposition of the additional virtual objects, the marker-based AR approach was used. Each AR marker represented a different planet. Robots also use markers and landmarks to detect and recognize objects easier [34]. In an Augmented Reality system, markers can be used to render a visualization of an augmented workspace area [4], as well as for localization purposes [24].

In our system the humanoid robot NAO of Softbank Robotics was chosen. The human-like characteristics of socially assistive robots, such as the NAO robot, can enhance positive emotions in young students [35]. The NAO robot used in our study is in version 5.0 with installed software NAOqi, version 2.1.0.19. The robot can connect and communicate through Wi-Fi.

NAO robot's landmarks, called NAOmarks, were used along with the AR markers. They were placed in a table-like surface between the standing robot and the users. Both the robot and the students pointed their attention in the same direction where the markers were placed. The robot prompted students to scan the marker with the mobile device. When the marker was detected, NAO robot shared interesting information, made gestures and provided students feedback in relation to the cognitive objectives of the activities. At the same time, the students observed the animated three-dimensional models of the planets in the mobile device through the AR application, as shown in Fig. 1.

This is a work-in-progress. We are currently examining the connection of the NAO robot with the AR application. The NAO robot is programmed using Python. The robot acts as a server and receives coded actions from the AR application. The AR application communicates with the robot using its IP address and sends messages, correlating the events with the actions we wish NAO to execute in order to interact both with the virtual elements of the AR application and with the users.

Fig. 1. Student interacting with the NAO robot, using Augmented Reality in a shared environment

4   Discussion and Conclusions

Robotics research has been prevalent in recent years due to technological advances, increased technological accessibility and reliability, as well as commercial availability [36]. Working with robots and understanding their intentions is crucial for human-robot collaboration, especially in the field of Industry [19]. Augmented Reality technology has been studied to supplement the real environment with virtual information and enhance communication between humans and robots [37]. Augmented and Virtual Reality provide users with immersive experiences, visualizing the procedures that occur during human–robot collaboration [38].

An important parameter that needs to be taken into consideration when designing an AR system for human – robot interaction (HRI) is the bi-directional communication, with both users and robots participating actively [2]. This is one of our goals while optimizing our proposed AR system.

Advances in Augmented, Virtual and Mixed Reality are laying the groundwork for an alternative solution of mediating human-robot communication [39]. The virtual elements that appear in the real world through Augmented Reality can be used to improve the communication [22] and the interactions between users and robots [40].

Augmented Reality systems may include a robot that aims at manipulating and handling a variety of objects [4]. In our study, we propose the handling of the virtual objects in the AR environment in a cognitive manner, aiming at more engaging learning experiences for students.

Previous studies regarding the utilization of Augmented Reality technology and social robots in educational settings is limited [16]. We are currently in the process of designing and setting all the needed parameters for our AR system for learning with a social robot. The robot has a socially assistive role, setting its attention in a common point of interest with the students. The social robot perceives what occurs in the augmented environment and acts accordingly. The environment that this paper describes will be the testbed for further researching the proposed approach; handling virtual objects as educational material and establishing joint attention in the context of an Augmented Reality shared world. In future studies, research and analysis of the characteristics and effectiveness of this approach will be conducted.

Acknowledgements. This work is part of a project that has received funding from the Research Committee of the University of Macedonia under the Basic Research 2020-21 funding programme.

References

1. Muhammad, F., Hassan, A., Cleaver, A., Sinapov, J.: Creating a shared reality with robots. In: 2019 14th ACM/IEEE International Conference on Human-Robot Interaction (HRI), pp. 614–615. IEEE (2019)
2. Qiu, S., Liu, H., Zhang, Z., Zhu, Y., Zhu, S.C.: Human-robot interaction in a shared augmented reality workspace. In: 2020 IEEE/RSJ International Conference on Intelligent Robots and Systems (IROS), pp. 11413–11418. IEEE (2020)
3. Bassyouni, Z., Elhajj, I.H.: Augmented reality meets artificial intelligence in robotics: a systematic review. Front. Robot. AI **296** (2021)
4. Chacko, S.M., Kapila, V.: Augmented reality as a medium for human-robot collaborative tasks. In: 2019 28th IEEE International Conference on Robot and Human Interactive Communication (RO-MAN), pp. 1–8. IEEE (2019)
5. Quintero, C.P., Li, S., Pan, M.K., Chan, W.P., Van der Loos, H.M., Croft, E.: Robot programming through augmented trajectories in augmented reality. In: 2018 IEEE/RSJ International Conference on Intelligent Robots and Systems (IROS), pp. 1838–1844. IEEE (2018)
6. Ong, S.K., Yew, A.W.W., Thanigaivel, N.K., Nee, A.Y.: Augmented reality-assisted robot programming system for industrial applications. Robot. Comput.-Integr. Manuf. **61**, 101820 (2020)
7. Ostanin, M., Mikhel, S., Evlampiev, A., Skvortsova, V., Klimchik, A.: Human-robot interaction for robotic manipulator programming in Mixed Reality. In: 2020 IEEE International Conference on Robotics and Automation (ICRA), pp. 2805–2811. IEEE (2020)
8. Cleaver, A., Tang, D., Chen, V., Sinapov, J.: HAVEN: a unity-based virtual robot environment to showcase HRI-based augmented reality. arXiv preprint arXiv:2011.03464 (2020)
9. Hernández, J.D., Sobti, S., Sciola, A., Moll, M., Kavraki, L.E.: Increasing robot autonomy via motion planning and an augmented reality interface. IEEE Robot. Autom. Lett. **5**(2), 1017–1023 (2020)
10. Makhataeva, Z., Varol, H.A.: Augmented reality for robotics: a review. Robotics **9**(2), 21 (2020)
11. Fang, H.C., Ong, S.K., Nee, A.Y.C.: Novel AR-based interface for human-robot interaction and visualization. Adv. Manuf. **2**(4), 275–288 (2014). https://doi.org/10.1007/s40436-014-0087-9
12. Lambrecht, J., Kruger, J.: Spatial programming for industrial robots based on gestures and augmented reality. In: IEEE/RSJ International Conference on Intelligent Robots and Systems (IROS), pp. 446–472 (2012)
13. Galin, R., Meshcheryakov, R.: Review on human–robot interaction during collaboration in a shared workspace. In: Ronzhin, A., Rigoll, G., Meshcheryakov, R. (eds.) ICR 2019. LNCS (LNAI), vol. 11659, pp. 63–74. Springer, Cham (2019). https://doi.org/10.1007/978-3-030-26118-4_7

14. Lahemer, E.S., Rad, A.: An adaptive augmented vision-based ellipsoidal SLAM for indoor environments. Sensors **19**(12), 2795 (2019)
15. Velentza, A.M., Fachantidis, N., Lefkos, I.: Human or robot university tutor? Future teachers' attitudes and learning outcomes. In: 2021 30th IEEE International Conference on Robot & Human Interactive Communication (RO-MAN), pp. 236–242. IEEE (2021)
16. Hennerley, J., Dickinson, M., Jiang, M.: Augmented reality enhanced human robot interaction for social robots as e-learning companions. In: Electronic Visualisation and the Arts (EVA 2017), pp. 1–6 (2017)
17. Pasalidou, C., Fachantidis, N.: Distance learning in the era of COVID-19: supporting educational robotics with augmented reality. In: Malvezzi, M., Alimisis, D., Moro, M. (eds.) EDUROBOTICS 2021. SCI, vol. 982, pp. 39–51. Springer, Cham (2021). https://doi.org/10.1007/978-3-030-77022-8_4
18. Gao, P., Reily, B., Paul, S., Zhang, H.: Visual reference of ambiguous objects for augmented reality-powered human-robot communication in a shared workspace. In: Chen, J.Y.C., Fragomeni, G. (eds.) HCII 2020. LNCS, vol. 12190, pp. 550–561. Springer, Cham (2020). https://doi.org/10.1007/978-3-030-49695-1_37
19. Bolano, G., Juelg, C., Roennau, A., Dillmann, R.: Transparent robot behavior using augmented reality in close human-robot interaction. In: 2019 28th IEEE International Conference on Robot and Human Interactive Communication (RO-MAN) (2019)
20. Materna, Z., et al.: Using persona, scenario, and use case to develop a human-robot augmented reality collaborative workspace. In: Proceedings of the Companion of the 2017 ACM/IEEE International Conference on Human-Robot Interaction, pp. 201–202 (2017)
21. Chandan, K., Kudalkar, V., Li, X., Zhang, S.: ARROCH: augmented reality for robots collaborating with a human. In: 2021 IEEE International Conference on Robotics and Automation (ICRA), pp. 3787–3793. IEEE (2021)
22. Williams, T., Hirshfield, L., Tran, N., Grant, T., Woodward, N.: Using augmented reality to better study human-robot interaction. In: Chen, J.Y.C., Fragomeni, G. (eds.) HCII 2020. LNCS, vol. 12190, pp. 643–654. Springer, Cham (2020). https://doi.org/10.1007/978-3-030-49695-1_43
23. Green, S.A., Billinghurst, M., Chen, X., Chase, J.G.: Human-robot collaboration: a literature review and augmented reality approach in design. Int. J. Adv. Rob. Syst. **5**(1), 1 (2008)
24. Bock, S., Klöbl, R., Hackl, T., Aichholzer, O., Steinbauer, G.: Playing Nine Men's Morris with the humanoid robot nao. In: Proceedings of the Austrian Robotics Workshop, vol. 22, no. 23 (2014)
25. Benitti, F.B.V.: Exploring the educational potential of robotics in schools: a systematic review. Comput. Educ. **58**(3), 978–988 (2012)
26. Clabaugh, C., Ragusa, G., Sha, F., Matarić, M.: Designing a socially assistive robot for personalized number concepts learning in preschool children. In: 2015 Joint IEEE International Conference on Development and Learning and Epigenetic Robotics (ICDL-EpiRob), pp. 314–319. IEEE (2015)
27. Fridin, M.: Storytelling by a kindergarten social assistive robot: a tool for constructive learning in preschool education. Comput. Educ. **70**, 53–64 (2014)
28. Petrov, P.D., Atanasova, T.V.: The effect of augmented reality on students' learning performance in stem education. Information **11**(4), 209 (2020)
29. Chang, C.W., Lee, J.H., Wang, C.Y., Chen, G.D.: Improving the authentic learning experience by integrating robots into the mixed-reality environment. Comput. Educ. **55**(4), 1572–1578 (2010)
30. Jording, M., Hartz, A., Bente, G., Schulte-Rüther, M., Vogeley, K.: The "social gaze space": a taxonomy for gaze-based communication in triadic interactions. Front. Psychol. **9**, 226 (2018)

31. Pereira, A., Oertel, C., Fermoselle, L., Mendelson, J., Gustafson, J.: Responsive joint attention in human-robot interaction. In: 2019 IEEE/RSJ International Conference on Intelligent Robots and Systems (IROS), pp. 1080–1087. IEEE (2019)
32. Cao, H.L., et al.: Robot-assisted joint attention: a comparative study between children with autism spectrum disorder and typically developing children in interaction with NAO. IEEE Access **8**, 223325–223334 (2020)
33. Pérez-Fuster, P., Herrera, G., Kossyvaki, L., Ferrer, A.: Enhancing joint attention skills in children on the autism spectrum through an augmented reality technology-mediated intervention. Children **9**(2), 258 (2022)
34. Figat, J., Kasprzak, W.: NAO-mark vs QR-code recognition by NAO robot vision. In: Szewczyk, R., Zieliński, C., Kaliczyńska, M. (eds.) Progress in Automation, Robotics and Measuring Techniques. AISC, vol. 351, pp. 55–64. Springer, Cham (2015). https://doi.org/10.1007/978-3-319-15847-1_6
35. Subin, E.K., Hameed, A., Sudheer, A.P.: Android based augmented reality as a social interface for low cost social robots. In: Proceedings of the Advances in Robotics, pp. 1–4 (2017)
36. Lambert, A., Norouzi, N., Bruder, G., Welch, G.: A systematic review of ten years of research on human interaction with social robots. Int. J. Hum.-Comput. Interact. **36**(19), 1804–1817 (2020)
37. De Pace, F., Manuri, F., Sanna, A., Fornaro, C.: A systematic review of Augmented Reality interfaces for collaborative industrial robots. Comput. Ind. Eng. **149**, 106806 (2020)
38. Dianatfar, M., Latokartano, J., Lanz, M.: Review on existing VR/AR solutions in human–robot collaboration. Procedia CIRP **97**, 407–411 (2021)
39. Williams, T., Szafir, D., Chakraborti, T., Ben Amor, H.: Virtual, augmented, and mixed reality for human-robot interaction. In: Companion of the 2018 ACM/IEEE International Conference on Human-Robot Interaction, pp. 403–404 (2018)
40. Walker, M., Hedayati, H., Lee, J., Szafir, D.: Communicating robot motion intent with augmented reality. In: Proceedings of the 2018 ACM/IEEE International Conference on Human-Robot Interaction, pp. 316–324 (2018)

Designing an Educational Point-and-Click Adventure Game About Cognitive Flexibility

Dirk M. Reyes, Julia J. Santos, and Andrea L. Tsai[✉]

Ateneo de Manila University, 1108 Quezon City, Metro Manila, Philippines
{dane.reyes,julia.santos,andrea.tsai}@obf.ateneo.edu

Abstract. Being an executive function, cognitive flexibility is one of the skills that allows a person to accomplish tasks, specifically the ability to change mental states. Proper executive function is essential in a society centered on work and productivity, especially with the increased demand due to the COVID-19 pandemic. This study aims to design and develop a point-and-click adventure video game that teaches players about the role and nature of cognitive flexibility, and to measure its effectiveness. Most people don't understand that one's surroundings and mental state can affect productivity and executive functioning, and instead it is stigmatized. By understanding the role that cognitive flexibility plays in everyday life, people can better understand their own capabilities and limits. The game is designed first by analyzing how cognitive flexibility is trained in childhood and adolescence, then enforced in adulthood. Certain concepts of cognitive flexibility are directly mapped to mechanics in the game, and puzzles are used to lead players to understand the applications of cognitive flexibility. The game will be playtested to measure whether participants gained any new insights after playing. They will also be given the option to be interviewed two weeks after to measure whether the techniques had any impact on their lives after the initial playtest. To illustrate points of interest, a player's mouse click activity while playing will be tracked. This highlights which puzzles the players struggled with and how they approached them, and can identify what aspects of the game's design were effective in relaying information.

Keywords: Game design · Serious games · Games for education · Cognitive flexibility · Executive function · Point-and-click adventure games

1 Introduction

Cognitive flexibility is the executive functioning skill defined as one's ability to switch between mental states, actions, and tasks, as well as the ability to quickly adapt to changes in a situation or environment [1]. Cognitive flexibility also allows one to identify the steps building up to a task and to switch from one step to the next. Hence, issues with cognitive flexibility result in getting stuck on a task and not knowing how to push forward or adapt to the new plan [9]. Other issues that can stem from poor cognitive flexibility are the inability to start on a complex task or switch between tasks in parallel. This can be particularly challenging in a capitalistic society that demands productivity, quick

© The Author(s), under exclusive license to Springer Nature Switzerland AG 2022
C. Stephanidis et al. (Eds.): HCII 2022, CCIS 1582, pp. 88–95, 2022.
https://doi.org/10.1007/978-3-031-06391-6_12

solutions, and the ability to juggle multiple tasks and heavy workload. Therefore, it is important that people are aware of cognitive flexibility, the role that it plays in their lives, the barriers that may hinder it, and ways to enhance or properly maintain it.

Consequently, the aim of this study is to create a point and click puzzle adventure video game and incorporate game mechanics that accurately communicate the different tools for enhancing cognitive flexibility. This game will be targeted towards the demographic of young adults aged 18 to 25 as executive functioning skills can be developed up until young adulthood, and it is during these years when the demand for performance in these skills becomes more pressing [7]. We aim to test whether the game is effective in educating players and helping them recognize the role of cognitive flexibility in their own lives. The goal is to teach players strategies for assisting cognitive flexibility, rather than enhancing their skills through simply playing the game.

Such strategies include breaking overwhelming complex tasks into smaller more manageable tasks [7]. Tasks are easier to start once the steps are first identified. Breaking tasks down into smaller tasks also makes progress easier to keep track of [9]. Another way of enhancing cognitive flexibility would be to manage and navigate the factors that inhibit it. It is true that genetics, learning disabilities, and brain injuries can cause issues with cognitive flexibility [12], but even those without such issues can struggle with cognitive flexibility due to their own circumstances. According to Diamond [3], proper physical, social, and emotional health are crucial in maintaining good executive function. Hence, lack of sleep, exercise, social activity, and emotional well-being are all factors that can hinder one's cognitive flexibility. Stress is also a common barrier that can involuntarily prompt executive functioning skills to go offline [5].

Through gameplay and storytelling, we aim to inform players that the experience of "getting stuck on a problem" or becoming overwhelmed by a big task is not a product of laziness or any inherent flaws, but rather a product of external barriers that hinder their cognitive flexibility. The game's mechanics and puzzles were carefully designed to reflect the factors that affect one's cognitive flexibility, as well as the different ways cognitive flexibility can affect one's life and productivity.

2 Game Design Process

"To-Do: Break Down", is a point-and-click adventure game that follows the protagonist, Moxie, throughout their day as they attempt to finish their to-do list. They utilize various coping mechanisms to overcome their struggles with cognitive flexibility, which are represented in the game's plot and mechanics.

The decision to educate using a point-and-click adventure game is inspired by Mayer's [10] suggestion that the gameplay loop—the series of actions that a game's core mechanics revolve around—can count as practicing an executive function skill when designed with that intention. As players are repeatedly exposed and practiced in the skills needed in the game, they gain a mastery of said skills as they continue to play. Rather than simulating the actual usage of cognitive flexibility, this study will utilize the gameplay loop to educate players on its nature and the tools they can use to develop it (Fig. 1).

Fig. 1. A portion of the game's storyline. The protagonist is struggling with an unexpected schedule change and acknowledges that this is due to an issue with cognitive flexibility.

The game itself was designed by analyzing how cognitive flexibility is trained in childhood and adolescence, then enforced in adulthood [1, 5, 7]. We then looked at the different techniques used, and with the assistance of a licensed psychologist specialized in this field, designed the game's mechanics around helping the player become aware of these practices and how they work.

The nature of the proposed point-and-click adventure game will require players to juggle multiple tasks at once and make use of previously gained clues to solve puzzles later on in the game. The genre's focus on exploration and experimentation [4] will allow them the space to make use of the tools they are given, and the focus on puzzles will afford them the chance to focus on figuring out the game's internal logic [8], which will in turn be based on the logic of cognitive flexibility.

The game's overarching structure follows an expand-collapse pattern. The puzzles would start out simple, with limited solutions as to allow the player to familiarize themselves with the game's mechanics. After learning how to navigate the gamespace, the puzzles would then 'expand', growing in number and gradually becoming more complex. As the player progressed through the game, the puzzles would then 'contract' once more as they are resolved one by one [6] (Fig. 2).

Fig. 2. A screenshot of the game. At this point in the game's progression, players are given multiple tasks to finish in parallel. The task displayed here is a bathroom that the players will need to clean.

2.1 Mapping of Game Design Elements to Psychology Concepts

Due to the educational nature of the game, when designing the mechanics and puzzles, we aimed to illustrate two things: how to improve cognitive flexibility and the role that cognitive flexibility plays in our lives.

The main in-game tasks were categorized and summarized in the Table 1 below:

Table 1. The game's mechanics and its associated concept on cognitive flexibility.

Associated mechanic	How to improve cognitive flexibility	Uses of cognitive flexibility
Energy Bar	Taking care of yourself improves brain functions	Finding alternative solutions to problems and working on several puzzles in parallel
Notepad	Breaking tasks down into smaller steps improves cognitive flexibility by making shifting between tasks more manageable	Requires cognitive flexibility to break down tasks and shift between them
To-Do List	Planning and arranging tasks make it easier to know where to start	Requires cognitive flexibility to make a plan
Puzzles	Solving in-game obstacles that reflect the real-life effect of unseen barriers to our cognitive flexibility skills can help players recognize their own personal barriers	

There are three techniques to enhance cognitive flexibility that the game focuses on. The first is breaking down large goals into smaller, clearly defined steps [7]. The game's puzzles require the player to complete their tasks one step at a time, using hints to clearly define the next steps they have to take. The second technique is encouraging the exploration of alternative solutions to problems [5]. Different puzzles may have different solutions, all of which require the player to be flexible in their thinking. The last is the ability to recognize barriers that can impede cognitive flexibility [2]. Solving the puzzles will require players to recognize that difficulty in completing goals may also be caused by the existence of 'barriers' like external distractions or unattended physiological needs.

These three techniques are reflected in the three main mechanics of the game. The point-and-click exploration, the 'Notepad' mechanic, and the 'Energy Bar' mechanic.

Point-and-Click Exploration. The player primarily interacts with the game using the mouse, which is used to point and click on what they want the character to interact with. The character will then either interact with the object, commentate on it, or pick it up. Items in the character's possession will be stored in their inventory, and can be used to interact with other objects onscreen.

The emphasis on trial-and-error and exploration encourages players to think of creative ways to solve the puzzles. This ties into how cognitive flexibility aids with thinking of alternative solutions to problems.

Notepad. For certain tasks, merely clicking on two objects is not enough to incite the proper reaction from the character. Instead, the player must give more granular instructions to help assist the character in understanding how to proceed. This is also meant to introduce the concept of breaking down tasks into smaller actions.

The interaction starts with the character expressing confusion at their intended action (ex. the player tries to interact with a washing machine, to which the character says "I don't know where to start with this."). It should be noted that this dialogue should be distinct from regular pieces of dialogue that indicate that the player is going in the wrong direction (ex. the player uses the wrong item, to which the character replies "I don't think that would work.").

The player is then meant to interact with it using their Notepad, which will pop out in the bottom-right corner with a list of set verbs. The screen will switch to a more zoomed-in version of the specified area. Rather than just clicking on the environment, the player must first pick a verb then interact with the environment (ex. clicking 'open' then clicking on a cabinet, rather than just clicking on the cabinet). Different scenarios may also produce different sets of verbs (ex. a segment about doing the laundry has different of verbs from a segment about repotting plants).

Moxie comments on each of the players actions, giving feedback as to whether they are making progress with the task or not (Fig. 3).

Energy Bar. Certain scenarios will require the player to expend energy in the energy bar. They will be given a choice between certain actions that cost varying degrees of energy and will produce varying results. This means the player must budget and manage their energy so that they get satisfactory results with their limited resources. For example, they will be given a choice between different methods of meal preparation, which require and replenish different levels of energy.

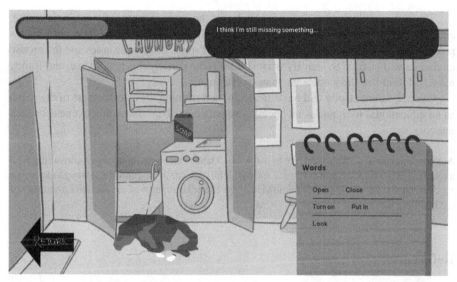

Fig. 3. A puzzle that makes use of the Notepad mechanic, in which the game's protagonist must launder their clothes in a washing machine. Players must perform this task step by step.

If the character runs out of energy, they will no longer be able to continue working and mention that they need a break. Energy can be replenished by doing relaxing activities or having a meal. This emphasizes how cognitive flexibility is reliant on a person's overall wellbeing.

3 Future Work

We have so far established a way to design a point-and-click adventure game as an educational tool on cognitive flexibility. The design proposed involves using a storyline to present players with the different tools for coping with issues in cognitive flexibility, and a series of puzzles meant to give them the opportunity to practice these tools. We discussed how these mechanics take full advantage of the strengths of point-and-click adventure games, as well as how the mechanics map to concepts of cognitive flexibility. The game has been fully developed, and so the next step is to proceed with the user testing sessions.

We will measure the game's effectiveness as an educational tool through a series of playtests. Each user testing session will consist of a pre-test, a playtest, a post-test, and a delayed post-test. These tests will be used to determine whether or not the participant was able to demonstrate a greater understanding of cognitive flexibility after playing the game. Participants will undergo a short interview after the post-test, in which they will be asked to identify which aspects of the game they struggled with or found helpful. Two weeks after their initial testing date, they may also opt to join a delayed post-test interview. This will be used to measure whether or not they were able to apply the game's concepts to their own lives.

The game will record each mouse click that the participant makes within the game, and those overseeing the user testing session will be taking notes of how participants react to and understand the game's mechanics and story. Both these notes and the mouse click data will be used to identify what solutions the participants tend to use, and if they managed to utilize the game's mechanics effectively.

Overall, future efforts will be dedicated to determining the effectiveness of the game as an educational tool, and what specific aspects contribute to its effectiveness or lack thereof.

Acknowledgements. We would like to thank Ms. Therese Ocampo for her work consulting with us on this study, and Mr. Neithan Casano and Ms. Jenilyn Agapito for guiding us through the design process. Lastly, we would like to acknowledge the financial support of the Ateneo Laboratory of the Learning Sciences.

References

1. Cañas, J.: Cognitive flexibility. In: Karwowski, W. (ed.) International Encyclopedia of Ergonomics and Human Factors, pp. 297–301. Taylor & Francis, Kentucy (2006). https://doi.org/10.13140/2.1.4439.6326
2. Carson, D.: Environmental storytelling: Creating immersive 3D worlds using lessons learned from the theme park industry (2000). https://www.gamedeveloper.com/design/environmental-storytelling-part-ii-bringing-theme-park-environment-design-techniques-to-the-virtual-world. Accessed 15 Mar 2022
3. Diamond, A.: Understanding executive functions: what helps or hinders them and how executive functions and language development mutually support one another. Perspect. Lang. Literacy **40**(2), 7–11 (2014)
4. Fernández-Vara, C., Osterwil, S.: The key to adventure game design: insight and sense-making. Paper presented at Meaningful Play, Michigan State University, East Lansing, 21–23 October 2010
5. Foy, N.: How Stress Affects Executive Function in Children — What Teachers Need to Know. https://medium.com/a-parent-is-born/how-stress-affects-executive-function-in-children-what-teachers-need-to-know-b67ac90fd3a6 (2020). Accessed 7 Dec 2021
6. Gilbert, R.: Puzzle Dependency Charts (2014). https://grumpygamer.com/puzzle_dependency_charts. Accessed 7 Dec 2021
7. Harvard University: Executive Function Activities for Adolescents. Harvard University. https://46y5eh11fhgw3ve3ytpwxt9r-wpengine.netdna-ssl.com/wp-content/uploads/2015/05/Activities-for-Adolescents.pdf. Accessed 7 Dec 2021
8. Kangas, P.: The pleasures of puzzle-solving in adventure games: close reading Day of the Tentacle. Master's thesis, Tampere University (2017). https://doi.org/10.13140/RG.2.2.31251.99367
9. Kelly, K.: Why Kids with Executive Functioning Issues Have Trouble with Planning. Understood for all Inc. https://www.understood.org/en/learning-thinking-differences/child-learning-disabilities/executive-functioning-issues/why-kids-with-executive-functioning-issues-have-trouble-with-planning. Accessed 7 Dec 2021
10. Mayer, R.E., Parong, J., Bainbridge, K.: Young adults learning executive function skills by playing focused video games. Cogn. Dev. **49**, 43–50 (2019). https://doi.org/10.1016/j.cogdev.2018.11.002

11. Understood: Trouble With Flexible Thinking: Why Some Kids Only See Things One Way. https://www.understood.org/en/learning-thinking-differences/child-learning-disabilities/executive-functioning-issues/flexible-thinking-what-you-need-to-know. Accessed 7 Dec 2021
12. Understood: Executive Functioning Issues: Possible Causes. https://www.understood.org/en/learning-thinking-differences/child-learning-disabilities/executive-functioning-issues/executive-functioning-issues-possible-causes. Accessed 7 Dec 2021
13. Understood: 8 Fun Games That Can Improve Your Child's Executive Functioning Skills. https://www.understood.org/en/school-learning/learning-at-home/games-skillbuilders/8-fun-games-that-can-improve-your-childs-executive-functioning-skills. Accessed 7 Dec 2021

Development of the Teaching Material Using a Tablet Device for Learning the Concept of Watersheds

Natsumi Sagara[✉] and Yu Suzuki

School of Project Design, Miyagi University, 1-1 Gakuen, Taiwa-cho, Kurokawa-gun,
Miyagi 981-3298, Japan
{p1820084,suzu}@myu.ac.jp

Abstract. Due to topographical and meteorological features, floods and landslides occur frequently in Japan. Therefore, disaster prevention education is essential. When considering natural disasters such as floods, it is important to learn the concept of watersheds. In this study, we developed the teaching material using a tablet device that enables students to learn the concept of watersheds by extending their learning about the action of running water in elementary schools. A three dimensional (3D) topographical map is displayed on the screen of the tablet device, and when a student touches the screen, a ball that looks like rainwater falls at the touched point. After the ball falls, it rolls over the topographic map, drawing a trajectory. In two learning modes, students learn by repeatedly observing the ball's path. In the basic learning mode, they learn about the basic properties of running water. In the developmental learning mode, they learn about watershed concepts and disaster prevention. This paper describes the development of two learning modes and a trial verification of the basic learning mode.

Keywords: Watershed · Teaching material · Tablet device

1 Introduction

Japan is located in one of the world's rainiest regions and has many steep mountainous terrains. These land conditions make Japan prone to floods, so dis-aster prevention education is essential [2].

With the revision of the Courses of study in 2019, the study of natural disasters was enhanced in elementary school science courses in Japan [1]. This revision provides increased opportunities for learning about the action of running water as part of disaster prevention education for such things as floods. In reality; however, it is difficult to learn about both of the effects of running water and in-depth disaster prevention in a limited amount of class time.

Since floods occur in watersheds, Sugawara et al. point out that if many people are aware of the concept of "watersheds," they will be able to think for themselves and evacuate proactively in the event of a disaster. In other words,

C. Stephanidis et al. (Eds.): HCII 2022, CCIS 1582, pp. 96–103, 2022.
https://doi.org/10.1007/978-3-031-06391-6_13

when considering natural disasters such as floods, it is important to learn the concept of watersheds. However, while the current Japanese course of study includes an elementary study of the concept of watersheds in units that deal with the action of running water in science, it does not specify the word "watershed" or the content of an in-depth study of watersheds.

The purpose of this study is to develop a teaching material that enables students to learn the concept of the watershed by extending their learning in elementary school about the action of running water.

2   Existing Teaching Materials

The following are existing teaching materials for learning the concept of watersheds, each of which has its problems for students to learn. The first is teaching materials using a 3D topographical map model and marbles. Generally, several students use one material during class time when using teaching materials using such large models. This makes it difficult for them to learn at their own pace. Furthermore, 3D topographic models have lines drawn in advance to indicate rivers and watersheds, so there is a little element of independent thinking by students.

The second is a water education program, Project Wet "Discover a Watershed." The use of this material requires qualified instructors, so it limits students' learning opportunities. In addition, learners must work within a limited time, so it is difficult for them to deepen their learning at their own pace.

The third is a video for study review. Using the video materials, students can reflect on their learning about the action of running water in science class and learn the concept of the watershed in relation to the content of the class. However, viewing videos is not a hands-on learning experience like experiments and observations, making it difficult for students to learn while thinking independently.

3   Guidelines and Design of the Teaching Material to Be Developed

3.1   Guidelines for the Teaching Material

To achieve better learning by following the purpose of this study and solving the problems of existing teaching materials, we developed the following guidelines for the development of teaching material.

① To enable students to acquire basic knowledge of the action of running water to study the concept of watersheds.

② To enable students to do developmental learning about the concept of watersheds and local disaster prevention.

③ Fewer restrictions on learning opportunities, allowing students to work at their own pace.

④ To enable students to learn independently, such as through experiments and observations.

3.2 Design of the Teaching Material

A Target Unit. According to the Japanese Courses of study, students learn about the action of running water in fourth and fifth grade. In the fourth grade unit "Where rainwater goes and how the ground looks," students acquire the knowledge that "Water flows from a high place to a low place and collects," which is the elementary knowledge to understand the concept of a watershed. As a result, we selected this unit as the target, and developed teaching materials that enable students to learn about the concept of watersheds by extending the basic study about "Water flows from a high place to a low place and collects."

Form of the Teaching Material. In the 2018 Programme for International Student Assessment by the Organization for Economic Co-operation and Development, the proportion of students who said they did not have access to the Internet at home was less than 5% [3]. It indicates that digital devices, such as access to the Internet, are familiar to students.

In Japan, through the GIGA School Initiative promoted by the Ministry of Education, Culture, Sports, Science, and Technology (MEXT), tablet devices for each student have already been delivered in more than 95% of Japan's regions.

Currently, tablet devices are standard learning tools for students with few restrictions on learning opportunities. Students can study independently at their own pace in an environment where each student has one device. Therefore, we select tablet devices as the form of the teaching material because it satisfies Guideline ③.

A Reference Teaching Material. The teaching material using a 3D topographic map model and marbles is close to the real phenomenon and concisely expresses the basic item to be learned, "water flows from a high place to a low place and collects." Despite its brevity, this teaching material is easy to implement, from the acquisition of basic knowledge to the developmental study of watershed concepts. As a result, we refer to teaching materials using a 3D topographic map model and marbles to develop the teaching material. Furthermore, by referring to teaching materials that allow for actual experiments and observations, students can have a similar experience on a tablet, so it satisfies Guideline ④.

4   Development of the Teaching Material

4.1   Outline of the Teaching Material

We refer to teaching materials using a 3D topographic map model and marbles, and develop the teaching material. First, a 3D topographical map is displayed on the screen of the tablet device. A ball that looks like rainwater falls at the touchpoint when a student touches the screen. After the ball falls, it rolls over the topographic map, drawing a trajectory. A student learns the basic properties of running water and the concept of watersheds by observing the path of a ball that resembles rain repeatedly.

4.2 Development Environment

Using the Unity game engine, we develop the teaching material. We use maps published as open data by the Geospatial Information Authority of Japan.

4.3 Composition of Teaching Materials

The teaching material have a basic learning mode and a developmental learning mode.

The basic learning mode is for acquiring the basic knowledge necessary to understand watershed concepts, and it satisfies Guideline ①. In the basic learning mode, students learn the following three study items.

(A) Water flows from a high place to a low place.
(B) Running water collects.
(C) At a certain point, water flows separately.

In addition to (A) and (B), which are to be studied in the target unit, students also learn (C), which is necessary to understand the concept of watersheds. At first, three study items (A), (B), and (C) are displayed on the screen. The appropriate terrain for each study is displayed when a student selects a study item. Students study by repeating observations.

The developmental learning mode is for learning about the concept of watersheds and disaster prevention, and it satisfies Guideline ②. Students select an area they want to study and observe the path of a ball on a topographic map of the respective area. Through repeated observations, they learn about the concept of watersheds and the composition of local watersheds.

4.4 Functions of Basic Learning Mode

To support students' learning, the basic learning mode has the following functions.

Switching perspectives
  A student switches between two perspectives by touching the icons on the screen (Fig. 1a, Fig. 1b). The perspective from above, with a broad view, is suitable for observing the confluence and separation of multiple balls. The perspective following the ball is suitable for observing how balls that resemble rainwater roll in more detail.

Multitouch viewpoint manipulation
  Students can move viewpoints with multitouch operations (Fig. 1c): one-finger swipe to translate, two-finger pinch-out to zoom in, two-finger pinch-in to zoom out, two-finger swipe to rotate around the horizontal axis, and two-finger rotate to rotate around the vertical axis. Students can observe the path of the ball at arbitrary positions and angles by operating in the same way as general map applications.

Display hints for study

When a student touches the icon for displaying hints, a sentence indicating the point of learning is displayed to clarify the points to be focused on in each item (Fig. 1d). By displaying hints in the middle of the study, a student can recognize the points to be focused on and repeat the observation of balls, so they acquire knowledge without fail.

(a) Perspective from above with a broad view (b) Perspective following the ball (c) Viewpoint manipulation (d) Display hints

Fig. 1. Functions of the basic learning mode

4.5 Functions of the Developmental Learning Mode

In addition to the same multitouch viewpoint manipulation as the basic learn-ing mode, the developmental learning mode has the following functions.

Display of watershed images

The watershed image can be switched between showing and hiding (Fig. 2a). When the image is hidden, students can learn independently by observing the ball while predicting where the watershed boundaries are. When the image is displayed, they observe balls while being aware of the actual watershed boundaries. Students confirm how rainwater collects within a watershed and can learn deeply to understand the concept and composition of watersheds.

Comment function

When students touch any point on the screen, an icon is placed at the touched point (Fig. 2b). When they touch the icon, a comment box for writing com-ments appears. Students write their repeated observations and predictions of possible disasters in the comment box.

Display of hazard maps

he hazard map for the selected area can be viewed (Fig. 2c). Students com-pare the hazard map to their predictions, which are written by the comment function. Students can determine whether their predictions were consistent or not, and notice risks that they were unable to predict.

Pen function

Students can freely draw lines on the screen when the pen function is enabled (Fig. 2d). They draw lines on the predicted trajectory of the balls and the predicted watershed boundaries. The pen function supports independent learning by making the student's predictions visible.

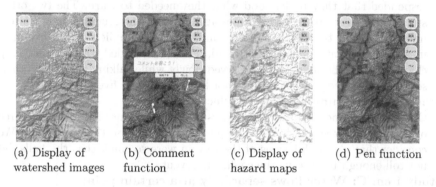

| (a) Display of watershed images | (b) Comment function | (c) Display of hazard maps | (d) Pen function |

Fig. 2. Functions of the developmental learning mode

5   A Trial Experiment of the Basic Learning Mode

A trial experiment was conducted with fourth-grade elementary school students to evaluate the user interface and the level of comprehension of the three study items in the basic learning mode.

5.1   Experimental Procedure

Students used each of the three study items in the basic learning mode for five minutes each. Three students use one device per person, and two students use one device per two people. In order to confirm that the students could operate the user interface without any confusion, their hands were recorded with a video camera.. Furthermore, we asked the students to fill out a questionnaire to test whether they could learn what they needed to learn while using each learning item.

5.2   Experimental Results

Evaluation of the User Interface. We confirmed the students' learning through video camera recordings. There was some misunderstanding about notation and the function of the user interface to switch perspectives. Regarding the notation, there were some situations in which the students had difficulty understanding the Japanese kanji notation and the meanings of words. The student had to drop the ball and then touch the icon for the perspective switching operation, but one student touched the icon and then drop the ball. Other operations were generally performed without difficulty, and we confirmed that the students were able to use the functions proactively.

Evaluation of the Level of Comprehension of the Three Study Items.
From the students' responses to the questionnaire, we examined whether they understood what they should learn in each study item.

Study item A: Water flows from a high place to a low place
  The three students who studied in the one device per person environment responded that they understood what they needed to learn. The two other students did not give specific responses. Three of the students immediately understood how to use the material and were fully studied within five minutes. Two students, on the other hand, initially struggled with reading kanji characters. Furthermore, they observed slowly while talking with each other, so it is considered that they could not learn enough in five minutes.

Study item B: Running Water collects
  One student responded that she understood what she needed to learn. Three of the four other students wrote about the phenomenon that balls stop. We consider that the undulations of the terrain were so small that the balls did not roll enough to observe the confluence event.

Study item C: Water flows separately at a certain point
  One student responded that she understood what she needed to learn. By displaying the hints at the beginning of the study, she understood what she needed to focus on. Three of the other four students saw the hint after about three minutes, and one student saw it just before the end of the study, but they did not notice anything that needed to be learned in the latter part of the study time.

5.3   Consideration

One reason for the lower comprehension of learning items B and C compared to learning item A might be the difference in the clarity of the terrain. The terrain used in study item A was relatively smooth, with clear differences in elevation, making it easier to clearly understand what was to be learned. On the other hand, the terrain used in study item B was less sloped and had many undulations, so the balls did not converge at the confluence that was assumed during the study's development.

  Differences in comprehension were also affected by differences in the properties of the study items. The students' responses to the questionnaire tended to focus on the properties of individual balls, such as rolling, stopping, and the speed of rolling. There were few descriptions of the relationship between multiple balls, such as their coming together or separation. While study item A is a property of a single ball, Study Items B and C are properties that are considered in terms of the relationship be-tween multiple balls. The reason for the differences in comprehension might be that the students could not consider the relationship between multiple balls due to the small number of balls they dropped, or that it is difficult for them to learn by focusing on the relationship between multiple balls.

6 Conclusions

We developed a teaching material using a tablet device that enables students to learn the concept of the watershed by extending their learning about the action of running water in elementary school. Students can acquire basic knowledge to understand the concept of watersheds in the basic learning mode. The developmental learning mode allows students to learn about watershed concepts and local watersheds.

The results of a trial experiment in the basic learning mode showed issues with the user interface and the topography and functions of each study item. In the future, some functions need to be improved based on the issues identified. Furthermore, to verify that the teaching materials are sufficiently useful, it is necessary to conduct large-scale evaluation experiment.

By using open data topographic maps of regions around the world, the developed teaching materials can be used for learning in other areas. It is expected that many students will learn the concept of watersheds in connection with their basic study of the action of running water and will acquire knowledge about disaster prevention.

References

1. Ministry of Education, Culture, Sports, Science and Technology: the courses of study for elementary. https://www.mext.go.jp/content/1413522_001.pdf
2. Ministry of Land, Infrastructure, Transport and Tourism: The white paper on land, infrastructure, transport and tourism in Japan (2020). https://www.mlit.go.jp/hakusyo/mlit/r01/hakusho/r02/pdf/np101100.pdf
3. Schleicher, A.: Pisa 2018 insights and interpretations. https://www.oecd.org/pisa/

Developing an English Rhythm Learning Support System Using Physical Exercise

Risa Segawa and Yu Suzuki[✉]

Miyagi University, 1-1, Gakuen, Taiwa-cho, Kurokawa-gun, Sendai, Miyagi, Japan
{p1720128,suzu}@myu.ac.jp

Abstract. Learning rhythm in a language, which is an element of pronunciation, is challenging when the rhythm differs from that of the native language. In this study, we developed Rhythm-Wan, which is a support system for learning English rhythm via physical exercise, to achieve an effective learning method for obtaining English rhythm using a computer-based method. This system focuses on the acoustically non-isochrony of the English language and supports the learning of English rhythm by linking the swaying movements of the body with reading English text aloud in the stressed syllables of the text. The results of the Rhythm-Wan experiment indicated a positive outcome. Although a more precise verification is required, the results are promising for the effect of rhythm acquisition.

Keywords: English prosody · Isochrony in English rhythm · Stress-timed language

1 Introduction

In terms of rhythmic typology, all languages can be classified as either syllable-timed or stress-timed [1]. In the former, each syllable is uttered simultaneously. In the latter, the time between the stressed syllable and the subsequent one is approximately the same. When native speakers of the syllable-timed rhythm learn a foreign language with a stress-timed rhythm (e.g., English), they find learning pronunciation difficult partly because of the rhythmic differences between the two languages [6].

Learning a language's rhythm is effective in improving speech intelligibility. However, when learning a language with a different rhythm, it is more difficult to master pronunciation than when learning a language with the same rhythm as one's native language. Acquiring a rhythm that differs from one's native language requires not only knowledge of the correct rhythm but also repeated practice and feedback. The best way to obtain feedback is to be guided by a teacher who is familiar with the language's pronunciation. However, there is a limited place and time for taking instructions. To address these problems, this study examines a computer-based method that is independent of the instructor. Further, this study achieves an effective learning method for acquiring the rhythm of language through computer-based methods.

© The Author(s), under exclusive license to Springer Nature Switzerland AG 2022
C. Stephanidis et al. (Eds.): HCII 2022, CCIS 1582, pp. 104–111, 2022.
https://doi.org/10.1007/978-3-031-06391-6_14

2   Acoustic Characteristics of English

English is a stress-timed rhythm language. Each syllable is uttered simultaneously in the syllable-timed rhythm. However, the time between a stressed syllable and the subsequent one has approximately the same utterance duration
in the stress-timed rhythm. Abercrombie [1] used the term foot to describe the
isochronous of English, where each time length between stress and the subsequent
stress is equal. The rhythmic structure of English is now explained theoretically
in the same way as that of music. In music, the measure corresponds to the foot.
However, actual foot lengths are extremely uneven when measured rigorously. In
Lehiste's view, native English speakers perceive the actual physical foot lengths
to be evenly spaced [4].

Chants are exercises, in which English words or sentences are re-cited repeatedly as music or rhythm. However, chants cannot cope with the acoustically
non-isochrony of the stress-timed rhythm. Chant-based rhythm education is well
known, but these rhythm-teaching methods assume that English is isochronous
at the foot level. Since English is not acoustically isochronous, the difference
between the rhythm of chants and natural English speech is problematic.

3   Related Research

Murao [5] examined the effect of learning language rhythm by reading sentences
aloud. The experimental results showed that neither parallel reading nor repetition was effective for learning the rhythm of the language. Thus, this study
employs an approach that incorporates multiple methods rather than just reading aloud. Additionally, this approach only provides feedback when the instructor
is present, limiting the place and time for taking instruction; thus, an approach
that does not require an instructor is used in this study.

Lappe et al. [3] demonstrated that using auditory and motor skills during
rhythm training is more efficient than using only auditory skills. Based on these
results, this study employs an approach that combines auditory and motor activities.

4   Rhythm-Wan, an English Rhythm Learning Support System

4.1   Approach

To address the issues of each study described in Chapter 3, this study eliminates
the need for an instructor. Additionally, physical exercise is incorporated into
the approach of this study because related studies have shown that combining
physical exercise and reading aloud is effective in acquiring rhythm.

4.2   Design Guideline to Solve the Problems of Existing Studies

To address the problems of the chants described in Chapter 2, this study follows guidelines that satisfy the following conditions:

- Make the user aware of isochrony
- No acoustic isochronism required

4.3   System Overview

Rhythm-Wan is a system for practicing English stress-timed rhythm by manipulating a dog character using body swaying movements and performing a well-timed vertical throw-up of a ball. Users read aloud the given English text and made the dog shoot the ball by swaying their body at the timing of each stressed syllable. A Balance Wii Board was used to obtain body sway.

4.4   System Configuration

The Rhythm-Wan system consists of a display, a computer, Google Cloud Platform Speech-to-Text, a wired microphone, and a Balance Wii Board.

The Balance Wii Board is used to obtain the user's body sway and is connected to the computer via Bluetooth; it uses OpenSound Control protocol to send data. The microphone is used to record the user's voice while reading aloud. The obtained voice is transcribed into text using Google Cloud Platform's Speech-to-Text, and the text data are used to evaluate the system's reading aloud. The screen is a large display; this enables the user to easily look at the screen while swaying. Unity was used to develop the system. The model speech voices from native speakers used in this system are from a dataset of native speakers of American languages in the database of Japanese students' spoken English (UME-ERJ) [2].

4.5   Usage

The system has two phases: ① and ②.

① This phase involves practicing reading aloud the target phrase or sentence in English.
② This phase involves practicing reading aloud the target phrase or sentence using body sway (Fig. 1)

In phase①, the user reads the target English phrase or sentence aloud into a microphone after a model speech voice. The user proceeds to phase② after reading aloud an arbitrary number of times. In the phrase, the same voice reading as in phase① is played first. The users read aloud and sway their bodies while looking at the English text, dog, and ball displayed on the screen. While reading aloud the English sentence displayed on the screen, the users manipulate the dog to hit the ball by swaying their body at the moment when each stress occurs in the sentence.

The ball flies over the dog's head at the timing of each stressed syllable. The ball rises vertically into the air when hit at that time. The time between the ball rising to the air and coming back over the dog's head represents the foot length. In other words, the longer the foot length, the higher the ball flies and the longer it suspends in the air.

For example, the sentence "This is the house that Jack built" stresses on "This," "house," "Jack" and "built." As the user reads this English sentence aloud, they make body swaying movements at the timing of these syllables being read aloud (Fig. 2).

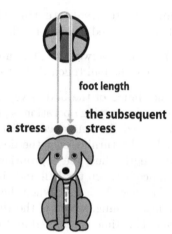

Fig. 1. A screen where the user performs rhythm learning

Fig. 2. An expression of isochrony

4.6 Function

Foot Length Calculation Function Based on User's Utterance Duration. The system calculates foot length based on the user's utterance duration. First, the foot length ratio of each target English sentences is calculated. As foot length is never uniquely determined, its ratio is calculated and recorded based on the number of seconds at which each syllable is pronounced in the audio file, which is manually recorded in advance. Further, the system obtains the time taken to read a sentence aloud from the user's speech during oral reading practice in phase①, as described in Sect. 4.5. The ratio of the time taken to read aloud to the pre-determined foot length is used to calculate the length of each foot in the target English sentence.

Foot length = time taken to read a sentence aloud × time taken to pronounce a particular foot in the audio file of the target English sentence ÷ the length of the audio file of the target English sentence.

The calculated foot length is reflected in the height at which the ball rises when moving from phase① to ②.

Function to Obtain Body Sway and Operate the System. A Balance Wii Board is used to obtain body sway and the user's centroid. As the centroid changes significantly when the body sways, the values of the centroid obtained in each frame vary from frame to frame, and swaying is determined when the values exceed an arbitrary threshold value. The centroid is expressed in two-dimensional coordinates in the vertical and horizontal directions. Because vertical swaying is more natural than horizontal in terms of body motion, the evaluation is based on the vertical values. The dog is manipulated to hit the ball based on the determined body sway.

Function to Evaluate the Timing of the User's Body Swaying. The following is used to evaluate the timing of the user's body swaying:

(A) distance between the ball and the dog's head
(B) time the ball touched the top of the dog's head overhead

If the timing of the body sway is earlier than the appropriate strength timing (i.e., if the swaying operation is performed when the ball is above the dog's head), (A) is used. As mentioned earlier, the distance between the ball leaving the dog's head and returning over the dog's head via a vertical throw-up represents the foot length; thus, the appropriateness of the timing can be calculated from the distance between the ball and the dog's head.

Further, (B) is used when the timing of the sway is later than the appropriate strength timing, which is the time since the ball touched the top of the dog's head. This time is retained and used for evaluation.

The user receives feedback from displaying effects that depict whether the timing of their body sway was appropriate or not, based on (A) or (B).

5   Evaluation Test

5.1   Test

Subjects and Evaluators. The subjects were 10 university students (six males and four females) and two native Canadian speakers (both males) as evaluators. The subjects were asked to experiment, and the evaluators were instructed to listen to the audio recordings obtained during the experiment for evaluation.

Experimental Procedures. The experiment consists of a pre-test, rhythm training, and post-test, simultaneously. First, in the pre-test, the subjects were instructed to read aloud the target phrases and sentences, and their speech was recorded. Next, in the rhythm training, they practiced the phrases and sentences 15 times each for three consecutive days using the Rhythm-Wan. Finally, in the post-test, they were instructed to read aloud the same Materials in the same way as the pre-test, which was then recorded. Furthermore, the evaluator compared the voice recordings between the pre-test and post-test and evaluated the results. The subjects were given a questionnaire survey after the post-test.

Target Phrases and Sentences. Experiments will be conducted on Materials 1, 2, 3, and 4. Materials 1 to 3 will be used throughout the pre-test, rhythm training, and post-test, whereas Material 4 will not be treated in the rhythm training but will be used for comparison.

Material 1 Market closing time
Material 2 This was easy for us.
Material 3 Please give us your name first.
Material 4 I will be ten years old this month.

Evaluation Items

- Intelligibility
- Idiomatically rhythmic

Intelligibility is the degree of agreement between the speaker's intended message and the listener's understanding. This can be measured on a five-point scale; one denotes "difficult to understand" and five is "easy to understand." Idiomatically rhythmic indicates the degree to which the speaker is rhythmic in terms of English speaking, which is a stress-timed rhythm language. It can be measured on a five-point scale; one means "not rhythmic" and five implies "as rhythmic as a native speaker." In the pre-test and post-test of the experimental procedure, the subjects' oral readings were recorded, respectively. These recordings were submitted to the evaluators who rated their intelligibility and idiomatically rhythmic. The average of all raters' scores on each item is used in the analysis.

5.2   Questionnaire Survey

The subjects were given a questionnaire after the post-test. On a five-point scale, the first item asked whether the subjects enjoyed learning with Rhythm-Wan to understand their effective evaluation of the Rhythm-Wan system. Furthermore, on a five-point scale, the second item asked whether the subjects think they have effectively mastered the rhythm using Rhythm-WanWan to understand how they perceive the learning effect. The other columns are for free-writing feedback. Additionally, the demographic items included whether the subjects had studied abroad and the duration of their study. They were asked whether they had taken the TOEIC (L&R) test and what their scores were, considering the possibility that the results might differ depending on their English proficiency level.

5.3 Result

Experiment

Tests Between Pre-test and Post-test. Wilcoxon signed-rank tests were conducted between the pre-test and post-test from Materials 1 to 4; a significant difference was observed for intelligibility in Material 2 with a 5% dominance level, but not for the others. We assumed that this is because the number of subjects was insufficient and that some subjects had mastered the rhythm from the beginning.

Tests Between Materials 1 to 3 and Material 4. The results of the test of the increase from the post-test to pre-test scores (post-test minus pre-test score) between Materials 1 to 3 and Material 4 demonstrated that the increase in the pre-test from the post-test scores was statistically significant in the case of either intelligibility or idiomatically rhythmic with a 5% dominance level. This comparison was effective because more subjects had a greater increase in the score for Materials 1 to 3 than for Material 4.

Observation of Rhythm Training During the Experiment. The following are the behavioral that managed and characterized the subjects' rhythm training during the experiment:

- Pattern in which the subjects mastered the correct rhythm
  - Cases in which the subjects skipped some syllables while reading aloud
- Pattern in which the subjects mastered incorrect rhythm
  - Cases in which the subjects could not synchronize body sway and reading aloud
  - Cases in which the subjects synchronized body sway and reading aloud, but misunderstood the rhythm

In the pattern of correctly learned rhythm, the most characteristic case was that a subject skipped some syllables while reading aloud. In the case of the dropout while reading aloud, the subject performed the swaying and reading aloud at the appropriate time, but occasionally skipped some syllables in the foot. When we inquired why this happened, the subject explained that she was too conscious of the timing of the swaying by gazing at the ball on the subtitle, and did not pay attention to the content of the text being read aloud.

In the case of the subject who failed to synchronize the swaying with the reading aloud, the subject correctly recognized the foot break and read aloud, but unsuccessfully synchronize the swaying with the stressed syllables until the end. As the target sentences were read aloud with the stress in the wrong position, it implies that the correct timing of swaying was not achieved because the timing of the stress was incorrectly recognized, although the respective foot break was recognized. In the case where the subjects synchronized swaying and reading aloud but misunderstood the rhythm, they learned with an incorrect understanding of the breaks in the foot. This may be because the position of the stressed vowel could not be accurately presented.

5.4   Analysis of Results

Although there was no significant difference between the pre-test and post-test for each Material, there was a significant difference between Materials in which the subjects conducted and did not conduct rhythm training, indicating that learning with Rhythm-Wan was effective. Precise verification is required by increasing the number of subjects. The effective evaluation in the questionnaire survey implies that the effect on the affective side was observed. Additionally, because the subjective evaluation of the learning effect in the questionnaire survey and the observations during rhythm training show that the correct rhythm information was not accurately presented, it is crucial to improve the method for presenting information on the foot break, making it more obvious.

6   Conclusion

In this study, we focused on the effects of isochronous and acoustically non-isochronous English and the effect of rhythm acquisition by the body, and we developed a device to support the learning of English rhythm through physical exercise. Further, we developed a system for learning English rhythm by mastering body sway using a Balance Wii Board and swaying the body at the timing of stressed syllables while reading English text aloud. The results of the experiment using Rhythm-Wan were effective. Although a more precise verification is required, there was a significant difference between the phrases and sentences that were practiced using Rhythm-Wan and those that were not practiced, indicating that there is an effect of rhythm acquisition.

References

1. Abercrombie, D.: Syllable quantity and enclitics in English, pp. 216–222. Longmans, Green, London (1964)
2. Consortium, S.R.: UME-ERJ. https://research.nii.ac.jp/src/UME-ERJ.html
3. Lappe, C., Trainor, L.J., Herholz, S.C., Pantev, C.: Cortical plasticity induced by short-term multimodal musical rhythm training. PLoS ONE **6**(6), 1–8 (2011)
4. Lehiste, I.: Isochrony reconsidered. J. Phonetics **5**, 253–263 (1977)
5. Murao, R., et al.: ARELE: does reading-aloud training facilitate the improvement of English stress-timed rhythm? A comparison between repeating and parallel reading. Annu. Rev. English Lang. Educ. Jpn. **29**, 289–304 (2018)
6. Otaka, H., Kamiya, A.: On the validity of the isochrony of feet in the English rhythm. Lang. Cult. **16**, 17–23 (2013)

Development of Instructional Model in Virtual Design Classroom

Sang-Duck Seo(⊠)

University of Nevada Las Vegas, Las Vegas, NV 89154, USA
sang-duck.seo@unlv.edu

Abstract. This study investigates a new design pedagogy with remote instruction in a virtual teaching and learning environment. Ever since the pandemic crisis forced shifting online and remote instructions, there were chaotical concerns about whether the present digital tools and instructional models were applicable to all disciplines in higher education. Design education is traditionally comprised of the studio hands-on basis where students interact with a peer group. Even though face-to-face in-person instruction replaced video conference in remote instruction, there were still limited interaction and communication tools for learning and teaching in a virtual environment. This study developed an experimental pedagogy and instruction model and measured the effectiveness of learning and teaching outcomes in comparison to three semesters. The analysis of implemented instruction models was compared with the in-person instruction and open-ended survey responses were discussed for improvements and developments of instructional tools and models. In finding, this study found that design discipline can be driven by remote instruction more effectively even though there is limited access for the physical facilities in their creativity. This study also addresses the significance of new design pedagogy in preparation for the new paradigm of a working environment in the design profession.

Keywords: Remote instructions · Virtual classroom · Self-directed learning

1 Introduction

The nature of art and design education refers to various "hands-on creativity studios" [3] as a part of the critical-thinking-development. "Studio Art and Design" is interpreted as a tangible space [9] not only providing facilities for creativity but also accommodating students to interact with each other for the group works in each course [5]. In pedagogical semantic, "Studio Art and Design" provides students' learning attitude with "attention, inspiration, and motivation" as an effective learning climate [2, 12, 15]. Since the COVID-19 pandemic enforced a higher education shifting to the 'emergency remote teaching' [1], 'emergency eLearning' [17], 'complex environment of online teaching' [18], studio art and design instructors have dealt with technology issues to accommodate students learning in virtual studio classroom which appears as a significant limitation of class activities and a lack of interaction in learning [4, 10]. A few video conferencing tools such as "Zoom," "Webex," and "Google Meet" introduced a new paradigm

C. Stephanidis et al. (Eds.): HCII 2022, CCIS 1582, pp. 112–119, 2022.
https://doi.org/10.1007/978-3-031-06391-6_15

of expanding virtual classrooms. Many instructors had to challenge remote-instruction guidelines given by their institute and it has become instructors' responsibility to learn how to use digital tools effectively for keeping students' learning activity as same as an in-person class. This learning environment, especially digital media education including graphic design disciplines has been critical to examine the viability of current programs towards the new technological resources and instruction [16, 19].

According to the report in 2016 from Princeonomics Data Studio, 75% of the top-ranked higher education institutes in the United States has offered online degree while offering online degree in art and design discipline appeared as low [8]. Moreover, the 2017 US News reported that only five colleges were offering an online undergraduate degree in Graphic Design discipline. This significant fact also depicted that many educators and design students could not see effective social interactions whether students may obtain equivalent quality in their learning experience through the online course [11]. Dreamson [6, 7] articulated that it is an appropriate time for adopting a digitally networked learning environment for learner's connective experiences such as "meta-, inter-, trans-, and extra-." Therefore, we need to revisit existing online courses to investigate the issues faced by instructors and students in teaching and learning through a virtual environment.

2   Method

This study focuses on the investigation of the current issues of remote instructions for online teaching and learning art and design education. Among several studies related to online design education, Fleischmann [8] demonstrated five key strategies for effective online design course through the investigation of students' attitudes towards online learning: *1) instant feedback from instructors; 2) idea exchanges between instructors and students; 3) receiving instant peer feedback; 4) checking work progress; 5) direct collaboration.* This study applied the five strategies to measure and analyze the limitation of the current graphic design studio-based learning and teaching. The research method for the comparisons between remote and in-person instruction was demonstrated by sequential analysis with three phases: *P1) Online instruction and tools: analysis effectiveness of interactive pedagogy in a virtual environment, P2) Experimenting a new pedagogy with remote instruction: Discussion for a new teaching and learning methods in various aspects of online studio art and design disciplines, and P3) Learning outcomes and assessment: Discussion with survey responses in regards to remote and self-directed learning in creativity.*

3   Analysis and Findings

The study measured and analyzed the effectiveness of remote teaching and learning instruction in the studio-based discipline. The data and samples were collected from GRC 470 Graphic Design Studio IV that was taught by the researcher in the 2020 Spring Semester.

3.1 Analysis of Online Instruction Tools and Methods

Prior to the COVID-19 pandemic, online courses in higher education appeared as mostly vocational disciplines by learning digital tools such as graphic design, illustrations, and web design [8]. It is not clearly specified yet between online and remote instruction even though the term the "remote instruction" was appeared by the online face-to-face meeting [13]. However, Bozkurt and Sharma [1] referred to 'distance education' as a process characterized by 'distance in time and/or space' and to 'remote education' as a context of 'spatial distance.' The concepts of online teaching and learning are significantly considered to redefine the characteristics of online environments and connectivity manipulated by technology [14]. Table 1 is an analysis of terms between online and remote instruction that describes different characteristics and conditions in teaching and learning. Remote instruction is more likely arranged by synchronized meeting time and place which is based on approaching the in-person class instruction. In contrast, online instruction provides students more flexible time and self-directed learning progress beyond assessment methods for students' learning accomplishments.

Table 1. Analysis of terms in instruction methods

Method	Online term	Remote term
Condition	Unsynchronized	Synchronized
Schedule	Flexible	Fixed
Meeting	Virtual Drive/Archive	Virtual Face-to-face Meeting room
Communication	Indirect	Direct and indirect
Resources	Indirect	Direct and indirect
Learning style	Self-directed	In-directed
Effective learning model	Tutorials and Lecture Basis	Critical-Thinking Problem-Solving, Critique

According to the nature of user-interaction and user-communication in a virtual face-to-face environment, audio and video access is a primary tool for exchanging information and content (Fig. 1). This is an essential standard to deliver effective communication and interaction of social, cognitive, and teaching [9]. Moreover, art and design classes demand dynamic interaction between students during a critique and brainstorming. Carrillo and Flores [4] recently conducted research to review the literature on online teaching and learning and analyzed 134 papers for educational experience based on the seven criteria. The findings show that only nine papers appeared most relevant with the 'use and effects of video,' but 27 papers discussed 'interaction among participants' in online learning. Referring to the result, this research collected further samples and data in communication tools and applications through online research. Several online applications have introduced common functions and tools, but it was found a little different feature in terms of competitive distinctions. Besides, instructors and students were given limited choices to meet their class from a few particular profit-oriented platforms in which resources remain more private enterprises than public goods [17].

Fig. 1. The current standard of virtual meeting room structure for instruction and communication methods between users.

3.2 New Experimental Pedagogy by Remote Instruction

Since all class shifted the online or remote instructions due to the pandemic emergency in March 2020, most schools considered one of the pre-oriented video conferencing tools as a top priority for replacing in-person instruction into the virtual learning environment. Schwartzman [14] discussed the phenomenon of pandemic pedagogy that importantly reflected next p as probing pandemic pedagogy. While asynchronous instruction has set for convenient accessibility and connectivity through several online education, synchronous instruction provided studio-based education with various advantages for engaging with classmates and instructors in real-time simultaneously interacting face-to-face communication with each other. Table 2 shows a comparison of the instructional model between two semesters (Spring and Fall 2020) shifted learning instructions for a major graphic design studio that focuses on User Experience Design (UXD) taught by the author.

Table 2. Comparison of Instructional model

Instruction	(I)* Spring 2020	(R)** Spring 2020	Fall 2020
Lecture	S	G	S
Brainstorming	S	G	S
Feedback (Process)	S, G	S, E, G	S
Critique	S	S, G	S
Assessment	E	E	G

S (Face to Face Synchronized), E (Email), G (Google Drive), *I (In-Person Instruction), **R (Remote Instruction)

This comparison is significant to be ongoing pedagogical development for the effective learning model. The color on the table cell indicates that there were significant differences in effective learning interaction based on the given condition of each instructional model. From the findings of ineffective instruction methods for learning and teaching with digital tools in Spring 2020, the class has introduced a revised instructional model in Fall 2020. The lecture was more effective in synchronized remote instruction because students appeared comprehension level better on the live lecture in which instructors can interact/engage with students for instant discussions and questions. Like the problem-solving process in the design discipline, developing design concepts and idea requires high demands in face-to-face live brainstorming. Even if students were given for further discussion with any suggestions and comment through the shared documents in "Google Slide" (Fig. 2) considering their flexibility, it appeared as not effective due to less engagement and commitments. Group critique and peer evaluation also appeared less effective in synchronized instruction. Flexible self-directed participant on the sharing documents was more successfully engaged with peer groups to continue discussions.

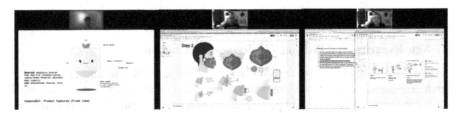

Fig. 2. WebEx virtual meeting room in screen shared mode and google online tools

3.3   Measuring Learning Outcomes and Accessing Remote Instruction Models

This study fundamentally identifies the importance of the effectiveness in student learning, and instructor teaching methods and tools because remote instruction has more limited interaction and communication compared to personal instruction. At the end of Spring 2020, the survey for learning effectiveness through remote instruction was distributed to 20 students, and 18 responses were collected.

Firstly, this study found a significant lack of self-motivation for making progress in their design process. Figure 3 was the survey responses from the question, *"Q1. During a remote instruction, what was the most/least your challenge to accomplish the learning objective?"* Most students felt that time management and self-directed work progress were the most challenging while given flexibility for face-to-face individual virtual-meeting and other communication methods regardless of class schedule appear less challenge for their learning.

Even though students were working alone at home, communication methods, or sharing their working progress and getting so feedbacks from the peer group became an important learning task. For the survey question, *"Q2. For getting some feedback from working progress, which communication tool was the most effective from your experience?"* 77.8% of students responded that written statements and visual descriptions through email and shared drive appeared as the most effective tool and method rather than a virtual live meeting. The reason was found from the following question, "Q3. what was the reason for your answer to Q2? Surprisingly students felt that online digital

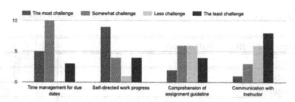

Fig. 3. Analysis of challenge in remote instruction

communication tools and methods were more rapidly delivered (72.2%) and effectively accessible as needed (83.3%).

Additional concerns and other issues were collected from the exit interview. Most students at the final group meeting expressed that virtual face-to-face meeting was working properly, but it was not preferred due to the unstable internet connection and lack of direct interaction through the video conferencing. A few students were positive with the virtual face-to-face meeting in terms of better attention to the computer screen without any interrupted circumstances. Also, many students believe that remote instructions can accommodate most graphic design disciplines as equivalent to the in-person design studio if accessibility, flexibility, and interactivity are considered for working progress in course instruction. This depicts those students would be engaged better with a studio group work if the instruction is more flexible and condensed rather than obligating entire class hours.

Another interpretation is that remote instruction may have an issue with only limited time consuming for the concentration to the work and discussion. Comprehension level of learning subject matter and the problem-solving process appeared as "effective." This finding addresses remote instruction as a positive method with supplemental resources delivered through an online environment such as live screen sharing and google drive. Moreover, most students responded to positive experiences in effective flexibility and accessibility by using "Google Slide" that provides interactive tools and functions to tack the communication in a peer group. This is another reason why most students prefer email and shared drive as the most effective communication tools in remote instruction. Synchronized virtual meeting such as video conferencing is necessary for a live lecture or individual/small group meetings on feedback and critique.

Table 3. Assessment summary of learning effectiveness of remote instruction methods

Effectiveness for Remote Instruction		ME	E	M	L	LE
Comprehension		▒	■			
Self-Motivation			▒		■	
Time-management				▒	■	
Synchronized virtual meeting	Lecture	▒	■			
	Feedback	▒	▒	▒		
	Critique			▒		
Unsynchronized Communication tools	Email	■	▒			
	Shared Drive	■				
Color density indicates the preference						

80%~	60~80%	40~60%	20~40%	0~20%	0%

M (Most effective), E (Effective), M (Mutual), L (Less effective), LE (Least effective)

From both big and small group meetings, students felt that a small group (4 students per group) is more effective to interact with online communication in limited time and space. A few students also expressed that missing shared camera views from some classmates are not easy to interact with a sense of effective responses such as body language, facial expression, and climate in dialogue. This author had the same experience with lectures and group critiques when the meetings were held on a shared screen.

4 Conclusion and Discussion

This study investigated a virtual learning environment for studio-based education. The "pandemic pedagogy" as becoming a new term in higher education, this study initially reviewed a few profit-oriented platforms that most instructors and learners were adopted by their institutes. Through collected data from the empirical teaching design studio and survey responses, this study found answers to the early research questions. Art and design studio-based learning activities have shown significant limitations in general due to the absence of accessing studio facilities and space, but learning and teaching activities such as lecture, critique, and group work are still possible to make it effective and tangible like in-person instruction. Another finding, comparing synchronized and unsynchronized class meetings in a design studio, has shown significant values that support the importance of developing new pedagogy for the face-to-face studio class through virtual meeting space and digital tools. Meeting characteristic as a "real-time" can be easily replaced in virtual spatial but interactive communication in "real-time" is not yet seen as effective values compared with in-person meetings or communication. This underpins that the virtual meeting environment is still lacked by other necessary or essential attributes of the n teaching and learning model, especially cognitive and perceptive interaction via video conferencing. This study, however, was difficult to find an assessment tool for students' learning outcomes due to the absence of accuracy in learning and teaching objectives based on different disciplines. According to the design studio-based disciplines without required studio space for their creativity, it is recommended to create an assessment rubric different from in-person class to be objectively measured for effective teaching and learning model. Therefore, the findings of various limitations and constraints in studio-based teaching and learning by remote instruction reflect the future study to develop a virtual studio-based learning environment and tools. This study continues cultivating new design pedagogy through virtual studio learning for art and design education.

References

1. Bozkurt, A., Sharma, R.C.: Emergency remote teaching in a time of global crisis due to corona virus pandemic. Asian J. Dis. Educ. **15**(1), i–vi (2020)
2. Brewer, G., Hogarth, R., ProQuest: Creative education, teaching and, learning : creativity, engagement, and the student experience. Palgrave Macmillan (2015)
3. Button, T.A.: Design and studio pedagogy. J. Architectural Educ. **14**(1), 16–25 (1987)
4. Carrillo, C., Flores, M.A.: COVID-19 and teacher education: a literature review of online teaching and learning practices. Eur. J. Teach. Educ. **43**(4), 466–487 (2020)
5. Demirbas, O.O., Demirkan, H.: Learning styles of design students and the relationship of academic performance and gender in design education. Learn. Instr. **17**(3), 345–359 (2007)
6. Dreamson, N.: Online design education: meta-connective pedagogy. Int. J. Art Des. Educ. **39**(3), 483–497 (2020)
7. Dreamson, N.: Critical understandings of digital technology in education: meta-connective pedagogy. Routledge, New York, London (2020)
8. Fleischmann, K.: Online design education: searching for a middle ground. Arts Humanit. Higher Educ. **19**(1), 36–57 (2020)
9. Garrison, D.R., Anderson, T., Archer, W.: Critical inquiry in a text-based environment: computer conferencing in higher education. Internet Higher Educ. **2**(2), 87–105 (1999)
10. Hart, J., Zamenopoulos, T., Garner, S.: The learning scape of a virtual design atelier, Compass J. Learn. Teach. Univ. Greenwich **2**(3), 1–15 (2011)
11. Ioannou, O.: Design studio education in the online paradigm: introducing online educational tools and practices to an undergraduate design studio course, IEEE Global Engineering Education Conference (EDUCON), pp. 1871–1875 (2017)
12. McIntosh, P., Warren, D.: Creativity in the classroom case studies in using the arts in teaching and learning in higher education. Intellect (2013)
13. Newman, G., et al.: Online learning in landscape architecture: assessing issues, preferences, and student needs in design-related online education online. Landsc. J. **37**(2), 41–63 (2018)
14. Schwartzman, R.: Performing pandemic pedagogy. Commun. Educ. **69**(4), 502–517 (2020)
15. Seitamaa-Hakkarainen, P., et al.: Pedagogical infrastructures of design studio learning. J. Textile Des. Res. Pract. **4**(2), 155–181 (2016)
16. Swann, C., Young, E. (eds.): Re-inventing Design Education in the University. In: Proceedings of the Perth International Conference. Perth: School of Design, Curtin University of Technology (2002)
17. Williamson, B., Eynon, R., Potter, J.: Pandemic politics, pedagogies and practices: digital technologies and distance education during the coronavirus emergency. Learn. Media Technol. **45**(2), 107–114 (2020)
18. Zhang, W., Wang, Y., Yang, L., Wang, C.H.: Suspending classes without stopping learning: china's education emergency management policy in the COVID-10 Outbreak. J. Risk Finan. Manage. **13**(58), 1–6 (2020)
19. American Institute of Graphic Arts and National Association of Schools of Art and Design (AIGA/NASAD) (2016) Technology Thresholds in Graphic Design Programs (2016). https://nasad.arts-accredit.org/wp-content/uploads/sites/3/2016/03/AIGA_N ASAD_technology.pdf. Accessed 6 Sep 2020

The Applied Study of Reverse Engineering: Learning Through Games Based on Role-Play

Yao Song[1], Hang Su[2], and Yuan Liu[3(✉)]

[1] Central Academy of Fine Arts, Beijing, China
[2] Central Saint Martins, London, England
suhangdesign@163.com
[3] Beijing Institute of Fashion Technology, Beijing 100029, China
yuan.liu@polimi.it

Abstract. Learning through Games is a mature teaching method, which has many applications in the field of e-learning through gamification, Intercultural learning or Promoting global empathy and interest. This study takes role-play as the main teaching idea and aims to understand the relationship between product and materials technology, structure design and appearance design from multiple perspectives by substituting students into different roles (designer, engineer and design director) in product engineering process.

This case work is a part of product design course of China Central Academy of Fine Arts (CAFA). It takes reverse engineering as the medium and teaches sophomores. In the process of dismantling and reconstructing products, the team members had a clear division of labor according to the requirements in advance, including project manager, engineer, designer and recorder. They worked closely with each other to interpret the pre-set problems of the course from different perspectives, so as to solve various problems encountered in reverse engineering. Finally, through the form of questionnaire, the teaching method of Learning through games based on role play has been verified by the form of evaluation questionnaire. The results show that most students have reached the cognitive level of reverse engineering.

We see this period of work as practical study, aiming to verify the possibility of using role-play to intervene in product design courses. In the second stage of the study, we will systematically deepen role-play characters, environmental scenes and design props.

Keywords: Role play · Learning through games · Reverse engineering

1 Introduction

In today's economic situation and complex social production relations, each individual needs to play the role in his own post, so as to ensure the smooth progress of socialized mass production. For instance, in the product design field, the birth of each product is actually the result of the close cooperation between designers, engineers, project managers and other roles. Cannot leave the "role" given by the society or the enterprise, many

C. Stephanidis et al. (Eds.): HCII 2022, CCIS 1582, pp. 120–127, 2022.
https://doi.org/10.1007/978-3-031-06391-6_16

graduates grow up quickly after leaving campus. And it is in such a real environment that talents in all walks of life can grow rapidly.

The way of communication between people (especially unfamiliar relationships), the efficiency of communication and teamwork will also have a profound impact on the whole design process, which is relatively lacking in school, especially in Chinese design education. However, the "strange relationship" in the society leads to the tendency of people to work with familiar people. In the "non-acquaintance" environment, people usually choose to keep a certain distance in body and language, and even a considerable number of people today suffer from social phobia. This, however, runs counter to the frequent communication that is common in design jobs.

Therefore, in the actual education process, compared with the traditional teaching mode of teachers speaking and students listening, we should try to use immersion learning to enable students to effectively learn professional knowledge. And learning through role play is a very good way. Through design to simulate a real character, and with other strange classmates in class based on the study of product design task, students can not only learn the necessary professional knowledge, but also exercise the comprehensive ability, such as team consciousness, cooperation ability and so on.

2 Literature Review and Theoretical Background

2.1 Role Play in Education

Role playing is a very effective teaching method, which has been proved by teaching cases in many countries in the world. Here we have three examples, from learning chemistry by playing the role of a game designer, learning the Code of Hammurabi by playing the various professions of ancient Mesopotamia, and developing global empathy by experiencing the lives of people around the world through computer games.

Between 2010 and 2013, about 40% of test takers in Malaysia were unable to achieve high grades due to the abstract nature of chemistry concepts, which is generally considered a difficult and undesirable subject. To solve this problem, the researchers put students in the role of game designers, trying to develop digital games while studying chemistry. Quasi-experimental non-equivalent control group and pre - and post-test control group were used in this study. The subjects were 138 middle school students. The results showed that the treatment group was superior to the control group in the chemical achievement test. The results suggest that involving students as game designers in chemistry learning can help students gain a deeper understanding of chemistry, develop chemistry skills for the 21st century, and improve students' motivation to learn chemistry.

In GameDesk's "Time- LARPs" course, students and teachers play fictional characters set in ancient Mesopotamian Settings during the reign of Hammuraby (1779 to 1715 BC). Students played the roles of the existing various professional, the businessman, the governor, astrologers, and the priest), Interacting with each other in the characters to achieve goals in the game, and a deeper understanding of the social norms and cultural practices. In essence, spontaneous, co-creation, role-playing involves scenes, and one of the best ways to introduce this concept into the classroom is through LARPs. LARPs stands for Live Action Role-play, which is part performance, part historical immersion/interaction, and part system modeling. Through this systematic teaching model, students are encouraged to enjoy and retain their knowledge in their experience. It uses emotion as a mechanism for students to personalize key knowledge, processes and concepts. It involves concretization and situational modeling, leading students not only to study the Code of Hammurabi, but to actually experience it (Fig. 1).

Fig. 1. The LARPs in GameDesk's "Time-LARp" course[1].

To cope with an increasingly interdependent world, empathy was seen as a particularly important ability to cross national boundaries and cultural divides, and to understand others. However, it is difficult for people to empathize with different people in different cultural and geographical contexts. "Real Life" is a computer simulation game in which players experience personal lives around the world. Compared with the control group, students who used simulation games as part of their course showed more global empathy and were more interested in learning about other countries. Identification with roles in real life is also positively correlated with global empathy. In this way, role-playing helps realize mutual identification among people from different cultural backgrounds and makes people more empathetic.

Through the above three cases, it can be found that role playing plays a strong role in enhancing people's cognition of unfamiliar areas. This learning method has been widely used around the world, especially in the field of education, with many successful cases and very high value.

Role playing has an important enlightening significance for learning, which can be summarized as follows:

In science teaching, chemistry is regarded as a boring subject due to the abstractness of its concepts. However, through the fun of role-playing and the immersive experience of

[1] Source: https://journals.sagepub.com/doi/abs/10.1177/1046878111432108.

letting students play as game designers, they can have a deep understanding of chemistry knowledge and become more enthusiastic.

In the field of religion, situational learning and role playing enable students to effectively learn the Code of Hammurabi.

In the field of culture, people from different regions can understand each other by experiencing the lives of people from different parts of the world, which solves the problem of mutual incomprehension and lack of empathy between different parts of the world.

2.2   The Necessity of Role Playing in Industrial Design Education

The complexity of today's society and design activities requires designers to have strong comprehensive ability, people who create products and services have to be generalists, they need to know something about everything. However, there is still a lack of enlightening and systematic teaching methods to train students' product cognition ability, structure understanding ability and other abilities centered on understanding and memory.

From an extensive literature review, few scholars have attempted to relate the concept of role-play-based learning through play to design learning. However, we find that this direction is very worthy of discussion, because through good experience, students can deeply understand the necessary knowledge at the undergraduate stage, so that they can adapt to the society more quickly in the future social practice and improve the speed of individual growth.

In the traditional teaching mode, for example, teachers use pdf. to impart knowledge to students. In fact, students get a single and boring experience. This leads to a lot of necessary knowledge cannot be effectively conveyed, or students' experience is not deep enough to effectively learn, resulting in poor information. In this reverse engineering class, students can learn the knowledge of industrial products from the game roles of designers, engineers, project manager and so on. This method not only enables students to quickly master the necessary knowledge and fill the gap of product cognition, but also exercises the ability to cooperate with each other and become more comprehensive talents.

3   Method

3.1   Experimental Method

As can be seen from the above theoretical basis, it is an effective method for students to learn in the form of role-playing in games. This experiment is a part of product design course of China Central Academy of Fine Arts (CAFA). It takes reverse engineering as the medium for the sophomores. In the process of dismantling and reconstructing products, the team members had a clear division of labor according to the requirements in advance, including project manager, engineer, designer and recorder. They worked closely with each other to interpret the pre-set problems of the course from different perspectives, so as to solve various problems encountered in reverse engineering.

In the process of the experiment, three kinds of problems that students may encounter are fully considered in advance, which are: (a) technical problem, (b) lack of knowledge reserve, and (c) teamwork problems. These categories of problems are the potential learning content of this project. By exposing random problems and solving them, the purpose of solving the cognitive gap problem of students is achieved, and it is also the simulation of common problems encountered in future practical projects.

3.2 The Experimental Process

First, the game is divided into four distinct roles, the product manager, the product engineer, the product designer and the recorder.

Each role has its own clear tasks, such as product engineers to solve complex research on product structure and materials, product designers to interpret product functions and man-machine design from the perspective of design, and so on.

The process of the experiment can be divided into three steps, which are divided into (a) Grouping, (b) Disassemble and (c) Restructuring (Fig. 2).

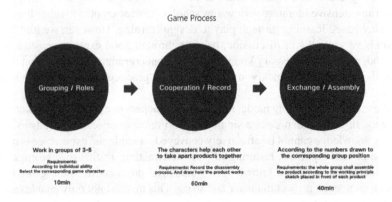

Fig. 2. The game process and work groups.

a) **Grouping**

This course is made up of sophomores from different freshman classes who are willing to learn product design. At the same time, the ratio of boys to girls in the class is close to 1:1. Therefore, the following principles are adopted in the grouping:

1. Do not form groups with your classmates (try to cooperate with strangers)
2. It must be a mix of boys and girls
3. Mix according to different characters/areas of personal expertise (learn through games) (Fig. 3)

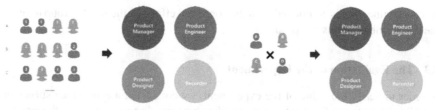

Fig. 3. The grouping and roles to choose.

In this way, the original relationship between classmates was broken, and the relationship between "groups" and cooperation is transformed into a new one. The grouping time was controlled within 10 min, and each individual matched with other members through self-introduction, thus breaking the inherent relationship for the first time and establishing a new partnership. Take a group of four as an example, two boys and two girls from four classes formed a temporary group based on their respective roles in a strange relationship with each other.

b) **Disassemble**

The process of disassembling is the main part of the game, After the joint research, and under the planning of the product manager, the "waste products" brought by the team members were disassembled. Because the knowledge of the product structure and material is not understood, the engineering aspects of the project are solved by the "engineer" role, and the students who play the role need to give the corresponding strategies, such as how to disassemble a part, or how the department is assembled in a fixed way to find the corresponding tools for disassembling. In the process of disassembly, designers need to analyze from the perspective of design, what function the parts of the product are composed to accomplish, and what component composition and structural design are supported by this function. The idea of realizing this function needs to be fully discussed with engineers and other team members. The product manager and the recorder are responsible for the overall task assignment and the auxiliary work/record dismantling process respectively.

After disassembly, each group will leave the disassembly process drawings recorded on the table, put the disassembled parts in order, and then draw lots in the hand of the professor. The whole group will be transferred to other group's table.

c) **Restructuring**

Now each team is faced with the task of disassembling and reassembling, which is an important part of reverse engineering. According to the left records from the former team (manuscripts and pictures, text), the product manager again leads the group to study the "explosion" of products, through reverse thinking, each role play to their advantages, engineer according to the basic principle of structure and material of "reconstruction", Designers push back from the point of view of function and design and so on. Finally, reverse engineering is completed with the concerted efforts of the whole group to restore the disassembled industrial products.

3.3 The Evaluation of the Experiment

In order to verify the value of the experiment, we conducted a centralized survey and sampling of students afterwards, so as to make a horizontal comparison with the results of the same type of courses in previous years. Mentioned by more than 86% of the students in this experiment, and shows the content of the learned to be lively, by disassembling, reassembling, touching the product itself, checking documents and learning in person, and cooperating with the teacher's PPT before class, the content they learned was deeply impressed and more solid. And in the whole process of disassembly and reorganization, the problems encountered and knowledge learned are actually dominated by comprehension, such knowledge is difficult to learn through simple explanation, but through active learning hands-on practice, namely exercise on the actual product, students can more deeply understand the knowledge, which also increased the interest in the product design.

4   Discussion

4.1 Discussion of Experimental Results

Based on observations and follow-up interviews, students found the tool to be very helpful in learning and to be able to stimulate their subjective initiative to some extent and achieve their learning goals in an immersive experience. Through role-playing, they can clearly see what they have to do and try to solve various problems based on the character's attributes. Most of the students can well integrate into each role, but due to the different professional background of each student, there will be different reactions and solutions to the problems, but due to the modular design of the task, finally achieve the goal of learning.

In conclusion, the toolbox is generally available, and the actual results of the experiment are close to the prediction. The user group of this toolkit is suitable for students just beginning their study of industrial design. Through this tool kit, students can master the necessary professional knowledge and cognition more quickly. Therefore, our task kit has more vivid and intuitive advantages than the traditional teaching methods.

To sum up, this study disassembled and analyzed the concepts and related theories of role-playing-based learning through games, and reflected them into corresponding toolkits to achieve the purpose of research and learning. Through the process of experiments, students have a preliminary understanding of purely theoretical knowledge, which can help their subsequent study and work in the future.

4.2 Future Works

At present, we have preliminarily verified the possibility and rationality of toolkit in teaching tasks, but there are still many unfinished parts, including the development of more role-playing-related models to adapt to different teaching contents and tasks. At the same time, the follow-up will strengthen the guidance of the game process, to help users better understand the task and scene. The effectiveness of teaching, including whether the tool kit can be used to stimulate students' learning and understanding of the profession as a whole, It needs to be verified and evaluated.

References

1. Andersson, N., Andersson, P.H.: Teaching professional engineering skills–industry participation in realistic role play simulation. Making change last: Sustaining and globalizing engineering educational reform (2010)
2. Boradkar, P.: Design as problem solving. The Oxford handbook of interdisciplinarity, pp. 273–287 (2010)
3. Casakin, H.P.: Factors of metaphors in design problem-solving: implications for design creativity. Int. J. Des. 1(2), 21–33 (2007)
4. Druckman, D., Ebner, N.: Onstage or behind the scenes? Relative learning benefits of simulation role-play and design. Simul. Gaming 39(4), 465–497 (2008)
5. Jonassen, D.H.: Instructional design as design problem solving: an iterative process. Educ. Technol. 21–26 (2008)
6. Liu, Y., Ricco, D., Calabi, D.A.: Immersive learning. from basic design for communication design: a theoretical framework. In: 6th International Conference for Design Education Researchers DRS LEARNxDESIGN 2021. Engaging with Challenges in Design Education, vol. 3, pp. 756–771. Design Research Society (2021)
7. Naidu, S., Ip, A., Linser, R.: Dynamic goal-based role-play simulation on the web: a case study. J. Educ. Technol. Soc. 3(3), 190–202 (2000)
8. Otto, K.N.: Product design: techniques in reverse engineering and new product development. 清华大学出版社有限公司 (2003)
9. Otto, K.N., Wood, K.L.: Product evolution: a reverse engineering and redesign methodology. Res. Eng. Des. 10(4), 226–243 (1998)
10. Sheng, I.L., Kok-Soo, T.: Eco-efficient product design using theory of inventive problem solving (TRIZ) principles. Am. J. Appl. Sci. 7(6), 852 (2010)
11. Wood, K.L., Jensen, D., Bezdek, J., Otto, K.N.: Reverse engineering and redesign: courses to incrementally and systematically teach design. J. Eng. Educ. 90(3), 363–374 (2001)

Logi-Corock: Learning Game Using Tangible Interfaces for Programming Education

Yu Suzuki$^{(\boxtimes)}$ and Fuka Iida

School of Project Design, Miyagi University, 1-1 Gakuen, Taiwa-cho,
Kurokawa-gun, Miyagi 981-3298, Japan
suzu@myu.ac.jp

Abstract. "Programming education" is an education to foster computational thinking. Children acquire the logical thinking skills necessary to have computers perform the intended process through hands-on programming experience. In this study, we developed a learning game "Logi-Corock" that can be played intuitively. This game supports the learning of computational thinking at home. We chose a simple physical phenomenon as the game' s subject to allow it to be played with little prior knowledge of the rules and language. Users play the game with block-shaped tangible interfaces. This game contributes to acquiring computational and logical thinking at home.

Keywords: Computational thinking · Programming education

1 Introduction

The demand for programming education is increasing in Japan, as programming education has become compulsory in elementary schools. Programming education refers to learning to develop "computational thinking," where children experience programming to make computers perform the intended processing and acquire the logical thinking skills necessary to do so. In programming education, children need to experience the fun of programming, using computers, and a sense of accomplishment. It is also necessary to promote "awareness" of the functions and advantages of computer programs and foster an "attitude" of attempting to solve problems by skillfully using computers.

In this study, we developed a learning game "Logi-Corock" that can be played intuitively. This game supports the learning of computational thinking at home. This paper reports on the design and implementation of our game.

2 Existing Methods of Programming Education

There are two main types of programming education: pseudo-language and unplugged methods.

Pseudo-languages are not programming languages for program development, such as C or Java, but for describing algorithms. Two types of pseudo-languages are used in programming education: visual and text-based programming languages. Visual programming languages, such as Scratch [4], allow easy programming by combining functions such as building blocks. Although these languages are easy to work with, even if the user is not accustomed to typing, the user is required to understand unique rules such as the types of blocks and their combination. Text-based programming languages are more versatile for skilled users but require basic skills with keyboard and other operations, and an understanding of the language.

Unplugged methods are programming education methods that do not use personal computers (PCs), such as Hello Ruby [3]. Unplugged methods are an easy way to start programming education at the elementary school because they do not require the use of PCs. In most cases, they use games, quizzes, puzzles, and stories. Thus, a user does not need to be consciously engaged in logical thinking and can begin without prior knowledge. Furthermore, since specialized knowledge is not required, differences among instructors are unlikely to arise. However, it is difficult to satisfy the learning of "awareness" and "attitude" because no computers are used.

3   Design of Our Learning Game

Based on the above-mentioned educational issues, we design a learning game with the following two points as design guidelines:

- Users can playfully take on tasks at their own pace.
- Users can experience hands-on programming with minimal prior knowledge.

3.1   Content Design

We adopted a simple physical phenomenon as the subject of the game to enable users to playfully take on tasks at their own pace. Specifically, the content involves creating a course that guides a falling sphere from the start to the goal according to physical phenomena.

3.2   Learning Flow

Computational thinking is the ability to think about the combination of functions corresponding to each movement to realize one's desired activity and think logically about improving such combinations. After discovering a problem to be solved, a user seeks to solve it through trial and error.

Figure 1a shows the learning model of computational thinking. Based on this model, we modeled the learning flow of this game, as shown in Fig. 1b. Based on the given mission, a user thinks about the path of the falling sphere from the start to the goal. The user uses blocks to create a path for the sphere to roll down, aiming to clear the stage.

(a) Computational thinking   (b) Our learning game

Fig. 1. Learning models.

3.3 Device and User Interface

A tablet PC is used as the device of our learning game. The tablet PC can be easily handled by children because it can be operated by simply touching the screen.

To minimize prior knowledge of the rules and language, a tangible user interface [2] is adopted for program input. In this research, a special block is developed to catch a sphere that falls under the action of gravity. By using blocks, a user need not learn most of the computer-specific operation rules, such as a mouse, keyboard, and various commands, and can apply the operation rules in the real world.

4 Development of the Learning Game "Logi-Corock"

4.1 Overview

"Logi-Corock" is a game in which players place special tangible blocks on a tablet PC and complete a course that leads a falling sphere from the start to the goal (Fig. 2). The game consists of several stages. A player discovers, analyzes, and solves problems in each stage, aiming to clear each stage through trial and error.

Fig. 2. Operating the Logi-Corock.

4.2 Special Block

Four types of blocks with different functions were developed specifically for this game: path, warp, jump, and condition blocks (Fig. 3). The path block catches the falling sphere and serves as a path to guide the sphere. The warp block instantly moves the sphere between two points when it touches the block. The jump block moves the sphere in the direction indicated by the block, and the distance traveled can be adjusted by extending or retracting the block. The conditional block can relate two path blocks so that one input state can be switched when another one is touched.

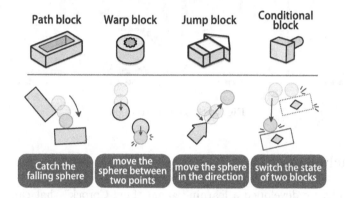

Fig. 3. Design and function of the special blocks.

These blocks were implemented using a capacitive marker [1]. The capacitive marker is a technology for detecting the position and orientation of a physical object based on the pattern of multiple conductive parts placed on it. In this research, a three-point marker was developed (Fig. 4).

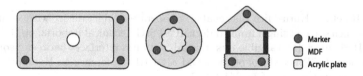

Fig. 4. Placement of capacitive markers in each block.

4.3 How to Play

The user first selects a stage and checks its mission. Next, the user plans a route to carry the sphere from the start to the goal and draws a line by tracing it with a finger. Then, based on the planned route, a user places the special blocks and starts to drop the sphere. If the mission is not completed, the route of the sphere is re-planned and the stage is cleared. Once a stage is cleared, the user moves on to the next stage.

4.4 Stage Construction

The game consists of the four stages shown in Fig. 5. Each stage has different restrictions on the use of special blocks and different goals for acquiring items. All stages were designed to encourage trial and error by users.

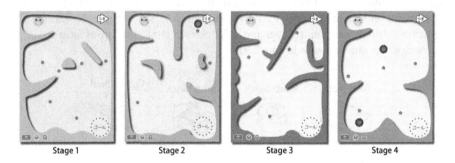

Fig. 5. Stage construction.

5 Conclusions

In this study, we developed a learning game "Logi-Corock" that can be played intuitively with a tablet PC and special blocks. This game supports the learning of computational thinking at home. We designed a game based on a physical phenomenon to cultivate computational thinking playfully with a minimum of prior knowledge. The input interface is a physical block implemented with electrostatic markers.

References

1. Aoki, R., et al.: Kuru-Miru that enables to operate a tablet device with a capacitive multi-touch screen using a frame object. IPSJ SIG Technical Reports, pp. 1–8 (2011)
2. Ishii, H., Ullmer, B.: Tangible bits: towards seamless interfaces between people, bits and atoms. In: Proceedings of the ACM SIGCHI Conference on Human factors in computing systems, pp. 234–241 (1997)
3. Liukas, L.: Hello Ruby: Adventures in Coding. Feiwel & Friends (2015)
4. Resnick, M., et al.: Scratch: programming for all. Commun. ACM **52**(11), 60–67 (2009)

Use of IoT Programming in Mudslide Disaster Prevention Education for Children

Mengping Tsuei[✉], Yuan-Chen Chang, and Jen-I. Chiu

Graduate School of Curriculum and Instructional Communications Technology,
National Taipei University of Education, Taipei, Taiwan
mptsuei@mail.ntue.edu.tw

Abstract. Disaster prevention education covers disaster risks and their management, and practice in disaster escape. The aims of this study were to integrate internet of things (IoT) programming education into mudslide disaster prevention education and to explore the effects of this approach on elementary students' mudslide concepts and computational thinking. This study had a quasi-experiment design. Four classes of fifth-grade students ($n = 105$) in one elementary school participated for 10 weeks. Two classes comprised the experimental group, and the other two classes comprised the control group. Students in the experimental group had significantly higher computational thinking test scores than did students in the control group; mudslide test scores did not differ significantly between groups. These results the use of IoT programming in mudslide disaster prevention education to improve children's computational thinking.

Keywords: Programming education · IoT programming · Computational thinking · Mudslide disaster prevention education

1 Introduction

Many countries are focusing on the promotion of STEM education for elementary-school students via the internet of things (IoT). Programmable IoT kits can enable children to make their own IoT tangibles, with an educational purpose. Many tools are available for children to employ programming languages to operate IoT objects. Physical computing interfaces for children, such as Scratch [1], and robotics toolkits have been used in primary schools [2]. The research and industry communities have worked actively on the development of blocks for IoT tangible programming, such as Project Block by Google [3] and Web:Bit programmable sensors [4].

IoT tangibles have become the edge of innovation in STEM education. The enjoyable and exciting challenges that they bring into the learning experience have been deemed instrumental for overall educational purposes [2]. Children display understanding and engagement during the design stage when performing IoT programming [2]. Moreover, children who have experience with different programming tools, such as Lego WeDo, MBot and Arduino, are strongly involved in dealing with complex challenges and have developed computational thinking [5]. Robertson et al. [6] found that children could

C. Stephanidis et al. (Eds.): HCII 2022, CCIS 1582, pp. 133–137, 2022.
https://doi.org/10.1007/978-3-031-06391-6_18

identify various devices containing chips, including tablets, smartphones, video cameras, traffic lights and watches. According to Piaget's cognitive development theory [7], children are entering a phase in which they begin to develop logical thinking and problem-solving skills, and thus can only understand and conceptualise programming associated with real-life contexts.

A mudslide is defined as the movement of a mixture of surface materials down a slope. Taiwan is a mountainous country underlain by the Eurasian and Philippine Sea plates; typhoons and heavy rains cause occasional mudslide disasters in several areas of the country. We found that a low-polygon virtual reality game developed for children to learn about mudslide disaster prevention improved fifth-grade students' motivation, presence and attitude questionnaire scores [8, 9], but that students need a more hands-on approach to learn about mudslide concepts. Thus, this study was performed to extend previous research, with the integration of IoT programming learning into mudslide disaster prevention education. We explored the effects of this approach on children's conceptualisation of mudslides and computational thinking.

2 Related Works

Lee, Liew, Khan and Narawi [10] reported that 13-year-old students who participated in an IoT programming and mBot robot operation workshop found the STEM learning experience to be very interesting and had slightly increased interest in the field of robotics. Five of the six student groups could use the IoT sensors, and two groups could solve very difficult problems involving multiple sensors. Saez-Lopez, Sevillano-Garcia and Vazquez-Cano [5] found that the integration of robotics and visual programming into didactic mathematics and science units for sixth graders significantly improved the students' understanding of mathematical and computational concepts. Mertala [11] reported that young children's perceptions of ubicomp and the IoT could be shaped and refined by providing them with computers and internet access, and having them apply this new knowledge to a design task, but that most children's perceptions were superficial, rather than profound. Research on the use of the IoT and mudslide disaster prevention interventions involving computational thinking for children is limited.

3 Methods

3.1 Design, Participants and Procedure

This study had a quasi-experimental design. Four classes of fifth-grade students ($n = 105$) in one elementary school in Taipei City, Taiwan, participated in it for 10 weeks. Two classes ($n = 50$ students) were allocated to the experimental group and used the Webduino programming language and the IoT Web:Bit microboard and sensors for mudslide simulation, and the other two classes ($n = 52$ students) were allocated to the control group, which learned Webduino without application to a specific context. The students learned about mudslides by watching videos and PowerPoint presentations. Each student was provided with a PC in the computer laboratory.

3.2   The Webduino Programming Language and Web:Bit Kits

The students in the experimental group used the block-based Webduino programming language to operate Web:Bit toolkits including a microboard and three sensors from their screens for mudslide simulation. An ultrasonic sensor measured the distance to a mudslide area by emitting ultrasonic waves and converting the reflected sound into an electrical signal; students used this information to escape the mudslide. For mudslide prediction, a temperature and humidity sensor collected rainfall data and a soil moisture sensor measured the soil volumetric water content. When the parameters were correct, the mudslide animation was displayed on the screen (Fig. 1).

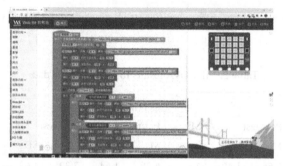

Fig. 1. The Webduino programming language interface. (1) Programming area (left) and (2) mudslide animation area (right).

3.3   Computational Thinking Tests

The Bebras Computing Challenge (International Challenge on Informatics and Computational Thinking) was administered to the students before and after the intervention. We administered the 12-item Benjamin task for fifth-grade students (total possible score = 300).

3.4   Mudslide Test

A 10-item test on mudslides was administered before and after the intervention (total possible score = 10). The discrimination index for this instrument ranged from .30 to .70, and the difficulty index ranged from .24 to .78.

4   Results

4.1   Students' Computational Thinking Performance

Students' scores on the computational thinking tests were analysed by the Analysis of covariance (ANCOVA). The results revealed that computational thinking scores were significantly higher in the experimental group than in the control group (M^a, 132.14 vs. 112.75; $F = 4.08$, $p < .05$; Table 1).

Table 1. ANCOVA results for computational thinking data

EG (n = 50)					CG (n = 52)					F
Pre-test		Post-test		M^a	Pre-test		Post-test		M^a	
M	SD	M	SD		M	SD	M	SD		
117.20	50.42	135.39	57.96	132.14	105.66	45.92	109.52	55.97	112.75	4.08*

Note: CG: control group; EG: experiment group

4.2 Students' Mudslide Knowledge Performance

Mudslide test scores did not differ significantly between groups (ANCOVA, $F = 1.29$; Table 2).

Table 2. ANCOVA results for mudslide test data

EG (n = 50)					CG (n = 52)					F
Pre-test		Post-test		M^a	Pre-test		Post-test		M^a	
M	SD	M	SD		M	SD	M	SD		
6.67	1.54	7.56	1.49	7.48	6.48	1.64	7.32	1.62	7.15	1.29

5 Conclusion

The present study revealed that the use of IoT programming in mudslide education significantly improves children's computational thinking. This result coincides with recent findings regarding the benefits of the IoT and programming in elementary education. Several studies have provided evidence that this approach improves students' motivation, leading to the promotion of its use in schools [5, 10, 11].

Our preliminary results indicate that the IoT design was more suitable for disaster prevention education than was traditional instruction. Additional research conducted with larger samples and various IoT tools for mudslide prevention education is needed to validate this approach.

Acknowledgments. This work was supported by funding from the Ministry of Science and Technology of Taiwan (MOST109-2511-H-152-006).

References

1. Scratch. https://scratch.mit.edu/
2. Gennari, R., Melonio, A., Rizvi, M., Bonani, A.: Design of IoT tangibles for primary schools. In: Paternò, F., Spano, L.D. (eds.) CHItaly 2017: Proceedings of the 12th Biannual Conference on Italian SIGCHI Chapter, pp.1–6. ACM press, New York (2017)
3. Google blockly. https://blockly.games/
4. Web: Bit. https://webbit.webduino.io/
5. Sáez-López, J.-M., Sevillano-García, M.-L., Vazquez-Cano, E.: The effect of programming on primary school students' mathematical and scientific understanding: educational use of mBot. Educ. Tech. Res. Dev. **67**(6), 1405–1425 (2019). https://doi.org/10.1007/s11423-019-09648-5
6. Robertson, J., Manches, A., Pain, H.: It's like a giant brain with a keyboard: children's understandings about how computers work. Child. Educ. **93**(4), 338–345 (2017)
7. Piaget, J.: The Principles of Genetic Epistemology. Routledge & Kegan Paul, London (1972)
8. Tsuei, M., Chiu, J., Peng, T., Chang, Y.: Preliminary evaluation of the usability of a virtual reality game for mudslide education for children. In: VRST 2019, Parramatta, NSW, Australia (2019)
9. Tsuei, M., Chiu, J.-I.: Effects of virtual reality mudslide games with different usability designs on fifth-grade children's learning motivation and presence experience. In: Stephanidis, C., Antona, M., Ntoa, S. (eds.) HCII 2020. CCIS, vol. 1294, pp. 319–323. Springer, Cham (2020). https://doi.org/10.1007/978-3-030-60703-6_41
10. Lee, B.Y., Liew, L.H., Bin Mohd Anas Khan, M. Y., Narawi, A.: The effectiveness of using mbot to increase the interest and basic knowledge in programming and robotic among children of age 13. In: Proceedings of the 2020 The 6th International Conference on E-Business and Applications, pp. 105–110 (2020)
11. Mertala, P.: Young children's perceptions of ubiquitous computing and the internet of things. Br. J. Edu. Technol. **51**(1), 84–102 (2020)

Towards Trustworthy Learning Analytics Applications: An Interdisciplinary Approach Using the Example of Learning Diaries

Hristina Veljanova[1] , Carla Barreiros[2,3](✉) , Nicole Gosch[1](✉) ,
Elisabeth Staudegger[1](✉) , Martin Ebner[2](✉) , and Stefanie Lindstaedt[2,3](✉)

[1] University of Graz, Graz, Austria
{hristina.veljanova,nicole.gosch,
elisabeth.staudegger}@uni-graz.at
[2] Graz University of Technology, Graz, Austria
{carla.soutabarreiros,martin.ebner,lindstaedt}@tugraz.at
[3] Know-Center GmbH, Graz, Austria

Abstract. Learning analytics (LA) is an emerging field of science due to its great potential to better understand, support and improve the learning and teaching process. Many higher education institutions (HEIs) have already included LA in their digitalisation strategies. This process has been additionally accelerated during the COVID-19 pandemic when HEIs transitioned from face-2-face learning environments to hybrid and e-learning environments and entirely relied on technology to continue operating. Undoubtedly, there was never a time when so much student data was collected, analysed, and reported, which brings numerous ethical and data protection concerns to the forefront. For example, a critical issue when implementing LA is to determine which data should be processed to fulfil pedagogical purposes while making sure that LA is in line with ethical principles and data protection law, such as the European General Data Protection Regulation (GDPR).

This article contributes to the discussion on how to design LA applications that are not only useful and innovative but also trustworthy and enable higher education learners to make data-informed decisions about their learning process. For that purpose, we first present the idea and methodology behind the development of our interdisciplinary Criteria Catalogue for trustworthy LA applications intended for students. The Criteria Catalogue is a new normative framework that supports students to assess the trustworthiness of LA applications. It consists of seven defined Core Areas (i.e., autonomy, protection, respect, non-discrimination, responsibility and accountability, transparency, and privacy and good data governance) and corresponding criteria and indicators. Next, we apply this normative framework to learning diaries as a specific LA application. Our goal is to demonstrate how ethical and legal aspects could be translated into specific recommendations and design implications that should accompany the whole lifecycle of LA applications.

Keywords: Learning analytics · Learning diaries · Ethical values · Data protection · GDPR · Human-centred design · Pedagogy · Educational technology

C. Stephanidis et al. (Eds.): HCII 2022, CCIS 1582, pp. 138–145, 2022.
https://doi.org/10.1007/978-3-031-06391-6_19

1 Introduction

Higher education institutions (HEIs) reveal a growing interest in Learning Analytics (LA) as the next step to digitalisation. Within the project "Learning Analytics - Students in Focus", we develop and evaluate LA tools that enable higher education learners to make data-informed decisions about their learning process and support self-regulated learning. To achieve our goals, we brought together an interdisciplinary team of LA and pedagogy researchers, TEL-practitioners, data scientists, and ethics and data protection experts.

When designing, developing, and using LA, a critical issue is to determine which data should be processed to fulfil pedagogical purposes while ensuring that LA is in line with ethical principles, the data protection law such as the European General Data Protection Regulation (GDPR) [4], and also beyond it considering, for example, the European Declaration on Digital Rights and Principles for the Digital Decade COM(2022)28 [5]. In the past years, there has been a rise in the number of ethical frameworks on LA proposing a set of principles, values or core issues regarding LA. Slade and Prinsloo [11], Drachsler and Greller [2], Slade and Tait [12], Khalil and Ebner [10] are just few of the many scholars who have developed such frameworks. While all these frameworks are relevant and provide a valuable contribution to the LA community, most of them generally focus on the level of principles. Against that background, our goal is to develop a normative framework in the form of an interdisciplinary Criteria Catalogue for trustworthy LA applications that goes beyond the level of principles.

The proposed Criteria Catalogue distinguishes itself from existing frameworks in three aspects. First, it places students in focus. It represents a tool that could help students assess the trustworthiness of LA applications that they are using or would like to use in a way that is easier and user-friendly. Moreover, it ensures that students have actual control over their own data. With this, students are given more power and knowledge regarding the LA products they are using to support their learning process. Second, even though data protection constitutes an integral aspect of the normative framework, the Criteria Catalogue does not represent a mere translation of existing legal requirements. It goes beyond the compliance level and examines what more could be done regarding the design and use of LA applications. The rationale for such an approach is that for designing trustworthy technologies and fostering trust among all affected stakeholders, acting within the bare legal minimum is just the first step. Namely, as Floridi argues in the context of the Digital "compliance is necessary but insufficient to steer society in the right direction" [6]. This means that legislation does not and cannot cover everything, and there are situations when it does not always give straightforward answers. This is something that digital ethics and digital governance could do. Third, the Criteria Catalogue follows the well-known "value-sensitive design" approach according to which moral and societal values should be considered throughout the whole life cycle of the product, including the design, implementation, and deployment phases. The approach uses a tripartite methodology consisting of conceptual, empirical, and technical investigation [7].

In this article, we present the idea and methodology behind the development of our normative framework in the form of a Criteria Catalogue for trustworthy LA applications, consisting of seven core areas, i.e., transparency, privacy and good data governance, autonomy, non-discrimination, respect, responsibility and accountability, and protection. Next, we exemplify the application of the core area responsibility and accountability to learning diaries (LDs) as a specific LA application, thus exposing the process of moving from abstract core areas to criteria and indicators of trustworthiness.

2 Proposing an Interdisciplinary Criteria Catalogue for Trustworthy LA Applications Intended for Students

The development of the proposed LA Criteria Catalogue will follow a hierarchical structure, as depicted in Fig. 1. On the first level are the core areas, which reflect the values that should be considered in the design, development, and implementation of LA tools. Since the core areas are very abstract, in the next step, they are broken down into criteria. The criteria are more concrete than the core areas, nevertheless, they are still not concrete enough to be easily measured. As a result, in a third step, the criteria are broken down into corresponding indicators.

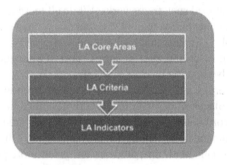

Fig. 1. The hierarchical structure of the LA Criteria Catalogue.

The process of identification of the core areas started by analysing prominent ethical LA frameworks in the literature, e.g., Slade and Prinsloo [11], Drachsler and Greller [2], Slade and Tait [12], Khalil and Ebner [10], Kay, Korn and Oppenheim [9], Slade and Boroowa [13], and creating a matrix with the principles and terms that dominate these frameworks. This matrix helped to identify any potential gaps in the frameworks. Next, an in-depth ethical analysis was conducted, where the most relevant ethical issues and challenges were analysed regarding the design and use of trustworthy LA applications. The research resulted in seven core areas, which were then defined from the perspective of each participating discipline in the project, i.e., ethics, law, pedagogy, computer science, and educational technology. Table 1 presents the definition of the interdisciplinary LA core areas, which combines the perspectives of the five disciplines.

Table 1. The interdisciplinary LA core areas.

Transparency: LA tools should be provided in line with HEIs information obligations for the purpose of achieving greater information transparency. This includes communicating information to all relevant stakeholders that is meaningful, comprehensible, useful, user-friendly, and easily accessible

---

Privacy and good data governance: LA tools should be designed to empower students and enable them to determine for themselves the disclosure and use of their personal data to prevent unjustified and uncontrolled surveillance practices. At the same time, privacy should be understood more than just in terms of data. Students should feel respected in their privacy and be given intimacy in their learning and thus enjoy space for personal development

---

Autonomy: Students should be considered as autonomous agents whose self-determination and self-organisation is respected by providing them the opportunity to make informed and voluntary decisions regarding the use of LA tools. One way to do so is by providing LA to students as a voluntary service that they can choose whether to use it or not. At the same time, the functional scope of the LA tools, i.e. their degree of automatisation and the range of possible automatisation-related tasks they can perform, should be appropriately considered and addressed

---

Non-discrimination: LA tools should be designed and implemented to avoid cases of algorithmic bias and unjustified (data-based) discrimination. Additionally, such an approach ensures the provision of discrimination-free LA recommendations and interventions which are sensitive to different groups of learners (accessibility)

Respect: LA tools should be designed to respect the students as autonomous persons with specific individual interests. Accordingly, students should not be regarded as mere data producers, but as agents actively involved in the design, implementation, and evaluation of LA tools. Additionally, when providing LA interventions or recommendations, students must not be reduced merely to their data. For establishing positive learning environment, teachers should ensure that the use of LA in course descriptions and examinations is transparent to (prospective) students. The ultimate decision to use LA tools ought to rest with the students

---

Responsibility and accountability: Whenever LA tools are used in an educational setting, there should be a clear allocation of roles and responsibilities among relevant stakeholders for the purpose of preventing harms and damages as well as ensuring accountability in cases when these occur. In that sense, HEIs should acknowledge their duties towards students arising from the implementation of LA, take appropriate measures to facilitate and promote responsible use of LA and are able to demonstrate this proactively (accountability). This includes not only compliance with legal obligations, but also consideration of ethical issues, didactic aspects as well as taking appropriate technical measures. Teachers should be considered responsible for the use of LA tools in their area of decision-making. At the same time, students as autonomous agents ought to retain a certain degree of self-responsibility for the organisation and success of their studies

---

Protection: HEIs should take appropriate measures to protect students from harm that could be caused by the implementation of LA tools. This includes measures to protect the data that is collected, processed, and made available as a result of interaction with LA tools. Moreover, it also includes the protection of students' mental health, students' motivation, and the need to ensure that their rights and interests are not violated

---

3 Application of Criteria Catalogue to Learning Diaries – from Core Areas to Criteria and Indicators of Trustworthiness

In this section, we exemplify the process of translating the core areas into criteria and indicators of trustworthiness and applying them to a particular LA application. For this purpose, we use as an example a Learning Diary (LDs) tool and the core area "responsibility and accountability". LDs are a didactical practice that fosters the learner's ability to reflect upon their learning process [1] and enhances awareness of their behaviour, enabling them to change learning habits [3]. LDs typically collect large amounts of data, e.g., the number of entries, time spent studying, details about a learning activity, thoughts and feelings, insights, and action plans. The data collected within LDs is considered personal data and thus must be guided by ethical and legal considerations to ensure a trustworthy, accepted, and successful LA application.

The design and use of LDs in an educational context come with the involvement of different actors with whom various obligations lie. Therefore, a clear and transparent allocation of roles and responsibilities between all relevant actors is required. Determining these roles and responsibilities is not only a matter of compliance with legal requirements but also consideration of ethical issues, didactic, and technical aspects. In what follows, we will briefly look into the concepts of responsibility and accountability in the context of LDs from an ethical, legal, didactic, and technical perspective. This will shed more light on how we arrived from the disciplinary to the interdisciplinary understanding of this core area, as depicted in Table 1.

In *philosophy,* a distinction is made between forward- and backward-looking responsibility. One way to talk about forward-looking responsibility is in the sense of responsibility as duty [14]. In the context of LDs, this would demand identifying the relevant stakeholders to whom responsibility could be allocated as well as their roles and tasks that derive from those roles. This would include, for example, (a) the HEI, which introduces LDs as a tool to support students in their studies and ensures that students' privacy and personal data is thereby protected, (b) the company or organisation developing the LA application and its developers, (c) teachers opting to use LDs in their courses as well as (d) students as prospective users from whom a certain self-responsibility as autonomous agents could be expected regarding the organisation and success of their studies. On the other hand, responsibility as accountability is one type of backward-looking responsibility, where the focus lies on the moral obligation of the agent to account for one's actions. To realise responsibility as accountability certain mechanisms should be put in place by the HEIs that would enable, for example, students to seek and gain redress for harms caused by the use of the LD. For both forward- and backward-looking responsibility, it is also essential that the allocation of responsibilities and the existence of mechanisms is clearly communicated by the HEIs to students and other affected parties.

Legal aspects of responsibility and accountability in the context of LDs can be found primarily in data protection law. The GDPR explicitly refers to an allocation of responsibilities (Recital 79 GDPR) and defines the concepts of controller (Article 4 (7) GDPR), processor (Article 4 (8) GDPR) and data subject (Article 4 (1) GDPR). From the perspective of data protection law, the controller is liable for material and immaterial damages incurred to data subjects due to data protection violations. The controller is the person or entity that decides on the purposes and means of the processing and is also accountable for compliance with the data protection principles (Article 5 GDPR) when processing personal data as part of an LD. Responsibility of any person who processes personal data on the controller's behalf and instructions, such as employees as subordinates or processors, is attributed to the controller in the sense of a central concentration of responsibility (Article 29 GDPR). However, if several individuals or institutions decide on processing personal data, they may also be considered jointly responsible (Article 26 GDPR). Suppose LDs are offered as a service in a higher education environment, providers, HEIs, and teachers can all be involved in deciding on the purposes and means of processing and thus be individually or jointly responsible. However, who is responsible under data protection law must always be agreed in the specific individual case. Where LA applications are offered as a service, the right to data portability (Article 20 GDPR) should be underlined, according to which the data subject can receive "his/her" personal data and reuse it for own purposes and for different services. The change of the service provider would subsequently entail a new (additional) controller under data protection law.

Responsibility and accountability from a *didactic* perspective are particularly relevant when LDs are used as LA service at HEIs. The allocation of roles in the higher education context reflects an interplay between HEIs, teachers, and students regarding the tasks and duties that arise in the teaching and learning process. HEIs must facilitate and promote the responsible use of new educational technologies, such as LA. However, HEIs should offer LA as a purely voluntary service [8], which teachers and students can adopt to enhance the teaching and learning processes. In this context, HEIs are responsible for offering further training measures for teachers and providing didactic support to ensure the pedagogically meaningful use of LA application. Teachers should provide students with suggestions and assistance to support their learning processes based on the data. It also implies a certain degree of student responsibility while using LA service.

From a *technical* point of view, responsibility and accountability arise in all phases of the LDs system development life cycle, i.e., requirement analysis, design, development and testing, implementation, documentation, and evaluation. Therefore, it is necessary to define the areas of responsibility of individual persons, e.g., team leaders, developers, testers in the sense of personal accountability. Also, it is vital to include the ethical, legal, and didactic requirements for the LA tool, which should be reflected in the design and development of the LD. These requirements compliance should be validated before rollout.

Having discussed responsibility and accountability from an ethical, legal, didactic and technical perspective, we can now move from the level of the core area to the level of criteria. Figure 2 illustrates few examples of criteria that we derived from the core area responsibility and accountability as well as few examples of indicators derived from one selected criterion. The indicators can be formulated either as statements or yes/no questions and should be easily understandable, operationalisable and measurable for developers to implement them into practice.

Based on what has been said so far, several observations can be made. First, the core area responsibility and accountability presents an important prerequisite in the efforts to design trustworthy LA applications. Nevertheless, as the disciplinary and interdisciplinary understanding(s) showcased, it also overlaps with aspects of the other core areas as presented in Table 1, in particular with transparency, privacy and good data

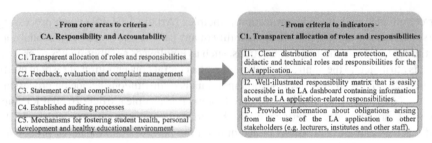

Fig. 2. Examples of criteria derived from the core area responsibility and accountability and examples of indicators derived from one selected criterion.

governance, and autonomy. Second, as the input from law demonstrated, the allocation of roles and responsibilities in relation to technology but also in particular with LA is not a new endeavour. The GDPR is very concise on this matter (e.g., Article 12 & 13 GDPR). What could be considered new is the need to communicate not only clearly and more transparently data protection specifications but also aspects concerning ethical, didactic and technical responsibilities and allocation of roles to affected stakeholders such as students. For example, this would require embedding the matrix of roles and duties allocation as a design requirement in the LDs application.

4   Conclusion

In this paper, we presented the idea and methodology behind the development of our normative framework in the form of a Criteria Catalogue for trustworthy LA applications. As part of the Criteria Catalogue, we identified seven core areas from which we derive corresponding criteria and indicators that should be considered in the technical development of LDs as an LA service, and thus should facilitate the implementation of values already in the design process. Moreover, it is important for the future that such core areas, criteria and indicators find their way into the specifications of LA applications in the form of design requirements that are easily understandable, operationalisable and measurable for developers to implement them into practice. At the same time, it should be ensured that they are preserved and taken into account throughout the entire life cycle of the system.

Acknowledgements. This work was co-funded by the Federal Ministry of Education, Science and Research, Austria, as part of the 2019 call for proposals for digital and social transformation in higher education for the project "LA – Students in Focus" (2021–2024, partners: University of Vienna, Graz University of Technology, University of Graz).

References

1. Clipa, O., Ignat, A.A., Stanciu, M.: Learning diary as a tool for metacognitive strategies. Soc. Behav. Sci. **33**, 905–909 (2012). https://doi.org/10.1016/j.sbspro.2012.01.253

2. Drachsler, H., Greller, W.: Privacy and analytics - it's a DELICATE issue. a checklist for trusted learning analytics. In: LAK16: Proceedings of the Sixth International Conference on Learning Analytics & Knowledge, pp. 89–98 (2016). https://doi.org/10.1145/2883851.288 3893
3. Dörrenbächer, L., Perels, F.: More is more? Evaluation of interventions to foster self-regulated learning in college. Int. J. Educ. Res. **78**, 50–65 (2016). https://doi.org/10.1016/j.ijer.2016.05.010
4. European Union. 2016. Consolidated text: Regulation (EU) 2016/679 of the European Parliament and of the Council of 27 April 2016 on the protection of natural persons with regard to the processing of personal data and on the free movement of such data, and repealing Directive 95/46/EC (General Data Protection Regulation) (Text with EEA relevance). RL 2016/679/EU
5. European Union. 2022. European Declaration on Digital Rights and Principles for the Digital Decade COM(2022)28 final
6. Floridi, L.: Soft ethics and the governance of the digital. Philos. Technol. **31**(1), 1–8 (2018)
7. Friedman, B., Kahn, P., Borning, A.: Value sensitive design and information systems. In: Zhang, P., Galletta, D. (eds.) HCI and Management Information Systems: Foundations. Advances in Management Information Systems, (Armonk: M.E. Sharpe, 2006), pp. 348–372 (2006)
8. Gosch, N., et al.: Learning analytics as a service for empowered learners: from data subjects to controllers. In: LAK21: 11th International Learning Analytics and Knowledge Conference (LAK21). Association for Computing Machinery, New York, NY, USA, pp. 475–481 (2021). https://doi.org/10.1145/3448139.3448186
9. Kay, D., Korn, N., Oppenheim, C.: Legal, risk and ethical aspects of analytics in higher education. CETIS Anal. Ser. 1(6) (2012)
10. Khalil, M., Ebner, M.: Learning analytics: principles and constraints. In: Proceedings of World Conference on Educational Multimedia, Hypermedia and Telecommunications 2015, pp. 1326–1336. Chesapeake, VA: AACE (2015)
11. Slade, S., Prinsloo, P.: Learning Analytics - ethical issues and dilemmas. Am. Behav. Sci. **57**(10) (2013). DOI:https://doi.org/10.1177/0002764213479366
12. Slade, S., Tait, A.: Global guidelines: Ethics in learning analytics (2019)
13. Slade, S., Boroowa, A.: Policy on Ethical Use of Student Data for Learning Analytics. Open University UK, Milton Keynes (2014)
14. Williams, G.: "Responsibility", The Internet Encyclopedia of Philosophy. Accessed Mar 2022

Peer-to-Peer Monitoring in Pandemic Times: Use of a Web Application to Improve the Academic Performance of Engineering Students at a University in Colombia

Derlis Villadiego Rincón(✉) ⓘ, Alex Castellar Rodríguez ⓘ,
Alejandro Valencia Pérez ⓘ, and Camilo Muñoz Gutierrez ⓘ

Universidad de la Costa, 58 street #55-66, Barranquilla, Colombia
Dvilladi3@cuc.edu.co

Abstract. The purpose of this research is to measure the effect of the Academic Monitoring Service between peers through a web application of the Universidad de la Costa on the academic performance of students. The academic results of 463 students from different engineering programs at the CUC university were analyzed for the periods 2021–1. Prior to the analysis, the permanence and the number of mentoring provided by the peer monitor to the student were taken into account in order to establish two (2) groups. A group with three or fewer mentoring sessions was compared to a group with four or more mentorings at three different times in the 2021–1 semester. For the data analysis, the statistical software SPSS version 22 was used. The Kolmogorov-Smirnov test was applied to determine if the data came from a normal distribution and the two groups were compared in each moment of the semester using Mann-Whitney U, which showed that for the first and second evaluation moments there were no significant differences between the groups; however, for the third evaluation moment, there were statistically significant differences with a p-value < 0.05. Findings suggest that the continuity and intensity of assistance in monitoring through the web application have a positive impact on the academic performance of students.

Keywords: Web application · Peer to peer mentoring · Online learning · Academic performance

1 Introduction

The World Health Organization stated COVID-19 as a pandemic [1], as a result, changes in education systems worldwide were required to reduce the impact at all levels of education and thereby hundreds of students [2]. This forced educational programs to transit to methodologies associated with the remote access modality to help meet the objectives of education.

The Universidad de la Costa conceives the evaluation of learning as a permanent and continuous process that allows decision-making aimed at the continuous improvement of teaching-learning processes. In this sense, institutional evaluation at the university has the following purposes:

- Analyze the performance of the students, in order to contribute to decision-making for the reorientation of didactic and pedagogical strategies.
- Reflect on the learning processes to contribute to their strengthening.
- Provide information to training programs and systems to strengthen their academic quality from curricular perspectives.

Within this framework, institutional efforts have been oriented towards an integration of actions around the formative and summative function of evaluation, recognizing that in the teaching-learning scenario, teachers and students are essential for its achievement. With remote learning, instruction extends beyond the teacher-students [3]; rather, students can support with other learning material available and with peers and mentors.

Taking into account the above, and as a result of the pressure exerted by the Covid-19 pandemic, the university moved from a face-to-face teaching-learning model to a remote virtual model, forcing, among other things, that many institutional processes be seen forced to travel in that direction. In accordance with this, in 2021 the TARA application (Tutorials, consultancies, reinforcement and accompaniment) is consolidated, which was born from the need to integrate into one place all the information regarding the students who are part of the strategy of monitories and thus optimize the method of consultation, attendance record and evaluation of satisfaction with the service offered.

The application was created and designed by instructors from the systems engineering program as part of a classroom project for one of their classes. In addition, it is born from the need to satisfy the need of the student community, which did not have a tool that would allow viewing the existing monitors by program and subject. It should be noted that information on each member was included in this tool, such as the hours of operation and interactive access icons to the institutional mail and chat of the Microsoft Teams application, which would allow the monitors to be contacted in an agile and effective manner and, in turn, to hold the meetings remote.

The Teams application made it possible to create interest and academic support groups to be able to exchange complementary material and video recordings that benefited students who could not connect to the meetings to see the explanations of these monitors in asynchronous time.

The TARA platform, in addition to displaying the information of the monitors in an organized and friendly way for students, also allows managing the academic offer of the subjects to establish the number of monitors according to trend analysis between subjects with the greatest loss and withdrawal and other aspects of their own. of each faculty and program. Nominate by the teachers the monitors who have the profile to exercise this role and accompany the process in a systematic and effective manner.

2   Methodology

The research approach of this study is quantitative (Hernández-Sampieri et al., 2014). In this sense, and considering that the objective of the research is to identify the effect of one variable on another, the scope of the study is descriptive and has an experimental design. The sampling is probabilistic, of an intentional type, since the students who will be part of the study are premeditatedly decided (Otzen and Manterola, 2017).

2.1 Sampling

In the 2021–1 period, a total of 5,179 visits were made by the academic monitors through the TARA platform, which represent 772 students who were taken as the study population. Of this total, a sample of 463 students was intentionally chosen, assigning as a criterion that after the engineering programs and also that the qualifications of the 3 evaluation moments applied by the university for each academic cut were obtained. It should be noted that these academic programs were chosen since they were the ones that reflected the platform with the highest number of students served.

2.2 Procedure

The present study was applied through the following steps:

STEP 1 - In the first step, the assistance registered by sessions in the TARA platform was downloaded, the information was organized and the sample represented in 463 students of the different engineering programs of the university in the analyzed period was taken. This sample was classified into two groups according to the number of visits made. In this sense, the first group consists of 411 students who attended three monitoring sessions or less at each evaluation moment of the semester versus a second group made up of 52 students who attended four monitoring sessions or more at each evaluation moment.

STEP 2 - Immediately afterwards, a descriptive analysis of the data was carried out, to determine the mean, median and standard deviation of each group at each evaluation moment, to contrast from this point of view in terms of trend and variability.

STEP 3 - The qualifications of the students of the selected sample were taken and an analysis was carried out taking into account the permanence of the students in the attention process within the framework of the monitoring and the results obtained at each moment of evaluation of the academic period 2021–1. We proceeded to analyze whether the scores of the two groups to be contrasted at each evaluation moment come from a normal distribution. For this, the Kolmogorov-Smirnov test was used at first.

STEP 4 - Subsequently, the non-parametric Mann-Whitney U test was used to check whether there were statistically significant differences by a group for each evaluation moment. The analyzes were performed using the statistical data analysis software SPSS version 22.

3 Results

A total of 463 students attended the engineering program distributed as follows: 2 from agroindustrial engineering, 36 from environmental engineering, 5 from civil engineering, 52 from systems engineering, 16 from electrical engineering, 19 from electronic engineering, 30 from industrial engineering and 9 mechanical engineerings (see Fig. 1). The classification was made into two groups according to the amount of attention received by the students, distributed as follows (see Fig. 2):

- Group 1: Less than 4 mentoring received.
- Group 2: 4 or more mentoring received.

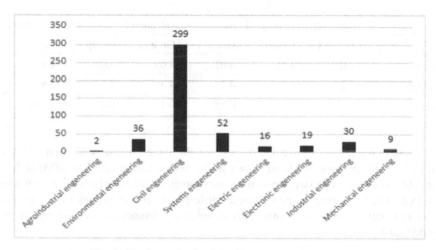

Fig. 1. Total sample distributed by academic programs.

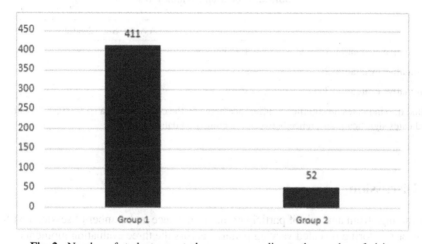

Fig. 2. Number of students per study group, according to the number of visits.

A descriptive analysis is carried out (see Table 1) where the means, medians and standard deviations of each group can be visualized at each evaluation moment analyzed. Observing that moment 1 and 2 of each group remains homogeneous without distinctive changes. But the 3rd moment we can glimpse an increase in both groups with respect to the first two.

It should be noted that it is always observed that group 2 is always above group 1 in the mean and median. Regarding the deviations, it can be noted that group 2 had a significant decrease in the 3rd moment, this being important in the following analysis of the results. Table 1 shows the grade's average for each summative evaluation respectively.

Table 1. Mean, Median and Std. Deviation (academic period 2021–1).

	Summative evaluation 1		Summative evaluation 2		Summative evaluation 3	
	Group 1	Group 2	Group 1	Group 2	Group 1	Group 2
Mean	4.07	4.05	4.07	4.09	4.09	4.3
Median	4.2	4.4	4.2	4.4	4.3	4.6
Std. Deviation	0.68	0.83	0.68	0.79	0.7	0.59

Through the Kolmogorov Smirnov test for the three cuts, it is inferred that the student's grades do not come from a normal distribution with p values at 0.000 all less than 0.05, so we proceed to work with the non-parametric U test of Mann Whitney where it is appreciated that there are no significant differences between groups 1 and 2 during the first two cuts; however, the statistically significant differences are evident in the third period (see Table 2).

Table 2. U de Mann Whitney Test

	Z	Asymp. Sig. (2-tailed)
Summative evaluation 1	-1.723	*0.085
Summative evaluation 2	-865	*0.387
Summative evaluation 3	-266	**0.008

*Value of p indicates no significant difference between the compared data ($p > 0.05$); **Value of p indicates significant difference between the compared data ($p \leq 0.05$)

4 Discussion

The findings from analysis of participation, permanence and number of sessions within the peer mentoring revealed varying patterns across the three evaluation moments.

To start with, data from analyzing the effect of the Academic Monitoring Service between peers through a web application of the Universidad de la Costa on the academic performance of students showed that the service has statistically significant differences on academic performance when considering the permanence and number of sessions through a range of time. However, literature in this field is limited; therefore, the growth has been proven on generic competencies such as leadership, self-awareness and confidence [6–8] rather than specific competencies.

In the same sense, the increase in the academic performance by the third evaluation moment might suggest a relation between the peer mentee and the topic-related knowledge, mainly when the topics addressed include learning activities [9]. This is coherent with research that suggests the relevance of peer mentoring to empower peers on engaging in their own learning and development [10–12].

Overall, results from the study reflect on the relevance of the web application as a tool to enhance peer mentoring. As stated by DeLamar and Brown, the web application facilitated the process of requesting and programing a session for mentoring those students who were having difficulties with a specific topic or were at risk of failing a course and needed additional interventions and support [13].

In the same sense, online mentoring provided an opportunity to reduce the gap between the students and the mentors; mainly, because of the overall availability and accessibility, both features reported by Murrell et al. [14]. The transition from face-to-face mentoring to online mentoring prompted a boundaryless scenario where the impacts of economic, social and cultural factors decreased [15–18].

5 Conclusion

Overall, research showed that for the summative evaluation 1 and 2 no statistically significant differences were found in the process between both the groups evaluated (see Tables 1 and 2). Contrary to this, for summative evaluation 3, statistically significant differences were evidenced, showing a greater increase in the medians of the academic performance of the group with 4 or more interventions carried out (see Table 1). However, evidence suggests that there is a degree of coherence among time transcurred and academic performance, as can be seen for summative evaluation number 3.

The greater the number of actions carried out, an increase in the results of the academic performance by subject is reflected.

Moreover, the web application helped to optimize the process and to have greater scope and coverage in the service provided. Prior to its implementation, the average of mentoring requested by students was 3000, whereas with the web application it went up to 5000 average.

To conclude, this study was relevant to identify that peer mentoring can be successfully employed in online settings as a strategy to develop student approach and understanding of knowledge in remote learning scenarios.

Finally, the study suggests that implementing the mentoring program online contributes to improving academic performance and wellbeing in university students, which could have an impact, yet to be explored, on the retention of students.

References

1. Who Timeline COVID-19 (archived). https://www.who.int/news/item/27-04-2020-who-tim eline---covid-19. Accessed 15 Mar 2022
2. UNESCO (2020) From COVID-19 learning disruption to recovery: A snapshot of UNESCO's work in education. https://en.unesco.org/news/covid-19-learning-disruption-recovery-sna pshot-unescos-work-education-2020. Accessed 15 Mar 2022

3. Goodrich, A.: Online peer mentoring and remote learning. Music. Educ. Res. **23**(2), 256–269 (2021)
4. Hernández-Sampieri, R., Fernández-Collado, C., Baptista-Lucio, P.: Metodología de la investigación. 6th ed. México D.F.: McGraw-Hill (2014)
5. Otzen, T., y Manterola, C.: Técnicas de muestreo sobre una población a estudio. Int. J. Morphol. **35**(1), 227–232 (2017)
6. Beltman, S., Schaeben, M.: Institution-wide peer mentoring: benefits for mentors. Int. J. First Year Higher Educ. **3**(2), 33–44 (2012)
7. Hogan, R., Fox, D., Barratt-See, G.: Peer to peer mentoring: outcomes of third-yearmidwifery students mentoring first-year students. Women Birth **30**(3), 206–213 (2017)
8. Fayram, J., Boswood, N., Kan, Q., Motzo, A., Proudfoot, A.: Investigating the benefits of online peer mentoring for studentconfidence and motivation. Int. J. Mentor. Coach. Educ. **7**(4) (2018)
9. Chilvers, L.: Communities of practice for international students: an exploration of the role ofpeer assisted study sessions in supporting transition and learning in higher education. J. Learn. Dev. High. Educ. **10**(1), 1–25 (2016)
10. Werder, C., Thibou, S., Kaufer, B.: Students as co-inquirers: a requisite theory in educational development. J. Faculty Dev. **26**(3), 34–38 (2012)
11. Bovill, C., Cook-Sather, A., Felten, P.: Students as co-creators of teaching approaches, course design, and curricula: implications for academic developers. Int. J. Acad. Dev. **16**(2), 133–145 (2011)
12. Chan, C.K.Y., Luo, J.: Towards an inclusive student partnership: rethinking mentors'disposition and holistic competency development in near-peer mentoring. Teaching in higher education (2020)
13. DeLamar, S., Brown, C.G.: Supporting transition of at-risk students through a freshman orientation model. J. At-Risk Issues **19**(2), 32–39 (2016)
14. Murrell, A.J., Blake-Beard, S., Porter, D.M., Jr.: The importance of peer mentoring, identity work and holding environments: a study of African American leadership development. Int. J. Environ. Res. Public Health **18**, 4920 (2021)
15. Kanchewa, S.S., Yoviene, L.A., Schwartz, S.E., Herrera, C., Rhodes, J.E.: Relational experiences in school-based mentoring: The mediating role of rejection sensitivity. Youth Society (2016)
16. Lane, S.: Addressing the Stressful First Year in College: Could Peer Mentoring Be a Critical Strategy? **22**(3), 481–496 (2020)
17. Masehela, M., Mabika, M.: An assessment of the impact of the mentoring programme on student performance. J. Student Aff. Africa **5**(2), 163–182, 2307–6267 (2017)
18. Larson, H., Aaron, S., Conn, S., Sinclair, E.: Striving for contribution: the five Cs and positive effects of cross-age peer mentoring. Mentor. Tutor. Partner. Learn. **28**(5), 522–535 (2020)

Exploring Sound Feedback for Deterring Unrelated Tasks During Online Lectures

Teamyoung Yun[1], Ren Imai[1], Yuji Kimura[2], Kenro Go[1],
and Akihiro Miyata[2(✉)]

[1] Graduate School of Integrated Basic Sciences, Nihon University, Tokyo, Japan
[2] College of Humanities and Sciences, Nihon University, Tokyo, Japan
miyata.akihiro@acm.org

Abstract. In universities, online lectures are becoming more common. Online lectures are advantageous but there is a problem that a certain number of students do things unrelated to their studies during lectures; this reduces the quality of learning. We focused on sound feedback because it allows students to notice warnings when they are looking at something other than the computer screen. To explore suitable sound feedback for warning during online lectures, we compared four types of sound feedback in terms of noticeability and pleasantness: 1) presenting a buzzer sound, 2) alternating between presenting and muting the lecture audio, 3) gradually reducing the lecture audio, and 4) muting the lecture audio. The experimental results confirmed that feedback types of 2–4 are preferable in terms of the balance between noticeability and pleasantness. This finding contributes to enhancing online lecture systems and improving the quality of online learning.

Keywords: Sound feedback · Unrelated task · Online lecture

1 Introduction

Online classes are becoming more common in academic institutions worldwide due to the change in learning styles and the pandemic. Particularly in universities, online lectures are becoming more common. Online lectures have two advantages. First, they prevent the spread of infections. During online lectures, students and a teacher are not in contact with each other because they gather in an online environment. This decreases the risk of infections. Second, online lectures can save commuting time as students can attend them from any location, such as their home. As previously stated, online lectures are advantageous, however, there is a problem with them. Due to the lack of in-person monitoring by teachers, a certain number of students do things unrelated to their studies during lectures and this reduces the quality of learning. It does not matter at face-to-face lectures because a teacher can monitor each student regardless of the number of students by glancing over a classroom. However, in online lectures, if there are a lot of students, it is hard for the teacher to monitor all of them

C. Stephanidis et al. (Eds.): HCII 2022, CCIS 1582, pp. 153–159, 2022.
https://doi.org/10.1007/978-3-031-06391-6_21

simultaneously. This is why the teacher cannot monitor each student easily in online lectures and students' temptation to do unrelated tasks follows on it.

In this paper, we solve this issue using sound feedback. We focus on warning students doing unrelated tasks during online lectures using sound feedback leading them to stop voluntarily. The sound feedback should be noticeable, but at the same time, it should not be overly unpleasant. In general, there is a trade-off between noticeability and pleasantness in sound feedback. To explore suitable sound feedback for warning during online lectures, we conducted a preliminary experiment to compare four types of sound feedback in terms of noticeability and pleasantness. Based on the experimental results, requirements of warning sound feedback for online lectures are discussed. This discussion contributes to enhancing online lecture systems and improving the quality of online learning.

2   Related Work

In previous studies, sound feedback is presented with many purposes. Kayukawa et al. used sound feedback to help blind people avoid collision with nearby people [1]. In their proposed system, the user and nearby people who have a potential risk of collision with the user are warned using sound. Some studies focus on sound feedback to use in situations related to vehicles. Fagerlönn et al. explored the usefulness of notifying drivers in the early stages of a threatening situation using sound [2]. According to this study, manipulating radio sound is useful to notify drivers. They also focused on combined auditory warnings to convey driving-related information [3].

3   Research Goal

As mentioned before in the first chapter, several students do things unrelated to their studies during online lectures. In this paper, we focus on using sound feedback to warn such students. Our goal is to explore suitable sound feedback for warning during online lectures in terms of noticeability and pleasantness.

4   Experiment

4.1   Purpose

In this experiment, we evaluated various types of sound feedback and analyzed how efficient these are for warning students doing unrelated tasks during online lectures.

4.2   Types of Sound Feedback

We selected four types of sound feedback as follows.

- Feedback 1: presenting a buzzer sound.
- Feedback 2: alternating between presenting and muting the lecture audio.
- Feedback 3: gradually reducing the lecture audio.
- Feedback 4: muting the lecture audio.

Feedback 1 was selected because of its noticeability. This feedback presents a loud buzzer sound for 5 s. Feedback 2, 3, and 4 were adopted with reference to related studies. Fagerlönn et al. used sound feedback that reduces the sound level of radio. They discussed that it can be used as an early warning in graded in-vehicle warning signals [2]. In Feedback 2, the lecture audio alters between presenting and muting for 15 s. In Feedback 3, the lecture audio gradually becomes quieter for 15 s and remains quiet for the next 15 s. In Feedback 4, the lecture audio is muted for 15 s.

4.3   Lectures for the Experiment

We prepared four lecture movies. Each movie comprises a lecture part of at least five minutes followed by an announcement part. The lecture part was performed by a professional lecturer specializing in information science. The topics of all lectures were related to programming methods to realize artificial intelligence. The spoken language was Japanese. The face and name of the lecturer were not disclosed. The content of the lectures differed in each movie. The announcement part announced the end of the lecture.

4.4   Participants

We recruited 100 participants for each feedback method using a crowdsourcing platform. This experiment was conducted in a between-subjects design. They were paid 250 JPY for each feedback method. Participants had to meet the following conditions.

1. University student or graduate student between the age of 20–40.
2. Be fluent in Japanese.

4.5   Environment

This experiment was conducted online. Each participant was in his or her own room and had access to a stable network. They used his or her own computer (desktop or laptop, with at least a 10-inch screen) and smartphone. They placed the computer on the desk and listened to the sound output from it through headphones (wired or wireless).

4.6 Procedure

The experimental procedure was as follows.

- Step 1. Each participant watched the movie describing the overview of the experiment.
- Step 2. Each participant started to watch the lecture movie on the computer.
- Step 3. Following the instruction of the text message that appeared on the computer screen two minutes after the start of the lecture movie, each participant began to perform an *unrelated task* (reading news articles) using the smartphone.
- Step 4. About four and a half minutes (4 min 40 sec for Feedback 1, 4 min 32 sec for Feedback 2, 4 min 20 sec for Feedback 3, and 4 min 35 sec for Feedback 4) after the start of the lecture movie, one sound feedback randomly selected by the experimenter was presented.
- Step 5. Each participant recorded the time they noticed the feedback.
- Step 6. Each participant completed the questionnaire described below.

4.7 Questionnaire

The questionnaire comprises seven questions.

- Q1. Did you notice the sound feedback? (yes / no)
- Q2. When did you notice the sound feedback? (time)
- Q3. Did you think the sound feedback was noticeable? (1: unnoticeable - 7: noticeable)
- Q4. Did you think the sound feedback was pleasant? (1: unpleasant - 7: pleasant)
- Q5. Did you think you were forced to stop doing the unrelated task? (1: forced - 7: unforced)
- Q6. Did you stop the unrelated task voluntarily? (1: involuntarily - 7: voluntarily)
- Q7. Describe how you felt about the sound feedback. (an open-ended format)

Participants who answered "no" to Q1 (i.e., did not notice the sound feedback) reviewed the scene of the sound feedback, and completed Q3-7.

4.8 Results

After eliminating invalid responses (e.g., responding a time much longer than the length of the lecture video in Q2), we obtained 80–90 valid responses for each feedback. In detail, 80 (male: 37, female: 43) responses for Feedback 1, 80 (male: 37, female: 41, other: 2) responses for Feedback 2, 82 (male: 36, female: 44, other: 2) responses for Feedback 3, and 90 (male: 43, female: 45, other: 2) responses for Feedback 4 were obtained.

Figure 1 shows the elapsed time from the time the feedback started to the time the participants noticed it, as derived from the responses to Q2[1]. The average elapsed time for Feedback 1, Feedback 2, Feedback 3, and Feedback 4 is one second, four seconds, 12 s, and four seconds, respectively. The one-way ANOVA test with EZR[2] at a significance level of 0.01 showed that there were significant differences between Feedback 3 and each of other types of feedback.

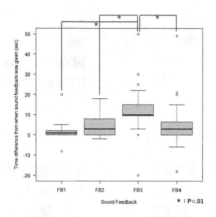

Fig. 1. Elapsed time from feedback start to noticing (Feedback 1: N = 65, Feedback 2: N = 49, Feedback 3: N = 63, Feedback 4: N = 67).

Figure 2(a) shows responses to Q3 (*Did you think the sound feedback was noticeable?*). Feedback 1 revealed the highest rating among all types of feedback. The Steel-Dwass test with EZR(see footnote 2) at a significance level of 0.01 showed that there were significant differences between Feedback 1 and each of other types of feedback.

Figure 2(b) shows responses to Q4 (*Did you think the sound feedback was pleasant?*). Unlike the case of Q3, Feedback 1 revealed the lowest rating among all types of feedback. The Steel-Dwass test with EZR(see footnote 2) at a significance level of 0.01 showed that there were significant differences between Feedback 1 and each of other types of feedback.

Figure 2(c) shows responses to Q5 (*Did you think you were forced to stop doing the unrelated task?*). Feedback 1 revealed the lowest rating among all types of feedback. The Steel-Dwass test with EZR(see footnote 2) at a significance level of 0.01 showed that there were significant differences between Feedback 1 and each of other types of feedback.

---

[1] Negative values indicate that participants mistakenly believed that the feedback was presented before it began.

[2] EZR [4] is a graphical user interface for R (The R Foundation for Statistical Computing, Vienna, Austria). More precisely, it is a modified version of R commander designed to add statistical functions frequently used in biostatistics.

Figure 2(d) shows responses to Q6 (*Did you stop the unrelated task voluntarily?*). Feedback 1 revealed the highest rating among all types of feedback. The Steel-Dwass test with EZR(see footnote 2) at a significance level of 0.01 showed that there were significant differences between Feedback 1 and each of other types of feedback.

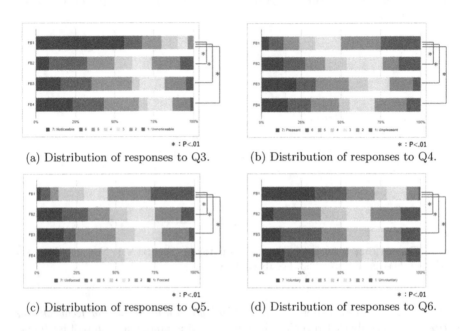

(a) Distribution of responses to Q3.   (b) Distribution of responses to Q4.

(c) Distribution of responses to Q5.   (d) Distribution of responses to Q6.

Fig. 2. Distribution of responses to Q3-6 (Feedback 1: N = 80, Feedback 2: N = 80, Feedback 3: N = 82, Feedback 4: N = 90).

4.9 Discussion and Limitation

Based on the experimental results, Feedback 1 is suitable in terms of noticeability. However, this feedback is not preferable in terms of pleasantness.

This indicates that Feedback 2–4 are preferable in terms of the balance between noticeability and pleasantness. At this moment, we cannot determine which feedback is suitable because the questionnaire results have not been fully analyzed.

5   Conclusion

In this paper, we explored suitable sound feedback for warning students who perform unrelated tasks during online lectures. The experimental results confirmed that the buzzer sound feedback is not suitable in terms of pleasantness. Other types of feedback need further detailed analysis.

References

1. Kayukawa, S., et al.: BBEEP: a sonic collision avoidance system for blind travellers and nearby pedestrians. In: Proceedings of the 2019 CHI Conference on Human Factors in Computing Systems (CHI 2019), No. 52, pp. 1–12 (2019)
2. Fagerlönn, J., Lindberg, S., Sirkka, A.: Graded auditory warnings during in-vehicle use: using sound to guide drivers without additional noise. In: Proceedings the 4th International Conference on Automotive User Interfaces and Interactive Vehicular Applications (AutomotiveUI 2012), pp. 85–91 (2012)
3. Fagerlönn, J., Lindberg, S., Sirkka, A.: Combined auditory warnings for driving-related information. In: Proceedings of the Audio Mostly 2015 on Interaction with Sound (AM 2015), No. 11, pp. 1–5 (2015)
4. Kanda, Y.: Investigation of the freely available easy-to-use software 'EZR' for medical statistics. Bone Marrow Transplant. **48**, 452–458 (2013)

The Relation Between Television Viewing Time and 4–7-Year-Old Children's Learning and Behavioral Habits

Ting Zhang📵, Yanan Chen📵, Yating Yu📵, and Hui Li$^{(\boxtimes)}$ 📵

Central China Normal University, Wuhan 430070, Hubei, People's Republic of China
{zhangting77,chenyanan,YatingYu}@mails.ccnu.edu.cn,
huilipsy@mail.ccnu.edu.cn

Abstract. With the spread of mass media such as televisions (TV) around the world, more young audiences watch television on various devices at an early age. Subsequently, researchers noticed that children in many countries watch television too much, which is unhealthy. It was indicated that television viewing is significantly associated with subsequent attention problems and poor academic performance. The current study focused on the relation between television viewing time and 4–7-year-old children's learning and behavioral habits. We used the data from the China Family Panel Studies (CFPS) in 2018, which is a national, large-scale, multidisciplinary social follow-up survey project. The result showed that children's television viewing time was significantly associated with their learning and behavioral habits. Thus, parents should realize the harm of excessive TV viewing and emphasis the limitation of children's TV viewing. The study seeks to remind parents that excessive TV viewing may be adverse to children's good learning and behavioral habits.

Keywords: Television viewing time · Learning habits · Behavioral habits · CFPS

1 Introduction

With the popularity of mass media such as televisions (TV), smartphones and tablets, the users have an irrepressible tendency towards younger age. Data show that 97% of families with young children aged 0–8 years have at least one smartphone, 75% of families have at least one tablet in their own home, 46% of children aged 2–4 years, and 67% of children aged 5–8 years have their own mobile devices [1]. This shows that a lot of young children have easy access to televisions or movies nowadays.

Digital devices and screens are now ubiquitous and universal in children's lives around the world. In many countries and regions of the world, there is a problem that children spend too much time watching TV. According to the results of the Common Sense Media (CSM) survey of media use in children aged 0–8 years, children aged 2–4 years reported 2.5 h of media use per day, while children aged 5–8 years reported 3.05 h of media use per day. Importantly, watching TV and videos as children's primary activity on screen devices accounted for 73% of the whole screen time. The American

C. Stephanidis et al. (Eds.): HCII 2022, CCIS 1582, pp. 160–167, 2022.
https://doi.org/10.1007/978-3-031-06391-6_22

Academy of Pediatrics (AAP) recommended that children aged 3–4 years spend no more than 1 h of sedentary screen time per day [2]. In 2016, the Canadian 24-h Movement Guidelines recommended that children aged 5 and over should not spend more than 2 h per day on screen entertainment [3]. Still, a Canadian survey showed that only 24.4% of children met this requirement [4]. A study focused on preschool children in Portugal showed that only 20.3% of children followed the guidelines' restrictions on screen time [5]. Years ago, a lot of 6–12-year-old children in India watched more than 2 h per day on television [6].

Coupled with the increase of social employment pressure and the boosting family economic pressure, lots of parents leave their children to television media, mobile phones, tablets, etc., thus squeezing out time to engage in their own work or other activities [1]. However, parents hardly recognize the danger of television parenting. The majority of parents keep a positive attitude towards the effect of mass media on children's development, including learning, behavioral performance, and so on. For example, most (72%) parents believed that their kids' use of media contributes to their kids' learning, while only 8% believed that using media could be harmful and adverse to learning [1]. It is indicated that, even though preschool education is a critical period to develop good habits [7], most parents are not yet aware of the negative impact of their children's excessive use of the screen on the development of children's learning during the preschool period, and they would hardly realize that children's poor academic performance in primary school later may relate to their own television parenting behavior in earlier years. Given that television viewing accounts for significant time of children and parents' attitude towards that, exploring the relation between television viewing time and children's development is especially necessary.

Many researchers have explored the relation between children's TV viewing time and children's development previously. On the one hand, previous studies have shown that children's TV viewing time is related to physical development, such as the relation between TV viewing time and childhood obesity [8], the relation between screen-usage time and children's brain development [9]. On the other hand, it has also been proved that screen viewing time is related to children's mental health [8], executive function [10], attention, etc. For instance, a survey found that infants who spent more than one hour watching TV per day had undesirable social-emotional outcomes (e.g. prosocial behavior, empathy) [11]. And it was indicated that excessive television viewing was adverse to individuals' development of creativity [12]. Another study found that the increase in TV viewing time of children aged 5–11 years was associated with attention deficit in adolescence [13]. Research by Tamana et al. [14] has shown that increased screen-time in preschoolers was associated with more severe inattention problems. Besides, there is a longitudinal research which indicated that both the time of TV viewing in young children at age 1 and 3 were able to predict their attention problems at age 7 [15]. In addition, some studies also explored the relationship between television viewing and relevant variables for child development in other aspects. For instance, there are studies exploring the relation between television viewing and children's academic performance, the results are not consistent. According to the result of a survey in Japanese, television viewing had no negative impact on children's academic performance in school [16]. On the contrary, the result of another study showed that television viewing time is negatively associated with preschoolers' school readiness skills [17]. School readiness requires good learning and behavioral habits, which could contribute to children's adaption to primary school life in advance [18]. The learning habits and behavioral habits of young children, who are confronting with transition from kindergarten to primary school, are quite plastic. Hence, parents and teachers should pay special attention to the factors that may affect children's habits [19], as far as possible to prevent the occurrence of adverse effects. However, according to Deng's [20] survey, both primary teachers and parents believed that the biggest problem with freshmen enrollment was not being equipped with good learning habits.

Habits refer to an individual's external and stable tendency during activities [7]. The definition of the concept of learning habits and behavioral habits by different researchers is different. One of the main points of view is the "behavioral tendency theory". Lin [21] believes that learning habits are individuals' automatic behavioral tendency to achieve good learning results, which is consistent with the way that behavioral habits are defined. Good behavioral habits also mean an individual's self-disciplined actions [7]. In addition, being equipped with good behavioral habits could contribute to adapting to social demands and promote an individual's positive development [22]. Besides, there are pieces of evidence showing that students' learning habits and academic performance are positively correlated [23]. Good learning habits are believed crucial as the basis of children's successful development [24], which could promote children's learning autonomy [25]. The purpose of school construction is to encourage and promote children to form good habits of individual development [26]. And good behavioral habits are the focus of schools' activities [27]. Forming good behavioral habits could contribute to an individual's development over a long period [28]. To sum up, developing learning habits and behavioral habits plays a sustained and essential role in education. Hence, it is of significance to focus on the relation between television viewing time and young children's learning habits and behavioral habits. Given that plenty of studies focusing on school-aged children has been conducted previously, the present study aims to focus on both school-aged children (7 years old) and preschool children (4–6 years old), not only tends to explore the correlation between television viewing time and learning habits and behavioral habits, but also seeks to respectively make a comparison of the differences in TV viewing time, learning habits and behavioral habits between children in different school stages.

In summary, the research focusing on the relation between the 4–7-year-old children's television viewing time and their learning and behavioral habits is highly crucial and urgently needed in China. By comparing the difference between children in different school stages and analyzing the relation between the children's television viewing time and learning and behavioral habits, this study aims to arouse parents' attention to the management of children's television viewing time and remind parents to encourage children to spend more time on other activities instead of TV viewing, which is extremely beneficial and essential to the development of children's good learning and behavioral habits.

2 Methods

2.1 Participants

The current study used data from the China Family Panel Studies (CFPS) in 2018. CFPS is a national, large-scale, multidisciplinary social follow-up survey project, which focuses on the economic and non-economic welfare of Chinese residents, as well as economic activities, educational achievements, family relations and family dynamics, population migration, health, and so on. Conducted by the Institute of Social Science Survey (ISSS), CFPS employs computer-aided Survey technology to meet diverse design needs, improve Survey efficiency and ensure data quality. As a major project funded by Peking University and the National Natural Science Foundation of China, CFPS aims to provide a data base for academic research and public policy analysis. Characteristics of 4–7-year-old children in the valid sample of the present study are: the average age of the children is 5.52 years old, the proportion of boys is 53.2%, and girls account for 46.8% of the whole children, 160 4-year-old children (17.1%), 288 5-year-old children (30.8%), 326 6-year-old children (34.9%), 160 7-year-old children (17.1%).

2.2 Measures

All the main variables were measured with the 2018 Child Proxy Questionnaire, which is one of four main questionnaire types in CFPS. The respondents of CFPS involved all members of the families under investigation, including children. Child Proxy Questionnaire was provided for those children who were under 10 years old, and the questions were answered by their guardians in Child Proxy Questionnaire.

The variables in this study include children's "television viewing time", children's "learning habits" and "behavioral habits". The "television viewing time" refers to the total time children spent watching TV, movies and other videos every week except holidays, which was obtained from a fill-in-the-blank question. Children's "learning habits" were measured by three questions, which focused on their homework habits, such as checking their work after finishing by themselves, etc. Children's "behavioral habits" were measured by four questions, which focused on their rule consciousness, attention, etc. Those seven questions all use 4-point scales, ranging from 1 to 4, referring to totally disagree, disagree, agree and totally agree. The higher the total score is, the better children's learning habits is, which is the same as behavioral habits.

2.3 Statistics Processing

Based on the demands of the study, we selected the data reported by family members of children aged 4–7 years, and we excluded invalid data by SPSS26.0, such as missing values and samples with equivalent values of "do not know", "refusal to answer" and "not applicable". Finally, a sample size of 934 was obtained. Also, we used SPSS26.0 and processed the descriptive statistics, correlation analysis, and difference testing.

3 Results

We obtained children's average score of learning habits and behavioral habits through a descriptive statistic. Children's average score of learning habits is 8.55 (SD = 1.55). Specifically, boys' average score of learning habits is 8.42 (SD = 1.54), and girls' is 8.69 (SD = 1.55). 4-year-old children's average score of learning habits is 8.30 (SD = 1.59), 5-year-old children's is 8.54 (SD = 1.49), 6-year-old children's is 8.71 (SD = 1.55), 7-year-old children's is 8.49 (SD = 1.61). The average score of behavioral habits is 11.42 (SD = 1.77). Specifically, boys' average score of behavioral habits is 11.23 (SD = 1.69), and girls' is 11.64 (SD = 1.84). 4-year-old children's average score of behavioral habits is 11.25 (SD = 1.80), 5-year-old children's is 11.51 (SD = 1.76), 6-year-old children's is 11.40 (SD = 1.78), 7-year-old children's is 11.47 (SD = 1.76).

We also obtained children's average television viewing time through descriptive statistic. Children's average television viewing time per week is 11.33h (SD = 9.73). Boys' average television viewing time per week is 11.87h (SD = 10.27), and girls' is 10.71h (SD = 9.05). Television viewing time of 4-year-old children per week is 11.7h (SD = 11.70), that of 5-year-old children is 10.95h (SD = 8.85), that of 6-year-old children is 11.7 h (SD = 10.41), that of 7-year-old children is 10.87h (SD = 8.22).

As independent-samples t-test on the gender differences in the learning and behavioral habits, there was a significant gender difference in the score of learning habits (t = 2.69, p < 0.01), and the score of girls' behavioral habits was significantly higher than that of boys (t = 3.49, p < 0.01). One-way ANOVA results showed that there was no significant difference in the television viewing time among children of different ages (p > 0.05), there was no significant difference in the learning habits and behavioral habits among different ages, either (p > 0.05).

A bivariate correlation between children's television viewing time and their "learning habits" and "behavioral habits" revealed that children's "television viewing time" and "learning habits score" were significantly negatively correlated (r = −.120, p < 0.01); and the children's "television viewing time" and the "behavioral habits score" were significantly negatively correlated (r = −.097, p < 0.01).

4 Discussion

To conclude, the analysis results showed that children who watched the television for more time had worse learning habits and behavioral habits. This may be due to the longer time children spend on TV and movies, the less time and energy they spend on learning [29]. In addition, children with a more average TV time would develop poor attention [30]. It has been shown that screen viewing time may aggravate young children's attention defects and further affect attention-related actions [31], such as learning activities, reading comprehension, etc. It was found that students with lower television viewing time had more learning motivations, although the internal mechanism needs further study[32]. Moreover, the information transmitted by mass media, such as televisions, tends to be intuitive, which is not conducive to the development of children's ability and habits of independent thinking, indirectly resulting in the reduction of their interest in learning and poor development of learning habits [33]. Hence, parents are supposed to spend more time with children instead of leaving them to televisions. Parents should also cultivate children's self-control ability, so that children can reasonably plan and manage TV viewing time and frequency on their own. In addition, the present study also found that girls scored significantly higher than boys in both learning habits and behavioral habits. This may be because girls are quieter and better than boys under social expectations and requirements [24]. Therefore, parents and teachers should strengthen the cultivation of good habits of boys. The results also showed no significant difference in television viewing time among different age groups, making cautions that parents are supposed to manage and guide children's TV viewing behavior from children's early age.

Importantly, the study also found no significant difference in learning habits and behavioral habits among different ages. The result shows that the effect of habit cultivation conducted by preschool teachers and parents seems to be limited, which means children's enrollment preparation is not sufficient. As mentioned before, bad learning habits and behavioral habits may lead to poor performance of new students in the lower grades of primary schools. On the one hand, before young children enter primary schools, preschool teachers and parents should pay attention to the cultivation of kid's habits to help young children adapt to the learning and life in primary schools in advance; on the other hand, for young children with poor learning habits and behavioral habits, primary teachers should also take effective measures to help them establish good learning habits and behavioral habits, such as encouraging young children to learn from others in the upper grades, giving a positive assessment of young children's behavior. In addition, teachers and parents are models for children, so they should manage their own words and deeds and insist on being a good example for children [21].

5 Strengths and Limitations

In summary, the study seeks to remind parents that excessive TV viewing may be harmful and adverse to children's good learning habits and behavioral habits, tending to attract parents' attention to limit and manage children's television viewing time. Initially exploring the national duration of children's TV viewing time and its relation with 4–7-year-old children's learning habits and behavioral habits, the study further provides an elementary basis for understanding how Chinese children are affected by TV viewing in the development of learning and behavioral habits, and further exploring the internal mechanism of human-computer interaction.

There are still several limitations in terms of the present study. First, the study didn't focus on children's television viewing contents. It has been found that the correlation between television viewing and children's development relies on the type of programs [34]. Future research could simultaneously focus on the relation between TV viewing time and content and young children's learning habits and behavioral habits. Moreover, there is another limitation which is also unavoidable in plenty of studies, the television viewing time is reported by informants instead of observed by researchers. However, due to the range and character of respondents of CFPS, the method is relatively appropriate. Future studies could further explore more objective measures else, such as reporting the videos time recorded by devices.

References

1. Rideout, V., Robb, M.B.: The Common Sense Census: Media Use by Kids Age Zero to Eight. Common Sense Media, San Francisco (2020)
2. Willumsen, J., Bull, F.: Development of WHO guidelines on physical activity, sedentary behavior, and sleep for children less than 5 years of age. J. Phys. Act. Health **17**(1), 96–100 (2020)
3. Tremblay, M.S., et al.: Canadian 24-hour movement guidelines for children and youth: an integration of physical activity, sedentary behaviour, and sleep. Appl. Physiol. Nutr. Metab. **41**(6), S311–S327 (2016)
4. Chaput, J.P., et al.: Proportion of preschool-aged children meeting the Canadian 24-Hour Movement Guidelines and associations with adiposity: results from the Canadian Health Measures Survey. BMC Public Health **17**(5), 147–154 (2017)
5. Vale, S., Mota, J.: Adherence to 24-hour movement guidelines among Portuguese preschool children: The prestyle study. J. Sports Sci. **38**(18), 2149–2154 (2020)
6. Arya, K.: Time spent on television viewing and its effect on changing values of school going children. Anthropologist **6**(4), 269–271 (2004)
7. Wu, X.F.: To realize the positive migration of living habits to children's learning habits. J. Shanghai Educ. Res. **12**, 89–90 (2011)
8. Nieto, A., Suhrcke, M.: The effect of TV viewing on children's obesity risk and mental well-being: evidence from the UK digital switchover. J. Health Econ. **80**, 102543 (2021)
9. Horowitz-Kraus, T., Hutton, J.S.: Brain connectivity in children is increased by the time they spend reading books and decreased by the length of exposure to screen-based media. Acta Paediatr. **107**(4), 685–693 (2018)
10. Martins, C.M.D.L., et al.: A network perspective on the relationship between screen time, executive function, and fundamental motor skills among preschoolers. Int. J. Environ. Res. Public Health **17**(23), 8861 (2020)
11. Lu, S., Cui, Y., Wang, Z.Y., Li, Y.Q., G, W.T., Liang, X.: The relationship between TV time and infant language and emotional social development: a follow-up study. Stud. Early Childhood Educ. **11**, 15–26 (2018)
12. Mukherjee, S.B., Gupta, Y., Aneja, S.: Study of television viewing habits in children. Indian J. Pediatrics. **81**(11), 1221–1224 (2014)
13. Landhuis, C.E., Poulton, R., Welch, D., Hancox, R.J.: Does childhood television viewing lead to attention problems in adolescence? results from a prospective longitudinal study. Pediatrics **120**(3), 532–537 (2007)
14. Tamana, S.K., et al.: Screen-time is associated with inattention problems in preschoolers: results from the CHILD birth cohort study. PLoS ONE **14**(4), e0213995 (2019)
15. Christakis, D.A., Zimmerman, F.J., DiGiuseppe, D.L., McCarty, C.A.: Early television exposure and subsequent attentional problems in children. Pediatrics **113**(4), 708–713 (2004)
16. Kureishi, W., Yoshida, K.: Does viewing television affect the academic performance of children? Soc. Sci. Japan J. **16**(1), 87–105 (2013)
17. Clarke, A.T., Kurtz-Costes, B.: Television viewing, educational quality of the home environment, and school readiness. J. Educ. Res. **90**(5), 279–285 (1997)
18. Liu, B.L.: Talk about the senior class enrollment work in the kindergarten. Stud. Early Childhood Educ. **05**, 32–33 (1995)
19. Sun, N.: The formation of behavioral habits of new primary school students. J. Teach. Manage. **29**, 8–10 (2012)
20. Deng, Y.: Research on the initial adaptation of primary school freshmen from the perspective of primary school connection. East China Normal University (2010)

21. Lin, C.D.: The Encyclopedia of Chinese Middle School Teaching. Education volume. Shenyang Press, Shenyang (1990)
22. Luo, S.L., Wang, Z., Zhang, D.J., Chen, W.F., Liu, G.Z.: The relationship between children's psychological traits and their good behavior habits and problem behaviors. Stud. Early Childhood Educ. **04**, 56–63 (2017)
23. Gong, J., Lu, Z.T., M, J.Y.: Does higher parental expectation means better child grades-empirical analysis? - based on CFPS (2016) data. Shanghai Educ. Res. **11**, 11–16 (2018)
24. Tian, L.: Empirical analysis of the learning habits of urban pupils—survey of 5,600 students in 17 schools in 5 provinces and cities. J. Shanghai Educ. Res. **09**, 46–49 (2010)
25. Liang, S.X.: Effective strategies for developing good study habits. J. Chin. Soc. Educ. **S2**, 123–124 (2016)
26. Gao, D.S.: Rethinking habit and habit forstering. J. Educ. Stud. **15**(03), 17–27 (2019)
27. Zhu, C.Y., Shi, X.H.: Construction and practice research of classes Self-Management mode in primary school. Theory Practice Educ. **35**(08), 24–26 (2015)
28. Mo, X., Wang, Z., Shao, J.: Parent-child attachment and good behavior habits among Chinese children: chain mediation effect of parental involvement and psychological Suzhi. PLoS ONE **16**(1), e0241586 (2021)
29. Ennemoser, M., Schneider, W.: Relations of television viewing and reading: findings from a 4-year longitudinal study. J. Educ. Psychol. **99**(2), 349 (2007)
30. Ray, M., Jat, K.R.: Effect of electronic media on children. Indian Pediatr. **47**(7), 561–568 (2010)
31. Calleja-Pérez, B., et al.: Trastorno por déficit de atención/hiperactividad: Hábitos de estudio. MEDICINA (Buenos Aires). **79**(1), 57–61 (2019)
32. Amin, S.N, Mattoo, M.I.: Influence of heavy and low television watching on study habits of secondary school students—a study. New Media and Mass Communication 3 (2012)
33. Li, M.Y., Wang, Q.: Investigation of three-to-six-year-old children's use of multimedia at home in Beijing. J. Educ. Stud. **10**(06), 95–102 (2014)
34. Wright, J.C., Huston, A.C., Murphy, K.C., St. Peters, M., Piñon, M., Scantlin, R., Kotler, J.: The relations of early television viewing to school readiness and vocabulary of children from low-income families: the early window project. Child Dev. **72**(5), 1347–1366 (2001)

HCI, Cultural Heritage and Art

Follow the Blue Butterfly – An Immersive Augmented Reality Museum Guide

Jessica L. Bitter, Ralf Dörner, Yu Liu, Linda Rau, and Ulrike Spierling[✉]

Faculty of Design, Computer Science, Media, Hochschule RheinMain, Unter den Eichen 5, 65195 Wiesbaden, Germany
{jessicalaura.bitter,ralf.doerner,yu.liu,linda.rau,
ulrike.spierling}@hs-rm.de

Abstract. We present our concept and prototypical implementation of an avatar guide that helps museum visitors to navigate to chosen points of interest. The prototype shows an animated butterfly with interactive behavior that is controlled by a state machine. The avatar's path can be pre-defined at an authoring stage, by walking the space with the head-mounted display and by placing path nodes interactively, or it can be generated at runtime, in which case the whole area needs to be scanned and processed beforehand. As the app is iteratively redesigned and tested with first-time users for accessibility, we report on first lessons learnt.

Keywords: Museum navigation system · Augmented reality · Head-mounted display · Avatar guide

1 Introduction

In the last decades, consumer use of Augmented Reality (AR) apps in museums and exhibitions has become more and more commonplace, while the current state of the art mostly allows employing off-the-shelf smartphones with simple touch interactions. In our project "presentXR", we extend this state of the art by exploring future applications of more advanced tracking and immersive technology, such as increased precise localization (SLAM and room scanning) and hands-free human-computer interaction styles of head-mounted displays. We design and prototype several museum use cases, using the Microsoft HoloLens 2 as an example hardware. We explore accessibility issues in the application domain of museums, where we cannot rely on user training. While the whole range of interaction possibilities needs to be simplified, the aim is to let visitors experience the fascination of being immersed in spatial AR overlays of the real world and museum artefacts.

One central use case of this concept is the real-world navigation while walking through an exhibition. We present our concept and prototype of an avatar guide – an animated 3D butterfly – that leads visitors to chosen points of interest in a museum. The abstract adaptable concept allows future authors to exchange avatar geometry and its locomotive movements, while the overall interactive behavior is controlled by a state machine. The avatar's paths can either be pre-defined at an authoring stage, by walking

C. Stephanidis et al. (Eds.): HCII 2022, CCIS 1582, pp. 171–178, 2022.
https://doi.org/10.1007/978-3-031-06391-6_23

the space with the head-mounted display and by placing path nodes interactively, or it can be generated at runtime, in which case the whole area needs to be scanned and processed beforehand. As the app is iteratively redesigned and tested with first-time users for accessibility, we report on first lessons learnt.

2 Related Work

Indoor navigation with AR so far has been mainly implemented on handheld devices (HHD) [1]. With new generations of such devices, an increased number of research endeavors propose guiding applications based on varieties of sensors [2]. Many of them use the game engine Unity [3] and its built-in navigation and pathfinding system called NavMesh [4]. One part of the NavMesh system is a Navigation Mesh ("NavMesh") that refers to geometry defined as a walkable area. Unity's NavMesh has also been used previously to create a guiding application for head-mounted devices (HMD) [5].

In the context of exhibitions, HMDs promise new immersive visiting experiences [6, 7]. For the Microsoft HoloLens 2 as a state-of-the-art example, indoor navigation also works with so-called spatial anchors, which are fixed points of reference in the physical world [8]. Bachras et al. [9] investigated their use for AR-based navigation. They found that while authoring a pathway with spatial anchors increases the development effort, it is essential to use them to avoid drift over longer distances.

Guiding applications for museum scenarios often consider the learning experience of visitors [10]. To enhance this experience, the integration of an avatar can be helpful [11]. These virtual museum guides often mainly present narrative content, as for example in the Egyptian MuseumEye project that includes four virtual characters as guides [12]. In these cases, the appearance of an avatar provides the main interface to the visitors, and its visual affordance plays an important role to support the understanding of interactions [13]. As avatars and navigation systems are there to help users, it is of utmost importance to make their behavior easily understandable [5]. For the display of situated behavior of animated characters, state machines as a concept are widely used in the games industry [14].

We base our work on several of these concepts and integrate indoor navigation and abstract avatar behavior on head-mounted displays to create an immersive navigation guide.

3 User Requirements for Real World Navigation in a Museum

Augmented Reality on head-mounted display so far has been mainly introduced in industrial or other professional fields, in which skilled users get training on how to act with the unusual interfaces. This is different from museum visitors, who come unprepared, and who do not want to spend a long time for learning how to interact. Their visit is usually framed in a short time leisure experience, and it is a voluntary action. If visitors encounter difficulties while using the application, they probably collect negative experiences and will stop using it, which is also contrary to the idea of providing them with the intended fascinating perception of the spatial augmentations of artefacts.

Using the avatar to get guidance can be enjoyable but also challenging. The visitor should first be able to interpret the behavior of the guide to be able to follow. Then, visitors walk through the museum at different individual speed, which the tour guide needs to take into account. Further requirements of visiting include that various exhibits next to the path may raise interest; the visitor may also be interrupted and inattentive, or needs to take breaks. The guiding logic should be adaptable to these situations and tolerate mistakes from user actions. Further, visitors may want to skip the guiding and ask for new destinations or topics to visit, which results in the necessity to converse with the guide. Consequently, a natural and lifelike behavior of a virtual guide may need to get complex. In our ongoing project, the first concept includes the options to start the guide, choose a destination and follow the avatar to the set goal.

To account for variations in walking speed and interruptions, we thought of several states in the adaptable avatar behavior, which we draft as a state diagram in Fig. 1. So far, the guiding functions of our prototype address the following basic use cases. The user starts the guiding app and finds the avatar at an idle position. The avatar offers to guide the visitor, who confirms and follows it, partly intermittently, partly with pausing and resuming, until arrival at the goal.

4   Behavior Concept of the Virtual Guide

For guiding a visitor to a point of interest, we developed a state machine concept for the avatar's behavior. The goal is an abstract framework that can be applied to various forms of guides. The avatar's shape currently consists of 3D geometry with several brief canned animation cycles that correspond to each behavioral state. Hence, different models with associated animations can be designed and easily exchanged. For example, a walking insect could replace our flying butterfly. We are in the process of defining the design parameters that need to be followed by avatar modelers to make new models fit into the framework. We first used role-playing methods to identify a minimum of necessary behavior states for a guide in a museum, so that it is easy to follow, taking into account possible interruptions or visitor concerns. We identified six states that we claim to be universal to a guide, be it virtual or physical.

We use an abstract blue flying butterfly that fits our environment of a natural history museum. The state diagram will be explained with this example in the following (Fig. 1). Before the butterfly starts, it should wait at a specified position for the visitor to join. We call this state "idle". This state includes an animation that makes the avatar look vivid. After starting the navigation, the avatar determines, depending on its distance to the user, whether it needs to move slowly, fast, or even needs to wait for the visitor to let them catch up. In the authoring phase, various reference distances between a visitor and the guide can be defined that trigger the transitions between these states when the values fall below or exceed that threshold. Throughout the guiding process, the system constantly calculates the distance and adjusts the speed accordingly. If the guide is already in the waiting state and the user moves even farther away, the guide will move back towards the user. When the avatar undercuts the maximal distance to the goal, it shows an arrival animation, and then returns into the idle state.

Figure 1 shows four values (a–d) that need to be defined for the state machine to work. The value (a) indicates the closest distance between the guide and the user that

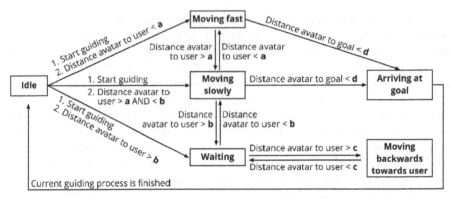

Fig. 1. State diagram of the guiding state machine.

makes the avatar move faster if fallen below, or conversely, more slowly if it is exceeded. Value (b) specifies a threshold that defines the limits for waiting, which should of course be a greater distance than (a). Therefore, with greater distance the avatar will first move slowly, before it enters a waiting state. Value (c), which again should exceed value (b), defines at what distance the avatar transitions from the waiting state to moving back towards the visitor. Lastly, value (d) sets a maximum distance from the final goal, defining arrival with some tolerance.

5   Authoring and Calculating Pathways

We explore two distinguished options to author and calculate the avatar's pathways. The first option is to pre-define all pathways at an authoring stage, by walking the space with the head-mounted display and by placing path nodes interactively. Our second option is to calculate navigation paths at runtime, in which case the whole area needs to be scanned and processed beforehand. We implement both options using the game engine Unity [3] and describe them in detail in the following.

5.1   Authoring Pathways Based on Nodes and Goals

Figure 2 (left) illustrates an example result of an authored path. This track is composed of four nodes, of which one is the final goal (number 4). At each corner or whenever the path changes direction, one node is placed and connected to the prior node. The last node is connected to the pathway's goal. The authoring application, running on the Microsoft HoloLens 2, visualizes nodes with location markers (Fig. 2, left).

The nodes are anchored in the real world using spatial anchors [15]. These are positioned by an author wearing a HoloLens, walking along an intended visitor trail in the real space and placing appropriate nodes directly at suitable positions. When a visitor starts the guiding process, the butterfly moves along the resulting path while automatically aligning itself with its defined front towards the goal.

The nodes from different pathways stay independent from each other and are not connected. Therefore, currently the avatar cannot calculate new ad-hoc paths based on nodes from different existing paths. Users can only follow one predefined pathway and switch to another one, if that starts near the user's current location. If a visitor leaves the track, the avatar waits, or the guiding process can be stopped. Our prototype cannot calculate yet if there is another (probably faster) pathway, or how to get back to the original pathway. This could be approached by implementing a wayfinding algorithm that calculates a new path based on existing nodes at runtime. To make this work, authors could specify possible cross-connections between close nodes, e.g., in a table. Care must be taken to prevent the avatar from flying through walls. This makes authoring more complex as it would be easy to forget certain connections when authoring the table.

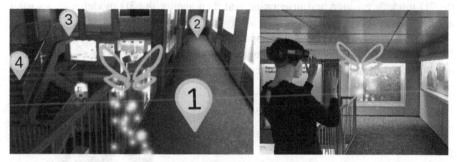

Fig. 2. Left: HoloLens 2 screenshot of the authoring app with four visible nodes and the butterfly avatar following the path. Right: The visitor's view with nodes invisible.

5.2 Navigation Based on a Pre-processed 3D Scan of the Environment

To be able to calculate a pathway at runtime, knowledge about the environment is necessary. Instead of connecting nodes on tracks as described before, we enable a less rigid navigation by scanning the environment beforehand and by using this scan data as a base for ad-hoc calculations. In this section, we describe our test implementation.

We scanned our office floor as test environment using an indoor mobile mapping system by NavVis [16] and created a 3D object from the scan data. We then processed the data to create a Vuforia area target [17]. Based on an area target, the tracking library Vuforia detects and tracks real-world areas so that virtual objects can be positioned into them. To achieve this, we place the avatar at a specific position on the virtual area target's floor in Unity, so that the avatar will appear at that corresponding position on the floor in the real world. Without an area target or a spatial anchor, virtual content appears in a position relative to the HoloLens' initial position. The area target allows to position and orient virtual content in the real world, regardless of the HoloLens' position and rotation.

When running the HoloLens app, Vuforia anchors the 3D model of our scan data to the area target, mapping its geometry with the real world to create an approximate overlay. The 3D model is then made invisible, while it enables to calculate the pathway at runtime based on Unity's NavMesh system [4]. By adding a NavMesh, we define our 3D model as a walkable area. Our prototype application bakes the NavMesh at runtime when the 3D model is overlaid with the real-world area. Figure 3 shows the 3D scan of our model in real-world colors with the floor as a NavMesh in blue. The illustrated path (the red line) from the avatar's position to the goal is then calculated at runtime.

Authors only need to author one or several goals, because the pathway can be calculated automatically based on the NavMesh. However, other challenges need further exploration. For example, calculating a path is only possible at places where there is a NavMesh. In case it would have large holes, this would lead to the calculation of strange paths from the point of view of a user, as the avatar always needs to be on the NavMesh. In our prototype, area targets demanded much computing power, partly making avatar calculations and rendering not satisfying. We then used the area target only to initialize the 3D model's position and orientation and then anchor the 3D model with a spatial anchor. We regularly check if position and rotation still fit and update it.

In the future, we expect that this approach is more flexible than the node-based one, for example to ad-hoc take into account variable optimized paths. These could depend on situational parameters, such as temporary crowds, or on individual needs, such as step height or pathway length.

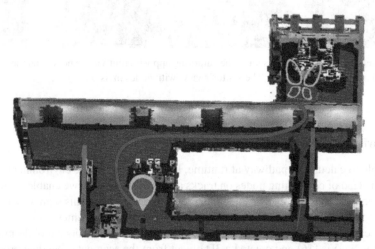

Fig. 3. Pathway calculations based on a pre-processed 3D scan. A 3D model of the environment is anchored to the real world using a Vuforia area target (real-world colors). This 3D model is then overlaid with a NavMesh (in blue), to calculate a pathway (red line). (Color figure online)

6 Evaluation

We tested the avatar guide application with the primary goal to understand whether visitors can follow the virtual avatar properly to the destination, and how the behavior with its different states can be understood and recognized. The tests so far have been performed with the prototype of the authored node-based path. We asked 30 students to serve as individual subjects. They were asked to follow the butterfly across a university corridor to find a goal, while wearing the HoloLens 2. In each individual walkthrough, two helpers took notes or served as support in case of problems. We used the qualitative results and comments of the testers for the iterative redesign of parameters and indications for future work. Further, we tested the guiding app in a big museum of Natural History with a longer distance navigation.

Overall, the test results confirmed that the concept of using the butterfly guide on a HMD is fascinating and enjoyable. It showed that a virtual avatar using our state-based behavior concept could support users to navigate through an indoor space, while it also revealed some challenges.

First, it is essential that there must be a reason to follow a guide, because the direction of a point of interest is unknown. With a goal within eyeshot, testers abandoned the butterfly and moved on independently. If several points of interest are in one room, it is more effective to present locative indicators to guide visitors, than an avatar moving between them.

The general moving speed of the butterfly influences the guiding experience. When the speed is too slow or too fast, users have difficulties following. In the first instance, the general speed was too slow, so that users did run into the avatar with the feeling to push it. Further, the initial parameter settings need to be different according to the room size. The parameters from the tests in the office floor did not work for the big museum space. With our authoring tools, these parameters can be tweaked while wearing the HoloLens, but still, it is necessary to start with reasonable default values.

Another confusion occurred with the state-based behavior when visitors were not moving. The users recognized that the avatar waits for them, but it did not change states when the distance stayed the same. Hence, our test showed a necessity to base the change of the waiting state also on the time passed while waiting, and to include even a further state, in order to show more liveliness or start to interact with the user.

Our test also illustrated the difficulties of novice users to handle the HoloLens' hand menu that is part of the operation system. For a future museum application, we plan to overcome these with the implementation of a kiosk mode with tailored interfaces.

7   Conclusion and Future Work

We presented early prototypes and concepts of immersive AR museum navigation that can be used to engage and guide visitors in museums. It is part of a project to analyze the possibilities and limitations of employing head-mounted displays in this domain. While the first prototype had the focus on the basic behavior possibilities of a guiding avatar, there are many important issues to solve before this navigation becomes feasible in any museum situation. For example, the guide should detect moving obstacles that block the path, e.g. other visitors, and circumvent them. We want to include spatial mapping into the navigation process so that the butterfly can recognize and sit on a surface on the way, or wait at corners for the visitor. On a more nice-to-have note, we want to extend the state machine to enable a richer, more lifelike behavior.

Acknowledgments. This work has been funded (in part) by the German Federal Ministry of Education and Research (BMBF), funding program "Forschung an Fachhochschulen", project "presentXR", contract number 13FH181PX8.

References

1. Joshi, R., Hiwale, A., Birajdar, S., Gound, R.: Indoor Navigation with Augmented Reality. In: Kumar, A., Mozar, S. (eds) ICCCE 2019. Lecture Notes in Electrical Engineering, vol. 570. Springer, Singapore (2019)
2. Hepzibah, S., Keerthana, S., Shruthi, C.S., Sindhuja, P.: Mobile application development for indoor navigation using slam and augmented reality. Int. J. Sci. Res. Sci. Technol. (IJSRST) **8**(3), 128–133 (2021)
3. Unity Technologies Website. https://unity.com/de. Accessed 12 May 2022
4. Unity Documentation: NavMesh. Unity Scripting API, Version 2020.3 (LTS). https://docs.unity3d.com/ScriptReference/AI.NavMesh.html
5. Tang, R.: A mixed reality solution for indoor navigation. Master Thesis, VRIJE Universiteit, Brussels, BE (2018)
6. Chung, H.L., Chin, K.Y., Wang, C.S.: Development of a head-mounted mixed reality museum navigation system. In: 2021 IEEE 4th International Conference on Knowledge Innovation and Invention (ICKII), pp. 111–114 (2021)
7. Liu, Y., Spierling, U., Rau, L., Dörner, R.: Handheld vs Head mounted AR Interaction Patterns for Museums or Guided Tours. In: Proc. INTETAIN 2020, LNICST, vol. 377, pp. 229–242. Springer, Cham (2021)
8. He, W., Xi, M., Gardner, H., Swift, B.: Spatial anchor based indoor assets tracking. In: 2021 IEEE Virtual Reality and 3D User Interfaces (VR), pp. 255–259 (2021)
9. Bachras, V., Raptis, G.E., Avouris, N.M.: On the use of persistent spatial points for deploying path navigation in augmented reality: an evaluation study. In: Lamas, D., Loizides, F., Nacke, L., Petrie, H., Winckler, M., Zaphiris, P. (eds.) INTERACT 2019. LNCS, vol. 11749, pp. 309–318. Springer, Cham (2019). https://doi.org/10.1007/978-3-030-29390-1_17
10. Ghouaiel, N., Garbaya, S., Cieutat, J.-M., Jessel, J.-P.: Mobile augmented reality in museums: towards enhancing visitor's learning experience. Int. J. Virtual Real. **17**(1), 21–31 (2017)
11. Campbell, A.G., Stafford, J.W., Holz, T., O'Hare, G.M.P.: Why, when and how to use augmented reality agents (AuRAs). Virtual Real. **18**(2), 139–159 (2013). https://doi.org/10.1007/s10055-013-0239-4
12. Hammady, R., Ma, M., Strathern, C., Mohamad, M.: Design and development of a spatial mixed reality touring guide to the Egyptian museum. Multimed. Tools Appl. **79**(5–6), 3465–3494 (2019). https://doi.org/10.1007/s11042-019-08026-w
13. Deng, S., Xu, X., Wu, C., Chen, K., Jia, K.: 3D AffordanceNet: a benchmark for visual object affordance understanding. arXiv e-prints. arXiv:2103.16397 (2021)
14. Millington, I., Funge, J.: Artificial Intelligence for Games, 2nd edn. Morgan Kaufmann, Burlington (2009)
15. Microsoft: Spatial anchors. Mixed Reality Structural Elements Documentation, Version (2021). https://docs.microsoft.com/en-us/windows/mixed-reality/design/spatial-anchors
16. NavVis: M6 Scanning System. https://www.navvis.com/de/m6. Accessed 12 May 2022
17. Vuforia Developer Portal: Area Targets. https://library.vuforia.com/features/environments/area-targets.html. Accessed 12 May 2022

Between Shanshui and Landscape: An AI Aesthetics Study Connecting Chinese and Western Paintings

Rong Chang[✉], Xinmiao Song, and Huiwen Liu

Beijing Institute of Graphic Communication, No. 1 (band -2) Xinghua Street, Daxing District, Beijing, China
changrong-bj@bigc.edu.cn

Abstract. As a preliminary study for painting AI development work, we conducted experimental creations based on human-AI collaboration. The materials for creation were from Chinese Shanshui paintings and Western landscape paintings. Various experimental methods, such as AI painting, human hand-painting, and human-AI collaboration painting, were tried. The creation themes included line drawing, colorization, deconstruction and reconstruction, and the experimental results were discussed from the aspects of visual cognition, visual expression, and visual imagination. Rethinking the relationships of human, AI and art probably help us find the better paradigm of painting AI. We suggest designing painting AI centered on the human-AI joint subject to stimulate more creativity and deepen aesthetic experience.

Keywords: Painting AI · Chinese Shanshui painting · Western landscape painting · Human-AI joint subject

1 Introduction

Although visual style transfer provides an effective means for picture simulating [1], it is not feasible to create professional hand-painting works. Researchers have tried the following approaches to improve the computing framework: training the model based on manually annotated categories for texture enhancement [2], or splitting the generation process into sketch transfer and pixel-to-pixel translation [3]. But the results were still unsatisfactory. We hypothesize that a framework based on human-AI collaboration would open ambitious applications for the professional painters. Therefore, the focus of this study is to explore the relationship between human and AI in painting creation.

Whether in the East or West, the driving force behind the development of painting art lies in the evolution of human's visual perception and cognition. The Song Dynasty and Yuan Dynasty were the critical periods for the maturity of Chinese Shanshui painting. Around the same stage, the West entered the Renaissance and landscape painting gradually developed into an independent art form. Western landscape painting at that time had a strong ability to depict the nature, while Chinese Shanshui painting had the

C. Stephanidis et al. (Eds.): HCII 2022, CCIS 1582, pp. 179–185, 2022.
https://doi.org/10.1007/978-3-031-06391-6_24

characteristic of non-realistic representation. The research on these classic works would lead to an understanding of human's visual imitation and representation in painting, thereby providing support for painting AI development work.

In this paper we present our explorations to this important new topic. First, we constructed a study framework for painting AI based on painting history and art style analysis theory. Second, we designed experiments involving different approaches to examine the performance of human and AI in different painting scenes. Third, we investigated different AI architectures and adapted the frameworks of Vgg19 [1], AC-GAN [2] and Pix2Pix [3] for painting.

The rest of the paper is organized as follows. Section 2 discusses the experimental results of line drawing together with our view on what the connecting of Chinese and Westen paintings could be. Section 3 presents the experimental results of different colorization pattern. The experimental results of deconstruction and reconstruction are discussed in Sect. 4. Finally, we conclude in Sect. 5. Due to space limitations, this paper mainly introduces the experimental creation part related to Chinese Shanshui painting.

2 Line Drawing

Chinese paintings are mostly made of lines. Chinese painters pay attention to the changes in the trajectory, length, width, twists, and turns of the lines, and change the combinations of lines to present the structure. Lines can further develop into line strokes, which are used to express the veins and textures of mountains, rocks, and trees. In the Five Dynasties, Dong Yuan created flexible and long line strokes named "Hemp-fiber". During the Yuan Dynasty, Ni Zan liked using neat and dry line strokes called "break-belt", and in the Qing Dynasty Yuan Ji draw line strokes like snakes. The patterns of lines and line strokes are the main features of Chinese Shanshui painting.

We trained AI to learn a variety of lines and line strokes from famous paintings (see Fig. 1). Based on the enhancement of human hand-drawn drafts, as well as model training, AI partly captured the outlines and the distribution of line strokes in classic works.

Line drawing plays an important role in both Chinese and Western paintings. As Wölfflin said, the Renaissance was the art of lines. Raphael's lines were elegant and gentle, Michelangelo's lines were powerful. Subsequently, lines blended with color and light. In the post-impressionist period, Gauguin's and Van Gogh's paintings had clear lines again. Some of Van Gogh's later paintings could even be seen as dynamic combinations of long and short lines. At this point, Eastern and Western paintings established an essential connection.

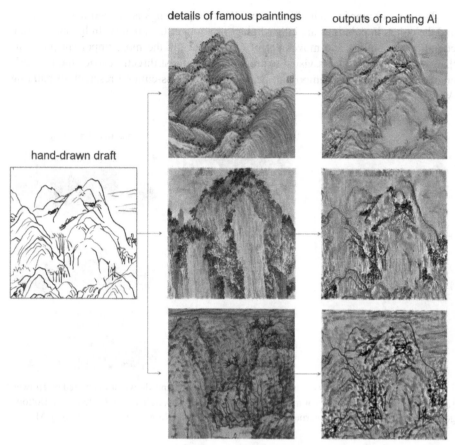

Fig. 1. Experimental creations of line drawing. Left column: hand-drawn draft created by Huiwen Liu. Middle column: examples of different lines and line strokes. Top, created by Hui Wang, Qing Dynasty. Middle, created by Yuanzhi Wu, Jin Dynasty. Bottom, created by Yuan Ji, Qing Dynasty. Photo credit: Taipei Palace Museum. Right column: Outputs of painting AI.

3   Colorization

Chinese painting often uses simple tones. The colorization of Chinese Shanshui painting can be roughly divided into several main modes, such as light wash ink, light ocher, teal, gold-and-teal. The light ocher Shanshui adds ochre and other colors on the light wash ink, and often expresses the scene of autumn. The teal Shanshui is thinly applied azurite and stone green. Gold-and-teal Shanshui is based on teal and depicts mountain profiles, pavilions, colorful clouds, etc. with mud and gold.

We trained AI to learn the main coloring mode. Part of the results are shown in Fig. 2.AI learned some rules of assigning colors to categories in Chinese painting, that is, dividing objects in paintings into several categories and assigning one color to each category.

The use of color in both Chinese and Western paintings is beyond natural scenes, and the colors in paintings are either lighter or stronger than reality. In human's visual cognition the outline and movement of objects occupy the more important positions than color; but in human's visual expression, color most directly carries the painter's emotions. This is also an important perspective for cross-cultural research of painting AI.

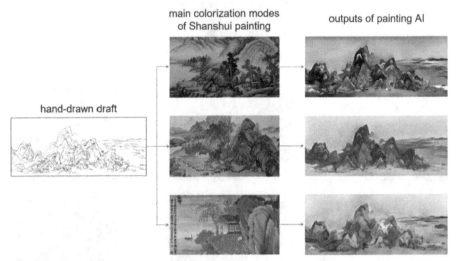

Fig. 2. Experimental creations of colorization. Left column: hand-drawn draft created by Huiwen Liu. Middle column: examples of main colorization modes. Top, light ocher. Middle, teal. Bottom, gold-and-teal. Photo credit: internet public resources. Right column: outputs of painting AI.

4   Deconstruction and Reconstruction

The above experiments are all based on hand-draw drafts. In viewing, people grasp the world and process it as a picture. A hand-draw draft is the person's cognition, construction, and visual representation of the world model. For AI, such a draft is the given semantic map that specifies the structure and elements of the image. AI still does not have the ability to create images with high-level semantics based on its own observations. This means that AI cannot complete creative painting independently.

To investigate deeply into the image consciousness of human painter, the study observed how human deconstruct and reconstruct images between Chinese and Western paintings. We tried experimental creations in two ways: one is to change Dong Yuan's famous work "Sandbanks in the Cold Forest" into a Western landscape painting; the other is to change Corot's famous painting "The Scenery of Fontainebleau Forest" into a Chinese Shanshui painting.

During deconstructing and reconstructing, the human painter extracted the key elements, such as mountains, sandbanks, trees, houses, and bridges from the original work and changed the Chinese vertical composition into a Western style composition which emphasizing on the fixed-point perspective (see Fig. 3). The ground that appears erect in the original work now is back to the level. The water surface in the near view and the sky in the far view each occupies about one-third of the picture. The sandbanks in the middle shot are the focus of the depiction. The trees on the left sandbanks break the symmetry, so that the picture is no longer monotonous and repetitive. The colorization way of impasto is also like the western landscape paintings. The bleak mood revealed by the original work turns to bright.

Fig. 3. Change Chinese Shanshui painting into Western landscape painting. Large picture: created by Xinmiao Song. Small picture: *Sandbanks in the Cold Forest* created by Dong Yuan, Five Dynasty. Photo credit: Japan Kurokawa Institute of Ancient Culture

When deconstructed the Western landscape painting "View of the Forest of Fontainebleau", the painter chose some elements in the original work and deleted the figure and the details of close-up depictions (see Fig. 4). Composition that emphasizing details and perspective changed into the composition of flat and far.

The new picture is sparse and open. The compositional units embedded to each other in the original work now are relatively independent. In terms of colorization, the oil painting impasto is changed to water ink lines and line strokes. The mountains and trees are thickly inked, and the rocks are represented with strokes named "Axe-cut". Water is outlined with few curves, combining with the white space and light ink. Thus, the sweet mood of the original picture is turned to plain and quiet.

Fig. 4. Change Western landscape painting into Chinese Shanshui painting. Large picture: created by Huiwen Liu. Small picture: *View of the Forest of Fontainebleau* created by Camille Corot, 1830. Photo credit: National Gallery of Art

Transcending the space at this moment with visual imagination has always been the common goal pursued by both Chinese and Western painters. Chinese painters use scatter perspective to construct flow scenes, and Western painters use fixed-point perspective to construct deep scenes. This is the third important perspective for cross-cultural research of painting AI.

5 Conclusion

Through experimental creations, our main findings are as follows: First, in terms of visual understanding, painting AI cannot create a new world model independently, and needs to refer to the semantic map provided by human painter, such as manuscripts or photographs. Second, in terms of visual expression, painting AI's outputs of Western landscape painting is more complete and better than that of Chinese Shanshui painting. This means that on the one hand, AI has certain visual imitation capabilities; on the other hand, AI does not have the ability of non-realistic representation. Third, as far as visual imagination, the proven AI imagination comes from combining pre-existing images, rather than deep foresight or serendipitous inspiration.

Jing Hao, the father of the majestic Shanshui style, once expressed his painting thoughts in "Bi Fa Ji": Taking the image and then extracting the truth. At present, painting AI can take the image to some extent, but it may not extract the truth. Human painters can create world model freely and express it in either Western or Chinese styles. The ability to transfer from concrete cognition to abstract concept and then to creative practice is the advantage of human painter. Therefore, human-AI joint subject is the more applicable subject for painting AI. It could be embedded in the heart flow of human painter, embodied physically, emotional, and sensitive to cultural background, which allow painting AI to retain its artistic origin and avoid from becoming a simple technical system.

The main research tasks from now to the future are as follows: 1) In terms of cross-cultural computing theory for painting, to find more inclusive representation and computing way for painting; 2) In terms of human-AI collaboration framework, to construct embodied and self-supervised framework centered on the human-AI joint subject. Our goal is to build AI aesthetics which can make aesthetic decisions in a similar taste as human, generate artworks extending creativity of human, and deepen aesthetic experience [7]. The methodology of Human-AI collaboration will help us achieve this object.

Acknowledgement. Funding from the Humanities and Social Sciences Research Foundation of the Ministry of Education (No. 21YJA760005) is gratefully acknowledged.

References

1. Gatys, L.A., Ecker, A.S., Bethge, M.: Image style transfer using convolutional neural networks. In: 2016 IEEE Conference on Computer Vision and Pattern Recognition (CVPR), pp. 2414–2423. IEEE, Piscataway (2016)
2. Tong, Y.: Research on the style transfer model of Chinese paintings based on deep network. Chinese Museum **142**(3), 139–145 (2020)
3. Alice, X.: End-to-End Chinese Landscape Painting Creation Using Generative Adversarial Networks. arXiv preprint arXiv:2011.05552 (2020)
4. Simonyan, K., Zisserman, A.: Very Deep Convolutional Networks for Large-Scale Image Recognition. arXiv:1409.1556 (2014)
5. Odena, A., Christopher, O., Shlens, J.: Conditional Image Synthesis with Auxiliary Classifier GANs. arXiv:1610.09585 (2016)
6. Isola, P., Zhu, J.Y., Zhou, T., Efros, A.A.: Image-to-Image Translation with Conditional Adversarial Networks. arXiv:1611.07004 (2016)
7. Chang, R., Huang, Y.: Towards AI aesthetics: Human-AI collaboration in creating Chinese landscape painting. In: Rauterberg, M. (ed.) HCII 2021. LNCS, vol. 12794, pp. 213–224. Springer, Cham (2021). https://doi.org/10.1007/978-3-030-77411-0_15

The Interactive Behavior Analysis of Integrated Augmented Reality and Gamification Museum Guide System

Zi-Ru Chen[✉] and Zhi-Yi Chen

Southern Taiwan University of Science and Technology, No. 1, Nan-Tai Street, Yungkang Dist., Tainan City 710, Taiwan, R.O.C.
zrchen@stust.edu.tw

Abstract. There are more and more previous works and mobile applications related to the cases of gamification deign and augmented reality applied to museum guide system. However, most of these studies only explored whether digital guide systems can improve users' learning effectiveness and attitudes, and seldom paid attention to the interactive design aspects of guide systems in museum spaces. Therefore, the objective of this study used a practical case of system prototyping, invited 12 users to use this guide system integrating gamification and augmented reality. After a set of behaviour coding analyses, this paper proposed and discussed the interactive behaviour modes of this system, which can be used as references for the development of museum guide systems.

Keywords: Mobile guide · Gamification · Augmented reality · Coding schema · Qualitative analysis

1 Introduction

The development and maturity of digital technology and mobile devices have an obvious influence on the way of museum guided tours. Technological tools can mediate visitors' experience with objects. Technology when used well they should disappear, letting the narrative come forward or object speak for itself (Thomas et al. 1998). Handheld museum guide tours dictate particular ways of navigating and experiencing a museum, to the exclusion of other ways (Thom-Santelli et al. 2005). The mobile guide system is mainly loaded on mobile devices which combine high portability with powerful computer functions and allow visitors to choose their favourite exhibits at any time and any place, so as to meet the needs of different visitors when selecting workshops. In addition, in recent years, augmented reality (AR) technology has matured and started to be applied in many different fields. There are more and more cases of introducing AR application into museum guide experience. This kind of immersive visiting experience is different from the traditional display mode, bringing novelty and participation to visitors, and often becomes the highlight in the exhibition hall. AR has the advantage of combining the virtual and real world. It can bring visitors in a three-dimensional environment to

© The Author(s), under exclusive license to Springer Nature Switzerland AG 2022
C. Stephanidis et al. (Eds.): HCII 2022, CCIS 1582, pp. 186–195, 2022.
https://doi.org/10.1007/978-3-031-06391-6_25

interact with objects that cannot actually be brought to the exhibition hall, cannot be touched or need to be enlarged in real-time, prolong the stay time of visitors in front of exhibits, and connect the knowledge that the museum wants to convey with the experience of visitors. It serves as a communication medium between the museum and visitors (Ma et al. 2017).

The application of gamification mechanism in learning situations are also important research topics. Sharma (2014) suggested that motivation and engagement are important factors driving learning through the application of gamification concepts. Quinn (2000) defined games as intrinsic motivation and interesting, which makes the potential cognitive process easier to understand and think about. In the game-oriented teaching method, computer games can arouse students' learning motivation because of their characteristics of challenge, curiosity, and fantasy (Malone 1980). Most studies held that gamification has a positive impact on learning (Lee and Hammer 2011; Simoes et al. 2013). In 2015, the New Media Consortium (NMC) put forward some examples of gamification applied to museums, and thought that this trend could enhance the audience's exhibition experience, and also pointed out that how to enhance the creative experience process is a great challenge for such tour design in the future (Johnson et al. 2015). The game system can stimulate learners' emotions and promote a better feeling and connection between people and technology interfaces (Roy et al. 2009). Besides, the integrated use of interactive technology and interactive design also involves the management of aesthetic experience (Locher et al. 2010). To some extent, the viewpoint of interactive aesthetic management can also provide considerable inspiration for how digital tools can be integrated and applied to gamification activities.

2 Problem and Objective

As there are more and more literature and preliminary applications on the research and case studies of the gamification concept and the application of AR techniques to museum guides, the diversity and importance of this research topic are observed. The vigorous development of museum education research in recent years, coupled with the impact of new technologies and concepts of AR and gamification on the experience of mobile guide service, museums, which play a vital role in social education, also try to find a new social orientation in this new era and seek to make the influence of museums penetrate the lives of the public. In addition, museum librarians or researchers also found that the application of digital technology can attract the attention of visitors, increase the diversity and interactivity of exhibitions, and improve exhibition satisfaction. In terms of museum education and learning functions, museums have a more attractive effect than static billboards and dynamic TV screen images. Through the display technology of interactive digital technology, museums can provide more vivid and interesting learning methods and entertainment effects, and digital technology has substantial effects on enriching visitors' experience in visiting museums.

At present, as there are more and more cases of the interactive mobile guide application in museums, the application of designing the gamification concept in museum education is also gaining popularity. However, most of these studies only discussed whether digital guide systems can improve users' learning effectiveness and attitude while paying little attention to the interactive design of guide systems. Therefore, this study used a practical case of system prototyping, invited 12 subjects to use this guide system integrating gamification and AR. After a set of behaviour coding analyses, this paper discussed the interactive behaviour mode of this system, which can be used as a design reference for the future development of museum guide systems. This system combines the concept of gamification, designs the museum guide service with the design of gamification mechanism and the adoption of game elements, and uses the new interactive technology of AR to enrich the experience situation of museum guides.

3 Methodology and Steps

3.1 The Selection of Guide Contents

In the museum selection of experimental field, the Chinese Wooden Architecture Exhibition Hall of the Ancient Mechanical Science and Technology Museum established by Southern Taiwan University of Science and Technology in 2016 was adopted as the main research field. The exhibits in the exhibition hall include the Dougong structure research and physical component design, the restoration of five-story wooden pavilions and day and night wheels, and the research and guide design of Song-style costumes. Two series of exhibits, namely exhibition walls and physical objects, were selected as the direction, which is the form of exhibits displayed in most museums. The contents of the exhibition wall include "Timeline Wall", which describes the life introduction of Sicheng Liang, a puzzle solver of Chinese wooden architecture, as well as "Song Dynasty Costume" with rich historical knowledge. The physical models include a 1: 3 Dougong model describing the ten styles of Dougong in Yingzao Fashi (rules of architecture), and an assembly experience model with high interaction of exhibits, "Dougong Instruction".

Table 1. Museum guide exhibits list and introduction.

No	Display form	Exhibition theme	Exhibition introduction	Exhibition contents
1	Display planes	Timeline Wall	Introduction to the life of Chinese wooden architecture puzzle solver Sicheng Liang	Sicheng Liang began to study Yingzao Fashi in 1930 and completed the first draft of Yingzao Fashi Notes in 1963, which made great contributions to the research and protection of Chinese traditional architecture. See Fig. 1a

(*continued*)

Table 1. (*continued*)

No	Display form	Exhibition theme	Exhibition introduction	Exhibition contents
2	1:3 physical models	Dougong Group	1:3 Dougong model-Yingzao Fashi ten Dougong styles	Dougong is a symbol of ancient Chinese traditional architecture and an important element in oriental architectural structure. See Fig. 1b
3	Display planes	Song Dynasty Costume	Song dynasty costume analysis	The clothing characteristics of officials in the Song Dynasty are divided into several main parts: scarves, official clothes, leather belts, fish symbol, and official shoes. See Fig. 1c
4	1:6 DIY models	Dougong Instruction	Dougong mouth assembly model	The Dougong mouth continues the rule of single Dougong, which is a horizontal one-way component. If it needs to be combined with longitudinal components, it needs to add Huagong in the longitudinal direction to become a cross, see Fig. 1d

The information and introduction of these four exhibits are sorted out in Table 1, and the situation presented by the exhibits is shown in Fig. 1.

3.2 The System Mode of Augmented Reality and Gamification System Design

Mobile guides are an experience situation formed by the real environment and virtual information. It can make visitors easily get exhibition-related information, search for information and conform to visitors' experience. In this study, the AR technology was presented to cooperate with the guide system. Visitors use smartphones to scan physical exhibits through the lens. When the system detects the corresponding pictures, digital icons will be augmented on the screen of smartphones to remind users to click on the icons

Fig. 1. Guide content exhibit. a. Timeline Wall; b. Dougong Settlement; c. Song Dynasty Costumes; d. Dougong Instruction.

and watch the guide information. The guide system designed in this study is divided into two modes. One is the guide mode. Users scan target exhibits through AR technology to obtain relevant exhibit introduction information. The other is a gamification mode. Users can understand the interactive mode of each game level through task prompts. When the corresponding exhibit is detected by a smartphone lens, the smartphone screen will display the game button. By click the game button, users can play the game and complete tasks.

Guide Mode. The guide mode of this system contains the initial screen at the beginning of the application, previous story plot, related guide function keys, and augmented reality guide content. The guide function icons include "task list" and "puzzle-solving illustration". The guide content can use augmented reality technology. When exhibits are detected, the symbol "⊕" will appear. After clicking, the interface will display more exhibit information. See Fig. 2.

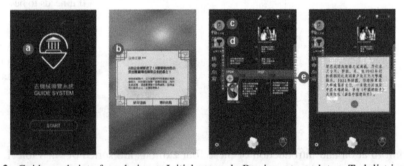

Fig. 2. Guide mode interface design a. Initial screen b. Previous story plot; c. Task list icon; d. Solving puzzles icon; e. Guide content icon detection and display.

Gamification Mode. In the gamification mode, when scanning exhibits with smartphone lenses through AR technology, a symbol of game button will appear. After clicking the symbol, users will enter the game task, which includes game task plot description, game task description, and game result reply. Figure 3 takes "Timeline Wall" as an example. When the user enters the game mode, a game task plot description will appear to guide the user into the game situation and explain the game progress mode according to the game task. Finally, the system judges whether the game passes or not, and gives a reply. If the task is successfully completed, it will be rewarded and the game will be ended. If the answer is wrong, you can choose to return to the game task page to continue challenging or end the game.

Fig. 3. Game interface of timeline wall

3.3 Coding System of Using Behavior

This study used AR technology and gamification concept to complete a prototype of an interactive mobile guide system. The purpose of this study was to understand how users use this guide system, and to observe and examine whether this system is usable through user behavior analysis, and to apply it to museum guides. Therefore, this step proposed a guide system behavior coding schema as the basis for analysis. This coding schema is referred to the coding system proposed by Chang et al. (2014) for the mobile guide system for art museum painting appreciation combined with AR. The topic of this study was the design purpose of a guide system applying AR and gamification. Therefore, see Table 2 for the codes of extended guide and gamification mode function operation.

Table 2. The code schema of augmented reality and gamification guide system behavior.

Code		Behavior of subjects	Behavior classification
A1		Look, observe, and focus on an exhibit (more than 5 s)	Human-situation (exhibits) interaction
A2		Browse an exhibit roughly (less than 5 s)	
A3		Touch and interact with the physical exhibits (assemble the bucket arch)	
B1		Operating mobile device	Human-computer (device) interaction

(continued)

Table 2. (*continued*)

Code			Behavior of subjects	Behavior classification
	B1-navi-1		Use the guide function keys (open the task list, open the puzzle guide)	
	B1-navi-2		Use guide content (click/close AR guide content)	
	B1-game-1		Use the game function keys (turn on the game button and turn off the game mode)	
	B1-game-2		Use the game task keys (perform game tasks, select/drag/pair objects)	
	B1-game-3		Use the game completion key (confirm the completion of the game task and judge whether it passes or not)	
B2	B2-game		Read and listen to the guide content (exhibit information)	
	B2-game		Read and listen to the game content (level task plot, level description)	
B3			Operate the image recognition function of the mobile device camera (AR detection and recognition)	
C1			Seek help from the exhibition servicer	Human-human interaction
D1			Walk/Move	
D2	D2-1		Other acts View other exhibits (view non-target exhibits)	
	D2–2		Watch the introduction of the main venue in the exhibition hall (instead of the introduction of a certain exhibit)	

4   The Results of Behaviour Analysis

This system was designed to guide users to visit museums, first observe and focus on the exhibits in the museum in the actual environment, then know the contents of the exhibits through the task list and puzzle-solving illustrations, and turn on AR to detect and identify exhibits. Then, guide content was used to read and listen to the guide information of relevant exhibits. After completing the guide mode stage, users may go back to AR to detect the situation, open the game function key to enter the game mode, start the game task level, read and listen to the game content, use the game button to select objects, drag objects or assemble teaching aids according to the game task content, and finally press the game completion button to judge whether they pass the game or not. fter analyzing these four exhibits through the behavior code schema, two user behavior patterns were obtained. One is for users in the process of game mode. There is the behavior pattern which did not touch the exhibits. The exhibits of Timeline Wall, Dougong Group, Song Dynasty Costume are all of this category. The other behavior mode that user touched the exhibits. The exhibits of Dougong Instruction is this category. Because in the game process, the physical model needs to be assembled before it would be detected and identified by the mobile device, and the game task would be passed after it was confirmed to be correct, so the game behavior will increase the behavior mode of touching and interacting with the physical exhibits (A3).

5 Conclusion

In this study, the design of the game-based guide system considered the interactive forms of different exhibits. It can be divided into two types of game levels: Human-situation/exhibitions interaction and human-computer/device interaction. Through behavioral coding analysis, the use of device and the use behavior of the game process interacting with exhibits were divided into two behavior patterns, and a preliminary model was put forward for developing a museum mobile guide system of augmented reality and gamification design. The behavior of its framework includes that users will browse the physical exhibits first, use the guide mode of the mobile guide system to watch the guide content of this exhibit, and finally enter the game mode to complete the game task developed for this exhibit. Please refer to Fig. 6 for detailed behavior flow, and this model can be used as a design reference for system developers to design an augmented reality and gamification system of museum guides in the future.

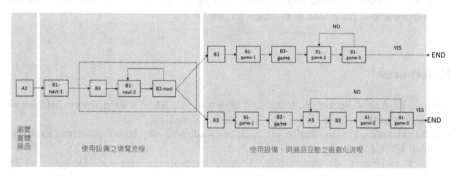

Fig. 6. Preliminary design model of augmented reality and gamification applied to museum mobile guide.

According to the user test, this study collated three aspects for discussion, including the suggestion of applying AR to guide system, the suggestion of applying gamification to the interface of AR guide system, and the suggestion of game content design, which are explained as follows:

- Application of AR to guide system: In the interview part of the subjects, it is difficult for subjects to eliminate the problems encountered during detection, so researchers should help them deal with them. It is suggested that the information of detection points of each exhibit should be displayed on the map of the guide system, or photos or icons of correct detection should be added in the guide system, which can reduce the detection problems encountered by users during the guide.

- Gamification application for the interface of AR guide system: The test results showed that because the subjects need to use smartphones to detect, their concentration will be scattered between the smartphones and exhibits, and the text introduction on the guide system is less thoughtful to read. It is suggested that the text should be presented in the form of voice or animation, which will make it easier for visitors to enter the situation when experiencing the exhibition.
- Game content design: Subjects prefer game content with high feedback, such as the game tasks of "Dougong Textbook" and "Song Dynasty Costume". The interactive mode of hands-on operation and pairing can give the subjects fun in the guide process, but the subjects deemed that the way of asking questions and finding parts is boring. It is suggested that the interactive mode with high feedback and easy understanding should be better when designing games so that visitors can have a good interactive experience when experiencing the exhibition.
- Future studies: In order to know whether the usage mode provided by the design of the game-based guide system in this study can meet the actual use of visitors and whether we can get information from this guide system combining augmented reality and gamification, future research can invite subjects to use this game-based guide system. Pre-test and post-test can be adopted to detect the learning effect of users. Future research can also investigate the usability of users in the operating system to further understand the design model of the guide mobile application developed by gamification thinking and AR proposed in this study, and its suitability for use behavior and applications in museum guides.

References

Johnson, L., Adams Becker, S., Estrada, V., Freeman, A.: NMC horizon report: 2015 higher education edition. Austin, Texas: The New Media Consortium (2015)

Lee, J.J., Hammer, J.: Gamification in education: what, how, why bother. Academic Exchange Quart. **15**(2), 146 (2011)

Locher, P., Overbeeke, K., Wensveen, S.: Aesthetic interaction: a framework. Design issues **26**, 70–79 (2010)

Ma, M., Hammady, R., Temple, M.: Augmented reality and gamification in heritage museums. In: Serious Games: Proceedings of Joint International Conference on Serious Games, Brisbane, Australia, pp. 181–190. Springer, Heidelberg (2017)

Malone, T.W.: What makes things fun to learn? A study of intrinsically motivating computer games. Technical report CIS-7. Palo Alto: Xerox PARC (1980)

Quinn, C.: mLearning: mobile, wireless, in-your-pocket learning. Retrieved December 31, 2018, http://www.linezine.com/2.1/features/cqmmwiyp.htm (2000)

Roy, M., Hemmert, F., Wettach, R.: Living interfaces: the intimate door lock. In: Proceedings of the Third International Conference on Tangible and Embedded Interaction, pp. 45–46. ACM, NY (2009)

Simoes, J., Redondo, R.D., Vilas, A.F.: A social gamification framework for a K-6 learning platform. Comput. Hum. Behav. **29**, 345–353 (2013)

Thomas, S.: In: Thomas, S., Mintz, A. (eds.) Introduction to the virtual and the real: Media in the museum. American Association of Museums (1998)

Thom-Santelli, J., Toma, C., Boehner, K., Gay, G.: eyond just the facts: museum detective guides. In Proceedings of the Int'l workshop re-thinking technology in museums: Towards a new understanding of people's experience in museums, pp. 29–30. IE: Interaction Design Centre, University of Limerick (2005)

Comparative Study on the Growth Power of Cultural and Creative Products in Museums

Wei Ding and Xinyue Yang[✉]

East China University of Science and Technology, No. 130 Meilong Road, Xuhui District, Shanghai, China
1730293864@qq.com

Abstract. By analyzing the development status of cultural and creative products of museums in China, this paper puts forward a set of theoretical framework that accords with national conditions and conforms to the growth power of cultural and creative products of museums. Based on the new growth theory, this paper applies it to the research on the power of cultural and creative products in museums. By comparing two excellent cultural and creative product design cases – the Palace Museum and the British Museum, this paper analyzes the development mode of their existing cultural and creative products in China, and verifies whether the theoretical framework of the hypothesis is practical. This study compares the advantages and disadvantages of the Palace Museum and the British Museum in terms of the growth power of cultural and creative products, and holds that the theoretical framework of the growth power of cultural and creative products of museums has certain feasibility, hoping to bring reference and learning value to museums in other provinces.

Keywords: Cultural and creative product power · Theoretical framework · New growth theory · Comparative study

1 Introduction

For now, the development of the museum itself is limited. The most critical limiting factor is the shortage of funds [1]. Since 2008, museums and memorial halls across the country have been open to the public for free. Now the era of "Internet Plus" has arrived, and 2020 is the first year of the birth of "5G". Cultural and creative products seem to embrace unprecedented new opportunities. The development of cultural and creative products of museums is no longer limited to the sales of physical cultural and creative shops, but begins to cooperate with new media to innovate and cooperate. Online marketing mode has become the main camp of museum development.

2 The Theoretical Framework of the Growth Power of Museum Cultural and Creative Products

2.1 The Basic Meaning of the New Growth Theory

New growth theory is a branch of economics that addresses the root causes of growth. In his book "Design and the Creation of Value", John Heskett has combed through the

© The Author(s), under exclusive license to Springer Nature Switzerland AG 2022
C. Stephanidis et al. (Eds.): HCII 2022, CCIS 1582, pp. 196–203, 2022.
https://doi.org/10.1007/978-3-031-06391-6_26

interpretation and refinement of the concept of the "new growth theory" by economists at various stages. The extended model of the theory produces innovation in three directions based on innovation strategy, namely product innovation, process innovation and transaction innovation. Innovation in these three directions is essential for growth, as is the growth power of cultural and creative products. Especially at present, cultural and creative products of museums are on the rise. It is of certain reference value to put forward a set of theoretical framework suitable for the growth of cultural and creative products of museums.

2.2 The Basic Meaning of the New Growth Theory

As shown in Figs. 1 and 2, on the basis of the new growth theory, we are going to product innovation, process innovation, transaction innovation is applied to the museum on the research of product creation, the "product innovation" corresponding "cultural and creative product innovation", "technological innovation" corresponding to the "technological innovation" and "Marketing model innovation" corresponding "marketing model innovation", The three innovations constitute the basic theoretical framework of the growth power of museum cultural and creative products.

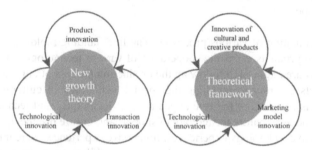

Fig. 1. The evolution of the corresponding relationship among the three innovations of the new growth theory

1. First of all, the most important thing in museum cultural and creative product design is the innovation of the concept of cultural and creative product itself, and excellent cultural and creative product innovation should conform to the following points:

    - Make full use of the museum's historical and cultural resources. Museums are not short of rich historical and cultural resources, and each museum has its own regional cultural characteristics. Therefore, every object displayed in the museum may become a source of inspiration for designers, but the design team should step by step when extracting creative elements. We can start from the "treasure of the museum" that consumers are familiar with, and analyze its shape, pattern, function and other multidimensional exploration.
    - Dig deep into the history behind the museum. Visitors to museums follow the guides to discover the stories behind their artifacts, not just skim them. In contrast,

as a design team, it should be more like this, simply copying the patterns of cultural relics is only superficial. In-depth excavation of cultural relics, more than curators and other senior people to exchange and understand the historical figures, customs and habits or anecdotes of that period, these will become exclusive creative resources in the hands of the design team [2].

– Design practical products in line with modern aesthetics. Cultural and creative products are always for the use of consumers and need to meet their aesthetic standards. This is illustrated by the revival of Chinese fad, which applies local Chinese culture to trendy brands and cutting-edge technology to achieve cross-border collaboration. Shan Jixiang, director of the Palace Museum, has stressed more than once that "cultural creation of the Palace Museum should be combined with the needs of the people" and "cultural creation should care about society and the people". No matter how precious cultural relics are, they are also preserved for people. No matter how gorgeous the culture is, it is also created for people. Therefore, the Palace Museum launched cultural and creative products, requiring a combination of functionality, practicality and culture.

2. Secondly, a good design scheme of cultural and creative products needs appropriate technology to present, so excellent technological innovation should conform to the following points:

– A combination of various processes. The final landing molding of cultural and creative products needs the cooperation of various technologies. In many cases, artisans are required to follow up the production process of cultural and creative products in order to highlight the special technology of cultural and creative products and restore the true appearance of techniques and techniques. It also needs modern mature technology to support and ensure product quality.

– Immersive technology experiences. Immersive experiences were initially used in 3D films, but have since expanded to games, exhibitions, restaurants and hotels. According to the 2020 White Paper on the Development of China's immersion Industry, the total output value of China's immersion industry reached 4.82 billion yuan in 2019. In recent years, the cultural industry has also embraced immersive experiences. On December 29, 2019, The Confucius Temple Scenic Area, in collaboration with Tencent, launched an immersive experience of traditional culture, attracting many visitors with its unique pavilion design. Then the collision between museum cultural and creative industry and immersive experience will be wonderful.

3. Finally, excellent cultural and creative products need the cooperation of multiple marketing modes. New media in the era of "Internet plus" provides strong background support for cultural and creative industries, and excellent marketing mode innovation should conform to the following points:

– Propaganda and education platform. If any product wants to sell well, the direct listing will certainly fail to achieve the expected effect, and the same is true for cultural and creative products. In the early stage of the official launch, cultural and creative products need large-scale platform publicity, such as online Wechat public account push, offline shopping malls and subway advertising space, etc. It is worth mentioning that, different from the cold marketing methods of other commercial products, the publicity of cultural and creative products can be combined with the regional cultural background to achieve the publicity effect of cultural and creative products while spreading history and culture [3].

- Preheat the platform before sales. When the publicity effect of cultural and creative products reaches the expected, it will be immediately upgraded to the product warm-up stage. Here have to mention Taobao double eleven preheating, one month in advance of the preheating period can be seen everywhere. The preheating of cultural and creative products can learn from Taobao and other platforms, but can not be scripted. The preheating of cultural and creative products only needs to be targeted at the youth groups mentioned above, and can be preheated through their frequently used apps, such as Taobao home page, Wechat video number, Tik Tok, Kwai, RED and other popular apps.
- Product sales platform. After two stages of publicity and education and presale warm-up, we are fully prepared for the preliminary work of improving the strength of cultural and creative products power. In the initial stage, cultural and creative products of the museum can be sold on designated authorized platforms or transferred to designated platforms through links from other platforms. On the one hand, large e-commerce platforms have wide traffic and high consumer recognition; On the other hand, the museum can save the investment cost, so that the investment capital can be quickly recovered. In the mature stage, when the museum has sufficient liquidity, the museum can consider establishing its own official e-commerce platform to create a big-name IP culture.
- Interactive feedback platform. In the era of "Internet plus", the museum establishes an interactive feedback platform to interact with users in a timely manner and select high-quality user feedback [4]. Consumers' feedback on the use of

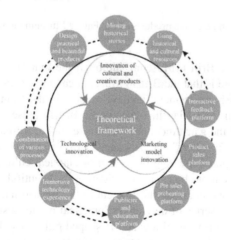

Fig. 2. The theoretical framework of the growth power of museum cultural and creative products

products can be said to be an important factor in the success or failure of products. Good feedback is the affirmation of cultural creation and design. Of course, there is no need to be discouraged by bad feedback.

3   Demonstration and Analysis of Excellent Museum Cultural and Creative Products Power

3.1   Cultural and Creative Product Innovation

China's youth group is a large and main consumer group, and the Palace Museum is the main consumer object. The Palace Museum is China's largest museum of ancient culture and art, mainly collecting cultural relics and treasures from the Ming and Qing dynasties. The unique advantages make it no problem for the Palace Museum to innovate cultural and creative products. Take the Palace Museum's Taobao as an example. Its Tmall flagship store mainly sells cultural and creative products of the Palace Museum. As shown in Fig. 3, the serious and dignified historical figures in the Ming and Qing Dynasties of the Forbidden City are "made cute". The royal cat and dog in the palace are "anthropomorphized", with an official hat on top of her head and a neon dress on her body, which poked at the adorable point of consumers [5]. The Palace Museum is rich in historical and cultural resources, which can be described as a source of inspiration for cultural and creative design. It is necessary to make full use of the precious cultural heritage resources to enhance the power of cultural and creative products.

Fig. 3. Cultural and creative products of the Palace Museum taobao flagship store

Compared with the British Museum, although the main reason for its entry into the Tmall flagship store is that the British Museum cannot sustain itself with the funds allocated by the British government, its development in the Chinese cultural and creative market is unequivocal. Flagship store in the British museum as an example, the store mainly selected the gaia Anderson cat bronze statue, Rosetta stone, Louis chess series, "fu yue thirty-six views" surf in kanagawa hokusai woodcut printmaking etc. Characteristics of coloured drawing or pattern of classical cultural relics as the main text and the development of object, and considering the beautiful sex and practicability of the product. As shown in Fig. 4, the element of the Bronze statue of Gaia Anderson cat is "adorable" into a series of derivatives: practical products such as mobile phone stand, shawl blanket, arm-warm pillow and U-shaped pillow, etc. Fun products such as weather bottles, stickers, key chains and trinkets are designed to match the shape of gaia Anderson.

China's youth group is a large and main consumer group, and the Palace Museum is the main consumer object. The Palace Museum is China's largest museum of ancient culture and art, mainly collecting cultural relics and treasures from the Ming and Qing dynasties. The unique advantages make it no problem for the Palace Museum to innovate cultural and creative products. Take the Palace Museum's Taobao as an example. Its Tmall flagship store mainly sells cultural and creative products of the Palace Museum. As shown in Fig. 4, the serious and dignified historical figures in the Ming and Qing Dynasties of the Forbidden City are "made cute". The royal cat and dog in the palace are "anthropomorphized", with an official hat on top of her head and a neon dress on her body, which poked at the adorable point of consumers. The Palace Museum is rich in historical and cultural resources, which can be described as a source of inspiration for cultural and creative design. It is necessary to make full use of the precious cultural heritage resources to enhance the power of cultural and creative products.

Fig. 4. Cultural and creative products featuring Gaia Anderson cat (photo from Tmall flagship store)

3.2 Technological Innovation

A product from the creative to the final landing, the quality of the process is a key factor in the presentation of high-quality cultural and creative products. Taking the embroidery calendar of the Palace Museum's flagship Store on Taobao as an example, the designer carefully selected more than 300 woven and embroidered cultural relics from the Palace Museum according to the seasons for the creative design of the calendar. As shown in Fig. 5, the embroidery calendar covers the combination of handicrafts and a variety of modern handicrafts, and is interpreted from the perspectives of patterns, colors and materials, fully demonstrating the beauty of the embroidery relics in the Palace Museum.

The British Museum has also launched an element calendar for 2021. As shown in Fig. 6, the Shell of the Rosetta Stone contains twelve themes, each of which represents a theme. Compared with the Palace Museum's taobao embroidered calendar, the British Museum's calendar is a little less creative, but its high-quality texture can be seen in the printing process.

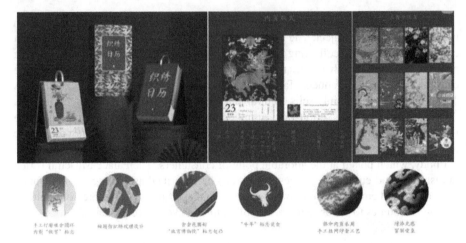

Fig. 5. Embroidery calendar (photo from Tmall flagship store)

Fig. 6. 2021 collection elements annual calendar (photo from Tmall flagship store)

3.3 Marketing Model Innovation

In domestic drama "the new, the Forbidden City," as an example, the national Palace Museum in addition to the joint Beijing television, also combined the headlines today launched the vote of innovative products, as long as a majority reach a certain audience can immediately on a new, so on the one hand, enhance the participation of the audience, on the other hand, ensures that the purchasing power of the new arrival. However, considering that the British Museum is a foreign culture, it is not easy to enter the Chinese market. It is one of the strategies to seek strategic partners to authorize its IP in the Chinese market, and high-quality joint cooperation can enable the British Museum to quickly obtain economic benefits. "Egyptian Culture" makeup series is the first collaboration between the British Museum and Chinese beauty makeup. The packaging design of one powder cake even won the German Red Dot Design Award. Its brand effect, star endorsement, design award and traffic platform publicity are all factors contributing to the success of this product, and it also achieves good sales volume every month.

4 Conclusion

The development of cultural and creative products of museums in China is still in its infancy, so many researchers or practitioners are constantly trying to promote the development of cultural and creative industry of museums in a faster and better way. Based on the three aspects of cultural and creative product innovation, technological innovation and marketing model innovation, this paper deeply analyzes the cultural and creative product strength of the Palace Museum and the British Museum, and explores whether their advantages conform to the theoretical framework set, and whether their disadvantages do not follow the theoretical framework set. Finally, it is concluded that the development of museum cultural and creative products needs to combine new ideas, new technology and new marketing mode to create a competitive model that can adapt to the development of The Times and improve the power of museum cultural and creative products. This paper hopes to bring some reference and inspiration to the development of cultural and creative products in museums around China through research and demonstration of the theoretical framework.

References

1. Jiang, N.W.: Exploration of marketing innovation strategy of museum cultural and creative products based on "Internet+." Collectors **04**, 74–76 (2019)
2. Zhou, M.Y., Sun, X.: Research on cultural and creative product design of museum. Packaging Eng. **41**(20),1–7 (2020)
3. Liu, X.: A brief analysis of the current situation of the development of cultural and creative products in museums. Public Relations World (24),60–61 (2019)
4. Wang, J., Zhang, R.L.: Research on museum cultural and creative products under the background of "Internet+". Packaging Eng. **41**(12), 132–138 (2020)
5. Cao, Y.Z.: New media marketing and promotion of cultural and creative products in museums – a case study of the Palace Museum Taobao. New Media Res. **4**(09), 54–55 (2018)

An HCI Experiment to Explore Interactive Artificial Life Art

Glare Dumo[1,2(✉)], Pedro G. Lind[1,2,3], and Stefano Nichele[1,2,3,4,5]

[1] Department of Computer Science, OsloMet – Oslo Metropolitan University,
P.O. Box 4 St. Olavs plass, 0130 Oslo, Norway
glare_dumo@yahoo.com
[2] AI Lab – OsloMet Artificial Intelligence Lab, Pilestredet 52, 0166 Oslo, Norway
[3] NordSTAR – Nordic Center for Sustainable and Trustworthy AI Research,
Pilestredet 52, 0166 Oslo, Norway
[4] Department of Holistic Systems, Simula Metropolitan Center for Digital
Engineering, Pilestredet 52, 0166 Oslo, Norway
[5] Department of Computer Science and Communication, Østfold University College,
B R A Veien 4, 1757 Halden, Norway

Abstract. We present an interface for creating art using tools from artificial intelligence and artificial life. The interface is tested and validated, through an online experiment with the aim of investigating how AI algorithms can be used for enabling humans - able or disabled - to express their artistic creativity. The interface uses evolutionary algorithms to generate images and videos of life-like patterns of pixels, based on rules describing local updates for cellular automata. Participants were asked to select a sequence of rules, either randomly generated (control group) or assisted by an interactive evolutionary algorithm which takes into account the participant's previous choices (test group). Our results show a significantly higher satisfaction of the test group with a significance level of 95% and a power of 82%. Finally, we also discuss the usefulness of such an interface for people with disabilities and limitations.

Keywords: Human-computer interface · Artificial life art · Cellular automata · Interactive evolution · Creative universal design

1 Introduction

Scientists and artists share one common ideal trait, being creative. As both must be able to come up with their own original concepts, they should have the ability to push boundaries to pursue greater knowledge and creativity. But what could possibly happen when science meets arts?

Some authors already talked about artificial life in art in the late 90s (Ascott 1993; Rinaldo 1998). Mitchell Whitelaw has provided an elaborated inspection of the emergence of artificial life art by undertaking an extensive study through a book called Metacreation: Art and Artificial Life (Whitelaw 2004), which was released in 2004. According to Whitelaw, "Artificial life (or ALife) is a young, interdisciplinary scientific field concerned with the creation and study of artificial systems that mimic or manifest the properties of living systems". Artificial life, over the years has been found quite engaging and people were fascinated especially with the none-player game called Game of Life (Berlekamp et al. 2004) created by the British mathematician John H. Conway. Since then, ALife inspired other studies focusing on a deeper perspective of what life is, how it functions and how it could be created in artificial systems. However, Whitelaw in his book was able to show how ALife could as well be stretched out to other fields, such as in the arts. Hence, artists could create some artworks where interaction between technology and the study of life is achievable.

Originally, the term artificial life was introduced by Christopher Langton, an American computer scientist considered one of the founder of the said field in the late 80s. According to Langton, artificial life is "the study of natural life, where nature is understood to include rather than to exclude, human beings and their artifacts" (Langton 1986). It is said to be a multidisciplinary field of research including computer scientists, philosophers, biologists, engineers, mathematicians, and artists among the many others. This paper aims to investigate a simulated artificial life environment where interactive evolution can be used as a tool for supporting the universal design for art creation. Through our online platform inspired by *MergeLife*[1], we aim at providing a possibility for art creation and understanding the process of human creativity, regardless of humans' disabilities and limitations, following equitable use principle from universal design.

In Sect. 2 we present the methodology and describe the experiment as well as how the interface is implemented (front end and back end). Section 3 includes the main results, and their statistical analysis and Sect. 4 concludes this article.

2 Methodology and Experimental Design

2.1 Evolutionary Algorithms for Artificial Life

One of the most significant models for investigating Artificial Life are cellular automata (CA) (Dorin 2014). A CA consists of a grid of cells with their internal states, which are updated based on their current state and that of the closest neighbors. In our experiment the cells are the pixels of an image and the CA rule governs how the color of each pixel evolves in time. Modern extensions to the simple elementary CA are so-called neural CA (Mordvintsev et al. 2020; Nichele et al. 2017; Variengien et al. 2021), where CA rules are replaced by a neural network, and Lenia (Chan 2020), a continuous CA capable of producing self-organizing life-like designs.

In this paper, we use a framework inspired by *MergeLife* (Heaton 2019), which allows to produce full color dynamic animations based on the aesthetic specifications by the users through an evolutionary algorithm, a bio-inspired algorithm that mimics the process of evolution by natural selection (Darwin 1859).

---

[1] https://github.com/jeffheaton/mergelife.

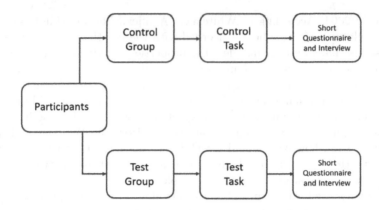

Fig. 1. Sketch of the experimental design for testing the HCI for artificial life art.

In particular, *MergeLife* CA are encoded as simple 16-byte update rules that are graphically rendered and selected through a fitness function which incorporates aesthetic guidelines from a user.

2.2   Experimental Setup

Each participant is exposed to a sequence of selections which may - or may not - appear aesthetically pleasing to the users. The sequence of selections is prepared in two different ways depending if the participant belongs to the control or to the test group. In the control group, the users will be provided with a sequence of randomly generated *MergeLife* rules producing life-like CA art where their choice will not influence the random generation. In the test group, participant's choices will be used through an interactive evolutionary algorithm to recombine the life-like CA rules and produce similar "offspring" in the next iteration. An overview of the experimental design is given in Fig. 1.

We have recruited a total of 28 participants, each one performing the experiment for both the control and the test group. The participants were in the age range 25–45 years old, mainly from an academic institution (Oslo Metropolitan University). All ethical requirements were approved by the Norwegian center of data protection *Norsk Senter for Forskningsdata* (NSD) under the application with reference number 885778. Prospective participants are directed to a consent form through where additional information such as the purpose of this experiment is introduced. Their names and email addresses have been asked for contacting purposes, only, and deleted after the data collection period. Figure 1 shows the experimental design used in this study.

The two experiments consist of the control and test group which are illustrated in Figs. 2a and 2b respectively.

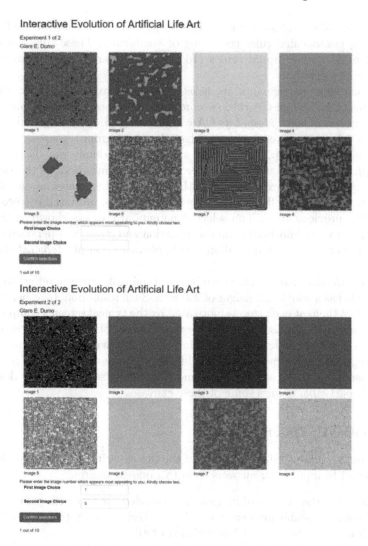

Fig. 2. Initial set of images, from which participants select two out of eight to evolve into a new set of images (see text). (Top) First part of the online experiment in the online interface (control group). (Bottom) Second part of the experiment (test group).

2.3   Implementation of the Experimental Interface

The interface is accessed online by the participants using their preferred browser. A short instruction will be shown, explaining how the experiment will be conducted. The 15 participants out of the total 28 started with the control group followed by the test group experiment. While the rest of the 13 participants started with the test group being followed by the control group experiment.

In the initial step of our online platform, the update rules are set randomly by generating hexadecimal rules consisting of 8 sub-rules. These rules correspond to random *MergeLife* update rules (16-byte digits derived directly from their hexadecimal strings).

At each step, participants are asked to select two, out of eight, real-time executions of *MergeLife* CA rules, according to their aesthetical evaluation. Ten subsequent sets of eight *MergeLife* CA will be provided, either randomly (control group) or following the evolutionary algorithm (test group).

For the control group, the CA rules are applied randomly. For the test group, *MergeLife* update rules will combine crossovers and mutations of the two rules generating the selected executions. In other words, one generates new executions, which are somewhat "offsprings" of the previous ones, produced by recombination of the previous rules. The selected parents are always shown in the next iteration. For more information on the mutation and crossover operations, please refer to the original work describing the implementation of *MergeLife* (Heaton 2019).

The canvas size that refers to each box containing its corresponding *MergeLife* update rule has a width and height of 250 cells. Such resolution, together with the usage of 8 of them at each step is motivated by the typical screen's compatibility. We want all the 8 canvases to be visible right away without using the scroll bars for the ease of the participants, requiring them only with less physical effort in using the mouse or the mousepad. In addition, we want all the *MergeLife* update rules' executions to be seen at the same time, while scrolling up or down will make the participants miss some of these canvases.

2.4 Follow-Up Questionnaire

A short online survey follows each one of the two experiments where participants are required to input their answers from this questionnaire:

Q1 Concerning the last set of images, how satisfied are you with your artwork's final result? Possible answers: (++) Very satisfied; (+) Satisfied; (0) Neutral; (−) Not so satisfied; (−−) Not satisfied at all.

Q2 How much do you feel that your selections influenced the process of selecting the sequence of images? Possible answers: (++) Strong positive influence; (+) Weak positive influence; (0) No influence; (−) Weak negative influence; (−−) Strong negative influence.

Q3 Concerning the last set of images, please select from the following characteristics THE ONE that best describes your artwork's final result. Possible answers: (i) Still images; (ii) Geometric images; (iii) Random images; (iv) Periodic or repeating patterns; (v) Lifelike patterns or shapes.

Questions Q1 and Q2 are quantitatively mapped into a score scale from 1 (lowest class) to 5 (highest class) to carry out power analysis and hypothesis testing.

3   Results and Discussion

Our test hypothesis is that the average score μ_t of the test group for questions Q1 and Q2 together is significantly higher than the average score μ_c for the control group. The null hypothesis is $\mu_t = \mu_c$. To better quantify these claims we carry out a power analysis (Schellenberg et al. 2021) of our results. The overall results are given in Table 1 and Fig. 3.

From the values of the means and standard deviations for both groups in Table 1, we can estimate the effect size D as

$$D = \frac{|\mu_c - \mu_t|}{\tilde{\sigma}}, \tag{1}$$

where $\tilde{\sigma}$ is the pooled standard deviation, $\tilde{\sigma} = \sqrt{(\sigma_c^2 + \sigma_t^2)/2}$. From power analysis standards, the value $D = 0.62$ of the obtained effect size points towards rejection of the null hypothesis. Indeed, assuming Z-scores with a significance level of $1 - \alpha = 0.95$ and a power of $1 - \beta = 0.8$, a minimum sample size in each group should be

$$N \sim \frac{(Z_\alpha + Z_{1-\beta})^2}{D^2} \lesssim 17. \tag{2}$$

Moreover, introducing in Eq. (2) $N = 28$ and fixing a significance level of 95%, yields a power Z-score of $Z_{1-\beta}$, i.e. a power of $1 - \beta = 0.82$.

Figure 3 shows the comparison of the control and test group's short survey scores from the 28 participants being presented in the two box plots where the first one on the left shows the average scores of the control and test group's question 1 and 2 while on the right shows the separate scores for each question 1 and 2 for the control and test group.

For question 3 comparison, the control group which has been provided with random images or random *MergeLife* update rules, a total of 3 out of the 28 participants chose the one that best describes their artwork's final result is with "Random images" and the majority answered that it's like "Lifelike patterns or shapes" with a total number of 9 participants. Since the *MergeLife* update rules are like animated images which start with a different color, pattern, shape, size and then evolve after a few seconds, thus, most participants might have

Table 1. Results of the online experiment (questions Q1 and Q2) for 28 participants.

	Control group	Test group
Mean	$\mu_c = 6.11$	$\mu_t = 8$
Stand. dev.	$\sigma_c = 3.47$	$\sigma_t = 2.67$
Pooled stand. dev. $\tilde{\sigma}$	3.07	
Effect size D [Eq. (1)]	0.62	
Sample size for $\alpha = 0.05$, $1 - \beta = 0.8$ [Eq. (2)]	17	
Power for $\alpha = 0.05$ **and** $N = 28$ participants	0.82	

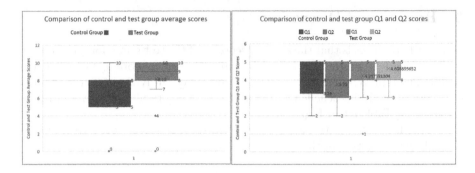

Fig. 3. Short survey of questions Q1 and Q2, comparing control and test groups. (Left) The sum of the scores of both questions. (Right) The score of each question separately.

interpreted these images as lifelike patterns or shapes. In the test group, the total number of participants who chose the characteristic "Lifelike patterns or shapes" is higher compare with the control group, with a total number of 10. There is also a total of 10 participants under the test group that perceived that their final artwork's result is with "Periodic or repeating patterns" simply because under this group, crossovers and mutations of their selected images would be provided, thus, the similarities of these said images are present.

4   Conclusions

We presented the results of an online experiment to test how evolutionary algorithms can help to assist humans in artistic expressions through combinations of images according to their preferences. From a total of 28 participants, the results reject our null hypothesis up to a confidence level of 95% and a power of 82%, having an effect size of $D = 0.62$.

While showing such promising results, our framework can serve as a benchmark to future developments towards interfaces for artists with special needs.

Acknowledgements. Authors acknowledge all students and employees at Oslo Metropolitan University, who participated in the experiment. GD thanks the Department of Computer Science of OsloMet for financial support. This project was done in collaboration with the project FELT - Futures of Living Technologies (Bergaust and Nichele 2019), funded by the Norwegian Artistic Research Programme, DIKU.

References

Ascott, R.: Telenoia: art in the age of artificial life. Leonardo **26**(3), 176–177 (1993)
Bergaust, K., Nichele, S.: FeLT-The Futures of Living Technologies (2019)
Berlekamp, E.R., Conway, J.H., Guy, R.K.: Winning ways for your mathematical plays, volume 4. AK Peters/CRC Press (2004)

Chan, B.W.-C.: Lenia and expanded universe. arXiv preprint (2020). arXiv:2005.03742

Darwin, C., a.O.: On the origin of species by means of natural selection or the preservation of favoured races in the struggle for life, vol. 2. Books, Incorporated, Pub. (1859)

Dorin, A.: Biological bits. A Brief Guide to the Ideas and Artefacts of Computational Artificial Life. Animaland, Melbourne (2014)

Heaton, J.: Evolving continuous cellular automata for aesthetic objectives. Genet. Program Evolvable Mach. **20**(1), 93–125 (2018). https://doi.org/10.1007/s10710-018-9336-1

Langton, C.G.: Studying artificial life with cellular automata. Physica D **221**–**3**, 120–149 (1986)

Mordvintsev, A., Randazzo, E., Niklasson, E., Levin, M.: Growing neural cellular automata. Distill **5**(2), e23 (2020)

Nichele, S., Ose, M.B., Risi, S., Tufte, G.: Ca-neat: evolved compositional pattern producing networks for cellular automata morphogenesis and replication. IEEE Trans. Cognitive Developmental Syst. **10**(3), 687–700 (2017)

Rinaldo, K.: Artificial life art. Leonardo **31**(5), 370–370 (1998)

Schellenberg, F., Gnad, D.R., Moradi, A., Tahoori, M.B.: An inside job: Remote power analysis attacks on fpgas. IEEE Design & Test (2021)

Variengien, A., Nichele, S., Glover, T., Pontes-Filho, S.: Towards self-organized control: using neural cellular automata to robustly control a cart-pole agent (2021). arXiv preprint arXiv:2106.15240

Whitelaw, M.: Metacreation: art and artificial life. Mit Press (2004)

A Model for Sustainable Design Curatorial Approach in the Post-epidemic Era

Siyang Jing[✉]

Central Academy of Fine Arts, Beijing, Wangjing 100102, People's Republic of China
jingsiyang@cafa.edu.cn

Abstract. In the post pandemic era, both design and design curation pay considerable attention on UN sustainable goals due to the social and environmental crisis. Based on the analyzing on nearly hundred exhibitions before and after the pandemic, this article concluded trends, methodologies and models for curatorial actives responding to emergencies and massive challenges of this era. Firstly, the author proposes the layer-cake model as the foundation of the curation. Secondly, the trends of the exhibition theme were concluded according to the analyze of typical sixty-six design exhibitions. Thirdly, the author innovates seven models of curatorial approaches dealing with uncertainty of the crisis age. The aim of this article is to draw attention of the necessity to bring up innovative and dynamic methods in face of the special era in both design and curatorial dialogue.

Keywords: Post-epidemic era · Design curation · Sustainability · Methodological model

1 Introduction

The 17 Sustainable Development Goals (SDGs) set by the United Nations in 2015 are a milestone of the world's development and environmental issues. Compared to the several rounds of relatively independent elements of goals set by the UN before, the goals of SDGs are interdependent with each other. Especially after the epidemic, a new wave of advancement and implementation of sustainability issues has been launched by all stakeholders in society, no exception with the field of design exhibition curation. The high frequency curatorial terms in the post-epidemic era are "restoration", "ecology", "margin", "community with a shared future of mankind" etc., as with the theme of the 59th Venice Biennale of Art, "The Milk of Dreams". Based on the analysis of nearly 100 design exhibitions, this paper, firstly, proposes the method of building value model of design exhibitions as the preparation of design curation. Secondly, it summarizes the trend of the themes of design exhibitions. Thirdly, it concludes s as well as innovates a new model of design curatorial methods.

2 Layer-Cake Model for Design Exhibition

To begin with, the author proposes the "Layer-cake Design Curatorial Value Model" in response to the complex and non-linear development in the social crisis context after

C. Stephanidis et al. (Eds.): HCII 2022, CCIS 1582, pp. 212–219, 2022.
https://doi.org/10.1007/978-3-031-06391-6_28

the epidemic. This model superimposes diverse layers of aspects to form the necessity and value of design exhibitions. On the one hand, the exhibition is the result of the overlapped layer-cake. On the other hand, the exhibition has reflection and suggestive effect on different layers. This model is based on the "layer-cake method", or "suitability analysis", which was coined by Ian McHarg, the father of ecological design. Originated in the 1960s, it is mainly applied in the field of landscape architecture. The value of this model is that different disciplines are integrated and discussed together to lead to the final design solution for the first time visually and spatially, involving layers such as hydrology, topography, biodiversity, etc.

As the model applies to design curation, different layers in the era interwove the background and foundation of the curation, which could consist of current social issues, economic issues, political environment, climate issues, pioneering technologies, site conditions, etc. Taking the present time as an example, factors listed in the layer-cake could be prominent social issues such as hunger, unstable educational conditions, rising inequality; economic downturn and prevalence of local protectionism; increased efforts to control carbon emissions and encouragement of employing new energy; frequent occurrence of extreme climate. One exhibition may cut one slice of the cake vertically, thick or thin, as the foundation. The layers should not less than five, nor the slice too thick. Otherwise, the effect of the layer-cake will not be achieved to generate a comprehensive enough model as the foundation of the exhibition.

The model could generate the following forms in design curation. First, curators arise from different fields. For instance, the 23rd Milan Triennale in 2022, "Unknown unknowns-an introduction to mysteries", will be curated by astrophysicist Ersilia Vaudo from the European Space Agency. Secondly, the exhibitions echo with important conferences. The World Economic Forum in Davos was held in conjunction with the design triennial "Nature", and exhibition "The Age of Waste" responded COP26. Finally, museums and institutions from various fields collaborates. A case is that the London Design Museum's national net-zero emissions research programme, namely *the Future Observatory*, works with the UK government's department of Business, Energy and Industrial Strategy, department of the Arts and Humanities Research Council, and the department of UK Research and Innovation. The project focuses on moving towards a net-zero emissions future, bringing design research to scenarios as a catalyst, linking it to industry development as well as policy to have a greater impact on the challenges facing the UK.

3 Trends in Curatorial Themes of the Design Exhibitions

In the last decades, design has completely transcended its initial role to become a tactical response to social challenges at different scales [1]. Design as an attitude in response to emergencies has become a consensus. As Alice Rawsthorn, former director of the Design Museum in London, has used design curation to respond to an era of intense economic, political, and ecological instability [2]. Similarly, Gustav Metzger, the former curator of Extinction Marathon of Serpentine Gallery, believed that artists and designers should create works that addresses the urgent dangers the society faced with [3]. Good contemporary design is about connection, empathy, anticipation, and projection of the real world [4], where both the live and the unlive are Hyper-Objects, leveraging in complex networks.

Based on the research and summary of the important design exhibition institutions till 2022, this paper finds shifts and trends in curatorial themes of the design exhibition. The study samples are drawn from 66 exhibitions at seven design museums that have thrived since 2010, including the Design Museum in London, the Cooper Hewitt Design Museum, MOMA, V&A, V&A Dundee, Het Nieuwe Instituut(HNI), and Z33 (see Table 1). Around 2010, there was a proliferation of design museums and exhibitions with disruptive influence, growing as with the establishment or restructure of several design galleries and museums. In 2008, exhibition "Design and Elastic Mind" opened in MOMA, expanded the meaning of design to the resilient, elastic, socially responsible and futuristic one. Around 2010, Z33 gallery began to take technology, fiction, fabrication, nature, and material as important curation aspects. In 2012, the NAi, Premsela and Virtueel design institutions in the Netherlands united as HNI, a comprehensive, interdisciplinary design museum and research institute. In the same year, the London Design Museum moved to new site to meet the growing demand.

First of all, the statistics reflect a clear tendency of the themes of exhibitions. Exhibitions about nature, materials, and resources account for 31% of the exhibitions, with as many as 17% of them in the materials category. For example, HNI curated a series of exhibitions about materials from 2013, including wood, glass, plastic, and lithium. Materials are also discussed in the new exhibition "Design for Our Times-Material innovation for our contemporary age" at the V&A dundee in 2021, and a special exhibition on plastics in 2022. The other major exhibitions are related to technology, machines,

Table 1. The Proportion of theme types of design exhibition. The data are collected from Design museum, HNI, Z33, Cooper Hewitt museum, MOMA, V&A museum, V&A Dundee museum etc.

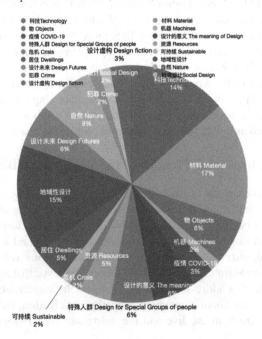

design for the future and design for special people, with technology accounting for 14%. Some representative exhibitions include "Thinking Machines: Art and Design in the Computer Age, 1959- 1989" curated by MOMA in 2017, and V&A Dundee's exhibition "Hello, Robot: Design Between Human and Machine" in 2019.There is also a large category of regional design, which accounts for 15%. For instance, in 2017 the Design Museum launched a discussion on the design phenomenon in Silicon Valley, titled "California: Designing Freedom". In addition, exhibitions on the meaning of design, objects, and dwelling also account for about 5%. Discussions on living focused on sustainable living and the future of living space. Niche but increasingly important topics include crisis, epidemic, crime, design fiction, etc. MOMA curated the exhibition "SAFE: Design Takes On Risk" in 2005 for the first time, and "Design and Violence" in 2013. Since 2020, almost every museum has curated exhibitions that address the social landscape of the post-epidemic era. Some of these are creative responses by designers to the crisis era, such as "Design and Healing: Creative Responses to Epidemics" by Cooper Hewitt Museum in 2021 and "@design.emergency" curated by Paola Antolini, senior curator of the design section at MOMA. Some are discussions of life-shifting and interpersonal relationships, such as the "Now Accepting Contactless-Design in a Global Pandemic" by V&A Dundee in 2021.

Secondly, the themes of exhibition emerged iteratively from the perspective of time. Topics related to sustainability were prevalent around 2010. Important exhibitions include "Design and Elastic Mind" at MOMA in 2008 and "Sustainable Futures" at the Design Museum in London in 2010. In 2013 and 2014, there was a focus on speculative design, such as "design fictions" and "social design for wicked problems". From 2019 onwards, the focus on nature, materials and resources becomes more intense. After 2020, reflections on epidemics gradually increase. The discussion of technology, started at 2001, range from internet to cyber intrusion, machines, and manufacturing, occurs intermittently over two decades. From another perspective, the given theme of annual residency has also been evolving since 2016 according to the hot topics of the year. Taking the London Design Museum as an example, the topic of residency from 2016 to 2020 were "Open", "Support", "Dwelling" and "Care".

To sum up, curatorial themes of design exhibition is a mapping of changes in the social order. Design exhibitions have shifted to the focus on social events, especially social emergencies that affect future human development, such as climate change, resource, social violence and security, sustainable development, epidemic and health, crisis and resilience, technology, and the future, etc. The exhibitions regarding to social emergencies thrive from scratch to phenomenon, acting as a thread linking problems and proposing solutions to major human challenges.

4 Seven Models of Design Curatorial Methods

To keep pace with the increasingly prominent sustainable issues, contemporary design exhibitions have innovated strategies that varied from traditional design curatorial approaches. The author summarizes these contemporary strategies as seven models, for addressing issues such as climate change, hunger and food security, new energy and materials, and the circular economy as seven models, borrowing ecologically relevant terms. It is undoubted that much of the wisdom in "ecology" is both a key to sustainable development and a reflection of the situation of the times, such as "dynamic balance", "decentralization", "evolution", etc.

The seven models are: Curate as successing, Curate as ecology, Curate as tipping point, Curate as landscape, Curate as process, curate as evolution, and curate as evolution (see Table 2).

Table 2. Models of Design Curation and key words

Curation Methods	Key words
Curate as Successing	Transformation, new structure
Curate as Ecology	Multi-players, dynamic balance
Curate as Tipping Point	Extreme condition, collapse
Curate as Landscape	Panorama, vision
Curate as Process	Open-ended, exploration
Curate as Evolution	Culture, grow
Curate a a Nutrient Flow	Role play, visible-invisible

4.1 Curate as Successing

Succession, in ecological terms, refers to the process by which the structure of a biological community evolves over time, namely the gradual replacement of old species structures by new ones. Curating as evolution is the result of the interaction between curators, designers and artists as inner factors, and the social environment as outer factors. There is a transformation of the focused attention area of them. Curators are asking bigger questions than "what is the good design", such as how climate change challenges the role of designers, scientists, and museums themselves [5]. Exhibitions have pushed designers to collaborate creatively with scientists working at the forefront to address fundamental issues such as habitat loss, mass extinctions etc. For example, marked by the Copenhagen COP15 in 2009, art and design activities at each subsequent COP have responded to multiple climate change issues, selected diverse creative sites, filtered complex creative media, built cross-disciplinary collaborative projects, and catalyzed multi-level institutional action [6]. As the focusing topics evolves, curating as a strategy for dealing with an uncertain future has gradually become a consensus among many curators [7]. Designer Eli Blevis observes that "We can think of a design as a plan for the future, making us responsible for our designs and the designs we choose." [8].

4.2 Curate as Ecology

One of the most striking features of ecology is the way in which countless elements interact and influence with each other in the environment. In contrast to the traditional museums as an isolated brand, contemporary design museums tend to being a part of a network of partners rather than inaccessible. Exhibitions transferred from "object-centered" to "education-centered" to "audience-centered" to "polycentric" finally [9]. For example, the curatorial principle of HNI is not focusing on the so-called "star designers", but rather shifting the focus from the designers to the viewers or users themselves [10]. Another case is that one initiative of Z33 is to create a platform to connect with different partners to collaborate in the long term. Usually, subsequent projects are much larger than the scale of the exhibition itself, with following activities such as temporary projects in public spaces, debates, performances, and education. These initiatives will allow the institution to go further.

4.3 Curate as Tipping Point

Ecological tipping point is a state that reaches the edge of equilibrium, beyond which the state collapses. The tipping point is uncontrollable, unpredictable, and unrecoverable. Guus Beumer, former director of HNI, argues that design curation should focus on massive conflicts in society to address tipping points in advance [10]. For example, exhibition "The Coming World: Ecology as the new Politics 2030–2100" discusses the tipping points of 2030 and 2100. In 2030, the remaining oil resources will be depleted. While in 2100, the human being will be forced to find dwellings on another planet. Another exhibition "Waste Age: What can design do?" divides waste into Peak Waste and Post Waste. Peak Waste includes plastics, rubber, steel, electronics, etc. Post Waste includes new materials such as mycelium, bioplastic PLA, and agricultural waste. The exhibition "Designing Scarcity: Design and Innovation in Times of Scarcity", on the other hand, discusses the extremes in times of resource scarcity.

4.4 Curate as Landscape

Landscape here is not related to scene nor territory, but rather vision, a panoramic insight in a certain field. Curate as landscape, is commonly an exhaustive list and summary. For example, the Cooper Hewitt Design Museum's triennial "Nature" summarizes the seven types of strategies designers can use to work with nature, namely "Understanding", "Stimulate", "Salvage", "Facilitate", "Augment", "Remediate", and "Nurture". Exhibition "Our Broken Planet: How We Got Here and Ways to Fix It" in 2021 listed three panels "Eating the Earth", "Nature for sale" and "Climate emergency". Another exhibition "Designing Scarcity: Design and Innovation in Times of Scarcity" will use 11 key words to conclude the design methods: extension, collage, recycling, multi-purpose, super-use, substitution, imitation, repair, conservation, and resilience throughout the exhibition.

4.5 Curate as Process

Curate as a process is not a retrospective or a summary of the design products of the market, but a new type of research ahead of the market. This is highlighted in the curatorial program of HNI, where research-based curation responds to the innovative ideas and the development of designers as researchers. For example, exhibition "FOOD: Bigger than the Plate" divides the study of food into four sequential processes, namely "compost", "farming", "trading" and "eating". The exhibition takes visitors on a journey through the food cycle, from reusing waste to producing, to growing food, transporting it, and serving as a meal. The research is not an answer but a discussion of possibilities that will need to be verified over a longer period. Some cases include how to cultivate food in harsh environments, how to grow underground salads in the lab, how to exact proteins from soil molds, how to make cheese from human bacteria, etc. On the other hand, the designers have designed futuristic foods according to human eating habits in the future. For example, there is a growing agreement on insects as an alternative source of protein. Also "digital condiments" allow us to experience the taste of food from the brain rather than the taste buds. The more speculative designers believe that humans will evolve into the species, with a modified digestive system that can digest wasted and decaying food.

4.6 Curate as Evolution

Exhibitions nurture as well as incubate design works, making them triggers, catalysts or facilitators [11]. In 2004, Bruce Mau's exhibition "Massive Change" posed the question "Will this be a design for destruction or for a sustainable new world that we can safely hand down to our children and our children's children?" [12] as a starting point for design thinking. The exhibition "Redesign for Circularity and Waste Age: What can design do?" are curated not to see wastes as the end of life, but rather to find value in the edge of application. The exhibition focuses on creative economic models that transform mined materials into planted materials, sparking a broader economic transformation.

4.7 Curate as Nutrient Flow

Nutrient flow refers to how different substances in the flow transmit information and transform energy, such as the transformation of nitrogen in the environment. It is to find out the visible and invisible clues to understand the elements in different scenarios. The point of this approach is to bring new perspectives to the narrative, driving the public's attention to new perspectives on old issues or new perspectives on new issues. For example, "the Edible Futures" exhibition offers a dual perspective on reality by providing a "consumer" and a "producer" view. Also, "Plastic: Remaking Our World", which will open in 2022 in V&A museum, re-tells the story of our lives through the lens of plastic.

In conclusion, these curatorial strategies are like Swiss Army Knives in the socio-cultural system, proposing strategies that are both diverse and precise, both local and international, both present and future oriented. As a result, a multi-dimensional think tank is formed rising from different contexts of industry, life, culture, society, and future, responding to contemporary crises with innovative approaches. In this open framework, the exhibition topics ferment and rebound, inspiring strong emotions of the audience, catalyzing innovative prototypes of interdisciplinary collaboration.

5   Conclusion

The epidemic has changed the order of human society, with all fields converted their original perceptions of health, resources, and life. If the second industrial revolution gave birth to modern design, with the peak of curatorial period since 1990s, then the epidemic was another turning point for design curation. In the era of crisis, a broader dimension of design exhibitions is urgent to develop, with continuous breakthroughs in form, content, audience, and impact to respond to the challenges of sustainable human development. As Bjarke Ingels said "A sustainable future is not a political dilemma, nor a typological dilemma, I really think it is a design challenge" [13].

This study hopes to initiate a new system of design curatorial research through a preliminary exploration of design curation in the post-epidemic era. The power of design curation will serve as a research method to gather imagination, speculation and hope to shape a better era in the midst of crisis.

References

1. Net Nieuw Institute home page. https://hetnieuweinstituut.nl/en/design. Accessed 10 Jan 2022
2. Alice Rawsthorn , Clément Dirié: Design as an Attitude, JRP|Ringier, 28 August 2018
3. Hans Ulrich Obrist: Ecology will be at the heart of everything we do, February 2020.https://www.theartnewspaper.com/2020/02/03/hans-ulrich-obrist-ecology-will-be-at-the-heart-of-everything-we-do. Accessed 01 Oct 2022
4. Antonelli, P., Tannir, A.: Broken Nature: Design Takes on Human Survival, Rizzoli Electa, 10 December 2019
5. The New York Times: Glimpsing Our Post-Consumption Future at the Cooper Hewitt.t-review.html. Accessed 01 Oct 2022
6. Jing, S.: Creative Responses to the Climate Crisis - The Art Movement at the UN Climate COP, Musuem Magzine, December 2021
7. Aldersey-Williams, H.: Peter Hall: Design and the Elastic Mind, The Museum of Modern Art, 1 March 2008
8. Blevis, E.: Seeing what is and what can be: on sustainability, respect for work, and design for respect. In: CHI '18: Proceedings of the 2018 CHI Conference on Human Factors in Computing Systems (New York: ACM, 2018), paper no. 370, 2. DOI: https://doi.org/10.1145/3173574.3173944
9. Zhang, Z.: Cross-border Survival: New Ideas for Art Museums, China Youth Publishing House, February 2014
10. Jing, S.: Interview with Guus Beumer, 01/22/2021
11. Razor Sharp: The Curator Known as HUO. https://www.damnmagazine.net/2017/05/31/hans-ulrich-obrist/. Accessed 01/10/2022 Bruce Mau, Jennifer Leonard: Massive Change, Phaidon Press, October 1, 2004
12. Mau, B., Leonard, J.: Massive Change, Phaidon Press, 1 October 2004
13. "Hedonistic" future could be better for the environment says Bjarke Ingels at COP26, 5 November 2021. https://www.dezeen.com/2021/11/05/cop26-hydrogen-powered-flights-bjarke-ing els-hedonistic-future/. Accessed 10 Jan 2022

Towards an Interactive Virtual Museum Visit: The Implementation of 3D Scanning, Virtual Reality, and Multimedia Technologies in Art Exhibits Conservation and Virtual Demonstrations

Savvas Koltsakidis[1,2]([⊠]), Konstantinos Tsongas[2,3], Dimitrios Tzetzis[1,2], Charisios Achillas[1,4], Alexandra Michailidou[1], Christos Vlachokostas[1], Vasilis Efopoulos[5], Vasilis Gkonos[3], and Nicolas Moussiopoulos[1]

[1] Laboratory of Heat Transfer and Environmental Engineering, Department of Mechanical Engineering, Aristotle University Thessaloniki, Thessaloniki, Greece
[2] Digital Manufacturing and Materials Characterization Laboratory, School of Science and Technology, International Hellenic University, Thermi, Greece
skoltsakidis@ihu.edu.gr
[3] Teloglion Fine Arts Foundation – Aristotle University Thessaloniki, Thessaloniki, Greece
[4] Department of Supply Chain Management, International Hellenic University, Katerini, Greece
[5] Tessera Multimedia S.A., Pefka, Thessaloniki, Greece

Abstract. The permanent collection of the Teloglion Fine Arts Foundation includes important artworks of Modern Greek and European art, constituting it one of the most important in Greece. The Foundation collects, records, and studies cultural heritage, organizes exhibitions in collaboration with other institutions in Greece and internationally, as well as provides the audience with the chance of getting familiar with artwork via tours and educational programs. In this light, the Foundation constitutes an extroverted, open, and -most of all- interactive Museum that combines research, education, art, culture, and science. To that end, the Teloglion Foundation, in close collaboration with Aristotle University of Thessaloniki and Tessera S.A., are developing innovative ICT applications in the framework of the ARTECH project ("digitAlize aRt and culTural hEritage for personal experienCe via innovative tecHnologies"), so as to highlight and promote its permanent collection to the wide public and specialized groups of visitors. The aim is to enhance the experience and the experiential learning – entertainment of visitors through interactive, modern educational and multimedia methods. One method employed to fulfill this ambitious task is by designing a Virtual Reality (VR) environment based on 3D data of Teloglion premises, captured through state-of-the-art laser scanners as well as a photogrammetry mapping drone. Furthermore, selected artworks are digitalized through a structured light 3D handheld scanner and are hosted in the given VR environment, forming 3D virtual tours where visitors and researchers can zoom, analyze and receive information at certain hot spots. The capabilities and advantages of 3D scanning and 3D printing in the conservation of artworks are also investigated by presenting case studies of digitalized damaged exhibits and restoration procedures in open workshops where participants will have the chance to conserve and synthesize a 3D copy work of art. Finally, experiential education and entertainment are further amplified through multimedia games that challenge and enrich visitors' knowledge, concerning the artist, the story and the symbolism of the artifacts.

Keywords: Digital culture · Virtual museum · Experiential education · Visitor-computer interaction

1 Introduction

The partnership of this project consists of a Research and Knowledge Dissemination Organization - the Aristotle University of Thessaloniki (AUTH) -, a company - TESSERA S.A. which is primarily active in the provision of research and development services for interactive multimedia applications - and Teloglion Fine Arts Foundation AUTH which is a center of art, research and culture in Northern Greece. The Collection of the Fine Arts Foundation is of historical importance, as it includes important works which mark key developments of Modern Greek and European art. The object of this project is the design and development of experiential actions and applications to highlight the iconic works of the permanent collection of the Teloglion Art Foundation SA. to the public and to specialized groups of visitors as well as to form training educational workshops. These actions will aim to enhance the visitor's experience as well as the experiential learning and entertainment through interactive, modern educational, multimedia methods. In particular, applications have been designed and implemented which will enable the following; three-dimensional virtual tour and interaction of the visitors within the premises and around the exhibits, learning experience of maintenance - digital and real - works of art and empirical education and entertainment via multimedia educational applications.

2 Methods

2.1 3D Virtual Exhibition

An application is being designed for virtual tour of visitors in the external and internal areas. The tour will initially allow the visitor to explore the Foundation's premises and will be accompanied by audio-enhanced descriptive information about the Foundation. For the three-dimensional rendering of the interior premises of the Technological Institute of Arts a laser scanner was used in combination with panoramic shots from a full frame 50 Mpixels camera attached to a mechanical stabilizer (gimbal) at two different heights in order to achieve the fairest photorealistic texture. In addition for the three-dimensional rendering of the surrounding space and the building exterior, a laser scanner was also used combined with an unmanned aerial vehicle with a full frame 45 Mpixels camera. Finally, for the 3D representation of the artifacts, a structed light scanner was employed. The technologies that were deployed as well as their purpose are summarized in Table 1.

Table 1. Different methods used for 3D rendering of premises and artifact's geometry and texture.

Technology	Purpose	Advantage	Model	Resolution
Laser scanner	Interior & exterior geometry	Large data capture	Focus 3D s120	3 mm
Camera photogrammetry	Interior & exterior texture	High quality texture	Canon EOS 5DSR	50 MPixels
Drone photogrammetry	Exterior texture & geometry	Unreachable data	Matrice 300 RTK	2 cm
Structured light scanner	Artifact's geometry & texture	High resolution	Artec Eva	0.1 mm

Results of the 3D rendered building are presented in Fig. 1. The following procedure was followed: Measurement of photo fixed control points (Ground Control Points or GCPs) inside and outside of the building, followed by scan with 3D laser scanner and aerial photographic images for the exterior of the building and its surroundings. As a final step, photographs of the facades of the building (external and internal) were taken along with panoramic photographic images for optimum texture quality. All the data are combined in the Reality Capture software to create the 3D model of the building and the surrounding area with a photorealistic texture.

(a)   (b)

Fig. 1. (a) View of the intersection of the model within the institution (b) view from the model that results photogrammetrically using DSS, the positions of aerial shots and photo stationary points in the courtyard of the institution are also shown.

Three-dimensional handheld scanners that emit light rays or laser beams for identification of a point cloud are widely used for cultural heritage reconstruction [1]. An example of an artifact and its final rendering is presented in Fig. 2. The procedure starts with repeated scans on different sides and angles until the number of points acquired can portray the exhibit. Through specific algorithms and point-deletion commands, unnecessary information is removed with the aim of facilitating later steps as well as reducing the volume of files. Mesh integration and scan alignment follows where the data are combined. Eventual holes due to incomplete data acquisition are filled. Finally, texture is implemented to form the final 3D model.

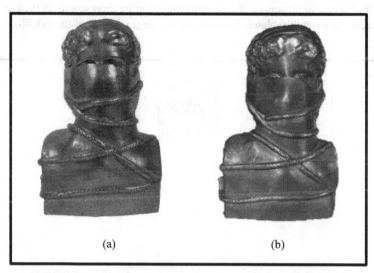

(a)   (b)

Fig. 2. (a) Photograph of an artifact (b) 3D representation produced by employing a structured light scanner.

2.2 Art Conservation

The 3D printing and scanning technology has been utilized to print exhibits with three-dimensional characteristics (e.g. carvings) and damaged parts, so that they can be maintained and restored [2]. This technique avoids much of the strain of authentic exhibits, as all the tests are carried out on printed copies. Moreover, the final application of the optimal solution to original works also involves significantly less stress compared to traditional methods of restoration. In this project digital 3D printer maintenance techniques will be exposed to visitors and researchers through educational workshops during which participants will be able to analyze, document, maintain and virtually compose a work of art on 3D replicas. A qualified conservator will guide the process and perform (both himself and the participants) the maintenance of the 3D copy - work of art in a natural way. This will further enhance the experience of trainees in the methodology and maintenance stages of an artwork (data identification, examination, diagnosis, development of maintenance methodology, maintenance) and acquire knowledge through practical engagement with the object. In addition the concept of preservation and maintenance of artifacts can be replaced by the concept of their reproduction in their digital forms (as an image, a digital or a three-dimensional representation). The contribution of digitization is crucial for collections that are heavily damaged and cannot be fully restored. The digital image and representation is also easier to manage, process or restore, without any intervention in the work itself which favors any educational or recreational process. Examples of the used techniques are presented in Fig. 3. Figure 3a presents a method for restoring an artifact. The procedure begins with 3D scanning and reconstruction of the artifact. The missing piece is then identified and 3D printing can be employed to recreate it. Figure 3b presents a digital reconstruction method where all broken pieces are scanned and smoothly blended to recreate the original form of the exhibit.

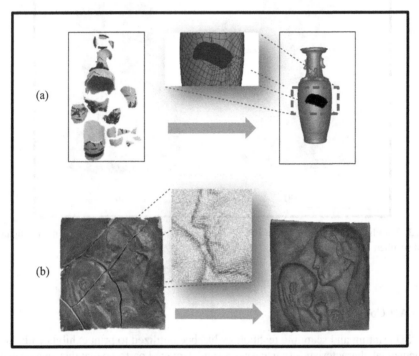

Fig. 3. (a) Digital restoration of an artifact by scanning its parts and identifying the missing piece. (b) Digital reconstruction of an artifact by smoothly blending the broken parts.

2.3 Multimedia Technologies

In recent years, serious games have been developing enormously. Serious games have been given several definitions, but they are mainly characterized as games with educational goals, supported by entertainment. Their purpose is more complicated than normal games, as they aim at providing fun combined with educational elements that lead to knowledge acquisition. [3]. Within the framework of the ARTECH project, multimedia educational applications were implemented. The applications facilitate the understanding of concepts related to culture and arts, thus contributing to enriching visitors' knowledge and cultivation of their personality. The educational applications developed are Art Explorer, Paint it, Smart Quiz, and hot spot presentation shown in Fig. 4 and are described below.

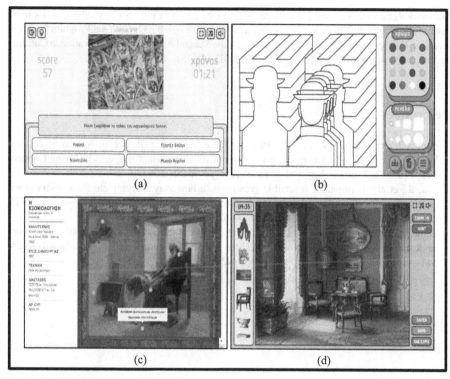

Fig. 4. Multimedia applications (a) smart quiz (b) paint it (c) hot spots presentation (d) art explorer.

Paint it: The player can either select the desired painting himself or press the 'random painting' option and display a painting. Once he has painted the painting, the original artwork can be compared with the 'new' and some educational content information are provided.

Smart Quiz: There will be multiple choice questions with sound rewarding the right response of the participant. Topics related to the style, art stream and theme of the work of art and the techniques used will be covered. The questions will be related to both morphological and conceptual issues (e.g. sections: religious scenes, still life, portraiture, urban landscape, landscape, war/peace, symbolism/allegories, expressionism, etc.). The trainee will also be able to interact with basic concepts and terms of the History of Art and understand the link between the visual creation and the historical context.

Art explorer: The user will observe the painting and try to find the objects that are requested. For greater assistance, there will be a magnifying glass, which will make it easier to see the board, while the contested spot will be shown brighter. The player will be able to zoom anywhere on the board. Any object found will be clickable. At the same time, there will be a button with important information (creator, style, art stream, theme etc.) for the painting to enhance his experience and knowledge.

Hot spot presentation: For selected projects, there is a possibility to focus on points of particular interest 'hot spots', to which the person concerned can draw his attention, bring closer to focus, and to analyze as well as to receive important information.

Acknowledgments. This work has been co-financed by the European Regional Development Fund of the European Union and Greek national funds through the Operational Program Competitiveness, Entrepreneurship and Innovation, under the Special Action "Open Innovation in Culture" (project acronym: ARTECH, project code: T6ΥΒΠ-00015).

References

1. Santos Junior, J.D.O., Vrubel, A., Bellon, O.R.P., Silva, L.: 3D reconstruction of cultural heritages: challenges and advances on precise mesh integration. Comput. Vis. Image Underst. **116**, 1195–1207 (2012). https://doi.org/10.1016/j.cviu.2012.08.005
2. Liu, S., et al.: Transparent reversible prosthesis, a new way to complete the conservation–restoration of a Black Ding bowl with application of 3D technologies. Heritage Sci. **10**(1), 1–14 (2022). https://doi.org/10.1186/s40494-022-00646-0
3. Gunter, G., Kenny, R., Vick, E.: Taking educational games seriously: using the RETAIN model to design endogenous fantasy into standalone educational games. Educ. Tech. Res. Dev. **56**, 511–537 (2008). https://doi.org/10.1007/s11423-007-9073-2

Exploration of Generous Interface Design Principles for Digital Cultural Heritage

Qiang Li[✉], Jingjing Wang, and Tian Luo

Shenyang Aerospace University, Shenyang, China
qiangli@sau.edu.cn

Abstract. Rapid advances in information technology have facilitated the development of cultural heritage, and digital networks have become the largest repository of cultural heritage information, containing millions of works and cultural knowledge data. The generous interface serves as the primary contact point for users to communicate with cultural heritage information, and its display form is essential for users to understand digital cultural information. Many designers have used the concept of generous interfaces for digital cultural heritage, but the design specifications of generous interfaces are still limited. Therefore, this study explores the design principles of generous interface for digital cultural heritage by case analysis and evaluation. Three design principles were identified: guiding principle, hierarchical principle, and information visualization principle. This research aims to provide a practical reference for the design of the digital cultural heritage interfaces and assess the role of the generous interface.

Keywords: Digital cultural heritage · Design principle · Generous interface

1 Introduction

Digital collections have become a common feature of many cultural heritage websites. It represents an important achievement of the transformation of global institutions from physical institutions to digital institutions over the past few decades. However, digital displays are different from those in traditional museums, galleries, etc., in that the users must deal with large and complex amounts of cultural data. At the same time, information researchers point out that many users do not have a fixed information goal when browsing the cultural heritage interfaces, but come from their curiosity or pursuit of new experiences [1]. Therefore, it is essential to provide users with effective information content in the cultural heritage interface, and Mitchell Whitelaw refers to generous interface design forms in his research [2]. The interface organizes and arranges the massive amount of digital cultural heritage information, adding information navigation tips so that users no longer seek functional satisfaction of the information they need, but also pursue a sense of spiritual pleasure. This interface design form is of great significance for the dissemination of cultural heritage information and strengthens the communication between the users and the interface. Therefore, the design specifications of the generous interface need to be explored.

© The Author(s), under exclusive license to Springer Nature Switzerland AG 2022
C. Stephanidis et al. (Eds.): HCII 2022, CCIS 1582, pp. 227–233, 2022.
https://doi.org/10.1007/978-3-031-06391-6_30

In digital collections, the interface is the window that makes digital cultural heritage information available to the general public [3]. When a large amount of information data comes together, it poses a massive challenge for users to explore and search [4]. Therefore, the design of the interface should take into account the rational layout of information as well as the usability and aesthetics of the interface. The usability principle is the basis for evaluating the interface prototype, which means that the interface must be easy to understand and use. In other words, the design of the interface should meet the three conditions: content visibility, easy accessing and easy browsing. At the same time, the good usability of the interface will bring users a good emotional experience initially. Beauty was defined by Alberti as "a great and sacred thing", explaining the importance of beauty in life [5], so the aesthetics of the interface is the first impression brought to the users. Aesthetics will affect users' participation and user's sense of experience to a certain extent [6]. In addition, Zhai Jiajia proposed that the interface design should be a combination of usability, interactivity and artistry [7]. Practicality and artistry can impress users and arouse their emotional resonance. It is clear that interface design is a process of continuous improvement and iteration, and the designers should focus on users and develop interfaces that meet users' needs and preferences [8]. In general, the generous interface is just a presentation of all the different information interface expressions. The difference lies in the vast and complex information system hidden behind the generous interface. Marian Dörk et al. have tried to visualize the substantial digital collection, presenting diverse cultural information from multiple dimensions [9]. The visualization of the interface has improved the efficiency of users' access to information and changed the public's perception of the traditional cultural collection interface.

The study explores the design principles of the generous interface. This concept was first proposed by Whitelaw, and then Taylor and others used the idea of the generous interface to design a web visualization system containing 17000 historical pictures [10]. Although the idea of a generous interface is well known, no one gives a precise answer on designing a generous interface. The paper lists the relevant cases of the generous interface; analyzes the design form of generous interface; and finds out the design points of generous interface. We deeply explore the profound connotation of "sharing spirit" contained in the generous interface, and finally assess the value and role of the generous interface.

2   Methodology

The generous interface is a new form of interface presentation. The word "generosity", however, has a different meaning. It is expressed as "generous and comprehensive", giving the spirit of "sharing" to the interface design of cultural heritage. The generous interface intends to present users with richer content and more exploratory interaction modes. Digital cultural heritage is a vast cluster of information, and the websites of institutions also pay attention to the diversity and novelty of digital displays. Then, we will make a profound analysis of the digital interface form by the following examples.

SORT BY	Name ⇕		WORK COUNT	
ROLES			0-1	1959
			1-5	1518
artist	3734		6-10	485
printer	482		10-20	328
publisher	210		20-50	305
print after	174		50-100	98
client	194		100-1000	88
engraver	95		SEX	
author	80		Male	2143
print workshop	104		Female	1359
other	286		Organisation	720
			None	0

Fig. 1. The interface of print and printmaking collection in national gallery of Australia.

The digital cultural heritage interface provides users with a comprehensive overview of information, including the category of creation, authorship, quantity, and gender of the collection (Fig. 1). All the information categories are grouped in one module for detailed division. All the information contained in the whole interface can be read out in this panel. For example, the number of works by artists; the number of works by female authors; and the possibility of an in-depth study and exploration of the results of each artist. This display mode breaks the limitations of the traditional interface, and it saves more display space and actively provides users with more information about the work. Users are free to browse all the ranges of the interface content instead of losing their sense of direction to retrieve specific content. The generous interface emphasizes the connection between the theme and the spatial visualization. It enriches our perception of the cultural heritage interface and strengthens the communication between the user and the interface through interface cues (see Fig. 2).

Fig. 2. Australian print and printmaking decade browser

This interface is from the website of the Australian printmaking museum. All works in the interface are arranged in chronological order. Each time period contains samples of the collection of the era, in order to show the style and characteristics of the era. The overall height of the histogram represents the number of pieces contained in that period. The interface clearly shows the structure of the collection and the relationship between the number of items. There is a timeline as the user browsing clue, which provides a good guide for the user browsing the interface.

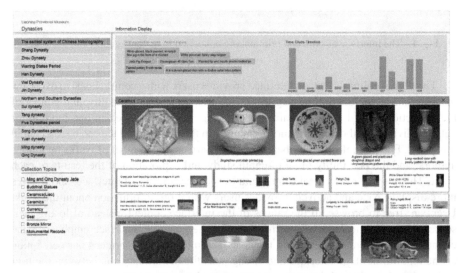

Fig. 3. Liaoning provincial museum interface

Based on the design characteristics of the generous interface analyzed above, this paper redesigned the interface of the Liaoning Provincial Museum. The picture above shows the general information of the museum collections (Fig. 3), including categories, chronology, timeline, etc. Each work is presented in thumbnail format, with all the work displayed by mouse touch or hover. The left side represents the chronology of all the pieces, expressing the number of components in that chronology by color shades and echoing the hints of the timeline on the right. The timeline is chronological, and the number of positions is expressed in a bar chart so that users can get a clear picture of the entire collection. In addition, the theme part of the collection on the left uses different color bars to distinguish different categories of groups. This visualization makes the collection categories easier to identify and distinguish, maximizing the information and presenting it to the users.

From the images shown above, the design form of the generous interface is significantly different from the traditional interface, which is all based on theoretical and visual ideas without practical verification. Therefore, in order to explore the differences between the two interfaces, we compared the museum's generous interface with the traditional interface. The experimental results show significant differences between the design forms of the generous interface and the traditional interface. The mean values of the generous interface are higher than those of the conventional interface in terms of aesthetics and user engagement. The expression of generous interface has a significant impact on improving the user experience. The generous interface provides a new design framework for the collection model of digital cultural heritage.

3 Principles

Through the analysis of the generous interface examples and the redesign of the interface of Liaoning Provincial Museum, the concept of generous interface and the form of displaying data information become clearer. The interface of Liaoning Provincial Museum displays a large amount of cultural information in a more integrated and visual way. This format enhances the dissemination of cultural knowledge and makes it easy for users to navigate. In summary, the principles of the generous interface are as follows:

3.1 Guiding Principle

Guidance in the interface is the primary principle of generous interface design. Most users enter the interface for the first time, they have not received training or learning. There is no clear purpose for everyone to view the content. After random browsing or clicking, you may enter a new content page. But it is not clear how to return to the previous page or jump to another interface. At this time, the interface guidance information is essential. The guiding information in the interface is the context connecting the whole cultural heritage collection. Guidance methods include but are not limited to timeline, color bar, and image. All guidance methods provide users with more explicit browsing ideas. The purpose is to let users learn culture-related knowledge in a pleasant and relaxed mood, and users can get the information they need to improve their experience.

3.2 Hierarchy Principle

Hierarchical relationships play an essential role in the design of a generous interface. It presents the logical connection of the whole interface, which consists of a general overview - work collection - single work details. The hierarchical design makes the content structure of the entire interface clearer and provides an explicit visual guide for users. The second collection of works is an interpretation of the general overview. On the other hand, the collection of works outlines the overall content of the interface and attracts users with novel content and unique typography to increase user engagement and reduce user bounce rate. When a user is interested in a work, he can view the details of the work by clicking on it. For untargeted users, this is a new way of presenting the page different from the traditional interface, which does not require the user to search through the search box, but it actively contributes all the content of the page for the user to choose. This display form gives users more freedom to meet their psychological and emotional needs.

3.3 Information Visualization Principle

The important reason for visualizing cultural heritage data is to engage users. Human vision is an essential sense for humans to extract information from the physical plane. Using images instead of words in interface design is more accessible for people to understand and this way can reduce the trouble caused by many words. The form of visualization strengthens the communication between people and the interface. The visualization principle of generous interface design takes advantage of this feature, which provides visual clues for users to browse the interface through images or lines. It displays the quantitative relationship of the work in a visual way to reduce the user's burden of use. When viewing an artwork image, the interface may send feedback signals to the user by clicking on the image or hovering over it - the image zooms in or out, stimulating the sensory system and increasing the chance of user interaction with the interface. The visual representation of digital collections represents a new trend in interface development and it is an essential theme for our future research.

The above three design principles clearly express the design guidelines for generous interface. The three design principles are summarized as a theoretical model (see Fig. 4) to guide the design of generous interface for cultural heritage.

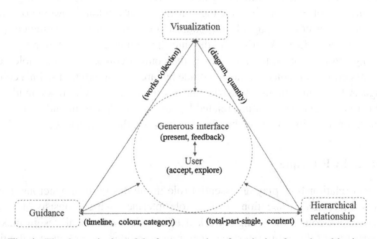

Fig. 4. The theoretical model of generous interface design for cultural heritage

4 Conclusion

The content of digital cultural heritage determines the presentation of the generous interface, the amount and type of cultural heritage information determines the overall framework structure design. In generous interface, the hierarchical structure form and information visualization are perfectly combined. The public can get more knowledge of cultural heritage from the interface and appreciate the more profound cultural atmosphere. This paper explored the research of relevant experts in generous interface design in recent years and analyzed the generous interfaces of relevant museums and art galleries. We summarized the three design principles of generous interface and proposed a theoretical model of generous interface design. The study evaluated users' experiences during the use of the generous interface utilizing a questionnaire and analyzed the role of the generous interface. The results of this study provided reference basis for the design of generous interfaces for digital cultural heritage.

Acknowledgement. The work was supported by Liaoning Province Education Department (JYT2020098), and teaching reform fund of Shenyang Aerospace University (2022).

References

1. Morse, C., Niess, J., Lallemand, C., Wieneke, L., Koenig, V.: Casual leisure in rich-prospect: advancing visual information behavior for digital museum collections. J. Comput. Cult. Heritage (JOCCH) **14**(3), 1–23 (2021)
2. Whitelaw, M.: Generous interfaces for digital cultural collections (2015)
3. Whitelaw, M.: Towards generous interfaces for archival collections. In: International Council on Archives Congress, pp. 20–24 (2012)
4. Petras, V., Hill, T., Stiller, J., Gäde, M.: Europeana–a search engine for digitised cultural heritage material. Datenbank-Spektrum **17**(1), 41–46 (2017)
5. Lavie, T., Tractinsky, N.: Assessing dimensions of perceived visual aesthetics of web sites. Int. J. Hum. Comput. Stud. **60**(3), 269–298 (2004)
6. Speakman, R., Hall, M.M., Walsh, D.: User engagement with generous interfaces for digital cultural heritage. In: Méndez, E., Crestani, F., Ribeiro, C., David, G., Lopes, J.C. (eds.) TPDL 2018. LNCS, vol. 11057, pp. 186–191. Springer, Cham (2018). https://doi.org/10.1007/978-3-030-00066-0_16
7. Jiajia, Z., Hui, Z.: Research on the design principle of "digital tangling" user interface. Packag. Eng. **37**(18), 67–71 (2016)
8. Trieschnigg, D., My Datafactory, M.: Supporting the exploration of online cultural heritage collections: the case of the Dutch Folktale database. DHQ **11**(4) (2017)
9. Dörk, M., Pietsch, C., Credico, G.: One view is not enough: high-level visualizations of a large cultural collection. Inf. Des. J. **23**(1), 39–47 (2017)
10. Arnold, T., Ayers, N., Madron, J., Nelson, R., Tilton, L.: Visualizing a large spatiotemporal collection of historic photography with a generous interface. In: 2020 IEEE 5th Workshop on Visualization for the Digital Humanities (VIS4DH), pp. 30–35. IEEE (2020)

The Evaluation of a Mid-Air Based Natural Interactive Installation on Cultural Heritage Learning

Qiang Li[✉], Tian Luoand, and Jingjing Wang

Shenyang Aerospace University, Shenyang, China
qiangli@sau.edu.cn

Abstract. To improve the efficiency of learning ancient art and cultural knowledge for users through cultural heritage, the interactive installation of Chinese traditional painting *Ruihe Tu* is designed by applying mid-air motion capture technology. Several factors which may affect learning efficiency are considered during the design, such as aesthetics, motivation, participation, usability and so on. In this study, these variables were evaluated by empirical and quantitative research methods. The results show that those users who experience the mid-air based natural interactive installation *Ruihe Tu* have a stronger interest in learning the original work. And users have a better performance in terms of engagement and exploration desire.

Keywords: Cultural heritage · Ancient painting · Mid-air based natural interactive installation

1 Introduction

Ancient painting is an important part of cultural heritage, which has always played an important role in transmitting art and historical and cultural knowledge. With the rapid development of the digital media technology, multi-carrier presentation has become an important part of the innovative design of cultural heritage. Many scholars believe that interdisciplinary cooperation is conducive to the protection and dissemination of Cultural Heritage [1]. The application of modern technology to the display of cultural heritage can fully mobilize the various sensory organs of the human body [9], which is conducive to the audience to obtain more information from interaction and good user experience [8]. For example, Fang Fang (2014) proposed that the application of new interactive methods to modern exhibitions can enhance the interest of exhibits and stimulate the excitement of the viewer [2]. Jessie Pallud (2016) proposed that when users perceive the interaction with technology as being intuitive and interactive, they experience higher levels of cognitive engagement [3]. Human-computer interaction and experience human-computer interaction are the key issues in the virtual experience. Due to the unique attributes of cultural heritage information, human-computer interaction is particularly important in the virtual experience of cultural heritage [4]. In recent years, many scholars are also

C. Stephanidis et al. (Eds.): HCII 2022, CCIS 1582, pp. 234–239, 2022.
https://doi.org/10.1007/978-3-031-06391-6_31

actively studying the role of various interactive technologies in cultural heritage display. Through comparison, Jinsheng found that the IVR environment significantly increased the learning effectiveness and motivation compared to the MTT system [7], Among various interaction technologies, mid-air natural interaction technology is an effective tool to realize interaction. mid-air natural interaction technology controls equipment with body action, which provides a revolutionary experience for human-computer interaction. Learning the relevant historical and artistic knowledge of works has always been one of the important purposes of cultural heritage display. It has always been the general responsibility of cultural heritage display to promote the public to learn art, history and cultural knowledge. Therefore, this paper attempts to analyze the influence of the application of mid-air natural interaction technology on the display of ancient paintings from the perspective of learning knowledge related to cultural heritage. Situational learning theory holds that "the essence of learning is the process of individuals participating in practice and interacting with others and the environment, it is the process of forming the ability to participate in practical activities and improving the level of socialization [5]." The digital display of ancient paintings can enable the audience to interact with ancient paintings, so as to improve their interest in learning.

In this study, we promote the study of art and history and culture through the construction of interactive media narration [1], and explore the interactive display form of the ancient Ruihe Tu with mid-air natural interaction technology as the carrier. To sum up, this paper puts forward the hypothesis that the application of mid-air natural interaction technology in ancient painting can effectively improve users' interest in learning relevant knowledge.

2 Research Method and Process

In order to prove that the application of mid-air natural interaction technology in ancient painting can effectively improve users' interest in learning historical and cultural knowledge, this study adopts the methods of observation and interview.

2.1 Experiment Materials

The interactive display device used in this experiment is mainly designed for the mid-air natural interaction technology display of the ancient painting Ruihe Tu. Most scholars believe that the painting of auspicious cranes was written by Zhao Ji of the Northern Song Dynasty [6]. This work is 138.2 cm long and 51 cm wide. It is now collected in Liaoning Provincial Museum. "The painting of auspicious cranes" depicts the spectacular scene of cranes hovering over the palace. The painting techniques are exquisite. The cranes in the picture are like clouds and fog, and they are various postures and characteristics. This work can express the author's beautiful expectations for the future of the country.

Based on the famous scholar Collins and others pointed out in Situational Cognition in culture: "knowledge is inseparable from activities, and situational activities are part of knowledge acquisition [5]." We divided the design framework of the work into two parts: visual expression and mid-air natural interaction technology. Our purpose is to present the dynamic elements in ancient paintings in a more direct animation form, and enhance the experiencer's memory of the whole work through the control of the experiencer's body movements. So as to promote the audience's appreciation of traditional art and the acquisition of historical art knowledge.

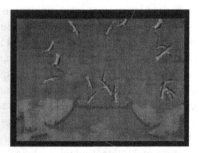

Fig. 1. The prototype was constructed by Unity 3D and C4D.

The mid-air based natural interactive installation Ruihe Tu was designed by unity 3D (see Fig. 1). Kinect was used to capture users' actions so as to control the "crane" in the Ruihe Tu. The cranes in the picture of Ruihe Tu are designed to follow the position of the audience's right hand. When the user lowers his arm, the cranes will stop following and hover freely. After the user steps out of the recognition range of Kinect, the artefact returns to a static state. (see Fig. 2).

Fig. 2. Schematic of the system framework

2.2 Participant Selection and Experiment Design

In this test, 30 undergraduates were selected as the experimental objects, and their learning interests were evaluated from the perspectives of emotional state, concentration and enthusiasm. In order to ensure reliability and validity, all participants had known the Ruihe Tu and its related knowledge before participating in this experiment. In this experiment, the experimental group and the control group were set, with 15 people in each group. Participants in the experimental group experienced the mid-air based natural interactive installation Ruihe Tu according to the usage methods provided above. The participants in the control group experienced the traditional painting display method of ordinary plane display. In this experiment, all participants were tested under the same conditions.

The experiment was conducted in digital media department of a university. The experimental steps are as follows: (1) The researcher explained the purpose and method of the experiment to the participants. (2) Let the two groups of subjects experience the traditional painting display methods of the mid-air based natural interactive installation Ruihe Tu and ordinary plane display respectively. (3) The researcher distributed the manual of art and historical and cultural knowledge related to the Ruihe Tu. (4) The researchers observed the participants' emotional state, concentration and enthusiasm when reading the relevant knowledge manually. (5) After the experiment, the participants in the experimental group were interviewed one-on-one (see Fig. 3).

Fig. 3. One-on-one interviews

3 Results and Analysis

3.1 Discussion on Experimental Results

By observing the experience process of the two groups of participants, it is found that: (1) The participants in the experimental group were more enthusiastic about learning the relevant knowledge of Ruihe Tu. After experiencing the interactive device, all 15 participants actively read the relevant knowledge Manual of Ruihe Tu, and all had a high degree of concentration in the reading process. Among them, five participants raised questions related to the Ruihe Tu and not mentioned in the knowledge manual, and said they would consult relevant materials after the experiment. The participants in this group showed a strong desire to explore during the experiment. (2) In the control group, only 10 of the 15 participants chose to actively read the relevant knowledge manually. The degree of attention in the reading process was not high, and 6 of them only read roughly. The test showed that the use of mid-air natural interaction technology to display ancient paintings could better stimulate the viewer's desire to explore the knowledge related to ancient paintings and improve the user's interest in learning (see Fig. 4).

Fig. 4. Usability test

3.2 Discussion of Survey Results

At the end of the experiment, we selected ten subjects from the experimental group for an interview. At the end of the experiment, we selected 10 subjects from the experimental group for a one-on-one interview. During the interview, each subject discussed the experience of the body feeling Ruihe Tu and the expectation of the interactive display form of ancient painting. According to the value of keyword frequency, the specific results are summarized as follows: (1) More than 90% of respondents said that effective interaction with ancient paintings could improve their desire to learn knowledge related to works. (2) 30% of the respondents said that in the process of interacting with the main body of the picture, they would ignore other details in the picture, resulting in insufficiently detailed observation of the work. (3) All respondents said that in the process of interacting with the works, they all focused on the works and felt the external interference. Most participants believe that mid-air natural interaction technology will be better used in the display of ancient paintings in the future.

4   Conclusion

The observation and interview results show that compared with the subjects experiencing the traditional display painting, the subjects experiencing the mid-air based natural interactive installation have a stronger interest in learning relevant history and culture. There is no significant difference observed in learning interest from the relevant ancient art. Therefore, we intend to conduct the follow-up study for verifying the difference between the mid-air natural interaction and the traditional display form on the long-term memory of users and their learning effect.

References

1. Sun, W.: Research on interactive media narrative. Nanjing Arts Institute (2011)
2. Wang, A., Wang, Z.: Diversified visual presentation of cultural heritage. Packag. Eng. 1–7 (2019)
3. Pallud, J.: Impact of interactive technologies on stimulating learning experiences in a museum. Inf. Manag, 465–478 (2017)
4. Wang, A., Wang, Z.: State of the art on the digital presentation and interaction of culture heritage. J. Zhejiang Univ. (Sci. Ed.) 261–273 (2020)
5. Wei, J., Luo, L.: Study on the design of children's literacy cards with augmented reality. Packag. Eng. (2022)
6. Liu, W.D.: Cranes dancing in the air, morning or evening—interpretions about auspicious cranes. J. Nanjing Arts Inst. (Fine Arts Des.) 112–113 (2004)
7. Jin, S., Min, F., Aynur, K.: Immersive spring morning in the Han Palace: learning traditional Chinese art via virtual reality and multi-touch tabletop. Int. J. Hum.–Comput. Interact. 213–226 (2022)
8. Yan, F.: Digital application of cultural heritage. Art Observ. 19–22 (2018)
9. Liu, Y., Zhang, L.: Innovative applications of multimedia technologies in digital display for intangible cultural heritage. Packag. Eng. 26–30 (2016)

Exploration of Urban Heritage Preferences in Chinese Context Using Computer Vision: An Analytic of Kulangsu International Settlement

Xiaoxu Liang[1]([✉]) [iD] and Guang Cai[2] [iD]

[1] Department of Architecture and Design, Polytechnic University of Turin, Viale Mattioli, 39, 10125 Turin, Italy
Xiaoxu.liang@polito.it
[2] Individualized Interdisciplinary Program, Hong Kong University of Science and Technology, Clear Water Bay, Kowloon, Hong Kong

Abstract. Social media plays a core role in inclusive heritage management and contains multi-potential values to structure the inner connection of stakeholders and express the preferences of users and non-users in urban landscape studies without distinction. However, engaging residents to cultural heritage sites and understanding their preferences through social media have not been well-evaluated and explored in the Chinese context. The article offers a method to understand the residents' preferences by identifying more than two thousand urban-heritage-linked images acquired from the dataset of Weibo. Both Google Cloud Vision detection and manual examination were utilized parallelly to ensure the validity of the result. Little difference was found in the comparison of results between the two judgement methods. The result revealed that residents in Kulangsu have a stronger interest in and concern more about the buildings and nature landscapes other than urban design. The study concludes with two points. First, the analysis of social media data is strongly recommended to be introduced in the decision-making process of urban heritage conservation as a strategy in the post-pandemic period. Second, computer vision can be a trustable tool to present residents' preferences and is worth being widely applied in Chinese urban heritage studies.

Keywords: Image recognition · Chinese urban heritage · Inclusive heritage management · Computer vision · Kulangsu

1 Introduction

Kulangsu is inscribed in the World Cultural Heritage List in 1997 after around ten years of preparation [1, 2]. Located in the Chinese southern coastal area, the Kulangsu island has a 316.2-hectare core zone and 886-hectare buffer zone [3]. The local settlements are formed in the early 20th century under the interweaving of multiple cultures and the long-term colonial history. The unique architectural typology, the Amoy-Deco style, coexisted and merged from the vernacular "red brick house", and various architectural styles from

C. Stephanidis et al. (Eds.): HCII 2022, CCIS 1582, pp. 240–246, 2022.
https://doi.org/10.1007/978-3-031-06391-6_32

Europe, such as Neo-Renaissance, Victorian Gothic, etc. [4, 5]. Getting through World War II and the political turmoil period in China, most of the buildings on Kulangsu were fortunately well-preserved due to the social, political and spatial environment. After the founding of the People's Republic of China in 1949, Xiamen Municipal Government and the Kulangsu District Government took over the buildings and neighbourhoods.

2 Background

Heritage conservation strategies should be designed based on the local situation instead of simply aligning with the global notion [6]. It is worth mentioning that during the last decades, heritage conservation in China is gradually transiting its focus from materiality to sustainable development with significance attached to community participation [7–9]. Effective actions adhering to wider international standards with better consideration of collective memory, the notion of authenticity, identity and the sense of belonging have been taken by China [10, 11]. In addition to the traditional participatory management discussions, scholars are interested in finding out how new forms of engagement with heritage in different cultural contexts are encouraged and enabled by social media [12–14].

Increasing the inclusiveness of cultural heritage conservation requires immense work. The challenges are complex and far different in most cultural contexts [15]. Over the past decade, the incipient collaborative planning and public participation through the internet in China have shown an increasingly vital influence [10, 11]. The Chinese government has tried to employ Information and Communication Technologies (ICTs) to increase the citizen's engagement and thus benefit cultural heritage conservation. Digital application and online communication have gradually become important methods of public consultation and supervision during the Dashilar renewal project [16]. What is more, experts and civic groups utilized social media spontaneously to criticize the large-scale relocation in the government-led regeneration of Beijing's bell and drum tower neighbourhood [17]. With the use of social media, these groups of activists can contest official propositions for the area and make suggestions to care for everyday life and alternative forms of memories that matter to its inhabitants based on scientific arguments [11, 17].

During the pandemic, face-to-face workshops and interviews are no longer the main approaches to listening to the voice from the bottom up. Many scholars contribute to enhancing community engagement by considering different stakeholders' opinions and experiences in Kulangsu using ICTs. Lin proposed an application design model involving Augmented Reality technology to improve the users' experience while following a guided tour [2]. The texts and images from social media posts have been used to evaluate the participatory level of the locals [18]. A pan island 3D digital model is used in the impact assessment and management system to assist the decision-making in the heritage conservation process [5]. However, in face of massive amounts of data, manual classification lack efficiency in support of studies and practices on people's urban and cultural landscape heritage preferences [19].

The study comparing the result on landscape preferences between computer vision algorithm and on-site-interview survey in the selected urban-proximate parks of Boulder,

Colorado, USA, is impressive [20]. A qualitative analysis of urban landscape perceptions in Berlin was conducted by a group of researchers with the use of computer vision and machine learning technologies [21]. Using computer vision algorithms technologies, such as Google Cloud Vision, to analyze social media photographs are becoming an important approach to promoting the values of destinations [22]. More than 20,000 images taken in the Camargue region in Southern France are collected from social media (Flickr) and analyzed by Google Cloud Vision [23]. After examining an accurate manual classification of more than 20,000 photographs from Singapore, Richards and Tunçer concluded that the result exported from accessing Google Cloud Vision is trustable and saved around 170 h of manual work [19]. However, a discussion and examination on the possibility of applying computer vision to understanding residents' preferences are still needed in the Chinese context.

3 Method

The whole process can be divided into three parts: data collection, data analysis and data examination.

To collect a sufficient amount of dataset, Web Scraping tools were used to extract data from targeted social media Weibo. The search expression was set according to urban heritage components such as historic city, traditional architecture, and the time window was set in the year 2020. Local residents, as our targeted research group, were selected by an additional restriction on personal address. This process was coded in Python. Multithreading and multiple requests methods were used to break the restriction of scraping set by Weibo. In this process, more than 1500 original Weibo posts were acquired, of which 285 posts are attached with images. Repetitive images with highly similar contents were removed by resizing and matching. Also, images with different sizes and minor differences, such as images with watermarks, were considered the same. Eventually, 1931 valid images from 2197 raw images were obtained.

Google Cloud Vision (GCV) API, an open CV application programming interface trained by Google company and widely applied in content-based image retrieval (CBIR), can be used for further analysis of the images [24]. It can also improve efficiency and give rather objective, exact and rich labelling results. Google Cloud Vision will give multiple possible labels and corresponding scores to each image. The score stands for confidence, ranging from 0 to 1. The closer the score to 1, the more trustable the label is [20]. With the use of Google Cloud Vision, 19260 labels with a score over 0.5 by default were generated from those images, and they could be merged into 1082 different kinds of labels such as building, plant, window, house. To understand the users' focus and preference, labels were sorted by count, picked up and classified into different categories. Therefore, identifying the literal meaning of each label and categorizing them are crucial in this process. When picking up, strongly irrelevant labels were picked out, and when categorizing, the classification of labels and the formulation of selection criteria were based on the different scales and constituent elements of the space: city, architecture, landscape. With this method, users who are interested in different aspects and hierarchies of urban heritage can be ascertained. As a result, the top 10 labels were selected as research objects, which covers 4277 labels of all 19260 labels (about 22%).

The final step was to manually examine the previous outcome by comparing it with Google Cloud Vision's result. To calculate the accuracy, two volunteers, one architectural professional and the other non-professional, were invited to participate in the examination to test the consistency of the images and matching labels. By doing so, the influence caused by educational background would be excluded. All images with the elected labels mentioned before were checked.

4 Result

The labels obtained through CV image recognition are roughly divided into two categories: urban and cultural heritage related and irrelevant, and the labels of related parts are further classified as shown in Table 1. The outcome shows that the overall concerns of residents on the architectural level are significantly higher than the city and landscape level. Interestingly, the most rated labels Building, Window, Facade, Architecture, House, and Interior design are all recognized as a certain aspect of buildings and architecture design. 805 images are marked with the label Building, which ranks as the first place in the list. While on the landscape category, the label Natural Landscape appears only 116 times which is barely 13% of Building.

Table 1. The image recognition analysis result and manual examination comparison

Label category	Label name	Total number	Candidate A (professional)	Candidate B (non-professional)	Average accuracy
Architectural level	Building	805	795	797	98.88%
	Window	407	395	388	96.19%
	Facade	230	228	227	98.91%
	Architecture	156	155	142	95.19%
	House	148	144	144	97.30%
	Interior design	133	132	129	98.12%
City level	Urban design	254	229	250	94.29%
	City	228	196	219	91.01%
	Neighborhood	127	126	123	98.03%
Landscape level	Natural landscape	116	113	111	96.55%

Seeing the result from the two testers, candidate A and candidate B shows just slightly difference on agreements with GCV analysis. The diverse reaction may result from the different degree of professional knowledge on the selected labels' definition. For example, the label Neighborhood for an architect means an urban settlement or complex, while for people from other occupation it means the relationship and memory with neighbors and other local communities. Judging from the average accuracy, the results of the GCV algorithm are highly consistent with the results of manual inspection by more than 90%. Eight out of ten labels even reached at a consistency at 95%. The label detection at the city level is relatively controversial, and the GCV false positive rate is slightly higher at 6% and 9%.

5 Discussion

Considering diverse values such as social, aesthetic, age, historic, economic, scientific, political, and ecological values could be embedded in heritage assets [25], it is necessary to conduct a comprehensive community-based survey to get rid of the current dictatorship dominated by the standard expert-based studies on urban heritage's material forms. The use of social media can add up knowledge on daily encounters with the historic urban landscape and on heritage assets and places that are neglected by experts.

Image annotation is largely operated manually in the cultural heritage conservation field, which is widely criticized for its low efficiency and the uncontrollable subjective examining criteria and could lead to less trustable authenticity of research results [26]. To make up for this shortcoming, the applicability of the GCV label recognition function to the field of cultural heritage protection was tested. After testing by two participants, GCV's identification images and labels were confirmed to be highly fit and accurate. However, the identified part of the image is not necessarily the subject content of the image, nor does it necessarily represent the subject of the image and the focus of the publisher. Therefore, the method can be improved on this basis to be used more widely in cultural heritage protection in the future.

However, some limitations appear in this study. Firstly, Google Cloud Vision is a platform based on English. The detected labels should be well-localized and translated into Chinese. Some language and cultural background barriers emerge in the practical process, for example, the labels namely Building, and Architecture are both translated as Jianzhu indiscriminately. It forces researchers and professionals to find a better way to investigate the utilization method of those two labels in the Chinese context. Secondly, the labels returned from Google Cloud Vision API are disorganized and most of them are not urban-heritage relevant ones. In a large extent, a personalized machine learning process is needed to apply in the future researches by training the CV tools according to needs.

6 Conclusion

In cultural heritage conservation, the use of social media can add up knowledge on daily encounters with the historic urban landscape and on heritage assets and places that are neglected by experts [13]. Therefore, combining traditional surveys and social media would increase the inclusiveness of the cultural heritage.

It is highly recommended to introduce the analysis of social media data when making decisions on urban heritage conservation as a strategy after the pandemic. What is more, computer vision can be a trustable tool to present residents' preferences and can be widely applied in Chinese urban heritage studies. The information extracted from images would be useful for the experts since it integrates folksonomies generated from tagging into their classification models. This would create a more collaborative and inclusive approach to agreeing on "what to protect" for the future generations.

References

1. Qian, Y.: From colonial veranda style to "Amoy Deco"-the evolution of contemporary Verandah architecture in Kulangsu. Arch. J. 108–111 (2011)
2. Lin, F., Chen, F., Zhu, M.: User experience centered application design of multivariate landscape in Kulangsu, Xiamen. In: Soares, M.M., Rosenzweig, E., Marcus, A. (eds.) HCII 2021. LNCS, vol. 12780, pp. 43–59. Springer, Cham (2021). https://doi.org/10.1007/978-3-030-78224-5_4
3. UNESCO: Kulangsu, a Historic International Settlement. https://whc.unesco.org/en/list/1541
4. Qian, Y.: The early development of Kulangsu before the middle of the 19th century and the development of original settlement and traditional architecture. J. Gulangyu Stud. 02, 1–33 (2020)
5. Yan, S.: HUL and conservation of the historic city of Kulangsu: a scoping case. Hist. Environ. Policy Pract. 9, 376–388 (2018). https://doi.org/10.1080/17567505.2018.1530495
6. Harrison, R.: Understanding the Politics of Heritage. Manchester University Press (2009)
7. Svensson, M.: Heritage 2.0: maintaining affective engagements with the local heritage in Taishun. In: Svensson, M., Maags, C. (eds.) Chinese Heritage in the Making, pp. 269–292. Amsterdam University Press, Amsterdam (2018)
8. Verdini, G., Frassoldati, F., Nolf, C.: Reframing China's heritage conservation discourse. Learning by testing civic engagement tools in a historic rural village. Int. J. Heritage Stud. 23, 317–334 (2017). https://doi.org/10.1080/13527258.2016.1269358
9. Liang, X.: Participatory management for cultural heritage: social media and Chinese urban landscape. In: Stephanidis, C., Antona, M. (eds.) HCII 2020. CCIS, vol. 1226, pp. 300–307. Springer, Cham (2020). https://doi.org/10.1007/978-3-030-50732-9_40
10. Cheng, Y.: Collaborative planning in the network: consensus seeking in urban planning issues on the Internet—the case of China: Planning Theory (2013). https://doi.org/10.1177/147309 5213499655
11. Deng, Z., Lin, Y., Zhao, M., Wang, S.: Collaborative planning in the new media age: the Dafo Temple controversy. China Cities 45, 41–50 (2015). https://doi.org/10.1016/j.cities. 2015.02.006
12. Giaccardi, E.: Heritage and Social Media: Understanding Heritage in a Participatory Culture. Routledge, Abingdon (2012)
13. Ginzarly, M., Pereira Roders, A., Teller, J.: Mapping historic urban landscape values through social media. J. Cult. Herit. 36, 1–11 (2019). https://doi.org/10.1016/j.culher.2018.10.002
14. Kitchin, R., Dodge, M.: Code/Space: Software and Everyday Life. MIT Press, Cambridge (2011)
15. Riva Sanseverino, E., Riva Sanseverino, R., Anello, E.: A cross-reading approach to smart city: a european perspective of chinese smart cities. Smart Cities 1, 26–52 (2018). https://doi. org/10.3390/smartcities1010003
16. Fu, Z., Bu, Y.: Constructing the research model of beijing neighborhood through the living lab method. In: Rau, P.-L. (ed.) CCD 2016. LNCS, vol. 9741, pp. 527–539. Springer, Cham (2016). https://doi.org/10.1007/978-3-319-40093-8_52
17. Bideau, F.G., Yan, H.: Historic urban landscape in beijing: the Gulou project and its contested memories. In: Maags, C., Svensson, M. (eds.) Chinese Heritage in the Making, pp. 93–118. Amsterdam University Press, Amsterdam (2018)

18. Liang, X., Hua, N., Zhang, Y.: Chinese social media (Weibo) as a tool to advance participatory management during the pandemic period. In: Yang, X.-S., Sherratt, S., Dey, N., Joshi, A. (eds.) ICICT 2021. LNNS, vol. 235, pp. 983–993. Springer, Singapore (2022). https://doi.org/10.1007/978-981-16-2377-6_89

19. Richards, D.R., Tunçer, B.: Using image recognition to automate assessment of cultural ecosystem services from social media photographs. Ecosyst. Serv. **31**, 318–325 (2018). https://doi.org/10.1016/j.ecoser.2017.09.004

20. Wilkins, E.J., Van Berkel, D., Zhang, H., Dorning, M.A., Beck, S.M., Smith, J.W.: Promises and pitfalls of using computer vision to make inferences about landscape preferences: evidence from an urban-proximate park system. Landsc. Urban Plan. **219**, 104315 (2022). https://doi.org/10.1016/j.landurbplan.2021.104315

21. Tian, H., Han, Z., Xu, W., Liu, X., Qiu, W., Li, W.: Evolution of historical urban landscape with computer vision and machine learning: a case study of Berlin. J. Digit. Landsc. Arch. 436–451 (2021). https://doi.org/10.14627/537705039

22. Taecharungroj, V., Mathayomchan, B.: Traveller-generated destination image: analysing Flickr photos of 193 countries worldwide. Int. J. Tour. Res. (2021). https://doi.org/10.1002/JTR.2415

23. Gosal, A., Geijzendorffer, I.R., Václavík, T., Poulin, B., Ziv, G.: Using social media, machine learning and natural language processing to map multiple recreational beneficiaries. Ecosyst. Serv. **38** (2019). https://doi.org/10.1016/j.ecoser.2019.100958

24. Chen, S.-H., Chen, Y.-H.: A content-based image retrieval method based on the google cloud vision API and WordNet. In: Nguyen, N.T., Tojo, S., Nguyen, L.M., Trawiński, B. (eds.) ACIIDS 2017. LNCS (LNAI), vol. 10191, pp. 651–662. Springer, Cham (2017). https://doi.org/10.1007/978-3-319-54472-4_61

25. Da Silva, A.M.T.P., Roders, A.R.P.: Cultural heritage management and heritage (impact) assessments. In: Proceedings of the Joint CIB W070, W092 & TG72 International Conference on Facilities Management, Procurement Systems and Public Private Partnership, 23–25 January 2012, Cape Town, South Africa (2012)

26. Hanbury, A.: A survey of methods for image annotation. J. Vis. Lang. Comput. **19**, 617–627 (2008). https://doi.org/10.1016/j.jvlc.2008.01.002

A Location-Based Mobile Guide for Gamified Exploration, Audio Narrative and Visitor Social Interaction in Cultural Exhibitions

Andreas Nikolarakis[✉], Panayiotis Koutsabasis[iD], and Damianos Gavalas[iD]

Department of Product and Systems Design Engineering, University of the Aegean,
84100 Syros, Greece
{dpsd15083,kgp,dgavalas}@aegean.gr

Abstract. Mobile guides comprise a valuable tool for cultural site visitors, as they may engage audiences in active exploration that enriches the cultural experience. This paper presents the design, development, and evaluation of a mobile guide app that features gamified exploration with exhibit recognition, audio narratives and co-located visitor encounters for a small-scale indoors exhibition space. The mobile guide-mediated experience is designed for selected exhibits and, at the same time, sustains a balance of user attention between the physical exhibition space and digital interactions. Self-guided visitors engage in locating and scanning exhibits with their mobile phone's camera in order to unlock audio narratives. A "meet-and-greet" activity based on a favorite exhibit selection has been introduced to encourage social interaction between visitors. The mobile app has been developed for Android OS and makes use of ARCore functionality to enable exhibit recognition; the app has been published in Google Play. Findings from empirical field evaluation with expert users reveal a very positive user experience in which visitors engage with the mobile guide and can be more attentive to various items of the exhibition.

Keywords: Mobile application · Cultural exhibition · Location-based · Image recognition · ARCore · Gamification · Storytelling · Social interaction

1 Introduction

An audience-centered approach for the curation of cultural exhibitions requires cultural heritage institutions to be sensitive to the needs of museum visitors throughout their user experience (UX). For a long time, mobile guide apps have been employed by many museums and cultural institutions to enhance visitor UX. Mobile guides have the role of a 'mediator' between the visitor (user) and the cultural content, and therefore their design must be carefully considered so that it fits the purposes of cultural institutions and their audience. In the last few years mobile guide apps are often enriched with storytelling techniques, gamification patterns and state-of-the-art immersive technologies, such as Augmented Reality (AR), to enhance visitor engagement and learning.

C. Stephanidis et al. (Eds.): HCII 2022, CCIS 1582, pp. 247–255, 2022.
https://doi.org/10.1007/978-3-031-06391-6_33

The design of mobile guides for cultural exhibitions considers several dimensions audience-related aspects, such as: visitors' profiles, anticipated visitor navigation within the space, anticipated time of exhibit examination; as well as the exhibition, such as: the exhibition theme, the artifacts' forms and sizes, possible semantic connections among exhibits, various aspects of the exhibition identity, etc. Our work is about the design of mobile audio guides in small-scale, "contextual exhibitions" [13], in which the artifacts are complementary to some accompanying informative, comparative and explicatory material, which determines their reading and interpretation.

Specifically, this paper presents the design, development, and empirical evaluation of a mobile guide app that features (i) gamified exploration with exhibit recognition, (ii) pre-recorded audio narratives, and (iii) co-located visitor encounters, for a smallscale indoors exhibition space. This exhibition space is under the direction of the Kyveli Institute[1], a theatrical cultural institution based in the island of Syros, Greece, and comprises a small-scale, indoors gallery of square displays that feature compositions of artifacts about art, theater, history and literature.

2   Related Work

Interactive systems that offer guided tour experiences in cultural heritage contexts act as 'mediators' between visitors and exhibits [3]. These systems range from traditional audio guides, multimedia mobile guide apps to mobile location-based games. Nowadays, a significant number of cultural institutions provide mobile guide applications that are either own-developed or third party (e.g. Smartify[2]). The provision of mobile guide apps usually relies on Bring-Your-Own-Device (BYOD) practice [9].

The explorative approach has become a prevalent aspect of the user experience (UX) shaped by many mobile guide apps as it encourages visitors to actively explore exhibitions and focus freely on what they are interested in. Storytelling techniques and gamification patterns are usually implemented not only to increase engagement, but also for navigation purposes [10]. A commonly used gamification pattern, which embraces active exploration, is the treasure-hunt model [2, 10].

The primary content delivery form in mobile guide apps is audio narrative, which is often accompanied with multimedia content (images, video, animations etc.), and these days, with advanced technologies, such as Augmented Reality (AR) [1, 5]. Mobile guide apps offer a single-user experience, which might discourage social interactions between visitors [3, 6, 8]. Some relevant interactive systems have addressed this by applying 'information gap' techniques and stimulating discussion among visitors with the aid of a human facilitator [1].

---

[1] Kyveli Institute. https://kyveli.eu/en/home/.

[2] Smartify. https://smartify.org/.

3 Design and Implementation of the Kyveli App

3.1 Contextual Research

Contextual research examines the ways in which the Kyveli Institute and its exhibition space is organized and operated. The exhibition space hosts a permanent and a temporary exhibition. Its main exhibits are custom-made square showcases (twelve and eight respectively), which comprise compositions of smaller artifacts. Other items in that room (e.g. theatrical costumes, art paintings, antiques etc.) play mostly a decorative role.

The principal methods employed during the contextual research phase involved observation of visitors in the exhibition space and interviews with the director of the Kyveli Institute. Field observation took place repeatedly during guided tours aiming to obtain detailed understanding on issues like: how the tour is formed, visitors' behavior during their tour and, more broadly, the identification of positives and negatives in the overall visitor experience.

To complement our understanding, a series of semi-structured interviews were conducted with the director of the Kyveli Institute, who is also in charge of curating exhibitions and providing guided tours. The main conclusions were related to visitors' motivations, the method of touring the exhibition space and exploring the possibilities for the technological enhancement of the tour as well as the relevant restrictions.

3.2 Conceptual Design

The conceptual design of the mobile guide app is depicted in Fig. 1. The main elements are:

Gamified Exploration of the Temporary Exhibition. Temporary exhibits are distributed within the exhibition space. Following a gamified explorative approach, visitors are challenged to search for "partially hidden" exhibits. Once they find an exhibit, they are prompted to either scan it with their mobile device's camera or to answer a three-choice visual quiz about nearby items (Fig. 4: "How many paper craft children dressed in Tsolias costume are there in the display above?"). In the former case, the mobile app is able to recognize exhibits using ARCore Image Recognition functionality; in the latter, the app simply checks whether the user answered the quiz correctly. In both cases, after the validation, the user unlocks the respective audio narrative.

Audio Narrative and Multimedia Content. The mobile app communicates the interpretive material mostly in the form of audio narrative, authored and voiced by the person in charge of exhibitions and tours. For every exhibit, the audio narrative is accompanied with background music as well as multimedia content: the text of the narrative, photographs of the exhibits or their showcase, and explanatory captions as appropriate.

Visitor Social Interaction. Taking into account that museum visits are essentially social experiences [4, 8], we made use of some design patterns for co-located social interaction discussed in [7]. Visitors are encouraged to select their favorite temporary exhibit, towards the end of their tour, and "meet-and-greet" another visitor at the exhibition space with the same choice. After successful verification of their physical presence in front of the common favorite exhibit, a video about the history of Kyveli Institute is unlocked.

4   Software Architecture and Implementation

The Kyveli Mobile Guide App has been developed with Android Studio using Java and Android Architecture Components. Furthermore, ARCore[3] (Google's platform for building AR experiences) has been integrated with "Augmented Images API" to enable exhibit recognition. The online database that facilitates visitors' social encounters based on their favorite exhibit was implemented with Google Sheets web service enhanced with Google App Scripts (a cloud-based scripting platform).

The mobile guide app has been developed based on the Model-View-ViewModel (MVVM) software architecture pattern (Fig. 2) recommended by Google[4]. This software design pattern effectively manages data exchange between User-Interface (View) and local data source(s) (Data Models); it takes advantage of Android native libraries (e.g. ROOM Database, LiveData); and it is fully compatible with the activity lifecycle. The final version of the app is available through the Google Play Store[5]. It works on mobile devices with Android 7.0 Nougat (API 24) or later (Figs. 3, 4 and 5).

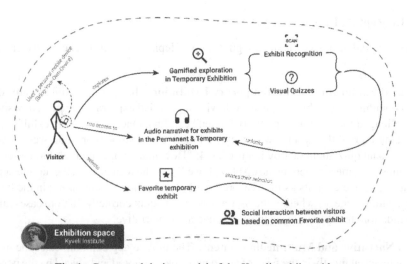

Fig. 1. Conceptual design model of the Kyveli mobile guide app

---

[3] Google Developers. ARCore. https://developers.google.com/ar.

[4] Android Developers. Guide to app architecture (last accessed 2021/12/09), http://web.archive.org/web/20210912072206/https://developer.android.com/jetpack/guide.

[5] Google Play. Kyveli mobile guide app. https://play.google.com/store/apps/details?id=com.cyb ele.application.

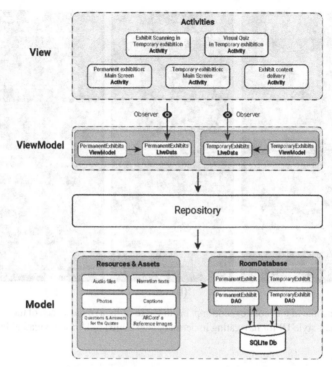

Fig. 2. Visualization of the Model-View-ViewModel (MVVM) pattern of the Kyveli mobile guide app

Fig. 3. Screenshots of the mobile guide app. From left to right: a) main screen of the mobile guide app; b) a keypad-style UI for navigating in permanent exhibits; c) UI for navigating in temporary exhibits.

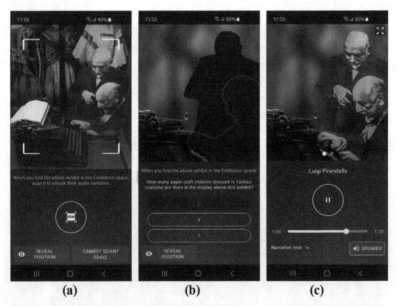

Fig. 4. Screenshots of the mobile guide app. From left to right: a) exhibit scanning & recognition screen; b) visual quiz screen; c) exhibit content delivery screen with audio player.

Fig. 5. Photos from evaluation with experts at the exhibition space of the Kyveli Institute.

5 Evaluation

5.1 Methods and Participants

We have conducted a formative empirical evaluation in the field [5] with the participation of nine (average age 42.5 years; four women) experts: three HCI researchers, three design engineering graduates and three cultural heritage professionals. The goal was to uncover issues related to usability, functionality, cultural content and the overall UX of the mobile guide app. The protocol of retrospective probing was employed, and thus researchers did not intervene, except upon participants' requests. Quantitative data included user analytics and participants' responses to the User Experience Questionnaire (UEQ) [11, 12], while qualitative data were findings from observation and comments.

5.2 Results

Participants used the mobile guide app at their own pace to navigate in both the Permanent and the Temporary exhibition (average time ~ 29 min). In general, the guiding experience was characterized as very interesting, while almost all participants expressed their appreciation for the expressive audio narrative. Some of them, also, highlighted that the UI design is consistent with the aesthetics of the exhibition space.

Feedback was mostly about minor usability issues (e.g. reveal position button had not been noticed on time). Concerning most frequent UX issues, 5/9 reported that it was time-consuming to locate some temporary exhibits and 2/9 felt temporarily embarrassed, when they were about to "meet-and-greet" another visitor, who might be a stranger.

The responses from the UEQ questionnaire (>0.8 for all dimensions, Fig. 6) reveal a very positive and captivating user experience [11], in which visitors engage with the mobile guide app and can be more attentive of various items of the exhibition.

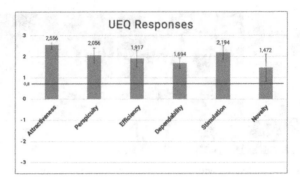

Fig. 6. Responses to the user experience questionnaire (UEQ).

6 Summary and Conclusions

This paper presented the design, implementation and empirical evaluation of a mobile guide for a small-size conceptual exhibition. The mobile guide app combines gamified exploration with exhibit recognition, pre-recorded audio narrative, and co-located visitor encounters. The app is fully developed with Android native technologies and it is available from Google Play.

The design of the Kyveli mobile guide app takes into account several aspects of the exhibition theme, space and artifacts, as well as user needs and requirements. It allows visitors to examine cultural exhibits 'freely' based on what attracts them the most. The feature of visual exhibit recognition (through the mobile device camera) adds an engaging challenge to the visitor UX, who are incited to explore the exhibition space in a playful manner. The interpretive content that has been authored and voiced by the person in charge of exhibitions and tours plays an equally important role to the UX. Last but not least, visitors have the chance to "meet-and-greet" others via selecting their favorite exhibit, which promotes the social dimension of museum visits.

We expect that future research in mobile guides for cultural exhibitions will take into account the requirements of the cultural institutions and their audiences in creative new ways that combine the affordances of mobile technologies with cultural content and digital media. Additionally, innovative design approaches, methods and interaction patterns for mobile apps should arise from the cooperative work of cultural heritage professionals and interaction designers that will jointly consider the types or styles of cultural exhibitions and advancements in mobile and other interactive technologies.

References

1. Badzmierowska, K., O Hoisin, N., Kopetzky, K. et al.: D3. 9–Pilot experience (s) based on platform final release (2019). https://emotiveproject.eu/wp-content/uploads/2019/12/EMO TIVE_D3.9_PilotExperiencesPrototypesFinal_v1.0.pdf. Accessed 17 Dec 2021
2. Damala, A., Hornecker, E., van der Vaart, M., van Dijk, D., Ruthven, I.: The Loupe: tangible augmented reality for learning to look at Ancient Greek art. Mediter. Archaeol. Archaeom. **16**(5), 73–85 (2016)

3. Economou, M., Meintani, E.: Promising beginnings? Evaluating museum mobile phone apps. In: Proceedings of the Re-thinking Technology in Museums: Emerging Experience Conference, Limerick, Ireland, pp. 87–101 (2011)
4. Falk, J.H., Dierking, L.D.: Learning from Museums: Visitor Experiences and the Making of Meaning. AltaMira Press, Walnut Creek (2000)
5. Koutsabasis, P., et al.: Field playtesting with experts' constructive interaction: an evaluation method for mobile games for cultural heritage. In: 2021 IEEE Conference on Games (CoG), pp. 1–9. IEEE, August 2021
6. Lanir, J., Kuflik, T., Dim, E., Wecker, A.J., Stock, O.: The influence of location-aware mobile guide on museum visitors' behavior. Interact. Comput. **25**(6), 443–460 (2013)
7. Paasovaara, S., Jarusriboonchai, P., Olsson, T.: Understanding collocated social interaction between Pokémon GO players. In: Proceedings of the 16th International Conference on Mobile and Ubiquitous Multimedia, pp. 151–163 (2017)
8. Perry, S., Roussou, M., Mirashrafi, S.S., Katifori, A., McKinney, S.: Shared digital experiences supporting collaborative meaning-making at heritage sites. In: Lewi, H., Smith, W., vom Lehn, D., Cooke, S. (eds.) The Routledge International Handbook of New Digital Practices in Galleries, Libraries, Archives, Museums and Heritage Sites, London, p. 144 (2019)
9. Petrelli, D., O'Brien, S.: Phone vs. tangible in museums: a comparative study. In: Proceedings of the 2018 CHI Conference on Human Factors in Computing Systems (CHI 2018). ACM, New York (2018)
10. Roussou, M., Katifori, A.: Flow, staging, wayfinding, personalization: evaluating user experience with mobile museum narratives. Multimodal Technol. Interact. **2**, 32 (2018). https://doi.org/10.3390/mti2020032
11. Schrepp, M.: User experience questionnaire handbook. All you need to know to apply the UEQ successfully in your project (2019). https://www.ueq-online.org/Material/Handbook.pdf. Accessed 10 Feb 2022
12. Schrepp, M., Hinderks, A., Thomaschewski, J.: Construction of a benchmark for the user experience questionnaire (UEQ). Int. J. Interact. Multimedia Artif. Intell. **4**(4), 40–44 (2017)
13. Vergo, P.: The reticent object. In: Vergo, P. (ed.) The New Museology, pp. 41–59. Reaktion Books, London (1989)

A System for Generating Interactive Japanese Traditional Comedy Using Smart Speaker

Shingo Otsuka[1]([⊠]) and Akiyo Nadamoto[2]

[1] Kanagawa Institute of Technology, Atsugi, Kanagawa, Japan
otsuka@ic.kanagawa-it.ac.jp
[2] Konan University, Kobe, Japan
nadamoto@konan-u.ac.jp

Abstract. Currently, the concept of Quality of Life (QOL) is in the limelight. For the elderly, attention is focused on efforts to extend one's "healthy life" expectancy. As for young people, attention is focused on removing the accumulated stress of living in a society where life can be difficult for young people. In response to these demands, local governments are making various efforts, and in particular, the solution of "laughing" is attracting attention. "Laughter" leads to improved respiratory health, stabilized blood pressure, and reduced stress, and anyone can easily apply this solution. However, this requires time and cost, such as the need to prepare a comedian. In this paper, we aim to improve QOL for the elderly and young people by building a system that allows users to easily access opportunities for "laughter." Specifically, we propose a system that automatically generates comic scenarios and easily presents audio media while interacting with humans using smart speakers.

Keywords: Smart speaker · Japanese Traditional Comedy (Manzai) · Support for the elderly and young people

1 Introduction

The average human age is rising with the development of medical care in Japan. On the other hand, the difference between life expectancy (i.e., death) and "healthy life" expectancy was 8.84 years for men and 12.35 years for women in 2016. Healthy life expectancy is the period during which an individual can perform daily activities and lead a healthy life. If this difference widens as the average life expectancy increases in the future, there are concerns not only about health problems but also about the impact on households due to increased medical and care costs. On the other hand, young people who support the elderly are constantly stressed due to the feeling of constraint and thus feel like giving up on the super-aging society. As a result, the number of people with mental illness is increasing, and the number of people who cannot think and act on their own is also increasing.

C. Stephanidis et al. (Eds.): HCII 2022, CCIS 1582, pp. 256–261, 2022.
https://doi.org/10.1007/978-3-031-06391-6_34

Under these circumstances, Quality of Life (QOL) is in the limelight, and attention is being focused on efforts to extend healthy life expectancy for the elderly and to support young people so they can live with as little stress as possible. Among the proposed solutions, "laughing" is attracting attention because it leads to reduced stress and anyone can easily apply it. Japan has begun to enter a super-aging society, so maintaining the health of both the elderly and young people is extremely important for society. In addition, with the recent development of AI and robot technology, people are becoming less uncomfortable about the integration of computers with humans and society.

In this paper, we purpose a way to improve the QOL for the elderly and young people. Specifically, we propose a system that automatically generates Japanese traditional comedy and presents the generated audio media while interacting with humans using a smart speaker.

2 Related Works

Research on laughter and health in Japan has attracted increasing interest since the 1970s, when a well-known report on laugh therapy was presented by journalist Norman Cousins [1]. This paper stated that patients with severe pain and the inability to sleep well could improve their situation by watching TV shows and laughing.

On the other hand, it is necessary to "remove anxiety" to support the rehabilitation of young people with mental illness. It is important to find the cause of anxiety through counseling and to provide effective treatment. Regarding Pokemon-loving mental illness, many cases have been reported in which the Pokemon GO game made it possible leave one's residence voluntarily, which then alleviated this condition's symptoms.

Numerous studies have presented jokes and humor using robots. Klaus et al. [2] proposed a real-time adaptation of a robotic joke teller based on the human social signals of facial smiles and vocal laughs. They implemented an entertainment robot shown to learn jokes that were in accordance with the user's preferences but without incorporating explicit feedback. Knight et al. [3] proposed Robot Theater as a novel framework to develop and evaluate the interaction capabilities of embodied machines. Vilk et al. [4] built a robotic stand-up comedian, which performed comedy in real environments. They concluded that the timing of robot joke-telling markedly improved the audience response. Katevas et al. [5] developed humanoid robots to perform stand-up comedy. They demonstrated the manner in which a humanoid robot could be useful by probing the complex social signals that contribute to the live-performance experience. For this study, we specifically examined the easily understandable and funny comedy genre of *traditional Japanese Manzai*, and we assessed a new style of observing an automatically generated *Manzai* scenario.

3   Automatic Generation of Manzai Script

3.1   What is Manzai?

Manzai, a traditional Japanese comedy genre, is usually presented by a duo of characters engaged in humorous dialogue. Generally, each of the *Manzai* characters takes up one of two distinct roles: *Boke* or *Tsukkomi*. The *Boke* makes a statement causing a misunderstanding, forming a funny remark or a joke, which elicits laughter from the audience. The *Tsukkomi* then points out the mistakes and misunderstandings made by the *Boke* and provides opportunities for humor. In our system, when a user inputs a keyword, the system creates a *Manzai* scenario based on web news related to that keyword. There are three parts of each act: "Introduction," "Body," and "Conclusion" (i.e., punch line). In these times, web news usually contains bad news, such as political discord and accidents. However, bad news should not be used for *Manzai* because *Manzai* is comedy. We set "stop" words such as "death" and "disaster" to prevent the generation of an inappropriate *Manzai* scenario. Such subjects are seldom the subject of appropriate humor.

3.2   Proposed System

We are building a system called "*Manzai* script automatic generation system" [6]. This system automatically generates a *Manzai* script from related news for the "theme" entered by the user. The script is composed of an introduction, a body, and a conclusion, and it is possible to easily create a wide variety of comic story material. We also propose a method to automatically generate a single *Manzai* script from multiple articles published in the headline news of a web news site [7]. In this case, the user only needs to say, "headline news," and no theme needs to be input.

First, there is the "Introduction" part. This part provides the opening greetings, the first laughter, and the topic for this story. The system starts with familiar topics related to the subject and then reads the title of an article to connect to the "Body" part. Next, the system executes the "Body" part, which is the main axis of *Manzai*. The flow of current affairs made in the "Introduction" part is inflated with this material and blurred. The "Body" part expands the story made in the "Introduction" part with the *Boke*. For the *Boke* of our system, we use "Wordplay *Boke*," which makes a mistake in reading that is shown by making a sound similar to a certain word from the database. In addition, this system can function as the uncertain "Nori *Tsukkomi*," where subtle timing is used to evoke temporary pondering of the *Boke*'s statement before correcting it. In this case, the role of *Tsukkomi* is synchronized once with the content of the *Boke*, and then the corrective *Tsukkomi* is performed again. Furthermore, "Conflict *Boke*" can be created to extract synonyms that are in conflict. Consequently, the "Body" part is the longest in the entire *Manzai*, and most of the *Boke*'s remarks are inserted using the above technique.

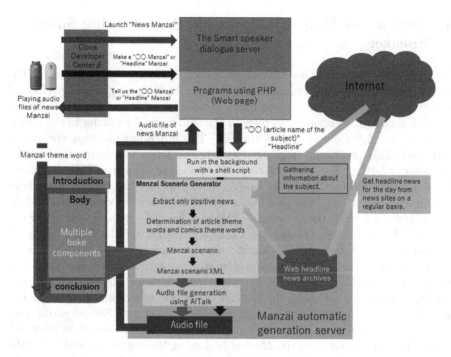

Fig. 1. System for Generating Interactive Japanese Traditional Comedy

Finally, the "Conclusion" (i.e., punch line) part presents a summary and a last laugh, and our method uses a riddle for the "Conclusion" part. The method prepares a format in advance using the riddle style of "Why is A like B?" and then "Because C(C')!". In the system, part A is used as input from current affairs, and homonyms C(C') and noun B are created from the information in the dictionary and Wikipedia. In the actual constructed system, the user inputs words such as "soccer" and "politics" as the "theme," and the system generates the *Manzai* script as an XML file.

In the case of creating a script using headline news, first, the headline news of the day is extracted in advance. Next, negative articles not suitable for the *Manzai* are removed from those articles, and the method selects the news articles to be converted into the *Manzai* scripts. Finally, the *Manzai* script is generated using the subject words of the entire headline news and the subject words of each news article. As a result, it is possible to produce a dialogue using the *Manzai* theme words, and, moreover, it is possible to make the flow of the *Manzai* story consistent.

4   Interactive *Manzai* Generation System using Smart Speaker

An outline of our interactive *Manzai* generation system is shown in Fig. 1. The smart speaker used in the system is LINE Clova. Skill development is performed using the "Clova Developer Center β," provided by LINE Clova. In order to activate a skill, it is necessary to register the skill name for talking to the Clova, and here the skill name is "News *Manzai*." The program runs when the skill is activated. This program is registered in advance when registering the skill by accessing a URL. This time, we created a program using the PHP language. When a user tells the Clova to "launch a news *Manzai*," the Clova gives a brief explanation. After that, the user issues one of the following commands: "Make a xxx *Manzai* (xxx is theme word)," "Make a headline *Manzai*," or "Play the *Manzai*." When the user commands "Make a xxx *Manzai*," the *Manzai* script is generated in XML format by executing a script that generates a *Manzai* with the theme of "xxx" in the *Manzai* automatic generation server. Based on this file, it is converted to an audio file using AITalk, which is synthetic speech reading software. In addition, the *Manzai* automatic generation server regularly acquires headline news. Therefore, it is possible to generate a *Manzai* script from the latest headline news when the user commands "make a headline *Manzai*." Then, the user can listen to the *Manzai* by issuing the user command "Play the *Manzai*," after which the system downloads the generated audio file from the *Manzai* automatic generation server and plays this audio.

In this way, the user can create a *Manzai* and listen to it by simply speaking with the Clova. As a result, even elderly people can easily listen to their favorite *Manzai* without using a smartphone or PC.

5   Conclusion

We propose a system that automatically generates a *Manzai* script and an audio file for a specified theme or for headline news. Furthermore, this system uses a smart speaker for audio output. Currently, the system only rarely succeeds in generating interesting *Manzai*, so we aim to improve its accuracy and performance in the future. In addition, we intend to explore ways of measuring the reactions of the people who are listening to the *Manzai*.

References

1. Cousins, N.: Anatomy of an Illness as Perceived by the Patient. W W Norton & Co. Inc., New York (2001)
2. Weber, K., Ritschel, H., Lingenfelser, F., Andre, E.: Real-time adaptation of a robotic joke teller based on human social signals. In: Proceedings of the 17th International Conference on Autonomous Agents and MultiAgent Systems (AAMAS 2018) (2018)

3. Knight, H., Satkin, S., Ramakrishna, V., Divvala, S.: A savvy robot standup comic: online learning through audience tracking. In: Workshop Paper (TEI 2010) (2011)
4. Vilk, J., Fitter, N.T.: Comedians in cafes getting data: evaluating timing and adaptivity in real-world robot comedy performance. In: Proceedings of the 2020 ACM/IEEE International Conference on Human-Robot Interaction (Cambridge, United Kingdom) (HRI 2020) (2020)
5. Katevas, K., Healey, P., Harris, M.: Robot comedy lab: experimenting with the social dynamics of live performance. Front. Psychol. 6 (2015)
6. Mashimo, R., Kitamura, T., Umetani, T., Nadamoto, A.: Implicit communication robots based on automatic scenario generation using web intelligence. Int. J. Web Inf. Syst. (2016)
7. Haraguchi, K., Yane, K., Sato, A., Aramaki, E., Miyashiro, I., Nadamoto, A.: Chat-type Manzai application: mobile daily comedy presentations based on automatically generated Manzai scenarios. In: The 18th International Conference on Advances in Mobile Computing and Multimedia (MoMM 2020) (2020)

Design and Research of Art Exhibition Information App Based on KANO Model

Rui Shen[✉]

School of Design, South China University of Technology, Guangzhou 510006,
People's Republic of China
1535338848@qq.com

Abstract. Purpose To meet the needs of art lovers to obtain exhibition information, explore more functional designs to enhance their exhibition experience. Methods Taking the interface design of the art exhibition app as an example, using competitive product analysis, user portraits and other methods to understand user demand, classify the design needs by attributes through the Kano model, complete the user demand segmentation, and construct the design based on the calculation results of the user satisfaction index The four-quadrant diagram of requirements is required, and important design requirements are refined, and the page design is carried out accordingly. Conclusion The Kano model method can improve design efficiency, help designers better understand the needs of visitors in the process of visiting the exhibition, and enhance the visitor experience.

Keywords: Kano model · Art exhibition · User demand · Attribute classification

1 Introduction

Viktor Shklovsky once wrote in "Art as Technique" that "art exists to restore a sense of life, to feel things, to make a stone stand out from a stone". The texture [1]. As a carrier of art works, art exhibitions provide a platform for the public to accept the edification of art. With the development of the social economy and the increasing aesthetics of the public, people need more forms of activities to enrich their spare time. Art exhibitions have become the first choice for the public to enrich their lives and cultivate their sentiments.

With the development of the Internet, the dissemination of art exhibition information has also changed. In the era of traditional media, the dissemination of exhibition information mainly relies on radio, newspapers, magazines, etc., which are often limited by time and place, resulting in a limited number of people who can obtain exhibition information. In the Internet era, the media and methods of exhibition information are becoming more and more abundant, showing a diversified trend. Websites, Weibo, etc. are all platforms for people to obtain exhibition information. In the context of the growing demand in the cultural market, art exhibition information APPs came into being, such as iMuseum, VART, ArtCalendar, Zaiyi, watching exhibitions, etc., all of which provide art lovers with the latest daily exhibition information, special special exhibitions, permanent exhibitions, etc. A high-quality app for art exhibition information such as special galleries.

C. Stephanidis et al. (Eds.): HCII 2022, CCIS 1582, pp. 262–270, 2022.
https://doi.org/10.1007/978-3-031-06391-6_35

2 Competitive Analysis

The author will elaborate from the aspects of product positioning, data performance, characteristic functions, interaction design and so on.

2.1 Zaiyi

"Zaiyi" is a mobile application that integrates art life services and commenting and socializing, providing information on art exhibitions and intra-city art events held by art galleries, museums, galleries and other organizers around the world. Art itself is a niche field. When it is delivered to more people in the form of art exhibitions, the audience it radiates will increase exponentially, so it is particularly important to promote exhibition information. Zaiyi provides an integrated service for online viewing of exhibition information and ticket purchase. The app has been downloaded 1.22 million times in the app market, with a score of 5 points, and has a large number of users.

The main content of this app includes exhibition information, art lectures, art community, live broadcast, etc. It is rich in content and practical. Users can inquire about art exhibitions around the world in the "Exhibition" module, and purchase tickets with one click on the ticketing system of the application; the "Course" module is highly knowledgeable and records the lectures or courses offered by experts in various fields of art. Video, which is convenient for users to obtain more professional learning methods without leaving home; "Home" is a community where everyone records and shares artistic life in the form of pictures, texts or short videos, and users can build their own art circles here. In addition, the live broadcast function of Zaiyi is unique. The platform invites institutions to settle in, live broadcast to watch exhibitions and live broadcast forums. Through these forms, a large number of users are accumulated, and the "interactive live broadcast" era of art communication is opened, allowing users to watch the interesting and interesting world from zero distance. Art scene. see picture 1 (Figs. 1 and 2).

Fig. 1. Zaiyi interface   **Fig. 2.** iDaily Museum interface

2.2 iDaily Museum

"iDaily Museum" is an app that focuses on global art exhibitions and museum activities. It publishes global exhibition information as comprehensively as possible, allowing users to keep abreast of the exciting exhibitions going on around them. The app has been downloaded 640,000+ times in the app market and has a score of 4.9.

iDaily Museum divides the app into four modules with the navigation at the bottom of the page: world, city, dynamic, and personal center. The "World" section displays exhibition information from all over the world and the introduction of museums and art galleries in various cities; the "Same City" section allows you to view exhibitions in custom cities, as well as select national museums, special museums, private museums, and commercial galleries in the city. In the "Dynamic" section, you can make your own exhibition plan, or learn about your friends' plans and travel together; in the "Personal Center", you can quickly view information such as trends, exhibition collections, venue collections, and article collections. The four sections work together to help users improve their efficiency in finding exhibitions and making plans.

The advantage of Zaiyi app is that exhibitions and lectures are rich in content, covering most of the art activities; the disadvantage is that the function is too powerful, resulting in too fragmented sections of the app, making it difficult for users to quickly find the functions they want. The advantage of iDaily Museum is that the function is highly targeted, focusing on the release of exhibition information. The interface is concise and clear, which is convenient for users to get started quickly; interactive requirements. The exhibition information is not classified into modules, and users can only browse the exhibition information in the order of push, and the search efficiency is low. The author will learn from experience to improve the interface design of art exhibition information apps.

3   Build User Portraits

The author conducted iodized salt for the art exhibition information app. According to the survey results, it was found that most of the users were college students or art lovers. Based on this, the user portraits were constructed: college students and young art lovers.

3.1   Current University Student

Zhang Tingting is a college student studying in a university in Guangzhou. She usually likes to visit high-quality art exhibitions, and after viewing the exhibitions, she shares and records the exhibitions in the form of pictures or videos. If the exhibition also sells related art peripherals, she is happy to help These art peripheral products are paid for. Zhang Tingting hopes that through a platform, she can comprehensively grasp the information of art exhibitions across the country and even around the world, so that she can inquire about and participate in exhibition activities in a timely manner, so as to improve her artistic quality (Figs. 3 and 4).

3.2   Arts Lover

Duan Zhenyu is the executive director of a company in Zhongshan City. After working hard in the workplace for a few years, his work has stabilized. He has already started a family and has a child. The husband and wife pursue a spiritual and quality life, and like to take their children to the art exhibition hall to receive the edification of art and increase their children's knowledge. However, due to his limited art knowledge, Mr. Duan could

Fig. 3. College students - role model   **Fig. 4.** Young art lovers - models

not provide a comprehensive explanation to the children in every exhibition. Since he did not live in a first- and second-tier city, there were few local art resources. Mr. Duan hoped to have a platform to solve the inquiries about the exhibition., works, etc.

4 Analysis of User Needs Based on KANO Model

In order to better understand the needs of users, the author conducted user interviews with art students before designing the questionnaire, in order to more accurately grasp the needs and pain points of users, and improve the accuracy of the analysis of the Kano model. The author marks the extracted 11 requirements as C1, C2...C11, see Table 2 for details.

Table 1. Kano model evaluation table

Demand realization	Need not fulfilled				
	like	deserves	doesn't matter	tolerable	dislike
like	Q	A	A	A	O
as it should be	R	I	I	I	M
It doesn't matter	R	I	I	I	M
tolerable	R	I	I	I	M
dislike	R	R	R	R	Q

Table 2. List of requirements

Types	Number	Requirements
Before the exhibition	C1	Recommended viewing strategies
	C2	Buy tickets online
	C3	View the online exhibition
	C4	Venue Notice
	C5	Book an offline experience class
In the exhibition	C6	Check-in interaction
	C7	Provide venue classification guide
	C8	Scan the code to view the introduction
After the exhibition	C9	buy art merchandise
	C10	Inquire and submit to the Art Contest
	C11	Live Art Lectures

4.1 Requirements Attribute Classification

Questionnaire Distribution and Inspection

A total of 63 online questionnaires were received in this survey, of which 86% of the respondents were between the ages of 18 and 25, and 22% had used art exhibition information apps. Some participants have less experience, which is similar to the user role characteristics targeted in this article. The author used SPSS software to conduct reliability analysis on the 63 questionnaires collected to study the reliability and accuracy of quantitative data responses. Among them, the Cronbach α coefficient of the forward question was 0.861, and the Cronbach α coefficient of the reverse question was 0.899. The coefficients of the forward and reverse problems are all greater than 0.8, indicating that the research data has high reliability and can be used for further analysis.

User Requirement Kano Attribute Classification

By comparing the evaluation table of the Kano model, see Table 1, the author classifies the attributes of the results of the returned questionnaires. The details of the Kano attributes of the design requirements are shown in Table 3. Among them, C1, C3, C5, C6, C9, C11 are indifference attributes, indicating that there is no obvious relationship between the presence or absence of these functions and user satisfaction.

4.2 Ranking of Important Needs

The core function of the four-quadrant model is to divide the design requirements into four quadrants according to the two dimensions of urgent and important, including four quadrants of important and urgent, important and non-urgent, non-important and urgent, and non-important and non-urgent. The urgency of the design requirements. Figure 5 The Better-Worse coefficient graph shows the coordinates of each requirement, the horizontal axis is the Worse value, and the vertical axis is the Better value, which intuitively shows the importance and emergency of all functions.

The first quadrant is the desired attribute, with a high Better value and a high absolute value of Worse, indicating important and urgent design requirements, including two requirements of C2 and C7, namely online ticket purchase and venue tours. The realization of these two requirements is of great help in providing user satisfaction, and is also a key element in building user loyalty.

Table 3. Demand Kanot attribute classification table

Number	KANO 属性	Better	Worse
C1	I	44.62%	-26.15%
C2	O	52.24%	-64.18%
C3	I	40.98%	-22.95%
C4	O	43.94%	-63.64%
C5	I	47.69%	-24.62%
C6	I	51.56%	-23.44%
C7	O	52.31%	-60.00%
C8	A	56.92%	-35.38%
C9	I	46.27%	-22.39%
C10	A	56.45%	-27.42%
C11	I	51.52%	-25.76%

A: 魅力属性,O: 期望属性,M: 必备属性,I: 无差异属性,R: 反向属性,Q: 可疑属性

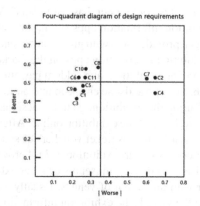

Fig. 5. Four-quadrant diagram of design requirements

The second quadrant is the charm attribute. The Better value is high and the Worse value is low in absolute value, indicating important but not urgent needs, including four needs of C6, C8, C10, and C11, that is, punch-in interaction, scan code to view work introduction, query and submit Art competitions, live art lectures, the realization of these needs can improve the user experience, and should be prioritized when developing and designing.

The third quadrant is the indifference attribute, with a low Better value and a low absolute value of Worse value, indicating non-important and non-urgent design requirements, including four requirements of C1, C3, C5, and C9. The functions of this quadrant are usually not provided.

The fourth quadrant is a must-have attribute, with a low Better value and a high absolute value of Worse, indicating non-important and urgent design requirements, including the C4 requirement, which is the venue notice. The functions in this quadrant must be satisfied, and the user satisfaction of the requirements in this quadrant must be continuously paid attention to.

In terms of the priority of function provision of the four-quadrant diagram, the usual implementation order is: required attribute > desired attribute > attractive attribute > indifference attribute. Both the first and second quadrants are important needs, and the first and fourth quadrants are urgent needs. The first quadrant is both important and urgent. The realization of these needs has a significant effect on improving user satisfaction., so the order of realization of the design requirements is determined as the first quadrant > the second quadrant > the fourth quadrant > the third quadrant.

5   Fourth, According to the Needs of the Order to Expand the Program Design

Seven important requirements were screened out through the four-quadrant diagram, namely C2, C7, C4, C6, C8, C10, and C11. It can be seen from the better values in Table 3 that C2, C6, C7, C8, C10, and C11 have a significant impact on improving user satisfaction. Among them, C2 is "online purchase of tickets". While providing exhibition information, art exhibition information apps should also attach a link to purchase exhibition tickets, which can provide users with great convenience. C6 is "check-in interaction". Currently, the exhibition information apps on the market pay more attention to the information push before the exhibition, and seldom pay attention to the user experience during the exhibition. The app adds the check-in interaction function to allow users to watch the exhibition. During the exhibition, go to the designated place to take photos and upload or share the experience of the exhibition online. After the card is successfully punched in, you can get rewards such as ticket vouchers or souvenirs, so as to increase the interaction between users and the art exhibition. C7 is "providing a classified tour of venues". When people visit art galleries, museums or other exhibition venues, most of them are very unfamiliar with the layout of venues. Usually, they must follow the on-site guidance to complete the visit. If the exhibition information app can The provision of electronic venue classification guides will allow users to understand the exhibition layout of the entire event in advance, and they can visit according to their interests when they arrive at the venue. C6, C7, and C8 are all to enhance the user experience during the exhibition.

C10 is "Inquiry and Submit Art Competition". According to the results of the questionnaire, college students and young art lovers account for the largest proportion of the groups who visit art exhibitions. Some of these groups have the needs to participate in art competitions. This requirement can provide convenience for these users. C11 stands for "Live Art Lectures". The application of Internet technology provides technical support for the development of all walks of life. The "Live Broadcast" function is added to the art exhibition app, allowing people who cannot attend art lectures and courses due to geographical and time constraints. Watch art lectures online to enrich the user experience.

From the worst value in Table 3, it can be seen that C4 has a significant effect on the reduction of dissatisfaction. C4 is "Reminder for Venues". Before arriving at the exhibition site, people usually want to know the basic information such as opening time, closing time, and exhibition address, as well as information on facilities such as luggage storage, public activity space, and toilets to meet this demand. It can improve the user's comfortable psychological experience.

Based on the seven design requirements in Fig. 5, the interface design of the art exhibition information app is carried out, and the design focuses on C2, C6, C7, and C10. The main interface renderings are shown in Figs. 6 and 7.

Fig. 6. Art exhibition information APP low fidelity

Fig. 7. Art exhibition information APP high fidelity

6   Epilogue

This paper takes the interface design of the art exhibition information app as an example to study, adopts the methods of competitive product analysis, user interviews and user portraits to obtain user needs, and completes the user needs segmentation through the Kano model analysis method, and combines the four-quadrant model to determine the important design requirements. Determine the order of requirement realization according to the schedule, and give priority to completing important and urgently needed design requirements when time is urgent; when time and resources are abundant, focus on important non-urgent design requirements to meet users' expectations and attractiveness needs. Kano model analysis method can shorten the development cycle, improve design efficiency, and improve user satisfaction, but this method focuses on user demand research, and the research content has limitations. In a complete design plan, it needs to be combined with other research methods. With the cooperation, in the future, more research methods can be combined to deeply explore more functional designs of the art exhibition information app.

References

1. Phantom Shadow, D.: Research on the Design of Art Guide APP "Exhibition Companion" Based on Sharing Economy. Beijing Institute of Graphic Printing, Beijing (2020)
2. Ning Xiner., D.: Research on user experience-oriented museum Internet product design. Hunan Normal University (2020)
3. Xiong, Y., He, R.J.: Interface design of business intelligence system based on Kano and four-quadrant model . Packag. Eng. **41**(10), 242–247 (2020)
4. Chen, P.D.: Research on the design strategy of museum service system. Hefei University of Technology (2019)
5. Zhang, F., Jia, C.J.: Research on product innovation method based on user demand classification and importance evaluation. Packag. Eng. **38**(16), 87–92 (2017)
6. Liu, R.D.: Research on dynamic visualization of art exhibition information release. Shanghai University (2017)
7. Li, M., Zhang, J., Pan, W., Tsao, J.: Integrating Kano model, AHP, and QFD methods for new product development based on text mining, intuitionistic fuzzy sets, and customers satisfaction. Math. Probl. Eng. **2021** (2021)
8. Dewi, S.K., Nugraha, A,J.: n Quality of service evaluation based on importance performance analysis method and the kano model. J. Phys. Conf. Ser. **1764**(1) (2021)
9. Wang, Y.D.: Research on the differentiated design of app interfaces centered on user experience Sichuan Academy of Fine Arts (2014)

Research on Qiang Culture Redesign Based on AR Technology

Juanjuan Shi[⊠], Jie Hao, and Qian Nie

Beijing Institute of Fashion Technology, Beijing 100029, China
sjjzgy@126.com

Abstract. In order to study the redesign of Qiang culture linking tradition and fashion, based on summarizing the connotation and design status quo of Qiang culture, combined with the characteristics of augmented reality technology and interactive expression, the AR picture book and IP image design of Qiang culture targeted at modern fashion users are studied. The picture book vividly shows the historical connotation of Qiang culture in a three-dimensional and visual way, and highlights the ethnic characteristics of Qiang by combining ethnic IP to enhance ethnic affinity and communication. For the key culture and rich cultural content of Qiang nationality, AR technology is combined with two interactive ways of 3D data superposition and video superposition to provide vivid digital display content. which stimulates users' exploration and thirst for knowledge, makes the pop-up book more lifelike, and forms an interactive experience combining the virtual and the real. It improves the exploration of knowledge, the interest and extension of the content, and opens up a new field for the learning and inheritance of Qiang culture.

Keywords: Qiang culture · Augmented reality technology · Interaction design

1 Introduction

The Qiang is one of the oldest ethnic minorities in China. As an important part of traditional Chinese culture, the Qiang people have left behind many unique and precious intangible cultural heritage, such as the Historical stories of the Qiang people, clothing, architecture, Shibi culture, festivals, Qiang flute, embroidery, etc. They are the symbol and crystallization of the wisdom of the Qiang people for thousands of years and have great artistic and cultural heritage value. And with the continuous development of new media technology, the audience's way of life is in constant change in the innovation, the traditional forms of Qiang cultural heritage are facing out modern user perspective and the situation of inheritance, how to use modern information interaction technology Qiang culture to meet the modern user perspective way better legacy is particularly important. Under the new media environment, augmented reality technology develops rapidly. Combined with the education industry, augmented reality can realize reality interaction, combine teaching with fun, and improve the exploration of knowledge and extension of content [1]. Based on summarizing the connotation and design status quo of

C. Stephanidis et al. (Eds.): HCII 2022, CCIS 1582, pp. 271–279, 2022.
https://doi.org/10.1007/978-3-031-06391-6_36

Qiang culture, this paper focuses on the AR picture book and IP image design of Qiang culture aimed at modern fashion users, combined with the characteristics of augmented reality technology and interactive expression. The AR picture book based on Qiang culture vividly shows the historical connotation of Qiang culture in a three-dimensional and visual way, highlights the ethnic characteristics of Qiang nationality with ethnic IP, and enhances ethnic affinity and communication. The design uses AR technology to add the interaction of moving the picture book and IP image through mobile phone scanning. Which creates an interactive experience that links tradition and fashion, and shapes a sustainable ecological model for intangible cultural heritage inheritance.

2   The Connotation and Design Status of Qiang Culture

2.1   Historical Connotation of Qiang Culture

Qiang people are the only ethnic group in China whose surname is written in oracle bones. In the long history of development, Qiang people have integrated their wisdom into all aspects of work and life, forming a unique ethnic culture and religious belief. Sheep is inseparable in the development of Qiang people. As one of the objects of worship of Qiang people, sheep not only lays a foundation for their economic life, but also makes a profound reflection in their national costumes [2]. Shibi is the most authoritative cultural and intellectual integrator of the Qiang nationality, which is a strange and primitive religious and cultural phenomenon left by the ancient Qiang nationality. The Qiang people believe in animism, and Shibi is respected as a person who can connect the realm of life and death, and direct to the gods. Shibi culture reflects qiang people's worship of God and longing for a peaceful life. The Qiang people are a non-literate people. The intelligent Qiang people have concentrated their wisdom and culture in the beautiful Qiang embroidery skills and the beautiful Qiang flute music, which have been passed down from generation to generation. Qiang embroidery was rated as a national intangible cultural Heritage in 2008. The Qiang embroidery culture, which has been dormant for thousands of years, has once again entered the world's attention through the new media of the new era, and has shaken the aesthetics and concepts of modern people through its distinctive style and expression form [3]. The Qiang clothing has many exquisite embroidery patterns, and the Qiang's famous "Yunyun shoes" are the classic moire embroidery. As an important part of the Qiang culture, the traditional clothes, and shoes of the Qiang people come from life and are higher than life, expressing the Qiang people's yearning for a better life in the future. The performance of the Qiang flute expresses the feelings of the Qiang people, who are positive, respect the natural things and love life. It has become an important channel for communication and inheritance of national culture. On May 20, 2006, Qiang Flute performance and production techniques were approved by The State Council to be listed in the first batch of national intangible cultural heritage list.

The Qiang people's history, totem belief, Shibi culture, Qiang flute, clothing, Yunyun shoes, stories and embroidery and other traditional culture have been accumulated by the Qiang people in the long historical process. They have their own unique cultural characteristics and national style, and are the symbol and crystallization of the wisdom of the Qiang people for thousands of years, and contain profound artistic and historical cultural connotations.

2.2 Design Status Quo of Qiang Culture Under Fashion Environment

The Needs of Fashion Users. According to Maslow's motivation model as shown in Fig. 1, modern fashion users pay more attention to cognitive, aesthetic and self-realization of high-level needs based on meeting life needs. Facing modern fashion users, Qiang culture with ancient culture and artistic value wants to occupy a place in the modern market with fierce competition. While insisting on its own national characteristics and artistic style, it must combine modern information interaction technology to seek innovation and development in line with the perspective of modern users.

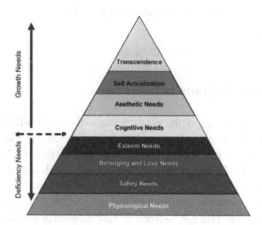

Fig. 1. Maslow's motivation model

The Design Status of Qiang Culture. The Qiang Culture Museum is shown on the left in Fig. 2. It is one of the conservation planning projects established after the Ministry of Culture organized experts to conduct investigation, research and rescue research on the Qiang intangible cultural heritage after the 2008 earthquake. The Qiang Culture Museum has a wealth of images and videos of The Qiang culture, as well as academic research and news reports, which are of great help to the induction and protection of the Qiang culture. As shown on the right of Fig. 2, 5D Immersive interactive Intangible Cultural Heritage Light and Shadow Restaurant is a project jointly created by Yang Huazhen, the national inhertor of Qiang Embroidery, and Pizza Hut. A large interactive light and shadow installation is combined with the traditional Culture of Qiang Nationality intangible cultural Heritage, and the peony pattern symbolizing reunion and happiness is integrated into the interactive light and shadow installation. Peonies are in full bloom and butterflies are dancing. Through new media technology, Qiang embroidery culture is naturally integrated into the dining environment to enhance the aesthetic feeling and value of the restaurant. This design not only matches traditional culture with modern aesthetics, but also integrates traditional culture into modern life and modern consumer market. The two cases have played a good role in the inheritance of Qiang culture by combining with the corresponding modern information exchange technology and adopting a way that meets the aesthetic and needs of modern young people. However, all users need to study on the spot, which is limited by regional space, so the audience is not large, and the spread is not enough.

Fig. 2. Design cases of Qiang culture

3   AR Interaction at Home and Abroad

Augmented reality technology is the clever fusion of virtual information simulation with the real world. The two kinds of information complement each other, to realize the "enhancement" of the real world. It has three characteristics: Combines Real and Virtual, Interactive in Real Time and Registered in 3-D [4]. AR interactive effects can be presented in various ways, including AR interactive mode based on mobile terminals, head-mounted, mirror, desktop, and holographic projection. The AR interaction mode based on mobile terminal takes the screen of mobile device as the medium of overlay virtual information world. Although this is a relatively basic AR interaction mode, other AR interaction devices have low penetration rate and high price. For fashionable users in the information age, smart mobile devices have long become their necessities. According to the usage habits of fashion users, based on analyzing the characteristics of AR interaction, the mobile AR interaction expression mode suitable for fashion users is studied.

3.1   Characteristics of AR Interaction Design

The characteristics of AR interaction design are studied from three aspects: First, the "enhancement" of real-world information. Virtual information such as text, picture, video, sound, and 3D data are used to fuse with real world information from width and depth to achieve "enhanced" effect. As shown on the left in Fig. 3, 3d dinosaurs in the virtual world integrate with paper books from depth information such as 3D vision, sound and hearing to enhance the effect of paper books. Second, the interactive display of virtual information should be correct, intuitive, and refined. Picture, video, or 3D data is better than text data, large font is better than small font, and local enlargement function is provided appropriately where information is large. Virtual information is often not limited by time and space, relatively flexible and free. Finally, AR interaction design should be user-centered and conform to the characteristics of users. The user is the controller of AR interaction, and the interactive feedback of virtual information should conform to the user's behavior habits in nature and the existing interaction design norms, so that the virtual information can be easily interacted and controllable by the user. According to people's nature of exploring the unknown, on the basis of security, virtual information with explorability can be appropriately introduced to meet users' nature of exploring, improve users' viscosity and unknown experience of AR interaction.

3.2 Interactive Representation of Mobile AR

According to the habits and characteristics of users using AR interactive devices, smart devices based on mobile terminals are the mainstream AR interactive devices of current fashion users. Mobile AR interactive representation includes three-dimensional data superposition, video superposition and AR game superposition. Both dynamic and static 3D models and 3D scene presentation are 3D data overlay. As shown on the left in Fig. 3, virtual 3D dinosaurs appear on paper books, while cracks appear in the floor tiles of the objective world in the mobile phone lens as the dinosaurs move. Dynamic 3D models interlock with realistic 3D scenes, which is one of the common and quite expressive ways of AR interaction. The video is characterized by rich content, detailed expression, and accuracy. The intermediate case in Fig. 3 shows the interactive effect of AR video superposition. The paper idiom picture book tells the story of the outing life familiar to modern children as the main line, and naturally quotes the idiom "row upon row" to describe the playing scene at that time. However, this idiom has a Ming Dynasty allusion which is worth further learning by users. In combination with mobile AR interaction, video animation superposition is used to show users the origin of this idiom and increase the possibility for users to explore the cultural origin of this idiom. The AR game overlay of Pokemon GO is shown on the right in Fig. 3. It takes the user's real world as the setting for the game. Many virtual superimposed Pokemon can appear in the real world through mobile devices, and users can play interactive games such as exploration, capture and combat in the virtual Pokemon, so that users can play in the real world with superimposed virtual things without being bound by the site and space.

Fig. 3. AR interaction

4   Interactive Design of Qiang Culture Based on AR Technology

4.1   The Overall Design of Qiang's Stereoscopic Picture Book

Based on the research of Qiang culture connotation, modern user characteristics and AR technology, the general framework of AR technology based Qiang culture interaction design is finally determined as shown in Fig. 4. Which is mainly composed of Qiang culture picture book and AR interaction APP. The picture book makes a visual and three-dimensional design of the extracted Qiang cultural connotation. The catalogue contains the history of the Qiang people, the ancient Sheep totem of the Qiang people, the religion of the Qiang people, the making of the Qiang flute, the Clothing of the Qiang people, Yunyun shoes and Qiang embroidery. The IP image with the typical characteristics of the Qiang people guides users to read the picture book interdynamically. For Qiang's key culture and rich cultural content, AR technology is combined with two interactive ways of 3-D data superposition and video superposition to provide vivid digital display content, to improve the interest, extensibility and user interaction and participation of picture book content.

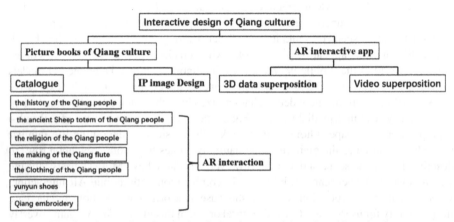

Fig. 4. Qiang culture interactive design framework based on AR technology

In the history page of Qiang nationality, the 3-D image of the ancestors of Qiang nationality standing between the blue sky and white clouds shows the long historical background of Qiang nationality. The IP image of Qiang nationality guides users to read the historical changes of Qiang nationality before and after THE A.D. at the bottom right of the page. The ancient Sheep totem page of The Qiang nationality embodies the sheep totem of the Qiang people's desire for peace and prosperity with the 3-D warm living picture between shepherds and sheep. In this page, the evolution process of the digital sheep totem with AR technology and the origin of the IP image design of the Qiang nationality are combined. On the religion page of Qiang people, the 3-D "Shibi" sacrificial scene shows the religious credibility of Qiang people. On the lower right corner of the page, the QIANG IP image guides users to interact with the dynamic scene of "Shibi" sacrificial scene combined with AR technology. The production page of The Qiang flute reflects the production steps of the Qiang flute by turning the inside page and visualizes the Qiang flute performance screen, and reproduces the dynamic performance screen and music of the Qiang flute with AR technology. The Qiang clothing page visualizes the typical clothing information of Qiang men and women, and extends the more detailed interactive information of clothing with AR technology. The page of Yunyun shoes visualizes the shape of Yunyun shoes and the hero and heroine images in the fairy stories related to Yunyun shoes, and interacts with the myth and legend of the love story of the carp fairy and the shepherd boy with AR technology. Qiang embroidery page is re-visualized to design the Qiang embroidery patterns with a sense of The Times and its introduction. The IP image of Qiang nationality on the upper left of the page guides users to understand the cultural characteristics and beautiful connotations of Qiang embroidery patterns with AR technology.

4.2 Qiang Nationality IP Image Design

Among the numerous natural artifacts, the ancestors of the Qiang people chose sheep as one of the objects of worship. The Qiang people regard sheep as their patron saint and have a special love and worship for sheep totem [5]. The design of IP image of Qiang nationality is based on the sheep totem, and the colors are selected from the representative sacred colors of Qiang embroidery and goat horn. The IP image of Qiang nationality designed in accordance with modern user aesthetics is shown in Fig. 5. Creating ethnic IP can highlight the characteristics of the ethnic group, enhance ethnic affinity, communication, so that users can understand and feel Qiang culture in a subtle way. The image of the picture book and the IP image of Qiang nationality are visualized in a 3-D form. When the book is opened, the image stands up, and the IP image guides users to perceive the cultural connotation of Qiang nationality.

Fig. 5. Qiang nationality IP image design

4.3 Application Research of AR Technology in Qiang Interactive Picture Books

The AR realization technology of the Qiang culture interactive picture book adopts the method of Unity3D combined with Vuforia. Unity3D is a fully integrated professional virtual interaction engine developed by Unity Technologies. Vuforia is a software development kit launched by Qualcomm for mobile device augmented reality applications. The corresponding AR interaction can be generated using the Vuforia plug-in, which is assembled in Unity. The specific use process is shown on the left in Fig. 6. Prepare the AR recognition target map, upload the target map to Vuforia website for detection and processing, and generate the corresponding Database. Download the Database to automatically generate a Unity package file. This file will be imported into Unity project and combined with the corresponding 3D data, video or AR game of the target map for subsequent AR design and development. The Qiang flute is inscribed with the genes of the ancient culture and expresses the aspirations of the Qiang people [6]. The AR interactive effect of the Qiang Flute page in the Picture book of Qiang culture is shown on the right in Fig. 6. The still picture of Qiang flute playing is visualized on the picture book page. This picture is taken as the target image of AR recognition, combined with the corresponding video, the dynamic performance picture of Qiang flute is reproduced by the mobile app and the ancient and beautiful music of Qiang flute is listened to. This method is used to achieve the corresponding AR interaction effect in other pages of picture books. On the basis of retaining users' habit of reading paper picture books, the AR interaction between the mobile app and picture books is realized to guide users to further explore the connotation of Qiang culture in a way consistent with modern users' habits and make the pop-up books more lifelike.

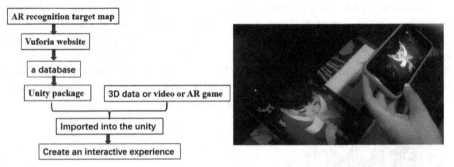

Fig. 6. The process of using AR technology and AR interaction of Qiang Flute

5 Conclusion

For modern fashion users, the research on interactive design of Qiang culture stereoscopic picture books can not only enhance the awareness of Qiang culture, but also break the limitations of regional space and better link tradition and fashion by combining the characteristics of augmented reality technology and interactive expression. It stimulates users' exploration and thirst for knowledge, so that users can understand and feel Qiang culture in a subtle way. This can not only play a role in inheriting Qiang culture, but also let users feel tangible and perceptive cognitive embodiment, and experience the connotation of Qiang culture in an interesting way. It enhances the user's interaction and participation, forms the interactive experience combining the virtual and the real, improves the exploration of knowledge and the extension of content, and opens up a new field for the learning and inheritance of Qiang culture.

References

1. Shi, J.J., Nie, Q., Wang, K.X.: Interactive design of fashion idioms based on AR technology. Educ. Teach. Forum **42**, 88–89 (2018)

2. Chen, H.: Research on the artistic symbols of the Sheep's horn pattern in Qiang people's clothing. Northwestern Univ. Westleather. **42**(16) (2020)
3. Yao, H., Pang, L.: Applied study of Qiang embroidery in cultural and creative products design. Ind. Des. **06**, 151–152 (2020)
4. Azuma, R.T.: A survey of augmented reality. Presence Teleoper. Virt. Environ. **6**(4), 355–385 (1997)
5. Fu, S.: National Image Memory: Cultural Interpretation and Design Wisdom of Sheep Image Symbols of Qiang Nationality, p. 04. Sichuan University Press, Chengdu (2020)
6. Huang, C.: Inheritance and innovation of Qiang flute music in the digital era. Shanxi Youth (Second Half) **10**, 232 (2013)

Contextual Behavior Evaluation Design
for an Artistic Research Setting

Cedric Spindler$^{(\boxtimes)}$, Jonas Kellermeyer , and Jan Torpus

Critical Media Lab, Academy of Art and Design, University of Applied Sciences
and Arts Northwestern Switzerland—FHNW, Freilager-Platz 1,
4002 Basel, Switzerland
{cedric.spindler,jonas.kellermeyer,jan.torpus}@fhnw.ch

Abstract. With this poster we propose the concept of "Contextual Behavior Evaluation Design" which was developed for the artistic research project *"Technology, Human, Design - Paradigms of Ubiquitous Computing"* (funded by the Swiss National Science Foundation, 2019-22). We present theoretical principles, the immersive research setup, and the mixed methods applied for data collection and evaluation. The focus is on the question whether it is possible to identify personal attitudes of people towards a sensor-technologically enhanced environment on the basis of behavioral patterns in key situations (without access to personal data). Subsequently, we discuss design strategies, exemplary algorithms and initial findings.

Keywords: Ubiquitous computing · Artistic research · Contextual behavior analysis · Environmental psychology · Techno-social hybridity · Responsive environment · Sensor actor network · Evaluation design

1   Introduction

The leading research question for this e-poster is: *"What appropriation processes do humans apply to cognitively and emotionally access technologically augmented environments and how can the involved computation help to identify human behavioral patterns and attitudes?"* To answer this question, we created a technologically responsive environment and invited participants to experience the walk-in installation and to report on it. By means of embedded sensors and actuators, we staged interactive scenes that make characteristics of ubiquitous computing experienceable and measurable. To gain insight into human appropriation processes and attitudes in this technologically augmented environment, the scenes were designed to create challenging situations that could be analyzed by an algorithmically implemented evaluation design. After concluding the user evaluations, we are currently analyzing the collected data, which we would like to present and discuss.

Supported by Swiss National Funds.

C. Stephanidis et al. (Eds.): HCII 2022, CCIS 1582, pp. 280–287, 2022.
https://doi.org/10.1007/978-3-031-06391-6_37

2   Related Work/Theoretical Foundation

Our research is situated in a theoretical field of tension between Science & Technology Studies (*Ubiquitous Computing, Techno-Social Hybridity, Affective Computing*), Design Research (*Critical Design, Sense-Making*) and contemporary psychology (*Environmental Psychology, Contextual Behavioral Science*).

Ubiquitous Computing (UbiComp) in itself is a rather antiquated concept that has been around since the early 1990s,s, deriving a lot of its shape and theoretical power from the initial writings of Mark Weiser. His text *The Computer for the 21st century* [1] marks the conceptual birth of an environment physically augmented by several mechanisms to provide practical assistance to everyday work tasks. The idea behind the primal form of UbiComp was to free workers from tedious small-scale work steps and allow them to focus on the bigger picture. Its potential is allegedly to be found in an ever extending networking condition, consequently leading towards a specific kind of *seamless*[1] integration of technology into the social realm and vice versa.

The radically human-centered vision that is UbiComp, calls for new interaction paradigms that structure the experiences with technologically augmented environments much "more like the way humans interact with the physical world" [2] (pp. 154). For this purpose, it seems all the more necessary for computing processes to become "invisible," which means that they successively merge with the environment. In this respect, computing power is becoming almost indistinguishable from plain physical configurations. The respective users do not have to be particularly tech savvy in order for such a system to work. The stated goal of UbiComp in general is that "both the interface and the computer would be invisible, subservient to the task the person was attempting to accomplish" [3] (pp. 216 ff.). The techno-social hybrid condition does not depend upon cognitive awareness, but rather works regardless of individual knowledge, concentrating much more on the situative context.

"The union of explicit and implicit input defines the *context* of interaction between the human and the [technologically enhanced] environment" [2] (pp. 156) and it is this very notion of *context* that is crucial for our research and the corresponding evaluation as well.

For this very reason, environmental psychology comes into play: the role of context in human functioning is one of the linchpins of environmental psychological endeavors [4,5]. Contexts play a prominent role on both the personal and on the environmental level: the individual in question certainly has contextual qualities as part of his/her personality: held beliefs, socialization and past experiences are just a few examples that can make a big difference. The environment on its part provides cultural clues and (physical) affordances like temperature, lighting conditions and acoustic ambiance that may or may not resonate with the respective participant.

---

[1] In later texts, Weiser discarded the idea of *seamlessness* in favor of a more sophisticated *seamful* approach.

The excessive contextual view leads us further to the issue of sense-making. In contrast to mere (technological) sensing of certain events, sense-making is closely connected to the narrative structure of social understanding. It implements a trajectory that is based on an extensive notion of time – *past* experiences become the basis on which new information, gathered in the *present*, can be categorized and *future* outcomes may be anticipated respectively (cf. [6] pp. 124 ff.). Since "[w]e humans want to understand and interpret our experiences" [6] (pp. 122), there is a need for an archival systematic structure that enables storing and subsequently helps us rating our experiences.

3   Research Objective and Design Approach

We applied strategies of New Media Art [7] and Speculative Design [8] to stage interactive key situations in a walk-in installation, to make them not only experienceable and debatable for participants, but also measurable and analyzable. As a starting point, we extracted intrinsic paradigms of UbiComp such as *omnipresence, immediacy, invisibility, seamlessness, interconnectedness* and *smartness* of devices and staged them in the research setting. By utilizing unfamiliar situations, subjective narratives, and cultural references, we created ambiguous experiences and forced participants to reframe their idiosyncratic attitudes and routines. Some situations were restrained, leaving room for the subjects to explore, others more confrontational or patronizing. The situations forced the subjects to react, make decisions, and adopt attitudes toward the computerized environment. To draw conclusions about the human experience, we interviewed the participants of the study but also implemented an evaluation design that automatically rated their behavior patterns on the basis of sensory measured interactions in a series of key situations. Applying the same semantic differentials using opposed pairs of adjectives, the participants rated their experience. At the same time, the computer system applied the same categories to the (semi-)automatized evaluation. For example: *"Does a subject behave rather restrained, playful, or refusing in a challenging situation?"* The consistency of the extracted characterizing adjectives is promising, because at first sight, they don't seem to fundamentally contradict each other. For verification, we compared these automated conclusions with the self-assessments of the participants obtained by the questionnaires.

4   Experimental Setup

The research setting consists of five honeycomb-shaped rooms (cf. Fig. 1 a), which we call *ubicombs* and offers a walk-through that lasts about 20 min. The scenic rooms (cf. Fig. 1 b–f), as well as the garment worn by the participants, are equipped with sensors that record their actions and behaviors (e.g. contact, weight, capacity, acceleration, position, head movement, galvanic skin response (GSR)). The acquired sensor values are used to drive different actuators (e.g. lamps, speakers, motors), thus enabling the responsiveness of the rooms. The test subjects can explore, solve puzzles or stage themselves, but are guided in time so that the different test runs are comparable. However, the sensory-measured data are not only used for the responsiveness of the technologically enhanced environment, but also recorded to analyze the behavior of the test subjects.

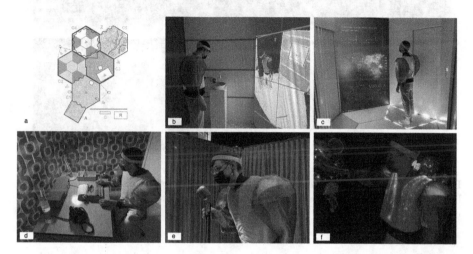

Fig. 1. Floor plan of the *ubicombs* setup (a, 8.70 × 6.50 × 2.50 m), Staged paradigms of UbiComp in five connected honey-comb-shaped spaces: *Zen Garden* (b), *SciFi* (c), *Office Anachronism* (d), *Echo Chamber* (e) and *Mycelium* (f)

5   Mixed-Methods Evaluation

In this research project we combine qualitative and quantitative data collection and analysis methods. On the one hand we asked the participants for interviews (recorded, transcribed, QDA-coded) and to fill out questionnaires (semantic differentials), on the other hand we collected sensory data of the subjects and their interaction with the installation that was subsequently analyzed it by means of the projects' own *Evaluation Viewer* (Fig. 2), and transformed using corresponding algorithmic rating implementations.

5.1   Participants and Evaluation Units

Three pre-tests were conducted with a total of 37 participants, which helped to optimize the research situation and the evaluation design. Subsequently, three evaluation blocks of 20 persons each were invited to explore the artistic installation. Diversity in age, gender and background was taken into account. Using an online pre-survey, all participants were asked to provide anonymous information about themselves and to conduct self-assessments regarding creativity and openness toward new things and technology. Since the participants can be grouped

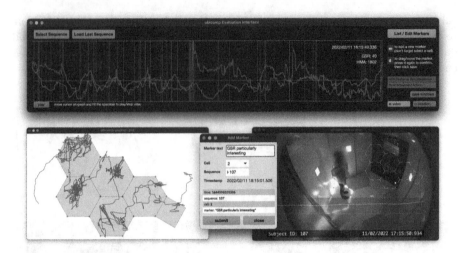

Fig. 2. The *Evaluation Viewer*: timeline with event markers and plots of GSR and head movement, position tracking on ground floor plan, video composed of camera recordings, editor for manual markers

into different categories dynamically by the pre-survey information, we did not define test groups.

All participants were asked to give consent to the use of anonymized data collection, camera and audio recordings as part of the pre-survey and again before entering the installation in situ. The anonymized data is stored on the database SWITCH (in collaboration with the FHNW), based on the Data Management Plan (DMP) agreed on with the Swiss National Science Foundation (SNSF).

5.2   Quantitative Data Collection and Visualization

The behavioral patterns of the participants were identified by the triggered events, by collecting and contextually referencing the sensor data. The data was used to evaluate key situations such as *"Does she take an apple [Yes/No]?"* or *"Does she solve the puzzle before time-out [Yes/No]?"*. In the *Evaluation Viewer*, sensor data is synchronized and displayed alongside video tracks recorded by wide-angle cameras installed in all rooms. All recorded events (interactions of the participants and temporally controlled changes) are displayed as markers on a time axis and allow retrieval of additional information in the context of the video recording. Special attention is paid to the measurements of skin conductivity (GSR[2] finger ring) and head movement (recorded with an IMU[3] worn on the head). All sensor and event data are stored in a database.

---

[2] *GSR*: Galvanic Skin Response, also *EDA*: Electro-dermal Activity.
[3] Inertial Measurement Unit.

5.3   Qualitative Data Collection

Central for this poster is the development of *semantic differentials* [9,10]. The participants were asked to rate the *ubicombs* using the same adjectives that were used for the evaluation of the collected sensory data (cf. 5.4). The semantic differentials are structured along the following dimensions: *atmosphere, affect, behavior, activity, attitude*, that were derived from studies in environmental psychology [11–13] and contextual behavior analysis [14]. For each of these dimensions, pairs of adjectives (antonyms) were compiled to investigate human behavior, appropriation and attitude in techno-social environments. On a scale of 1–5, the participants had to rate antonyms such as: networked/disconnected (for atmosphere); calm/anxious (for affect); unconcerned/cautious (for behavior); involved/excluded (for activity); consenting/refusing (for attitude).

5.4   Data Analysis and Interpretation

In order to relate the quantitative and qualitative approaches, the same antonyms that the subjects had used for self-assessment during the interviews, were used to evaluate the sensory data collected: four researchers (a psychologist, a media theorist, a designer, and a media artist) subjectively classified the participants recorded actions (subsequently called *conditions*) by assessing the video recordings and entering the rating for each condition in terms of every semantic differential in the rating matrix. In the first *ubicomb* the rating could, for example, indicate: *"The subject perceives the apple bowl but does not interact with it"* corresponds to a rather anxious, passive, and/or refusing behavior. *"The subject takes an apple"* corresponds to a rather calm, active, and/or consenting behavior. The rating-matrix consists of 77 *conditions* and 25 *semantic differentials*.

In the summarizing process, the average values of the four rating matrices are used. The individual ratings contributed by the team members were discussed and changed when the respective values were deviating until the matrix of average rating values reflected consensus (minimizing standard deviation, Fig. 3). The summarizing process entails averaging the rating values of only the activated conditions per subject, first by *ubicomb* and finally in respect to the entire run. The processed ratings exceeding an empirically determined threshold are used to select the semantic differentials used to identify behavioral patterns and attitudes of the participants. In a next step, the personality expressions determined by the rating system are compared with those determined by the subjects in their self-assessments.

6   Findings and Discussion

We call the design of these evaluation situations "Contextual Behavior Evaluation Design". The study is not intended to be commercially applicable. Rather we intend to critically assess how easy it is to make statements about people's

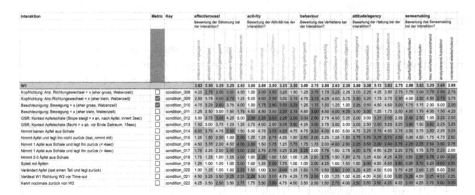

Fig. 3. Superimposed rating matrices. Consensus variation is calculated and visualized by color: The more the ratings differ, the higher the numbers and the darker the color representing a lower rating reliability.

personal behavioral patterns and attitudes using ubiquitous, environmentally embedded measurement technologies. Since this procedure is very intrusive, it has to be said that we are aware of the ongoing ethical debate about privacy issues. However, the current state of the discourse seems to be mostly concerned with smart data analysis on personal devices. Another important aspect however, is the automatic analysis of behavior in sensory equipped public space (cf. [15]).

The developed semantic differentials were also reviewed to draw conclusions on their effectiveness. Analyzing the data will help to reduce redundancies, increase comprehensibility for the participants, and sharpen the validity regarding the assessment of attitudes towards technologically enhanced environments.

We computed the consensus variation (Fig. 3) leading to rating confidence. For the extraction of the characterizing adjectives we plan to evaluate the inclusion of a confidence factor: adjectives that are selected by a high rating confidence get more weight. However, adjectives that were rated under ambiguous conditions (i.e. interactive scenes with ambiguous rating potential) leading to a low rating confidence, would have their influence in the selection reduced. Consensus variation should therefore also be used to identify design aspects. Situations, the four researchers rated with a high level of consensus, proved to be suitable to identify personal behavior patterns and attitudes. We will further analyze these aspects and derive design principles for Contextual Behavior Evaluation Design.

The algorithmically derived behavioral patterns and attitudes (1) (Fig. 3) are compared to the subjective assessments of the participants (2). Furthermore, we will add the human expert observer reviewing the video recordings (3) to judge the participants' behavioral patterns and attitudes. This third perspective is crucial to find out whether the complex process of human observation and assessment can be reduced to specifically designed and rated key interactions.

We will go on analyzing and documenting the collected data according to the discussed issues. The findings of our research may be valuable to future scientific endeavors and data driven new media art. In general, the findings from our research may be of value to whoever is trying to convey new information to a largely heterogeneous public.

References

1. Weiser, M.: The computer for the 21st century. In: Scientific American special issue on Communications, Computers, and Networks, pp. 94–104 (1991)
2. Abowd, G., Mynatt, E.: Designing for the human experience in smart environments. In: Cook, D., Das, S. (eds.) Smart Environments. Technology, Protocols, and Applications, pp. 153–174. John Wiley & Sons Inc., Hoboken, NJ (2005)
3. Norman, D.: Why interfaces don't work. In: Laurel, B. (Eds.) The Art of Human-Computer Interface Design, pp. 209–219. Addison-Wesley Publishing Company Inc. (1990)
4. Mehrabian, A., Russell, J.A.: An Approach to Environmental Psychology. The MIT Press, Cambridge, MA (1974)
5. Bechtel, R., Churchman, A.: Handbook of Environmental Psychology. John Wiley & Sons Inc, New York, NY (2002)
6. McCarthy, J., Wright, P.: Technology as Experience. The MIT Press, Cambridge, MA (2004)
7. Wilson, S.: Information Art. The MIT Press, Cambridge, MA (2002)
8. Dunne, A., Raby, F.: Speculative Everything. Fiction, and Social Dreaming. MIT Press, Cambridge, MA, Design (2013)
9. Osgood, C.E., Suci, G.J., Tannenbaum, P.H.: The Measurement of Meaning. University of Illinois Press, Urbana, IL (1957)
10. Rosenberg, B., Navarro, M.: Semantic differential scaling. In: The SAGE Encyclopedia of Educational Research, Measurement, and Evaluation, pp. 1504–1507. SAGE Publications, Thousand Oaks, CA (2018)
11. Bakker, I., van der Voordt, T., Vink, P., de Boon, J.: Pleasure, arousal, dominance: mehrabian and russell revisited. Curr. Psychol. **33**(3), 405–421 (2014). https://doi.org/10.1007/s12144-014-9219-4
12. Gifford, R., Steg, L., Reser, J.P.: Environmental psychology. In: Martin, P.R., Cheung, F.M., (eds.) et al. IAAP Handbook of Applied Psychology, pp. 440–470. Wiley Blackwell, Hoboken, NJ (2011)
13. Stern, P. C.: Toward a coherent theory of environmentally significant behavior. J. Soc. Issues **56**(3), 407–424 (2000)
14. Hayes, S.C., Barnes-Holmes, D., Wilson, K. G.: Contextual behavioral science: creating a science more adequate to the challenge of the human condition. In: The Act in Context, pp. 280–317. Imprint Routledge, New York (2012)
15. Zuboff, S.: The Age of Surveillance Capitalism. The Fight for a Human Future at the New Frontier of Power. PublicAffairs, New York, NY (2019)

Understanding Speleology and Paleoanthropology Through Digital and Interactive Technologies

Emmanouil Tzimtzimis[1,2(✉)], Dimitrios Tzetzis[1,2], Charisios Achillas[1,3], Sokratis Poulios[4], Petros Tzioumakis[4], Andreas Darlas[5], Athanasios Athanasiou[5], Dimitrios Aidonis[1,3], and Dionysis Bochtis[1]

[1] Institute for Bio-Economy and Agri-Technology, Centre for Research and Technology Hellas (CERTH), Volos, Greece

[2] Digital Manufacturing and Materials Characterization Laboratory, School of Science and Technology, International Hellenic University, Thermi, Greece
m.tzimtzimis@ihu.edu.gr

[3] Department of Supply Chain Management, International Hellenic University, Katerini, Greece

[4] Polytech S.A., Larisa, Greece

[5] Ephorate of Palaeoanthropology and Speleology, Ministry of Culture and Sports, Athens, Greece

Abstract. The Petralona Cave, which is considered one of the most impressive and important caves throughout Europe, is located near the village of Petralona, Chalkidiki, Greece. The cave was found in 1959 and became well known all over the world in 1960 as the home of the oldest human remains ever found in Greece, when the skull of Arhanthropos was found. The cave was approximately formed a million years ago in the limestone of Katsika Hill, stretches across an area of 10,400 m^2 and consists of a series of stoas, chambers, high ceilings and pools, full of stalactites, stalagmites, curtains and shields, columns and other formations. Within the proximity of the Petralona Cave, the Petralona Museum is also operating. In the framework of the Cave3 project and in collaboration with the Hellenic Ministry of Culture and Sports and Polytech S.A., the Centre for Research & Technology Hellas (CERTH) is developing innovative mechanisms and state-of-the-art, digital tools, open labs and serious games in order to provide an interactive experience to the visitors, including also people with special needs. This project presents the process of digitalization of the Petralona Cave and various paleontological findings from the Cave's Museum, including the human skull of Arhanthropos, as well as several bones from different species lived inside the cave throughout its existence. Using different 3D scanning methods and techniques, such as photogrammetry and laser scanning, both the inner and the outer of the cave has been digitalized. Moreover, paleontological findings with special interest in their historical heritage have been selected for the implementation of a digital library. The digitalization of these findings was conducted with white light and laser 3D scanning methods, as well as state-of-the-art 3D software for photorealistic illustration. The aforementioned digital models of the Petralona Cave and the paleontological findings are merged in a virtual reality environment to interact with visitors and enrich their experience, while serious games have been developed for educational purposes.

C. Stephanidis et al. (Eds.): HCII 2022, CCIS 1582, pp. 288–295, 2022.
https://doi.org/10.1007/978-3-031-06391-6_38

Keywords: Virtual reality · 3D scanning · Human-computer interaction · Culture

1 Introduction

1.1 A Subsection Sample

In the framework of the Cave3 project four collaborative partners, contribute on the design, research and development of innovative interdisciplinary applications. Cooperation between the project partners should lead to the activation of know-how transfer activities and thus to the strengthening of cooperation between them.

The Cave3 project aims at the utilization of modern digital technologies, virtual reality and three-dimensional printing for the development of innovative navigation mechanisms in the Cave and the Museum of Petralona, with the specific purpose of the experiential & interactive experience of the visitor.

Modern three-dimensional technologies (three-dimensional scanning and printing, virtual reality) can turn the visit to the cave and museum into real entertainment and medium pedagogy through the operation of demonstration workshops in the form of "open-sighted laboratories" (open labs).

The test operation of the demonstration facility is valuable both to the general public (adults and schools) and to specialist scientists, since the information will be "classified" in such a way that one can refer to it according to the extent that one wants to deepen.

The project has carried out a thorough bibliographical survey and a survey of the current technological situation in the subjects related to the Cave3 project. Relevant definitions are incorporated [1], themes related to the development and historical evolution of virtual reality are described, while the main characteristics of virtual museums are analysed. An analysis of the use of virtual reality in the educational and learning process is carried out [2], the advantages of using virtual reality in education, the virtual reality application areas for educational purposes are given, and indicative areas for exploiting the relevant technology are presented.

The research incorporates information on technologies and requirements for the use of virtual reality technologies, both in hardware and software. Indicative training games (Serious games) are presented and categorized [3], reference is made to their historical development and development capabilities.

Finally, information on three-dimensional digitization technologies is provided, which is a key parameter for the implementation of the project, namely issues of reverse engineering, three-dimensional scanning and equipment of three-dimensional scanners, while the basic principles of their operation are analysed, and a related categorization of the available equipment is carried out.

2 User Requirements

As a necessary element for the success of the project, the Ephorate of Paleoanthropology-Speleology (YPO.A.) conducted a survey of user requirements regarding the type of services that would be desirable from potential future visitors to the Cave and the Museum of Petralona. The survey was designed with the cooperation of the project partners and was in the form of a questionnaire, which included thirteen simple and understandable questions with multiple predefined answers. The participants were given the opportunity to choose one or more answers, depending on the nature of the question. The survey took place from 24 July to 21 December 2020 and involved a total of 117 people of various ages, educational levels, etc.

The questions were of two kinds: a) completion of certain personal data (gender, age, place of residence, frequency of visits to museums and the Cave and Museum of Petralona), and b) concerning the desired experience of a future visit to the Cave and the Museum of Petralona, the reasons for visiting the museum, type and format of the exhibition and the knowledge it provides.

The answers which emerged, and analyzed using simple statistical methods, led to the following conclusions:

- The Cave and the Petralona Museum are not sufficiently well known to the general public and efforts should be made to make the importance of the cave and its findings more widely known.
- It is preferable to use modern display techniques, using short texts and more supervisory material.
- Innovative technologies are needed to highlight the findings of the cave, as well as their integration into a single narrative framework.
- The use of educational games is welcome, and therefore their creation should be an immediate priority of the Project.

3 Methods

3.1 3D Scanning of Paleontological Findings

In the framework of the Cave3 project four collaborative partners, contribute on the design, research and development.

Paleontological Findings suitable for the 3D Scanning Process. For the 3D scanning and the implementation of the virtual reality environment, findings of the Cave were selected with a particular interest in their geometric and physical condition and their historical heritage. For this reason, the digital library contains a diverse range of pale-ontological findings including skulls of various species (goat, rhinoceros, equidae, hy-ena, etc.) with the most characteristic of all the human skull molding found in the Cave (Fig. 1).

Fig. 1. 3D scanning of human skull

As seen in Fig. 2 some of the findings were mounted and glued onto a rigid column, making it difficult to scan the bottom surfaces of them. Hence, they were chosen due to the particular interest in their historical background.

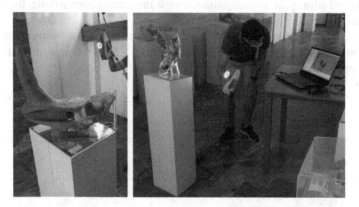

Fig. 2. 3D Scanning of mounted findings

3D Scanning Process. The 3D scanning process consists of four main stages. The generation of the point cloud with the help of the three-dimensional scanner is the first step to digitize the physical object in the digital environment. The natural object (finding) is scanned from different sides and angles (Fig. 5) in order to capture a large number of points that will help in the digital construction of the finding (Fig. 3).

The individual point clouds are then cleared of any noise that may be around them and are aligned with each other through various common user-defined reference points. Aligning scans creates a common coordinate system, useful for later processing.

The third step of the processing consists of creating the mesh and modify it. By aligning all the necessary point clouds, through special algorithms and commands, the triangular grid (wireframe) is created. Afterwards the points are joined together to create

Fig. 3. Three-dimensional scan of find from different sides and angles

the three-dimensional digital copy of the finding. The number of these points affects the precision of a 3D model; the more points the resolution of the final copy (larger mesh) gets, the better the accuracy, but at the same time the data (Gigabytes) of each digital copy enlarge.

At the final stage of processing, the texture (the natural colors) of the physical object is added onto the digital copy. As in the previous stages, there are a variety of options for adding and editing the texture, with the most important characteristic, the quality of the desired resolution.

Finally, Fig. 4 illustrates all the important stages to create a three-dimensional digital model from an early cave bear skull (Ursus Spelaeus), from the implementation of the cloud point to the addition of the natural colors to the final copy.

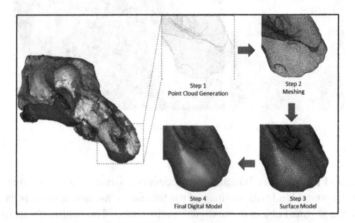

Fig. 4. The processing steps for the digital model

3.2   3D Scanning of the CAVE

As part of the Cave3 project, the research team of the National Center for Research & Technological Development - Institute of Bio-economy and Agro-technology scan the entire route (Fig. 5) of the Petralona Cave, but also areas outside the route using ground scanners and unmanned flying devices – drones (Fig. 6). With the aim of maximizing the promotion and demonstration of the findings of the Cave and the Petralona Museum, photogrammetry of the Cave's terrain was imprinted, as well as excavations, which can be presented digitally to visitors for the first time.

Fig. 5. 3D scanning process inside the cave

A total of three flights were made, one out of 110 m to quickly capture the ground on site and create a digital terrain model. This model was then uploaded to the UAV system remote control and two more flights were made, following this time a fixed height of 35 m from the ground model obtained from the first flight. Thus, the analysis on the ground remains as stable as possible and particularly high.

Fig. 6. 3D Scan of the outer area (left) and a digital reconstruction of it (right)

3.3 Virtual Reality and Serious Games

The serious games have thematic units related to the findings of the cave. The system is essentially a platform for developing 2D and 3D games and applications, with the ability to expand and add supplementary functionality. It provides the ability to operate across mobile-Android (iOS) environments. The Serious Game application is aimed to visitors, of the cave, mostly under 12 years old with the main purpose of having fun when visiting the cave while providing knowledge and information of the findings of the cave.

The application is deployed in Unity Engine and programmed in C#. MeshLab was also used to modify the size of some objects, as well as GIMP to create some graphics. The main part of the application is to navigate a predetermined route within the cave from a predetermined "A" point to a predetermined "B" point in order to complete the game.

The user controls the character using the touch screen. The right part of the screen controls the camera and the left the movement of the character. During the journey, there are objects/finds that the user must collect. During the collection of the finding, a window with information about it emerges, with the possibility of penetrating more information and starting games on some of them.

So far, a number of serious games have been developed within the application such as:

- Game with matching cards (memo game). Depending on the time it took the user to match all the cards with their pairs, as well as how many times he tried to turn the cards, he will receive a corresponding score.
- Game by organizing an image that is split into multiple pieces and each piece is not in the correct rotation position on the Z axis, having rotated in addition to 90°.
- Game with multiple choice questionnaire (Fig. 7).

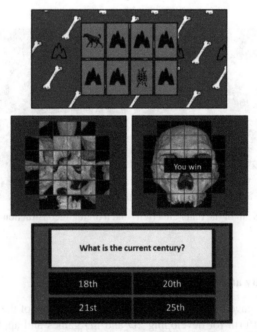

Fig. 7. Serious games. matching cards (Top), puzzle pieces (Middle), multiple choice questionnaire (Bottom)

3.4   Virtual Reality OPEN Lab

The OPEN Lab system is used to create a virtual reality lab for the cave finding maintenance processes. It consists of a high-specification computer system with an integrated
interface instrument used by the operator to actively interact with the virtual laboratory environment imitating the mechanical behavior of a series of virtual tools that can
be used by the user for virtual representation of actual tasks performed within a real
speleological and paleontology laboratory.

The VR laboratory is illustrated inside an area, which is the laboratory of a paleontologist. Up to this point the workshop area consists of multiple objects such as workbench,
lighting and findings (Fig. 8). The user can navigate through this area and explore it either
through the screen or through the three-dimensional glasses. In terms of paleontologist
work, a simulated carving of an object using the mouse pointer has been achieved. It will
then be tested and validated to further improve the algorithm in terms of user performance
and experience. Finally, an Undo-Redo system has been designed while processing the
object to determine if there has been an incorrect movement, to allow the user to change
over time and thereby change the morphology of the object.

Fig. 8. The VR environment of the OPEN Lab

References

1. Laamarti, F., Eid, M., el Saddik, A.: An overview of serious games. Int. J. Comput. Games
   Technol. (2014). https://doi.org/10.1155/2014/358152
2. Christou, C.: Virtual reality in education. In: Affective, Interactive and Cognitive Methods
   for E-Learning Design: Creating an Optimal Education Experience, IGI Global, pp. 228–243
   (2010). https://doi.org/10.4018/978-1-60566-940-3.ch012
3. Gunter, G.A., Kenny, R.F., Vick, E.H.: Taking educational games seriously: using the RETAIN
   model to design endogenous fantasy into standalone educational games. Educ. Tech. Res. Dev.
   56(5), 511–537 (2008). https://doi.org/10.1007/s11423-007-9073-2

Narrating the Story of a Digitized Old Historical Map

Evgenios Vlachos[1,2(⊠)] ⓘ, Jakob Povl Holck[1] ⓘ, and Mogens Kragsig Jensen[1] ⓘ

[1] University Library of Southern Denmark, University of Southern Denmark,
Campusvej 55, 5230 Odense, Denmark
evl@bib.sdu.dk

[2] The Mærsk Mc-Kinney Møller Institute, University of Southern Denmark,
Campusvej 55, 5230 Odense, Denmark

Abstract. We describe the process to create an interactive digital artifact out of a physically born material that would assist the interactive cultural heritage experience, as well as the pedagogical practice through artifact-oriented learning and digital storytelling. Our main aim is to reconceptualize, reuse and reintroduce physically born materials that were previously only known to a small group of scholars, students, and specialists to the general public. In our pilot study, we present a graphical interactive map which is an enriched depiction of the Battle of Lützen (1632) that includes geographical information, cultural products inspired by the depicted event (e.g., paintings, music, museum artifacts, documentaries), technological artifacts illustrated at the map, and elements to assist the digital narration (e.g., buttons, captions, sound and text). Our proposed low-cost solution demands no programming skills at all, is based mostly on open-source tools, and requires -ideally- only a touch-screen. The ease of implementing this solution enables it to be applied in a plethora of digitized artifacts and be used at schools, libraries, museums, and universities.

Keywords: Old maps · Cartography · Interactive art and design · Digital humanities · Digital storytelling · Artifact-oriented learning

1 Introduction

With the rise of digital humanities, the current developments concerning the usability of digital objects have increased the expectations on the extent of available features, and on the general user interface. Digitizing physically born materials and enhancing them with audiovisual elements admittedly assists greatly the interactive cultural heritage experience. If storytelling processes are included in addition, then the digitized materials can also include a pedagogical dimension [1].

For classical library collections to renew their relevance, efforts towards digital storytelling should be considered. Concerning old maps and similar graphics, the digital storytelling perspective calls for a detailed analysis of the printed elements before choosing the means of virtual enhancement. The wealth of information contained in an old historic map is extended beyond what meets the eye. Digitizing the map and capturing

© The Author(s), under exclusive license to Springer Nature Switzerland AG 2022
C. Stephanidis et al. (Eds.): HCII 2022, CCIS 1582, pp. 296–303, 2022.
https://doi.org/10.1007/978-3-031-06391-6_39

all its graphical details is one thing; but being able to digitally narrate the story of the map including all its elements is another quite challenging one.

In this case-study, we present a graphical interactive war map[1] which is an enriched depiction of the Battle of Lützen (1632) [2] between the Protestant troops commanded by Swedish king Gustav 2. Adolph, and the imperial Catholic army under Wallenstein during the Thirty Years War. Apart from information of the main characters that appear in the original map, we have included geographical information, cultural products inspired by the depicted event (e.g., paintings, music, museum artifacts, documentaries), technological artifacts illustrated at the map, and last but not least graphical elements to assist the digital narration (e.g., buttons, captions, sound and text). It should be noted that it takes a significant amount of effort to gather valid scientific information concerning the artifact, and then additional effort to figure out what is the best possible way to illustrate that information, and then actually create the illustration.

Smith and Smith [3] have shown that people spend on average 27.2 s observing a work of art in a museum, while Heidenreich and Turano [4] found that observations last from 20 to 82 s. Our method of digitizing physical artifacts and enhancing them with audiovisual storytelling elements may increase the observation time, while making the experience more interactive, thus reintroducing the artifact. Our proposed low-cost solution adds a complementary digital twist in the whole aesthetic experience of observing printed artifacts without reducing it or intending to replace it. Last, but not least, it can be used in the classroom as artifact-oriented learning [5] is a valid interdisciplinary educational method combining arts, science and learning literature in a holistic way.

2   Reconceptualization, Reuse, and Reintroduction

Rare old maps, and topographical engravings are often part of the special collections in research libraries. The format of physical maps, e.g., very large sizes, and the frequently fragile condition of these materials, calls for digitization initiatives. However, there are other reasons for digitization. At the University Library of Southern Denmark (SDUB), the enhanced accessibility, that comes with a digitization, fits nicely into the general Open Science policy of the university that follows the FAIR principles [6]. Reborn-digital objects [7] can also be considered a pillar in the ongoing efforts to reconceptualize, reuse and reintroduce library materials that were previously only known to a small group of scholars, students, and specialists.

The *Diocese Library of Funen* (SDUB collection) contains hundreds of rare maps and topographical etchings. One of them is the copper engraving *Instructio aciei caesareanorum et Suecorum prope Luzzenam* […] (c. 1633), (likely engraved and) published by Matthäus Merian in Frankfurt, Germany – originally as part of Johann Philipp Abelinus: 'Theatrum Europaeum', volume 2 (1st edition) [8]. In its analog format, the SDUB's engraving is uncolored and measures c. 29 × 36.5 cm. The engraving has the call number: mv 90.2 Ve 56 nr. 8. Due to its historical importance as an event, we have chosen this engraving as a case study for reconceptualization, reuse, and reintroduction, thus creating an interactive map.

---

[1] Demo of the interactive map as viewed in a tablet https://youtu.be/t-WJgm7azT4, last accessed 15 Mar 2022.

2.1 Reconceptualization

The reconceptualization aims at aligning the chosen library materials with current behavioral and 'immersive technologies' trends in modern society, considering the fact that university students, and other library patrons are well versed in the use of computers, and corresponding software. Phenomena like AR (Augmented Reality), VR (Virtual Reality), XR (eXtended Reality), mixed reality, along with 'gamification', or even robotics have become increasingly important tools for learning [9, 10].

While the physical old map, or topographical material, typically requires the reader/scholar to look in reference works to decode the content, the new generations of library users are accustomed to a plug-and-play-like, instant access to multiple layers of information in the form of Linked Open Data (LOD) [11]. Apart from the idea of using standards for the representation, and the access to data on the Web, LOD involves the setting of hyperlinks between data from different sources. The reconceptualization of the rare old library maps and engravings takes this into consideration.

2.2 Reuse

The reuse of the library materials is, in fact, a transformation of the format from a 2D product into 5D – with the fifth dimension being the applied interactivity with the interlinked information structure.

The digital interactivity draws strength from the combination of several stimuli, both visual, auditive and tactile: You push a button (by touchscreen, or PC mouse), and you get an animated action on your monitor, accompanied by the recorded sound from your loudspeakers, or headset.

By placing links that point to other parts of the Internet, the user of the interactive map experiences "gateways" in real-time to new historical facets and, in principle, endless study. In other words, the interactive map is not a closed entity but a complex of informational, web-based threads into the World that may stimulate further scholarly engagement.

2.3 Reintroduction

The reintroduction of the library materials is the promotion of the once analog items as digitally reborn objects with enhanced functionality (Interactive Virtual Objects – IVOs) [12]. The reborn-digital objects have some of the same features as the analog ones, but also come with the above-mentioned extradimensional application(s).

Of course, the researcher who is interested in the paper quality, or ink analysis will not be satisfied – unless the results of such analyses have already been digitized and added to the interactive layers of the reborn-digital object. Libraries and similar institutions may choose different types of digital platforms – digital libraries – to reintroduce materials that could previously only be used in a reading room.

In comparison to our map study, the concept of reintroduction has manifested itself in similar types of work, e.g., in museums [13] with new ways of communicating museum artefacts and enhancing the learning experience [14]. In a cultural heritage perspective [15], the digital reintroduction provides a possibility of providing equal access to cultural content, as an important element in the general democratic discourse [16]. Concerning maps in general, the application of immersive technologies for visualization purposes [17] is well-known, in addition to other creative uses of digital map objects [18] that may function as a means of reintroducing once analog materials, also deploying web-geographic information systems and LOD [19].

3 Historical Perspective

The Battle of Lützen unfolded on November 16th 1632 in the vicinity of the small town of Lützen, not far from Leipzig, in the Electorate of Saxony in Germany. The battle is generally considered as one of the most memorable in the long string of conflicts and battles that ripped Europe apart in the decades between 1618 and 1648, and later known as the Thirty Years War. Not because of the impact of the battle, nor for any other military, or political reason, since Lützen was just one major battle among several. The special legacy of this battle is closely connected with the fact that the Swedish king Gustav 2. Adolph died on the battlefield, which in the long aftermath earned him hero status [20]. Due to that fact, we believe it could serve well as our prototype interactive map.

The Thirty Years War rooted in religious conflicts between the catholic south and the protestant north. The main antagonist was the Holy Roman Empire with the Habsburg emperor struggling to maintain Catholicism, at the one side, opposed to the German protestant states, who wanted to fight for their religious freedom, gained in the Reformation, which they, a century earlier, had achieved. As in 1630, the catholic forces were victorious when the Swedish king, as one of the major protestant monarchs, entered the European scene with his armies, and in the next two years convincingly continued the war, and gained several spectacular victories [21].

At Lützen the belligerents were the catholic party, namely the Holy Roman Empire, added by the Catholic League, with the renowned generalissimo Albrecht von Wallenstein, Duke of Friedland (1583–1634), as the supreme commander. His subcommanders were Field Marshal Gottfried, Count von Pappenheim (1594–1632) and Major General Heinrich von Holk (1599–1633). In this battle they commanded an army consisting of infantry and cavalry, in total 19.175 men, of which 2/3 were made up of cavalry. His opponents on the protestant side, first and foremost Sweden, supported by Saxony and Hessen-Kassel, was commanded by the Swedish king, Gustav 2. Adolph (1594–1632) in person. His subcommanders were Major General Dodo Baron of Innhausen and Knyphausen (1583–1636) and General Bernard, Prince of Saxe-Weimar (1604–1639). The strength of their army were 18.738 men, of which 1/3 were cavalry [21].

The battle began at first light at 7.30 a.m. and lasted the whole day, at least until darkness fell at 5 p.m. There were 38.000 men at the battlefield this day, and close to 1/3 of them died, or were wounded. The losses on the protestant side amounted to about 6.000 killed and wounded men, where the catholic side amounted to 5.160 killed, wounded, and captured. Due to these facts, the battle can be described as a narrow Swedish victory [21].

The death of the Swedish king was of course unpredictable, but also remarkable for its age. At midday he saw his army short of commanders, and he decided to personally intervene instead of waiting for reinforcement. In this turmoil the king was suddenly struck by a bullet, which broke his left arm above the elbow, after which he fell back with a small entourage. His stablemaster took the reins of the king's horse and began to lead him back to the Swedish lines, when suddenly a group of enemy cuirassiers appeared out of the mist and fired a pistol in the king's back. He fell off his horse and received several rapier thrusts through his body. When the Swedish reinforcements approached, someone quickly delivered the mortal pistol shot in the king's temple [22].

While the memory of battles normally fades after a century or so, Lützen is a different case. From the bicentenary and onwards, the battle has been commemorated in Germany and Sweden, supporting various forms of nationalism expressed through Protestantism, and so has its natural place in European remembrance culture [20, 21].

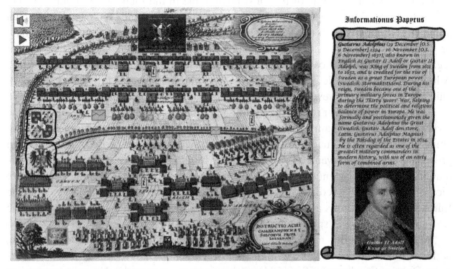

Fig. 1. Snapshot of the interactive digitized map of the Battle of Lützen, with additional information appearing after pressing the Swedish Coat of Arms button.

4 Development

We made an intended effort to include no programming and coding at all when developing the interactive map. We are aware that the main user groups who could utilize best the interactive map are librarians, museum curators, researchers from the humanities, and students, all of whom could face great difficulties in programming, as well as lack coding skills. Thus, we resorted in using Microsoft PowerPoint, and took advantage of the animations, and transitions tabs. We also wanted to keep the costs close to zero, therefore we used available open-source solutions whenever possible. All buttons were created in Microsoft Paint, all four animated GIFs (graphic interchange format) were created by Gifmaker[2] (cannon fire; fire at the city of Lützen; windmill turning; German

---

[2] Gifmaker, https://gifmaker.me/, last accessed 15 Mar 2022.

soldier moving), and the banner was created with DesignEvo[3] free logo maker (see Fig. 1). Table 1 shows all the buttons and their actions.

Table 1. Buttons and their actions.

Button	Category	Action
	Image	(x3) Opens up an image with either a caption or additional text with possible links to external resources.
	Video	Opens up a 30-minute documentary about the battle of Lützen[4].
	Audio	Opens up an audio file with war sounds (muskets and cannons) from that era[5].
	Information	(x4) Opens up an information panel with details on a specific person, place or artifact with possible links to external resources.
	Additional Art	Opens up the painting "The battle at Lützen" from Peter Snayers (1632) depicting the same event.
	Coat of Arms	Opens up information on Swedish king Gustav 2. Adolph, while playing "Motetto - Salve decus suecorum Rex Gustave Adolphe", by Jacob Preaetorius (1586-1651)[6].
	Coat of Arms	Opens up information on Albrecht von Wallenstein, the supreme commander of the Imperial Army of Roman-German Emperor Ferdinard II, followed by the song "Wallenstein" by dArtagnan (2019)[7].

5   Conclusion

We have presented our low-cost solution to reconceptualize, reuse, and reintroduce reborn-digital objects under an educational and cultural prism via the interactive maps concept. The ease of implementing this solution -as it demands no programming skills- combined with the fact that is based on open-source tools, enables it to be applied in a number of digitized artifacts and be utilized at schools, libraries, museums, or universities.

This was our first attempt towards an interactive map. Future work includes turning more maps and paintings into an interactive form, collaborating with graphic designers to create better illustrations, and engaging website developers to move the interactive maps project online on its own website. We would also like to run workshops on teaching how to create such maps where users would come with their own digital artifacts, learn how to search for valid scientific literature, and then explore software tools and programmes that would help them illustrate their ideas.

---

[3] DesignEvo, https://www.designevo.com/, last accessed 15 Mar 2022.

References

1. Coulter, C., Michael, C., Poynor, L.: Storytelling as pedagogy: an unexpected outcome of narrative inquiry. Curriculum Inq. **37**(2), 103–122 (2007). https://doi.org/10.1111/j.1467-873X.2007.00375.x
2. Britannica. The Editors of Encyclopaedia. Battle of Lützen. Encyclopedia Britannica, 9 November 2021. https://www.britannica.com/event/Battle-of-Lutzen. Accessed 20 Jan 2022
3. Smith, J.K., Smith, L.F.: Spending time on art. Empir. Stud. Arts **19**(2), 229–236 (2001). https://doi.org/10.2190/5MQM-59JH-X21R-JN5J
4. Heidenreich, S.M., Turano, K.A.: Where does one look when viewing artwork in a museum? Empir. Stud. Arts **29**(1), 51–72 (2011). https://doi.org/10.2190/EM.29.1.d
5. Peppler, K., Davis-Soylu, H.J., Dahn, M.: Artifact-oriented learning: a theoretical review of the impact of the arts on learning. Arts Educ. Policy Rev. 1–17 (2021)
6. Wilkinson, M., Dumontier, M., Aalbersberg, I. et al.: The FAIR guiding principles for scientific data management and stewardship. Sci. Data **3**, 160018 (2016). https://doi.org/10.1038/sdata.2016.18
7. Brügger, N.: Digital humanities in the 21st century: digital material as a driving force. Digit. Hum. Q. **10**(3) (2016)
8. Abelinus, J. P., Merian, M.: Historische Chronick Oder Warhaffste Beschreibung aller vornehmen und denckwürdigen Geschichten : so sich hin und wider in der Welt/ von Anno Christi 1629. biß auff das Jahr 1633. zugetragen ; Insonderheit/ was auff das im Reich publicirte Kayserliche/ die Restitution der Geistlichen von den Protestirenden in Teutschland eingezogenen Güter/ betreffende Edict/ für Jammer und Landsverwüstung erfolget: Was die Evangelische für Trangsalen von den Römisch-Catholischen erleyden müssen/ und wie sie endlichen durch Göttlichen Beystand/ und Ihrer Mayest. Gustavi Adolphi, Königs zu Schweden [...]. Frankfurt am Main (1633). Cf. German online edition: http://diglib.hab.de/per iodica/70-b-hist-2f/start.htm?image=00802, http://diglib.hab.de/periodica/70-b-hist-2f/start. htm?image=00803
9. Niermann, P. F.J., Palmas, F.: Extended Reality Training: Ein Framework für die virtuelle Lernkultur in Organisationen (1. 2021 ed.). Springer Fachmedien Wiesbaden (2021)
10. Vlachos, E., Hansen, A.F., Holck, J.P.: A robot in the library. In: Rauterberg, M. (ed.) HCII 2020. LNCS, vol. 12215, pp. 312–322. Springer, Cham (2020). https://doi.org/10.1007/978-3-030-50267-6_24
11. Bizer C., Vidal M.E., Skaf-Molli H.: Linked open data. In: Liu L., Özsu M.T. (eds.) Encyclopedia of Database Systems. Springer, New York, NY. (2018) https://doi.org/10.1007/978-1-4614-8265-9_80603
12. Banfi, F., Mandelli, A.: Interactive virtual objects (ivos) for next generation of virtual museums: from static textured photogrammetric and hbim models to xr objects for vr-ar enabled gaming experiences. In: International Archives of the Photogrammetry, Remote Sensing and Spatial Information Sciences - ISPRS Archives 46(M-1–2021) 47–54 (2021). https://doi.org/10.5194/isprs-Archives-XLVI-M-1-2021-47-2021
13. Alinam, M., Ciotoli, L., Koceva, F., Torre, I.: Digital storytelling in a museum application using the web of things. In: Bosser, A.-G., Millard, D.E., Hargood, C. (eds.) ICIDS 2020. LNCS, vol. 12497, pp. 75–82. Springer, Cham (2020). https://doi.org/10.1007/978-3-030-62516-0_6
14. Butcher, K.R., et al.: Museum leadership for engaging, equitable education: the transformative potential of digitized collections for authentic learning experiences. Curator (New York, N.Y.) **64**(2), 383–402 (2021)

15. Makropoulos, C., et al.: DiscoVRCoolTour: discovering, capturing and experiencing cultural heritage and events using innovative 3D digitisation technologies and affordable consumer electronics. In: Moropoulou, A., Korres, M., Georgopoulos, A., Spyrakos, C., Mouzakis, C. (eds.) TMM_CH 2018. CCIS, vol. 961, pp. 232–249. Springer, Cham (2019). https://doi.org/10.1007/978-3-030-12957-6_16

16. Seifert, C., et al.: Ubiquitous access to digital cultural heritage. J. Comput. Cult. Heritage **10**(1), 1–27 (2017)

17. Lochhead, I., Hedley, N.: Designing virtual spaces for immersive visual analytics. KN – J. Cartography Geo. Inf. **71**(4), 223–240 (2021).https://doi.org/10.1007/s42489-021-00087-y

18. Koeva, M.N., et al.: Integrating spherical panoramas and maps for visualization of cultural heritage objects using virtual reality technology. Sensors **17**(4), 829 (2017)

19. Nishanbaev, I., et al.: A web GIS-based integration of 3D digital models with linked open data for cultural heritage exploration. ISPRS Int. J. Geo Inf. **10**(10), 684 (2021)

20. Oredsson, S.: Historische Jubiläen – Gefahren und Möglichkeiten am Beispiel Lützen. In: Krieger, M., Krüger, J. (eds.): Regna firmat pietas. Staat und Staatlichkeit im Ostseeraum, pp. 433–442 (2010)

21. Wilson, P.H.: Great Battles Series. Oxford University Press, Lützen (2018)

22. Brzezinski, R.: Lützen 1632. Osprey Publishing, Climax of the thirty years War (2001)

Infographic Design Skills Applied to the Heritage Sector: An Experience from O-City's Pathway in the Orange Economy to Acquire Competences

Valentina Volpi[(✉)] [ID]

Link Campus University, Via del Casale di San Pio V 44, 00165 Rome, Italy
v.volpi@unilink.it

Abstract. Recent evolutions in global economy and society demonstrate that creative competences are a key asset for competing and succeeding in local and international markets. In this sense, there is a need for investments in the creation of an integrated system of relations between entrepreneurship and culture that is generally referred to as the orange economy. In this framework, education is the first step of a process aiming at properly using creativity for achieving social, economic, and environmental development. On the one hand the aim of this short paper is presenting the O-City project's Pathway in the Orange Economy to Acquire Competences as a tool for creating environmental and social sustainability in cities and territories by preserving and promoting heritage. On the other hand, it intends to assess some results obtained in implementing the learning pathway, through a specific course among those developed during the project and available on the O-City learning platform, i.e., the II.6 Infographic course, dealing with user experience (UX) and information design. In detail, the focus is on some specific learning experiences that allowed the realization of creative products in the O-City World, as a way to acquire competences and create value for natural and cultural heritage, as well as for cities and citizens. The short paper will mainly provide insights from qualitative research on the perceived effectiveness and satisfaction about two classroom learning experiences and from expert evaluation about the whole course achievements.

Keywords: User experience · Information design · Creative economy · Natural and cultural heritage

1 Introduction

In front of the wicked problems and the complexity of the global ecosystems, creativity represents a fundamental resource for improving quality of life in cities and territories, because it helps in finding new solutions for the social innovation and the sustainable development of communities at different scales. Therefore, the development of creative competences is required as a key asset, not only in the core sector of the traditional arts, but also in the wider economy, especially for enterprises and regions looking for

C. Stephanidis et al. (Eds.): HCII 2022, CCIS 1582, pp. 304–311, 2022.
https://doi.org/10.1007/978-3-031-06391-6_40

competing and succeeding in local and international markets [1–4]. In this sense, many initiatives in the so-called orange economy, i.e., that sector of the economy that has talent and creativity as leading inputs [5], have been investing in creating an integrated system of relations between entrepreneurship and culture for offering better products and services and for incentivizing the capacity building of workers and professionals. In this framework, education is the first step of a process aiming at activating an increasing number of public and private actors in using creativity for achieving social, economic, and environmental development. According to Peters and Besley [6], universities can make a central contribution, because of their role in transmitting and developing new ideas by creating interconnections between arts and sciences.

So, several research and innovation projects have been developing by several parties with the goal of improving entrepreneurial and creative skills in the heritage sector. In this short paper, the focus will be on the O-City [7] project, and especially on a specific learning product it developed, the II.6 Infographic course. Like the whole project, the course has the aim of building useful skills to create value in the heritage sector, referring both to natural and cultural assets, in the view of boosting the orange economy. In this regard, the short paper will present and discuss some results derived by qualitative research about the effectiveness of two specific classroom learning experiences based on the course and about the perceived satisfaction of the beneficiaries attending them. Further considerations will include expert evaluation about the whole course achievements, also including the results from the students enrolled on the O-City e-learning platform.

2 Related Work About the Role of Creativity and Design Skills in the Heritage Sector

The importance of supporting and fostering urban projects based on creative solutions and culture has recently been made evident in Europe by the New European Bauhaus (NEB) movement, launched by the European Commission [8] to reimagine sustainable living based on circular economy and co-design. In the past, several localized projects and broader studies had shown the fundamental connection between creativity and sustainable development [9–11], directly involving cultural heritage, too [12].

In this regard, design practice and thinking are key assets and competences in deploying creativity, especially when the process is focused on creating better user experiences and positive impacts on the whole ecosystem. This applies even to the city context, where designers and citizens can collaborate at different levels [13]. Indeed, creativity and design skills can be fundamental for the development of the cultural and artistic sectors by promoting or creating added value. At the same time, cultural and artistic perspectives allow us to go beyond mere functionality in design and let the human emerge. Going further, the work of Capello, Cerisola, and Perucca [12] highlights that there is a concurrent mutually reinforcing relationship between cultural heritage and creativity. Therefore, on this basis, the creation of creative and design competences applied to the cultural heritage becomes a trigger that can foster the development of the sector and of the wide orange economy and city well-being as well.

3   The Contribution of the O-City Project in Creating Competences for the Heritage Sector

O-City, Orange City in full, is an Erasmus + project involving 13 partners from Spain, Italy, Greece, Serbia, Slovenia, and Colombia. Its main goal is to discover and promote heritage by encouraging the creation of creative items, i.e., multimedia products such as photography, video, comics, etc., about the natural and cultural realities of a city. The value generated by this process is expected to boost the orange economy and the city's well-being. To achieve this goal, the O-City project created a pathway to train young people, professionals, and organizations in entrepreneurship and in the use of creative technologies. Besides, it also provided universities with innovative teaching tools. The training pathway created by the project is mainly based on the use of two online platforms with different, but integrated goals: on the one side the O-City World platform [14] is used to spread culture and city heritage, along with creative products; on the other side the O-City Learn platform [15] is an open e-learning environment aiming at building competences and innovating learning methodologies, that can be spent in O-City World or in the larger orange economy sector. The O-City Pathway in the Orange Economy to Acquire Competences consists of four main areas of knowledge corresponding to the four different modules of the training program available on the O-City Learn platform, built on the Learning Management System (LMS) of the Polytechnic University of Valencia (UPV): Cultural Heritage and Intellectual Property, Technical, Business, and Soft Skills. All the modules provide basic contents to be acquired through different courses to fairly and effectively create multimedia products and businesses, as well as improving as professionals. Put in practice, the O-City pathway is developed through three main phases. The first one concerns the teachers training on the O-City Learn platform. Here teachers can find different types of open access resources, such as learning materials (e.g.: lectures, factsheets with instructions to develop activities for students, etc.), suggestions on applying innovative learning methodologies (e.g.: project-based learning, flip teaching, e-scrum, etc.), and rubrics for the assessment of students' project works. The second phase is addressed to train the students by transferring knowledge and skills. For technical courses there is a third step consisting in the upload on the O-City World platform of the multimedia created by students during the implementation of the course (step 2). In addition, during the project duration, teachers and students had the possibility to enroll in the courses available on the LMS platform to have more support and tutoring.

Also, a schema of competences is provided for students' evaluation by the teacher. It has been built on EU Digicomp [16] and Entrecomp [17] frameworks for developing and understanding digital and entrepreneurial skills, adapted to the specificities of the O-City project. According to it, students can reach 4 different levels on each competence: Knowledge, when demonstrating basic understanding of concepts, facts, and techniques; or Ability level 1, 2, and 3 while creating a multimedia item, in class guided step by step or only supported by the teacher (level 1 and 2), or by their own with the final feedback of the teacher (level 3). The different levels also reflect the ability to work on given examples rather than to elaborate or create something new.

Besides, each course allows to develop specific abilities. The Infographic course presented in this short paper aims to create digital, communication, and design skills. In detail, it is a technical course developed by Link Campus University in Rome. It deals with basic knowledge and skills on user experience (UX) and information design, allowing the creation of a multimedia based on infographics, i.e., a way of visually representing information and data to make them more readable and easily understandable. In detail, after acquiring some basic principles of user-centered design, visual communication, and information visualization, that can be applied in different real situations, students learn by doing some basic skills for the realization of an infographic for the heritage sector, such as: properly identifying and taking into account different types of requirements; correctly and usefully collecting and organizing information and data; suitably representing them through adequate visualization techniques, first by creating and evaluating prototypes, then by realizing an effective and usable infographic through a graphic software. In addition, they can work in a collaborative way, so developing the related competences. Indeed, by being able to develop this kind of products, students can provide an engaging experience that guarantees the knowledge and subsequent promotion of natural and cultural heritage.

4 Classroom Learning Experiences to Build Infographic Design Skills Applied to the Heritage Sector

Classroom learning experiences represented a way to implement the O-City pathway (second and third steps) with the aim of validating and improving it by assessing the results obtained. So, the implementation of the Infographic course with classrooms was a planned step in the strategy created by the project. In detail, both the classroom experiences presented in this short paper let learners work on real infographic projects about a natural or cultural heritage, going through the different phases of the design process, with the aim of contributing to spread awareness about the heritage and promote it. To acquire the eligibility for the course, learners were required to work in groups for creating a static infographic about a specific heritage assigned during the training. The infographic had to respect the multimedia technical requirements and quality standards to be published on the O-City World platform. In the classroom, the teacher presented the theoretical and practical notions that students should follow in order to complete the infographic. Learning materials had been adapted to the schedule and the type of attendees by making a selection among the resources available on the e-learning platform and by elaborating the activities, based on the provided guidelines. After realizing the paper prototype or other kinds of low fidelity prototypes in the classroom, the students finished their projects by using a graphic software, that they were previously introduced to or a similar one, on their own or with the help of tutors/teachers (2 for the first experience and 4 for the second one) coming from the related organizations involved. The teacher was the same for both the experiences. She works for the Italian university taking part in the O-City project and had previous experience in the fields concerning the topics of the course, besides being well-trained for the O-City classroom learning experience.

The first classroom learning experience, Youth Training Exchange "Know The Heritage!", had been realized in collaboration with another Erasmus + project working on the relationship between cultural heritage and territory, Culture.EDU [18], that had contacts with some cultural sites in Bulgaria and Italy. The learning experience involved

14 undergraduate and graduate students (university education level) being expert in cultural heritage, 6 from Italy and 8 from Bulgaria (about 19–29 years old). Experience 1 was delivered in English and on occasion in local language (Italian) for the individual tutoring. It was in presence and online, even if most of the students were physically in the classroom. The training was scheduled in 3 lessons (18 h in total). For the realization of the final infographic the learners selected one of the cultural sites they visited thanks to the Culture.EDU project in the Sabina, an internal area in the center of Italy. In the end, 6 static infographics (4 in English language about 4 different cultural sites from 3 different cities, and 2 infographics translated in Italian among those created in English) were delivered by 4 groups, with 10 students out of 14 that completed the given assignment. All infographics have been evaluated as suitable to be published on the O-City World platform.

The second learning experience, Designing Digital Products in the Creative Economy Sector, was realized as Soft Skills and Orientation Path (Percorso per le Competenze Trasversali e l'Orientamento) with Istituto S. Orsola in Rome. The learning experience involved 25 fourth grade high school students (upper secondary school education level), 8 from Liceo classico, i.e., classics, and 17 from Liceo artistico, i.e., artistic lyceum (about 17–18 years old). Experience 2 was delivered in presence in English and Italian, to develop skills in both languages, using the local one (Italian) to clear concepts or tasks. The training was scheduled in 3 lessons (14 h in total), plus 12 h of group work (at home or at school with the support of tutors/teachers) to complete the project works. For the realization of the final infographic the learners selected one of the cultural sites in the Sabina area among those that had not already been picked in the first experience. In the end, 9 static infographics (8 in Italian language about 10 different cultural sites from 4 new cities and 1 already present in the O-City World, and 1 infographic translated in Italian among those created in English) were delivered by 8 groups, with all the 25 students having completed the given assignment. All infographics have been evaluated as suitable to be published on the O-City World platform.

After concluding the two classroom learning experiences, their results have been evaluated. The main attention has been put on the suitability of the learning modalities and the benefits perceived by students. Further issues investigated concerned the success level in acquiring competences and other benefits produced for the heritage sector. Several research tools have been used in the evaluation phase, even though a systematic approach has not been possible. In general, the feedback was gathered through qualitative research tools (i.e., observation, structured and unstructured surveys) to evaluate the perceived effectiveness and satisfaction about the course and the experience. Moreover, further insights were based on expert evaluation of the outputs produced during the classroom experiences and on data analysis about the course attendance on the e-learning platform.

5   Evaluation of Learning Experiences and Results Discussion

In this Section the results from the evaluation about the learning experiences with the Infographic course are presented and discussed. It must be said that a systematic approach had not been possible because of the fragmentation and limited extension of the samples, as well as for the lowering in rate response after the completion of the activities. In any case, students and teachers/tutors' feedback has been collected through the teacher delivering the Infographic course by asking for first impressions and opinions at the end of the lessons. Then, once received the final infographics, she asked students and teachers/tutors to provide more structured feedback about their experience, and especially about their satisfaction level with learning topics, resources, contents, and methodologies. In addition, she asked for general considerations about positive aspects and things that can be improved. Participants gave a collective response. In detail, for the first experience a representative of the tutors/teachers and one of the students intervened as spokespersons during a project event about the results of the learning experiences expressing a general satisfaction. Students' spokesperson reported that they were taught about interesting and cross-cutting topics that they can also apply in their working and ordinary activities. It was acknowledged as a challenging and fun experience, producing very good results. In this regard, they considered it important to develop these kinds of skills. One of the main difficulties perceived concerns the lack of graphical skills, but it was not considered as invalidating to realize an effective infographic. Referring to the second experience, tutors/teachers sent a collective written note, while students sent 4 videos reporting the classes' feedback. Among the main points of strength, they mentioned the fact that it was a very challenging (stimulating) experience presenting topics, contents, and modes useful for students' future professional life. They highlighted the clearness and effectiveness of learning materials, especially for the activities, and the high level of contents. Also working in groups was appreciated. On the contrary, the main points to improve concerned the short time available to work in the classroom with the graphics software and to review and discuss the project works. Another negative aspect was the lack of specific indications about where to retrieve information on the heritages. All the gathered feedback was consistent with first impressions and opinions. Finally, after a few months since the delivering of the classroom experiences, an online survey was conducted with students about what had motivated (e.g.: working on real projects, visibility in the O-City World of the final multimedia projects, student digital resume) or demotivated (e.g.: restrictions by the O-City World, limitation on creativity due to the topic on heritage, academic experience) them in creating their multimedia projects. Unfortunately, despite the positive feedback (since most of the solutions implemented were considered as motivating and not demotivating), the number of respondents is too low to consider it a representative sample.

In the end, assuming that some benefits have been produced, to better develop their competences, students would had need more time and support, especially with the use of digital tools. However, the course succeeded in keeping students motivated and objective oriented, as 35 out of 39 students successfully completed their project works. Indeed, to create more engagement and motivate students some extrinsic incentives and rewards have been used (even if there is not an actual validation of their impact). For example, a student digital resume was introduced to learners after they completed their learning pathway as a tool for the accreditation of competences based on the O-City schema. In the evaluation according to the O-City schema of the competences (reported in the digital resume) acquired by students at the end of the classroom experiences it resulted in a prevalence of ability level 2 and 3 acquisition by all students for most of the competences. In general, university level students demonstrated greater autonomy than secondary school students, while the latter were more skilled with graphics, except for digital techniques. A last consideration about the achievements from the Infographic course refers to the results from attendees on the e-learning platform. They have been 12 coming from the other four universities that took part in the O-City project. Again, the course obtained positive results, since 10 students did the final test to get the certification allowed for who enrolled on the UPV LMS platform and all the 12 students uploaded their final infographic.

6 Conclusions

This short paper intended to present insights and results from some learning experiences building creative competences for the heritage sector, with the final goal of boosting the orange economy, considered as a positive element for the sustainability of cities and territories. However, it must be pointed out that there are some flaws and shortcomings affecting the presented results. The main limitation consists in the lack of a structured methodology for data collection, as well as a limited response rate by the participants in the presented experiences. In any case, the aim of this short paper is not to provide scientific results, but to report and share a work that can inspire other ones by representing a basis for further experimentations and good practices. So, it contributes to the acknowledgement and dissemination of a capacity building approach applied to the heritage sector. Indeed, since the approach has been implemented in different Countries and with different targets, generally achieving good results, it is expected that it could likely generate positive impacts in other contexts too. In details, the O-City Infographic course can be used to create creative competences, such as digital, communication, and design skills, that are lacking or that need to be reinforced, as they are not so advanced in people not taking a specific educational pathway in communication and design, especially for the use of digital technologies.

These conclusions have been derived from qualitative research about the perceived effectiveness and satisfaction by the attendees, expert evaluation of results, and analysis of data from the O-City platforms. The main outputs of the presented experiences were the creation of new multimedia based on infographics and their uploading on the O-City World platform, together with the new cities and their cultural elements showed by infographics. In this sense the course contributes to building the skills required by professionals to design, develop, and promote creative products in the heritage sector. In the end, 7 new cities, 14 new cultural sites, and 15 (32 if also considering the attendees on the e-learning platform) infographics (including translations in other languages) were added in the O-City World platform.

References

1. UNESCO. The World Bank: Cities, Culture, Creativity: Leveraging culture and creativity for sustainable urban development and inclusive growth (2021). http://hdl.handle.net/10986/35621. Accessed 18 Mar 2022
2. Florida, R.: The creative class and economic development. Econ. Dev. Q. **28**(3), 196–205 (2014)
3. Cunningham, S.D., Higgs, P.L.: Creative industries mapping: where have we come from and where are we going? Creat. Ind. J. **1**(1), 7–30 (2008)

4. Comunian, R., Gilmore, A., Jacobi, S.: Higher education and the creative economy: creative graduates, knowledge transfer and regional impact debates. Geogr. Compass **9**(7), 371–383 (2015)
5. Buitrago Restrepo, F., Duque Márquez, I.: La economía naranja, una oportunidad infinita. Banco Interamericano de Desarrollo (2013). https://publications.iadb.org/es/la-economia-naranja-una-oportunidad-infinita. Accessed 18 Mar 2022
6. Peters, M., Besley, T.: Academic entrepreneurship and the creative economy. Thesis Eleven. **94**(1), 88–105 (2008)
7. O-City - Orange-CITY: Creativity, Innovation & Technology. European Commission, Project Reference: 600963-EPP-1–2018–1-ES-EPPKA2-KA. https://o-city.webs.upv.es/. Accessed 18 Mar 2022
8. New European Bauhaus Homepage. https://europa.eu/new-european-bauhaus/index_en. Accessed 18 Mar 2022
9. Kozina, J., Bole, D.: Creativity at the European periphery: spatial distribution and developmental implications in the Ljubljana region. In: Chapain, C., Stryjakiewicz, T. (eds.) Creative Industries in Europe, pp. 227–254. Springer, Cham (2017). https://doi.org/10.1007/978-3-319-56497-5_11
10. Sacco, P.L., Segre, G.: Creativity, cultural investment and local development: a new theoretical framework for endogenous growth. In: Fratesi, U., Senn, L. (eds.) Growth and Innovation of Competitive Regions. Advances in Spatial Science. Springer, Berlin, Heidelberg (2009)
11. Ratiu, D.E.: Creative cities and/or sustainable cities: discourses and practices. City Cult. Soc. **4**(3), 125–135 (2013)
12. Capello, R., Cerisola, S., Perucca, G.: Cultural heritage, creativity, and local development: a scientific research program. In: Della Torre, S., Cattaneo, S., Lenzi, C., Zanelli, A. (eds.) Regeneration of the Built Environment from a Circular Economy Perspective. Research for Development. Springer, Cham (2020)
13. Mueller, J., Lu, H., Chirkin, A., Klein, B., Schmitt, G.: Citizen design science: a strategy for crowd-creative urban design. Cities **72**(A), 181–188 (2018)
14. O-City World platform. https://ocityplatform.webs.upv.es/dashboard/map. Accessed 18 Mar 2022
15. O-City e-learning platform. https://poliformat.upv.es/portal/site/OCW_CUR1157407_2020/tool/27e5294e-830f-41ee-9679-92b0cb9469a5. Accessed 18 Mar 2022
16. Bacigalupo, M., Kampylis, P., Punie, Y., Van den Brande, G.: EntreComp: The Entrepreneurship Competence Framework. EUR 27939 EN. Publication Office of the European Union, Luxembourg (2016)
17. Ferrari, A.: DIGCOMP: a framework for developing and understanding digital competence in Europe. In: Punie, Y., Brecko, B., (eds) EUR 26035 EN. Publication Office of the European Union, Luxembourg (2013)
18. Culture.EDU - Culture Experiences through Digital environment Using. European Commission, Project Reference: 2020–2-BG01-KA205–079402

Understanding Affordances in Short-Form Videos: A Performative Perspective

Yiting T. Wang[✉] ⓘ and Daniel D. Suthers ⓘ

University of Hawai'i at Mānoa, Honolulu, HI 96822, USA
{yitingw,suthers}@hawaii.edu

Abstract. What would be a good system to explain short-form videos holistically? Building on a previous method paper (multimodal analysis), this paper outlines the following arguments. Short-form videos are in part a theatrical and dramatic medium; hence we present a performative analysis that draws on concepts from these fields. Creators of short-form videos use the affordances of multiple modes (audio, textual, spatial, etc.) to achieve theatrical devices such as situation, suspense, and mimesis; hence we present a multimodal analysis of affordances. Bridging modes and these theatrical devices, affordances are multi-layered: the outcomes of affordances at one level become affordances at a new level. In particular, audiencing is achieved through situation, suspense and mimesis.

Keywords: Short-form video · Affordance · Performative

1 Introduction

When talking about affordances in short-form videos, on the one hand, we talk about the interface of a platform that offers video creation or video sharing functions; on the other hand, we talk about the relationship between users and short-form videos. This paper focuses on the latter by using multimodal analysis to answer the question: what kind of relationship is between users and short-form videos?

As part of a wider research project, this paper demonstrates the use of multimodal analysis, a suitable method for analyzing short-form video data [1], and then applies theoretical ideas from theater to demonstrate how exactly affordances are multi-layered, contributing to the discussion of affordances in the field. Illuminated by previous discourse about affordances in multimodal analysis, we propose our own theory of multi-layered affordances illustrated by media-level affordances and high-level affordances, and explain how they build on each other.

2 Background

Short-form videos are short in length. They are usually 15 to 60 seconds long, but no more than 5 min [2]. More and more platforms utilize short-form videos, including TikTok,

© The Author(s), under exclusive license to Springer Nature Switzerland AG 2022
C. Stephanidis et al. (Eds.): HCII 2022, CCIS 1582, pp. 312–319, 2022.
https://doi.org/10.1007/978-3-031-06391-6_41

Instagram Reels, YouTube Shorts, and Taobao. For simplicity, we will call these videos user-generated short-videos (UGSVs) or SVs.

The terms *performance, performative,* or *theatrical* are increasingly used in the social media research literature. This paper will apply three theater theories, situation & suspense (S&S), mimesis, and audiencing, that are commonly used to discuss the ontology of performative activities, then merge them with multimodal analysis to show how affordances are generated in a multi-levelled fashion.

First, we briefly introduce the three theories with examples. *Situation* is the essence of a story, it is a context, or a circumstance. Users may employ writing textual annotations in a video to build a situation. For example, "when you go to airport in Hawai'i." By seeing this, a suspense is naturally created, with an audience wondering, what about it? *Suspense* is naturally generated out of a situated performer, it shows the twists of the story, or the punchline. A video may document the realization of a prank. Imaginative reactions to the set-up fuel suspense. Situation and suspense are indivisible.

Mimesis is the theatrical term for imitation. UGSV platforms are imitation publics [3]. Mimesis is used to remind people of the often-impoverished and narrow understanding of imitation. It is defined as "a multi-leveled series of repetitions and reproductions" [4]. There is an inseparable relationship between mimesis and memes. Deriving from the Greek word *mimema,* defined as "something which is imitated" [5], mimesis not only sees imitation as repetition but also representations. The biologist Richard Dawkins, who introduced the term "meme", states that today's cultural evolution requires a new noun that "conveys the idea of a unit of cultural transmission, or a unit of imitation" [6].

3 Multimodal Analysis and Affordance

Although this paper is mainly theoretical, it is necessary to introduce the method of multimodal analysis in order to continue discussion. Multimodal analysis centers on modes in each video. A mode is a medium of communication. Short-form videos interchangeably and repetitively use textual, audio, visual, gestural, or spatial modes. How a mode has been used, when it is repeated, what a mode means and does, and what social convention informs such use are all part of the affordances of a mode [7].

3.1 Multimodal Analysis

The steps of analysis in this paper follows the work of Jewitt [7] and Wang [1]. Multimodal analysis has been used widely in video data, and it has proved to be an appropriate method for analyzing user-generated short-form videos. This method analyzes modes, the components of a video and modalities. We address the problem of reporting analysis of video in a textual paper by treating videos as a set of moving images. This requires a sampling criterion. For this paper, our criterion is the emergence of storylines, marked by newly emerged modes. Step 2 transcribes data. By transcribing data, or by spelling out the details of the video, readers will know the content of a video. Step 3 analyzes individual modes and step 4 analyzes across modes. The last step is to link with theories.

Fig. 1. Meet *Brittany* (Left-right, top-down), respectively, the original video (nestled closely), Toy gun Pointing at Brittany, Adding Brittany Roped up, Adding right arm for man, Adding Legs for man and Brittany, FBI involved, Negotiator involved, Reporter reports news, and friends see news at home, shocked (not shown in this figure).

3.2 Examples

In this paper, we use a 2021 viral video *Meet Brittany* [8] and its sequels as video examples (Fig. 1). It starts with a man nestled closely to a woman and vocalized: "today is also my birthday, because it's my birthday, I get to introduce you to my girlfriend, who is amazing!" The original video was composed of spatial relationship (SR: two performers squeeze close), hand gesture (HG: five fingers spread), narration (N: "birthday"), and facial expressions (FE: woman with a faint smile, nervous). Seemingly banal, the odd spatial relationship (nestled), the forceful, emphatic gesticulating, and the dodging eye contacts become suspense that generates discussions and nurtures situations, all centered with the girlfriend as a hostage. Sequentially, performers started adding new situations including the girlfriend's hands being roped up, or the FBI being involved.

In terms of mimesis, the first type is *mannerism*. Performers imitate the careful maneuver of an FBI agent, or how a reporter talks through camera, to name a few. Another type of mimesis is *imitation with devices*: a TV remote held as a gun, a paper cone as a megaphone, and the rolled-up paper as a microphone. These imitations are normally undertaken to make-believe rather than make-belief. Developed by the performance theorist Richard Schechner, make-belief showcases the authenticity of a professional role, or identity. It creates the very social realities performers enact [9]. A president during a national crisis makes-belief to give a powerful speech, with a strong-willed gaze to the audience, performing the make-belief of authority, trustworthiness, and the public's confidence. Conversely, a performer plays a role in a play, or fiction, "highlights and foregrounds their own inauthenticity" [10] with a clearer boundary between the real and the pretended. The pretentious props in *Brittany* copies the form, but that is enough to deliver the message (content).

4 Audience and Audiencing

Social media is to be social and to engage with an audience. The absence of an audience may cease interaction and circulation.

A major proposal in research on audiences is the concept of *audiencing* [11, 12]. Emphasizing interactivity or initiation but not passivity, audiencing refers to "the process by which a visual image has its meaning renegotiated, or even rejected, by particular audiences watching in specific circumstances" [14]. Audiencing is listed one hierarchy higher than S&S and mimesis, in that audiencing functions as the ultimate outcome of affordances while S&S and mimesis function as the means of that outcome. Another reason is because audiencing focuses on context while the others focus on content, assisting contexts.

What are audiences doing while watching UGSVs? We argue while watching UGSVs, audiences are colluding with the context. We take *collusion* from context collapse [15] to emphasize the *intentionality* in which this audience subscribes to such a situation, or recognizes the use of a meme or a stereotypical situation. In other words, suspense and situation settings require colluded audiences.

How do audiences respond to a performance in a UGSV? Common responses include: 1) audience promotes/circulates the performance, 2) audience transforms to performer, 3) performer answers performer [13].

That audiences promote or circulate a post is not novel. This happens on other social media platforms that use media other than short-form videos. The promotion or circulation is usually manifested by likes, reposts, and quoted comments. The audience-performer transformation happens when a user decides to jump into the created situation to either create a new storyline, or elaborate. An audience is no longer a passive viewer; they have a stake in the video creation. When creators (spectators) interfered in the performance, the "performance transformed the involved spectators into actors" [16]. An audience is no longer a lurker: something in the video triggered them to become an actor rather than a watcher. The prior audience members decided to become a performer.

Performers answering performers usually happen when content creators use popular trends to gain traffic for themselves. This phenomenon is salient among UGSVs. The term to use on platforms such as TikTok, and Vine is *duet* (aforementioned sequels are duets): answering videos by adding their own videos.

Meet Brittany is a fine example for audiencing. It shows a collection of circulation, transformation, and answering. More circulation invited more transformation and answering, creating a performative discourse. The UGSV affordances allow the audience to transform between being an audience to a performer, and the affordances allow performers to answer performers.

5 Media-Level and High-Level Affordances

So far we have demonstrated multimodal analysis, how modes relate to the theatrical theories, and how the theories can be used to analyze UGSVs. How do we scale them into a system via affordances that are widely explored in multimodalities?

Numerous literature have done analysis of affordances, from Gibson [17], to Norman [18], to Gaver [19], and more. This paper employs a simple definition: affordances are possibilities for interaction between users and devices [20]. Prior literature has introduced modal affordance and multimodal affordances. *Modal affordance* refers to the potentialities and constraints of different modes: some are overt and some are covert [21]. Hurley uses *multimodal affordances* to link with imagined affordances, discussing how different modes come together to impact the conscious and unconscious expectations of technology [22]. Regardless, the term *affordance* is a complex concept linking with both the material and the cultural, social, and historical use of a mode [7].

Here we use the observation that affordances are layered [23] to analyze how modes manifest media-level and high-level affordances, and use three criteria [24] to judge our proposed affordances: 1) an affordance is neither the object nor a feature of the object; 2) an affordance is not an outcome; 3) an affordance has variability. These three criteria imply that affordances bridge from the object and features of the object to outcomes. We want to discuss media-level and high-level affordances that manifest a performative-level affordances.

5.1 Media-Level Affordances

As aforementioned, there are different modes in UGSVs (e.g., FE, HG, SR). These modes are repetitively yet interchangeably used for situation building, suspense transition, or mimesis. Working with S&S and mimesis to create content, they help shape the context to build audiencing.

Individual modes offer media-level affordances. Similar to low-level affordances, media-level affordances are typically in the materiality of the medium, in specific features, buttons, screens and platforms. When modes are used, they are capable of creating situation and suspense, and mimetic activities. Each individual mode may involve objects or has features, but they are hardly objects or features of an object: they are the media of communication. For example, individual modes such as the extreme nestled spatial relationship and the hand gesture (emphatic gesticulation, finger pointing forcefully towards the camera) are communicative.

Modes are not outcomes either: they are the means by which the outcome is achieved. Modes are repeatedly used to accomplish different outcomes. They are also highly variable. For example, a text mode may serve a means of situation building, but can still be a means of suspense. "When you say the wrong thing" is a situation, but also brings in what's happening next (suspense). At this level, situation, suspense, and imitation *are* the outcomes of media-level affordances.

5.2 High-Level Affordances

When it comes to high-level affordances, we notice that one layer's outcome becomes another layer's means of achieving an outcome. In this sense, it is critical to understand that neither situation nor suspense are the high-level outcomes; they are the *means* to the outcomes. Mimesis also becomes the means of replication. Audiencing becomes the grand outcome of all three.

In digital media, the environment does not have intrinsic features such as props, body movements, or sound: *users shape the medium to put these modes in there*. Therefore, the environment is not a fixed set of features; *it is the possibility of creating features*.

S&S is an affordance of short-form videos. It is achieved by objects or features of objects in modes, and can be used to achieve audience stickiness, story linearity, and coherence. Modes at the media-level may be swapped or altered under different circumstances; but ultimately, short-form videos often tell a coherent linear story: due to time limitations, users usually accomplish one *major* suspense within one *major* situation. Further, situation growth and suspense setting are frequently sequential. Rarely do we see flashbacks or interspersed timelines. However, since platforms are allowing longer and longer story telling time (e.g., TikTok extends to 10 min), videos afford flashbacks now.

Individually, situation and suspense as affordances have variability. *Meet Brittany* showcases how different creators elaborate the same starting situation to different situations and suspenses (e.g., Brittany is a hostage, the FBI is involved, it was on the news, and friends saw the news) while remaining loyal to the original story.

Mimesis, powered by modes, affords imitability (the possibilities of repetition) and meme-ability (the representational possibilities). Imitation is an activity to be perceived. Imitation is thus a more specific version of imitability in that the affordance of imitability offers different ways to imitate.

Mimesis is not an outcome; the outcomes are (for example) humor, contemplation, ridicule, or gaining pleasure. Mimesis affords different levels of imitability too, influencing behavior; thus mimesis is variable. For some people, the imitability remains entertaining (e.g., imitating an annoying brother); for others, it is political (e.g., Sarah Copper imitates Trump), only to name two.

Aside from imitability, mimesis affords meme-ability. It is recognized that videos on TikTok become memes that one can replicate. Shifman agrees that memes are produced by various means of imitation. "Means" here are different modes we have discussed. Modes invite endless possibilities of being used to imitate. As a consequence, memes are passed on by imitation [25], and imitation creates more memes; thus imitation affords meme-ability.

At this point, *media-level affordances* refer to the modes that are capable of creating situation and suspense, affording coherent and linear stories on a high-level. S&S as an affordance for short-form videos leads to audience stickiness; mimesis as an affordance leads to imitability and meme-ability. Coherence, linearity, stickiness, imitability, and mimetically are the high-level affordances. Two levels working together, create audiencing as the ultimate outcome: audiences "uptake" [26] or renegotiate what was offered and then elaborate. We argue that by taking features and objects within short-form videos and taking audiencing as an outcome, we witness that short-form videos afford performativity.

6 Conclusion

We return to our original question: what kind of relationship is there between users and short-form videos? The preliminary proposal here is a performative relationship. We reach this conclusion by multimodal analysis of affordances in four stages.

First, we used multimodal analysis to identify modes and analyzed how they work with each other. Then second, we showed the presence of the theatrical ontology by linking modes with situations, suspense, and mimesis. Third, modes as affordances realize situation, suspense, and mimesis; therefore, provoking a media-level affordance that is located in the materiality of the medium. Lastly, situation, suspense and mimesis as affordances leads to audience stickiness, story coherence, linearity, imitability and meme-ability. Understanding these aforementioned terms as performative, and affordances as layered, while putting the media and high-level together, audiencing is the last outcome of this entire equation.

References

1. Wang, Y.: Multimodal analysis: researching short-form videos and the theatrical practices. In: Proceedings of the 104th Association for Education in Journalism and Mass Communication (2022)
2. Kong, D.: Research Report on Short Video Industry., 36kr Research Center (2018). http://www.199it.com/archives/672181.html
3. Zulli, D., Zulli, D.J.: Extending the Internet Meme: Conceptualizing Technological Mimesis and Imitation Publics on the TikTok platform. New Media & Society, p. 146144482098360 (2020). https://doi.org/10.1177/1461444820983603
4. Gruber, W.E.: Non-aristotelian theater: brecht's and plato's theories of artistic imitation. Comp. Drama **21**(3), 199–213 (1987). https://doi.org/10.1353/cdr.1987.0007
5. Shifman, L.: Memes in a digital world: reconciling with a conceptual troublemaker. J. Comput. Mediat. Comm. **18**(3), 362–377 (2013). https://doi.org/10.1111/jcc4.12013
6. Dawkins, R.: The Selfish Gene, 30th, Anniversary Oxford University Press, Oxford; New York (2006)
7. Jewitt, C.: Multimodal analysis. In: Georgakopoulou, A., Spilioti, T. (eds.) The Routhledge Handbook of Language and Digital Communication, pp. 69–84. Routledge, NY (2016)
8. chris (ツ),, Meet Brittany, @Iameaschris. 09 May 2021. https://twitter.com/Iameaschris/status/1391207396979007488. Accessed 14 Jun 2021
9. Schechner, R., Brady, S.: Performance Studies: An Introduction, 3rd edn. Routledge, London; New York (2013)
10. Bäcke, M.: Make-believe and make-belief in second Life role-playing communities. Convergence **18**(1), 85–92 (2011). https://doi.org/10.1177/1354856511419917
11. Fiske, J.: Audiencing: a cultural studies approach to watching television. Poetics **21**(4), 345–359 (1992). https://doi.org/10.1016/0304-422X(92)90013-S
12. Ginters, L.: On audiencing: the work of the spectator in live performance. In: About Performance, p. 10 (2010)

13. Park-Fuller, L.M.: Audiencing the audience: playback theatre, performative writing, and social activism. Text Perform. Q. **23**(3), 288–310 (2003). https://doi.org/10.1080/104629303 10001635321
14. Rose, G.: Visual Methodologies: An Introduction to the Interpretation of Visual Materials, 2nd ed. Thousand Oaks, Calif: SAGE Publications, London (2007)
15. Davis, J.L., Jurgenson, N.: Context collapse: theorizing context collusions and collisions. Inf. Commun. Soc. **17**(4), 476–485 (2014). https://doi.org/10.1080/1369118X.2014.888458
16. Fischer-Lichte, E.: The Transformative Power of Performance, 0 ed. Routledge (2008). https://doi.org/10.4324/9780203894989
17. Gibson, J.J.: The Ecological Approach to Visual Perception. Psychology Press, New York, London (2015)
18. Norman, D.A.: The Design of Everyday Things, Revised and, Expanded Basic Books, New York, New York (2013)
19. Gaver, W.W.: Technology affordances. In: Proceedings of the SIGCHI conference on Human factors in computing systems Reaching through technology - CHI 1991, New Orleans, Louisiana, United States, pp. 79–84 (1991). https://doi.org/10.1145/108844.108856
20. Garlach, S., Suthers, D.D.:. I'm supposed to see that?' adchoices usability in the mobile environment. In: HICSS Proceeding, p. 10 (2018)
21. Kress, G.R.: Multimodality: a Social Semiotic Approach to Contemporary Communication. Routledge, London; New York (2010)
22. Hurley, Z.: Imagined affordances of instagram and the fantastical authenticity of female gulf-arab social media influencers. Soc. Media + Soc. **5**(1), 205630511881924 (2019). https://doi.org/10.1177/2056305118819241
23. Bucher, T., Helmond, A.: The affordances of social media platforms. In: The Sage Handbook of Social Media, 1st edition., Thousand Oaks, CA: SAGE Publications Ltd. (2018)
24. Evans, S.K., Pearce, K.E., Vitak, J., Treem, J.W.: Explicating affordances: a conceptual framework for understanding affordances in communication research: explicating affordances. J. Comput.-Mediat. Commun. **22**(1), 35–52 (2017). https://doi.org/10.1111/jcc4.12180
25. Blackmore, S.: Meme Machine. Oxford University Press (2000)
26. Suthers, D.D., Dwyer, N., Medina, R., Vatrapu, R.: A framework for conceptualizing, representing, and analyzing distributed interaction. Comput. Support. Learn. **5**(1), 5–42 (2010). https://doi.org/10.1007/s11412-009-9081-9

Design Strategy for the Curation of Digital Exhibition Experience

—Cases of the Graduation Exhibition for Art & Design Colleges

Zitong Wang and Han Han[✉]

Shenzhen University, Shenzhen, China
wangzitong2020@email.szu.edu.cn, han.han@szu.edu.cn

Abstract. The catalyst of the epidemic has transformed college graduation exhibitions with digital changes. College graduation exhibitions are driving the deep integration of traditional physical exhibitions with the Internet and technology, and the development of VR and AR has gradually become a new form of art & design industry development, offering new possibilities for artworks and virtual spaces. This study conducts both quantitative and qualitative research method, firstly classifying the current college graduation exhibitions based on open resource data, then summarizing the three analytical dimensions of the study based on the classification combined with cases, and finally constructing the design strategies of the three dimensions according to the characteristics of different kinds of exhibitions. Making it cross the limits of time and space, it expands the scope of communication of design academia and industry, and rethinks the connection between art and display. This strategy provides an initial exploration of the implications of online exhibitions, expanding the scope of communication between design education and industry, and rethinking the connection between artwork and display.

Keywords: Virtual digital exhibition · Graduation exhibition · Experience design

1 Introduction

Being affected by the COVID-19 pandemic since 2020, people's life consumption and production are facing rapid transformation to digitalization scenarios. At the same time, with the widespread application of 5G, virtual reality, artificial intelligence and other new technologies in various fields, digitalization is gradually leading the industrial transformation for different disciplines in the post-epidemic era. For the cultural industry, digital technology has greatly improved the efficiency of its transformation and becoming the main path for the dissemination of cultural content. Because of art exhibitions is a specialized form of displaying research in the field of art and intervention in modern culture construction [1], therefore, digital technology has enriched the exhibition experience in a multi-dimensional manner, and to a large extent demonstrated the value of cultural industry transmission, communication, and art & design education. The graduation exhibition of art colleges is a kind of exhibition strongly related to education, it is a

C. Stephanidis et al. (Eds.): HCII 2022, CCIS 1582, pp. 320–327, 2022.
https://doi.org/10.1007/978-3-031-06391-6_42

professional platform for students to display their degree works, communicate with the public and industries for the future career development of graduates' professions. Exhibitions in the physical space in colleges mainly provide exhibition experience for visitors through multi-sensory experience, texture creation of content space, and face-to-face social interaction. While under the influence of the epidemic, as university campuses are facing increasing challenges when opening to the outside, the educational and aesthetic attributes of graduation exhibitions are gradually being explored, and graduation exhibitions are extending its experience to online forms. Its essence relies on the development of new technologies that integrate cloud computing, big data, XR technology and mobile Internet technology, and then build a digital virtual exhibition space by interconnecting with entities such as universities (organizers and curators), the fresh graduate students (exhibitors), exhibition visitors (the public), etc., so as to construct a new type of exhibition experience and service model.

2 Literature Review

The concept of digital exhibition curation was originated from the beginning of the 21st century, and was mainly applied in the field of cultural information management to record and archive cultural heritage more efficiently. With the development of technology, digital curation not only improves the efficiency of information management, but also needs to pay attention to the experience of multiple users. Therefore, it is vital for the applicability of digital curation to study all the involved roles of the exhibitions, such as the cognitive activities of curators and exhibition audiences [2]. At the same time, previous researches provided possible method in extending the life cycle of digital curation management. For example, they suggested recording user's experience, observing interaction behavior, and tracking user's data, meanwhile constantly adding new content to the digital repository, which represents user's feedback and knowledge update. Any additional content implies evolution, resulting in a hierarchy of digital resources [3]. Digital curation can achieve digital preservation, electronic records and digital asset management at the information management level, because it is rooted in digital normative methods and serves management. But considering the diversity of digital curation practices, various elements, including curated contents, personal information, hierarchical catalogues, require public execution by a wide range of participants, including technologists, researchers, artists, users, and organizational communities, to uniformly build digital facilities suitable for curation [4]. Previous studies have raised the need for multi-dimensional technologies for digital curation, the establishment of digital infrastructure is to archive and disseminate datasets, and the application of 3D technology in curation is to allow visitors access these data in multiple dimensions, thereby enhancing the viewing experience [5].

From digital curation to exhibition experience, the experience economy perspective highlights digital experience strategies for improving services. The experience economy proposed by Pine and Gilmore in 1998 pointed out that a more attractive consumer experience should be created by improving services. Based on this statement, the further explore the relationship between experience and specific environment in two aspects: one is to attract the viewer through the experience; the other is to immerse the viewer into the experience. Based on experience economy concept, continuous efforts have been made in creating unique and innovative experiences for the art & design exhibitions disciplines [6]. In recent years, exhibitions have entered the experience economy and continued to develop [7], bringing new experiential and interactive elements to exhibitions by adding digital exhibits and digital forms [8]. While the digital world offers the viewer more experience value, the integration of digital technology, social tools, and physical elements adds complexity to the user experience. Different viewers have different feelings and behaviors towards digitalization, which also reflects the boundaries between physical and digital [9].

In addition, in order to enrich the experience of different products in the entertainment industry, the digital world joined the meaning of communication, Marsha Kinder created and introduced the concept of transmedia in 1991 [10]. With the transmedia experience of exhibitions are enhanced, more application methods are gradually realized, such as virtual reality, augmented reality and other new technologies [11, 12].

3   Research Objectives and Research Methods

Faced with the current situation of such exhibitions, the goal of this paper is to understand the possibility of digital transformation of graduation exhibitions, and to provide a design framework and inspiration for the construction of more exhibition platforms to enhance the digital experience.

In order to achieve the research objectives, on the basis of theoretical exploration and empirical support, the researcher selected the online graduation exhibitions of 40 art & design colleges as representative cases for data collection (Table1: Table 1 as a sample version, full version is with 40 cases). This is a schematic table of representative cases selected from the cases investigated by the researcher. Preliminary case classification was carried out according to its exhibition forms, platforms and technology. The exhibition forms are divided into online exhibition and offline exhibition. Platform refers to the carrier of the exhibition, such as the school's official website, self-built platform and third-party website, as well as the technology required to build the platform, including Virtual Reality, 3D modeling and so on.

4   Experience Design of Digital Graduation Exhibition

Based on the analysis of the above empirical data, the study found from the online graduation exhibitions of the selected colleges that digital technology and virtual space give exhibitions more possibilities. Its display platforms, dissemination methods, and browsing methods are constantly being adjusted with the new digital technology. According to different digital needs, the research summarizes three main models of online graduation exhibitions at this stage. Different models create a sense of experience through a variety of interactive interface design.

① Panoramic digital exhibition reproduction——Digital technology needs.
② Interactive Interface Exhibition——Digital experience.
③ Immersive virtual exhibition space——Digital communication needs.

Table 1. The sample of the 2020–2021 Online Graduation Exhibition of Art Universities' chart

College	Form	Platform	Technology
Central academy of fine arts (China)	Online exhibition	Online platform	3D panoramic virtual showroom 2D Web
School of Arts Peking University	Online exhibition	WeChat official accounts	Graphic communications
Taipei National University of the Arts	Online exhibition	ARTOGO	Virtual reality 3D modeling Dynamic web
Academy of arts & Design, Tsinghua University (China)	Online exhibition	Online platform (AliCloud resources)	2.5D exhibition Dynamic interaction Panoramic roaming
University of California, Los Angeles	Online exhibition	Online platform	Dynamic catalog
School of architecture	Online exhibition	Online platform	Game interaction

The first type (*Panoramic Digital Exhibition Reproduction*) mainly uses multifarious technologies to restore the physical exhibition space, and offers visitors the online navigation instructions to view the exhibition content in the virtual spaces just as same as in the real spaces. For example, the online graduation exhibition of the Central Academy of Fine Arts (China) in 2020 is mainly divided into "Cloud Online Graduation Exhibition" and "3D Virtual Graduation Exhibition" (Fig. 1). Viewers can choose to view the exhibition in two ways: graphic browsing and virtual digital browsing. Exhibits of different majors through five virtual exhibition halls, and browse the exhibits by clicking on the floating text and cursor (Fig. 2).

Fig. 1. The central academy of fine arts (China)

Fig.2. Virtual digital browsing

The second type (*Interactive Interface Exhibition*) is subdivided into two subtypes, one is to display works by using the existing online platform for curation tools (e.g. ArtVR), this is the current 3D digital virtual platform chosen by most universities. For example, the graduation exhibitions of most Chinese institutions such as Hubei Institute of Fine Arts and Xi'an Academy of Fine Arts (China) in 2020 were done through a digital virtual platform with relatively mature technology. However, in the process of implementation, users still face many problems that affect the viewing experience, such as web pages overload.

In addition, some universities use social platforms such as official websites, WeChat and microblogs to carry out simple interactive exhibitions with two-dimensional interfaces in combination with the application of H5 or plug-in programs. For example, the Art Institute of Peking University (China) curated the exhibition through the WeChat public platform since 2020 in the form of flat graphic browsing, combined into four comprehensive thematic exhibition halls, and used the official media website as the carrier of the exhibition to achieve the effect of its own dissemination. (Fig. 3).

Fig. 3. The art institute of Peking University

Another subtype is the school-enterprise cooperation to build a new interactive platform, mainly based on mobile interaction of the two-dimensional interface display, using 2.5D visual effect, which are mostly in the form of H5, panoramic roaming, dynamic interactive directory and other forms of interaction with the viewer. For example, the online platform built by the "Alibaba Human-Machine Natural Interaction Experience Lab" of Tsinghua Academy of Fine Arts and supported by AliCloud resources can be used to view the entire exhibition with a simple right-click operation, while the springboard navigation is displayed in a simple and clear manner on the left side, giving people a clear and smooth visual experience. (Fig. 4).

At the same time, dynamic web pages also form part of the interactive design of the virtual exhibition with various interaction methods and visual styles. For example, the home page of the thesis exhibition at the University of California, Los Angeles, consists of several blue bubbles that collide and jump around each other, and the names of different authors in the bubbles can be clicked to view the personal information and artworks of the students, which provides users clearly browse while adding some interesting. (Fig. 5).

   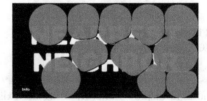

Fig. 4. Tsinghua academy of fine arts   **Fig. 5.** The University of California, Los Angeles

The third type (*Immersive full-scale virtual scene space*) combines the exhibition theme to create a virtual space, which is no longer just a copy of a physical projection, but combines concept, interaction and media to create a fully virtual immersive space. For example, the School of Architecture's (Taliesin) 2021 online exhibition features an online game that showcases student work in an immersive, virtual "shelter world" where exhibits appear as landmarks in virtual space and visitors can click on exhibits at any time while roaming the exhibition in a 360-degree panorama. Visitors can also choose their own role in the exhibition and add their favorite elements to create their own shelter world (Fig. 6). This immersive virtual exhibition effectively combines theme, interaction and media in a more interactive and storytelling way, making the viewer more involved, and in this way, the exhibition itself has become a communication content and communication channel.

Fig. 6. The school of architecture's (Taliesin)

5   Strategies to Integrate the Digital Exhibition Experience

This study summarizes three design strategies from the functional level of digital needs of graduation exhibition: ① platform construction ② technical support and ③ communication strategy (Fig. 7). In turn, the empirical data and qualitative analysis summarize and categorize the current online graduation exhibitions in colleges, which provides framework for the design strategy to integrate the digital exhibition experience.

In the platform construction, the three modes of digital exhibition rely on different platforms to bring different viewing experiences to the viewers. The first and third types mentioned above are Panoramic digital exhibition reproduction and Immersive virtual exhibition space, they require the use of virtual reality technology, physical projection and 3D modeling to build the scene. The first type aims to develop a platform to fully recreate realistic scenes through technical support, while the third type also creates virtual spaces, but with focus on combining content ideas to create fully virtual immersive spaces. The second type is Interactive interface exhibitions, which rely more on existing digital virtual platforms and web pages, for example, ArtVR[1] and a series of social platforms.

In the technical support dimension, different digital technology provides a variety of ways to display exhibits. Panoramic digital exhibition reproduction is built with physical projection, map shooting and realistic rendering art technology as the main platform so that the viewer can immerse themselves in the scene. The interactive interface exhibition uses interactive technologies such as H5, panoramic roaming, and dynamic catalog that can be operated within a two-dimensional web page, in the form of graphics and text is

---

[1] *ArtVR is an application that combines virtual reality, artificial intelligence, big data, blockchain, Internet and other technologies to construct a 3D/VR virtual art museum.*

more convenient for viewers to browse exhibits on mobile. Immersive virtual exhibition space connects creative concepts and artwork to build a concept space, in turn, provides a surreal virtual experience.

In the communication strategy, the digital exhibition exerts the maximum effect of communication through different media platforms, linking various online and offline communication methods such as graphic, video, live broadcast, forum and workshop to enrich the capacity of the exhibition and expand the scope of communication.

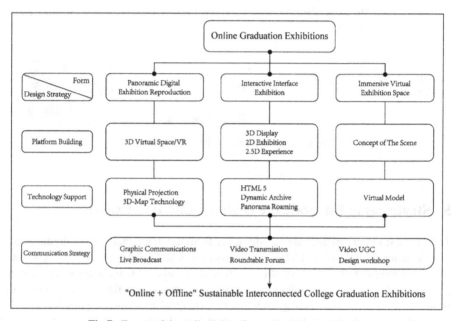

Fig.7. Forms of the collages' online graduation exhibitions

6 Conclusion

To sum up, as a form of digital exhibition, the online experience of graduation exhibition relies on the promotion of cyberspace as the extended interface of the exhibition, in which the construction of the experience is no longer limited to the provision of artworks, but creates a sense of technology through innovative and promotes creative human-computer interaction, and "across time and space" network communication. These elements provide new exploration paths for the future development of exhibition curation. In addition, since the graduation exhibition is also a professional platform to communicate the intelligence of graduates with the industry and the whole pubic, the design strategies revealed in this study are also important when supporting the design of exhibition platforms with similar functions. At the same time, the curation of digital exhibitions provides strategic clues for future research, constructs future digital knowledge forms, guides the design of interactive behaviors, and enriches communication models.

The limitation of this study lies in the collection of data samples. To some extent, the graduation exhibition of international art&design collages is also a manifestation of cross-cultural experience. Users in different countries will be more rigorous in future research expansion.

Acknowledgment. The author Zitong Wang and corresponding author Han Han would like to express sincere appreciation to all the participants who contribute advise and data to this study.

References

1. Cao, Q.: Digital Exhibition Resources (2010–2019) and research trends of Chinese modern art. Fine Arts **6**, 27–33 (2020)
2. Dallas, C.: An agency-oriented approach to digital curation theory and practice. In: ICHIM 2007, International Cultural Heritage Informatics Meeting (2007)
3. Constantopoulos, P., et al.: DCC&U: An extended digital curation lifecycle model. Int. J. Digit. Curation **4**(1) (2009)
4. Dallas, C.: Digital curation beyond the wild frontier: a pragmatic approach. Arch. Sci. **16**(4), 421–457 (2016)
5. Selden, R.Z., Perttula, T.K., O'Brien, M.J.: Advances in documentation, digital curation, virtual exhibition, and a test of 3D geometric morphometrics: a case study of the Vanderpool vessels from the ancestral Caddo territory. Adv. Archaeol. Pract. **2**(2), 64–79 (2014)
6. Pine, B.J., Gilmore, J.H.: Welcome to the experience economy, 29–36 (1998)
7. Mossberg, L., Sundqvist, A.A.: Att skapa upplevelser: från OK till WOW!. Studentlitteratur (2003)
8. Oppermann, R., Specht, M.: A nomadic information system for adaptive exhibition guidance. Arch. Mus. Inform. **13**(2), 127–138 (1999)
9. Mele, C., et al.: The millennial customer journey: a Phygital mapping of emotional, behavioural, and social experiences. J. Consum. Mark. (2021)
10. Kinder, M.: Playing with Power in Movies, Television, and Video Games. University of California Press (1991)
11. Kidd, J.: Museums in the New Mediascape: Transmedia, Participation, Ethics. Routledge (2016)
12. Hall, S.: Creating Strong Cross Media Concepts for Museum Exhibitions (2013)

eGovernment and eBusiness

Social Network Analysis: How Twitter Social Media Used in Raising Tax Awareness During the COVID-19 Pandemic

Maisarah Mitra Adrian[1][✉], Achmad Nurmandi[1], Isnaini Muallidin[1],
and Eko Priyo Purnomo[1,2]

[1] Department of Government Affairs and Administration, Jusuf Kalla School of Government,
Universitas Muhammadiyah Yogyakarta, Yogyakarta, Indonesia
`Maisarahmitra@gmail.com`, {`nurmandi_achmad,eko`}`@umy.ac.id`
[2] E-Governance and Sustainability Institute, Yogyakarta 55183, Indonesia

Abstract. This study analyzes how Twitter social media affects the invitation to pay taxpayers through Social Network Analysis. Taxes have an essential role in the country's development so that the income from the tax sector can help increase state revenues. This research method uses qualitative analysis with the type of data obtained by this study using secondary data sourced from Twitter social media with the hashtag #PajakKitaUntukKita and official government documents related to the results of the APBN and Taxpayer reports in the 2020–2021 period. Data analysis visualization was carried out with the help of Nvivo 12 Plus software, especially the Twitter Sociogram dataset tool and Netlytics, to identify research variables. The results of the analysis show that; 1) Dissemination of information carried out by the Directorate General of Taxes is very intensive, dominantly carried out by the Twitter social media account @DitjenPajakRI; 2) The results of the information response to #PajakKitaUntukKita which is shown by the dominant users' responses to government agencies, while the private sector and the community have a low response rate 3) The hashtag #PajakKitaUntukkita as a Campaign in increasing taxpayer awareness carried out by the Directorate General of Taxes has not run optimally in providing a significant influence on taxpayer awareness but is quite good at providing information and education related to taxes.

Keywords: Twitter · Social media · Network analysis · Tax awareness

1 Introduction

This article aims to identify and analyze the strategy of the Directorate General of Taxes in increasing public awareness of the obligation to pay taxes through social media. Social media has an essential role in providing information and communication to the general public [1]. The existence of social media provides easy access to information and communication so that it is often used by the public, private sector, and even the government. The function of social media for the government can be used as material for analysis related to the public's response to an issue or problem [2] to be used in making a

C. Stephanidis et al. (Eds.): HCII 2022, CCIS 1582, pp. 331–339, 2022.
https://doi.org/10.1007/978-3-031-06391-6_43

decision or to make or implement a policy. The Directorate General of Taxes (DJP), as a government agency, also uses social media to interact and exchange information related to problems or services related to taxation [3]. As the primary source of state financing, taxes contribute around 75%, according to the State Budget (APBN) [4]. Taxes have an essential role in the country's development [5], so that the tax sector income can help increase state revenues [6].

Since the COVID-19 pandemic has impacted the economic sector, marked by a decrease in the number of people's incomes, various business sectors, both from Micro, Small, and Medium Enterprises (MSMEs) and even large industries, have not run as they should [7]. This impact on the economic sector is due to the imposition of restrictions on human mobility to deal with the COVID-19 pandemic, which causes a decrease in work productivity [8]. The decline in the community's economic sector due to the COVID-19 pandemic has impacted the tax revenue sector [9]. However, in Indonesia, state revenues to realize the state budget in 2020 have increased in the tax revenue sector. The realization of the state budget in 2020 in Indonesia has increased from 2019 in the tax revenue sector.

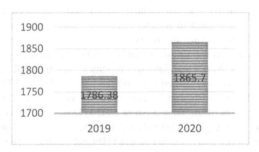

Fig. 1. Realization of the provisional state budget for the taxation sector for 2019–2020 Source: (DJP Annual report, 2019)

Figure 1 shows the details of the realization of the APBN in the tax revenue sector for 2019 to February 29, 2020, which includes; 1) tax revenue reached IDR 177.96 trillion or 9.54% of the 2020 APBN target, an increase of 0.29% year-on-year (YoY) compared to the realization in 2019 which was IDR. 177.44 Trillion: 2) Realization of Tax Revenues reached Rp. 152.92 trillion or 9.31% of the 2020 APBN target, 4.97% (YoY) lower than in 2019 of Rp. 160.91 trillion; 3) Realization of Customs and Excise Revenue reached Rp. 25.04 trillion or 11.22% of the 2020 APBN target, growing by 51.52% YoY from 2019, Rp 16.53 trillion [5, 10]. Based on the data, Fig. 1 shows that taxes have a major influence on the Indonesian State Budget.

Taxes are obtained from the contribution of the taxpayer community directly or by using a self-assessment system [11]. In this system, people report their taxes to taxpayers supervised by tax officials [12]. Self-Assessment is a system reform presented by the Directorate General of Taxes to increase public confidence in tax management. The existence of a self-assessment system is not enough to encourage public confidence in tax reporting. There needs to be a strategy to increase public awareness in providing taxpayer reports independently (self-assessment).

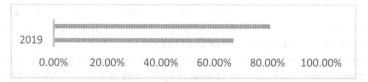

Fig. 2. Percentage of taxpayer revenue in 2019–2020 Source: (DJP Annual Report, 2019)

Figure 2 depicts an increase in reported Taxpayer income between 2019 and 2020. There was a 13.64% increase in 2020 compared to 2019, amounting to 67.20% of the 18.3 million taxpayer data that must be submitted in 2019 [5]. However, in 2020, there will be a decrease in taxpayers, particularly in the corporate sector. According to Finance Minister Sri Mulyani, the COVID-19 pandemic at the end of 2019–2020 is still putting a strain on corporate taxpayers [10].

The Ministry of Finance reported that the realization of tax revenues until the end of October 2020 was Rp. 826.9 trillion or 69.0% of the target in Presidential Regulation 72/2020 of Rp. 1,198.8 trillion. Meanwhile, the realization of tax revenue is minus 18.8% on an annual basis. The realization of corporate income tax (PPh) revenue is still the most significant contributor [10]. However, the realization was minus 35.01%, much deeper than the performance until the end of October 2019, minus 0.71% [5].

On the other hand, personal non-employee income tax receipts are still growing positively. However, the realization of growth was only 1.18%, much slower than the performance in the same period last year of 16.35%. Although the data on taxpayer receipts shows an increase in the reporting of notification letters (SPT) of taxpayer receipts, this is still very far from being realized from around 19 million taxpayers who are required to report SPT. However, until the deadline for submitting SPT, the Directorate General of Taxes only received 11.9 million SPT [5]. The low target of tax revenue shows how public awareness of taxpayers is still low. Moreover, the Directorate General of Taxes has implemented reforms in paying taxpayers through an integrated Self-Assessment through Information and Communication Technology (ICT).

This study uses Social Network Analysis (SNA) to identify Twitter social media accounts' dominant status and interactions. This article aims to analyze the role of social media in disseminating information, responding to information, and identifying the dominant status of Twitter social media accounts through the hashtag #PajakKitaUntukkita which affects invitations to pay taxpayers in Indonesia. The results of data analysis are visualized through the Twitter sociogram tool from the Nvivo 12 Plus and Analytics software. This study uses descriptive qualitative research methods to analyze research variables related to responses to information, identify dominant account interactions through #PajakKitaUntukKita.

2 Literature Review

2.1 Social Media and Social Network Analysis (SNA)

Social media is a type of online media where users can easily participate, share, and create virtual social networks and forums [13]. The use of social media as a strategy for rationalizing, directing, and making decisions more easily [14]. Social media creates a forum for dialogue among diverse audiences, including individuals, organizations, governments, the private sector, and others [15].

Twitter is one of the social media platforms that the general public frequently uses as a medium of dialogical communication [14]. Twitter is a social media platform that the general public uses to obtain information and communicate quickly, effectively, and efficiently. Integrated social media fosters new communication patterns among various audiences, including government agencies, the general public, and the private sector. It has a significant influence on communication patterns and responses [16]. As a result, it is not uncommon for the government to use social media to increase dialogue communication interactions with other actors involved in a particular issue or policy. The Social Network Analysis analysis approach Analysis can analyze the pattern of dialogical communication interactions via social media [16].

Social Network Analysis (SNA) is a sociological approach to analyzing patterns of relationships and interactions between social actors to uncover underlying social structures such as nodes or centers that serve as leader or employee relationships, related groups, and patterns of interaction between groups [17]. SNA has been used to investigate social interactions in a variety of contexts. Articles titled "Mixed Methods Analysis of the #Sugar Tax Debate on Twitter," "E-Cigarette Themes on Twitter: Dissemination Patterns and Its Relationship to Online News and Search Engine Questions in South Korea," and "Analyzing Public Discourse on Social Media with Geographical Context: A Case Study 2017 Tax Bill" are examples of previous studies that used SNA analysis of tax policy. Based on previous research, the use of SNA to explore and identify the actors involved, their connections, and the topics of discussion was investigated using content, sentiment, and thematic analysis, so that the results of the SNA analysis can be used as material for government analysis in developing jak-related strategies or policies.

3 Methods

The author uses a descriptive qualitative method with a theoretical approach to social media network analysis to identify the intensity of interactions carried out through Twitter social media. Data analysis visualization was carried out with the help of Nvivo 12 Plus software, especially the Twitter Sociogram dataset tool and Netlytics, to identify research variables. The type of data obtained by this study uses secondary data sourced from Twitter social media with the hashtag #PajakKitaUntukKita and official government documents related to APBN and Taxpayer reporting with the time series model for 2020–2021. The stages of data analysis carried out in this study were collecting data from data sources which were then classified and analyzed using the twitter sociogram tools on Nvivo 12 plus software. The author will compare the findings from data analysis visualized with netlytics software so that the data obtained can be compared and become material for a more in-depth and accurate analysis (Fig. 3).

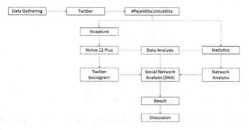

Fig. 3. Data collection process

The stages of this research were carried out; 1) data collection through Twitter social media with the data source from the hashtag #PajakKitaUntukKita through the N-Capture Tweet as dataset extension for data processed using Nvivo 12 Plus software. 2) Data from each account is collected through the netlytics dataset. 3) Analyze each data collected through twitter sociogram on Nvivo 12 plus software. At the same time, Netlytics through Network Analysis tools to identify social network analysis. 4) The next stage is the data visualization stage as material for study and discussion.

4   Result and Discussion

The presence of the COVID-19 pandemic has impacted the economic sector, resulting in a decrease in the number of people's income [18]. This is due to restrictions on human mobility, causing a decrease in the intensity of community economic activity [19]. The achievement of tax revenues until November 2020 reached 77.2% of the target according to Presidential Regulation 72 of 2020 of IDR 1,198.8 trillion. Tax revenue from Income Tax (PPh). Oil and gas tax revenues until the end of November 2020 reached Rp29.2 trillion, down 44.8% compared to the previous year's period of Rp52.8 trillion. Meanwhile, non-oil and gas taxes also fell 17.3% from Rp. 1,083.3 trillion last year to Rp. 896.2 trillion. The decrease in tax revenue is an evaluation material for the government to increase taxpayer awareness during the COVID-19 pandemic.

The research findings show that Twitter's social media role in increasing taxpayer awareness is based on the analysis of social networks from the hashtag #PajakKitaUntukKita to show the intensity of using the hashtag as a taxpayer campaign. The hashtag #PajakKitaUntukKita is a taxpayer campaign to increase public awareness in making taxpayer payments. Taxpayer awareness includes awareness of the rights and obligations to pay taxes for state financing [20]. To increase taxpayer awareness, the government uses social media as a campaign media in providing information related to taxes. The findings on the intensity of the use of #PajakKitaUntukKita as a taxpayer campaign were analyzed using Netlytics from 18/10/2021 to 27/10/2021, which can be seen in Fig. 5.

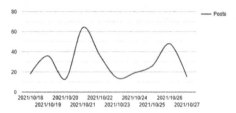

Fig. 4. Intensity of use of the hashtag #PajakKitaUntukKita

Based on Fig. 4 shows the use of hashtag #PajakKitaUntukKita which is seen based on Twitter social media analysis shows the intensity of posts related to the taxpayer campaign #PajakKitaUntukKita shows fluctuating results. The highest post value with #PajakKitaUntukKita seen in Fig. 5 occurred on 21/10/2021, reaching its peak with a value of 76 posts. The next day, the use of hashtags decreased drastically on 23/10/2021 and slowly increased again until 26/20/2021. Posts with the volatile hashtag #PajakKitaUntukKita show that the daily tax campaign is not carried out intensively. The dominant mention in the hashtag #PajakKitaUntukKita is seen in Fig. 6.

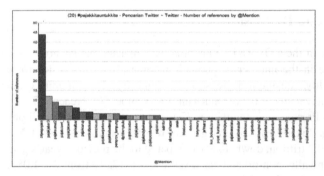

Fig. 5. Intensity of mentions using the hashtag #PajakKitaUntukKita

Figure 5 shows the mention of the hashtag #PajakKitaUntukKita shows that it is dominant on the social media account @ditjenpajakri with the highest position. The dominant value analysis results obtained using the Nvivo 12 plus software show that the intensity of the Twitter social media account @ditjenpajakri ranks first, with the highest mention intensity when compared to other accounts. The Twitter social media account @pajakjabar3 is in second place, and the Twitter account @pajaksumut2 is third. Meanwhile, the Ministry of Finance's social media account occupies the 9th position. The analysis results in Fig. 6 show that the government dominates the majority of mentions of the hashtag #PajakKitaUntukKita. Where is the dominance of the intensity of using the hashtag #PajakKitaUntukKita on the twitter media account of the Indonesian Directorate General of Taxes (@ditjenpajakri). It is only natural that the Twitter account @ditjenpajakri is dominant in conducting taxpayer campaigns to increase public awareness in paying taxes. Because it has become the responsibility and one of the strategies of the Indonesian Directorate General of Taxes to increase awareness of taxpayers through a campaign with the hashtag #PajakKitaUntukKita on Twitter social media. Meanwhile, the interactions and responses to the hashtag #PajakKitaUntukKita are based on social network analysis (SNA) of the hashtag's retweet (RT), which can be seen in the following image;

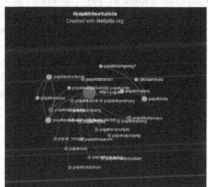

Fig. 6. Network analysis #PajakKitaUntukKita

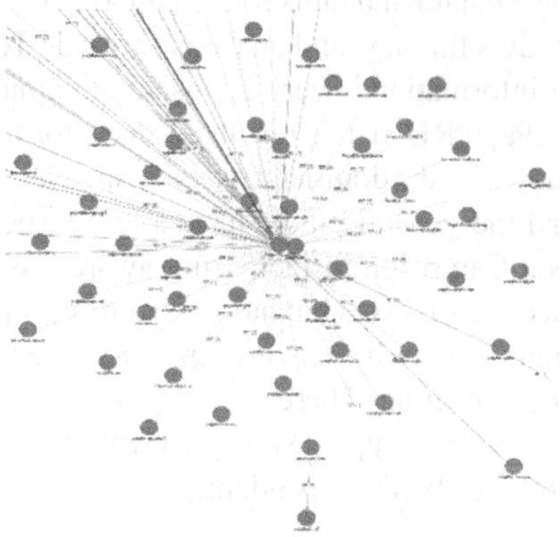

Fig. 7. Twitter sociogram #PajakKitaUntukKita

Figures 6 and 7 are the social network analysis (SNA) results, where Fig. 7 is analyzed using Netlytics software. In contrast, Fig. 8 results from analysis findings from the Twitter Sociogram tool on Nvivo 12 Plus software. Figures 6 and 7 have been divided into 6 clusters by looking at the intensity and response through retweets (RT) to the hashtag #PajakKitaUntukKita. These findings indicate that the interaction of taxpayer awareness campaigns is dominated by social media accounts belonging to government agencies, while social media accounts belonging to private sector agencies and even the public are not as intensive as government media accounts. It can be seen in the data in Fig. 8, which shows that there is one Twitter media account belonging to the private sector, namely the @redaksi_ortax account. At the same time, there are two media accounts for netizens that retweet (RT) against #PajakKitaUntukKita issued by the Twitter media account @ditjenpajakri.

The analysis findings are visualized through the pattern of information dissemination using Social Network Analysis (SNA) analysis. These results are shown in Figs. 7 and 8 that the role of social media in disseminating information with the hashtag #PajakKi-taUntukKita campaign has been carried out well by various government agencies in the tax sector. However, the role of social media as an interactive response in the #PajakKitaUntukKita campaign did not build public enthusiasm for taxpayer aware-ness by seeing the lack of response from the public and the private sector. The hashtag #PajakKitaUntukkita as a campaign to increase taxpayer awareness carried out by the Directorate General of Taxes of the Republic of Indonesia, has not run optimally in giving a significant impact to the public on taxpayer awareness but is quite good at pro-viding information and education related to taxes. So that efforts to increase taxpayer awareness need to be carried out with more complex strategies with policies that affect tax revenues, especially in the era of the COVID-19 pandemic.

5   Conclusion

The low tax revenue target shows how public awareness of taxpayers is still low. So that one strategy in increasing awareness of taxpayers is by utilizing the role of social media as a medium of communication. The strategy of using Twitter social media with the hashtag #PajakKitaUntukKita as a campaign can increase public taxpayer awareness. The study's findings and analysis show: 1) The Directorate General of Taxes' dissemination of information is very intensive, dominated by the Twitter social media account @DitjenPajakRI; 2) The results of the information response to #PajakKitaUntukKita, as has shown by the dominant users' responses to government agencies, while the private sector and the general public have a low response rate. 3) The hashtag #PajakKitaUntukkita as a Campaign in increasing awareness of taxpayers is carried out by the Directorate General of Taxes but has not been appropriately implemented. Maximum in providing a significant influence on taxpayer awareness, but quite good in providing tax information and education. Therefore, efforts to increase taxpayer awareness need to be carried out with more complex strategies with policies that affect tax revenues, especially in the era of the COVID-19 pandemic.

References

1. Prastya, D.E., Nurmandi, A., Salahudin: Analysis of website quality and city government's Twitter accounts in East Java Province, Indonesia. In: Yang, X.S., Sherratt, S., Dey, N., Joshi, A. (eds.) Proceedings of Sixth International Congress on Information and Communication Technology. Lecture Notes in Networks and Systems, vol. 216. Springer, Singapore (2022). https://doi.org/10.1007/978-981-16-1781-2_12
2. Pratama, I., Nurmandi, A., Muallidin, I., Kurniawan, D., Salahudin: Social media as a tool for social protest movement related to alcohol investments in Indonesia. In: Ahram, T., Taiar, R. (eds.) Human Interaction, Emerging Technologies and Future Systems V. IHIET 2021. Lecture Notes in Networks and Systems, vol. 319. Springer, Cham (2022). https://doi.org/10.1007/978-3-030-85540-6_18
3. Waluyo, T.: Pemeriksaan Terhadap Wajib Pajak Yang Tidak Menyampaikan SPT, Ketentuan dan Pemilihannya Sesuai Se-15/PJ/2018, p. 677 (2020)
4. Oktaviani, N.T., Nurmandi, A., Salahudin: Study of official government website and Twitter content quality in four local governments of Indonesia. In: Yang, X.S., Sherratt, S., Dey, N., Joshi, A. (eds.) Proceedings of Sixth International Congress on Information and Communication Technology. Lecture Notes in Networks and Systems, vol. 236. Springer, Singapore (2022). https://doi.org/10.1007/978-981-16-2380-6_69
5. Pajak, D.J.: Laporan Kinerja DJP tahun 2019 (2019)
6. Syaifuddin, M., Purnomo, E.P., Salsabila, L., Fathani, A.T., Adrian, M.M.: Development of Aerotropolis in Kulon Progo with green infrastructure concept. In: IOP Conference Series: Earth and Environmental Science, vol. 837, no. 1, p. 12014 (August 2021). https://doi.org/10.1088/1755-1315/837/1/012014
7. Kumala, R., Junaidi, A.: Strategi Bisnis dan Pemanfaatan Kebijakan Pajak di Masa Pandemi COVID-19 dan Era New Norman (Studi Kasus Pelaku UKM Marketplace). In: Prosiding Seminar STIAMI, vol. 3, no. 2017, pp. 54–67 (2020)
8. Malawani, A.D., Nurmandi, A., Purnomo, E.P., Rahman, T.: Social media in aid of post disaster management. Transform. Gov. People Process Policy 14(1), 237–260 (2020). https://doi.org/10.1108/TG-09-2019-0088

9. Siregar, N.Y.: Dampak Covid-19 Terhadap Penerimaan Pajak Negara Pada Sektor Umkm Di Indonesia. J. STIE Ibmi Medan **51**(51), 1–7 (2021)
10. Kementerian Keuangan RI: APBN Kita Maret 2020. Kemenkeu. Go. Id, no. April, p. 82 (2020)
11. Asrinanda, Y.D.: The effect of tax knowledge, self assessment system, and tax awareness on taxpayer compliance. Int. J. Acad. Res. Bus. Soc. Sci. **8**(10), 539–550 (2018). https://doi.org/10.6007/ijarbss/v8-i10/4762
12. Agustiningsih, W., Isroah, I.: Pengaruh Penerapan E-Filing, Tingkat Pemahaman Perpajakan dan Kesadaran Wajib Pajak Terhadap Kepatuhan Wajib Pajak Di KPP Pratama Yogyakarta. J. Nominal **5**(2), 107–122 (2016). https://doi.org/10.21831/nominal.v5i2.11729
13. Li, X., Zhou, M., Wu, J., Yuan, A., Wu, F., Li, J.: Analyzing COVID-19 on online social media: trends, sentiments and emotions. arXiv (2020)
14. Park, J., Tsou, M.H.: Analyzing public discourse on social media with a geographical context: a case study of 2017 tax bill. In: ACM International Conference Proceeding Series, pp. 14–20 (2020). https://doi.org/10.1145/3400806.3400809
15. Gruzd, A., Paulin, D., Haythornthwaite, C.: Analyzing social media and learning through content and social network analysis: a faceted methodological approach. J. Learn. Anal. **3**(3), 46–71 (2016). https://doi.org/10.18608/jla.2016.33.4
16. Mirzaalian, F., Halpenny, E.: Social media analytics in hospitality and tourism: a systematic literature review and future trends. J. Hosp. Tour. Technol. **10**(4), 764–790 (2019). https://doi.org/10.1108/JHTT-08-2018-0078
17. Pérez-Dasilva, J.-Á., Meso-Ayerdi, K., Mendiguren-Galdospín, T.: Fake news and coronavirus: detecting key players and trends through analysis of Twitter conversations. Prof. la Inf. **29**(3), 1–22 (2020). https://doi.org/10.3145/epi.2020.may.08
18. Hernat, O.P.: Intensif Perpajakan di Indonesia Selama Pandemi COVID-19. MABIS **4**(1), 6 (2021)
19. Lindiasari, P.: Potensi Penurunan Pajak dan Strategi Kebijakan Pajak untuk Mengatasi Dampak Pandemi COVID-19: Perspektif Ketahanan Nasional. J. Ekon. Kebijak. Publik **11**(2), 93–108 (2020)
20. Wardani, D.K., Rumiyatun, R.: Pengaruh Pengetahuan Wajib Pajak, Kesadaran Wajib Pajak, Sanksi Pajak Kendaraan Bermotor, dan Sistem Samsat Drive Thru Terhadap Kepatuhan Wajib Pajak Kendaraan Bermotor. J. Akunt. **5**(1), 15 (2017). https://doi.org/10.24964/ja.v5i1.253

Public Trust on Policy for Mobility Restrictions Policy in Indonesia an Analysis from Social Media Twitter

Paisal Akbar[1] , Achmad Nurmandi[1]([⊠]) , Bambang Irawan[2] , Zuly Qodir[1] ,
and Hasse Juba[1]

[1] Doctoral Program in Political Islam-Political Science, Jusuf Kalla School of Government,
Universitas Muhammadiyah Yogyakarta, Bantul, Indonesia
achmad_nurmandi@yahoo.com
[2] Masters Department of Public Administration, Universitas Mulawarman, Samarinda,
West Kalimantan, Indonesia

Abstract. Social media has become a liaison for all sources of information for
social media users. The exchange of information on social media becomes crowded
with various types of information. The focus of this study is the identification of
public confidence in the implementation of Indonesia's Mobility Restriction Policy
(PPKM). In this study, we use Twitter as a source of research data and discussions
regarding the issue of the extension of the PPKM policy in Indonesia. This study
uses a qualitative approach, using a qualitative data analysis mining approach
(QDA Miner) to analyze the resulting content, network, and cloud. We use Social
Network Analysis (SNA) software, namely NodeXL Pro, as a data search tool to
generate communication networks and tweet content from observed conversations
and Qualitative Data Analysis (QDA) software, namely Nvivo 12 Plus, for further
and comprehensive analysis. Understand qualitative data. The findings show that
public trust in implementing the Mobility Restrictions Policy in Indonesia reaps
more negative sentiment from Twitter social media users. In addition, the intensity
of the accounts involved in responding to the policy is relatively high, accompanied
by the resulting communication network.

Keywords: Mobility restrictions · Public trust · PPKM · Indonesia

1 Introduction

Due to the limited public activities outside during the Covid-19 pandemic, social media
became the hub for all sources of information for social media users (Shahi et al. 2021).
As a result, social media exchanges became lively with various details information. This
data can be analyzed to give stakeholders a new perspective on public trust in crises
and the best measures to pursue. According to the most recent studies, social media's
impact as a communication tool during Covid-19 can be divided into the following categories, which include coordination and communication tools (Machmud et al. 2021),
risk assessment, and analysis (Park et al. 2021), healthcare news (Park et al. 2020),

C. Stephanidis et al. (Eds.): HCII 2022, CCIS 1582, pp. 340–348, 2022.
https://doi.org/10.1007/978-3-031-06391-6_44

misinformation communication (Islam et al. 2020), conversations of Covid-19 policy initiatives through social media (Haupt et al. 2021; Irawan 2022), And also as a communication transmission device for medical groups whose functions are comparable to those of other organizations but which put a higher importance on public communication to enhance community participation (Park et al. 2016).

The focus of this study will be on public trust in the implementation of Indonesia's Policy for the Implementation of Mobility Restrictions (PPKM). The public trust score provides an overview of the general public acceptance of government policies. This public reaction data was collected after the Indonesian government, for the umpteenth time extended the deadline for implementing the PPKM policy in the country. On August 2, 2021, the Indonesian government announced the extension of the PPKM policy's functionality.

Twitter is the social media platform used to collect data for this study. According to Emeraldien et al. (2019), Twitter has developed into one of the social media platforms capable of bridging political communication channels at a faster rate. As a consequence, social media improves the effectiveness of public-government communication (Tromble 2018). In the case of an emergency or crisis, social media can be used to provide diverse information from the public authority or the community (Anson et al. 2017). In this study, we use Twitter as a source of research data and my conversations related to the issue of the extension of the PPKM policy in Indonesia.

2 Literature Review

2.1 Social Media for Public Policy Communication

Along with the advancement of information and communication technology, social media is a part of Web 2.0, a platform for people to exchange information (Delerue et al. 2012). As a modern communication tool, social media is designed to connect anybody in digital communication (Antony 2008; Madakam et al. 2015). Even nowadays, social media has become an indispensable component of all human activities (Kosasih 2016). Social media can facilitate users' access to information by leveraging electronic devices (Kaplan and Haenlein 2010; Näkki et al. 2011; Song and Lee 2016). He information circulating on social media is current or responsive (Ho and Cho 2016). At the moment, social media is used to communicate for practical policy campaigns (Akbar et al. 2021; Irawan 2022). Witanto et al. (2018) concluded that social media had evolved into a public information medium for reporting current events and issues.

With all the benefits that Belkahla Driss et al. (2019) assess, social media can provide valuable knowledge for the government, which can be considered throughout the decision-making stage. Because, at its core, policy communication is government communication that is understood as an effort to disseminate information about programs or ideas to the general public (Irawan 2022). Effective policy communication enables the implementing components of the policy and the policy targets to communicate with one another and create the desired results (Nurati 2016). As a result, it is indisputable that social media has evolved into the primary medium of communication capable of effecting change (Batara et al. 2018). Social media can provide statistics to stakeholders on the public response to government actions (Gintova 2019; Tari and Emamzadeh 2018; Witanto et al. 2018).

3   Research Method

This study employs a qualitative approach to investigate how social media users in Indonesia responded to the adoption of the Mobility Restriction policy during the Covid-19 pandemic. Social media communication has formed a communication network between each social media user (Himelboim et al. 2013). We employ a qualitative data analysis mining (QDA Miner) approach to analyze the generated content, network, and cloud. To investigate the facts and data available on the social media platform Twitter. We use Social Network Analysis (SNA) software, specifically NodeXL Pro, as a data search tool to generate communication networks and tweet content from observed conversations, as well as Qualitative Data Analysis (QDA) software, specifically Nvivo 12 Plus, to further and thoroughly understand qualitative data (Brandão 2015). Because studying information on Twitter social media requires the use of a data analysis tool to comprehend large amounts of data (Ranjan and Sood 2016).

The keywords used in the data search are the hashtag #Extended. The hashtag #Extended was included in the data search because it symbolizes Twitter user discussion in response to Indonesia's implementation of the PPKM extension policy. This Twitter user's comment then sparked a range of reactions to the policy.

RQ1: What is the intensity of the Twitter community's response to Indonesia's PPKM policy?
RQ2: Does the Twitter community trust the PPKM policies that have been implemented?

4   Finding and Discussion

4.1   Intensity of Public Response to #Extended

The implementation of the PPKM extension for the umpteenth time by the Government of the Republic of Indonesia resulted in various responses from Twitter social media users. This response is represented or characterized by the use of the hashtag #Extended which became one of Twitter's trending topics on August 2, 2021 in Indonesia. By using NodeXL Pro, we capture activity data using the hashtag #Extended on Twitter Social media. From the processing of the resulting data, we found a total of 16,250 accounts that had conversations related to the issue of the PPKM period extension. As well as producing as many as 19,023 communication links that are linked to each other and then create a communication network related to this issue.

In the intensity of other components, namely the activity intensity of Tweets, Retweets, Replies, Mentions, and MentionInRetweets, the amount of activity is directly proportional to the activity of the account in carrying out conversations. In Tweet Intensity, the number of occurrences generated is 6,873 tweets, and in Retweet activity the number of occurrences is 9,428 tweets. Meanwhile, in Replies activity there were 1910 tweets, Mentions had 141 tweets, and MentionsInRetweet had 12 tweets. In detail this can be seen in Table 1 above.

Table 1. Public response occurrences intensity by component.

Componen	Number of occurrences
Account	16.250
Edges	19.023
Tweet	6873
Retweet	9428
Replies	1910
Mentions	141
MentionsInRetweet	12

4.2 #Extended Communication Network

As mentioned in the previous section, the public response to the implementation of PPKM in Indonesia has resulted in 19,023 communication networks. This communication network is then divided into groups in which each group has an account of mutual influence (see the picture below). The total number of communication groups generated during the hashtag #Extended was 1083 groups. Each communication group raised the issue of extending the PPKM period by sharing various perspectives. The highest group of communication networks generated using the hashtag #Extended shows that Twitter has become a medium of information for users to share content with each other(Suryadharma and Susanto 2017) (Fig. 1).

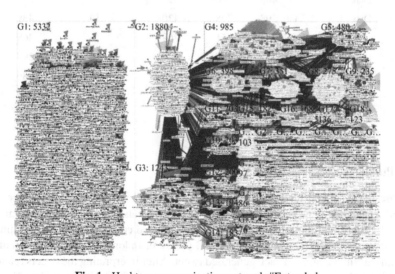

Fig. 1. Hashtag communication network #Extended.

Using NodeXL Pro, communication researchers can present network visualizations to enable more massive network analysis and open up various opportunities to analyze communication networks formed on social media (Purnama 2015). The number of responses regarding the PPKM extension policy in Indonesia shows that the PPKM extension is a policy that has a vast impact on people in Indonesia. In addition, this case also clarifies the strategic position of social media Twitter, namely as a means to create interaction in providing social support and relationships with one another (Ciszek 2013; Xiong et al. 2019). The relationship that occurs in the hashtag #Extended also shows that social media Twitter is a communication network among users to share content, depictions of individuals and people involved can be delivered with nodes or dots. In contrast, the resulting relationships between nodes that appear are referred to as edges or links (Susanto et al. 2012). The total edges in each group are shown in the Table 2 below.

Table 2. List of ten communication network groups with details of account appearance and link edges.

Group	Vertex shape	Label	Vertices	Unique edges	Edges with duplicates	Total edges
G1	Disk	G1: 5332	5332	5136	437	5573
G2	Disk	G2: 1880	1880	1933	15	1948
G3	Disk	G3: 1243	1243	1702	93	1795
G4	Disk	G4: 985	985	1151	155	1306
G5	Disk	G5: 480	480	522	10	532
G6	Disk	G6: 398	398	420	19	439
G7	Disk	G7: 351	351	369	0	369
G8	Disk	G8: 275	275	277	20	297
G9	Disk	G9: 235	235	310	26	336
G10	Disk	G10: 203	203	247	0	247

4.3 Public Trust Against PPKM Policy

The use of the Social network analysis (SNA) method will provide researchers with an understanding of the relationships between individuals or groups (Ramadhani et al. 2019). Furthermore, the relationship that occurs indeed contains particular sentiments, the sentiments that arise against the PPKM policy in Indonesia can then be identified through careful meaning in each generated tweet. After interpreting the tweets related to the hashtag #Extended, the resulting sentiment is categorized into four: Very Negative reaching 24.17%, Moderately Negative reaching 36.01%, Moderately Positive going 26.88%, and Very Positive reaching 12.94% (See Figure below). The sentiment formed in the use of #Extended shows a tendency to have a negative view, which illustrates that the public's response to the PPKM policy tends to be unfavourable, resulting in public acceptance of the policy not as expected by the Indonesian government. Because the presence of PPKM has a negative impact on social and economic conditions (Rizal et al. 2021; Rusiadi et al. 2020; Saputra and Salma 2020). Even so, on the other hand, the implementation of PPKM has a positive impact on reducing Covid-19 cases in Indonesia (Fig. 2).

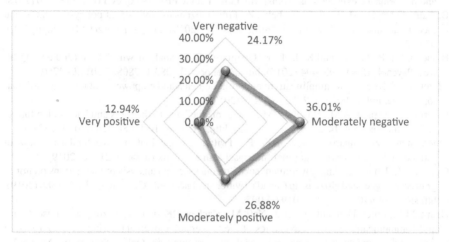

Fig. 2. Percentage of Twitter users sentiment against hashtag #Extended.

5   Conclusions

From identifying the hashtag #Extended above, public trust in the implementation of the Mobility Restrictions Policy in Indonesia has resulted in more negative sentiments from Twitter social media users. The negative sentiment that emerged gave an understanding that the Twitter user community in Indonesia did not entirely accept the policies implemented. The intensity of the accounts involved in responding to the procedure is relatively high, accompanied by the communication network that occurs, which can explain the communication relationships that arise between each communication group. This research also illustrates that public trust must be considered in the approaches taken in implementing policies. The extension of the PKKM term for the umpteenth time created a sense of disappointment and negative sentiment towards the extension policy being implemented.

References

Akbar, P., Irawan, B., Taufik, M., Nurmandi, A., Suswanta: Social media in politic: political campaign on United States election 2020 between Donald Trump and Joe Biden. In: Stephanidis, C., Antona, M., Ntoa, S. (eds.) HCI International 2021 - Late Breaking Posters. HCII 2021. Communications in Computer and Information Science, vol. 1499. Springer, Cham (2021). https://doi.org/10.1007/978-3-030-90179-0_46

Anson, S., Watson, H., Wadhwa, K., Metz, K.: Analysing social media data for disaster prepared-ness: understanding the opportunities and barriers faced by humanitarian actors. Int. J. Disaster Risk Reduct. **21**, 131–139 (2017). https://doi.org/10.1016/j.ijdrr.2016.11.014

Antony, M.: What is social media. London: iCrossing (2008). https://ebooks.publish.csiro.au/aut hor/Antony%2CLucilleM.K

Batara, E., Nurmandi, A., Warsito, T., Pribadi, U.: Are government employees adopting local e-government transformation?: The need for having the right attitude, facilitating conditions and performance expectations. Transform. Gov.: People Process Policy **11**(3), 343–376 (2018)

Belkahla Driss, O., Mellouli, S., Trabelsi, Z.: From citizens to government policy-makers: social media data analysis. Gov. Inf. Q. **36**(3), 560–570 (2019). https://doi.org/10.1016/j.giq.2019.05.002

Brandão, C.:. P. Bazeley and K. Jackson, Qualitative Data Analysis with NVivo (2nd ed.). Qual. Res. Psychol. **12**(4), 492–494 (2015). https://doi.org/10.1080/14780887.2014.992750

Ciszek, E.: Advocacy and amplification: nonprofit outreach and empowerment through participa-tory media. Public Relat. J. **7**(2), 187–213 (2013)

Delerue, H., Kaplan, A.M., Haenlein, M.: Social media: back to the roots and back to the future. J. Syst. Inf. Technol. **14**(2), 101–104 (2012). https://doi.org/10.1108/13287261211232126

Emeraldien, F.Z., Sunarsono, R.J., Alit, R.: Twitter Sebagai Platform Komunikasi Politik di Indonesia. SCAN-Jurnal Teknologi Informasi Dan Komunikasi **14**(1), 21–30 (2019)

Gintova, M.: Understanding government social media users: an analysis of interactions on immi-gration, refugees and citizenship Canada Twitter and Facebook. Gov. Inf. Q. **36**, 101388 (2019). https://doi.org/10.1016/j.giq.2019.06.005

Haupt, M.R., Jinich-Diamant, A., Li, J., Nali, M., Mackey, T.K.: Characterizing twitter user topics and communication network dynamics of the "Liberate" movement during COVID-19 using unsupervised machine learning and social network analysis. Online Soc. Netw. Media **21**, 100114 (2021). https://doi.org/10.1016/j.osnem.2020.100114

Himelboim, I., Smith, M., Shneiderman, B.: Tweeting apart: applying network analysis to detect selective exposure clusters in Twitter. Commun. Methods Meas. **7**(3), 169–197 (2013). https://doi.org/10.1080/19312458.2013.813922

Ho, A.T., Cho, W.: Government communication effectiveness and satisfaction with police perfor-mance: a large-scale survey study. Public Adm. Rev. **77**(2), 228–239 (2016). https://doi.org/10.1111/puar.12563.Government

Irawan, B.: Policies for controlling the covid-19 pandemic through social media communications by the East Kalimantan provincial government. Int. J. Commun. Soc. **4**(1), 125–136 (2022)

Islam, A.K.M.N., Laato, S., Talukder, S., Sutinen, E.: Misinformation sharing and social media fatigue during COVID-19: an affordance and cognitive load perspective. Technol. Forecast. Soc. Chang. **159**, 120201 (2020). https://doi.org/10.1016/j.techfore.2020.120201

Kaplan, A.M., Haenlein, M.: Users of the world, unite! the challenges and opportunities of Social Media. Bus. Horiz. **53**(1), 59–68 (2010). https://doi.org/10.1016/j.bushor.2009.09.003

Kosasih, I.: Peran Media Sosial Facebook dan Twitter Dalam Membangun Komunikasi (Persepsi dan Motifasi Masyarakat Jejaring Sosial Dalam Pergaulan). Lembaran Masyarakat: Jurnal Pengembangan Masyarakat Islam **2**(1), 29–42 (2016). https://doi.org/10.1017/CBO978110741 5324.004

Machmud, M., Irawan, B., Karinda, K., Susilo, J., Salahudin: Analysis of the intensity of commu-nication and coordination of government officials on Twitter social media during the Covid-19 handling in Indonesia. Acad. J. Interdiscip. Stud. **10**(3), 319 (2021). https://doi.org/10.36941/ajis-2021-0087

Madakam, S., Ramaswamy, R., Tripathi, S.: Internet of Things (IoT): a literature review. J. Comput. Commun. **03**(05), 164–173 (2015). https://doi.org/10.4236/jcc.2015.35021

Näkki, P., et al.: Social media for citizen participation report on the somus project, no. 755. VTT Publications (2011)

Nurati, D.E.: KOMUNIKASI KEBIJAKAN PUBLIK DALAM PENGELOLAAN PEDAGANG KAKI LIMA BERBASIS PADA KEARIFAN LOKAL (Kajian Pengelolaan Pedagang Kaki Lima di Kota Surakarta). JPAP: Jurnal Penelitian Administrasi Publik **2**(01), 93–106 (2016). https://doi.org/10.30996/jpap.v2i01.701

Park, H., Reber, B.H., Chon, M.G.: Tweeting as health communication: health organizations use of twitter for health promotion and public engagement. J. Health Commun. **21**(2), 188–198 (2016). https://doi.org/10.1080/10810730.2015.1058435

Park, H.W., Park, S., Chong, M.: Conversations and medical news frames on twitter: Infodemiological study on COVID-19 in South Korea. J. Med. Internet Res. **22**(5), e18897 (2020). https://doi.org/10.2196/18897

Park, S., et al.: COVID-19 discourse on twitter in four Asian countries: case study of risk communication. J. Med. Internet Res. **23**(3), 1–17 (2021). https://doi.org/10.2196/23272

Purnama, F.Y.: NodeXL dalam Penelitian Jaringan Komunikasi Berbasis Internet. Jurnal ILMU KOMUNIKASI **12**(1), 19–34 (2015). https://doi.org/10.24002/jik.v12i1.441

Ramadhani, D.P., Alamsyah, A., Wicaksono, M.B.: Eksplorasi Pemimpin Opini Untuk Alternatif Pendukung Pemasaran Pt. Net Mediatama Indonesia Menggunakan Metode Analisis Jejaring Sosial Di Twitter. Sosiohumanitas **21**(1), 73–78 (2019). https://doi.org/10.36555/sosiohumanitas.v21i1.1002

Ranjan, S., Sood, S.: Exploring Twitter for large data analysis. Int. J. Adv. Res. Comput. Sci. Softw. Eng. **6**(7), 325–330 (2016)

Rizal, M., Afrianti, R., Abdurahman, I.: Dampak Kebijakan Pemberlakuan Pembatasan Kegiatan Masyarakat (PPKM) bagi Pelaku Bisnis Coffe shop pada Masa Pandemi Terdampak COVID-19 di Kabupaten Purwakarta The Impact of the Policy for Implementing Community Activity Restrictions for Coffee Shop Busi. Jurnal Inspirasi **12**(1), 97–105 (2021). http://inspirasi.bpsdm.jabarprov.go.id/index.php/inspirasi/article/view/198

Rusiadi, R., Aprilia, A., Adianti, V., Verawati, V.: Dampak Covid-19 Terhadap Stabilitas Ekonomi Dunia (Studi 14 Negara Berdampak Paling Parah). Jurnal Kajian Ekonomi Dan Kebijakan Publik **5**(2), 173–182 (2020)

Saputra, H., Salma, N.: Dampak PSBB dan PSBB Transisi di DKI Jakarta dalam Pengendalian COVID-19. Media Kesehatan Masyarakat Indonesia **16**(3), 282–292 (2020). https://doi.org/10.30597/mkmi.v16i3.11042

Shahi, G.K., Dirkson, A., Majchrzak, T.A.: An exploratory study of COVID-19 misinformation on Twitter. Online Soc. Netw. Media **22**, 100104 (2021). https://doi.org/10.1016/j.osnem.2020.100104

Song, C., Lee, J.: Citizens use of social media in government, perceived transparency, and trust in government. Public Perform. Manag. Rev. **39**(2), 430–453 (2016). https://doi.org/10.1080/15309576.2015.1108798

Suryadharma, B., Susanto, T.D.: Faktor penerimaan media sosial instansi pemerintah di Indonesia. Inf. Technol. **2**, 1–10 (2017). http://ejurnal.itats.ac.id/index.php/integer/article/view/174

Susanto, B., Lina, H., Chrismanto, A.R.: Penerapan social network analysis dalam Penentuan Centrality Studi Kasus social network Twitter. Jurnal Informatika **8**(1), 1–13 (2012). https://doi.org/10.21460/inf.2012.81.111

Tari, Z.G., Emamzadeh, Z.: An analysis of the media messages during the 2016 U. S. presidential election: a thematic comparison between CNN News and Donald Trump's Tweets. J. Polit. Law **11**(2), 78–87 (2018). https://doi.org/10.5539/jpl.v11n2p78

Tromble, R.: Thanks for (actually) responding! How citizen demand shapes politicians' interactive practices on Twitter. New Media Soc. **20**(2), 676–697 (2018). https://doi.org/10.1177/1461444816669158

Witanto, J.N., Lim, H., Atiquzzaman, M.: Smart government framework with geo-crowdsourcing and social media analysis. Futur. Gener. Comput. Syst. **89**, 1–9 (2018). https://doi.org/10.1016/j.future.2018.06.019

Xiong, Y., Cho, M., Boatwright, B.: Hashtag activism and message frames among social movement organizations: semantic network analysis and thematic analysis of Twitter during the #MeToo movement. Public Relat. Rev. **45**(1), 10–23 (2019). https://doi.org/10.1016/j.pubrev.2018.10.014

Swedish Recreational Businesses Coping with COVID-19 Using Technologies

Ala Sarah Alaqra$^{(\boxtimes)}$ and Akhona C. Khumalo

Karlstad University, Karlstad, Sweden
as.alaqra@kau.se

Abstract. Restrictions imposed on societies across the world due to the COVID-19 pandemic have had direct and indirect consequences to the public's health and well-being. Unlike many countries, Sweden's restrictions were significantly milder. Businesses offering recreational services provide activities that are important to the well-being of the public. This study explores the status and perspectives of 34 Swedish businesses that provide recreational activities during COVID-19 and the role of technology on recreational services. Results show that businesses comply with guidelines and recommendations, have trust in the government despite lack of sufficient support, and have special considerations for youth. Technology was significant in aiding businesses to cope with COVID-19. Trends reported are: adoption of new remote technologies, increase of digital tools use, offerings of online services, and openness to new solutions.

Keywords: COVID-19 · Recreational activities · Well-being · Sweden · Technology · Digitalization · Coping with COVID-19

1 Introduction

COVID-19 and Sweden. The COVID-19 pandemic is an unprecedented crisis, and to this point (March 2022) there are approximately 450.23 million confirmed cases and over 6 million deaths worldwide [1]. Presently in Sweden, it is reported that there are 2.46 million confirmed cases and over 17.7 thousand deaths [2]. Around the world, there have been tight regulations and restrictions implemented to tackle the COVID-19 infection spread. Sweden was a special case, since it is known for not implementing tight restrictions unlike its neighboring countries. The government of Sweden encourages the public to take responsibility to follow guidelines and recommendations, without coercion, thus demonstrating its trust in the public. The impact of COVID-19 has not only adverse effects on the physiological health of individuals, but also indirect health effects as it may seriously affect the mental health and well-being of individuals [9]. Recreation businesses are at risk of pent-up demand during times of crisis and

The original version of this chapter was revised: this chapter was previously published non-open access. The correction to this chapter is available at
https://doi.org/10.1007/978-3-031-06391-6_76

C. Stephanidis et al. (Eds.): HCII 2022, CCIS 1582, pp. 349–357, 2022.
https://doi.org/10.1007/978-3-031-06391-6_45

often as a result of denied access to a market; meaning demand shifts from discretionary products and services [15]. Businesses and services such as restaurants, bars, sports, concerts, movies, and entertainment are at risk of facing an economic downturn even outside of lock-downs or pandemic-related operational restrictions. The government of Sweden has offered financial support, SEK 175 million, to increase supervision to ensure eating and drinking establishments adhere to restrictions. However, funds were also released by the government to support other services, at this time a total of SEK 3,53 billion was to go towards culture [3] and a total of SEK 1,995 billion towards sport [4].

Technological Trends Among Businesses. Despite the COVID-19 consequences on businesses, COVID-19 effects are shown to present digitalization opportunities for businesses [8]. In the wake of a pandemic, healthcare and retail have found ways to provide goods and services and to keep afloat. To overcome the limitations that come with COVID-19, consumer behaviors have changed to the use of modern technology to easily access and acquire products from the comfort of their homes [15]. Technology may have also benefited recreation businesses, but technology can be expected to have a limited impact on a number of these businesses. Beauty salons, spas, bars, theaters, movie houses, and entertainment places, for instance, can take bookings online, but cannot, for the most part, offer their products and services online. For example, gyms can offer virtual cardio exercises, but the use of gym equipment requires one to be in the gym premises [14]. COVID-19 has sped up the uptake of technology-based service offerings and has made the public more aware of technological options that can make their lives easier. "Innovation processes that would previously have been incremental and taken years have been forced by the global health crisis to move to a more radical model" [8, p. 4]. Many of the technologies used have existed before the COVID-19 pandemic but the limitations brought about by COVID-19 have expedited their adoption and use. COVID-19 has contributed to the acceleration of digitalization trends, and is thought to be a "catalyst" for the adoption of technological solutions for work places and organizations [5]. However, one main consequence is the restrictions imposed on people's lifestyles, limiting their activities, and therefore it poses a risk to their overall well-being. Inactivity leads to sedentary lifestyles which can have serious consequences to one's physical and mental health [6,12]. Studies show recommendations to help counter risks to physical and mental well-being [12,13]. Recreational activities, often considered as leisure activities, are essential for the overall well-being. Recreation does not only associate with cultural activities, but according to Metin et al.'s categories recreational activities include, to name a few, basic entertainment, mental activities, sports and exercises, music, art, and dance [11]. Since public health is given precedence over recreational activities during this crisis, our interest is to explore how recreational businesses cope with the COVID-19 restrictions and whether technological innovations or solutions have been adopted.

Research Objective. In this study, we explore the effects of COVID-19 on businesses, how they cope with the crisis, and the role of technologies, e.g., digitalization in Sweden. Specifically, we target businesses providing recreational/

leisure services and activities in effort to explore the support for such activities, essential for well-being.

2   Methodology

The study was conducted as an online-targeted survey, using the Survey & Report tool supported by Karlstad University. The survey consisted of 18 questions. Five demographic questions which collected information on which municipality the business is located, whether the business is municipality owned or private, the type of recreational business, the type of services offered, and the professional position of the participant. We asked close-ended questions about type of business and recreational activity provided, impact of COVID-19 on the business, measures and conformity to guidelines, and the role of technology. We also included comment-fields (open-ended responses) for most questions. The recreational businesses that were approached include the following categories: gym/pool, restaurant/pub, theatre/opera/cinema, museum/gallery, cafe/bakery, spa/hairdresser, and games/sports. The list of recreational activities was based on the activities and classifications by Metin et al. [11]. Two businesses were selected in each category in each of the 21 municipalities and these businesses were contacted by email containing information letter as well as the link to the online survey, provided in both English and Swedish. Two consecutive reminders were sent to non-respondents. Participation was voluntary, and a consent form was included at the beginning of the survey and participants proceeded only upon giving consent. No personally identifying information were collected[1]. Descriptive analysis is used to present the results of the closed-ended questions, and thematic analysis [7] is used for the open-ended responses, i.e., comments. Data was translated to English and Nvivo software was used to code the results and preliminary categorize data. During each stage of the analysis (coding, categorization, theme generation), both authors would process the analysis independently and then meet up to discuss and resolve conflicts. This study was conducted during the pandemic, this negatively affected the response rate from the relevant types of businesses. Despite the limited responses, the results are consistent with literature and can be assumed to give an accurate depiction of the state and experiences of businesses at the time of the survey.

3   Results

3.1   Statistical Descriptions of Closed Ended Questions

Our study yielded 34 responses sharing businesses' perspectives from 20 Swedish municipalities, see Fig. 1. The voluntary responses are from individuals holding managerial and executive positions at their recreational businesses. Twenty-five (73.5%) of the businesses are private businesses and 9 (26.5%) are municipality-owned. We asked participants about the categories of activities they provide, and

---

[1] This study received the approval from the ethical advisor at Karlstad university.

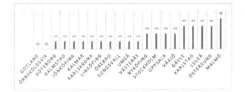

Fig. 1. Responses per municipality.   **Fig. 2.** Recreational activities provided.

the following activities are reported by the corresponding number of businesses: sports and exercises 14 (41.2%), basic entertainment 12 (35.3%), other social activities 11 (32.4%), mental activities 9 (26.5%), art & hobbies 5 (14.7%), play & games 5 (14.7%), music & dance 3 (8.8%), nature activities 3 (8.8%), and hedonic activities 2 (5.9%), as depicted in Fig. 2.

The results show that both the national guidelines (31, 91.2%) and municipality-specific guidelines (22, 64.7%) are being followed by the recreational businesses to ensure safety. The majority of the participants (28, 82.4%) indicate that their businesses were operational at the time of the survey (peak of restrictions), while 6 (17.6%) were closed. Five of the closed businesses indicate that closures were due to COVID-19 restrictions as opposed to revenue loss or resource unavailability.

It is reported the significant decrease of: the number of operating hours 25 (80.6%), number of staff 19 (63.3%), number of services 18 (60%), number of customers 29 (90.6%), and revenue 27 (90%). However, a small number of businesses, in the categories gyms/pools, and museum/gallery, report a positive outlook: 3 (9.7%) cite an increase in operating hours, 2 (6.7%) cite an increase in the number of services, number of customers, and increase in profits respectively. When asked about the importance of remaining open, 5 (14.7%) responses indicated "no" for moral consciousness e.g., public safety reasons. The rest indicated "yes" with the following reasons: 25 (73%) responses were for social well being purposes, 21 (61.8%) for economical purposes, and 4 (11.8) stated there is no reason to be closed. 19 (55.9%) of the responses mention that they have adopted new technologies to aid their work during the COVID-19 pandemic and 14 (43.8%) have adopted new remote services specifically. It is also reported that there is a need for technological development to serve new demands 8 (23.5%). Twenty participants (5, 14.7% strongly agree and 15, 44.1% agree) express having trust in the government, 11 (32.4%) remain neutral, 2(5.9%) disagree, and 1(2.9%) strongly disagrees. The majority (22, 64.7%) feel safe in Sweden, 10 (29.4%) are neutral, and 2 (5.9%) disagree. Though a few participants (3, 8.8%) are doubtful about the future of their businesses, many (22, 64.7%) remain positive. To the statement that the support from the state is sufficient participants: strongly disagree (6, 17.6%), disagree 8 (23.5%), neutral (10, 29.4%), agree (9, 26.5%), and strongly agree by 1 (2.9%).

3.2   Thematic Analysis of Open Ended Responses

Business Safety Measures. In addition to the majority indicating that they follow national and municipal guidelines, 2 participants mention following recommendations from authoritative bodies such as the Swedish Sports Confederation and the Special Sports Federation. One participant adds that their business also performed a risk analysis and made the necessary adaptations for staff and customers, while another highlights that the business added its own considerations to the national and local guidelines. According to one participant, their gyms reduced the number of visitors allowed at the time to ensure social distancing (10 sqm rule). They also reduced group training from 20–28 to 10–12 people.

COVID19 Impact on Business Status. Though only about a handful of participants (6) indicated that their businesses were closed at the time of the survey, 7 operated under special conditions. One business had closed and reopened on 2 different occasions. Of the businesses that operated on certain conditions, 3 participants mention that they were open for shorter that usual operating hours (2 businesses, operating at 20% and 33.3% of their usual work week). Two participants mention that they faced partial closures where certain services ceased and others continued to operate, such as providing outdoor or digital alternatives. Nine comments indicate that some institutions also continued to provide services where certain exceptions applied, such as for the youth (18 and younger), schools, rehabilitation, and associations. Other comments cite facing reduced services (1), reduced customers (2), and reduced revenues (1). The closures and restricted business operations resulted in a loss of revenue but businesses remained hopeful that they would soon open their doors to the public again. One participant cites that the loss of revenue was about 30% every month compared to 2019. According to 2 participants, businesses received financial support which went towards temporary lay-offs and staff retention. Three participants elaborate that financial support, reduction of services and conversion of operations to digital offerings are means by which businesses continued operations.

> *"Thanks to redundancy support (permitteringsstöd), we have been able to retain the staff so far. However, it is starting to get tougher now that we continue to lose revenue..." - PID07*

The Importance of Remaining Open. Two participants express that as long as safety measures were followed and that there was no risk of contagion then businesses could remain open. Priority to children, youth, and associations is indicated (2), as one highlights the importance to be available for schools and one mentions the importance of movement and exercise.

> *"It is important that children/young people have the opportunity for exercise/movement, it benefits all forms of motor skills and the social community is also important." - PID06*

Adoption of Remote Services. Due to the COVID-19 restrictions, recreational businesses adopted the use of technology to keep their businesses running. Fifteen participants list the adoption of remote services as a way in which technology has played a role during the pandemic, and one highlights that the pandemic encouraged more use of existing digital services. Digital team meetings intra- and inter-organizationally as well as the tools to facilitate digital meetings constitute over 50% of the additional comments given by participants regarding technology use. The businesses have used remote services such as online booking and queuing systems (2), broadcast lectures and programs (2), app-based delivery food service (1), posting of training films (2), and digital meetings and tools (8).

Required Technology Development to Serve New Needs. Participants identified the need for technology development to serve new needs that became apparent during the pandemic, which can be used in the recreational setting in the future. The key highlights are the digitalization of services and processes (13) and the need for alternatives (6). Online content sharing such as webcast workouts (1), video on demand (1), web training (1), digital concerts (1), online screenings and lectures (1), online games (1), hosting a Spring market online (1) are some examples technology serves new needs of recreational businesses. The need for digital equipment to support digital services is also highlighted (2) and using technology as a means to reach more customers (1). Furthermore, an opportunity is presented during the pandemic to learn from others how technology can serve their businesses.

> *"The digital can be developed and it is going on right now... We take part in other people's methods and see where we land... For example, the National Heritage Board, which collects good examples and broadcasts via its website."*
> - PID32

Expectations of Vaccination on Business Operations. The plans of the vaccine starting brought some recreational businesses hope, 2 participants cite getting back to normalcy, 7 participants looked forward to people (and especially the elderly) going out more again, 1 participant highlights that it would result in less services, while 3 participants still viewed it with uncertainty.

4   Discussions

The Swedish government's unique approach during COVID-19 with restrictions is to trust the public. Though the COVID-19 measures are known to not have been very stringent in Sweden, our results show that guidelines from respective authorities, are taken seriously by recreational businesses, thus prioritizing the health and safety of the public. No differences are seen between private and municipality controlled recreational activities. However, municipal recreational areas are more likely to oblige with closure recommendations. Our results indicate that the majority of our participants have trust in the government, feel safe in Sweden and have a positive outlook for the future. This is the case despite that businesses suffered a decrease in revenue and did not all receive financial aid, yet followed measures and remained hopeful for better days to come. Our results additionally enlighten that a small number of recreational businesses experienced more customers and more revenues, and offered more services during COVID-19

- an interesting outcome that highlights that the public continued to visit operational recreational establishments that contribute to their physical and mental well-being, even during a pandemic.

Inactivity or high level of sedentary lifestyle is associated with poor physical and/or mental health, and possibly lead to serious illnesses [6,12]. One of the major COVID-19 health concerns due to isolation is the overall inactivity of the public [12]. Our results illustrate the considerations to the public's well-being through recreational activities. The need for keeping recreational businesses running follow the important consideration on the effects of sedentary behaviors that result from measures enforced to maintain social distance during the COVID-19 pandemic. Additionally, psychological benefits are expected derivatives from the consumption of products and services of recreational businesses. However, the COVID-19 safety measures take precedence. Sweden considered continued social and physical activity in youth and children a benefit outweighing the potential risk of COVID-19 in children [10]. Thus the national public authorities allowed continued access to recreational activities such as sports for children born in or later than 2002. Another important consideration highlighted by our participants is continued access to recreational services for rehabilitation purposes. Thus at the regional, municipal, and at business level, exceptions were made that would accommodate these groups, also confirmed by our results. It must be noted however, that the political system in Sweden is such that regions and municipalities can make their own rulings on a matter and variations to the stringency or leniency of restrictions may exist. In addition, alternatives such as outdoor activities, online exercise activities and access to gyms based on bookings and limited allowable numbers that allowed for sufficient spacing, allowed individuals the opportunity to maintain active lifestyles. These measures contribute to society wellness during a daunting pandemic.

The pandemic opens doors to new technology aids and uses. In endurance sporting events in Sweden, for example, digital alternatives started to gain traction during the pandemic, and are likely to open up new opportunities in the future, albeit being viewed as less satisfying by some of the participants of digital races [16]. Our results show that during COVID-19, technology has played an important role in keeping the businesses running and forcing businesses to consider alternatives to the norm. Participants have indicated that they have found technology useful in aiding communication, better reaching customers, and providing online content. Many highlighted the adoption of new remote services, digitized internal processes, and digitized services thus offering new solutions that could continue after the COVID-19 pandemic.

5   Conclusions and Future Work

Our study gives insight on how recreational businesses cope with COVID-19 with the aid of technology. Given the unique governmental approach in Sweden to restrictions, trust is shown to be reciprocal from the majority of the participants' responses. Considerations to public's well-being are significant given public's safety is in place. Overall, participants express significant adoption of new digital solutions, and openness to future digital solutions for various recreational activities. Future studies could further investigate other contexts, i.e., countries with tighter restrictions. Upcoming innovative solutions could facilitate remote recreational activities especially for priority groups such as youth and associations.

Acknowledgments. We would like to express our thanks to the participants, representing recreational businesses, for their valued contribution to this study. We also like to extend our thanks to John Sören Pettersson for helping with the translations.

References

1. WHO Health emergency — WHO coronavirus (covid-19) dashboard with vaccination data. https://covid19.who.int/. Accessed 03 Oct 2022
2. WHO: Sweden— WHO coronavirus (covid-19) dashboard with vaccination data. https://covid19.who.int/region/euro/country/se. Accessed 03 Oct 2022
3. Ministry of Culture - Emergency support and incentives to culture (2021). shorturl.at/opxJV. Accessed 2 Sep 2021
4. Ministry of Culture - Emergency support and incentives to sport (2021). shorturl.at/dkqJ9. Accessed 2 Sep 2021
5. Amankwah-Amoah, J., Khan, Z., Wood, G., Knight, G.: Covid-19 and digitalization: the great acceleration. J. Bus. Res. **136**, 602–611 (2021)
6. Booth, F.W., Roberts, C.K., Thyfault, J.P., Ruegsegger, G.N., Toedebusch, R.G.: Role of inactivity in chronic diseases: evolutionary insight and pathophysiological mechanisms. Physiol. Rev. **97**(4), 1351–1402 (2017)
7. Braun, V., Clarke, V.: Using thematic analysis in psychology. Qual. Res. Psychol. **3**(2), 77–101 (2006)
8. Brem, A., Viardot, E., Nylund, P.A.: Implications of the coronavirus (covid-19) outbreak for innovation: which technologies will improve our lives? Technol. Forecast. Soc. Chang. **163**, 120451 (2021)
9. Druss, B.G.: Addressing the covid-19 pandemic in populations with serious mental illness. JAMA Psychiatry **77**(9), 891–892 (2020)
10. Helsingen, L.M., et al.: The covid-19 pandemic in Norway and Sweden-threats, trust, and impact on daily life: a comparative survey. BMC Public Health **20**(1), 1–10 (2020)
11. Metİn, T.C., Katırcı, H., Yüce, A., Sarıçam, S., Cabuk, A.: An inventory study on the categorization and types of recreational activities. J. Acad. Soc. Sci. Stud. **59**, 547–561 (2017)
12. Narici, M., et al.: Impact of sedentarism due to the covid-19 home confinement on neuromuscular, cardiovascular and metabolic health: physiological and pathophysiological implications and recommendations for physical and nutritional countermeasures. Eur. J. Sport Sci. **21**(4), 614–635 (2021)
13. Peçanha, T., Goessler, K.F., Roschel, H., Gualano, B.: Social isolation during the covid-19 pandemic can increase physical inactivity and the global burden of cardiovascular disease. Am. J. Physiol.-Heart Circ. Physiol. **318**(6), H1441–H1446 (2020)

14. Piotrowski, D., Piotrowska, A.I.: Operation of gyms and fitness clubs during the covid-19 pandemic-financial, legal, and organisational conditions. J. Phys. Educ. Sport **21**(2), 1029–1036 (2021)

15. Sheth, J.: Impact of covid-19 on consumer behavior: will the old habits return or die? J. Bus. Res. **117**, 280–283 (2020)

16. Svensson, D., Radmann, A.: Keeping distance? Adaptation strategies to the covid-19 pandemic among sport event organizers in Sweden. J. Glob. Sport Manag. 1–18 (2021). https://doi.org/10.1080/24704067.2021.1936592

The Use of Social Media in Controlling of Corruption During the Covid-19 Pandemic in Indonesia

Aslam[⊠], Achmad Nurmandi, Isnaini Muallidin, and Danang Kurniawan

Department of Government Affairs and Administration, Jusuf Kalla School Government,
University of Muhammadiyah Yogyakarta, Yogyakarta, Indonesia
aslam.aslam2107@gmail.com, nurmandi_achmad@umy.ac.id

Abstract. Social media is now close access for communication and dialectics. This study aims to examine the role of social media in eradicating corruption that occurred during the COVID-19 pandemic in Indonesia because during the pandemic there was an increase in corruption carried out by state officials. This study uses descriptive qualitative research methods, data processing using Nvivo 12 plus software, with the stages of data collection, data import, data coding, data classification, and data display the data is taken through Twitter social media by looking at the public discussion of corruption in Indonesia, to enrich the data, researchers target news in the media and see what news appears related to corruption in Indonesia. pandemic period. So that the results of the study will show how and what models of corruption eradication emerged during the pandemic. At the end of the research, the researcher will present knowledge of corruption crimes committed by state officials so that the public can anticipate the occurrence of corruptionKeyword: Corruption, Social Media, Covid-19.

Keywords: Corruption · Social media · Covid-19

1 Introduction

The condition of all countries in the world is ravaged by the presence of a coronavirus outbreak known as Corona Virus Diseases-19 or commonly called COVID-19 [1]. This condition is also felt in Indonesia, in addition to attacking Health Covid-19 also attacks the economy, social order, and also the education system. However, what people feel the most is the impact on the economy. The government has disbursed a large number of funds to tackle this outbreak, at least the government has disbursed additional funds for the 2020 State Budget for handling Covid-19, which totals Rp.405.1 trillion [1]. Various forms of social assistance have been issued by the government, especially during this pandemic. This assistance is provided through various programs from each ministry. These programs include the Family Hope Program (PKH), Basic Food Cards or Non-Cash Food Assistance (BPNT), and Direct Cash Assistance (BLT) [2]. The size of the budget allocated for the prevention of Covid-19 provides opportunities for certain actors to commit corruption [3]. One of the biggest corruption cases during the pandemic was

C. Stephanidis et al. (Eds.): HCII 2022, CCIS 1582, pp. 358–364, 2022.
https://doi.org/10.1007/978-3-031-06391-6_46

the corruption of social assistance funds carried out by the Indonesian Ministry of Social Affairs.

Corruption and bribery are common occurrences in local life where urban communities emerge, permanently forming a mechanism for interaction with civil society. It is also noted that local people's struggles with bribery cases have had practical results [4]. The people must bear the consequences of corruption. There-fore, the people need to control every public official in their neighborhood or state officials who have the potential to become corrupt. The supervision of corruptors in Indonesia has not been carried out strictly. For this reason, the community, institutions, and the office environment must be a good control for state officials or public officials, especially during the Covid-19 pandemic because, in a survey conducted by the Indonesian Survey Institute on the trend of corruption, the results showed that 39.6% stated the level of corruption. increased during the Covid-19 pandemics [5].

Anti-corruption as a type of social case activity from civil society authorities and institutions, which aims to increase public awareness about the nature of corruption as a negative social phenomenon [6], the main causes: the community is not ready to build the state (weak state traditions; lack of qualified personnel, economic resources, and industrial base; high levels of corruption [7].corruption is a large and clear breach of trust [5], Some analyzes suggest that political dynasties are the cause of corruption. However, corruption at the local level is carried out by regional heads of both dynasties Thus, minimizing corruption is not achieved by limiting political dynasties but by strengthening government control [6]. Social media is considered by many to be a very helpful tool in facilitating the process of public services, reducing the cost of public services, increasing transparency, and reducing corruption [8].

Public attention A big factor in efforts to eradicate corruption in a certain way is an effort to reduce corrupt practices, in modern times, social media has become an important part of controlling corruption [7]. By using electronic media, the public becomes an important part of unraveling corruption cases in Indonesia. Corruption in Indonesia is still very high when viewed from the existing data. According to the 2019 Corruption Perceptions Index, Indonesia got a score of 40 out of 100, with a score of 100 meaning that it is free from corruption [9]. If the public does not participate in monitoring corruption, corruption cases will increase. So in this research, the author will focus on discussing the role of social media in overseeing corruption in the pandemic era. Social movements, in this case, anti-corruption, are an inseparable part of social media by using hashtags as part of the communication strategy for encoding information content [10].

2   Literature Review

2.1   Controlling of Corruption During the Covid-19 Pandemic

Supervision of corruption is an effort to eradicate corrupt behavior that occurs in the community. The government, the private sector, and civil society are fighting against 'evil corruption' to free the world from corruption [10].

The digitization of information developed by digital technology can make anything possible, has put the logic of signs in the search for human truth into a matter of massification of symbol games. [11]. If it is associated with surveillance, digitalization provides a wide space for monitoring, taking into account social behavior or the sustainability of social media [6]. So the author concludes that the community has the power to monitor acts of corruption. if referring to Michel Foucault's theory of power that, power is owned by every individual who is not bound by a legitimacy that functions to monitor one another both between individuals and between groups, but if individual power is united in a relationship then that power can be more dominant in supervising [12].

From Michel Foucault's theory of power the author draws the first indicator is "Participation" through public participation can monitor corruption, participation can be done by using social media as a medium to channel power possessed by individuals, The two authors draw indicator "Relation" there are many meanings about relations in today's modern era, but in the context of using social media, relationships can be interpreted as a group of people who are united in one goal. Like the similarity of using Hashtag in controlling corruption. From here Foucault began to give a limitation or definition of power as the core of his main idea. According to Foucault, power is a variety of power relationships that exist within the scope in which the relationship runs [13]. In its implementation, participation is divided into Criticism, Information, and Solutions. Specifically, participation in responding to corruption by using social media of the three indicators is often done by social media users. The second indicator is a reaction in which there are actors and forces. Relationships can be formed intentionally and unintentionally but still with the same goal.

2.2 Controlling Through Social Media

According to Andreas and Michael Haenlin (2010), social media is a group of Internet-based applications that build on the ideological and technological foundations of Web 2.0 and enable the creation and exchange of user-generated content [14]. The basic benefit of social media is that users can easily participate, ac-cess information, and convey ideas [15]. The for m of power is supervision, so it is very closely related to social media because supervision is not rigid. the importance of Foucault's thoughts on power and knowledge in the context of the rapid growth of the country's mass media industry. The very rapid development of mass media has now become a tool of power for certain purposes so that supervision which is the embodiment of power is present during social media [12]. Likewise, it was proposed by Foucault that relations can be built with the transmitting tower for the exchange of messages for a purpose [13]. So that the author analyzes social media today as a tool that is used as a force to realize power by using social media can also build a relationship so that power can be combined in a goal.

3 Research Methods

This research uses descriptive qualitative research. Data analysis using Nvivo 12 plus software, data retrieval via Twitter account using the hashtags #Pandemidi-korupsi, #korupsiperkayapejabat, and # Hukummatikorupsi. via NCapture from NVivo 12 Plus with Chrome Web. The data is processed with the Crosstab feature to automatically calculate the necessary main statistical tests with significant comparisons and indirect variables. Crosstab Query feature is to enter code (manual, generate, etc.), text data, and numeric data on variable and pattern data. At this stage, automatic calculations were found among all data regarding hashtag user activities in monitoring corruption during the pandemic. The mention feature is used to see the pattern of relationships in the discussion. Furthermore, by using the Word Cloud feature, the most frequently used words or terms can be revealed. This study looks at the extent to which social media is used to monitor corruption during the COVID-19 pandemic in Indonesia.

4 Results and Discussion

The high number of corruption cases in Indonesia should be accompanied by high levels of oversight of corruption. Twitter is a social media that can be used to monitor corruption. In responding to corruption cases during the Covid-19 pandemic in Indonesia, Indonesian people use Twitter to carry out a social movement. The emergence of hashtags #Pandemidikorupsi #Pandemiperkayapejabat, and #Hukummatikoruptor is a response to corruption cases that occurred during the Covid-19 pandemic (Fig. 1).

Fig. 1. #Pandemidikorupsi, #Pandemiperkayapejabat, #Hukummatikoruptor word cloud

It can be seen from the results of the Word Cloud that was stated using Nvivo, the dominant words that emerged from the three hashtags were the word Zaman and @Jokowi (the name of the Indonesian president) meaning that many netizens mentioned the word Zaman and many netizens tweeted the account of the Indonesian president in response to corruption cases in Indonesia during the pandemic. covid-19. By using these three hashtags, there are many narrations conveyed by netizens, of course, these narratives are a form of participation and relations (Fig. 2).

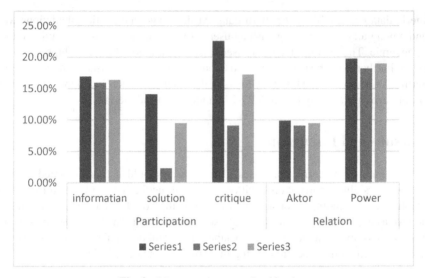

Fig. 2. Movement content classification

After processing data on activities in the use of Twitter, there is a separation from the indicators of participation and relations, the author explains in pictures about the grouping of narrative content made by netizens when using the hashtags #Pandemidiko-rupsi #Pandemiperkayapejabat, and #Hukummatikoruptor. The grouping is based on the theoretical indicators used so that the results show that Criticism and Strength are the highest activities. And not many netizens provide solutions in responding to the problem of corruption. And not many netizens provide solutions in responding to the problem of corruption.

No	Participation	Relationship
1	Criticism: In the use of twitter, many netizens criticize the realization of social assistance funds given to the community. Netizens criticized the small amount of help given to the community	Actors: President of Indonesia, CNN Indonesia, Detik.com, students, and workers are actors who are widely admired by netizens in conveying criticism, information, and solutions
2	Information: The information that is mostly conveyed by netizens is the mechanism for collecting data on beneficiaries which is considered not transparent. So that the distribution of aid is not well-targeted	Power: high number of mansions against the President of Indonesia and the media is a force in monitoring
3	Solutions: Applying the death penalty to corruptors is the dominant solution presented by netizens	

The results of data processing using Nvivo, criticism which is part of participation is the highest activity carried out by netizens, various narratives submitted by netizens in criticizing corruption cases during the pandemic. Criticism of the state, especially the government regarding the management of social assistance funds, and also criticism of the dismissal of kpk employees became the dominant narrative conveyed by netizens using the three hashtags. On the contrary, what happened to the solution indicator, social media users were still minimal in providing solutions to the problem of corruption, but some netizens conveyed several solutions in solving corruption cases, the dominant solution being delivered was the death penalty for corruption. Netizens think that with the implementation of the death penalty, corruption can give fear to corruptors addition to the accounts of the Indonesian president, CNN Indonesia, and Detik.com media accounts are also the goals of netizens who use hashtags because the media is an important part and has the power to provide information related to corruption in the community. With the presence of the media, information about corruption or the anticorruption movement can be reached among the wider community. The student movement is considered a movement that can change a civilization by using the hashtag #pandemi-dikorupsi, there is a mansion, a student movement that uses a mobile UGM account. The presence of the student movement in responding to corruption cases (Fig. 3).

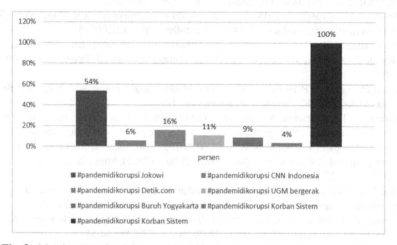

Fig. 3. Mention #Pandemidikorupsi #Pandemiperkayapejabat, #Hukummatikoruptor

5 Conclusion

Use Participation in monitoring corruption using social media is mostly done in the form of criticism, and information is only general about the information on the occurrence of corruption, only a few netizens can provide solutions in solving corruption problems during the Covid-19 pandemic. The case that received the most response from the public was the case of corruption in social assistance funds. The public demands the responsibility of the Indonesian president in solving corruption problems.

References

1. Sefriani, R., Sepriana, R., Wijaya, I., Radyuli, P.: Menrisal, blended learning with edmodo: the effectiveness of statistical learning during the covid-19 pandemic. Int. J. Eval. Res. Educ. **10**(1), 293–299 (2021). https://doi.org/10.11591/IJERE.V10I1.20826
2. Mykhailenko, G.M., Cheremisin, A.V.: Corruption and bribery in towns of the south of Ukraine during the period of 1785–1870. Public Policy Adm. **18**(4), 509–523 (2019). https://doi.org/10.13165/VPA-19-18-4-10
3. Vikhryan, A.P., Fedorov, M.V.: Anti-corruption education as a factor of social security*. Rudn J. Soc. **20**(4), 967–976 (2020). https://doi.org/10.22363/2313-2272-2020-20-4-967-976
4. Tolstykh, V., Grigoryan, M., Kovalenko, T.: Legal systems of the post-soviet non-recognized states: structural problems. Russ. Law J. **7**(2), 81–100 (2019). https://doi.org/10.17589/2309-8678-2019-7-2-81-100
5. Sapsford, R., Tsourapas, G., Abbott, P., Teti, A.: Corruption, trust, inclusion and cohesion in North Africa and the Middle East. Appl. Res. Qual. Life **14**(1), 1–21 (2017). https://doi.org/10.1007/s11482-017-9578-8
6. Purwaningsih, T., Widodo, B.E.C.: The interplay of incumbency, political dinasty and corruption in indonesia: are political dynasties the cause of corruption in Indonesia? Rev. UNISCI **2020**(53), 157–176 (2020). https://doi.org/10.31439/UNISCI-89
7. Brannum, K.: Guatemala 2018: facing a constitutional crossroad. Rev. Cienc. Polit. **39**(2), 265–284 (2019). https://doi.org/10.4067/S0718-090X2019000200265
8. Simarmata, M.H., Ham, D., Hukum, K.: Peranan e-Government dan media sosial untuk Mewujudkan Budaya transparansi dan Pemberantasan Korupsi. J. Integritas **3**(2), 203–229 (2017)
9. Balimula, S., et al.: Perancangan Kampanye Media Sosial tentang Nilai-Nilai Anti Korupsi untuk Anak-Anak Sekolah Dasar di Surabaya (2019)
10. Kurniawan, D., Nurmandi, A., Salahudin, S., Mutiarin, D., Suswanta, S.: Analysis of the anti-corruption movement through twitter social media: a case study of Indonesia. In: Antipova, T. (eds) Advances in Digital Science. ICADS 2021. Advances in Intelligent Systems and Computing, vol. 1352, pp. 298–308. Springer, Cham (2021). https://doi.org/10.1007/978-3-030-71782-7_27
11. Eka, A.G., Wuryanta, W.: Digitalisasi masyarakat: Menilik kekuatan dan kelemahan dinamika era informasi digital dan masyarakat informasi. J. Ilmu Komun. 131–142 (2013)
12. Kebung, K.: Membaca kuasa michel foucault dalam konteks kekuasaan di Indonesia. Melintas **33**(1), 34–51 (2018). https://doi.org/10.26593/mel.v33i1.2953.34-51
13. Syahputra, I.: Post media literacy: menyaksikan kuasa media bersama michel foucault. J. ASPIKOM **1**(1), 1 (2017). https://doi.org/10.24329/aspikom.v1i1.4
14. Syauket, A., Lestari, S.P., Simarmata, R.P.: Inovasi Birokrasi Pemerintahan Anti Korupsi Berbasis Teknologi Informasi Dan Komunikasi (Melihat Kebijakan E-Procurement). Jurnal Manajemen Publik dan Kebijakan Publik (JMPKP), **2**(2), 92–99 (2020)
15. Setiawan, R.E.B., Nurmandi, A., Muallidin, I., Kurniawan, D., Salahudin, S.: Technology for governance: comparison of disaster information mitigation of COVID-19 in jakarta and West Java. In: Ahram, T., Taiar, R. (eds.) Human Interaction, Emerging Technologies and Future Systems V. IHIET 2021. Lecture Notes in Networks and Systems, vol. 319. Springer, Cham. https://doi.org/10.1007/978-3-030-85540-6_17

A User-Driven Self-service Business Intelligence Adoption Framework

Sean de Waal[(✉)] and Adheesh Budree

University of Cape Town, Western Cape, Cape Town, South Africa
Sean.dewaal@myuct.ac.za

Abstract. Cost management and operational efficiencies play a critical part in both the financial institution's ability to grow as well as their overall profit margins. For a financial institution to stay competitive in this era of fast-paced decision making, driven not only by local competition but by competitors at a global scale requires the ability to make rapid and accurate decisions based on all the available data. This can only be achieved through the effective use and adoption of BI and SSBI across all areas of the business. Through a thorough systematic literature review (SLR), this paper evaluated various adoption frameworks that have been used in past research relating to BI and SSBI. The synthesis process focused primarily on academic publications drawn via accepted databases and literature search engines for the period of 2000 to 2021. BI and SSBI were found to be primarily examined from an organisational stance while adoption from the humanistic stance of individuals was missing within the literature. Therefore, the Model of PC Utilisation (MPCU) has subsequently been proposed as a potential framework to examine the adoption of SSBI from a humanistic stance within a financial institution.

Keywords: Self-service business intelligence · Business intelligence · Adoption framework · Model of PC utilisation

1 Background

Cost management and operational efficiencies are driving factors that financial institutions constantly need to consider. Their need to observe trends while making adjustments to their products and strategies can not only set one institution apart from the rest but can also have significant consequences on their profits [1]. Recently an exponential shift in the value of data to a business has been observed and can be considered one of its greatest assets for potential growth and profits [2].

As new technologies are continuously introduced into the banking industry, they bring with them the ability to generate a substantial amount of data relating to the customers, their activities, and financial behaviours [3]. With the increase in the volume of raw data, the financial institution's need for a group of specialised systems that can handle the sheer volume of the data while also catering for a flexible user-friendly approach to analytical reporting increases [4–7].

© The Author(s), under exclusive license to Springer Nature Switzerland AG 2022
C. Stephanidis et al. (Eds.): HCII 2022, CCIS 1582, pp. 365–372, 2022.
https://doi.org/10.1007/978-3-031-06391-6_47

The concept of Business Intelligence (BI) is nothing new and has been around for many years. Numerous developments in the field have been observed, calling for the topic to be constantly researched in order to obtain a concise understanding of its concepts, processes, deployment and adoption [8]. BI plays a fundamental role in how decisions are made by the various business users through its ability to present information in a manner that is both required and acceptable to the business [7, 9]. A recent shift from the traditional reporting methodologies of BI has brought about Self-Service Business Intelligence (SSBI), which was driven by influences such as 1) costly Business Intelligence specialists, 2) the pace at which strategies in the organisations need to change, 3) the need for rapid information consumption and 4) the shift from judgemental to analytical decision-making [10, 11].

SSBI is a vehicle that offers self-reliance to the consumers of information and at its core is fundamentally similar to the traditional BI methodology. The main advantage that SSBI provides is that it caters for the dynamic aspect of data representation where the consumers are able to access, manipulate, and extract business information without the need of a BI specialist [4, 12–14]. By increasing the adoption rate of SSBI with the financial institutions the BI specialists are able to concentrate on their core responsibilities while creating area-specific and business-critical reporting data models [10, 12, 14].

This paper aims to synthesise the adoption frameworks previous utilised within BI and SSBI research to identify whether the frameworks have catered for the humanistic aspect of adoption.

2 Literature Review Method

Systematic literature reviews (SLR) as a methodology have been utilised for many years to gain a greater understanding of a particular topic while reducing the possibility of bias during the research process through the construction of a detailed "plan of action" which is strictly adhered to throughout the search and selection process [15–17]. The importance of developing this well-structured and documented SLR plan is to ensure replicability and that sufficient focus is directed to the research objectives throughout the research process [18].

The SLR methodology applied was guided by a model proposed by [18] in which academic publications in the form of journal articles and conference proceedings were extracted via Google Scholar from a combination of the top IS journals as well additional sources as represented in Table 1.

For inclusion, the literature was initially evaluated based on their titles and keywords using the search terms: "Adoption", "Adopt", "Business Intelligence", "Self Service Business Intelligence", "Self-Service Business Intelligence" and "SSBI" with the language defaulted to English and the publication timespan set for 2000 to 2021. This initial search produced 87 peer-reviewed articles, each article was subsequently briefly reviewed to ensure that the focus of the article's remained squarely on the predefined search terms, excluding any article that drifted from this agenda. From the remaining 67 articles, a final section process was conducted selecting only articles where an adoption framework was stated and utilised, leaving 17 articles that formed part of the analysis

Table 1. List of additional journal and conferences.

Journal Title	Conference Title
Journal of Big Data Research	Central European Conference of Information and Intelligent Systems
Journal of Decision Systems	Asian Conference on Intelligent Information and Database Systems
International Journal of Innovation	
Journal of Theoretical and Applied Information Technology	
Journal of Systems Integration	
International Journal of Computer Applications	
Business Intelligence Journal	
Journal of Organizational Computing and Electronic Commerce	
Journal of Advances in Computer Engineering and Technology	

process. Figure 1 below provides a visual illustration of the search and selection process followed within the SLR methodology.

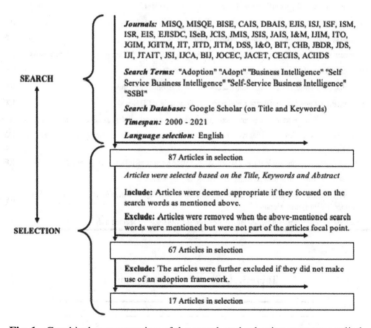

Fig. 1. Graphical representation of the search and selection strategy applied

3 Findings

Table 2 illustrates the 17 articles and their frameworks under review. Based on the results from Table 2 and Table 3 we are able to extrapolate that the Technology-Organisation-Environment (TOE) framework as formulated by [19] is the prevailing framework of choice, used in 11 (64.7%) articles within the review. Both the Technology Acceptance Model (TAM) by [20] and the Diffusion on Innovation (DOI) by [21] were only used in a single instance (5.8%). A combination of the TOE and DOI frameworks was the second most predominant framework of choice, used in 3 (17.6%) of the articles. In an article by [11], a combination of the TAM and the Delone & McLean IS success model was developed to incorporate an aspect of quality assurance into the adoption of the technology via the TAM model.

Table 2. List of articles reviewed.

Author(s) Details	Article Title	Framework Used
[22]	Adoption of Business Intelligence in the South African public social sector Department	TOE
[23]	Adoption of cloud business intelligence in Indonesia's financial services sector	DOI and TOE
[24]	An integrated model of business intelligence adoption in Thailand logistics service firms	TOE
[25]	Business intelligence adoption in academic administration: An empirical investigation	TOE
[26]	Business Intelligence Adoption in Developing Economies: A Case Study of Ghana	TAM
[27]	Business intelligence adoption: a case study in the retail chain	DOI
[28]	Business intelligence systems adoption model: an empirical investigation	TOE
[29]	Determinants of business intelligence systems adoption in developing countries: An empirical analysis from Ghanaian Banks	DOI and TOE
[30]	Determinants of Cloud Business Intelligence Adoption Among Ghanaian SMEs	TOE
[31]	Elucidating the determinants of business intelligence adoption and organizational performance	TOE
[32]	Exploring Risks in the Adoption of Business Intelligence in SMEs Using the TOE Framework	TOE
[33]	Investigating the factors affecting business intelligence systems adoption: A case study of private universities in Malaysia	DOI and TOE
[11]	Self-service business intelligence adoption in business enterprises: the effects of information quality, system quality, and analysis quality	TAM and IS Success model
[34]	Statistical Assessment of Business Intelligence System Adoption Model for Sustainable Textile and Apparel Industry	TOE
[35]	Survey of the Determinations of Business Intelligence Systems Adoption in SMEs	TOE
[36]	Technology, Organizational and Environmental Determinants of Business Intelligence Systems Adoption in Croatian SME: A Case Study of Medium-Sized Enterprise	TOE
[37]	Understanding the determinants of business intelligence system adoption stages: An empirical study of SMEs	TOE

Table 3. Utilised framework summary.

Frameworks Used	Number of Occurrences	Percentage
TOE	11	64.71%
DOI	1	5.88%
TAM	1	5.88%
Combination of TOE and DOI	3	17.65%
Combination of TAM and IS Success Model	1	5.88%
Total	17	100%

4 Discussion

Numerous frameworks have over the years been formulated to examine the adoption of Information Technology (IT) from a variety of stances, each focusing on a specific aspect of the adoption process [38]. There are two main groups which the frameworks can be classified into namely an Enterprise or Individual level framework. The Enterprise level frameworks focus on IS adoption from an organisation stance concentrating on the constructs relating to the organisation itself, the environment in which the organisation operates and how the technology can be used to improve the organisation's overall success [39]. The Individual level frameworks focus on how the technology is presented to the individuals in order to determine their level of adoption [40].

This review has found that over the last two decades research relating to BI and SSBI adoption has primarily been focused on the organisation and how the technology can be integrated into the current business strategies (88%). Similar findings were noted in a review conducted by [41], showing that TOE and DOI frameworks have remained to be the predominant lens through which the adoption of BI continues to be investigated despite the fact that the natural progress of BI and SSBI is centred around a cohort of information consumers within the organisation. Focusing the research predominantly from an Enterprise level fails to acknowledge the individuals and the importance of their role played within the adoption of the IS technology. Within each organisation, various levels of users will interact with the BI and each of the users are faced with particular human factors that will play an intricate part in their acceptance and ultimate adoption of the SSBI methodology [14].

There is however an adoption framework that is geared at examining the humanistic aspect of IT adoption which seems to have been overlooked which is the Model of PC Utilisation (MPCU) as developed by [42]. According to [42], "behavior is determined by what people would like to do (attitudes), what they think they should do (social norms), what they have usually done (habits), and by the expected consequences of their behavior" (p. 126). The MPCU framework has six primary constructs covering most importantly a variety of humanistic factors that influence an individual's adoption of the technology. These constructs are briefly defined as follows: i) Long-term consequences measures the user's ability to foresee the future benefits that the system might provide, ii) Job-fit refers to the belief that the system will improve the user's job, iii) Complexity is the degree of difficulty that the technology increases the user's task, iv) Affect towards use measures the user's feelings while using the systems, v) Social factors refers to the influences other have on the user's acceptance of the technology, and vi) Facilitating conditions relate to how easily the system has been created to ensure success [42, 43]. The MPCU framework focuses on investigating the behavioural influences that affect the use of the IS rather than determining whether the design aspects influence the intention to make use of the technology [44–46].

5 Conclusion and Recommendations

The frameworks utilised to evaluate the phenomenon of BI adoption has been extensively explored by making use of existing published literature on the topic. Primarily there has been a drive to examine the adoption of BI from an organisational stance to ensure that they are able to incorporate the technology into their current environments which has inadvertently created a significant gap in the literature. This gap relates to the individuals and how their humanistic factors could play an important and significant part in the overall successful adoption of BI within the organisation.

Based on this research and its observations, the implications of this paper to academia would be to further investigate this gap by conducting research in which the MPCU framework is utilised to evaluate the adoption of SSBI within the finance sector of South Africa. The aim of this research would be to obtain empirical evidence of the MPCU framework's ability to determine whether the various humanistic aspects in fact play a significant role in the adoption of the SSBI methodology.

References

1. Aničić, D., Aničić, J., Miletić, V.: Cost management efficiency factors of enterprises in Serbia. Ekonomika **66**(1), 37–51 (2020)
2. Hartl, K., Jacob, O., Jacob, F.L., Budree, A., Fourie, L.: The impact of business intelligence on corporate performance management. In: Proceedings of the Annual Hawaii International Conference on System Science, pp. 5042–5051. IEEE Computer Society, Hawaii (2016)
3. Pal, T., Brar, S.: Business intelligence in banking: a study of bi technology implementation and challenges. CGC Int. J. Contemp. Technol. Res. **1**(1) (2018)
4. Weiler, S., Matt, C., Hess, T.: Understanding user uncertainty during the implementation of self-service business intelligence: a thematic analysis. In: Proceedings of the Annual Hawaii International Conference on System Sciences, pp. 5878–5887. IEEE Computer Society, Hawaii (2019)
5. Lennerholt, C., van Laere, J.: Data access and data quality challenges of self-service business intelligence. In: 27th European Conference on Information Systems - Information Systems for a Sharing Society, pp. 1–13 (2019)
6. Maryska, M., Doucek, P.: Self-service business intelligence. Inf. Technol. Pract. 259–269 (2017)
7. Masouleh, M.F.: The impact of the adoption business intelligence among Iranian banks. J. Adv. Comput. Eng. Technol. **4**(1), 13–20 (2018)
8. Olszak, C.M.: Toward better understanding and use of business intelligence in organizations. Inf. Syst. Manag. **33**(2), 105–123 (2016)
9. Owusu, A.: Business intelligence systems and bank performance in Ghana: the balanced scorecard approach. Cogent Bus. Manag. **4**(1), 1–22 (2017)
10. Immhoff, C., White., C.: Self-Service Empowering Users to Generate Insights. TWDI Research (2011)
11. Daradkeh, M., Al-Dwairi, R.M.: Self-service business intelligence adoption in business enterprises: the effects of information quality, system quality, and analysis quality. In: Operations and Service Management: Concepts, Methodologies, Tools, and Applications, pp. 1096–1118. IGI Global (2018)
12. Schuff, D., Corral, K., St. Louis, R.D., Schymik, G.: Enabling self-service BI: a methodology and a case study for a model management warehouse. Inf. Syst. Front. **20**(2), 275–288 (2018)
13. Lennerholt, C., van Laere, J., Söderström, E.: Implementation challenges of self-service business intelligence: a literature review. In: 51st Hawaii International Conference on System Sciences, pp. 5055–5062. IEEE Computer Society (2018)
14. Alpar, P., Schulz, M.: Self-service business intelligence. Bus. Inf. Syst. Eng. **58**(2), 151–155 (2016). https://doi.org/10.1007/s12599-016-0424-6

15. Maher, N.A., et al.: Passive data collection and use in healthcare: a systematic review of ethical issues. Int. J. Med. Inform. **129**(1), 242–247 (2019)
16. Ul-ain, N., Giovanni V., Delone W.: Business intelligence system adoption, utilization and success - a systematic literature review. In: Proceedings of the 52nd Hawaii International Conference on System Sciences, pp. 5888–5897 (2019)
17. Aromataris, E., Pearson, A.: The systematic review: an overview. Am. J. Nurs. **114**(3), 53–58 (2014)
18. Oosterwyk, G., Brown, I., Geeling, S.: A synthesis of literature review guidelines from information systems journals. In: Proceedings of 4th International Conference on the, pp. 250–260 (2019)
19. Tornatzky, L.G., Fleischer, M.: The Process of Technology Innovation. Lexington Books (1990)
20. Davis, F.D.: A technology acceptance model for empirically testing new end-user information systems: Theory and results (1985)
21. Rogers, E.M.: Diffusion of Innovations: modifications of a model for telecommunications. In: Die diffusion von innovationen in der telekommunikation, pp. 25–38 (1995)
22. Masha, H., Adeyelure, S., Jokonya, P.O.: Adoption of business intelligence in the south African public social sector department. In: Proceedings of 4th International Conference on the Internet, Cyber Security and Information Systems, pp. 157–168 (2019)
23. Indriasari, E., Wayan, S., Gaol, F.L., Trisetyarso, A., Saleh Abbas, B., Ho Kang, C.: Adoption of cloud business intelligence in Indonesia's financial services sector. In: Nguyen, N.T., Gaol, F.L., Hong, T.-P., Trawiński, B. (eds.) ACIIDS 2019. LNCS (LNAI), vol. 11431, pp. 520–529. Springer, Cham (2019). https://doi.org/10.1007/978-3-030-14799-0_45
24. Chaveesuk, S., Horkonde, S.: An integrated model of business intelligence adoption in thailand logistics service firms. In: International Conference on Information Technology and Electrical Engineering, pp. 604–608 (2015)
25. Sujitparapitaya, S., Shirani, A., Roldan, M.: Business intelligence adoption in academic administration: an empirical investigation. Issues Inf. Syst. **13**(2), 112–122 (2012)
26. Kester, Q., Preko, M.: Business intelligence adoption in developing economies: a case study of Ghana. Int. J. Comput. Appl. **127**(1), 1–8 (2015)
27. Olexová, C.: Business intelligence adoption: a case study in the retail chain. Inf. Syst. Manag. **11**(1), 95–106 (2014)
28. Rouhani, S., Ashrafi, A., Zareravasan, A., Afshari, S.: Business intelligence systems adoption model: an empirical investigation. J. Organ. End User Comput. **30**(2), 43–67 (2018)
29. Owusu, A., Tijjani, D., Agbemabiese, G.C., Soladoye, A.: Determinants of business intelligence systems adoption in developing countries: an empirical analysis from Ghanaian Banks. J. Internet Bank. Commer. **8**(6), 1–25 (2017)
30. Owusu, A.: Determinants of Cloud business intelligence adoption among Ghanaian SMEs. Int. J. Cloud Appl. Comput. **10**(4), 48–69 (2020)
31. Bhatiasevi, V., Naglis, M.: Elucidating the determinants of business intelligence adoption and organizational performance. Inf. Dev. **36**(1), 78–96 (2020)
32. Stjepić, A.M., Pejić Bach, M., Bosilj Vukšić, V.: Exploring risks in the adoption of business intelligence in SMEs using the TOE framework. J. Risk Financ. Manag. **14**(2), 1–18 (2021)
33. Owusu, A., Ghanbari-Baghestan, A., Kalantari, A.: Investigating the factors affecting business intelligence systems adoption: a case study of private universities in Malaysia. Int. J. Technol. Diffus. **8**(2), 1–25 (2017)
34. Ahmad, S., Miskon, S., Alabdan, R., Tlili, I.: Statistical assessment of business intelligence system adoption model for sustainable textile and apparel industry. IEEE Access, **9** pp. 106560–106574 (2021)

35. Stjepić, A.M.: Survey of the determinations of business intelligence systems adoption in SMEs. In: Proceedings of the Fourth Central European Conference of Information and Intelligent Systems, pp. 177–185 (2017)

36. Stjepić, A.M., Sušac, L., Vugec, D.S., Bis, A.: Technology, organizational and environmental determinants of business intelligence systems adoption in croatian SME: a case study of medium-sized enterprise. Int. J. Econ. Manag. Eng. **13**(5), 737–742 (2019)

37. Puklavec, B., Oliveira, T., Popovič, A.: Understanding the determinants of business intelligence system adoption stages an empirical study of SMEs. Ind. Manag. Data Syst. **118**(1), 236–261 (2018)

38. Oliveira, T., Martins, M.F.: Literature review of information technology adoption models at firm level. Electron. J. Inf. Syst. Eval. **14**(1), 110–121 (2011)

39. Ilin, V., Ivetić, J., Simić, D.: Understanding the determinants of e-business adoption in ERP-enabled firms and non-ERP-enabled firms: A case study of the Western Balkan Peninsula. Technol. Forecast. Soc. Chang. **125**(1), 206–223 (2017)

40. Koul, S., Eydgahi, A.: A systematic review of technology adoption frameworks and their applications. J. Technol. Manag. Innov. **12**(4), 106–113 (2017)

41. Hatta, N.N.M., et al.: Business intelligence system adoption theories in SMEs: a literature review. ARPN J. Eng. Appl. Sci. **10**(23), 18165–18174 (2015)

42. Thompson, R.L., Higgins, C.A., Howell, J.M.: Personal computing: toward a conceptual model of utilization. MIS Q. Manag. Inf. Syst. **15**(1), 125–142 (1991)

43. Andreas, C.: UTAUT and UTAUT 2: a review and agenda for future research. Winners **13**(2), 106–114 (2012)

44. Alkhwaldi, A., Kamala, M.: Why do users accept innovative technologies? a critical review of models and theories of technology acceptance in the information system literature. J. Multidiscipl. Eng. Sci. Technol. **4**(8), 7962–7971 (2017)

45. Gunasinghe, A., Hamid, J.A., Khatibi, A., Azam, S.F.: Academicians' acceptance of online learning environments: a review of information system theories and models. Glob. J. Comp. Sci. Technol. **19**(1), 31–39 (2019)

46. Taherdoost, H.: A review of technology acceptance and adoption models and theories. Procedia Manufact. **22**(1), 960–967 (2018)

Application of Online Single Submission in Increasing Investment (Case Study in the Special Region of Yogyakarta)

Erlangga Hikmah Budhyatma[✉], Achmad Nurmandi, Isnaini Muallidin, and Danang Kurniawan

Master Government Affairs and Administration, Universitas Muhammadiyah Yogyakarta, Yogyakarta, Indonesia
jackssteven03@gmail.com

Abstract. This research is intended to see the impact resulting from the Online Single Submission (OSS) licensing system service in increasing investment in the Special Region of Yogyakarta. The Special Region of Yogyakarta is the centere of education, culture and tourism. By using a qualitative descriptive research approach, this research takes a case study in the Yogyakarta Special Region Government. This study obtained data from online media, the website of the OSS institution (oss.go.id), Licensing and Investment Office www.jogjainvest.jogjap rov.go.id, stakeholder statements, and government documents. The results of this study indicate that the establishment of regulations in terms of ensuring legal certainty for the ease of licensing services has raised Indonesia's ease of doing business (EODB) ranking from 91 in 2015 to 73 in 2019. The ease of doing business has encouraged the implementation of the OSS system to provide impact in increasing investment in the Special Region of Yogyakarta. The OSS system has an impact on increasing the realized value of the investment in the Special Region of Yogyakarta by Rp. 7,221,697.000,00 in 2018, Rp. 6,518,285,700,000 in 2019, Rp. 2,823,382,580,000.00 in 2020. Finally, in 2021 in the second quarter, the value of the increase in investment in the Special Region of Yogyakarta is Rp. 1,207,133,520,000.00.

Keywords: Online single submission · e-government · Investment

1 Introduction

As a developing country, Indonesia has problems in terms of economic development. What is often a problem in carrying out economic development is the limited or lack of funding. One that is often used as a source of financing to carry out economic development in Indonesia is through investment [1].

One of the most attractive investment climate criteria is the ease of business licensing. This happens because it is easier to take care of business licenses, it will encourage more business licenses which will also encourage more investment in a country or a region [2].

C. Stephanidis et al. (Eds.): HCII 2022, CCIS 1582, pp. 373–381, 2022.
https://doi.org/10.1007/978-3-031-06391-6_48

To create a favorable investment climate to support economic development efforts, the government issued Presidential Regulation no. 91 of 2017 concerning the Acceleration of Business Implementation and established the Economic Policy Package Task Force (PKE) and the Task Force for the Acceleration of Business Implementation (PPB). In addition, the government also issued Government Regulation No. 24 of 2018 concerning Electronically Integrated Business Licensing which is the basis for making Online Single Submission commonly known as OSS. OSS is a system that provides easy investment through the implementation of an electronically integrated business licensing system. What is expected is to change services related to licensing to be fast, cheap, and easy, so that they can attract a lot of investment.

Based on Government Regulation Number 24 of 2018 concerning Electronically Integrated Business Licensing Services, it is known that the Online Single Submission (OSS) is a system that can be used to carry out all kinds of registration processes and business legality proposals as well as other licensing proposals, which are listed on the service. business legality with the website address http://oss.go.id. Online Single Submission (OSS) is a business license issued by the OSS institution for and on behalf of the minister, head of the institution, governor, or regent/mayor through an integrated electronic government system (e-government) [3].

OSS was first launched by the central government on July 8, 2018, which was then implemented one month later in various regions, including the Special Region of Yogyakarta. The system in Online Single Submissions (OSS) is the amalgamation of 6 systems that exist in the government service system contained in the ministries/agencies as well as those in local governments, be it districts/cities or provinces, into a portal. The system in the Online Single Submissions is also a single reference (main guide) in making business legalities. If the K/L and Local Government have several electronic legality systems, the Online Single Submissions system will merge into one electronic legality system portal determined by the relevant K/L and Local Government [4].

Previous research related to the implementation of e-government in terms of the implementation of Online Single Submission (OSS) found; First, the research reveals the salient factors of the organization in the implementation of OSS in the city of Yogyakarta, Second, the implementation of OSS has an impact on bureaucratic and business behaviour which then has an impact on increasing investment, Third, the business license issued by OSS provides legal certainty [3, 5, 6, 1]. From all these studies, there is an underlying issue related to regulation which is an important factor in the implementation of OSS [3, 7]. So that this research can explain the main factors that cause OSS implementation to increase investment.

This business license is one of the government policies instruments to be able to exercise control over economic activities that cause negative impacts on third parties or known as negative externalities, which may arise due to social and economic activities [8, 9]. Licensing can also be used as a tool to obtain legal force/legality over ownership or operation of business activities. As a tool to control, licensing needs to be based on logical considerations and listed in government regulation as one of the guidelines [10]. Therefore, without logical considerations and explicit regulatory drafts, the legality of business will lose its value as a tool to defend business needs for behaviour caused by individuals [11]. Based on these regulations, now all business legality services are centralized through a system that we know as Electronic Business Licensing or in a foreign language called Online Single Submission (OSS) [9, 11]. So, this research is aimed at revealing regulation as the main factor in implementing OSS as the implementation of e-government services that have an impact on increasing investment in the Special Region of Yogyakarta.

2 Literature Review

E-government is another name for internet government, digital government, connected government, and online government. In simple terms, e-government is the use of ICT by government agencies, such as the internet, wide area networks and mobile computing, which can be used to improve relations between one government agency and other government agencies, the private sector, and the public [12–14].

The expansion of digital transformation, digitization of information, and the development of big data is known as artificial intelligence. Public sector organizations are specifically involved in the provision of public policies and services by leveraging the capabilities of artificial intelligence. An integrated data related to business licensing services collect and covers 25 ministries/agencies, 34 provinces, 514 districts/cities, 13 exclusive economic zones, 4 free trade zones and 111 industrial zones in Indonesia using online single submission (OSS) [15, 16, 17]. The goal is that the relationship in governance that involves the government, businesspeople and the community can be created more efficiently, effectively, productively and responsively. Thus, the results obtained through E-Government are the creation of good governance, preventing corruption, increasing transparency, better convenience, increasing state revenues, and/or reducing costs [18].

One of the promising solutions and alternatives to create transparency is an electronic government management system (e-government) [19, 20]. The implementation of e-government services in the city of Yogyakarta shows four indicators in the implementation of e-government; first, the use of IT in e-government services must have regulations governing procedures, powers and obligations, second, the application of IT requires sophisticated technology, third, the implementation of e-government services must provide benefits to the government, private sector, and society, fourth, application deployment requires a flexible organizational structure, adaptive leadership and adequate resources [3].

3 Method

This paper uses qualitative research methods to explain, understand and describe the government's involvement in public services in the Special Region of Yogyakarta in the application of online single submission (OSS) which is a form of service in terms of licensing and the impact of implementing online single submission (OSS) in increasing investment. in the Special Region of Yogyakarta. Data is collected from government documents that can be accessed through the website www.jogjainvest.jogjaprov.go.and

in-depth interviews with resource persons regarding the implementation of online single submission (OSS) in the Yogyakarta Special Region Government. The descriptive analysis approach uses the concept of electronic government (e-government).

4   Results and Discussion

4.1   Licensing System Change

Old Regime	Regime
Permits are issued after all conditions are met	Licensing issued With Commitment
Distributed and Uncoordinated Licensing	Licensing Only through OSS As Single Portal
No Licensing Standard yet	Business Process Standardization of Business Registration Number and License Format
Not yet integrated with other ministries/agencies electronically	Integrated with other Ministries/Institutions Electronically
No Control	Establishment of a Task Force for Escort

Fig. 1. Difference between old licensing system and licensing using OSS

OSS is the integration of electronic business licensing services to increase capital and business. Where the principle permit for investment in licensing is replaced by a Business Identification Number (NIB) which has a function as a Company Registration Certificate (TDP).

This form of service is focused on restructuring licensing, end-to-end assistance, and escorting and accelerating the resolution of obstacles through the creation of task forces (Satgas) at tiered levels from the centre to the regions. Licensing services are equal and equitable, not discriminating between large entrepreneurs and small entrepreneurs, between families of officials and ordinary people, as well as between private entrepreneurs and business entities and legal entities.

The change in the form of the licensing service system shows that regulation has an influence in terms of procedures, authorities and obligations in terms of licensing services. This situation causes the implementation of e-government in the form of OSS to work.

The technology in OSS that puts all licensing mechanisms in one application has made it easier to do business licensing which is presented in the OSS system. This is an important indicator for the implementation of e-government.

Figure 2 explained that OSS groups the types of services into individual, non-individual and other business entities. Of the four types of services, OSS oversees licensing services for as many as 20 business sectors except for the financial, mineral, coal and natural gas sectors. The many types of services carried out by OSS illustrate how

individual Example: Trade and Micro, Small and Medium Enterprises (MSMEs)	Non-Individual Example: Business Entities with Legal Entities and Non-Legal Entities, both foreign investment and domestic investment	Representative Example: Foreign corporation	Other Business Entities Example: Certificate of Recipient of Foreign Franchise

Fig. 2. Type of licensing service

the flexibility of a government organization has encouraged the implementation of e-government through the implementation of OSS applications which also provide benefits to the community, private sector and government.

4.2 Legal Certainty for Ease of Doing Business (EODB) Services Has Raised the Ease of Doing Business (EODB) Rating

The World Bank ranks the countries in the world based on the ease of doing business in an index which was later named the ease of doing business (EODB). This index created by the World Bank has been implemented since 2002. Providing business actors with an objective basis regarding the ease of doing business in a country is the goal of the World Bank in making this index. One of the indicators used by the World Bank in assessing the index is the ease of obtaining various permits that need to be done to start a business.

Aware of this, the Indonesian government issued regulations to ensure legal certainty for the ease of doing business in Indonesia which is manifested in various regulations ranging from central to regional governments. As a result, the regulation has raised Indonesia's ease of doing business (EODB) rating.

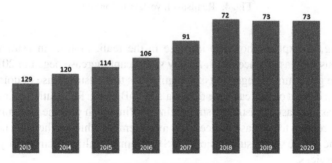

Fig. 3. Indonesia EODB ranking

From Fig. 3. It can be seen that Indonesia's EODB experienced a significant increase in 2017 when the government issued Presidential Regulation No. 91 of 2017 concerning the Acceleration of Business Implementation which was also followed by the establishment of a task force (SATGAS) for the Economic Policy Package (PKE) and the

SATGAS for the Acceleration of Business Implementation (PPB). As a result of the policies outlined in the regulation, Indonesia's EODB index increased from position 106 in 2016 to position 91 in 2017. Next in 2018, Indonesia's EODB index experienced a very significant increase to position 72 in the World. This happened because the government issued a regulation in the form of Government Regulation No. 24 of 2018 concerning Electronically Integrated Business Licensing.

4.3   Application of the Online Single Submission (OSS) System in Increasing Investment in the Special Region of Yogyakarta

The increase in Indonesia's ranking in the ease of doing business (OSS) index released by the World Bank has encouraged business players to do business in Indonesia by investing. It also encourages increased investment in Indonesia. regions in Indonesia, including the province of the Special Region of Yogyakarta.

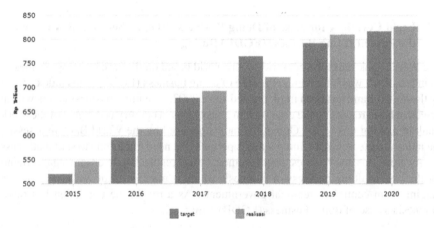

Fig. 4. Realisasi Investasi Indonesia

Next Fig. 4. explains how the increase in the realization of investment value in Indonesia has increased since 2015. A very significant increase began in 2017 wherein that year the government began to issue regulations that ensured ease of doing business which had an impact on increasing Indonesia's EODB index. Realization of investment in Indonesia has increased drastically starting in 2018 in which year the government issued a regulation related to the ease of licensing management which is the legal umbrella for the use of the online single submission (OSS) system to realize electronically integrated licensing services.

The increase in the realization of investment value in Indonesia has had an impact on increasing investment in its regions. In the Special Region of Yogyakarta, the increase in realized investment value is reflected in the data below:

Figure 5 shows the value of the investment in the Special Region of Yogyakarta has increased in 2018, in which year the government of the Special Region of Yogyakarta issued various regulations as implementers of Government Regulation No. 24 of 2018

No	Element	2018	2019	2020	2021	Unit
1	Accumulated Investment Realization Value	20.075.671,00	26.593.957,00	29.417.339,00	31.867.736.163.970,90	Trillion Rupiah
2	Investment Realization Value	7.221.697,00	6.518.285.700.000,00	2.823.382,00	2.450.396.509.169,00	Trillion Rupiah
3	Community Satisfaction Index Value	-	87,86	86,68	86,99	Mark
4	Business License Completion Time	-	5,00	4,00	4,00	Day

Fig. 5. Performance of cooperation and investment agency

which is the basis for the implementation of the use of the OSS system. In 2018 the realization of the investment value in the Special Region of Yogyakarta amounted to Rp. 7,221,697.000,00, then later in 2019 the realization of the investment value in the Special Region of Yogyakarta decreased to Rp. 6,518,285,700,000.00. And in 2020 it experienced a very significant decrease, which was 2,823,382,580,000.00. However, in 2021 there will be a very significant increase wherein a pandemic situation the realization of the investment value in the Special Region of Yogyakarta in the second quarter amounted to Rp. 1,207,133,520,000.00. Although there was a decline from 2019 to 2020, the realization of investment value in the Special Region of Yogyakarta has increased cumulatively every year. Explaining that the cumulative realization of investment in the Special Region of Yogyakarta has increased from year to year, especially since the implementation of online single submission (OSS) in business licensing services in the Special Region of Yogyakarta.

5   Conclusion

The ease of running a business can occur apart from the implementation of regulations, also due to the application of IT that uses sophisticated technology that can be carried out as a result of a flexible implementing organizational structure under adaptive leadership and adequate human resources which in the end have provided e-government services that provide benefits for the government, private sector and society. This has created a conducive investment climate to encourage the implementation of the OSS system to have an impact on increasing investment in the Special Region of Yogyakarta. The OSS system has an impact in increasing the realization of the investment value in the Special Region of Yogyakarta by Rp. 7,221,697.000,00 in 2018. In 2019 the increase in the realized value of the investment in the Special Region of Yogyakarta amounted to Rp. 6,518. 285,700,000.00 with a community satisfaction index value of 87.86. Then in 2020, the increase in the investment value is Rp. 2,823,382,580,000.00 with a community satisfaction index of 86.68. Finally, in 2021 in the second quarter, the value of the increase in investment in the Special Region of Yogyakarta was Rp. 1,207,133,520,000.00 with a community satisfaction index value of 86.99. Online Single Submission (OSS) also has an impact on improving the quality of service as shown in terms of the completion time of business licenses which can be completed within 5 days in 2018, 4 days in 2019, 2020 and 2021. Challenges also arise in its implementation, especially related to the lack of public understanding of the Online Single Submission (OSS) system. Then in 2020, the increase in the investment value is Rp. 2,823,382,580,000.00 with a community satisfaction index of 86.68. Finally, in 2021 in the second quarter, the value of the increase in investment in the Special Region of Yogyakarta was Rp. 1,207,133,520,000.00 with a community satisfaction index value of 86.99. Online Single Submission (OSS) also has an impact on improving the quality of service as shown in terms of the completion time of business licenses which can be completed within 5 days in 2018, 4 days in 2019, 2020 and 2021. Challenges also arise in its implementation, especially related to the lack of public understanding of the Online Single Submission (OSS) system. Then in 2020, the increase in the investment value is Rp. 2,823,382,580,000.00 with a community satisfaction index of 86.68. Finally, in 2021 in the second quarter, the value of the increase in investment in the Special Region of Yogyakarta was Rp. 1,207,133,520,000.00 with a community satisfaction index value of 86.99. Online Single Submission (OSS) also has an impact on improving the quality of service as shown in terms of the completion time of business licenses which can be completed within 5 days in 2018, 4 days in 2019, 2020 and 2021. Challenges also arise in its implementation, especially related to the lack of public understanding of the Online Single Submission (OSS) system. Finally, in 2021 in the second quarter, the value of the increase in investment in the Special Region of Yogyakarta was Rp. 1,207,133,520,000.00 with a community satisfaction index value of 86.99. Online Single Submission (OSS) also has an impact on improving the quality of service as shown in terms of the completion time of business licenses which can be completed within 5 days in 2018, 4 days in 2019, 2020 and 2021. Challenges also arise in its implementation, especially related to the lack of public understanding of the Online Single Submission (OSS) system. Finally, in 2021 in the second quarter, the value of the increase in investment in the Special Region of Yogyakarta was Rp. 1,207,133,520,000.00 with a community satisfaction index value of 86.99. Online Single Submission (OSS) also has an impact on improving the quality of service as shown in terms of the completion time of business licenses which can be completed within 5 days in 2018, 4 days in 2019, 2020 and 2021. Challenges also arise in its implementation, especially related to the lack of public understanding of the Online Single Submission (OSS) system.

References

1. Kumalasari, G.W.: Kebijakan Hukum Perizinan Sebagai Instrumen Penguatan Investasi Pada Sektor Ekonomi Kreatif Guna Meningkatkan Kesejahteraan Masyarakat. Perizinan di Era Citiz. Friendly, 224–241 (2017)
2. Maslihatin, E.: Dampak Kualitas Pelayanan Perizinan Terhadap Peningkatan Investasi pada UPT Pelayanan Perizinan Terpadu Provinsi Jawa Timur. J. Kebijak. dan Manaj. Publik 4(2), 27–33 (2016)
3. Pribadi, U., Iqbal, M., dan Saputra, H.A.: Implementation of online single submission software application in yogyakarta city: identifying prominent factors of organizational aspects. In: in 10th International Conference on Public Organization, ICONPO 2020, vol. 717, no. 1 (2021). https://doi.org/10.1088/1755-1315/717/1/012025

4. Dawud, J., Abubakar, R.R.T.: Implementasi Kebijakan Online Single Submission pada Pelayanan Perizinan Usaha (Studi Kasus di DPMTSP Kota Bandung & Kabupaten Bandung). Publica J. Pemikir. Adm. Negara **12**(2), 83–92 (2020)
5. Sanjoyo, S., Sapriani, S., Setiawan, A., dan Suroyya, S.: Perizinan Berusaha Melalui Online Single Submission Sebagai Ketaatan Hukum Dalam Rangka Meningkatkan Investasi. Borneo Law Rev. **4**(1), 64–78 (2020). https://doi.org/10.35334/bolrev.v4i1.1397
6. Orywika, M.F.: Pengaruh Penerapan Online Single Submission (Oss) Terhadap Perilaku Birokrasi Dan Pelaku Usaha Serta Dampaknya Bagi Percepatan Investasi Di Kabupaten Bangka Selatan Provinsi Kepulauan Bangka Belitung. J. Adhikari **1**(2), 88–93 (2021). [Daring]. Tersedia pada: http://dx.doi.org/https://doi.org/10.53968/ja.v1i2.31
7. Kurnia, T.S., Rauta, U., dan Siswanto, A.: E-Government Dalam Penyelenggaraan. Masal. Huk. **46**(2), 170–181 (2017)
8. Asmara, G.: Strengthening Ombudsman institutions of the republic of Indonesia to increase protection of citizens' rights in public services. Mediterr. J. Soc. Sci. **8**(5), 51–57 (2017). https://doi.org/10.1515/mjss-2017-0023
9. Izhandri, S., Kn, M., dan Agustina, D.: OSS dan Perkembangannya di Indonesia OSS and its Development in Indonesia 1 (2018)
10. Iskatrinah, I., dan Supriyo, D.: Urgency of the Ombudsman in the District in monitoring the Operation of Public Services **317**, IConProCS, 256–259 (2019). https://doi.org/10.2991/ico nprocs-19.2019.53
11. Hermawan, Online single submission (OSS) system: a licensing services breakthrough in local government?. Int. J. Innov. Creat. Chang. **10**(11), 284–296 (2020). [Daring]. Terse-dia pada: https://www.scopus.com/inward/record.uri?eid=2-s2.0-85079614945&partnerID= 40&md5=f9f0c9432063e0c7b8bee825fd8c71ca
12. Nurhidayati, D.: Does digital public service complaint promote accountability? a comparative analysis of Upik Yogyakarta and Qlue Jakarta. Policy Gov. Rev. **3**(2), 127 (2019). https://doi. org/10.30589/pgr.v3i2.139
13. Pratama dan, A.B., Imawan, S.A.: A scale for measuring perceived bureaucratic readiness for smart cities in Indonesia. Public Adm. Policy **22**(1), 25–39 (2019). https://doi.org/10.1108/ pap-01-2019-0001
14. Aritonang, D.M.: The impact of e-government system on public service quality in Indonesia. Eur. Sci. J. ESJ **13**(35), 99 (2017). https://doi.org/10.19044/esj.2017.v13n35p99
15. Paltieli, G.: The political imaginary of National AI strategies. AI Soc. 1–12 https://doi.org/ 10.1007/s00146-021-01258-1
16. Pudjiastuti, L., Indrawati, H.A., Arrum, D.A., dan Pudjiastuti, L.: Integrated E-supply chain management systems services as a form of acceleration of development in Indonesia. Int. J. Supply Chain Manag. **9**(3), 426–434 (2020). [Daring]. Terse-dia pada: https://www.scopus.com/inward/record.uri?eid=2-s2.0-85087789059&partnerID= 40&md5=a36da2fd93acdf3cb31f282c56fba2d5
17. Purnomo, E.P., Obisva, G., dan Astutik, Z.A.: Smart government: the involvement of govern-ment towards public services in Yogyakarta for smart development. SSRN Electron. J. 28–30 (2020). https://doi.org/10.2139/ssrn.3515036
18. Yusriadi, Y., Sahid, A., Amrullah, I., Azis, A., Rachman, A.A.: E-government-based bureau-cratic reform in public service **165**, Iccsr, 66–70 (2018). https://doi.org/10.2991/iccsr-18.201 8.15
19. Maulana, R.Y.: Collaborative governance in the implementation of E-government-based pub-lic services inclusion in Jambi Province, Indonesia. J. Gov. **5**(1), 91–104 (2020). https://doi. org/10.31506/jog.v5i1.7317
20. Hadian, D.: The relationship organizational culture and organizational commitment on public service quality; perspective local government in Bandung, Indonesia. Int. Rev. Manag. Mark. **7**(1) 230–237 (2017)

Indonesia Railway Public Transport Information Services Through Social Media in the Covid-19 Pandemic Era

Syifa Izdihar Firdausa Asfianur[✉], Achmad Nurmandi, Dyah Mutiarin, Isnaini Muallidin, and Mohammad Jafar Loilatu

Department of Government Affairs and Administration, Jusuf Kalla School Government, University of Muhammadiyah Yogyakarta, Yogyakarta, Indonesia
syifa.izdihar27@gmail.com

Abstract. The purpose of this paper is to examine the transformation of Indonesian Railways Public Transport Information Services Through Social Media in the Covid-19 Pandemic Era. The existence of social media makes it easier for people to know the rules that need to be met when traveling. The social media platform used in writing is an twitter account. The analysis of this research uses 4 Twitter social media accounts from KAI Airport, KAI Commuter, Kereta Api Kita, and Kereta Api Indonesia. The method used his Qualitative Data Analysis Software and analysis through Nvivo. From the results of the research of the four accounts, KAI Airport's monthly tweets are accounts that are often used by users in finding information in the era of globalization of Covid-19, while KAI Commuters is a search for information through the hashtag #rekancommuters, and the word that often appears in the four accounts is #rekancommuters. via word cloud.

Keywords: Public transportation · Passenger information · Sharing information · Covid-19

1 Introduction

The balance of information in this digital era, especially social media, affects the formation of public perceptions of the coronavirus. The meaning of information is a source of knowledge, and knowledge is a source of power [1]. After understanding the information, passenger information needs to be conveyed based on the truth, and these passengers are easy when searching for information. Information technology is a means and infrastructure (hardware, software, user) systems and methods for managing, transmitting, processing, interpreting, storing, organizing, and using meaningfully. The development of information and communication technology (ICT) and the increasing use of the Internet have changed the process of online communication in the public sphere [2]. ICT to create more transparent information mechanisms [3]. Information with public alerts delivers coordinated, fast, reliable, and actionable information to the entire community using straightforward, consistent, accessible, and culturally appropriate methods to inform effectively.

C. Stephanidis et al. (Eds.): HCII 2022, CCIS 1582, pp. 382–388, 2022.
https://doi.org/10.1007/978-3-031-06391-6_49

The importance of information will affect how people respond to it. The new Information and Communication Technology enables significant new types of exchange and collaboration for the world of politics. There is a need to understand the role of information in making users believe in the information conveyed [4]. Information technology can provide a powerful means to manage the flow of information and drive changes in knowledge management (KM) systems, which can then be linked to improving performance [5]. Information covers a broad discussion, one of which is the relationship between information and public transportation. Both of these discussions are exciting things to discuss. The linkage of information and public transportation is a compelling case to address. The nature and form of communication between public transit service providers and their customers have changed dramatically with the advent of GPS, smartphones, and digital social networks [6]. The existence of public transportation in human life will make it easier for humans to carry out activities. During the Covid-19 pandemic, public transit also has limitations and special conditions for traveling.

Social media is a communication tool that provides all information to users [6]; with this function, social media creates transparency in services [3]. Moreover, it considers that the process of social media is also an early warning tool. Become a supervisory tool for all human activities, especially in public facilities like transportation, markets, and roads [7]. Social media is a source of information about health crisis conditions that can quickly respond to all interactions on social media [8]. Social media can be used as a source of information in policymaking [9]. Based on this function, social media becomes an essential component in human life because it can connect aspects.

Social media are a medium through which individuals utilize these networking sites to share information, ideas, and personal messages [10]. Social media refer to any social networking site with all three aspects, one of which is not structured like Facebook and Twitter [11]. Modern social media applications, which have achieved considerable penetration into the daily lives of many users, provide an invaluable source of data on users' thoughts, beliefs, and opinions[12]. Social media serves as a supervisor for the information conveyed. Based on previous research, social media is a tool for sharing information with users. One of the unstructured social media is Twitter. Twitter social media as a means of public transportation sees the function of social media. Also, looking at the function of social media, this study can see whether the information provided is related to public transportation.

Transportation is closely related to aspects of life, essential in planning at an early stage [13], regional transport systems to adopt innovative strategies [14]. Twitter social media has become a tool in delivering information from public transportation to make it easier for people to access directly through gadgets without crowding to get information. The information presented also follows the community's need to share information. Based on the description above, the formulation of the problem in this study is how public transportation provides services through social media. At the same time, the purpose of this study is to look at passenger information provided to rail public transportation providers for users in providing information related to services during the pandemic. The analysis in this analyze four official Twitter accounts of Indonesian trains' social media accounts: KAI Airports, KAI Commuters, Kereta Api Kita, and Kereta Api Indonesia, and the four accounts use social media as a transmitter of information in providing services.

2 Theoretical Framework

The popularity of the Internet and the advent of Web 2.0 technologies have transformed web content from publishers to user-generated content [11]. Social media are a means for people to interact by creating, sharing, and exchanging information and ideas through words, pictures, and videos in a virtual network and community. Social media are essential in communication regarding disasters and health crises [8]. Social Media shows that Information Technology (IT) and constituent data are the basis of collaboration, communication, and inclusive relationships [15]. Social media refers to internet-based applications that allow users to communicate and share user-generated content between individuals [7]. The impact of social media on the dissemination of sustainable mobility opinions is not well-understood given the current lack of data [7]. Therefore, social media is a means of communication and information delivery [9]. Social media are emerging as an important information-based communication tool for disaster management [10]. Social media users have diverse backgrounds and can encourage user aggregation, providing a unique substrate for researchers to understand people's behavior patterns [12]. While the social media platform used his Twitter is widely regarded as a potentially valuable source of information for respondents during a crisis, the issue of extracting relevant Twitter posts remains a complex and largely open problem.

3 Research Method

This study uses the method by looking at the formulation of the problem under research and analyzing it through the Nvivo application. The use of Nvivo as an analytical tool has stages starting with (1) capturing data, (2) importing data, (3) coding data, (4) classifying data, and (5) displaying data [16]. Nvivo in this study was used to analyze KAI's Twitter social media users from the four accounts studied. Researchers also collect information using capture (N-Capture), data related to KAI, covid-19 information, data collection. The next stage is importing data, where the results of N-Capture will be analyzed into the Nvivo application. Furthermore, data analysis is in the form of graphs and tables. The researcher also analyzed using the Word cloud to see which words were the most used and influential in the Covid-19 era [17].

4 Results and Discussion

This study will analyze four official Twitter accounts of Indonesian trains' Twitter social media accounts related to information services provided in the Covid-19 era. Researchers chose social media accounts for Kereta Api Indonesia, Kereta Api Kita, KAI Airport, and KAI Commuter. Then, the researchers analyzed 4 KAI Twitter social media accounts that users often look for in finding information in this Covid-19 era. Researchers manually processed and analyzed the researchers' findings and Nvivo input data related to meticulous researchers. After processing the data that has been researched with Nvivo and analyzing it manually, the researcher will show a graph from the careful researcher, as follows (Fig. 1):

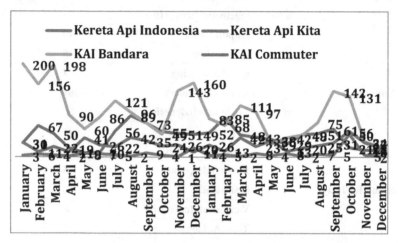

Fig. 1. Timeline of tweets by month

The picture above shows that of the 4 KAI Twitter social media accounts, the most tweeted by users from 2020 to 2021 is the Airport KAI account. Kereta Api Kita's Twitter social media account ranks second, the 3rd place is on the KAI Commuter account, and the last social media account is Kereta Api Indonesia. From the analysis above, all of KAI's Twitter social media accounts have increased and decreased tweets made by users. In addition, the social media account that has increased or is most prevalent in searching for information on KAI I in the Covid-19 era is the KAI Airport account, with a total of 200 tweets used by users to reach information during the Covid-19 period. After the researchers processed and analyzed through tweets from 4 social media accounts, the researchers analyzed the hashtags that the researchers chose; There are five hashtags from 4 accounts that will be explored, as follows (Figs. 2 and 3):

The researchers chose five hashtags on 4 KAI Twitter social media accounts with the number of hashtags presented. From the data that the researchers examined, there are 4 KAI Twitter social media accounts, each of which has five hashtags that users in the Covid-19 era often use. On the KAI Airport social media account, the most popular hashtag is #sestepkebandara, while on the KAI Commuter Twitter account, the most popular hashtag is #rekancommuters. The third social media account is Kereta Api Indonesia. In this account, users often use #friendskai. The last KAI Twitter social media account is Kereta Api Kita which has the most popular hashtag, namely our train. On the 4 KAI Twitter social media accounts, the hashtag that social media users most often use is #rekancommuters which is found on the KAI Commuters Twitter social media account. The last analysis that the researcher conducted was the world cloud, as follows (Figs. 4 and 5):

Table 1. Popular Hashtag

Account	Hashtags	Number
KAI Airport	step-airport	401
	togetherwithcovid19	77
	Airport soetta	46
	Coronavirus	18
	social distancing	7
KAI Commuter	fellow commuters	484
	Covid safe Indonesia	66
	Opponent corona	41
	Bumn for Indonesia	39
	Bumn fight covid	33
Indonesian Railways	best friend	10
	Wonderfull Indonesia	8
	Train Airlangga	2
Our Train	our train	159
	rail friends	174
	Bumn for Indonesia	16
	your train	52

Fig. 2. Frequency of words in Airport KAI account

Fig. 3. Word frequency in KAI commuters account

Word Cloud Analysis of Twitter data shows 20 keywords that seem to be used most related to KAI and Covid-19 [18]. The KAI Airport social media account and KAI Commuters Twitter account stated that the word that often appears is #rekancommuters. On the KAI Airport social media account, it is stated that the words airport and accept are words that often occur, while on the KAI Commuters Twitter account, it is noted that #ourtrain and #friendreska are words that users often use when looking for information related to public transportation in the COVID-19 era. Next, we will analyze the Twitter social media accounts of the Kereta Api account and the Twitter account of Indonesia Railways using the word cloud, as follows:

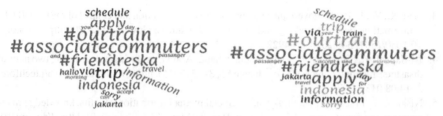

Fig. 4. Frequency of words in our Kereta Api account

Fig. 5. Frequency of words in the Indonesian Railways account

The word cloud data that the researcher processed on the Kereta Api Kita account said that the words #associatecommuters, #ourtrain, #friendreka are words that often appear in searches for users of this social media account. The Indonesian Railways Twitter social media account gave rise to 3 popular hashtags that users often use in searching for information in the COVID-19, namely era, #associatecommuters, #ourtrain, and #friendreska. #associatecommuters is a word that often appears on KAI's Twitter social media account. On the four Twitter social media accounts for public transportation, KAI stated that many people seek information through #associatecommuters. From the four KAI Twitter social media, it can be concluded that #associatecommuters, #ourtrain, and #friendreska are the words that often appear from the social media accounts that the researchers researched. The word #associatecommuters often appears on every KAI Twitter social media account, where users often search for information in the Covid-19 era.

5   Conclusion

The results of this study were that the four Twitter social media accounts, KAI in providing information services in the Covid-19 era were outstanding. The monthly tweet data that the researcher presents, the KAI Airport social media account is the top account that is often used by KAI's information services during the Covid-19. On the 4 KAI Twitter social media accounts, the hashtag most frequently used by social media users is #rekancommuters which is found on the KAI Commuters Twitter social media account. From the four KAI Twitter social media, it can be concluded that #associatecommuters, #ourtrain, and #friendreska are words that often appear from social media accounts that the researchers researched. The phrase #associatecommuters often appears on every KAI Twitter social media account, where users often look for information in the Covid-19 era.

References

1. Sukhwani, V., Shaw, R.: Operationalizing crowdsourcing through mobile applications for disaster management in India. Prog. Disaster Sci. **5**, 100052 (2020). https://doi.org/10.1016/j.pdisas.2019.100052
2. Haro-de-Rosario, A., Sáez-Martín, A., del Carmen Caba-Pérez, M.: Using social media to enhance citizen engagement with local government: Twitter or Facebook?, New Media Soc. **20**(1), 29–49 (2018). https://doi.org/10.1177/1461444816645652

3. Gao, X., Yu, J.: Public governance mechanism in the prevention and control of the COVID-19 : information, decision-making and execution. J. Chinese Gov. 1–20 (2020).https://doi.org/10.1080/23812346.2020.1744922
4. Al-Saggaf, Y., Simmons, P.: Social media in Saudi Arabia: exploring its use during two natural disasters. Technol. Forecast. Soc. Change **95**, 3–15 (2015). https://doi.org/10.1016/j.techfore.2014.08.013
5. Nisar, T.M., Prabhakar, G., Strakova, L.: Social media information benefits, knowledge management and smart organizations. J. Bus. Res. **94**(May), 264–272 (2019). https://doi.org/10.1016/j.jbusres.2018.05.005
6. Cottrill, C., Gault, P., Yeboah, G., Nelson, J.D., Anable, J., Budd, T.: Tweeting Transit: an examination of social media strategies for transport information management during a large event. Transp. Res. Part C Emerg. Technol. **77**, 421–432 (2017). https://doi.org/10.1016/j.trc.2017.02.008
7. Borowski, E., Chen, Y., Mahmassani, H.: Social media effects on sustainable mobility opinion diffusion: model framework and implications for behavior change. Travel Behav. Soc. **19**, 170–183 (2020). https://doi.org/10.1016/j.tbs.2020.01.003
8. Yu, M., Li, Z., Yu, Z., He, J., Zhou, J.: Communication related health crisis on social media: a case of COVID-19 outbreak. Curr. Issues Tour. **24**(19), 2699–2705 (2021). https://doi.org/10.1080/13683500.2020.1752632
9. wa Fu, K., Zhu, Y.: Did the world overlook the media's early warning of COVID-19?, J. Risk Res. 1047–1051 (2020). https://doi.org/10.1080/13669877.2020.1756380
10. Ngamassi, L., Ramakrishnan, T., Rahman, S.: Use of social media for disaster management: a prescriptive framework. J. Organ. End User Comput. **28**(3), 122–140 (2016). https://doi.org/10.4018/JOEUC.2016070108
11. Ghani, N.A., Hamid, S., Targio Hashem, I.A., Ahmed, E.: Social media big data analytics: a survey. Comput. Human Behav. **101**, 417–428 (2019). https://doi.org/10.1016/j.chb.2018.08.039
12. Jamali, M., Nejat, A., Ghosh, S., Jin, F., Cao, G.: Social media data and post-disaster recovery. Int. J. Inf. Manage. **44**, 25–37 (2019). https://doi.org/10.1016/j.ijinfomgt.2018.09.005
13. Majumdar, S.R.: The case of public involvement in transportation planning using social media. Case Stud. Transp. Policy **5**(1), 121–133 (2017). https://doi.org/10.1016/j.cstp.2016.11.002
14. Porru, S., Misso, F.E., Pani, F.E., Repetto, C.: Smart mobility and public transport: opportunities and challenges in rural and urban areas. J. Traffic Transp. Eng. (English Ed.) **7**(1), 88–97 (2020). https://doi.org/10.1016/j.jtte.2019.10.002
15. Martin, N., Rice, J., Arthur, D.: Advancing social media derived information messaging and management: a multi-mode development perspective. Int. J. Inf. Manage. **51**, 102021 (2020). https://doi.org/10.1016/j.ijinfomgt.2019.10.006
16. Loilatu, M.J., Irawan, B., Salahudin, S., Sihidi, I.T.: Analysis of Twitter's function as a media communication of public transportation. J. Komun. **13**(1), 54 (2021). https://doi.org/10.24912/jk.v13i1.8707
17. Hasti, I., Nurmandi, A., Muallidin, I., Kurniawan, D.: Pros and Cons of Vaccine Program in Indonesia (Social Media Analysis on Twitter). In: Ahram, T., Taiar, R. (eds) Human Interaction, Emerging Technologies and Future Systems V. IHIET 2021. Lecture Notes in Networks and Systems, vol. 319. Springer, Cham. (2022). https://doi.org/10.1007/978-3-030-85540-6_13
18. Pratama, I., Nurmandi, A., Muallidin, I., Kurniawan, D.: Social Media as a Tool for Social Protest Movement Related to Alcohol Investments. In: Ahram, T., Taiar, R. (eds) Human Interaction, Emerging Technologies and Future Systems V. IHIET 2021. Lecture Notes in Networks and Systems, vol. 319. Springer, Cham (2022). https://doi.org/10.1007/978-3-030-85540-6_18

Analysis on Open Government in Southeast Asia During Pandemic

Tiara Khairunnisa[✉], Achmad Nurmandi, Isnaini Muallidin, and Danang Kurniawan

Department of Government Affairs and Administration, Jusuf Kalla School Government,
University of Muhammadiyah Yogyakarta, Yogyakarta, Indonesia
tiarakhairunnisa1607@gmail.com

Abstract. This study aims to analyze how to provide information on countries with a high distribution level in Southeast Asia, namely Indonesia, Malaysia, and Singapore, to implement open government during the COVID-19 pandemic. This paper used qualitative research methods to describe and further analyze the government's website for political, critical and descriptive problems explanations and descriptions of information and data. Data retrieval was through observations and analyzed official government websites from 3 countries, Indonesia, Malaysia, and Singapore, with a questionnaire. The assessment tests used the framework E-Government Assessment work on the website. This assessment test used the Benchmark Model for Evaluating Data Openness and E-Government Assessment on the government's official website regarding COVID-19. This study found that of the five variables used in the assessment of the official website, Singapore excelled in three variables, transparency with an index of 1.06, openness with an index of 0.93, and basic data set with an index of 0.67. In addition, Malaysia had the highest participation rate of these three countries, with an index of 0.95. These three countries had the same index in the collaboration variable, which was 0.75.

Keywords: Evaluating Data Openness · E-Government Assessment · Indonesia · Malaysia · Singapore · COVID-19

1 Introduction

This study aims to analyze how to provide transparent, accountable, and accessible information in countries with the most serious cases in Southeast Asia, namely Indonesia, Malaysia, and Singapore, to implement open government during the COVID-19 pandemic. Open government is a concept whereby a country's government provides free, open, and readily available data used in projects or integrated with new products, applications, or services (Scala and Pota 2021). The openness of data presented by the government is an application of the concept of "Open Government," which was initiated by eight countries in the world with the signing of the Open Government Partnership (OGP) in 2011 (Klein et al. 2018; Nikiforova 2021; OECD, 2016). The government website is one of the products of the open government concept. Therefore it is important to need a website assessment to measure the quality of the website (Fan et al.

2020; HUANG et al. 2019; Jayasinghe et al. 2020). .Assessments through government websites measure the effectiveness of websites using the E-Government Assessment framework or assessment of government websites based on content and management perspectives (Ahmad et al., 2021; Erhan et al., 2017). E-government uses information technology to change the relationship with citizens, the private sector, and government agencies (Bank, 2020). This concept has an important role in improving services and has excellent efficiency potential, reducing corruption, promoting revenue growth, increasing transparency, convenience, and facilitating public sector cost efficiency in developed and developing countries (Cumbie and Kar 2016; Nunes et al. 2021). The measurement results can later be a reference to formulate recommendations for improvement for government websites, especially during the current COVID-19 pandemic (Buyle et al. 2021).

The rate of spread of the Coronavirus in Southeast Asia is fast compared to other countries in Asia. In the past two weeks, Southeast Asia has recorded 38,522 deaths from COVID-19 (IFRC 2021), twice as many as North America, according to the COVID-19 Dashboard by the Center for Systems Science and Engineering (CSSE) at Johns Hopkins University (JHU). The distribution of the COVID-19 cases can be seen from the data below.

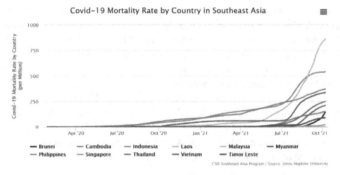

Fig. 1. The distribution of covid cases in Southeast Asia

Figure 1 shows that the distribution as of October 6, 2021, Malaysia is at 861.41 million people, Indonesia is 539.44 million people, and Singapore is 23, 16 million people (CSIS 2021). With such a high distribution rate, it is important to have data openness to increase public awareness in dealing with the outbreak caused by this Coronavirus (Budiyanti and Herlambang 2021). In today's digital era, people will find it easy to get information, while one of the benefits of information technology is that it can take advantage of space and time limitations (Suri 2019). The government's official website is one of the main sources for the public to obtain information regarding the development of this virus proven by the level of visitors from the official government websites of the three countries, as seen below.

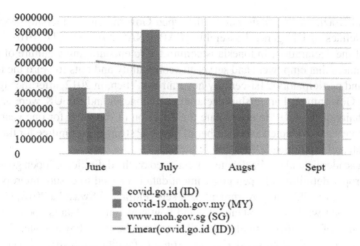

Fig. 2. Visitors to the government covid website

From Fig. 2, during the vulnerable period of June to September, 13% of Indonesians and 25% of Malaysians visit the website, and 50% of Singaporeans visit the website every month. In addition to knowing the high level of spread of COVID-19, the role of the government website as a source of information is also to become the official website to avoid hoaxes. The Indonesian Ministry of Communication and Informatics noted that from the beginning, this virus was detected until May 2020, more than 1,401 hoax content about COVID-19 was spread on social media (Malawani et al. 2020; Yusuf 2020). Thus, the government must provide a quality information platform with a high level of validity as evidence of providing adequate public services. The quality of information is vital to note, seen from the quality of the website as one of the outputs of the distribution of the information (Handayani et al. 2020).

This study answers the quality of information through the government's official platform to provide policy recommendations to reduce the spread of COVID-19. The researchers took a qualitative method approach through a literature review, aiming to find the various gaps or findings that have not been found. Previous research becomes a comparison material in conducting the latest research and formulating a model. In addition, this research analyzes government websites with a specific assessment theory on the website. There are two main analyses in this research; how is the quality of the information contained in the site by looking at its accountability, transparency, and ease of access? These studies aim to find the novelty of literature in open government studies and information assurance during the pandemic.

2   Literature Review

2.1   Data Openness During the COVID-19 Pandemic

Open Government practice was initiated in 2011 with eight countries in the world, including the United States, Britain, Indonesia, Mexico, Norway, the Philippines, South

Africa and Brazil, with the signing of the Open Government Partnership Declaration on the sidelines of UN general assembly (BAPPENAS 2015; OECD 2016). With the signing of the declaration, Indonesia is committed to encouraging a culture of government openness that empowers and serves the community and puts forward the ideals of an open and participatory 21st-century government. Then, in 2012, after the signing of the Open Government Partnership declaration, Indonesia and the UK were appointed as lead chairs of the OGP to coordinate the direction of the OGP for one year then in 2015, Indonesia was elected as a member of the OGP steering committee for three years (Zafarullah and Siddiquee 2021).

Much academic and public debate has centered on the definition of open government data. A proper definition of open government data is needed to ensure interoperability and evaluation of different government data sets (Putra and Swastika 2016).Open data must be defined well to understand why and how government data is open. Open data is a collection of data that is freely accessible and can be reused by anyone. Costa et al. (2012) stated that open data's underlying reason is to facilitate unrestricted access to raw data, enabling reuse and knowledge creation of Open Knowledge Base (OKF).

The open government consists of six main pillars in its implementation: transparency, accountability, participation, collaboration, inclusive policy-making, and technology (ADB 2016; Alderete 2018; Otter et al. 2015) done by working together to integrate an effective democratic system that responds to "more informed and assertive citizens" and strengthen governance mechanisms, hold public institutions accountable for their actions, and secure integrity in the civil service (Tydd 2018). The broader interpretation of the OG conveys that "the whole construction is meant to ensure an enlightened discourse between citizens" (Bergström and Routusi 2018). Such discourses require citizens to have accurate government activities, from planning and budgeting to social security issues and human resource management. Of course, there are exceptions for classified information (national security and intelligence, defense data, citizen privacy concerns, commercial secrecy, for example) to be hidden from public view. Citizens' access to information requires legal guarantees either from constitutional provisions or special laws to be enforced properly (Klein et al. 2018; Ratner and Ruppert 2019).

2.2 Website Assessment on the Government's Official COVID-19 Platform

Open Data has been praised for its ability to increase transparency. Open data has been praised for its ability to increase transparency (Park et al. 2016); increase citizen participation (Nam 2015); increase democratic accountability (van Veenstra and van den Broek 2013); and enhance governmental and non-governmental value-added services for citizens, industry, research and others. Data transparency is an important issue for the statistical systems of many countries, especially in developing countries. Even if the government wanted it, data did not become "open" overnight. There are several components to openness. To begin with, one must address legal issues regarding disclosure (Belkindas and Swanson, n.d.; Jin and Kwon 2016). In this case, it is important to have a website assessment that is commonly used to improve the quality of E-government in a government (Jung and Oh 2019; Putra and Swastika 2016). Concerns are site structure, conformance with web design guidelines, content, and overall site performance (Kelibay et al. 2020). Website usability and performance are the two most important elements to consider (Ahmad et al. 2021; Zahra et al. 2021).

3   Research Method

This research used mixed qualitative research methods, in which two different types of research methodologies, namely qualitative and quantitative, are combined. This method explains and further evaluates government websites to explain political, critical, and descriptive issues and illustrate data and information to collect more extensive, valid and reliable data. Data was collected using a matrix and carefully examined the official websites of three countries: Indonesia, Malaysia, and Singapore, and then evaluated the information collected. Conduct assessment tests using the E-Government Assessment framework, which can be found on government websites. The working steps are as follows and are seen in Fig. 3.

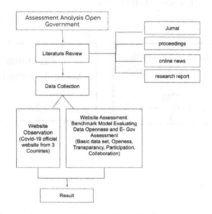

Fig. 3. Framework assessment analysis open government

The weighting of variables is carried out according to the priority content of the official website (Table 1). In addition, the instrument assessment rubric of the variables is used to classify each variable (Table 2) which will be measured in the next step.

Table 1. Thickness

Variable	Thickness
Basic Data Set	15%
Transparency	25%
Openness	25%
Participation	20%
Collaboration	15%

Table 2. Rating weight

Category	Score
Complete/ very good	5 (✅)
Incomplete/ good	4 (✅)
Fairly complete/ moderate	3 (✅)
Incomplete/ poor	2 (✅)
None/ very bad	1 (✅)

The assessment will be accumulated using the calculation formula for each variable, then the results of the calculation of the Government's COVID-19 website using a questionnaire instrument derived from the E-Government Assessment framework are obtained using the E-Gov framework formula

Rumus perhitungan setiap variable:

$$Vi = \frac{\sum Xi}{Yi} Z$$

Pengujian kerangka kerja E-Gov:Total Skor $= \sum_{i}^{n} Vi \times 20\%$

Information:
Vi = Variable
Xi = Total Value
Yi = Number of
questionnaire items
Z = Weight of variables

The scores obtained from the assessment results are then converted into criteria that state the condition of the website, in this study assessing the websites of three countries (Table 3).

Table 3. Official website and descriptions

No	Source	Descriptions
1	https://covid19.go.id/	The official website of the Indonesian government, which contains information about COVID-19
2	https://covidnow.moh.gov.my/	Malaysia's official government website, which contains special information about COVID-19
3	https://www.moh.gov.sg/	Singapore government official website, which contains information about government, including COVID-19

The researchers analyzed the data using two discreet analyses, graphical analysis to determine relevant content on official government websites using website assessment and word cloud analysis to explore key issues.

4   Results and Discussion

This study uses the "Benchmark Model" assessment for the Evaluation of Data Disclosure and Assessment of E-Government on the website by using five main variables, such as basic data sets, openness, transparency, participation, collaboration, which can be seen from the picture below (Table 4).

Table 4. Country comparison of open data

	Variable Assessment	Indo-nesia	Ma-laysia	Singa-pore
Basic data set	Country Identity on the home page (Country name & logo)	✓	✓	✓
	Office address at the beginning of the website (email, telephone no., fax)	✓	✓	✓
	Contact information Website institution (admin/state official)	✓	✓	✓
	Using domain state and security Website (https)	✓	✓	✓
	Total Variables	**0.49**	**0.49**	**0.56**
Transpar-ency	Institutional profile (vision, mission, job desk, organizational structure, or information on Institutional officials)	✓	✓	✓
	Include regulations/policies issued	✓	✓	✓
	News columns, articles, developments daily case, vaccine data, and various COVID-19 content	✓		✓
	Statistical data on work program achievements	✓	✓	✓
	Total Variables	**0.88**	**0.93**	**1.06**
Openness	File download facilities (pdf/doc/etc)	✓	✓	✓
	Easy-to-find searching facilities	✓	✓	✓
	Multimedia services (video, photos, etc.) which describes the activities of the institution	✓	✓	✓
	Website design is easy to understand	✓	✓	
	Another version of the website in the form of a mobile app	✓	✓	✓
	There is budget information/reports financial	✓	✓	✓
	Has a web-based service	✓	✓	✓
	Accessed via various browsers (IE, Mozilla, Opera, Chrome)	✓	✓	✓
	Total Variable	**0.84**	**0.84**	**0.93**
Participa-tion	Institutional contact and functioning well	✓	✓	✓
	A discussion forum that is active every day		✓	✓
	Complaint service has facilities chat and functions well on the website Website	✓	✓	✓
	visitors 1 million/month	✓	✓	✓
	Total Variable	**0.90**	**0.95**	**0.90**
Collabora-tion	Having links with equivalent institutions (Ministries/National level institutions)	✓	✓	✓
	Having links with lower institutions (local governments/lower agencies)	✓	✓	✓
	Having links with private institutions (private hospitals / etc)	✓		✓
	Has links with academics	✓	✓	✓
	Total Variable	**0.75**	**0.75**	**0.75**

From the above calculation, the following results are obtained.

Table 5. Data openness level

County	Index of data openness	DO level (Description)
Indonesia	Index = Variable × 20% = 3.86 × 20% = 77.2%	3- openness (the majority of data are published in RFD, XML, and other sematic formats, available to anyone and linked to other data
Malaysia	Index = Variable × 20% = 3,96 × 20% = 79.2%	3- openness (the majority of data are published in RFD, XML, and other sematic format, available to anyone and linked to other data
Singapore	Index = Variable × 20% = 4.20 × 20% = 84.0%	3- openness (the majority of data are published in RFD, XML, and other sematic format, available to anyone and linked to other data

Table 5 contains five main variables: the basic data set, openness, transparency, participation, and collaboration, which can be seen below (Fig. 4).

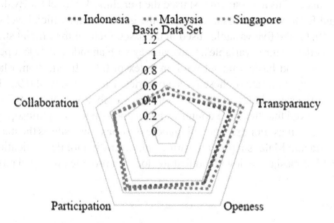

Fig. 4. Open data assessment

From these five variables, the official Singapore state website excels in three variables, transparency with an index of 1.06, openness with an index of 0.93, and basic data set with an index of 0.67, seen from the completeness of the content related to information needs during the COVID-19 pandemic. The -19 period starts from news, articles, death data, confirmation of virus infection, vaccine data and various other information related to the development of the pandemic. On the Malaysian side, Malaysia excels in the variable participation with an index of 0.95. In addition, these three countries have a high level of collaboration, as can be seen from the availability of links that are directly connected with related agencies, ranging from private, academic, and national and regional level institutions, with an index of 0.75. When viewed from the official website for handling COVID, Indonesia has the same index as Malaysia in several aspects, such as the *basic data set* with an index of 0.49 (ID) and 0.49 (MY), as well as the openness variable, which gets an index of 0.84 (ID) and 0.48 (MY).

These three countries run a good open data concept, seen from the quality of the websites provided. Existing information is provided on the website and has other media platforms that are more friendly to the community (Pratama et al. 2022) through social media. However, there are still shortcomings. For example, Singapore only has a website as the main door, while Indonesia and Malaysia provide other platforms in mobile applications. In addition, Singapore provides a download feature found, in contrast to two other countries, Malaysia and Indonesia, which have not provided this feature as a form of data disclosure.

5   Conclusion

Open government or the practice of open government is a collection of data that can be accessed freely and can be reused by anyone to increase transparency in government, one of which is through the official website. It is important to have a website assessment commonly used to improve the quality of E-government in improving quality of government performance. This assessment test used the Benchmark Model for Evaluating Data Openness and E-Government Assessment on the government's official website regarding COVID-19. Of the five variables used in the assessment of the official state website, Singapore excelled in three variables, transparency with an index of 1.06, openness with an index of 0.93, and basic data set with an index of 0.67. In addition, Malaysia had the highest participation rate of these three countries, with an index of 0.95. These three countries have the same index in the collaboration variable, which was 0.75. The websites offered showed that the three countries had a good open data philosophy, but there were still shortcomings. For example, Singapore only has a website as the main gateway, while Indonesia and Malaysia provide various platforms in mobile applications. Unlike Malaysia and Indonesia, the download feature does not provide this as a data disclosure.

References

ADB: How Information and Communication Technology Can Fast-Track Development (2016). https://www.adb.org/sites/default/files/publication/213206/how-ict-fast-track-development.pdf

Ahmad, J., Hardianti, H., Nilwana, A., Muliani, Hamid, H.: Digitalization era: website based e-government. IOP Conf. Ser. Earth Environ. Sci. **717**(1) (2021). https://doi.org/10.1088/1755-1315/717/1/012047

Alderete, M.V.: The mediating role of ICT in the development of open government. J. Glob. Inf. Technol. Manag. **21**(3), 172–187 (2018). https://doi.org/10.1080/1097198X.2018.1498273

Bank, W.: The World Bank New-Economy Sector Study Electronic Government and Governance: Lessons for Argentina (Issue July) (2020). http://documents.worldbank.org/curated/en/527061468769894044/pdf/266390WP0E1Gov1gentina1Final1Report.pdf

BAPPENAS: Laporan Akhir Reviu implementasi open government indonesia (2011–2014), p. 129 (2015). https://www.google.com/search?q=final+review+implementasi+OGI&rlz=1C1GGRV_enID751ID751&oq=final+review+implementasi+OGI&aqs=chrome..69i57j33i 160l2.38538j1j7&sourceid=chrome&ie=UTF-8

Belkindas, V.M., Swanson, V.E. (n.d.). International Support for Data Openness and Transparency. 2

Bergström, C.F., Routusi, M.: Grundlag i gungning? En ESO-rapport om EU och den svenska offentlighetsprincipen (an ESO report on the EU and the Swedish principle of public access to information). Expert Group on Public Economics (2018). https://eso.expertgrupp.se/wp-content/uploads/2016/12/ESO-2018_1-Grundlag-i-gungning.pdf

Budiyanti, R.T., Herlambang, P.M.: Disclosure of Coronavirus Disease-19 (Covid-19) Patient Data: Ethical and Legal Perspectives in Indonesia. Crepido 3(1), 22–32 (2021). https://doi.org/10.14710/crepido.3.1.22-32

Buyle, R., et al.: A Sustainable method for publishing interoperable open data on the web. Data, 6(8), 93 (2021). https://doi.org/10.3390/data6080093CSIS. *Southeast Asia Covid-19 Tracker*. https://www.csis.org/programs/southeast-asia-program/projects/southeast-asia-covid-19-tracker

Cumbie, B.A., Kar, B.: A Study of local government website inclusiveness: the gap between e-government concept and practice. Inf. Technol. Dev. 22(1), 15–35 (2016). https://doi.org/10.1080/02681102.2014.906379

Erhan, N., Mardiyono, Hermawan, R., Ohta, H.: Evaluation of e-government implementation in indonesian local government (case study of the implementation of electronic monitoring and evaluation in balangan local government). JPAS (J. Pub. Adm. Stud.) 1(4), 9–15 (2017). https://jpas.ub.ac.id/index.php/jpas/article/view/34

Fan, K.S., et al.: COVID-19 prevention and treatment information on the internet: a systematic analysis and quality assessment. BMJ Open, 10(9) (2020). https://doi.org/10.1136/bmjopen-2020-040487

Handayani, K., Juningsih, E.H., Riana, D., Hadianti, S., Rifai, A., Serli, R.K.: Measuring the quality of website services covid19.kalbarprov.go.id using the webqual 4.0 method. J. Phys. Conf. Ser. 1641(1), 0–6 (2020). https://doi.org/10.1088/1742-6596/1641/1/012049

Huang, J., Guo, W., Fu, L.: Research on e-government website satisfaction evaluation based on public experience. In: DEStech Transactions on Social Science, Education and Human Science, icesd (2019). https://doi.org/10.12783/dtssehs/icesd2019/29844

IFRC: COVID-19: Southeast Asia Battles World's Highest Deaths (2021). https://www.ifrc.org/press-release/covid-19-southeast-asia-battles-worlds-highest-deaths?utm_campaign=covid-19-southeast-asia-battles-worlds-highest-deaths&utm_medium=rss&utm_source=rss

Jayasinghe, R., Ranasinghe, S., Jayarajah, U., Seneviratne, S.: Quality of online information for the general public on COVID-19. Patient Educ. Couns. 103(12), 2594–2597 (2020). https://doi.org/10.1016/j.pec.2020.08.001

Jin, Y., Kwon, O.: Developing data openness evaluation index for intelligent IT service. J. Korea Soc. IT Serv. 15(3), 97–114 (2016). https://doi.org/10.9716/kits.2016.15.3.097

Jung, H.J., Oh, K.W.: Exploring the sustainability concepts regarding leather apparel in China and South Korea. Sustain. (Switzerland), 11(19) (2019). https://doi.org/10.3390/su11195389

Kelibay, I., Nurmandi, A., Malawani, A.D.: e-Government adoption of human resource management in Sorong City, Indonesia. J. Asian Rev. Pub. Affairs Pol. 1(2) (2020). http://dx.doi.org/10.222.99/arpap/2020.62

Klein, R.H., Klein, D.B., Luciano, E.M.: Open government data: concepts, approaches and dimensions over time. Revista Economia Gestão 18(49), 4–24 (2018). https://doi.org/10.5752/p.1984-6606.2018v18n49p4-24

Malawani, A.D., Nurmandi, A., Purnomo, E.P., Rahman, T.: Social media in aid of post disaster management. Transf. Govern. People Process Pol. **14**(2), 237–260 (2020). https://doi.org/10.1108/TG-09-2019-0088

Nam, T.: Challenges and concerns of open government: a case of government 3.0 in Korea. Soc. Sci. Comput. Rev. **33**(5), 556–570 (2015). https://doi.org/10.1177/0894439314560848

Nikiforova, A.: Smarter open government data for society 5.0: are your open data smart enough? Sensors **21**(15), 5204 (2021). https://doi.org/10.3390/s21155204

Nunes, F., Monteiro, M.H., Sequeira, S.: Big data analytics to support digital government public policies. In Top 10 Challenges of Big Data Analytics, pp. 125–159. Nova Science Publishers, Inc. (2021). https://www.scopus.com/inward/record.uri?eid=2-s2.0-85109237213&partnerID=40&md5=e217dd0b5d2cada49ee1d3f45d4c89d5

OECD: OECD Kajian Open Government - Indonesia Hal-Hal Pokok. OECD Publishing, pp. 1–24 (2016)

Otter, T., Sevciuc, I., von Lautz - Cauzanet, E.: Analytical Framework for Inclusive Policy Design - UNESCO. November (2015). https://doi.org/10.13140/RG.2.1.4335.2406

Park, M.J., Kang, D., Rho, J.J., Lee, D.H.: Policy role of social media in developing public trust: Twitter communication with government leaders. Public Manag. Rev. **18**(9), 1265–1288 (2016). https://doi.org/10.1080/14719037.2015.1066418

Pratama, D., Nurmandi, A., Muallidin, I., Kurniawan, D., Salahudin: Information Dissemination of COVID-19 by Ministry of Health in Indonesia, pp. 61–67 (2022). https://doi.org/10.1007/978-3-030-85540-6_8

Putra, I.G.L.A.R., Swastika, I.P.A.: Analisis Kerangka Kerja E-Government Assessment Pada Situs Website Pemerintah Daerah Di Indonesia. Seminar Nasional Teknologi Informasi Dan Komunikasi, **2016**(Sentika), 18–19 (2016)

Ratner, H., Ruppert, E.: Producing and projecting data: aesthetic practices of government data portals. Big Data Soc. **6**(2), 1–16 (2019). https://doi.org/10.1177/2053951719853316

Scala, P., Pota, G.: Elastic places and intermediate design. Festival Dell'Architettura Mag. **52–53**, 92–97 (2021). https://doi.org/10.1283/fam/issn2039-0491/n52-2020/501

Suri, D.: Pemanfaatan Media Komunikasi dan Informasi dalam Perwujudan Pembangunan Nasional. Jurnal Komunikasi Pembangunan **17**(2), 177–187 (2019). https://doi.org/10.46937/17201926848

Tydd, E.: Why "Open Government"? **34**(3), 28–31 (2018)

Yusuf, Y.: Kominfo Temukan 1.401 Sebaran Isu Hoaks terkait Covid-19 (2020). https://aptika.kominfo.go.id/2020/05/kominfo-temukan-1-401-sebaran-isu-hoaks-terkait-covid-19/

Zafarullah, H., Siddiquee, N.A.: Open government and the right to information: Implications for transparency and accountability in Asia. Public Administration and Development, January 2021. https://doi.org/10.1002/pad.1944

Zahra, A.A., et al.: Bibliometric analysis of trends in theory-related policy publications. Emerg. Sci. J. **5**(1), 96–110 (2021)

Analysis the Success of Government Twitter Use in Increasing Vaccine Participation (Case Study of Surabaya City Government, Indonesia)

Tatryana Rendi Ziar Zhafira[1]([✉]), Achmad Nurmandi[1], Danang Kurniawan[1], Isnaini Muallidin[2], and Mohammad Jafar Loilatu[2]

[1] Government Affairs and Administration, Jusuf Kalla School of Government, Universitas Muhammadiyah Yogyakarta, Bantul, Indonesia
Tatryanarendi@gmail.com
[2] Master Government Affairs and Administration, Universitas Muhammadiyah Yogyakarta, Bantul, Indonesia

Abstract. This study aims to find out how social media provides information related to COVID-19 Vaccination, especially the dissemination of Vaccination information in the City of Surabaya through the Twitter account @Command-Surabaya; this account is a social media that is quite active in providing vaccination information. In today's digital era, governments, like individuals, use social media to interact with the public virtually to increase participation and accountability. Social media users have changed their behavior in the context of personal and group communication, as well as government and political communication. The government requires In the Covid-19 situation, social media is very important for communication between the government and the general public in Indonesia. Social media has the following characteristics: intense, massive, interactive, and fast. The research method combines qualitative analysis with secondary data collected from the Twitter social site @CommandSurabaya as well as official government news. To visualize the data analysis, Nvivo12 plus software was used, specifically the Twitter Sociogram data collection tool. Based on these findings, the Twitter account @Commandsurabaya is more active in providing information about vaccinations in the city of Surabaya. Cities use Twitter to communicate with the public.

Keywords: Government communication · Media sosial · Covid – 19

1 Introduction

At the beginning of 2020 the world was shocked by the outbreak of Corona Virus Disease 19 or having a wide impact socially and economically, many countries took the decision to lock down or maintain social distancing policies. When information about a positive case of Covid-19 in Indonesia which was detected on March 2, 2020 was reported to the public, when two people were confirmed to be infected from Japanese citizens (Oktariani and Wuryanta 2020). At that time, the first information was reported by the Indonesian

C. Stephanidis et al. (Eds.): HCII 2022, CCIS 1582, pp. 401–410, 2022.
https://doi.org/10.1007/978-3-031-06391-6_51

government regarding the Covid-19 case. In the current digital era, which uses social media other than individuals, the government also uses social media to interact with the community virtually to increase participation and accountability. New media such as the internet, applications and media create a new style of interaction between government and society (Nurmandi et al. 2020). Government agencies and political elites use social media actively to interact and to inform their citizens of a policy that has been made (Nurmandi et al. 2018). In the conditions of Covid-19, communication between the government and the public In Indonesia, social media is crucial. The characteristics of social media are: intense, massive, interactive and fast. Of the population, more than half of the population is also actively using social media. Therefore, social media is an effective public space in conducting virtual interactions. Because at this time, people more often use social media as a means of communication and seeking information.

The following is data on social media users in Indonesia:

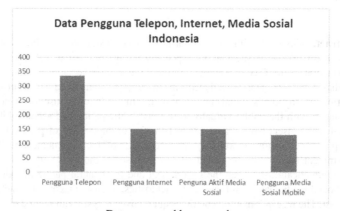

Data processed by researchers

Fig. 1. Indonesian telephone, internet, social media user data

Making it one of the effective and efficient media choices (Watie 2016). The presence of social media as a platform digital communication is able to create interactive communication and can disseminate information quickly between the community and the government. In addition, the government at this time is important to place social media as a platform communication to involve the community in building active interactions where seeing the popularity of social media is currently soaring (Graham et al. 2015) As at this time, where the world is experiencing a major pandemic, namely the Covid-19 and This requires communication that can be conveyed informatively and quickly related to various government policies. As stated by the government, the government will experience a communication crisis when the world experiences a pandemic and government communication needs to be carried out in an informative manner. Due to the spread of misinformation during the Covid-19 pandemic, it is a challenge for the government to be able to provide clarification (Mueller et al. 2020). Therefore, social media is needed to communicate between the government and the community. Communication has 3 elements, namely: communication of policies, institutions and disaster communication patterns and strategies for disseminating information/feedback on the dynamics of disaster issues (Oktariani and Wuryanta 2020). As a public communication strategy related to information about the Covid-19 pandemic which is being carried out by the Surabaya City government. this city uses twitter as a medium to provide information about Covid-19 which is done through vaccination. Dissemination of information through twitter in Indonesia is relevant to the number of Twitter users in Indonesia which is ranked ninth in the world according to the Social & Hootsuite Survey in 2019 (Tareq Ahram 2021). The Surabaya City Government during the COVID-19 pandemic provided significant information to the Surabaya City Community.

In addition, the @Commandsurabaya account is an official account used to provide information and coordinate between the Surabaya city government and the public regarding COVID-19. Social media also needs to pay attention to various aspects through message strategies to disseminate information related to Covid-19 mitigation (Eckert et al. 2018). Social media also pays attention to various aspects through message strategies. Communication between the government through social media and the public is connected via Twitter. This two-way communication model is done by retweeting and commenting (Setiawan et al. 2022). For example, California and San Francisco use twitter as a means of public communication and information related to disaster mitigation (Zeemering 2021). The purpose of the explanation above, this study aims to find out information about the COVID-19 pandemic, especially information related to vaccines in the city of Surabaya.

2 Literature Review

2.1 Social Media in Government Communication

Social media is an online media, where users can easily interact, convey ideas and access information (Cahyono 2016). Social media is also a tool for government communicators to communicate with the public. With social media, the government can connect with the public at any time. Both can occur because of adaptation and innovation for the work of a progressive government (Mergel 2016). The government needs good communication in the delivery of the policy process from conception to policy implementation (Gregory 2006). Because this will later lead to public perception related to the information submitted by the government. Poor public perception can weaken the success of government communication (Vos 2006) Social media is an online medium in which users can easily participate. The development of social media has the potential to disseminate information widely and has an image and reputation that can be influenced by harmful and inaccurate media (Rosselló et al. 2020). Collaboration between social media and government in e-government can have a positive impact on the government's public responsibility and trust (Song and Lee 2016). The important role of social media for the government is as a disaster communication medium and to provide disaster preparedness messages as public information (Tagliacozzo and Magni 2018). Research that has been done on the use of social media in government communication has produced several findings, namely: Users of social media as a government communication platform are able to have an impact on improving communication to the public (Driss et al. 2019).

The most widely used social media in government communications are Facebook and Twitter, although both are used for different purposes (Bossetta 2018).

Social media is an online media where users can easily participate. Its development makes the potential for the dissemination of information even greater. Disseminating information through social media has advantages and disadvantages, depending on how social media is used. Using social media appropriately can increase information for internet users who read and follow (Eckert et al. 2018). Social media is also used by government departments in various countries to control and implement government policies for the benefit of the community and increase productivity and public services as a whole is the core of government-community coordination (Nurmandi et al. 2018). Social media is one of the effective means for the government to increase citizens' trust in the government related to government transparency (Song and Lee 2016). Communication has a good influence on the ideas, goals and tasks of government, including in maintaining the relationship between communicators and communicants (Flabianos 2019). So that the use of social media as a government communication tool is able to reduce the gap in policy making made by the government. This is like the concept of government to citizen (G2C), where this concept makes social media a supporter to form relationships between the community and the government (Pardo et al. 2012).

2.2 Government Communications in Handling Covid-19 Through Social Media

In this study, it was found that through Twitter the mayor of Seoul, can be used as a communication bridge between the government and citizens and vice versa. Where the mayor's role as a bridging center in the Twitter network contributes to increasing government responsiveness by enabling it to overcome disconnection between citizens and local governments, and information asymmetry among mayors, public officials, and citizens. In addition, the role of social media is important in crises. communication (Eom et al. 2018). The use of social media at the local government level shows that it is still minimal, even though this needs to be done by the government for the adoption and use of social media tools for crisis communication and the social media section in managing crises (Campos-Domínguez 2017). Government communication, especially through Twitter social media during the Covid-19 pandemic, has not yet been conceptualized, so that the communication made seems less effective and results in a lack of enthusiasm for netizens for uploaded information. So that it can be said that communication through social media still seems unplanned, as a result communication through social media is less effective and structured (Talita and Legarano 2020).

Covid-19 which has been infecting Indonesia and various other countries for more than a year, this virus outbreak originating from Wuham China attack the respiratory tract through the air. Based on www.covid 19.go.id as of October 10, 2021, the number of positive cases in Indonesia was 4,227,932 and around 4,60,851 recovered. This figure shows that the decline in Covid cases in Indonesia is influenced by the Indonesian people who carry out vaccinations (Pratiwi et al. 2021). One of the government's efforts to break the chain of spread of Covid-19 and death caused by the Covid-19 virus is vaccination, achieved Herd Immunity is the main goal of vaccination to control the Covid-19 Pandemic (Widayanti and Kusumawati 2021).

2.3 Social Media in Vaccination Promotion

In early 2021 the Indonesian government seeks to start a vaccination program to reduce Covid-19 patients. Using the COVID-19 vaccine will significantly reduce the overall Covid-19 disease (Reiter et al. 2020). Several vaccine programs in Indonesia are trending on Indonesian Twitter. In this case, it is proven that the Indonesian people understand about public issues such as the issue of vaccination in Indonesia. Social media is the right place to see the public's response to public policies such as: social media is the right place to voice public policies, then social media gives people choices to access information more easily and cheaply (Kaldy 2015). Social media is a place to voice people's voices. Social media is also a prayer platform to respond to several government programs, one of which is vaccination that occurred in Indonesia. For now, the most popular ones used on social media are using hashtags to share content that is on the rise so that it is trending on social media.

In the use of social media to help deal with Covid-19, especially in the promotion of vaccination, the use of social media can easily access health-related information circulating on various platforms (Purike and Baiti 2021). By using social media, information about vaccinations related to the importance of Covid-19 vaccination to overcome the pandemic is easier to convey to the public (Kehumasan 2021).

3 Research Method

This study uses a qualitative description approach to explain how the government uses social media to disseminate information related to vaccines in the city of Surabaya through the Twitter account (@CommandSurabaya). In addition, it is coded using the Nvivo 12 plus application to determine the classification of Twitter account metadata. Researchers describe the process of Nvivo results to select how to deliver information related to vaccines in the city of Surabaya.

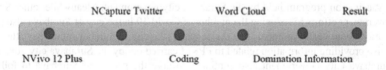

4   Result and Discussion

Figure 1 Word Frequency @CommandSurabaya The Surabaya City Government uses Twitter to provide information to the public regarding Covid-19 in the City of Surabaya. The Surabaya City Government also cooperates in providing information related to Vaccines by several agencies through social media. This image shows that the government uses Twitter to inform regarding the handling of Covid-19 in the city of Surabaya. In the @Commandsurabaya account the word that often appears is the word "Vaccination" to carry out campaigns related to the Covid-19 vaccine in the City of Surabaya during Covid-19. In addition, the words "Protkol and PPKM" are also often used to provide wider information related to Covid-19 on the @Commandsurabaya account. It is necessary to review the government's efforts in providing information regarding the Covid-19 Vaccine to suppress Covid-19 cases in the city of Surabaya

Fig. 2. Crosstab Query – rate Nvivo 12 Plus (Providing information related to the Covid-19 pandemic in the City of Surabaya) The Surabaya City Government provides information related to Vaccines, Implementation of Health Protocols and PPKM through Twitter social media. The biggest percentage is vaccination with 46%, the second is PPKM about 36% and the last is Health Protocol with 18%. The Surabaya City Government is more active in providing information related to the Vaccination program held by the Surabaya city government. Meanwhile, other Surabaya city government efforts in reducing the number of Covid-19 in the city of Surabaya also provide information about health protocols that the people of the city of Surabaya must pay attention to, while also providing information related to PPKM carried out by the Surabaya city government. The Surabaya City Government also continues to urge the people of Surabaya to follow the Health protocol which includes washing hands, maintaining a safe distance and wearing masks. To reduce the number of COVID-19 cases in the city of Surabaya, the government continues to provide information related to vaccines

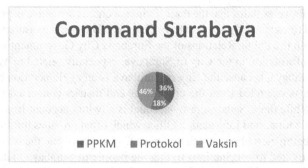

Fig. 3. Explains how the City of Surabaya cooperates with several nearby local agencies in disseminating information on vaccinations. The decline in the number of Covid-19 cases in Indonesia cannot be denied and the government continues to provide vaccine information. The Surabaya City Government also cooperates with several nearby areas in disseminating information on vaccinations. The decline in the number of Covid-19 cases in Indonesia is undeniable, and the government continues to provide information about the importance of vaccination. The Surabaya City Government also regularly interacts with the community to educate about the importance of vaccines and maintain protocols. The Surabaya City Twitter account @CommandSurabaya also uses the unusual #used to inform about vaccinations, Health Protocols, and PPKM. Outside of Covid-19, the Twitter account @CommandSurabaya provides information such as accidents in the Surabaya City area, current traffic jams, and Surabaya City weather

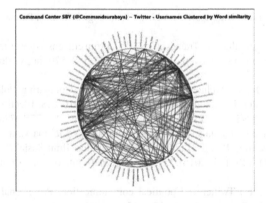

Table 1. Actors who cooperate in providing information on Covid-19 in the City of Surabaya

Government	NGO
@BanggaSurabaya	@Petabencana
@Sapawargasby	

The table above explains that the three Twitter accounts are active in providing information related to vaccines for the Surabaya City area. The @Banggasurabaya account is an account from the Public Relations of the Surabaya City Government which is active in providing information in the City of Surabaya, especially related to Vaccine info in the City of Surabaya, because the City of Surabaya is an agglomeration city where the city or district is extended from the city center and district connected by sustainable urban areas. While the @Sapawargasby account is a twitter account from the Surabaya City Communications and Information Office which often provides information regarding activities being carried out by the Surabaya City government, the two accounts also often retweet related to vaccine info so that the people of Surabaya understand which agency or institution will carry out the vaccine for the people of Surabaya Table 1).

5 Conclusion

The Surabaya City Government uses Twitter to inform about vaccinations in the city of Surabaya. Several Surabaya City Government Accounts are active in providing information related to Vaccines in the City of Surabaya which have caused the decline in the number of Covid-19 in the City of Surabaya.

References

Nurmandi, A., Kurniasih, D., Supardal, A.N.K.: Teknologi Informasi Pemerintahan. UMY Press (2020)

Belkahla Driss, O., Mellouli, S., & Trabelsi, Z. (2019). From citizens to government policy-makers: Social media data analysis. Govern. Inf. Quart. **36**(3), 560–570. https://doi.org/10.1016/j.giq. 2019.05.002

Bossetta, M.: The Digital Architectures of Social Media: Comparing Political Campaigning on Facebook, Twitter, Instagram, and Snapchat in the 2016 U.S. Election. Journalism Mass Commun. Quarterly **95**(2), 471–496 (2018). https://doi.org/10.1177/1077699018763307

Cahyono, A.S.: Pengaruh media sosial terhadap perubahan sosial masyarakat di Indonesia. Jurnal Ilmu Sosial & Ilmu Politik Diterbitkan Oleh Fakultas Ilmu Sosial & Politik, Universitas Tulungagung **9**(1), 140–157 (2016). http://www.jurnal-unita.org/index.php/publiciana/article/download/79/73

Campos-Domínguez, E.: Twitter and political communication. Profesional de la Informacion **26**(5), 785–793 (2017). https://doi.org/10.3145/epi.2017.sep.01

Eckert, S., et al.: Health-related disaster communication and social media: mixed-method systematic review. Health Commun. **33**(12), 1389–1400 (2018). https://doi.org/10.1080/10410236. 2017.1351278

Eom, S.J., Hwang, H., Kim, J.H.: Can social media increase government responsiveness? a case study of Seoul Korea. Government Inf. Quart. **35**(1), 109–122 (2018). https://doi.org/10.1016/ j.giq.2017.10.002

Flabianos, H.: Pengaruh Komunikasi Pemasaran Politik Partai Solidaritas Indonesia Melalui Media Sosial Instagram Pada Pemilu 2019 the Influence of Indonesian Solidarity Party Political Marketing Communications Through Instagram Social Media in 2019 Election, pp. 3–4 (2019)

Graham, M.W., Avery, E.J., Park, S.: The role of social media in local government crisis communications. Public Relations Rev. **41**(3), 386–394 (2015). https://doi.org/10.1016/j.pubrev.2015. 02.001

Gregory, A.: A development framework for government communicators. J. Commun. Manag. **10**(2), 197–210 (2006). https://doi.org/10.1108/13632540610664742

Kaldy, J.: Policy remedies for social media headaches. Caring Ages **16**(6), 11 (2015). https://doi.org/10.1016/j.carage.2015.05.016

Karya Tulis Ilmiah Kehumasan, K., Indrayani Rita Nurlita Tiara Kharisma, H.: Proceeding Komunikasi dan Kehumasan Dinamika dan Strategi Humas Pemerintah di Indonesia (2021)

Mergel, I.: Social media institutionalization in the U.S. federal government. Government Inf. Quart. **33**(1), 142–148 (2016). https://doi.org/10.1016/j.giq.2015.09.002

Mueller, I., et al.: Crisis Communication and Public Perception of COVID-19 Risk in the Era of Social Media. Cadernos de Saúde Pública, **12**(1), 1–30 (2020). http://dx.doi.org/10.1016/j.ijpara.2016.09.005%0Ahttp://dx.doi.org/10.1016/j.vaccine.2015.09.060

Nurmandi, A., et al.: To what extent is social media used in city government policy making? case studies in three asean cities. Public Policy Administration **17**(4), 600–618 (2018). https://doi.org/10.13165/VPA-18-17-4-08

TarerOktariani, R., Wuryanta, A.E.W.: Komunikasi pemerintah melalui media center gugus tugas percepatan penanganan Covid-19 kepada publik. Expose: Jurnal Ilmu Komunikasi **3**(2), 113 (2020). https://doi.org/10.33021/exp.v3i2.1196

Pardo, T.A., Nam, T., Burke, G.B.: E-government interoperability: interaction of policy, management, and technology dimensions. Soc. Sci. Comput. Rev. **30**(1), 7–23 (2012). https://doi.org/10.1177/0894439310392184

Pratiwi, T.S., Insani, P., Fitrianti, L., Sari, C. nur indah, Siburian, N., Wardi, J.: Pengaruh media terhadap opini milenial tentang vaksinasi. Seminar Nasional Karya Ilmiah Multidisiplin **1**(1), 60–64 (2021)

Purike, E., Baiti, A.: Informasi vaksin di media sosial dan program vaksin Covid-19: Langkah Apa Yang Dapat Dilakukan Oleh Pemerintah Republik Indonesia? Cross-Border **4**(2), 58–69 (2021). http://journal.iaisambas.ac.id/index.php/Cross-Border/article/view/635

Reiter, P.L., Pennell, M.L., Katz, M.L.: Acceptability of a COVID-19 vaccine among adults in the United States: how many people would get vaccinated? Vaccine **38**(42), 6500–6507 (2020). https://doi.org/10.1016/j.vaccine.2020.08.043

Rosselló, J., Becken, S., Santana-Gallego, M.: The effects of natural disasters on international tourism: a global analysis. Tourism Manage. **79**, April 2019. https://doi.org/10.1016/j.tourman.2020.104080

Setiawan, R.E.B., Nurmandi, A., Muallidin, I., Kurniawan, D., Salahudin: Technology for governance: comparison of disaster information mitigation of COVID-19 in Jakarta and West Java. In: Lecture Notes in Networks and Systems, vol. 319 (2022). https://doi.org/10.1007/978-3-030-85540-6_17

Song, C., Lee, J.: Citizens use of social media in government, perceived transparency, and trust in government. Public Perform. Manag. Rev. **39**(2), 430–453 (2016). https://doi.org/10.1080/15309576.2015.1108798

Tagliacozzo, S., Magni, M.: Government to Citizens (G2C) communication and use of social media in the post-disaster reconstruction phase. Environ. Hazards **17**(1), 1–20 (2018). https://doi.org/10.1080/17477891.2017.1339012

Talita, G., Legarano, C.: Peran Komunikasi Pemerintahan Dalam Menyampaikan Informasi Tentang Add (Alokasi Dana Desa) Di Desa Mariri Satu Kecamatan Poigar Kabupaten Bolaang Mongondow (2020). https://Ejournal.Unsrat.Ac.Id/

Ahram. T., Human Interaction, Emerging Technologies and Future Systems V (U. of C. Florida, ed.) (2021)

Vos, M.: Setting the research agenda for governmental communication. J. Commun. Manag. **10**(3), 250–258 (2006). https://doi.org/10.1108/13632540610681149

Watie, E.D.S.: Komunikasi dan media sosial (communications and social media). J. Messenger **3**(2), 69 (2016). https://doi.org/10.26623/themessenger.v3i2.270

Widayanti, L.P., Kusumawati, E.: Hubungan Persepsi Tentang Efektifitas Vaksin Dengan Sikap Kesediaan Mengikuti Vaksinasi COVID-19 Linda Prasetyaning Widayanti 1, Estri Kusumawati 2. J. Kesehatan Masyarakat **9**(2), 78–84 (2021)

Zeemering, E.S.: Functional fragmentation in city hall and Twitter communication during the COVID-19 Pandemic: evidence from Atlanta, San Francisco, and Washington. DC. Government Inf. Quart. **38**(1), 101539 (2021). https://doi.org/10.1016/j.giq.2020.101539

Effectiveness of the Electronic Government of the Public Administration. Case: José Leonardo Ortiz District Municipality – Peru

Luis Eden Rojas Palacios[1](✉) ⓘ, Moisés David Reyes Pérez[2] ⓘ,
Danicsa Karina Espino Carrasco [1] ⓘ, Carmen Graciela Arbulú Pérez Vargas[1] ⓘ,
and Alberto Gómez Fuertes[3] ⓘ

[1] Cesar Vallejo University, Pimentel, Peru
Rojaspal2@ucvvirtual.edu.pe
[2] Mayor de San Marcos National University, Lima, Peru
[3] National University of Trujillo, Trujillo, Peru

Abstract. This research work is descriptive; and it has been set as a goal to determine if the electronic government has been effective for the public administration in the District Municipality of José Leonardo Ortiz, during the 2019 period; for which we worked with a population of 46 workers that was equal to the sample, therefore there were no sampling techniques. The inclusion criteria considered were: belonging to the Municipality of JLO and working during the research period; using a "Checklist of fulfillment of objectives of the electronic government of the MDJLO" that included a preliminary questionnaire on the level of knowledge about Electronic Government. As results, an adequate awareness of the concepts related to electronic government was evidenced; showing a perception referring to the internal and external dimensions as adequate processes; but not conclusively, so the need to generate policy guidelines necessary for continuous improvement is assumed; which focus on sensitization, awareness, empowerment of the dimensions and application of the results-based municipal management strategy.

Keywords: Electronic government · Municipal management · Continuous improvement

1 Introduction

1.1 Problematic Reality

It is necessary to recognize the paradigm shift that accompanies the construction of electronic government, where the existing administrative structure is changing. This at the level of institutionalization and the legal framework to achieve EG under the tonality of promoting the development of urban public management, including the involvement of all collaborators, including the use of ICT, to participate as the protagonist of the process, not only of the users. In this sense, the Municipality of José Leonardo Ortiz

C. Stephanidis et al. (Eds.): HCII 2022, CCIS 1582, pp. 411–417, 2022.
https://doi.org/10.1007/978-3-031-06391-6_52

emphasizes the comparative differences with the management of information technology and accessibility to the Web, clarifying the different geographical, cultural, economic, gender reasons and other techniques used.

To the extent that administrative access is based on these principles, it limits citizens and parameterizes their use of the Internet, which varies according to taxpayer income levels, given the growing resistance to innovation, it is common in human society (comfort zones). Thanks to the use of advanced technology, the results are very ideal, allowing the acceptance of users and their critics, but it can be said that the urban center of José Leonardo Ortiz has digital streets and resistance to change. It is not yet known how effective, empowering and innovative the use of e-government mechanisms will be and support the needs of this work.

1.2 Literature Review

Electronic Government as the Basis of Contemporary Public Administration. The use of ICTs increases day by day due to the high income they generate. Thus, the public sector can gradually change its relationship with citizens. ICTs are a tool to develop organizational structures and governance models (open in this case), providing agile, efficient, transparent and high-quality responses to users of government services. go from a bureaucratic system to a flexible system with consequences.

This system is necessary to link municipal governments, citizens and companies in the provision of services and to develop higher levels of efficiency in municipal management and thus strengthen the dynamics of governance. However, this concept is not complete and not all of the above characteristics exactly define that the e-government of the municipal government must be efficient to the extent that it uses information technology to manage its municipal processes with quality. (Deyas 2012).

Structuring. Electronic government has essential elements. Some of them are: develop an efficient municipal government focused on transparency. The development of public services using the Web is fundamental, this based on the application of electronic forms for more efficient transactions, and that can be achieved for public management purposes. Therefore, a digital democracy is required to efficiently make all processes transparent.

Own Relationships. Community participation is understood as the interaction between elected representatives as citizens who participate at a horizontal level in an adequate interaction between the actors of the municipal process, which makes management more robust and therefore better results are obtained.

Dimensions of Electronic Government

The External Dimension. It is a gradual process where technological interfaces are continuously implemented with friendly environments that allow the mayor user to interact and obtain relevant results in the management that he is carrying out. This contemplates an intra relational dimension; where one of the areas of e-Government that has the greatest potential is reciprocity, which allows them to interconnect to improve existing practices. Not only for the process, but for the new generation. These aspects are essentially inter-organizational in the broadest sense of the community and include the different governing bodies of companies and social entities.

Internal Dimension. At the level of municipal management there is a great impact. Strongly being the key to change, creating the momentum for change in ICT implementations; which also presents an intra dimension of promotion, in which the particularities of the local public sector require that the model consider a fourth dimension. In other words, it is an aspect of public relations that deals with the development of sufficient culture, infrastructure and equipment, and is another essential integrator of regional activities in the field of e-government.

Objectives. Determine to what extent the electronic government of the public administration of the District Municipality of José Leonardo Ortiz has been effective, during the period 2021.

Apply the appropriate instrumentation to characterize the electronic government of the public administration of the District Municipality of José Leonardo Ortiz, during the 2019 period.

Propose the policy guidelines to implement an improvement of the electronic government for the public administration of the District Municipality of José Leonardo Ortiz.

2 Method

This research is descriptive because it responds directly to revealing the characteristics of the phenomenon to be studied (Hernández et al. 2019), it has a cross-sectional design because a cut-off point will be used to parametrically assess the dimensions of the electronic government of the MDJLO.

The collaborators of the Sub Management of Information Technology and Computer Processes formed the population that were 4 servers that participate in the electronic government of this commune; also the workers of the associated areas that were a total of 46 people, the population of 46 workers was equal to the sample, therefore there were no sampling techniques. The inclusion criteria considered were: belonging to the municipal entity and working during the research period. The exclusion criteria were: Not working during the research period, and not belonging to areas related to Electronic Government.

3 Results

When asked, do you know what Open Government means? It was evidenced that 31 of the workers of the municipality know about the question, 11 of the workers know little and 4 of these are unaware of the reagent; Regarding the question, do you know what Interinstitutional Articulation means? It was possible to show that 25 workers know this category, in addition 12 know little about it, while 9 workers are unaware of the reagent (Tables 1 and 2).

This presupposes that the workers of the MDJLO present adequate knowledge of the most important indicators of the internal dimension at a conceptual level, but operationally they show that a greater level of awareness is needed in the processes, considering that the level of transparency that is established is adequate. acquires by adequately

Table 1. Level of knowledge about the implementation of the Electronic Government in the MDJLO by the workers of said entity

Knowledge level	Alternatives			
	Known	Knows little	Does not know	Total
Do you know of the existence of the National Policy for the Modernization of Public Management in Peru?	28	13	5	46
Do you know what Open Government means?	31	11	4	46
Do you know what Electronic Government means?	32	5	9	46
Do you know what Inter-institutional Articulation means?	25	12	9	46
Do you know if Open Government policies are being implemented in your institution?	12	9	25	46
Do you know if Electronic Government policies are being implemented in your institution?	13	12	21	46
Do you know if Interinstitutional Articulation policies are being implemented in your institution?	12	9	25	46

Table 2. Perception that MDJLO workers assign to the internal dimension: public service and process improvement

Perception of workers according to dimensional indicators	Frequency		
	Suitable	Not suitable	Total
PUBLIC SERVICE: Offer public services efficiently, simply, timely, at low cost	29	17	46
PUBLIC SERVICE: Guarantees probity and transparency in each state action	34	12	46
IMPROVEMENT OF PROCESSES: Improvement of internal management processes by reducing the time it takes to process files	23	23	46
IMPROVEMENT OF PROCESSES: Improvement of attention to neighbors, reducing waiting times both online and in person	20	26	46

developing the electronic government process; the other elements still need to be worked on; which supposes a deviation of responses, for example, in the attention to the neighbor where it seems that there is a lack of awareness about the direct implication of an adequate electronic government with said activity of attention to the user.

Given the IMPROVEMENT OF PROCESSES dimension in its first indicator, it was evidenced that 23 workers considered it adequate, while 23 considered it inadequate, considering a tie criterion; and the PROCESS IMPROVEMENT dimension with its second Improvement indicator, it was shown that 20 workers considered it adequate, while 26 workers considered it inadequate.

This presupposes that the workers of the MDJLO present adequate knowledge of the most important indicators of the internal dimension at a conceptual level, but operationally they show that a greater level of awareness is needed in the processes, considering that the level of transparency that is established is adequate. acquires by adequately developing the electronic government process; the other elements still need to be worked on; which supposes a deviation of responses, for example, in the attention to the neighbor where it seems that there is a lack of awareness about the direct implication of an adequate electronic government with said activity of attention to the user.

Table 3. Perception that the MDJLO workers assign to the external: promotion of neighborhood participation and promotion of citizen participation

Perception of workers according to dimensional indicators	Frequency		
	Suitable	Not suitable	Total
NEIGHBORHOOD PARTICIPATION: Promotion of neighborhood participation through technological means	26	20	46
NEIGHBORHOOD PARTICIPATION: Effective neighborhood participation through technological mean	22	24	46
CITIZEN PARTICIPATION: Promotion of citizen participation for the next participatory budget for various processes	20	26	46
CITIZEN PARTICIPATION: Effective citizen participation for the next participatory pre-post for various processes	24	22	46

Therefore, Table 3 shows us the Perception that the MDJLO workers assign to the external: promotion of neighborhood participation and in terms of the processes of promotion of citizen participation; and the respective indicators of the external dimension, both in theoretical and effective evidence, as well as before the indicator that belongs to the NEIGHBORHOOD PARTICIPATION dimension, which is a promotion through technological processes of the community in the municipal services, it was possible to show that 26 workers considered it adequate and 20 as inadequate; but before the indicator of the NEIGHBORHOOD PARTICIPATION dimension: where the use of technological means that guarantee effective neighborhood participation can be seen, it was observed that 22 of the workers considered this process adequate and 24 workers considered it inadequate.

Given the indicator of the CITIZEN PARTICIPATION dimension: Promotion of citizen participation for the next participatory budget for various processes, it was shown that 20 workers considered it adequate, while 26 considered it inadequate, finally, before the indicator of the CITIZEN PARTICIPATION dimension: Effective citizen participation for the next participatory budget for various processes, it was observed that 24 workers considered it adequate and 22 considered this process inadequate.

The difference in perception between neighborhood participation and citizen participation is evident in terms of levels of acceptance of how the process is carried out in the MDJLO; and effective electronic government is therefore a faithful reflection of these processes. In other words, if they are perceived well, it is because they really have a good impact in the context of study.

4 Practical Contribution

This research provides as a practical contribution the following guidelines to be taken into account according to the third objective of our research, taking into account the definition that public services related to information technology and the Internet must have a clear mission to be very useful. to provide effectiveness and transparency to the municipal processes. (Lagos 2011).

Based on the definition presented and the results obtained, the following guidelines are proposed as their implementation in the MDJLO is progressive:

Guideline 1: Generate an awareness plan – awareness that starts from the Electronic Government Unit (which must be generated to maintain and provide operational service to the Municipal Electronic Management); which must be aggressive until the collaborators at the same time internalize the concepts of electronic government; put them into practice by gaining process visibility.

Guideline 2: Organize the procedural algorithms of the Electronic Government by means of User Operational Manuals where you specify the technical files to be used to access the most important procedures and user attention and follow-up, since the mayoral quality of service may be more easily parameterized.

Guideline 3: Promote the external dimension with neighborhood and citizen participation through strategies to approach electronic government under information transparency measures, which will ensure a forceful effect of legalization and a frontal fight against corruption; always applying to the indicators of effectiveness or de facto.

Guideline 4: Promote the internal dimension under the parameterization of the quality public service and the continuous improvement of processes (using the bases of Deming's continuous improvement); This will very effectively strengthen the Electronic Government of the MDJLO since it will provide it with the tools by making a specific regulation for its application effective; which must be linked to the Manual of Job Profiles - MPP and Regulation of Organization and Functions of the municipality.

Guideline 5: Electronic government should be strengthened through the strategy focused on results-based municipal management, in this way the budget defined for the operational maintenance of the Municipal Electronic Management System will be subject to specific changes in favor of improvement. keep going; because, as was clarified in a timely manner, one of the greatest aspirations of municipal management is user satisfaction.

The researchers are aware that by complying with the proposed guidelines, the levels of achievement of municipal management will improve because they will be anchored to an efficient electronic government; transparent, robust, free of corruption; That is why there is an urgent need to strengthen the institutional future here and now with technological support.

5 Conclusions

The characteristics of the electronic government of the municipal administration were identified, during the 2021 period; which presented an adequate awareness of the concepts related to electronic government; showing a perception referring to the internal and external dimensions as adequate processes; but not conclusively, so the need to generate policy guidelines necessary for continuous improvement is assumed.

The appropriate instrumentation was applied to characterize the electronic government of the municipal administration, using a "Checklist for the fulfillment of the objectives of the electronic government of the MDJLO" that included a preliminary questionnaire on the level of knowledge about the Electronic Government of the MDJLO and a checklist to indicate whether the workers considered the indicators of each dimension studied adequate or not.

5 policy guidelines have been proposed to implement an improvement of the electronic government for the public administration of the District Municipality of José Leonardo Ortiz, which focus on awareness, awareness, empowerment of the dimensions.

4. It is concluded that the electronic government of the public administration of the District Municipality of José Leonardo Ortiz, during the period 2021 has presented little effectiveness, for which it is suggested to propose policy guidelines to implement continuous improvement.

References

Deyas: United Nations Study on Electronic Government, USA, New York. Recovered from (2012). www.unpan.org/egovernment

Hernández, R., Fernández, C., Baptista, M.: Metodología de la investigación (8a ed). McGraw-Hill, México D.F (2019)

Lagos, R.: Municipal electronic government. Santiago, Chile: CIPOD editorial (2011)

Web Analytics: How VisitingJogja.com Used in Tourism Recovery Due to the COVID-19 Pandemic

Delila Putri Sadayi[1]([envelope]), Achmad Nurmandi[1], Isnaini Muallidin[1],
Eko Priyo Purnomo[1,2], and Danang Kurniawan[1]

[1] Department of Government Affairs and Administration, Jusuf Kalla School of Government,
Universitas Muhammadiyah Yogyakarta, Yogyakarta, Indonesia
`Delila.putri.psc21@mail.umy.ac.id`, {nurmandi_achmad,
eko}@umy.ac.id, isnainimuallidin@gmail.com,
kurniawand949@gmail.com
[2] E-Governance and Sustainability Institute, Yogyakarta 55183, Indonesia

Abstract. Visitingjogja.com, a website dedicated to restoring tourism in the Yogyakarta Special Region after the COVID-19 pandemic, is examined in this article. The presence of the COVID-19 pandemic has had a significant impact on the tourism sector. Digital tourism, which incorporates ICT, the internet of things (IoT), and artificial intelligence (AI), as well as other emerging technologies, is one way to revitalize the tourism industry (AI). This study employs a qualitative method and an exploratory research methodology to investigate the use of the website to create a digital tourism system. Web analysis using the rank watch software tool to collect data aid in the investigation. Web Analytics is a methodological study or technique used to collect, measure, report, and analyze illustrated websites based on sentiment analysis, grouping, and topic modeling. Use of Web Analytics to analyze website performance and optimize website usage. We use the Web Analytics analysis method to track organic keywords and analyze performance, activity, and traffic flow on the VisitingJogja.com website. The results of the analysis of the data findings show; 1) Website VisitingJogja.com performance is excellent to use; 2) The promotion strategy carried out by the Yogyakarta Special Region Tourism Office through the VisitingJogja.com website has become an effective information medium. 3) The activity of using the VisitingJogja.com website has not been maximally used as a tourism recovery strategy in the Special Region of Yogyakarta.

Keywords: Web Analytics · Tourism recovery · COVID-19 pandemic

1 Introduction

Visitingjogja.com, a website dedicated to restoring tourism in the Yogyakarta Special Region after the COVID-19 pandemic, is examined in this article. The presence of the COVID-19 pandemic has had a significant impact on the tourism sector (Purnomo et al. 2021). This impact occurs due to restrictions on human mobility through the Large-Scale

Social Restriction (PSBB) or Lockdown policy set by the government to minimize the spread of the COVID-19 pandemic (Dewi et al. 2020). The COVID-19 pandemic has become a deadly virus because of the spread of infections easily transmitted through droplets, causing disturbances to the human respiratory system (Assaf and Scuderi 2020). Restrictions on human mobility im-posed in response to the rapid spread of the COVID-19 pandemic illness were one of the factors contributing to Yogyakarta's decline in tourist traffic.

The COVID-19 pandemic, which had a significant impact on the tourism sector, resulted in a decrease in economic income in the tourism sector (Buheji and Ahmed 2020). There was a reduction in income for businesses in the tourism industry, including hotels, apartments, travel companies, travel brokers, tourist destinations, and other tourism business sector players (Vărzaru et al. 2021). The number of hotels and restaurants that went bankrupt has increased, with 1,557 hotels and restaurants in total. In addition, hotel and restaurant tax revenues decreased significantly in 2019 by 12.72% to 7.17% in 2020 (Tim Perumusan Kebijakan Ekonomi dan Keuangan Daerah 2021). Mean-while, the growth in the accommodation and food and drink provision sector GRDP in the third quarter of 2019–2020 is minus (−5.55%) (Tim Perumusan Kebijakan Ekonomi dan Keuangan Daerah 2021).

The decrease in hotel and restaurant tax revenues and the growth in the accommodation and food and beverage sector contributed to a decrease in the tourism sector's regional revenue. To deal with the COVID-19 pandemic, travel restrictions and human mobility limitations have severely limited tourism operations. Restrictions negatively impact the earnings of the tourism business on regulation (Pambudi et al. 2020). So that to increase the income of the tourism sector, one of the efforts to restore tourism is through digital tourism.

The COVID-19 pandemic has caused restrictions on human mobility. So that there is a digital transformation into a virtual human mobility media by utilizing technology, information, and communication (ICT) through the integration of the Internet of Things (IoT) and Artificial intelligence (AI) (Vargas 2020). Many industries, including education, financial services, and government, have undergone a digital revolution in recent years (Rizky et al. 2019). So, it is undeniable that tourism can also be digitized. Digital tourism is a form of creation from the Internet of Things (IoT) and Artificial Intelligence used to solve problems in the tourism sector by increasing tourism activities through technology. Digital tourism facilitates access to information and communication to increase business, income and create a digital culture in the tourism sector (Happ and Ivancsó-Horváth 2018).

This study aims to analyze the use of the visitingjogja.com website as one of the digital tourism media used by the Special Region of the Yogyakarta government in carrying out tourism recovery. The presence of the digitalization era and changes to the trend pattern of information and communication dissemination are challenges for the government in tourism recovery, which is why this research is essential (Saura et al. 2020). The analysis of this research shows the website's performance and the effectiveness of using the website as a digital tourism media managed by the Yogyakarta Special Region government in tourism recovery due to the COVID-19 pandemic. The analysis of this research uses web analytics software tools to facilitate data retrieval and website analysis. Sentiment and topic modeling can be analyzed and reported using web analytics tools.

2 Literature Review

2.1 Tourism Recovery and Digital Tourism

Tourism is a leading sector that contributes a lot to regional and state revenues (Wang et al. 2021). However, tourism has weaknesses, especially nature-based tourism, which is prone to disasters (Saito and Ruhanen 2017). Disasters can be natural, manufactured, or a combination of the two that harm the survival of life. Disasters are categorized into three disaster elements (Musaddad et al. 2019); 1) The existence of events caused by nature or man-made; 2) The timing of the incident suddenly; 3) These elements are interrelated with one another. The three sorts of catastrophes are natural, social, and non-natural disasters, which are combined.

Rapid action is needed to minimize the damage and restore the situation to its pre-disaster form as rapidly as possible when a disaster occurs. Reviving the tourism business is the method used. Communities, governments, and individuals all work together in the aftermath of a disaster to help restore tourism to the area (Kuo 2021). As a non-natural disaster, the COVID-19 pandemic significantly affects the tourism sector, especially in the tourism business afflicted by COVID-19 (Svirydzenka 2021). One of the efforts to restore tourism due to the COVID-19 pandemic is to reconstruct tourism through digital tourism.

Digital tourism is a form of creation from the Internet of Things (IoT) and Artificial Intelligence, used to solve problems in the tourism sector by increasing tourism activities through technology (Zsarnoczky 2018). Internet of Things (IoT) connects objects and environments in the digital world to offer applications and services for various stakeholders (Kasiwi et al. 2021; Ramdani et al. 2021). In addition, the presence of IoT is not only about connecting sensing devices but also includes creating insights or knowledge from data that can help solve problems and automate processes without human intervention (Agustiyara and Ramdani 2021). The large volume of data collected by IoT devices connected with algorithms and Artificial Intelligence (AI) techniques can analyze from data to create public services and value (Dzinnun et al. 2021). So that digital tourism is a form of digital transformation in the tourism sector that utilizes the sophistication of the development of integrated information technology through the Internet of Things (IoT) and Artificial intelligence (AI). Digital tourism facilitates access to information and communication to increase business, income and create a digital culture in the tourism sector. One form of digital tourism's role is to introduce tourism through technology platforms (Happ and Ivancsó-Horváth 2018). Digital tourism introduces tourism potential through a virtual tourism platform and becomes a business platform for the tourism industry (Khurramov and Boboqulov 2019). The tourism industry in the digital era provides the promising potential to be developed.

2.2 Web Analytics

The utilization of information and communication technology (ICT) through the website as a promotional and information media has overgrown and is in demand. Website is an information page provided via the internet to be accessed worldwide if it is connected to the internet (Rizky et al. 2019). Website is one of the most popular promotional media with unlimited scope and time (Gour et al. 2021). Through the website, every manager can promote and offer various products or services in an easier, faster, and more effective way and reach all countries globally (Awichanirost and Phumchusri 2020). The website as an effective medium in delivering information requires the application of specific strategies so that promotional activities through the website can be carried out optimally. Efforts made to formulate a website as an effective media strategy are analyzed using web analytics methods.

Web Analytics is a methodological study or technique used in collecting, measuring, reporting, and analyzing data on illustrated websites based on sentiment analysis, grouping, and topic modeling (Gour et al. 2021). Web analytics tools or software are required to analyze the website's performance and optimize its utilization (Putra 2019). Web Analytics tools are used to track organic keywords and analyze visitors, activity, and traffic flows on the website (Putra et al. 2018). As a result, website analytics can serve as an effective media strategy in the digital age.

3 Methods

This study uses exploratory qualitative research methods to analyze how the government uses the visitingjogja.com website to recover tourism due to the COVID-19 pandemic. The data source of this study used secondary data sources (Michopoulou and Buhalis 2008) obtained from website analysis which were collected and analyzed using web analytics soft-ware tools, namely Rank watch. After the required data is obtained, the data reduction stage is carried out. The author carries out the data analysis stage by testing the validity of the data based on research indicators to determine the effect of the Visit-ingJogja.com website in the recovery of the tourism sector.

Use of Web Analytics to analyze website performance and optimize website use (Gour et al. 2021). We use the Web Analytics analysis method to track organic keywords and analyze visitor activity and traffic flow on the VisitingJogja.com website. The analysis data obtained from the website uses a time series model for the last two years, namely January 2020 to September-2021. The following is a description of the flow of research methods carried out in this study.

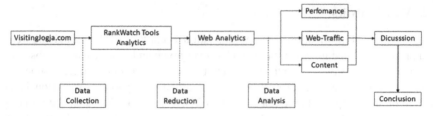

Fig. 1. Flow of research methods.

4 Result and Discussion

The use of digital tourism to promote tourist destinations, and the tourism industry uses a website platform (Putra et al. 2018). Website as a form of Internet of Things (IoT) and Artificial Intelligence (AI) is used to form a digital tourism system. The website has a significant influence on the development of tourism development (Mengkara and Saraswati 2014). One form of digital tourism's role is to introduce tourism through technology platforms. Digital tourism introduces tourism potential through a virtual tourism platform and becomes a business platform for the tourism industry (R. A. Putra 2019). The Special Region of Yogyakarta is a city that has been significantly affected by the COVID-19 pandemic in the tourism sector.

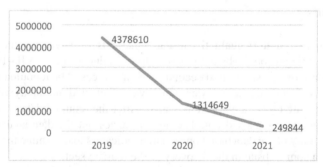

Fig. 2. Number of Tourist Visits from the Special Region of Yogyakarta in 2019- April 2021 Source: (Dinas Pariwisata Daerah Istimewa Yogyakarta 2020)

Figure 2 shows a significant decrease in local and foreign tourist visits from 2019 to April 2020. The number of visits in 2020 decreased by almost 3 million visitors from 2019 (Dinas Pariwisata Daerah Istimewa Yogyakarta 2020). Meanwhile, in 2021 a significant decline occurred again to 249844 in April 2021. Increased COVID-19 instances led to a regional restriction policy, which decreased tourist arrivals in the Yogyakarta Special Region. Because of this, the tour-ism industry's revenue is affected when the number of visitors drops. The Special Region of Yogyakarta is the city that generates the most revenue from tourism be-cause most of its residents rely on the sector for their livelihood (Kusuma et al. 2021).

One of his efforts in tourism recovery is integrating website technology based on the Internet of Things (IoT) and Artificial Intelligence (AI) through the visitingjogja.com website. The presence of a website www.visitingjogja.com provided by the Tourism Office of the Special Region of Yogyakarta, which contains portal material about tourism, social media tourism, official web, monitoring and internal evaluation of the service, as well as mapping the tourism potential of the Special Region of Yogyakarta (Rizky et al. 2019). This internet-based activity used as a tourist information medium is carried out as a form of implementation of Government Regulation No. 61 of 2010 concerning the Implementation of Law No. 14 of 2008 concerning Public Information Disclosure (KIP) and Law No. 11 of 2008 concerning Information and Trans-actions. Electronic to realize electronic-based tourist information services to the public.

The public information service, especially in this case regarding tourism, was chosen to use the website because the website is an online communication channel (Gour et al. 2021). This website is used as a distributor of information to make it easier for tourists to find out where the access process can be seen directly (Awichanirost and Phumchusri 2020). By accessing the website, every visitor can easily find out the content (information) anytime, anywhere on any digital device in real-time.

Fig. 3. Display of the Main Page of the visitingjogja.com website

Figure 3 shows the main page of the visitingjogja.com website; when analyzed in terms of content, the visitingjogja.com website has presented various menu options for website visitors to facilitate access to information. On the top view of the main page, website visitors can choose which language access website visitors want to use. Ease of access This language is set to facilitate access to information for local and foreign tourists. In addition, the Yogyakarta Special Region government has integrated technology based on the visitingjogja.com application so that visitors or tourists can access tourist and other information not only based on the website but also using the visitingjogja.com application(Fauzi and Setiawan 2020). The Yogyakarta Special Region government provides a direct chat menu through the WhatsApp application in the Tourism Center information section. It is integrated with other social media such as Facebook, Twitter, Instagram, and YouTube, to make it easier for visitors to browse information quickly.

Figure 3 also shows eight menu options including: 1) Tourist destinations; 2) Culinary; 3) Events; 4) Accommodation; 5) Tourist Map; 6) Virtual Tours; 7) Download E-Documents; 8) Office Profile. Based on content analysis on the visitingjog-ja.com website, it is categorized in full to support the creation of digital tourism in the Special Region of Yogyakarta. The menu choices on the visitingjogja.com website is integrated with other tourism industries, such as the accommodation options menu integrated with dozens of accommodation provider tourism industries. In this menu, visitors can search for references and even choose travel accommodation or travel agents and order them through the menu.

The target of the visitingjogja.com website is the entire community or tourists, both domestic and foreign tourists. The goal is to increase the number of tourist visits and increase the length of stay of tourists (PSPPR UGM 2016). There is no age limit in targeting this website because the content on the website contains general information about tourism that has the right to be known by the entire community. Access to information on the visitingjogja.com website can be seen on the Tour Destinations, Culinary, and Event menus. Each submenu link provides various information on natural and cultural tourism in the Special Region of Yogyakarta.

In addition, there is also a map sub-menu on this website. This is one of the advantages of this website because information on tourist, hotel, and culinary maps is contained in this map, making it easier for information seekers to visit the Special Region of Yogyakarta. The Yogyakarta Special Region Tourism Office breaks new ground by making available for download a variety of files and documents related to Yogyakarta Special Region tourism, such as e-brochures, statistical e-books, tourism study documents, performance reports from DIY Tourism Office agencies, and tourist policies and regulations and regulations.

The visitingjogja.com website has been around since 2015 and continues to develop to realize digital tourism, one of which is the presence of a virtual tourism sub-menu (PSPPR UGM 2016). This sub-menu provides virtual based tours, where visitors can enjoy them virtually. COVID-19 epidemic and the policy of limiting social mobility have impacted tourism and have resulted in a decrease in the number of tourist visits (Dzinnun et al. 2021). With the presence of this menu, it can be an attraction for tourists to visit to promote tourism after the COVID-19 pandemic.

The visitingjogja.com website is designed as a web containing a tourism portal. The community needs elements as domestic and foreign tourists, namely content elements or news information that is easily accessible, concise, clear, and up to date. However, the content on the sub-menu of the visitingjogja.com website is still incomplete. The website does not include all lodging options for tourists. There is only one virtual tour of Jomblang Cave to choose from when it comes to tour content. Tourist spots in Yogyakarta's Special Region remain under development, in any case. This suggests that the government is still not exploiting the internet as a tourism promotion strategy to its full potential. It is possible to use web analytics software to monitor the number of visitors to the visitingjogja.com website.

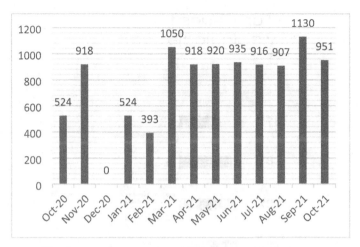

Fig. 4. Organic keyword used in website Visitingjogja.com

Web analytics software is used to track and improve the performance of websites. Visitors visitingjogja.com frequently utilize organic keywords, as seen in Fig. 5. To help search engines understand the information, an organic keyword is inserted into the text. The number of organic keywords accessed in 2020–2021 ap-pears unpredictable, peaking at 1,180 in September 2021. The organic search system uses a method of entering several search terms as a link to a website, which results in organic keywords (Awichanirost and Phumchusri 2020). The results of an organic search are generated at random, but search engines use this data to determine which websites have the most relevant content and use organic keywords to do so (Gour et al. 2021). In addition to increasing traffic and website visibility, organic search also can boost online marketing sales and raise consumer awareness of your brand.

Figure 6 shows the popular pages visited by website visitors. The tourist in-formation visit page by the Yogyakarta Special Region Tourism Office occupies the first position with a value of 37%. The Tourism Event Agenda occupies the second position at 18%, and the tourist map occupies the third position at 13%. The Top Page of this visit shows website visitors' interest related to tourist information and tourist events in the Special Region of Yogyakarta. This shows that effective tourism promotion is carried out through the visitingjogja.com website.

In contrast, the Tourism Event Agenda occupies the second position, and the tourist map occupies the third position. Tourist information and Yogyakarta-specific activities are of appeal, as seen on the website's front page. Visitors to visitingjog-ja.com can rest assured that the site's tourism promotion efforts are well-executed.

Figures 6 and 7 show an analysis of the performance of the visitingjogja.com website in terms of website speed and traffic. The speed of the visitingjogja.com website based on the analysis results of web analysis software shows an A+ value, which means it has a good performance value with a total page load time of 2.551 s and a total page size of 0.02 kb. While the global traffic rank website visitingjogja.com 1944 was the most visited globally, it was in the position of 435 most visited websites in Indonesia for the country

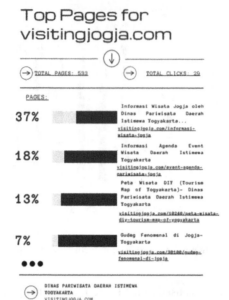

Fig. 5. Top pages for Visitingjogja.com

Fig. 6. Website Speed Visitingjogja.com   **Fig. 7.** Website traffic Visitingjogja.com

rank. Even though the global rank and country rank traffic of the visitingjogja.com website is still low, using the website provides easy access to the world. Through the website, every manager can promote and offer various products or tour packages in an easier, faster, and more effective way and reach all countries worldwide. So that the existence of a website that utilizes the Internet of Things (IoT) and Artificial Intelligence (AI) technology has significantly influenced the tourism industry after the COVID-19 pandemic.

Based on the results of the web analysis, the author visualizes the concept of tourism recovery due to the COVID-19 pandemic in the Special Region of Yogyakarta-ta City, shown in Fig. 8. Figure 8 shows the recovery of tourism in the Special Region of Yogyakarta by implementing digital tourism to realize smart tourism by integrating the internet of things (IoT) and Artificial Intelligence (AI) in the form of visit-ingjogja.com website. The visitingjogja.com website is a form of tourism recovery efforts in digital branding, tourism information, and virtual tourism. This medium is expected to establish interactive communication between the government, private sector, and the public

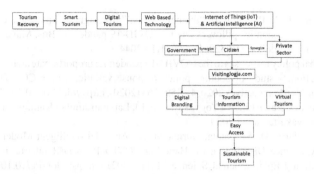

Fig. 8. Concepts of Tourism recovery in the special region of Yogyakarta through Digital Tourism

(tourists), then create a communication channel that can be reached by the whole society easily, cheaply, and accurately.

5   Conclusion

The tourism industry in the digital era provides the promising potential to be developed. Moreover, the impact of the COVID-19 pandemic on the tourism sector has had a significant impact on the tourism industry. The use of digital tourism is very effective compared to conventional media. Digital tourism technology makes it easier for tourists to have a seamless customer experience in finding, ordering, and paying for tourism services.

The use of digital tourism is also a form of digital branding for tourism potential and the tourism industry that is mutually integrated with the use of the Internet of Things (IoT) and Artificial Intelligence (AI). Using digital tourism through the visitingjogja.com website by the Yogyakarta Special Region government based on website analysis is one of the efforts to restore tourism due to the COVID-19 pandemic. The results of the analysis of the data findings show; 1) Website VisitingJogja.com performance is excellent to use; 2) The promotion strategy carried out by the Yogyakarta Special Region Tourism Office through the VisitingJogja.com website has be-come an effective information medium. 3) The activity of using the VisitingJog-ja.com website has not been maximally used as a tourism recovery strategy in the Special Region of Yogyakarta.

References

Agustiyara, Purnomo, E.P., Ramdani, R.: Using Artificial Intelligence Technique in Estimating Fire Hotspots of Forest Fires. IOP Conference Series: Earth and Environmental Science, 717(1) (2021). https://doi.org/10.1088/1755-1315/717/1/012019

Assaf, A., Scuderi, R.: COVID-19 and the recovery of the tourism industry. Tour. Econ. **26**(5), 731–733 (2020). https://doi.org/10.1177/1354816620933712

Awichanirost, J., Phumchusri, N.: Analyzing the effects of sessions on unique visitors and unique page views with google analytics: a case study of a tourism website in Thailand. In: 2020 IEEE 7th International Conference on Industrial Engineering and Applications, ICIEA 2020, pp. 1014–1018 (2020). https://doi.org/10.1109/ICIEA49774.2020.9102094

Buheji, M., Ahmed, D.: Planning for "the new normal": foresight and management of the possibilities of socio-economic spillovers due to COVID-19 pandemic. Bus. Manage. Strat. **11**(1), 160 (2020). https://doi.org/10.5296/bms.v11i1.17044

Dewi, A.: Global policy responses to the COVID-19 pandemic: proportionate adaptation and policy experimentation: a study of country policy response variation to the COVID-19 pandemic. Health Promotion Perspectives **2020**(4), 359–365 (2020). https://doi.org/10.34172/hpp.2020.54

Dinas Pariwisata Daerah Istimewa Yogyakarta. (n.d.). Laporan Jumlah Kunjungan Wisata Daerah Istimewa Yogyakarta Tahun 2020

Dzinnun, Y., Mutiarin, D., Suswanta, Nurmandi, A.: Artificial Intelligent Model: The Mapping of Social Assistance Distribution for Handling COVID-19 in DKI Jakarta. IOP Conference Series: Earth and Environmental Science 717(1) (2021). https://doi.org/10.1088/1755-1315/717/1/012045

Fauzi, E.A., Setiawan, A.: Accountability Jogya Smart Service Application in Public Sector Services in Yogyakarta 2019. SSRN Electron. J., 28–30, August 2020. https://doi.org/10.2139/ssrn.3528951

Gour, A., Aggarwal, S., Erdem, M.: Reading between the lines: analyzing online reviews by using a multi-method Web-analytics approach. Int. J. Contemp. Hosp. Manag. **33**(2), 490–512 (2021). https://doi.org/10.1108/IJCHM-07-2020-0760

Happ, É., Ivancsó-Horváth, Z.: Digital tourism is the challenge of future–a new approach to tourism. Knowl. Horizons. Econ. **10**(2), 9–16 (2018)

Kasiwi, A.N., Nurmandi, A., Mutiarin, D., Azka, M.F.: Artificial Data Management in Reaching Conditional Cash Transfer of Program Keluarga Harapan (PKH) Utilizing Simple Addictive Weighting. IOP Conference Series: Earth and Environmental Science, 717(1) (2021). https://doi.org/10.1088/1755-1315/717/1/012013

Khurramov, O.K., Boboqulov, A.A.: Digital tourism plays an important role in economic development. НАУКА-ЭФФЕКТИВНЫЙ ИНСТРУМЕНТ ПОЗНАНИЯ МИРА, 9–10 (2019)

Kuo, C.: Can We Return to Our Normal Life When the Pandemic Is under Control ? A Preliminary Study on the Influence of COVID-19 on the Tourism Characteristics of Taiwan (2021)

Kusuma, P. A., Mutiarin, D., Damanik, J.: Strategi Pemulihan Dampak Wabah Covid Pada Sektor Pariwisata Di Daerah Istimewa Yogyakarta. J. Tourism Econ. **4**(1), 47–59 (2021). https://doi.org/10.36594/jtec.v4i1.110

Mengkara, A., Saraswati, E.: Pemetaan obyek wisata berbasis web dalam rangka promosi pariwisata pulau bangka. Jurnal Bumi Indonesia 3(4), 1–9 (2014)

Michopoulou, E., Buhalis, D.: Performance measures of net-enabled hypercompetitive industries: the case of tourism. Int. J. Inf. Manage. **28**(3), 168–180 (2008). https://doi.org/10.1016/j.ijinfomgt.2007.07.003

Musaddad, A.A., Rahayu, O.Y., Pratama, E., Supraptiningsih, Wahyuni, E.: Pariwisata Berkelanjutan di Indonesia. Dinamika Administrasi: Jurnal Ilmu Administrasi Dan Manajemen **2**(1), 73–93 (2019)

Pambudi, A.S., Masteriarsa, M.F., Dwifebri, A., Wibowo, C., Amaliyah, I., Ardana, K.: Strategi pemulihan ekonomi sektor pariwisata pasca Covid-19. Majalah Media Perencana **1**(1), 1–21 (2020)

PSPPR UGM: Road Map Kota Yogyakarta Menuju Smart City. Jurnal Online Universitas Gadjah Mada 1, 1–27 (2016)

Antipova, T. (ed.): ICADS 2021. AISC, vol. 1352. Springer, Cham (2021). https://doi.org/10.1007/978-3-030-71782-7

Putra, F., Saepudin, P., Adriansyah, E., Wahyu Adrian, I.: Digital tourism: A content analysis of West Java tourism websites (2018). Putra, FKK, Saepudin, P., Adriansyah, E., Adrian, IGAW.: Digital Tourism: A Content Analysis of West Java Tourism Websites. Journal of Indonesian Tourism and Development Studies **6**(2), 73–84 (2018)

Putra, R.A.: Evaluasi usability terhadap sistem promosi pariwisata berbasis android dan web. J. Rekursif **7**(2), 170–178 (2019)

Ramdani, R., Agustiyara, Purnomo, E.P.: Big Data Analysis of COVID-19 mitigation policy in indonesia: democratic, elitist, and artificial intelligence. IOP Conference Series: Earth and Environmental Science **717**(1) (2021). https://doi.org/10.1088/1755-1315/717/1/012023

Rizky, F., Frinaldi, A., Putri, N.E.: Penerapan E-Government Dalam Promosi Pariwisata Melalui Website Oleh Dinas Kebudayaan Dan Pariwisata Kota Padang. Ranah Res. J., 507–514 (2019). https://jurnal.ranahresearch.com/index.php/R2J/article/view/85

Saito, H., Ruhanen, L.: Power in tourism stakeholder collaborations: power types and power holders. J. Hosp. Tour. Manag. **31**, 189–196 (2017). https://doi.org/10.1016/j.jhtm.2017.01.001

Saura, J.R., Reyes-Menendez, A., Palos-Sanchez, P.R.: The digital tourism business: a systematic review of essential digital marketing strategies and trends. Digital Marketing Strategies for Tourism, Hospitality, and Airline Industries, pp. 1–22 (2020)

Svirydzenka, K.: Policy Advice to Asia in the COVID-19 Era Policy Advice to Asia in. Imf.Org, 21/04, 1–8 (2021). https://www.imf.org/-/media/Files/Publications/DP/2021/English/PATACEEA.ashx

Tim Perumusan Kebijakan Ekonomi dan Keuangan Daerah. (2021). Laporan Perekonomian DIY. https://www.bi.go.id/id/publikasi/laporan/lpp/default.aspx

Vargas, A.: Covid-19 crisis: a new model of tourism governance for a new time. Worldwide Hospitality Tourism Themes **12**(6), 691–699 (2020). https://doi.org/10.1108/WHATT-07-2020-0066

Vărzaru, A.A., Bocean, C.G., Cazacu, M.: Rethinking tourism industry in pandemic covid-19 period. Sustainability (Switzerland) **13**(12) (2021). https://doi.org/10.3390/su13126956

Wang, X., Ka, I., Lai, W.: Regional Travel as an Alternative Form of Tourism during the COVID-19 Pandemic : Impacts of a Low-Risk Perception and Perceived Benefits (2021)

Zsarnoczky, M.: The digital future of the tourism & hospitality industry. Boston Hospitality Rev. **6**, 1–9 (2018)

Socialization Strategy in the Disability Vaccination Program Through Social Media in Indonesian

Elsa Septia[✉], Achmad Nurmandi, and Isnaini Muallidin

Department of Government Affairs and Administration, Jusuf Kalla School of Government,
Universitas Muhammadiyah Yogyakarta, Yogyakarta, Indonesia
elsaseptia08@gmail.com

Abstract. This study aims to determine the role of the Indonesian government in disseminating the disability vaccination program through social media, especially on Twitter. This research data is seen and analyzed in the social media accounts of @KemenkesRI, @KemensosRI, and @Kemkominfo. The method in this study uses Q-DAS (Qualitative Data Analysis Software) Nvivo 12 plus. The data obtained are tweets from the Twitter accounts of the Ministry of Social Affairs, Ministry of Health, and Ministry of Information Technology. This study found that the Ministry of Health was very intensive in disseminating information and distributing vaccination programs compared to the social media accounts of the Ministry of Social Affairs and the Ministry of Communication and Information. Dissemination of vaccination information for persons with disabilities on social media Twitter @ Ministry of Social Affairs in Vaccination Distribution information. Meanwhile, in conveying information, the Twitter social media account @Kemkominfo is more dominant in using symbols or hashtags.

Keywords: Social media · Vaccination · Disabillity · COVID-19

1 Introduction

In the last decade, governments in the world have implemented strategies to overcome the COVID-19 pandemic in various ways. The Indonesian government, in particular, has not made long or short policies in tackling COVID-19 (Covid19.go.id 2020). The COVID-19 prevention approach is currently one of the strategies carried out through vaccination programs, which have been shown to reduce the risk of being infected with the virus according to studies compared to people who have not been vaccinated, and with vaccines also reducing symptoms if infected with COVID-19 (Nasir et al. 2021). So that currently, the Government of Indonesia is conducting a campaign on the importance of vaccination in the community. One of how the government disseminates vaccination information is using social media.

The success of the vaccination program must be supported by the participation of all levels of society. The government is also obliged to pay attention to inclusion groups

C. Stephanidis et al. (Eds.): HCII 2022, CCIS 1582, pp. 430–437, 2022.
https://doi.org/10.1007/978-3-031-06391-6_54

in providing and distributing vaccinations. In (Grehenson 2021), persons with disabilities will be a priority group for vaccination programs by the government. Based on (Nurhasanah 2021) Data from the United Nations in 2020, 46% of the elderly 60 years and over are people with disabilities. Meanwhile, 1 in 5 women are likely to experience a disability in their life, and also for children, 1 in 10 children in the world are people with disabilities. In addition, according to recent research, the inclusion group category with severe mental illness and developmental or intellectual disabilities is particularly vulnerable to the ravages of COVID-19 and is essential to consider for priority vaccination (Shevzov-Zebrun and Caplan 2021). So this is a challenge for the government in providing a unique strategy related to the implementation of vaccination in the inclusion group.

The provision and implementation of a vaccination program in the inclusion group must have a particular strategy. The existence of access to a disability/inclusion-friendly location is an essential part of supporting inclusion group participation (Covid19.go.id 2021). This condition is influenced by their limitations, persons with disabilities related to accessibility. The inclusion/disability vaccination program in Indonesia is carried out responsibly by the Ministry of Health, Social Affairs, and the Ministry of Communication and Information based on the President's instructions (Rokom 2021). HK.02.01/MENKES/598/2021 related to COVID-19 vaccination services for the entire community, especially vulnerable groups such as people with disabilities and the elderly. Then in the Ministry of Social Affairs scope, affirming the commitment to provide access to COVID-19 vaccinations for all Indonesian people, especially for people with disabilities who are a vulnerable group affected by the COVID-19 pandemic (YH 2021). The Ministry of Social Affairs also cooperates with the Ministry of Health by utilizing one of the UPT (Technical Service Units) owned by the Ministry of Social Affairs (ARVI).

Providing and implementing a vaccination program for the disabled group have different challenges. Information problems related to clarity and accessibility are of substance (Grehenson 2021), and the inclusion vaccine program still relies on the help of others in obtaining information from the environment, for example, for the blind and the limited access to information they get about COVID-19 (Nurhasanah 2021). The clarity of information on vaccination programs in the disability group has different characteristics (Astutik 2021), so that the government in this condition must take a practical communication approach in increasing the vaccine program for inclusion/disability groups (Qonita 2021).

Based on several studies related to vaccination programs, the government is currently disseminating health information and vaccine programs through ICT, popular social media websites that have proven effective and practical for disseminating health information (Leonita 2018), including COVID-19 vaccination. So that information on related vaccination programs and health can be easily obtained on various forms of existing social media platforms (Purike and Baiti 2021) so that the government, in supporting the implementation of vaccination, needs to make use of social media as part of the strategy for delivering vaccination information, especially for persons with disabilities.

2 Methodology

This study will explain the function of social media as an essential part of the vaccination program. This research uses a Q-DAS (Qualitative Data Analyzing Software) approach, which uses Nvivo 12 plus for data analysis (Arrisy et al. 2021). Nvivo 12 Plus is used to analyze data and collect data from social media. Nvivo 12 plus in this study are Chart analysis, cluster analysis, and Word cloud analysis (Kurniawan et al. 2021) (Table 1).

Table 1. Data sources

No	Ministry	Social media account
1	Ministry of Social Affairs	@KemensosRI
2	Ministry of Information Technology	@Kemkominfo
3	Ministry of Health	@KemenkesRI,

The use of Nvivo as an analytical tool has five stages: (1) data retrieval, (2) data import, (3) data coding, (4) data classification, and (5) data display. The use of data in this study is from data, social media, Twitter accounts of the Ministry of Social Affairs, the Ministry of Health, and the Ministry of Informatics which have an essential role in the disability/inclusion vaccination program.

3 Literature Review

3.1 Social Media in Vaccination Promotion

Amid this increasing COVID-19 case, the availability of information about COVID-19 to prevent the spread of COVID-19 and deal with COVID-19 is very important because, with this information related to COVID-19, the public can find out what is happening. What they have to do and comply with the recommendations from the government, while the government can also carry out program innovations in providing information to the public to deal with COVID-19 jointly, because to stop the spread of COVID-19 and deal with COVID-19, cooperation and cooperation are needed. Cooperation from the government and the community (Rokom 2021) Thus, the government is also required to be more open or transparent in providing information related to the COVID-19 pandemic. Good governance must create mutual trust between the government and the community by providing information and ensuring the ease of obtaining accurate and adequate information (Wibawa 2020).

Then, in terms of using social media to help deal with COVID-19, especially in the promotion of vaccinations, social media users can easily access health-related information widely circulated on various forms of existing social media platforms (Purike and Baiti 2021). Community interaction with social media has made people more critical of media literacy. Information about the importance of COVID-19 vaccination to overcome the pandemic is undoubtedly easier to convey to the public (Azzahra 2020).

Media literacy can be understood as a series of abilities to understand, use, learn, and strategically communicate about the behavior of media users in utilizing and providing complimentary access to communicating messages (symbols) given by the mass media with their media literacy "literacy." media education and media education (Sukmana et al. 2021). This has also been explained in (Kurniawan and Jorgi Sutan 2021), which in his research said that "the vaccination program in Indonesia has received public attention, especially in the social media Twitter application. The trending of the vaccine hashtag can explain this public attentionn Indonesia, 18,1869 Twitter social media users respond to the vaccination program being held".

In addition, social media, especially in providing information and providing access to two-way communication, can be likened to a double-edged knife (Nanggala 2020), namely the socialization of vaccine promotions on social media can provide good benefits for accelerating vaccination programs, but can also be a barrier in accelerating vaccination programs. A vaccination program, namely the number of hoaxes and confusing information spread (Ma'ruf 2021). Then the use of social media and artificial intelligence (AI) to help deal with COVID-19, especially in the promotion of vaccinations, has long been present and has become a means of support; however, each of them lacks support from the Indonesian government or the community in its use due to lack of communication between stakeholders., weak community support and government policies are often not supported by local governments, even though Indonesia still has tremendous challenges in applying these technologies with good data management practices. This can be seen from the number of hoaxes created about COVID-19 to the spread of patient personal data distributed by a public official (Shafira 2020).

3.2 Disability Vaccination

The COVID-19 vaccine or SARS-CoV-2 is a crucial component to end the COVID-19 pandemic because it can reduce the spread of the virus and increase people's immunity to the disease (Latkin et al. 2021). Therefore, to break the chain of the spread of COVID-19, the Indonesian government has issued a policy regarding the administration of vaccines by all Indonesian citizens (Kesehatan 2021). However, on the other hand, this vaccination program did not run smoothly according to what was aspired; this was because many people did not want to be vaccinated against COVID-19, so that the chain of the spread of COVID-19 continued to increase (Ma'ruf 2021). In addition, the vaccination program, which aims to vaccinate all Indonesian citizens, at least means that the provision of this vaccine must be inclusive and reach all Indonesian citizens so that supporting policies or regulations are needed to help achieve the vaccination objectives. These supportive policies can at least help and pay attention to vulnerable groups, such as children, pregnant women, disability groups, and so on.

Then focusing on vulnerable groups, people with disabilities are vulnerable groups affected by COVID-19 either directly or indirectly due to infection because people with disabilities have difficulty doing physical distance, especially those who need physical assistance (Nurhasanah 2021). Then the World Health Organization (WHO) has also supported and explained that vaccination for people with disabilities, such as physical and mental disabilities, is essential because they are a very vulnerable group from COVID-19;

this group needs to be considered a priority in the program. Vaccination (Shevzov-Zebrun and Caplan 2021).

4 Discussion

Social media has an important impact on the dissemination of information. A comprehensive social media strategy in communicating with social media users allows social users to access anything on social media (Pedersen et al. 2020). In this section, we use analysis using the nVivo 12 plus Software to see the activity of the three accounts we analyzed, namely the Twitter social media account belonging to the Ministry of Social Affairs @KemensosRI, the Ministry of Communication and Information @Kemkominfo, and the Ministry of Health @KemenkesRI. Based on the results of the analysis we got from importing data in nVivo 12, the Twitter social media account belonging to the Ministry of Health is more dominantly active in disseminating information about vaccinations when compared to the Twitter social media account belonging to the Ministry of Social Affairs and the Ministry of Information and Communications (Fig. 1).

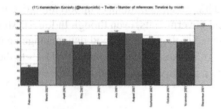

Fig. 1. Ministry of Communications and Information

Fig. 2. Ministry of Social Affairs

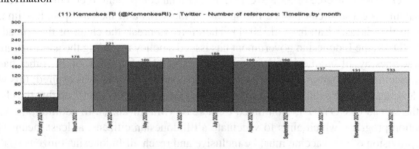

Fig. 3. Ministry of Health

In the fig diagram, it is the @KemenkesRI account belonging to the Ministry of Health's social media; in the table analyzed through the nVivo 12 Plus Software, the @KemenkesRI social media account is active in disseminating information during a very high pandemic from January to October. In April 2021, the most tweets reached around 230 tweets. In the Fig. 2 diagram, it is the @Kemensos Ministry of Social account, in that account from April 2020 to October 2021, and in September and November 2020 and May 2021, the most active tweets on Twitter. Moreover, table 3 is an account from the

Ministry of Communication and Information @Kominfo in an active intensive account during the COVID 19 pandemic from October 2020 to October 2021 and the most active in January 2021, with around 150 tweets (Fig. 3).

In the success of vaccination can be seen through several aspects, one of which is related to vaccination distribution, collaboration, use of symbols, and planning (Pedersen et al. 2020). In this case, social media accounts belonging to the Ministry of Health, Ministry of Communication and Information, and the Ministry of Social Affairs have their intensity in disseminating disability vaccination information. Like the nVivo 12 Plus Software data below (Fig. 4);

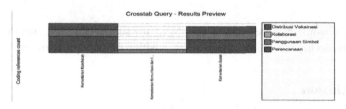

Fig. 4. Vaccination success

Based on the data obtained from the nVivo 12 Plus Software above, the Ministry of Health's social media accounts of the four indicators regarding the distribution of vaccines are the highest in disseminating disability vaccination information than other indicators. Meanwhile, the Twitter social media account belonging to the Ministry of Communication and Information in disseminating information on disability vaccinations focuses more on symbols. As well as the social media Twitter account belonging to the Ministry of Social Affairs in disseminating information more emphasis on the distribution of vaccinations. So, it can be concluded from the three social media accounts @Kemensos, @Kemkominfo, and @KemensosRI that the distribution of vaccines in disseminating information for disability is the most intensive.

In Twitter social media, researchers also analyzed using Nvivo 12 Plus with hashtags related to the spread of disability vaccination, based on word cloud analysis using word cloud analysis by showing the 17 words that appeared the most on the three Twitter social media accounts @ Ministry of Health, Kominfo, and @ Ministry of Health RI as follows (Fig. 5):

The most important word in the word cloud above is "Vaccination and Covid" The hashtag that appears the most is the word "Vaccination and Covid." On the other hand, phrases like #infosocial #covid19 #kemensos present are the most prominent hashtags in this topic. Not only that, phrases like "disability" are one of the most important words that appear in the word cloud analysis above.

In these two words, the words Vaccination and Covid are the most prominent because, at present, the COVID-19 pandemic is the government's concern, including these three Ministry accounts. The vaccination itself is one way to reduce the number of COVID-19, especially the disability group because the disability group is a priority group (Grehenson 2021). Why are the most powerful words like vaccination and covid used by the Ministry of Information and Communication, Health, and Social Affairs, because the expressions

Fig. 5. Word cloud@Kemensos, @Kemkominfo dan @KemensosRI

of these two words become subject and object, the subject is Covid, and the subject is vaccination. So the two words appear as the position of the topic narrator.

5 Conclusion

Twitter was chosen as one of the social media in conveying information to the public regarding the spread of disability vaccination. As a media platform that is frequently visited and has up-to-date news, the Twitter social media accounts at @Kemensos, @KemensosRI, and @Kominfo, it can be concluded that the Government of Indonesia uses social media as a promotional medium for information on Disability Vaccinations in particular. The government's strategy for delivering information includes four indicators: vaccine distribution, collaboration, use of symbols, and planning. Of the four indicators, the distribution of vaccines is mainly carried out by the three accounts @Kemensos, @KemensosRI, and @Kominfo in promoting the dissemination of disability vaccination information.

References

Covid19.go.id. Apakah Vaksin COVID-19 adalah Obat? covid19.go.id (2020)

Nasir, N.M., Joyosemito, I.S., Boerman, B., Ismaniah: Kebijakan Vaksinasi COVID-19 : Pendekatan Pemodelan Matematika Dinamis Pada Efektivitas Dan Dampak Vaksin Di Indonesia. J. ABDIMAS (Pengabdian Kpd. Masy. **4**(2), 191–204 (2021)

Grehenson, G.: Mensos: Penyandang Disabilitas Jadi Sasaran Prioritas Vaksinasi Covid-19. Universitas Gadjah Mada (2021)

Nurhasanah, Y.: Penyandang Disabilitas Berhak Divaksin Covid-19 (2021). http://indonesiabaik. id/infografis/penyandang-disabilitas-berhak-divaksin-covid-19

Shevzov-Zebrun, N., Caplan, A.L.: Priority vaccination for mental illness, developmental or intellectual disability. J. Med. Ethics 1–2 (2021). https://doi.org/10.1136/medethics-2021-107247

Covid19.go.id. Keterbukaan dan Kesetaraan Akses Vaksinasi Bagi Penyandang Disabilitas. covid19.go.id (2021)

Rokom: Cakupan Vaksinasi Dosis Pertama Untuk Penyandang Disabilitas di Jawa-Bali Hampir 100%. sehatnegeriku.kemkes.go.id (2021)

YH, A.: Sukseskan Program Vaksinasi Nasional, Penerima Manfaat Balai 'Melati' Ikut Divaksinasi. Kementerian Sosial Repbublik Indonesia (2021)

Astutik, Y.: Penyandang Disabilitas Punya Kesetaraan Akses di Vaksin Covid. CNBC Indonesia (2021)

Qonita, N.A.: Pentingnya Informasi COVID-19 dan Vaksin Bagi Penyandang Disabilitas. Humas Dit. Penyandang Disabilitas Kementerian Sosial (2021)

Leonita, E.N.: Peran Media Sosial dalam Upaya Promosi Kesehatan. urnal Inov. Vokasional dan Teknol. **18**(2), 25–34 (2018)

Purike, E., Baiti, A.: Informasi Vaksin Di Media Sosial Dan Program Vaksin Covid-19: Langkah Apa Yang Dapat Dilakukan Oleh Pemerintah Republik Indonesia? Cross-border **4**(2), 58–69 (2021). http://journal.iaisambas.ac.id/index.php/Cross-Border/article/view/635

Sutan, A.J., Nurmandi, A., Mutiarin, D., Salahudin, S.: Using social media as tools of social movement and social protest in omnibus law of job creation bill policy-making process in Indonesia. In: Antipova, T. (eds.) ICADS 2021. AISC, vol. 1352, pp 261–274. Springer, Cham (2021). https://doi.org/10.1007/978-3-030-71782-7_24

Kurniawan, D., Nurmandi, A., Salahudin, Mutiarin, D., Suswanta: analysis of the anti-corruption movement through Twitter social media: a case study of Indonesia. In: Antipova, T. (eds.) ICADS 2021. AISC, vol. 1352, pp. 298–308. Springer, Cham (2021). https://doi.org/10.1007/ 978-3-030-71782-7_27

Wibawa, K.C.S.: Peranan Komisi Informasi Dalam Mengawal Keterbukaan Informasi Publik di Masa Kedaruratan Kesehatan (Pendemi) COVID – 19. Adminitrative Law Gov. (2020). https:// doi.org/10.14710/alj.v3i3.481%20%20-%20%20493

Azzahra, R.: Peran Media dalam Upaya Edukasi Masyarakat Soal Vaksinasi. radiordk (2020)

Sukmana, R.A., Iyansyah, M.I., Wijaya, B.A., Kurniawati, M.F.: Implementasi Strategi Komunikasi Kesehatan dalam Meyakinkan Masyarakat untuk Pelaksanaan Vaksinasi COVID-19 di Kabupaten Barito Kuala. J. Sains Sosio Hum. **5**(1), 409–419 (2021). https://online-journal.unja. ac.id/JSSH/article/view/13933

Kurniawan, D., Jorgi Sutan, A.: Penggunaan Sosial Media Dalam Menyebarkan Program Vaksinasi Covid-19 Di Indonesia. Kebijak. Publik **12**(1), 27–34 (2021)

Nanggala, A.: Peran Generasi Muda Dalam Era New Normal. Widya Wacana J. Ilm. (2020). https://doi.org/10.33061/j.w.wacana.v%25vi%25i.3827

Ma'ruf, S.A.: Upaya Pemenuhan Vaksin COVID-19 untuk Memutus Rantai Penyebaran COVID-19. OSF Preprints (2021)

Shafira, I.: Penggunaan Teknologi Baru (Big Data, Artificial Intelligence, Cloud dan Internet of Things) Sebagai Upaya Mitigasi Pendemi COVID-19 : Kontemplaso Pengaplikasin Kebijakan Berbasis Teknologi Baru di Indonesia. Univ. Gadjah Mada (2020)

Latkin, C.A., Dayton, L., Yi, G., Konstantopoulos, A., Boodram, B.: Trust in a COVID-19 vaccine in the U.S.: a social-ecological perspective. Soc. Sci. Med. **270**, 113684 (2021). https://doi.org/ 10.1016/j.socscimed.2021.113684

Kesehatan, D.: Efektivitas Vaksinasi Dalam Pemutusan Rantai Penularan Covid-19. dinkes.bulelengkab.go.id (2021)

Pedersen, E.A., Loft, L.H., Jacobsen, S.U., Søborg, B., Bigaard, J.: Strategic health communication on social media: insights from a Danish social media campaign to address HPV vaccination hesitancy. Vaccine **38**(31), 4909–4915 (2020). https://doi.org/10.1016/j.vaccine.2020.05.06

Comparison of Indonesian and India Government Vaccination Policy Campaigns via Twitter Social Media

Anang Setiawan[1]([⊠]), Achmad Nurmandi[1], and Herdin Arie Saputra[2]

[1] Program Studi Doktor Politik Islam-Ilmu Politik, Program Pascasarjana,
Universitas Muhammadiyah Yogyakarta, Yogyakarta, Indonesia
`Ananggsetiawan2016@gmail.com`
[2] Program Studi Ilmu Pemerintahan, Universitas Muhammadiyah Semarang, Semarang,
Indonesia

Abstract. The covid-19 pandemic that attacks the whole world cannot be separated from Indonesia and India, there are many cases of covid in these two countries, this must be anticipated in terms of giving vaccines, of course Indonesia and India must have quite difficult challenges in the vaccination program, this requires a Policy Campaign Vaccination via Twitter Social Media, This study aims to analyze and determine the use of Twitter social media as a medium for the Indonesian and Indian Government Policy Campaigns in providing information to optimize vaccination strategies in relation to the start of the campaign, vaccination coverage, vaccination schedule, vaccination rate, and vaccine efficiency in Indonesia. each country. The research method combines qualitative analysis with secondary data collected from the Indonesian government's social media accounts used are @kemenkesri and @bnpb_indonesia while the Indian government twitter accounts are @mohfw_india and @pib_india. To visualize the data analysis, Nvivo12 plus software was used, specifically the Twitter Sociogram data collection tool. Based on these findings, the Indonesian and Indian governments were successful in their Vaccination Policy Campaign through Twitter Social Media.

Keywords: Vaccination · Policy · Campaigns · Indonesia · India

1 Introduction

The COVID-19 epidemic was declared a public health emergency of international concern by the World Health Organization in the last week of March 2020 (Schumacher et al. 2021). This disease that originated in China in December 2019 has caused havoc around the world, including Indonesia and India (Williams et al. 2021). This pandemic has caused more than 80,000 deaths with 3 million recoveries. The strict lockdown of the country for two months, the immediate isolation of infected cases and app-based tracking of infected people are some of the proactive steps taken by the authorities (Boey et al. 2020). For a better understanding of the evolution of COVID-19 in the world, a study of the evolution and growth of cases in Indonesia and India is inevitable (Cardenas 2021).

C. Stephanidis et al. (Eds.): HCII 2022, CCIS 1582, pp. 438–447, 2022.
https://doi.org/10.1007/978-3-031-06391-6_55

In January 2021, WHO has announced that a COVID-19 vaccine has been granted an emergency distribution permit (Weintraub et al. 2021).

Widespread uptake of the SARS-CoV-2 vaccine will be critical for the resolution of the COVID-19 pandemic (Shimizu et al. 2021). The government has the potential to influence vaccine sentiment and uptake through vaccine-related communications with the public (Adil Mahmoud Yousif et al. 2021). The vaccination movement is currently on the rise, spreading information online about vaccine safety and causing a decline in vaccination rates worldwide (Choudhary et al. 2021). In this period of history, it is critical to understand the reasons for vaccine hesitancy, and find effective strategies to dismantle the anti-vaccination rhetoric of proponents (Mathieu et al. 2021). Indonesia and India have similarities in the number of transmission of Covid-19 cases (Yoak et al. 2021). It is interesting to see how the vaccination targets of the two countries are supported by strategic policies.

Indonesia with a population of 272,229,372 people certainly has difficulties in implementing the vaccination program, plus the number of vaccines that are obtained is not much. Indonesia, which recorded the number of daily cases of Corona virus infection exceeding 40 thousand cases, daily cases of covid 19 in Indonesia experienced a decrease in active cases of Covid-19 in Indonesia reaching 4.21 million. This is also supported by the vaccination program in Indonesia which is quite high until September 27, 2021. Total Vaccination Dose 1 reached 87,742,907 doses (42.13%) and Vaccination Dose 2 reached 49,198,111 doses (23.62%) of the vaccination target of 208,265,720 people (Fig. 1).

Fig. 1. Of Indonesia's covid-19 vaccination data Source: https://vaccines.kemkes.go.id/#/vaccines

The same is true for India with a population of 1,383,440,000 people. Free vaccination against COVID-19 began in India on January 16, 2021, and the government is urging all its citizens to be immunized, in what is expected to be the largest vaccination program in the world. Of the eight COVID-19 vaccines currently in various stages of clinical trials in India, four were developed in the country. India's drug regulator has approved limited emergency use of Covishield (the name used in India for the Oxford-AstraZeneca vaccine) and Covaxin, a homemade vaccine manufactured by Bharat Biotech (Fig. 2).

Hoaxes related to the covid 19 vaccine are the main things experienced by the government in carrying out vaccination policies, related to the safety and efficacy of the vaccine (Liu et al. 2021). Vaccines are still relatively new and public doubts about the

Fig. 2. India's covid-19 vaccination data Source: https://www.mygov.in/covid-19

politicization that arose during the Vaccine manufacturing process were also raised. Many myths and hoaxes have circulated in the community about the COVID-19 Vaccine which is also a factor that raises public doubts about undergoing vaccination (Yoak et al. 2021).

This study aims to analyze and determine the use of social media Twitter as a medium for the Indonesian and Indian Government Policy Campaigns in providing information to optimize vaccination strategies in relation to the start of the campaign, vaccination coverage, vaccination schedule, vaccination rate, and vaccine efficiency in their respective countries.

2 Literature Review

2.1 Policy Campaigns

A public communication campaign can be defined as an attempt aimed at informing or influencing behavior in a large audience over a certain period of time using an organized set of communication activities and displaying a series of messages mediated in various channels generally to produce non-commercial benefits for individuals and society (Shimizu et al. 2021). Campaigning as a process is universal across topics and places, making systematic use of the frameworks and fundamental strategic principles developed over the last half century. The campaign designer conducts a situation analysis and sets goals that lead to the development of a coherent set of strategies and implements the campaign by creating persuasive information and messages that are disseminated through traditional mass media, new technologies, and interpersonal networks. Specific central theory of Policy Campaigns that can be applied to various aspects of public communication strategy, process, and implementation of campaigns (Ren et al. 2020).

The presence of social media cannot be separated from the study of new media. In general, new media theory assesses a change in access to technology that is seen from the limited way of community adoption, and slowly turns into a mass adoption pattern. The relationship of new media with social media can also be traced in studies related to communication networks (Choudhary et al. 2021). Communication networks are considered as intermediaries in a community that aims to maximize every information flow. The use of social media networks is also considered to have an impact on the

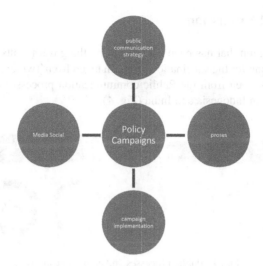

Fig. 3. Concept of policy campaigns

democratization process in many countries including Indonesia. This is largely based on the development of communication and information technology which is considered to facilitate interaction between individuals and groups. The use of social media, especially Twitter in providing education and policy campaigns to the people of Indonesia or India, is the key to the success of vaccination policies in each country.

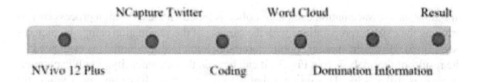

3   Research Methods

Penelitian ini menggunakan pendekatan kuatitatif dengan sumber data berasal dari studi dokumen dan media sosial Twitter Pemerintah Indonesia dan India. Akun media social pemerintah indinesia yang digunakan adalah @kemenkesri dan @bnpb_indonesia sedanykan akun twitter pemerintah india adalah @mohfw_india dan @pib_india. Data dikumpulkan dari tanggal 1 januari 2021 hingga 30 september 2021. Data dikumpulkan menggunakan fitur Ncapture for Nvivo. Analisis penelitian dilakukan dengan pengkodean data, analisis konten dan visualisasi data menggunakan Software analytics Nvivo 12 Plus.

4 Results and Discussion

Public communication that has been carried out by the governments of Indonesia and India in campaigning for the vaccination program taken from Twitter has obtained quite satisfactory results, seen from the Public communication processes and strategies for vaccination policy in Indonesia and India (Fig. 4).

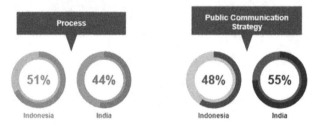

Fig. 4. Public processes and communications

Based on the picture above, it shows that the public communication strategy in Indonesia has an intensity of 48%, and the vaccination campaign process is 51%. Meanwhile, in India, it shows that public communication strategies in social media Twitter are 55%, and the vaccination campaign process is 44%.

5 Public Processes and Communications in Indonesia and India

In Indonesia, the vaccination campaign policy is based on the campaign process by prioritizing the existing preparations with the support of the vaccination campaign pictures (see Fig. 5). However, strategic public communication is still minimal, as evidenced by the results of the analysis (see Fig. 3), it can be seen that the intensity of public communication is still at 48%. This initiates that with the social media campaign, Twitter still does not have room for all circles of society. Only the majority of those who can access Twitter social media are young, because there are still many who have not empowered Twitter social media technology to capture information provided by the government. This lack of public communication creates information inequality and is vulnerable to the presence of false information (hoax).

The importance of the process and communication of vaccine campaigns carried out in the form of photos in supporting changes in society.

This public communication is also emphasized at every location and place outside the Twitter social media, where it can disseminate vaccine campaigns and more in the implementation process. As has been done by the government, the social implication is that every spectator who will enter the basketball venue, must have been vaccinated, and show the vaccine result letter and identity card (KTP) to the officer. Other social media, such as Instagram are also often used in disseminating information. The Instagram account @kemluRi has not been used adequately to convey information regarding the latest achievements of the Ministry of Foreign Affairs of the Republic of Indonesia.

Fig. 5. Vaccination campaign

In addition, there is no two-way communication on social media between institutions and the public. As a result, the two-symmetric communication mechanism has been abandoned (Maulida 2021). Dissemination of information by public communication, in this study by strengthening the vaccination policy there is also a continuous two-way communication (see Fig. 7). Two-way communication is very important to get and know, because in this communication stakeholders are obliged to know what kind of response is given by the community related to the implementation of the vaccination policy.

Meanwhile in India, policy campaigns based on public communication strategies in social media Twitter are more intense. The results of the analysis (see Fig. 4) show that the Indian government is very focused on public communication strategies to support the vaccination policy campaign. Of the three Twitter social media accounts, namely the ministry of health, the ministry of communication, the ministry of electronics and information technology, twitter is very empowering social media as public communication for vaccination policy campaigns. Governments and health authorities should consider the need for public information when trying to increase public engagement. This can lead to increased public awareness of disease outbreaks (Alhassan and AlDossary 2021). The preparation process of the Indian government also has several strategies in providing vaccination campaigns, by distributing posters and pictures (see Fig. 6) that can attract the attention of the Twitter social media community.

The process and public communication strategy as a public understanding of the importance of information that is highly required, in this case the vaccination policy to minimize the spread of Covid-19. The implication is that in Indonesia and India, there are

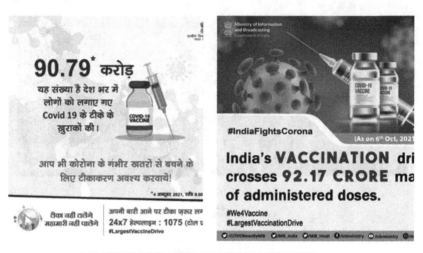

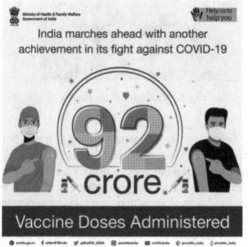

Fig. 6. Vaccination campaign in India

differences based on analytical values, but they have similarities in minimizing the spread of Covid-19 as a non-natural disaster. As an effort to build a common understanding of various matters relating to the changes made by the two countries to a very serious concern for the wider community. The understanding gained by the Twitter community about the existence of an official government account to campaign for policies indicates a change for the better for the future situation, by maximizing the long term. And it can slowly change every individual's attitude, values, and perspective, and show support from the government.

Communicator and communicant in social media twitter of the Ministry of Health of the Republic of Indonesia and the Ministry of Health of India.

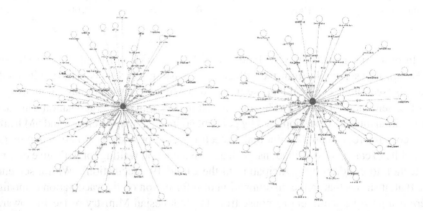

Fig. 7. Two-way communication from the Ministry of Health of the Republic of Indonesia and the Ministry of Health of India

Two-way communication carried out by the Ministry of Health of the Republic of Indonesia and the Ministry of Health of India is very varied and always provides the appropriate, two-way communication theory can be expected. This supports some information dissemination, so that the public can understand, accept, and have a broad view in the long term to understand the information provided by the government in each country. But not only that, two-way communication can interact with other Twitter social media account users, between individuals who carefully use the Twitter platform, and can share some information about Covid-19.

Two-way communication carried out by the Ministry of Health of the Republic of Indonesia with several Twitter accounts. This of course really helps in disseminating information and can campaign for vaccination policies, so that they can be massively spread throughout the country. A successful communication strategy is a two-way street that begins with a clear message delivered through the right media, adapted for a variety of audiences, and shared by trusted individuals. Ultimately, long-term success depends on building and maintaining public trust. Through greater and sustained community interaction, government policymakers can garner broad public support and participation. Engagement events should cover a wide variety of community groups (Hyland-Wood et al. 2021). Thus, they can interact and exchange information with others. In this approach, perceived mental content can be examined to characterize phenomenological experiences and cognitive capacities (Konkoly and Paller 2020).

From the dissemination of this information, it is inseparable from what is called sentiment towards the public, which is carried out by the official twitter accounts of the Ministry of Health of the Republic of Indonesia and the Ministry of Health of India.

Table 1. Sentiment of the Ministry of Health of Indonesia and India

	Positive	Negative	**Total**
Indonesia	66.67%	33.33%	100%
India	100%	0%	100%

Information carried out by the Indonesian Ministry of Health and the Indian Ministry of Health is inseparable from the influence of existing sentiments. The results of the analysis (see Table 1) reveal that the Indonesian Ministry of Health has an intensity of positive sentiment of 66.67%. This means that in disseminating "vaccination campaign information must also be supported by going hand in hand with 3T efforts and 5M health protocols, in order to provide optimal protection". And provide information that invites the public to carry out vaccinations, such as "what are you waiting for, let's give optimal protection to children by participating in the Covid-19 vaccination". With a sentence like that, it shows that in the dissemination of information on the vaccination campaign there is a positive sentiment response from the Indonesian Ministry of Health towards the process of running the vaccination campaign in Indonesia.

However, not only the positive response given by the Indonesian Ministry of Health. There is also a negative response given, it gives a total intensity of 33.33%. The negative sentiment given is "family support to involve parents in Covid-19 vaccination activities, it is very important so that the elderly as the most vulnerable group can be protected from the potential transmission of Covid-19". The creation of information marked with positive sentiment is influenced by good and good condition factors, as well as actors (admins) who have distinctive communication patterns. The most successful actors demonstrate specific communication patterns, setting the basis for the theoretical foundation of communication competence (Wen et al. 2020). A post's sentiment is determined by the number of "Love" and "Angry" reactions it receives (Eberl et al. 2020). In contrast to the information provided by the Indian Ministry of Health, there is positive sentiment in the dissemination of vaccination information in 2021. This supports the communication pattern and the condition of the perpetrators (admins) on the twitter account of the Indian Ministry of Health.

6 Conclusion

Governments of Indonesia and India in using. Social media twitter in campaigning for vaccination programs is successful, in indicators of strategic public communication, processes, implementations supported by social media, which can be seen from the content that is made quite interesting and makes people interested in vaccinating, two-way communication is very important to get as well as This is known, because in this communication, stakeholders are obliged to know what kind of response is given by the community regarding the implementation of the vaccination policy.

References

Yousif, N.A.M., et al.: The impact of COVID-19 vaccination campaigns accounting for antibody-dependent enhancement. PloS One 16(4), e0245417 (2021). https://doi.org/10.1371/journal.pone.0245417

Alhassan, F.M., AlDossary, S.A.: The saudi ministry of health's twitter communication strategies and public engagement during the COVID-19 pandemic: content analysis study. JMIR Public Health Surveill. 7(7), 1–14 (2021). https://doi.org/10.2196/27942

Boey, L., Roelants, M., Vandermeulen, C.: Increased vaccine uptake and less perceived barriers toward vaccination in long-term care facilities that use multi-intervention manual for influenza campaigns. Hum. Vaccin. Immunother. 00(00), 1–8 (2020). https://doi.org/10.1080/21645515.2020.1788327

Cardenas, N.C.: 'Europe and United States vaccine hesitancy': leveraging strategic policy for 'Infodemic' on COVID-19 vaccines. J. Public Health 1–2 (2021). https://doi.org/10.1093/pubmed/fdab228

Choudhary, M., Solomon, R., Awale, J., Dey, R., Singh, J.P., Weiss, W.: Effectiveness of a community-level social mobilization intervention in achieving the outcomes of polio vaccination campaigns during the post-polio-endemic period: evidence from CORE Group polio project in Uttar Pradesh, India. BMC Public Health 21(1), 1–14 (2021). https://doi.org/10.1186/s12889-021-11425-0

Liu, R., Zhang, Y., Nicholas, S., Leng, A., Maitland, E., Wang, J.: COVID-19 vaccination willingness among Chinese adults under the free vaccination policy. Vaccines 9(3), 1 (2021). https://doi.org/10.3390/vaccines9030292

Mathieu, E., et al.: A global database of COVID-19 vaccinations. Nat. Hum. Behav. 5(7), 947–953 (2021). https://doi.org/10.1038/s41562-021-01122-8

Maulida, R.A.: Public communication strategies of the ministry of foreign affair of republic Indonesia on Instagram account @ kemlu _ri. Int. J. Multicultural Multireligious Understanding 98–107 (2021). https://doi.org/10.18415/ijmmu.v8i6.2669

Ren, X., et al.: Knowledge, attitudes, and behaviors (KAB) of influenza vaccination in China: a cross-sectional study in 2017/2018. Vaccines 8(1), 1–13 (2020). https://doi.org/10.3390/vaccines8010007

Schumacher, S., Salmanton-García, J., Cornely, O.A., Mellinghoff, S.C.: Increasing influenza vaccination coverage in healthcare workers: a review on campaign strategies and their effect. Infection 49(3), 387–399 (2020). https://doi.org/10.1007/s15010-020-01555-9

Shimizu, K., Teshima, A., Mase, H.: Measles and rubella during covid-19 pandemic: future challenges in Japan. Int. J. Environ. Res. Public Health 18(1), 1–11 (2021). https://doi.org/10.3390/ijerph18010009

Weintraub, R.L., Subramanian, L., Karlage, A., Ahmad, I., Rosenberg, J.: Covid-19 vaccine to vaccination: why leaders must invest in delivery strategies now. Health Aff. 40(1), 33–41 (2021). https://doi.org/10.1377/hlthaff.2020.01523

Williams, V., Edem, B., Calnan, M., Otwombe, K., Okeahalam, C.: Considerations for establishing successful coronavirus disease vaccination programs in Africa. Emerg. Infect. Dis. 27(8), 2009–2016 (2021). https://doi.org/10.3201/eid2708.203870

Yoak, A.J., et al.: Barriers and opportunities for canine rabies vaccination campaigns in Addis Ababa, Ethiopia. Prev. Vet. Med. 187, 105256 (2021). https://doi.org/10.1016/j.prevetmed.2020.105256

Use of the "BARUGA SULSEL" Application to Increasing Public Participation and Services in South Sulawesi, Indonesia

Umi Umairah Suhardi[1]([✉]), Achmad Nurmandi[2], and Isnaini Muallidin[1]

[1] Government Affairs and Administration, Jusuf Kalla School of Government, University of Muhammadiyah Yogyakarta, Yogyakarta, Indonesia
umyumayrahh03@gmail.com
[2] Master Government Affairs and Administration, University of Muhammadiyah Yogyakarta, Yogyakarta, Indonesia
nurmandi_achmad@umy.ac.id

Abstract. This study aims to describe the Baruga Sulsel application service system as a forum for the public to submit complaints and aspirations online to the government. The research method used is qualitative with descriptive data analysis techniques, researchers use effectiveness theory with effectiveness measurement according to Duncan which consists of 3 aspects, namely goal achievement, integration, and adaptation. The results obtained from the research are the Baruga Sulsel application has been effective in serving public services in South Sulawesi Province. This can be seen from the 2 objectives set out in the formation of the South Sulawesi Baruga application, namely facilitating public aspirations and complaints and improving the quality of public services. Both have been realized and run well, but the completion period which takes days has resulted in the community not actively participating through applications and application socialization efforts are still lacking considering the community as the main target of public services. The application of the Baruga Sulsel application is managed and developed by the Department of Communication, Informatics, Statistics and Encoding, South Sulawesi Province as a provider of applications and reports will also be integrated with LAPOR! (People's Online Aspirations and Complaints Service) which applies nationally, so that the follow-up of public complaints in a system disposition to resolve, based on the authority of the district, city, province, and relevant ministries.

Keywords: E-Government · Public service · Government to citizent · Baruga Sulsel

1 Introduction

The presence of technology and the development of information have changed the way of interaction between government and society [1]. Technology plays an important role in the Indonesian government's digital transformation. Currently, Information Technology

(IT) has developed significantly in various fields not only closely related to Information Technology or Information Systems but also penetrated into various fields including government policy and business [2]. According to [3] that the use of information and communication technology affects the organization's public sector to shift organizational culture and activities that were previously manual or traditional then turn into technology-based organizational activities.

The implications for the fast-paced development of modern society and coupled with demands for the dynamics of the government order provide a new concept of the paradigm of governance called Good Governance so that the roles and functions of conventional government institutions transition to a modern orientation [4]. In the public sector, the use of ICT is interpreted as Electronic Government (E-Government) which in practice the government uses digital media and sophisticated terminologies such as mobile government, flexible government, and smart government [5]. The dimensions of smart governance related to participation include participation in decision-making, public and community services, and transparency in government [6]. With these three things, it allows the community and stakeholders to be integrated into the government process and modification based on feedback from the community [7]. For effective citizen participation in planning and decision-making processes, various social sites, public forums and online platforms [8] can be used.

The existence of ICT forces the government to be able to manage and produce innovations that are then implemented in providing public services [9]. [10] seeing that innovation has very broad benefits for government institutions including having advantages over other policies (Relative Advantage), Being able to follow the flow of people's desires (Compartbillty), Easy to understand (Complexity), can be tested before being implemented by the community (Triabilty), and can be developed to improve the performance of the innovation (Observability). Seeing the growth of internet users in the people of South Sulawesi Province, the government looks to where the needs of the community are in this digital era. For this reason, the government takes advantage of opportunities by improving public services based on technological innovation in increasing service satisfaction. By applying technology in public service complaints based on *e-government*, one form of *E-Government* made by the regional government of South Sulawesi Province is the Baruga Sulsel, the application was created to provide a forum for the community to submit complaints and aspirations that developed in the community. The service on the Baruga Sulsel application is the commitment of the South Sulawesi Provincial Government to continue to improve the quality of public services that are getting better quickly, precisely, and completely. The Baruga Sulsel application is expected to be able to create an effective public complaint service that is easily accessible to the public.

2 Literature Review

2.1 Smart City and Smart Governance

The concept of a smart city is to create sustainable urban growth and have a good quality of life [11]. [12] simply defines smart governance as "the capacity to use intelligent and adaptive actions and activities to maintain and make decisions about things." From this definition, it is clear that smart governance is about: (a) efficiency in decision-making, (b) effective resource management, (c) promoting intelligent society, (d) effective use of information and technology, (e) advancing the needs of society. citizens, (f) accountability and transparency, and (g) fostering a culture of good governance and effective leadership. The existence of actors involved in Smart Governance will create harmony in achieving sustainable development in the effort to implement smart cities [13]. [14], stated that a city is considered smart if investments in human resources, social capital, and infrastructure of traditional and modern communication systems are able to increase sustainable economic growth and quality of life by resource management. Public assessment of the response and resolution of the problems submitted is an important part of the internal cooperation carried out by the government with the support of ICT [15].

2.2 The Use of E-Government for Intelligent Service Design

E-government is a synonym for internet government, digital government, connected government, and online government. E-government is the use of ICT by government agencies, such as the internet, wide area networks, and mobile computing, which can be leveraged to improve relations between government agencies and other government agencies, businesses, and citizens [16]. The use of technology is to improve organizational performance [13]; [17]. The expansion of digital transformation, digitization of information, and the development of big data is known as artificial intelligence. Public sector organizations are particularly involved in policy provision and public services by leveraging the capabilities of artificial intelligence [18]. In order to design and develop intelligent services, city planners and administrators must seek the views and needs of citizens [19] to resolve local priorities and citizens' needs. New policies and regulations are needed to facilitate smart services in an easy way in smart cities [20] overview of smart city services and application areas).

3 Methods

This research conducted a study on the use of the "BARUGA SULSEL" application in increasing public participation and services in South Sulawesi Province. This study uses a qualitative approach with descriptive analysis. In this study, there are three things the author did to explore the use of the Baruga Application as a public complaint service, namely by looking at the effectiveness of the use of the Baruga South Sulawesi application, using the effectiveness theory according to Duncan, in this case, the achievement of goals, integrity, and adaptation. library research data collection, where the author collects various data from news, books, official websites, journals, official reports, articles, and internet sources. From the various sources above, it is hoped that it can help the author conduct research on the steps and analysis of the research object. The data was obtained from exploring the Baruga Sulsel application through a *smartphone*.

4   Results

4.1   Application Baruga SulSel

Baruga application is a public service application for the South Sulawesi Provincial Government. The application was made to accommodate every aspiration and public procurement. This application is present in the process of supporting the Smart Government concept in providing public services that can be accessed quickly and easily. The Government to Citizens concept through the Baruga Sulsel application is used by the South Sulawesi provincial government to make it easier to interact with the community so that the community can supervise the government in making policies and in improving policies that have been provided by the government. The application of the Baruga Sulsel application by the South Sulawesi Provincial government has been implemented since October 2018 until now (Fig. 1).

Fig. 1. The South Sulawesi Baruga Application

In the picture above it can be seen that in submitting a complaint there are several steps that must be taken, namely:

1. The public as complainants must "register" first by entering their Email, Full Name, Address, and lastly Password.
2. Upload the e-KTP document, by taking a selfie picture holding the e-KTP with the e-KTP note that it can be read and the whole face is visible.
3. The public submits their complaint by filling out the existing complaint form, namely the category, subject, and complaint.

4.2   The Effectiveness of the Application Baruga SulSel

To measure effectiveness in the implementation of the program can be seen from 3 aspects: others as follows:

1. Achieving goals

In the findings in the field, it was found that the purpose of the Baruga Sulsel application was in accordance with the provisions described above, namely facilitating public aspirations and complaints, this was evidenced by the number of public complaints that had been entered in the South Sulawesi Baruga application and were disposed of to the relevant service for handling and resolving of reported problems. All of this can be seen on the official website of Baruga Sulsel, which provides all reports that have been submitted, those that have been disposed of, followed up, and also those that have not been followed up (Fig. 2).

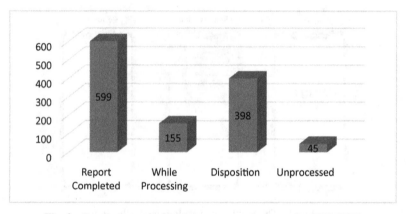

Fig. 2. Graph of new application report management for 2018–2019

From the information above, it can be seen that the reports that came in from the start of the South Sulawesi Baruga Application launched in October 2018 until the end of 2019 were divided into 4 groups, namely reports completed (599 reports), while being processed (155 reports), disposition (398 reports) reports), and have not been processed (45 reports). Unprocessed reports are reports that are considered unclear and repeated reports or reports that have been previously reported so that they cannot be processed further. A disposition report is a report that has been verified by the admin so that it can be processed further. Interim reports in the process are reports that have been verified by the admin, but there is still a lack of evidence from the complainant so that it requires re-confirmation to the reporter. The most complaints are related to road infrastructure, around 43%. In addition, there are reforms in the bureaucracy and governance of around 37% and the rest are education and health issues. Every incoming report will go through a verification process. If the report is deemed clear, it will be directly disposed of, which means the report is forwarded by the admin to the relevant agency through the liaison officer for follow-up (Fig. 3).

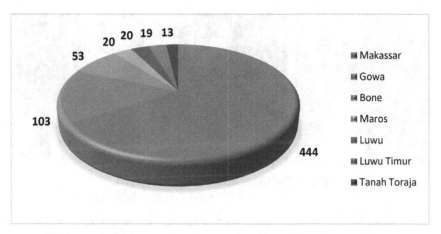

Fig. 3. Aspirations and complaints report of South Sulawesi Province 2020

In the diagram above, it can be seen that the incoming reports in 2020 were 672 reports, for the districts/cities that received the most aspirations and complaints were Makassar City with 444 aspirations or complaints, then Gowa 103 complaints, Bone 53 complaints, Maros 20 complaints, Luwu 20 complaints, East Luwu 19 complaints and Tana Toraja 13 complaints. Improving the quality of public services in South Sulawesi Province can improve thanks to the Baruga Sulsel application and that the community response also feels helped regarding the availability of the South Sulawesi Baruga application as a means of channeling aspirations and complaints from the community to the government, it is based on access which is considered quite easy and fast to use.. Then the application for the complaint of Baruga Sulsel is also integrated with the Application Lapor Sp4m complaint application which is valid nationally, so that the follow-up of public complaints in a system disposition to resolve, based on the authority of the district, city, province, and relevant ministries.

The Baruga Sulsel application can also be used to make it easier for the community or government to find out and solve problems that exist and are felt by the community and can make it easier for the community to express their aspirations directly to the government. Where the problems and aspirations submitted by the community can certainly be justified, because as soon as there are reports or aspirations that come in, the relevant agency will immediately respond to it, and be quick to follow up on the report, besides that the agency can provide concrete evidence of the follow-up to the report. Thus, this certainly can improve the performance of the government and can be a reference for evaluation for the government in terms of development and the provision of public services. An example of a follow-up report to the Drainage Task Force regarding drainage in Monginsidi that is filled with waste is shown in the following Fig. 4.

From the picture above, it can be seen that reports from the public have been followed up by the relevant agencies, because there is real evidence in the form of photos before being followed up and after being followed up, and also for the reporter and other people to quickly find out that the report has actually been followed up. This is indicated by the achievement of the objectives of the report. Based on the results of the research, the

Fig. 4. The follow-up to the complaint report.

intended target here is the community itself as the user and right-holder in channeling aspirations and complaints. Regarding the implementation of targets, the government is more specifically targeting people who are 'technology literate' or understand how to operate gadgets or gadgets.

5 Integration

Integration is a measurement of the level of ability of an organization to carry out activities from an agreed work program and conduct socialization with other parties. Integration consists of indicators, namely socialization procedures and processes. Socialization is also assessed from the extent to which the government provides services and counseling to the community [21]. In carrying out complaints services in Baruga Sulsel, the community must go through several stages that have been regulated according to service procedures that have been created and regulated in the Baruga Sulsel application according to the following image (Fig. 5):

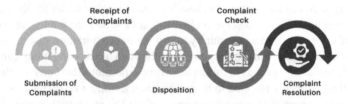

Fig. 5. Stages of settlement of public complaints

2. Adaptation

In developing countries, lack of resources, accountability, and government structures are some of the main causes of public service failure. Adaptation in this study consists of indicators, namely capacity building, and infrastructure. Based on the results of the research, the Office of Communication, Information, Statistics and Encoding of

South Sulawesi Province has made efforts in order to improve the capacity of Human Resources and existing infrastructure in the Office of Communication, Information and Statistics of South Sulawesi Province, namely by implementing 6 main programs and 2 support programs, as well as 24 activities, both on mandatory affairs in the field of communication and informatics as well as on elective matters. The 6 main programs compiled by the Office of Communication, Informatics, Statistics and Encoding, South Sulawesi Province are as follows:

1. Development of communication, information, and mass media
2. Facilitating the improvement of human resources in the field of communication and information
3. Information and Mass Media Cooperation
4. Development of Regional Data/information/statistics
5. Information Data Development
6. Improving the Quality of Information Services

Based on research results, government agencies have achieved performance targets and targets by prioritizing budget allocations for priority programs, as well as implementing efficiency through increasing human resources, improving facilities and infrastructure, as well as taking anticipatory steps and solutions to various problems in quality improvement service.

6 Conclusion

From the data that has been presented in the discussion. Researchers concluded that the Baruga Sulsel application has been effective in serving public services in South Sulawesi Province. This can be seen from the 2 goals set in the formation of the South Sulawesi Baruga application, namely facilitating public aspirations and complaints and improving the quality of public services. Both have been realized and run well, but the completion period which takes days has resulted in the community not actively participating through applications, and application socialization efforts are still lacking considering the community as the main target of public services.

References

1. Ghosh Roy, S., Upadhyay, P.: Does e-readiness of citizens ensure better adoption of government's digital initiatives? A case based study. J. Enterp. Inf. Manag. 30(1), 65–81 (2017). https://doi.org/10.1108/JEIM-01-2016-0001
2. Susanto, A., Bahaweres, R.B.: Preliminary research on e-government development overview: an assessment on e-Government capabilities in Indonesia. In: 2013 International Conference of Information and Communication Technology, ICoICT 2013, pp. 444–447 (2013). https://doi.org/10.1109/ICoICT.2013.6574617
3. Alghamdi, I.A., Goodwin, R., Rampersad, G.: Ready, set, govern: readiness of Saudi Arabian organizations for e-Government. Int. J. Electron. Gov. Res. 12(1), 69–98 (2016). https://doi.org/10.4018/IJEGR.2016010104

4. Trommel, W.: Good governance as reflexive governance. In praise of good colleagueship. Public Integr. **22**(3), 227–235 (2020). https://doi.org/10.1080/10999922.2020.1723356

5. Manoharan, A.P., Ingrams, A.: Conceptualizing e-government from local government perspectives. State Local Gov. Rev. **50**(1), 56–66 (2018). https://doi.org/10.1177/0160323x18763964

6. Mwaura, J.: Digital activism in the social media era: critical reflections on emerging trends in sub-Saharan Africa. Afr. J. Stud. **38**(1), 152–155 (2017). https://doi.org/10.1080/23743670.2017.1329249

7. Aziz, F.N., Roziqin, A.: The Perspective of Bureaucratic Reform (Kang Yoto's Leadership) in Bojonegoro. JAKPP (Jurnal Anal. Kebijak. Pelayanan Publik) 126–142 (2020). https://doi.org/10.31947/jakpp.vi.10014

8. Kumar, H., Singh, M.K., Gupta, M.P., Madaan, J.: Moving towards smart cities: solutions that lead to the smart city transformation framework. Technol. Forecast. Soc. Change **153**, 1–16 (2020). https://doi.org/10.1016/j.techfore.2018.04.024

9. Clarke, A.: Digital government units: what are they, and what do they mean for digital era public management renewal? Int. Public Manag. J. **23**(3), 358–379 (2020). https://doi.org/10.1080/10967494.2019.1686447

10. Singhal, A., Svenkerud, P.J.: Flipping the diffusion of innovations paradigm: embracing the positive deviance approach to social change. Asia Pac. Media Educ. **29**(2), 151–163 (2019). https://doi.org/10.1177/1326365X19857010

11. Greedharry, M., Seewoogobin, V., Gooda Sahib-Kaudeer, N.: A smart mobile application for complaints in Mauritius. In: Satapathy, S.C., Bhateja, V., Somanah, R., Yang, X.-S., Senkerik, R. (eds.) Information Systems Design and Intelligent Applications. AISC, vol. 863, pp. 345–356. Springer, Singapore (2019). https://doi.org/10.1007/978-981-13-3338-5_32

12. Scholl, H.J., Alawadhi, S.: Creating smart governance: the key to radical ICT overhaul at the city of Munich. Inf. Polity **21**(1), 21–42 (2016). https://doi.org/10.3233/IP-150369

13. Work, J.D.: Evaluating commercial cyber intelligence activity. Int. J. Intell. Counter Intell. **33**(2), 278–308 (2020). https://doi.org/10.1080/08850607.2019.1690877

14. Sellnow, T., Parrish, A., Semenas, L.: From Hoax as crisis to crisis as hoax: fake news and information disorder as disruptions to the discourse of renewal. J. Int. Cris. Risk Commun. Res. **2**(1), 121–142 (2019). https://doi.org/10.30658/jicrcr.2.1.6

15. Kim, H., Xu, H.: Exploring the effects of social media features on the publics' responses to decreased usage CSR messages. Corp. Commun. **24**(2), 287–302 (2019). https://doi.org/10.1108/CCIJ-10-2017-0095

16. Mensah, I.K., Adams, S.: A comparative analysis of the impact of political trust on the adoption of e-government services. Int. J. Public Adm. **43**(8), 682–696 (2020). https://doi.org/10.1080/01900692.2019.1645687

17. Mahmood, M., Weerakkody, V., Chen, W.: The influence of transformed government on citizen trust: insights from Bahrain. Inf. Technol. Dev. **25**(2), 275–303 (2019). https://doi.org/10.1080/02681102.2018.1451980

18. Kyalo Makau, G., Daudi, N., Omwenga, E.I.: The critical organizational factors of e-government in Kenya. Int. J. Comput. Appl. Technol. Res. **4**(4), 246–252 (2015). https://doi.org/10.7753/ijcatr0404.1007

19. Gao, X., Lee, J.: E-government services and social media adoption: experience of small local governments in Nebraska state. Gov. Inf. Q. **34**(4), 627–634 (2017). https://doi.org/10.1016/j.giq.2017.09.005

20. Novotny, R.W., et al.: Response of the S hashlyk Forward Spect rometer of PANDA to Ph otons below 800 MeV Energy, pp. 14–17 (2014)

21. Salinding, R., Posumah, J., Palar, N.: Efektivitas Pengelolaan Sampah Oleh Dinas Kebersihan Dan Pertamanan Kota Manado. J. Adm. Publik UNSRAT **3**(41), 1–12 (2016)

The Success of Socialization Vaccination Program Policies in DKI Jakarta Through Social Media

Dwi Jazimah Wijayati[(✉)], Achmad Nurmandi, and Isnaini Muallidin

Department of Government Affairs and Administration, Jusuf Kalla School of Government, Universitas Muhammadiyah Yogyakarta, Yogyakarta, Indonesia
dwijazimah07@gmail.com, nurmandi_achmad@umy.ac.id

Abstract. This paper aims to see the success of the socialization of the COVID-19 vaccine program policy from the DKI Jakarta Provincial Government. This study analyzed data from #vaksindulu created by the Twitter account of the Jakarta Special Capital Region (DKI) Provincial Government (@PemprovDKIJakarta) which is a form of socialization of the COVID-19 vaccine through social media. This research used descriptive qualitative research. Data analysis was implemented using NVivo 12 Plus software, data retrieval from #Vaksindulu created by the DKI Jakarta Provincial Government Twitter account via NCapture from NVivo 12 Plus with Web Chrome. The data was the content of vaccine socialization taken from the Twitter account @PemprovDKIJakarta with the hashtag #vaksindulu. The results found that the highest use of #vaksindulu was from June to August. The DKI Jakarta Provincial Government's strategy most often used socialization mechanisms, socialization materials, collaboration socialization, and participation. The DKI Jakarta Provincial Government, in its socialization orientation, communicates more often with government sectors than the private sector and NGOs. This research will be a benchmark for the success of the DKI Jakarta Provincial Government's socialization through social media and can be a reference for further research.

Keywords: Socialization · Policies · COVID-19 · VaccinePrograms

1 Introduction

The COVID-19 vaccine is an important component to end the pandemic because it can reduce the virus's spread and increase people's immunity to the disease [1]. The provision of this vaccine is one of the efforts to reduce morbidity and mortality due to COVID-19 [2, 3]. The vaccines given include Sinovac, Sinapharm vaccine, Moderna vaccine, and AstraZeneca [4]. The vaccination program turned out to cause many problems in the community, many pros and cons related to this vaccination program [5]. Thus, evidence-based health communication strategies are needed to effectively address vaccine doubts and grow vaccine confidence [6].

The vaccination program in supporting its success needs to be supported by high community participation, so the government needs to take a special strategic approach

C. Stephanidis et al. (Eds.): HCII 2022, CCIS 1582, pp. 457–465, 2022.
https://doi.org/10.1007/978-3-031-06391-6_57

to the community in communicating, especially related to the COVID-19 vaccination program [7]. Meanwhile, government challenges in the vaccination program are caused by the spread of fake news or hoaxes circulating in the community [8]. Unclear information can hinder the success of the vaccine program, so the government needs to use official social media accounts to disseminate the COVID-19 vaccine. In today's digital and internet era, all parties can use social media (including the government) to convey various information to all people [9].

Social media can respond to situations by sharing information through public authorities or the public[10]. Social media is a substitute for communicating and sharing data related to disease [11]. The pandemic in which social distancing is restricted and activities that gather large numbers of people are also restricted, so the government disseminates information on vaccine policies through several social media platforms [12]. With the great enthusiasm of the public in accessing social media, it is hoped that information regarding vaccine policies can be accessed as widely as possible by the public to get support from the community [13].

The DKI Jakarta government also uses social media as a public information communication strategy related to the vaccine program through the @PemprovDKIJakarta social media account. The vaccination program in DKI Jakarta must be carried out optimally because the COVID-19 cases in DKI Jakarta are among the provinces with the highest COVID-19 cases, with an additional 428 cases bringing the total to 853,359. DKI Jakarta cases were higher than in other provinces because it had become a corona hotspot in Indonesia and recorded up to 14,000 cases per day[14]. Thus, the vaccination program in DKI Jakarta must run optimally, supported by information and communication technology (ICT) social media.

2 Literature Review

2.1 Vaccination Program Policies

Vaccines are antigens of dead microorganisms, still alive but attenuated, still intact, or processed parts. They are microorganism toxins that have been processed into toxoids, recombinant proteins that will cause active specific immunity against disease when given to a person with certain infections [15]. Vaccines are carried out through active immunization, which aims to prepare the body to be more immune. When exposed again, the body can recognize and respond to it [16]. Currently, the government is intensively implementing a COVID-19 vaccine for the community [17].

In dealing with the COVID-19 pandemic, the Indonesian government stipulates Presidential Regulation No. 99 of 2020 concerning the Procurement of Vaccines and Implementation of Vaccinations in the Context of Combating the Coronavirus Pandemic Disease 2019 (COVID-19) as amended by Presidential Regulation No. 14 of 2021 concerning Amendments to Presidential Regulation No. 99 of 2020 concerning Vaccine Procurement and Vaccination Implementation in the Context of Combating the 2019 Corona Virus Disease (COVID-19) Pandemic[18]. One of the provinces that apply sanctions if citizens refuse the Corona vaccine is DKI Jakarta. In Article 30 of Regional Regulation No. 2 of 2020 concerning the Prevention of the Coronavirus [18], the people of DKI Jakarta must follow the COVID-19 vaccine.

2.2 Social Media as Socialization

Many researchers have studied the interaction between social media and COVID-19 misinformation from various aspects, such as information seeking and user sharing behavior [19]. Social media is online media, where users can easily participate, access information, and convey ideas [20]. Socialization is the process by which a person acquires the knowledge, abilities, and basics that make them able or unable to become members of a group [21]. James W. Vander Zanden defined socialization as a process of social interaction in which people acquire knowledge, attitudes, values, and behaviors essential for effective participation in society [22]. David B. Brinkerhoff and Lynn K. White defined socialization as learning the roles, status, and values necessary for social institutions. All socialization is carried out to achieve indicators of successful socialization. It can be said indicator of successful socialization visits from agents of socialization, socialization materials, mechanisms of socialization, and community participation [23].

When the world is amid the 19th pandemic, social media has consistently flooded with content related to the virus. Twitter plays a more prominent role in the medical world, with the hashtag (#) accumulating thousands of tweets per hour [24]. Twitter has played an important role in spreading medical information and misinformation during the COVID-19 pandemic [24]. Twitter, in particular, has an advantage over some other social media platforms providing short, real-time content availability with access to similar discussion networks via hashtags. Twitter has been used to assess the success of vaccination programs [25–27].

3 Research Methods

This research used descriptive qualitative research. Data analysis was implemented by NVivo 12 Plus software, data retrieval from #Vaksindulu created by the DKI Jakarta Provincial Government Twitter account via NCapture from NVivo 12 Plus with Web Chrome. The data was processed with the Cross Tab feature to automatically calculate the required key statistical tests with meaningful comparisons and analysis of indirect variables. The feature of Crosstab Query is to enter code (manual, generated, etc.), text data, and numeric data in variable and pattern data. At this stage, an automatic calculation was found between all data related to the spread of COVID-19 information. Next, the Word Cloud feature will discuss the words that often appear from the data search or view the terms. This study reveals the tweets of the DKI Jakarta Provincial Government regarding the COVID-19 vaccine.

4 Results and Discussion

4.1 Vaccination Information Strategy in DKI Jakarta

Social media has recently played an important role in the COVID-19 pandemic, and almost all activities have been shifted to online media to reduce the spread of COVID-19. This social media is more effective as a means of communication or socialization of the COVID-19 vaccine [28]. The DKI Jakarta Provincial Government has also turned to social media. Social media for the DKI Jakarta Provincial Government is consistently and actively disseminating the COVID-19 vaccine on social media, especially Twitter.

The DKI Jakarta government in utilizing social media as part of a successful vaccination strategy can be seen in the activity of the @PemprovDKI social media account in Fig. 1. Social media communication conveys to the public to participate in the COVID-19 vaccine program quickly and effectively. The socialization carried out by the DKI Jakarta provincial government can be seen from #vaksindulu on the @PemprovDKI-Jakarta Twitter account. The success of the socialization of the DKI Jakarta provincial government can be seen from #vaksindulu, which is the largest result. Since the creation of #vaksindulu in June to August, the hashtag has been the most. The results can be seen in Fig. 1. In June, #vaksindulu is still a little later. The hashtag increases rapidly due to the ongoing socialization and daily updates about the COVID-19 vaccine by the Provincial Government of DKI Jakarta. Until the following months, it begins to decline because the people of DKI Jakarta have socialized it.

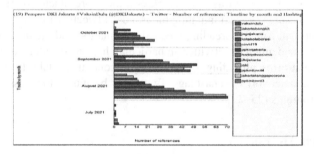

Fig. 1. .

The information submitted through #vaksindulu by the DKI Jakarta Provincial Government has some substance in the information submitted. The message can be an aspect of success. As for viewing the socialization content using #vaksindulu made by the DKI Jakarta Provincial Government is measured by four factors using hashtags, namely community participation, socialization collaboration, socialization materials, and socialization mechanisms.

The DKI Jakarta Government's strategy in providing socialization to the community through #vaksindulu, in substance, the information conveyed focused on the socialization mechanism, the data processed by researchers reached 16.2%, and the lowest seen from the socialization participation was only 1%. DKI Jakarta Provincial Government uses more socialization mechanisms. An example of a tweet made by the DKI Jakarta Provincial Government as an indicator of the socialization mechanism is information on the specific developments of Covid-19 in Jakarta so that people are moved to follow the Covid-19 vaccine. Especially for DKI Jakarta, the success of this factor can measure the direction of success or socialization strategies carried out by the DKI Jakarta Provincial Government. From the processed data, the researchers found that the DKI Jakarta Provincial Government's strategy most often uses socialization mechanisms, socialization materials, collaboration socialization, and participation can be seen in Fig. 2. Therefore, the DKI Jakarta Provincial Government prioritizes socialization with mechanisms that are considered effective for the people of DKI Jakarta.

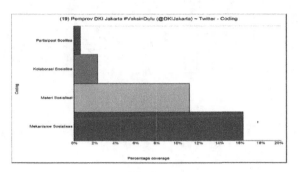

Fig. 2. .

4.2 Relations in Vaccination Socialization in DKI Jakarta

Having a communication relationship with government agencies in conveying information related to the vaccination program in DKI Jakarta through various relationships is necessary to achieve an effective and efficient strategy. Cooperation in this communication relationship can make it easier for the government to disseminate the COVID-19 vaccine. By strengthening relations with the government, people can be more motivated and spread information more evenly.

From Fig. 3, the DKI Jakarta Provincial Government Twitter account has an integrated institutional communication relationship with several sectors such as the intergovernmental sector, the private sector, and the NGO sector. This communication is done for the effective dissemination of information. The DKI Jakarta Provincial Government, in its socialization orientation, communicates more often with government sectors. The government sectors that communicate with the DKI Jakarta provincial government are the DKI Jakarta Environmental Service, the DKI Jakarta Provincial Food, Marine and Agriculture Security Service, the DKI Jakarta Water Resources Service, the DKI Jakarta BPDP, the DKI Jakarta Youth and Sports Service, and the DKI Jakarta Provincial Education Office, DKI Jakarta Provincial Social Service, Jakarta Provincial Health Office, DKI Jakarta PDAM, DKI Jakarta Culture Service, Communication, Information and Statistics Office of DKI Jakarta Provincial Government (Fig. 4).

The government uses Twitter to socialize the COVID-19 vaccine. The analysis using Word Cloud is to find words that are often discussed in research topics. Using Word Cloud, the type of story that appears on the DKI Jakarta Provincial Government Twitter account is information about the state of COVID-19 in Jakarta in the past year. The 50 most visible words on this topic come from the DKI Jakarta Provincial Government Twitter (Table 1).

The service provided by the government is to facilitate the community to make it easier to get information about the COVID-19 vaccine. The DKI Jakarta Provincial Government makes it easier to get information by socializing using social media and

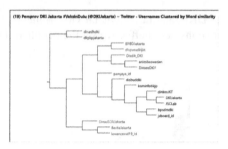

Fig. 3. .

Fig. 4. .

Table 1. Dose 1 vaccine coverage (November 1, 2021).

Regional health facility	Target number	Accumulated Dose 1	Persentase
Jakarta Barat	2,058,825	1,716,872	83.39%
Jakarta Pusat	905,537	1,990,672	219.83%
Jakarta Selatan	1,913,001	2,690,021	140.62%
Jakarta Timur	2,581,887	2,136,176	82.74%
Jakarta Utara	1,459,664	1,562,206	107.03%
Kepulauan Seribu	22,297	21,081	94.26%
Total	8.941.211		

Sumber: [29]

using WEB as one of the services to the community. The success of the COVID-19 vaccination in DKI Jakarta Province can be a success from the data taken by researchers from the WEB service created by the DKI Jakarta Provincial Government to make it easier for the public to access information related to the COVID-19 vaccine. From the data above, the achievement obtained by each district is good, although it is still in the process of being able to receive vaccinations as a whole. The socialization strategy of the DKI Jakarta Provincial Government has been successful. However, it needs to be done continuously until all people in DKI Jakarta can get the COVID-19 vaccine. The realization of Corona vaccination in Jakarta reached the highest number compared to other regions in Indonesia until Tuesday, September 14, 2021. Corona vaccination in Jakarta reached 113.2% of the target set by the provincial government of DKI Jakarta [30]. The national average that has been vaccinated is 28.17%. Some areas do have higher achievement. For example, Jakarta has more than 100%, Bali has also almost reached 100% for the first dose, Riau Islands is also above 60%, Yogyakarta and so on [31]. Achievement vaccination COVID-19 in Jakarta shows good progress because the number continues to rise. As of September 3, 2021, 9,821,061 people have been vaccinated, or 109.8% of the target 8,941,211 people [32].

5 Conclusion

Social media by the DKI Jakarta Provincial Government is carried out consistently and actively in socializing the COVID-19 vaccine on social media, especially Twitter. The success of the socialization of the DKI Jakarta provincial government can be seen from the use of #vaksindulu, which is the largest user. Viewing the socialization content using #vaksindulu made by the DKI Jakarta Provincial Government is measured by four factors: hashtags, community participation, socialization collaboration, socialization materials, and socialization mechanisms. Since #vaksindulu in June to August has been used the most, the DKI Jakarta Government's strategy in providing socialization to the community through #vaksindulu, in substance, the information conveyed focused on the socialization mechanism, the data processed by researchers reached 16.2%, and the lowest seen from the socialization participation was only 1%. By prioritizing socialization with a mechanism that is considered effective for the people of DKI Jakarta. Cooperation in communication relations can also facilitate the government in socializing the COVID-19 vaccine. This communication is done for the effective dissemination of information. The DKI Jakarta Provincial Government, in its socialization orientation, communicates more often with government sectors.

References

1. Latkin, C.A., Dayton, L., Yi, G., Konstantopoulos, A., Boodram, B.: Trust in a COVID-19 vaccine in the U.S.: a social-ecological perspective. Soc. Sci. Med. **270** (2021). https://doi.org/10.1016/j.socscimed.2021.113684
2. Asyafin, M.A., Virdani, D., Kasih, K.D., Arif, L.: Implementasi Kebijakan Vaksinasi Covid-19 Di Kota Surabaya. J. Publicuho **4**(2), 501–510 (2021). https://doi.org/10.35817/jpu.v4i2.18061

3. Lukiyani, L.: Kompas.com. Manfaat Vaksin Covid-19 yang Penting Diketahui (2021). https://www.kompas.com/sains/read/2021/07/25/113200423/manfaat-vaksin-covid-19-yang-penting-diketahui-?page=all

4. Rahayu, R.N., Sensusiyati: Vaksin covid 19 di Indonesia: analisis berita hoax. Intelektiva J. Ekon. Sos. Hum. Vaksin **2**(07), 39–49 (2021)

5. Widayanti, L.P., Kusumawati, E.: Hubungan Persepsi Tentang Efektifitas Vaksin Dengan Sikap Kesediaan Mengikuti Vaksinasi Covid-19. J. Kesehat. Masy. **9**(2), 78–84 (2021)

6. Chou, W.Y.S., Budenz, A.: Considering emotion in COVID-19 vaccine communication: addressing vaccine hesitancy and fostering vaccine confidence. Health Commun. **35**(14), 1718–1722 (2020). https://doi.org/10.1080/10410236.2020.1838096

7. Dewi, S.A.E.: Komunikasi Publik Terkait Vaksinasi Covid 19. Heal. Care J. Kesehat. **10**(1), 162–167 (2021). https://doi.org/10.36763/healthcare.v10i1.119

8. Jennings, W., et al.: Lack of trust, conspiracy beliefs, and social media use predict COVID-19 vaccine hesitancy. Vaccines **9**(6), 1–14 (2021). https://doi.org/10.3390/vaccines9060593

9. Febty, I.M., Nurmandi, A., Muallidin, I., Kurniawan, D., Salahudin: The effectiveness of social resilience in Indonesia. In: Ahram, T., Taiar, R. (eds.) IHIET 2021. LNNS, vol. 319, pp. 166–173. Springer, Cham (2022). https://doi.org/10.1007/978-3-030-85540-6_22

10. Anson, S., Watson, H., Wadhwa, K., Metz, K.: Analysing social media data for disaster preparedness: understanding the opportunities and barriers faced by humanitarian actors. Int. J. Disaster Risk Reduct. **21**, 131–139 (2017). https://doi.org/10.1016/j.ijdrr.2016.11.014

11. Pratama, D., Nurmandi, A., Muallidin, I., Kurniawan, D., Salahudin: Information dissemination of COVID-19 by ministry of health in Indonesia. In: Ahram, T., Taiar, R. (eds.) IHIET 2021. LNNS, vol. 319, pp. 61–67. Springer, Cham (2022). https://doi.org/10.1007/978-3-030-85540-6_8

12. Junaedi, D., Arsyad, M.R., Salistia, F., Romli, M.: Menguji Efektivitas Vaksinasi Covid-19 di Indonesia Dedi. Relig. Educ. Soc. Laa Roiba J. **3**, 227–235 (2021). https://doi.org/10.47476/reslaj.v4i2.558

13. Froehlich, R., Rüdiger, B.: Framing political public relations: measuring success of political communication strategies in Germany. Public Relat. Rev. **32**(1), 18–25 (2006). https://doi.org/10.1016/j.pubrev.2005.10.003

14. KH, R.: Dipimpin Jateng, Ini 5 Provinsi Dengan Kasus Covid Tertinggi. CNBC Indonesia (2021). https://www.cnbcindonesia.com/news/20210908174637-4-274756/dipimpin-jateng-ini-5-provinsi-dengan-kasus-covid-tertinggi

15. Rahman, Y.A.: Vaksinasi Massal Covid-19 sebagai Sebuah Upaya Masyarakat dalam Melaksanakan Kepatuhan Hukum (Obedience Law). Khazanah Huk. **3**(2), 80–86 (2021). https://doi.org/10.15575/kh.v3i2.11520

16. Prastyowati, A.: Mengenal Karakteristik Virus SARS-CoV-2 Penyebab Penyakit COVID-19 Sebagai Dasar Upaya Untuk Pengembangan Obat Antivirus Dan Vaksin. BioTrends **11**(1), 1–10 (2020)

17. Dahlan, D.N.: Upaya Petugas Kesehatan Dalam Menumbuhkan Semangat Vaksin Pada Masyarakat (Fenomena Ledakan Minat Vaksin Covid 19) Kota Tulungagung Jawa Timur, vol. xx, no. x, pp. 70–76

18. Ramadhan, R.S.S., Purba, N., Akhyar, A.: Analisis Yuridis Terhadap Penolakan Vaksinasi Covid-19 Ditinjau Dari Hukum Pidana (Suatu Analisis Terhadap Peraturan Daerah Dki Jakarta Nomor 2 Tahun 2020 Tentang Penanggulangan Covid-19 Di Dki Jakarta). J. Ilm. Metadata **3**(14), 12–26 (2020)

19. Laato, S., Islam, A.K.M.N., Islam, M.N., Whelan, E.: What drives unverified information sharing and cyberchondria during the COVID-19 pandemic? Eur. J. Inf. Syst. **29**(3), 288–305 (2020). https://doi.org/10.1080/0960085X.2020.1770632

20. Kurniawan, C., Nurmandi, A., Muallidin, I.: Economic recovery for tourism sector based on social media data mining. In: Ahram, T., Taiar, R. (eds.) IHIET 2021. LNNS, vol. 319, pp. 174–180. Springer, Cham (2020). https://doi.org/10.1007/978-3-030-85540-6_23

21. Brice, R.G.: Connecting oral and written language through applied writing strategies. Interv. Sch. Clin. **40**(1), 38–47 (2004). https://doi.org/10.1177/10534512040400010301

22. Damsar: Pengantar SOSIOLOGI PENDIDIKAN Edisi Pertama. Kencana Prenada Media Group, Jakarta (2011)

23. Sumantri, D.: Sosialisasi Politik Pasangan Calon Kepala Daerah Oleh Kpu Kabupaten Bekasi Pada Pilkada Tahun 201. Cendikiawan, p. 1226 (2018). www.trijournal.lemlit.Trisakti.ac.id

24. Rosenberg, H., Syed, S., Rezaie, S.: The Twitter pandemic: the critical role of Twitter in the dissemination of medical information and misinformation during the COVID-19 pandemic. Can. J. Emerg. Med. **22**(4), 418–421 (2020). https://doi.org/10.1017/cem.2020.361

25. Kwon, J., Grady, C., Feliciano, J., Fodeh, S.: Defining facets of social distancing during the COVID-19 pandemic: Twitter analysis. J. Biomed. Inf. (2020). https://doi.org/10.1016/j.jbi.2020.103601

26. Su, Y., Venkat, A., Yadav, Y., Puglisi, L.B., Fodeh, S.J.: Twitter-based analysis reveals differential COVID-19 concerns across areas with socioeconomic disparities. Comput. Biol. Med. **132** (2021). https://doi.org/10.1016/j.compbiomed.2021.104336

27. Younis, J., Freitag, H., Ruthberg, J., Romanes, J., Nielsen, C., Mehta, N.: Social media as an early proxy for social distancing indicated by the COVID-19. JMIR Public Heal. Surveill. (2020). https://doi.org/10.2196/21340

28. Herliana, M., Tazkiyah, D.: Kesantunan Pragmatik Ridwan Kamil Dalam Sosialisasi Vaksinasi Covid-19 Di Media Sosial. SPHOTA J. Linguist. dan Sastra **13**(2), 31–42 (2021). https://doi.org/10.36733/sphota.v13i2.1496

29. Corona.jakarta.id. Layanan Darurat COVID-19. corona.jakarta.id (2021). https://corona.jakarta.go.id/id

30. Ashar, S.: Update Vaksinasi Corona di Jakarta Mencapai 10.124.301 Penerima Vaksin Dosis Pertama. Ragional Kontan.co.id (2021). https://regional.kontan.co.id/news/update-vaksinasi-corona-di-jakarta-mencapai-10124301-penerima-vaksin-dosis-pertama?page=all

31. Merdeka: Menkes Sebut Vaksinasi di DKI dan Bali Sudah 100%, Tapi Masih Ada 5 Provinsi Terendah. Merdeka.com (2021). https://www.merdeka.com/peristiwa/menkes-sebut-vaksinasi-di-dki-dan-bali-sudah-100-tapi-masih-ada-5-provinsi-terendah.html

32. Paat, Y.: Capaian Vaksinasi Lebih dari 100%, Pemprov DKI: Hasil Kolaborasi Semua Pihak. Berita Satu, Jakarta (2021)

Digital Commerce and the Customer Experience

A Comparative Study: Influence on Real-World Consumer Perception of Products Presented in Augmented Reality

Kaiyuan Chen[(✉)] [ID] and Young Mi Choi

School of Industrial Design, Georgia Institute of Technology, Atlanta, USA
kchen477@gatech.edu

Abstract. With the development of the mobile device, augmented reality (AR) is moving from the laboratory into the consumer market. Product presentation in the augmented environment has become a compelling function that helps consumers have a better perception of the product. In this article, we proposed a comparative study to figure out how users perceive the product model in the AR environment and the difference compared with the real-world product. Through this research, we will further understand which attributes of the product can be better perceived in AR. The product semantic differential method was used here to build the product evaluation metrics and compare the user perception of 3 types of product presentation based on product semantic.

Keywords: Augmented reality · Product presentation · Semantic

1 Introduction

Augmented reality (AR) integrates computer-generated objects with the real environment and allows real-time interactions [4]. AR is moving from the laboratory into consumer markets after many years of development [5]. For the consumer market, AR plays an important role for retailers to engage with customers in a unique and vivid way [18]. Many online shopping platforms have started to experiment with AR-assisted shopping due to its one way to bridge the gap between online and offline shopping. For example, IKEA place, it provides an interactive AR experience by placing 3D models of products in a given space, helping consumer evaluate the product and allowing consumer to purchase these products within the application itself [2]. Firms such as Sephora, Loreal, Nike have implemented AR functions to enhance the consumers' shopping experience and help make shopping decisions [12]. As consumers' use of AR increases, there is a growing need to understand how users perceive the product model in the AR environment and the difference compared with the real-world

Supported by organization x.

product. Also, from the perspective of the product, attributes of the product can be better perceived in an AR scenario. In this paper, a comparative study method was proposed to measure user perception towards product and product performance under real word and AR system based on product semantic.

2 Conceptual Development

2.1 AR Characteristics and Product Presentation

VR and AR are comparable in that they allow users to perceive coexisting environments as immersive technologies that deliver extensive high-quality sensory input [13]. When the research focuses on the user perception and product presentation, the features of AR may be more specific. Three dimensions of the AR features and product presentation are considered here. There are many different definitions of AR's attributes based on the goal of each research. For example, Mclean proposed the interactivity, vividness, and novelty as three main attributes of the AR. However, when we focus on AR in the shopping scenario, the attributes of AR that are related to product presentation become more important. Therefore, the definition of these features becomes more detailed [12].

Mixed Virtual/Real. Javornik suggested that AR differs from other interactive technologies in its so-called augmentation, which refers to its ability to overlay physical environments with virtual elements [9]. From product presentation perspective, AR combines the real and virtual world by overlaying virtual products onto the consumer or their surroundings, which enables them to try a product 'as if' it is there [13]. The goal of the consumer is to take the product and use it in real life, not to use a virtual product. However, AR is based on reality, this feature shows the potential of AR in the consumer realm. Given the range and extent of manipulation between the actual world and AR, the user is likely to be confronted with fresh stimuli each time they use AR [12], which would be an effective way for consumer to perceive the product under such kind of AR presentation.

Interactivity. Under the AR environment, the user can interact with the objects in real time [4]. There are so many definitions of interactive of AR. However, some studies give a holistic definition of interaction in AR, namely as a technological consequence and as a user perception [18].

Scholars that emphasize the significance of technological characteristics define interactivity as an outcome of the technology's attributes [6]. Thus, interactivity arises from the capacity of technological systems to facilitate individual interaction and engagement with content [7]. From consumer's perspective, their perceptions may be influenced by sub-components of the technology involving the speed, such as how quickly users can manipulate content; mapping, the similarity of the control in the virtual world to the real world; and range, the extent to which the content can be manipulated by the user. However, from the perspective of product presentation, the interactivity becomes more specific. Consumers can inspect a product from a range of angles when manipulating it and causing it to interact with the environment in real time [11]. This is the process by which the consumer evaluates and perceives the details of the product, such as its form and function.

Space Placement. The objects in AR can be placed freely as well as fixed [16]. This feature helps the 3D display of products in the environment, and even based on image recognition technology, can be combined with the human body, such as some AR-based wear applications [8]. These distinct qualities of AR result in online product presentations that more closely mirror an in-person product experience [17]. For example, Apple store provide AR product presentation function for consumers to place related product on the desk or other location. When the new generation product is placed in a real environment, the consumer will notice and perceive the new design change or size change. Therefore, for the user, the placement and fix functions enable them to inspect the fixed product from various angles relative to their current location in order to gain a better understanding of the size and space matching in a real-world scenario.

3 Methodology

The overall research approach based on product semantics was inspired by previous work of product and user perception evaluation. The whole research was held in 3 phases. Phase i: define the semantics of the product for evaluation; Phase ii: analyse the perception differences between the real product and the different types of graphical representation (still image & augmented reality) and user recall research of the product's attributes. Phase iii: data analysis and discussion.

3.1 Product Selection

The product selection was considered from three perspectives: functionality, consumer familiarity and industrial design. Final product selection: DJI Osmo Action (see Fig. 1), a sports camera. This sports camera is highly functional and comes with many interactive innovations, such as the forward and reverse screen display. The sports camera is a relatively hot product in recent years, but it is still far from popular, so it is a reasonable product choice in terms of audience. In addition, the industrial design level, consumer electronics has always focused on industrial design research, DJI's products are more recognizable in terms of product appearance, and the surface of this product also uses a variety of materials to give consumers more dimensions that can perceive the appearance.

Fig. 1. Dji Osmo action

3.2   Phase I: Define the Semantics of the Product for the Product Evaluation

Identify Product Semantics Space

Semantic Differential Method (SDM). SDM [15] consists in listing the semantic attributes of the product to analyse and carry out user tests in which the user must assess the product according to these attributes. The attributes are often defined by pairs of antonymous adjectives which lie at either end of a qualitative scale. A semantic space, Euclidean and multi-dimensional, is then postulated. Factor analysis and principal components analysis may be used to reduce the dimensionality of the space and to find the underlying dimensions. SDM is used for example for the analysis of families of products [10] or for the design of a new product [14]. In this study, we used the SDM similar to Artacho's and Alcantara's research [1,3].

Build Initial Semantic Universe. The first session was held to build an initial semantic universe (ISU). 47 (23 product design/design background students and 24 business background students) participants were provided with 10 different sport cameras' images to help them brainstorm product descriptions. Adjectives about design, shape, function, and market were collected. Data collection was accomplished through an online questionnaire that provided adjective fill-in-the-blank positions. These words formed the initial semantic universe (ISU) and were collected from the following sources. Finally, we collected 451 semantic words to generate the initial ISU.

Narrow Down the ISU. Second, the collection of words and expressions were condensed to avoid a loss of reliability due to participant fatigue during the evaluation phase. Identical words were eliminated, and the vocabulary of this product semantic universe was condensed to the maximum extent possible. At the same time, the most common adjectives were collected first. The goal of this work is to reduce the words to 30–60. After that, 10 Industrial design students were divided into two groups to join in this work to help narrow down the ISU and generate a reduced version of the semantic universe. Finally, the semantic universe was narrowed down to 50 words, and then they were divided into 8 semantic axes. Each participant in this phase was asked to judge the final semantic words by online survey (the scale ranged between 1and 5, 1 subject

Table 1. Product semantic axis

AXIS 1 refers to the product shape/form/size		AXIS 2 refers to the features on the use of the product		AXIS 3 refers to the description of product quality	
Semantic word	Mean	Semantic word	Mean	Semantic word	Mean
Rounded	4.63	Portable	4.29	Durable	4.13
Small	4.50	Handy	4.13	High Quality	4.12
Light	4.13	Operational	4.13	Sturdy	4.10
Square	3.88	Easy to use	3.88	Steady	3.88
Geometric	4.88	Intuitive	3.63	Resilient	3.63
Heavier	3.00	Efficient	3.50	Integrity	3.50
		Convenient	3.25		
AXIS 4 refers to the description of product material		AXIS 5 refers to functional features		AXIS refers to the product design features	
Semantic word	Mean	Semantic word	Mean	Semantic word	Mean
Glassy	4.88	Stable	4.50	Technical	4.25
Plastic feel	4.20	Manageable	4.50	Pure	4.25
Hard	4.13	Functional	4.38	Eexquisite	4.14
Grainy	4.13	Attachable	3.88	Pure	4.00
Water-proof	3.83	Secure	3.75	Integrated	3.86
		Multifunctional	3.00	Simple lines	3.50
AXIS 7 refers to the innovation of the product		AXIS 8 refers to the most intuitive overall feeling of the product			
Semantic word	Mean	Semantic word	Mean		
Modern	4.38	Powerful	4.50		
Normal	3.88	Affordable	4.25		
low innovation	3.86	Cool	3.88		
Traditional	3.63	Dynamic	3.63		
Innovative	3.25	Speed	3.50		
Classical	3.25	Smooth	3.38		
Futuristic	3.25	Casual	3.25		

totally disagreed with the affirmation, 5 totally agreed and 3 neither agree nor disagree). The final result is as follows. Table 1 For each axis, the three highest rated words will be selected for further analysis.

3.3 Phase II, Perception Test and User Recall Research

Dji Osmo Action 3D model presentation based on augmented reality and physical product was used in this phase. The 45 participants were divided into 3 groups randomly. The first 15 people group was directly observing the product graphic from different angles. The second group used the AR system that only allow them to fix the product on a certain location and use device to observe the product. The final group evaluated the product model under AR environment. The AR environment allowed them to rotate, zoom in and zoom out, display, and interact with the product (see Fig. 2).

Fig. 2. Three types of product presentation

Each of them had 3 min to observe and evaluate the product according to the instruction. After the evaluation, they were allowed to fill the survey based on the semantics defined on the first round. People answered whether they agreed or not with the statement of the product semantic words of each axis (the scale ranged between -2 and 2, -2 subjects totally disagreed with the affirmation, 2 totally agreed and 0 neither agree nor disagree). After that, they finished another survey of the product attributes. The survey let them fill out the question related to the specific product details. For example, what's the colour of the surface? Where is the start shooting button located on the camera body? All the questions were related to the product evaluation dimensions such as product appearance, size and shape.

4   Data Analysis and Discussion

After collecting the data, a basic analysis was conducted to compare the differences between the three different product presentation types (Type 1: Real product graphic, Type 2: AR product presentation without interactive functions and Type 3: AR product presentation with full interactive functions). Based on the evaluation of the three terms for each semantic axis, to calculate the mean of a single axis for each participant. Finally, the three forms were collated to form a total of 135 data and a box-line plot was drawn (see Fig. 3)

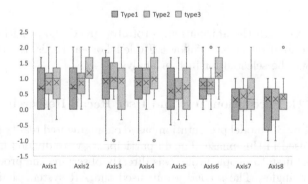

Fig. 3. Box plot of 3 types product presentation method

The overall rating of the real picture-based product presentation is slightly lower than Type 2, but reflects a larger difference. Direct product display with images is the way that the consumer perceives the product in online shopping, and due to the fixed number of images and content, the different cognitive abilities of users can lead to significant differences in their observation and understanding of the products, which reflects a certain degree of reasonableness. The second way of product display, because only the object is allowed to be fixed, through the different angles of the device to observe the different angles of the object in AR, which simulates the process of the human eye to observe the product, so the rating of the Type 2 is relatively concentrated and the differences are small. For Type 3, the overall performance is the best, but the individual dimensions reflect a large variability. Also, it was found that the two types of AR have stronger user perceptions in terms of the basic form of the product (Axis 1), the features of product use (Axis 2), product design (Axis 6), and product innovation (Axis 7) than the direct use of pictures of real-world products, and Type 3 is relatively more fully perceived by users due to its higher interactivity.

In a brief analysis of the recall questionnaire, all three had a good performance in terms of recall accuracy of product colour information. The difference is the size of the product, with Type 1: 52.1%, Type 2: 85.3% and Type 3 87.2%. In addition, on the recall of product materials, users were provided with four different materials to recall, among which the least rubber was mentioned in the responses. Due to the lack of tactile feedback, AR has some limitations in the restoration of some special materials. However, in the recall analysis, both AR presentation types have better performance for product appearance details as well as product size.

5   Conclusion

Based on the traditional product semantic-related research methods, this study investigated whether AR could better enhance users' perceptions of the product. It can be seen that through basic analysis, AR does have better performance in user perception of products. Of course, this is an ongoing project, and more data will be collected and discussed in the next phase of the study.

References

1. Alcántara, E., Artacho, M.A., González, J.C., García, A.C.: Application of product semantics to footwear design. Part I - identification of footwear semantic space applying differential semantics. Int. J. Ind. Ergon. **35**(8), 713–725 (2005). https://doi.org/10.1016/j.ergon.2005.02.005
2. Alves, C., Luís Reis, J.: The intention to use e-commerce using augmented reality - the case of IKEA place. In: Rocha, Á., Ferrás, C., Montenegro Marin, C.E., Medina García, V.H. (eds.) ICITS 2020. AISC, vol. 1137, pp. 114–123. Springer, Cham (2020). https://doi.org/10.1007/978-3-030-40690-5_12

3. Artacho-Ramírez, M.A., Diego-Mas, J.A., Alcaide-Marzal, J.: Influence of the mode of graphical representation on the perception of product aesthetic and emotional features: an exploratory study. Int. J. Ind. Ergon. **38**(11–12), 942–952 (2008). https://doi.org/10.1016/j.ergon.2008.02.020

4. Azuma, R.T.: Survey of augmented reality (October), 355–385 (2021)

5. Daponte, P., De Vito, L., Picariello, F., Riccio, M.: State of the art and future developments of the augmented reality for measurement applications. Meas. J. Int. Meas. Confederation **57**, 53–70 (2014). https://doi.org/10.1016/j.measurement.2014.07.009

6. Downes, M.J., Brennan, M.L., Williams, H.C., Dean, R.S.: Development of a critical appraisal tool to assess the quality of cross-sectional studies (AXIS). BMJ Open **6**(12), 1–7 (2016). https://doi.org/10.1136/bmjopen-2016-011458

7. Hoffman, D.L., Novak, T.P.: Marketing in hypermedia computer-mediated environments: conceptual foundations. J. Mark. **60**(3), 50–68 (1996). https://doi.org/10.1177/002224299606000304

8. Huang, T.-L., Liao, S.: A model of acceptance of augmented-reality interactive technology: the moderating role of cognitive innovativeness. Electron. Commer. Res. **15**(2), 269–295 (2014). https://doi.org/10.1007/s10660-014-9163-2

9. Javornik, A.: 'It's an illusion, but it looks real!' Consumer affective, cognitive and behavioural responses to augmented reality applications. J. Mark. Manag. **32**(9–10), 987–1011 (2016)

10. Vandersypen, L.M.K., Steffen, M., Breyta, G., Yannoni, C.S., Sherwood, M.H., Chuang, I.L.: Experimental realization of Shor's quantum factoring algorithm using nuclear magnetic resonance. Nature **414**(1976), 883–887 (2001)

11. Lee, T., Hollerer, T.: Handy AR: markerless inspection of augmented reality objects using fingertip tracking. In: 2007 11th IEEE International Symposium on Wearable Computers, pp. 83–90. IEEE (2007)

12. McLean, G., Wilson, A.: Shopping in the digital world: examining customer engagement through augmented reality mobile applications. Comput. Hum. Behav. **101**(November 2018), 210–224 (2019). https://doi.org/10.1016/j.chb.2019.07.002

13. Milgram, P.: A taxonomy of mixed reality visual displays. Ind. Eng. **12**, 1–14 (2011)

14. Nakada, K.: Kansei engineering research on the design of construction machinery. Int. J. Ind. Ergon. **19**(2), 129–146 (1997). https://doi.org/10.1016/S0169-8141(96)00009-1

15. Osgood, C.E., Anderson, L.: Certain relations among experienced contingencies, associative structure, and contingencies in encoded messages. Am. J. Psychol. **70**(3), 411–420 (1957)

16. Smink, A.R., Frowijn, S., van Reijmersdal, E.A., van Noort, G., Neijens, P.C.: Try online before you buy: How does shopping with augmented reality affect brand responses and personal data disclosure. Electron. Commer. Res. Appl. **35**(April), 100854 (2019)

17. Verhagen, T., van Nes, J., Feldberg, F., van Dolen, W.: Virtual customer service agents: using social presence and personalization to shape online service encounters. J. Comput.-Mediat. Commun. **19**(3), 529–545 (2014). https://doi.org/10.1111/jcc4.12066

18. Yim, M.Y.C., Chu, S.C., Sauer, P.L.: Is augmented reality technology an effective tool for e-commerce? An interactivity and vividness perspective. J. Interact. Mark. **39**, 89–103 (2017)

Korb: Design and Development of a User Interface that Presents an Expense Comparison Across Supermarkets with Online Delivery Service

Tanay Dalvi and Swati Chandna[✉]

SRH Hochschule Heidelberg, Heidelberg, Germany
tanay.dalvi09@gmail.com, swati.chandna@srh.de

Abstract. Even though we have been home for more than two years due to the COVID outbreak, the issue remains uncontained. As a result of the pandemic, people's buying habits have shifted. Several of us are curiously purchasing items online, which resulted in massive increases in demand for these websites. People want the convenience of buying groceries online and delivering them to their homes. While some shops offer this service, not everyone does. Due to the large number of supermarkets operating in Germany, prices of products may vary from one store to another. This value variance is beneficial for average consumers, as they will compare the prices and order the product accordingly. Furthermore, product evaluation is practical for items containing specific credits relevant to the purchasing decision. Keeping this in mind, Korb has been created to solve these approachable problems to an average person. The Korb web application scrapes data from many grocery websites and stores it in the MongoDB Atlas. This data is then compared for comparable names and displayed to the user, where the user can conveniently select the desired product and have it delivered to them. This study aims to create a user interface that addresses the issues mentioned earlier and enhances the user experience for everyday users. Additionally, the study examines the customer-to-customer delivery system, a novel concept on an e-commerce website in which users can assist one another in delivering food to their neighbor's homes. According to the findings of this study, customers can compare product prices to save money, and different people can earn part-time money while doing their work.

Keywords: Comparison website · Customer-to-customer delivery system · Web scrapping · E-commerce · ReactJS · MongoDB Atlas

1 Introduction

When you relocate to a new place, a local supermarket will likely be one of the first places anyone would visit from their house. It presumably will not feel like the supermarkets we are used to but do not let that throw you away. Step inside,

C. Stephanidis et al. (Eds.): HCII 2022, CCIS 1582, pp. 477–484, 2022.
https://doi.org/10.1007/978-3-031-06391-6_59

and you will discover an entire universe of tastes and flavors that you may not have even known about previously. There will be at least one grocery store in every town, village, and neighboring community. A conventional supermarket and a discounter are the two types of supermarkets found in most cities. In the major cities, there are stores to suit every budget and need. Supermarkets in city centers are often compact, but you'll be astonished at how much they cram into the aisles [1].

As there are so many choices for their daily supplies, the prices differ from one supermarket to another. Rather than undergoing the tedious process of comparing products manually, Korb can allow anyone to compare similar products on one single page and have them delivered to their home.

One makes every effort to save money and only spend it when necessary; this is true when purchasing daily food supplies from supermarkets. However, each store has its own set of prices for the products they sell, and as an understudy, it's critical to know where one can get reasonably priced products of high quality. As a result, they purchase food supplies in bulk, which saves time and money, but transporting these products is complex and frequently requires assistance from others. This study aims to develop an interactive web application that expands on the concept of comparing grocery products across many supermarkets and an online customer-to-customer delivery system.

- Facilitating the process of comparing grocery products.
- Delivering products to consumers in a timely and hassle-free manner.
- To optimize user's digital interactions by considering the most appropriate user interface for a comparison website.

The pricing differential between supermarkets in the EU countries has been progressively increasing over the last few years. In other regions of the world, some successful attempts have been made to assist low-income people in resolving this issue. Without resolving this issue, regular people will be compelled to pay a premium for items available for less elsewhere. Resolving this issue would benefit both the general public and the businesses that produce these products.

This thesis intend to address three primary questions that will point in the right route for resolving the above mentioned issues.

1. Is there a way to compare products from several supermarket websites in order to save money?
2. How can we ensure that the information is represented in a way that is understandable and perceptible to people, especially when it comes to UX/UI?
3. Is it conceivable to engage the public in assisting others with groceries delivery to their homes with the help of web development?

2   Related Work

Nowadays, e-commerce websites have become a primary source for purchasing various products. However, due to the proliferation of e-commerce websites, it becomes difficult for users to find the best offer on the desired goods. In addition, the vast numbers of e-commerce websites make it difficult for visitors to look for and purchase a single product across several e-commerce websites.

The study [9] describes how comparing E-commerce products with web mining helps customers compare prices and purchase desired products at the best possible price. Web crawlers and web scraping techniques are used to collect precise information from e-commerce websites to find the best discounts. Utilizing web crawlers and web scrapers makes it harder to reduce the website's response time; additionally, it contains a comparison engine, making it much more difficult to decrease its load time. This type of website will always require additional data to compare them and provide users with further possibilities. Several alternative websites operate on a similar premise; let us examine their benefits and drawbacks with competitive analysis.

2.1   Kaufda

The website provides brochures for all of Germany's markets, including supermarkets. Due to the fact that it simply displays brochures, customers must manually compare each product across multiple supermarket brochures. The Korb application eliminates this time-consuming task [8].

2.2   Idealo

Users can use the idealo website to compare costs on various products from hundreds of merchants. The idealo sites build a unique database of product offers that is filtered by a combination of screen scraping retailers' websites and CSV files supplied by the retailers. Nevertheless, Idealo does not have its own shipping service [6].

2.3   Instacart

Customers can order goods from partnering merchants and deliver them by a personal shopper. Orders are processed and provided by a personal shopper who selects, packs, and delivers the item according to the customer's specified time frame within one hour or up to five days in advance. Instacart is a delivery service; unlike the Korb application, it does not allow users to compare product costs across many supermarkets [7].

2.4   Basket

The basket website is similar to idealo in that it compares product costs from several stores and enables users to choose which one they prefer; however, this website has the drawback of not having a delivery mechanism [4].

The previous study completed lacked a few functionalities that might be improved with a few adjustments. Additionally, new elements can be introduced to these studies in order to enhance the application's aim; Korb concentrates on enhancing earlier studies while keeping the research objectives in mind.

3   System Design and Implementation

The agile technique aided this project in iteratively improving the application. The project's requirements and solutions were developed collaboratively by self-organizing usability testing participants. Adopting an agile methodology enabled more excellent responsiveness to changing business requirements and, hence, focusing on the project's feature modification. Due to this project's continual updating, the agile methodology was deemed appropriate.

3.1   System Architecture

The three-tier architecture is a well-known system architecture that divides applications into three logical and physical processing tiers:

1. The presentation tier, or user interface.
2. The application tier processes data.
3. The data tier stores and manages the application's data.

The web presentation tier of this project is built using ReactJS, HTML, and CSS and serves as the graphical user interface (GUI) via which users engage with the website. In this project, the application tier is built using NodeJS and interfaces with the data tier using API calls. While developing data models in this project for MongoDB apps, the primary consideration is the document structure and how the application depicts relationships between data. MongoDB enables the embedding of relevant data within a single document [3]. For example, Kaufland products are stored in the model "Kauf," and Netto products are stored in "Netto," which contains information about the products. This information includes the product's name, brand, price, and image, all of which are used to compare the product to each model. When the comparison between the previous two models is complete, goods with similar names will be included in the "products" model. Customer information is saved in the "shopper" model, while Kaüfer information is recorded in the "shoppernew" model. And the order data "ShopperDashboard" consists of a list of products, the quantities of each product, the pricing of each product, and the total amount of the order.

3.2   Information Architecture

After brainstorming, a list of concepts and functionalities was finalized and gathered together to build the project's layout. The two users have distinct capabilities and activities available on their separate dashboards. For example, both users can browse the application from this page; they can examine the products and their associated pricing, but they cannot add any products to their carts or even place orders before logging in (Fig. 1).

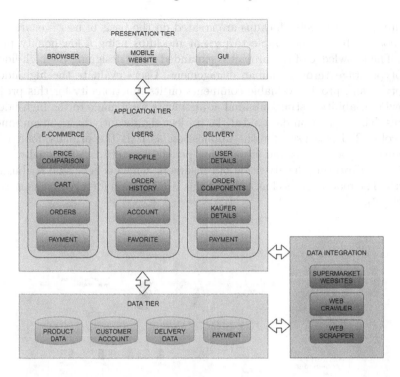

Fig. 1. System architecture

3.3   Design Thinking

This process was used to stimulate creative discovery, foster innovation, and develop new services and strategies that provide users with value and purpose [10]. An in-person interview is required to learn how participants feel about the project and empathize with them. However, due to the COVID epidemic, this interview could not take effect. The survey was primarily performed in Germany and India, with participants ranging in age from under 15 to over 56 years. The majority of participants were between 26 and 35, accounting for 47.1%, while 17.6% were 56 years and older. The pain points and solutions were analyzed, and similar frustrations were categorized better to better understand the potential remedy for the problem. Brainstorming sessions are conducted throughout Ideate stage to generate new concepts. The objective is to create as many new viewpoints and perspectives as possible before settling on a few core ideas [10].

With the help of developing a prototype it was easy to track users move around the project and execute specified activities. This project required the development of both a Sketch and a Wireframe from a low-fidelity perspective, which resulted in a tidy user experience. Instead of using modern stencils, conventional pencil and paper were used to design paper prototypes. Clickable wireframes were designed as a more cost-effective alternative to developing a website in this project. Mockups are created on the basis of user scenarios and storyboards. It became simple to present mockups using a low-fidelity prototype. The knowledge of the project is expanded while designing the high fidelity prototype stage through human engagement. Users evaluate the high-fidelity prototype and provide valuable comments on its functionality for this project. Following usability testing, minimal adjustments were made to the high-fidelity designs. The evaluation data aided the project significantly in its advancement. The color Red was used for the application as it is the primary food color, arousing our taste buds and stimulating people's appetite. Additionally, red is efficient in capturing the attention of consumers, which is beneficial for business growth. The food business has asserted this combination for a reason as it works [5] (Fig. 2).

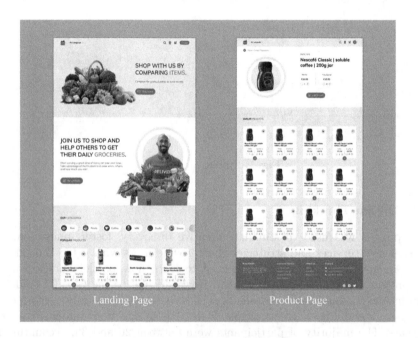

Fig. 2. High fidelity prototype

4   Evaluation

All tests were conducted via video conferencing in accordance with COVID regulations. The participants were made to feel more comfortable and acquainted with the strategies that will be employed. The five participants, one female and four male, were on average 35.80 years old. Germany and India were represented by participants. Participants represented a variety of occupations, including computer science students, craftsmen, retired service officers, and an information technology manager (Table 1).

Table 1. List of participants

Name	Age	Gender	Profession
Vishal Pokharne	28 years	Male	Student
Blazej Wieliczko	38 years	Male	Craftsman
Nilima Sawant	56 years	Female	Retired
Patrick Lozinski	30 years	Male	IT Manager
Karan Dulloo	27 years	Male	Student

The think-aloud technique was utilized in this research to comprehend participants' thoughts while they interacted with the program, allowing them to think aloud while they perform. Participants were asked to think and express their feelings on the application using this technique. After conducting usability testing, the results were evaluated on the basis of application's Effectiveness, Efficiency, and Satisfaction.

4.1 Effectiveness

The effectiveness test was used to determine the extent to which Korb interface enables a user to accomplish the task for which it was designed. As the average suggests, three out of five tasks are completed successfully, while tasks 3 and 5 are completed at an 80% completion rate.

4.2 Efficiency

To measure the speed with which users can complete tasks, efficiency test was used. Because the results of time on task are almost always positively skewed, the geometric mean is utilized rather than the arithmetic mean. Tasks 1 and 4 take the longest on average to accomplish. The time spent on task number two is the shortest of all.

4.3 Satisfaction

The System Usability Scale Survey was filled by the participants after the usability test to measure the satisfaction score. Participants were given set of 10 questions to rate the application in all aspects. The SUS score was then converted into a graph which suggest that the average SUS score of the application lie between 81–90 which is an Acceptable score [2].

After the usability testing was over the participants were asked to suggest any changes to the application so that it can help them access it more easily. One of the participant suggested that the size of the addition and subtraction buttons in the product card can be increased. One such suggestion was to add the Kaüfer login button as a separate section on the landing page so that users can know about this better.

5   Conclusion

After presenting frequent user concerns and obstacles, previous work was evaluated in this study and highlighted contemporary techniques in the field of E-commerce and delivery systems. In this proposal, the system's user-friendliness and its capacity to connect members of the same community in order to facilitate the exploration of online purchasing was emphasized. After conceptualizing and detailing the system's software structure, the approach was demonstrated through a proof-of-concept implementation that received a positive reaction during usability testing. One of the drawbacks is the scarcity of data available from grocery websites for scraping. Due to the fact that not all grocery websites allow for scraping due to their firewalls, users could only compare the pricing of products at the two supermarkets. The current implementation utilizes data from only two supermarkets; this number can be increased to provide users with more possibilities. Enhancing the web scraping component of this project can aid in expediting the process of product comparison. The customer-to-customer delivery system can also be used in a variety of different industries, including healthcare and utilities. Order tracking is another function that might be added to this program, allowing users to track the kaüfer's actual location.

References

1. A supermarkets and grocery stores in Germany (2021). https://www.expatica.com/de/living/household/supermarkets-germany-252069/
2. Bangor, A., Kortum, P., Miller, J.: Determining what individual SUS scores mean: adding an adjective rating scale. J. Usabil. Stud. **4** (2009). https://uxpajournal.org/determining-what-individual-sus-scores-mean-adding-an-adjective-rating-scale/
3. Atlas, M.: Guide to MongoDB Atlas (2021). https://docs.atlas.mongodb.com/
4. Basket (2021). https://mycircular.basket.com/
5. David, J.: Colors that influence food sales (2021). https://jenndavid.com/colors-that-influence-food-sales-infographic/
6. Idealo (2021). https://www.idealo.de/
7. Instacart (2021). https://www.instacart.com/store
8. Kaufda (2021). https://www.kaufda.de/webapp/?lat=49.435&lng=8.682
9. Shah, R., Pathan, K., Masurkar, A., Rewatkar, S., Vengurlekar, P.: Comparison of e-commerce products using web mining. Int. J. Sci. Res. Publ. **6** (2016)
10. WayPath: a comprehensive guide on design thinking (2021). https://waypathconsulting.com/what-is-design-thinking/

The Effect of Colors Used in E-Commerce Websites: An Analysis of Japanese Consumers

Kioka Goto[1], Jean-Eric Pelet[2], and Kayo Iizuka[1]([⊠])

[1] Senshu University, 2-1-1 Higashi Mita, Tama-ku, Kawasaki, Kanagawa 2400085, Japan
iizuka@isc.senshu-u.ac.jp
[2] Universite de Paris Saclay, 8 Av. Cauchy, 92330 Sceaux, France

Abstract. Online shopping usage exceeded 50% in 2020 in Japan [1]. Website design for e-commerce is one of the most important factors in the customer's purchasing process. In this study, we focused on the color of websites. This study presents the results of research on the effect of colors in an e-commerce website on consumer mood in Japan. As the experimental environment, we created eight different charts with varied hues, brightness levels and saturation based on a survey conducted in France [2]. We used these graphic charts to investigate how colors effect memorization, buying intention, mood, and emotion. This research enabled us to bring to the fore the effects of the colors used on e-commerce websites on consumer mood, emotion, memorization and buying intention. Mood and emotion have a significant effect on buying intention on e-commerce websites. In the research results, we found the effects of the colors used in e-commerce websites on consumer mood, emotion, memorization and buying intention. Mood and the emotion have a significant effect on buying intention on e-commerce websites in Japan. In addition, we found a different result compared to the survey result conducted in France.

Keywords: E-commerce website · Color · Achromatic colors

1 Introduction

Online shopping usage exceeded 50% in 2020 in Japan [1]. Website design for e-commerce is one of the most important factors in the customer's purchasing process, and color is involved in this process. Pelet conducted research on e-commerce website on consumer mood in France, 2012 [2]. In our study, we targeted consumers in Japan. Because people live in different countries and have different colors of eyes, their favorite colors are different [3]. In addition, people who live in the same environment like the same color [4]. A particular palette of colors is predominantly used for website design in different countries [5]. Thus, we researched the best colors for e-commerce for Japanese consumers.

C. Stephanidis et al. (Eds.): HCII 2022, CCIS 1582, pp. 485–491, 2022.
https://doi.org/10.1007/978-3-031-06391-6_60

2 Related Work

Pelet's study found direct effects of the colors of the graphic chart on memorization [2]. Moreover, free recall had a positive effect on buying intentions. The more information an individual memorizes about a product, the stronger the buying intention. In addition, the colors of graphic chart are very influential on buying intention. Brightness has a significant positive effect on buying intentions. However, the effect of brightness on buying intention is only significant with a chromatic color hue. A black and white hue chart does not have this effect. The colors of the chart affect emotion in a negative way, while a low brightness enhances stimulation. Moreover, Pelet found that stimulation has a significant effect on buying intention [2]. Hue and brightness have a significant interaction effect on negative mood. Negative mood does not have any effect on memorization, but it has a significant and negative impact on buying intention.

According to Hsieh's study in Taiwan [6], low-brightness backgrounds are associated with high patronage intention regardless of whether prices are high or low. The high-brightness backgrounds are sensitive to merchandise prices and react significantly negatively to high prices.

3 Research Method

As the experimental environment, we created eight different charts (Fig. 1) with varied hues, brightness and saturation (Table 1) based on the study in France, in order to measure the differences in color perception. These graphic charts are designed for e-commerce websites selling confectionary for gifts. For each confectionery, participants would see the package, the name, the price, drive charge, quantity and information about the item. We used these graphic charts to investigate memorization, mood, emotion, and buying intention.

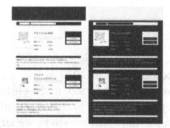

Fig. 1. Graphic chart for research use

We conducted experiments with 888 participants, and 741 valid responses were used for the analysis. The participants looked at one of the eight graphic charts, and imagined that they wanted to buy gifts on the internet for friends. They were asked their age, their sex and six questions about graphic charts. These six questions were intended to examine memorization and emotion, mood, and buying intention. The participants were asked two questions about recognizing two types of confection in order to measure

Table 1. Color design of the experiment

	plan	background(Dominant)				foreground(Dynamic)			
		name	H	B	S	name	H	B	S
chromatic colors- Green and Yellow	1	Magonlia Yellow		60	100	20	Newsvine Green		120	40	100
	2	Magonlia Yellow		60	100	20	Granny Apple Green		90	80	100
	3	Newsvine Green	120	40	100	Magonlia Yellow		60	100	20
	4	Newsvine Green	120	40	100	Sunflower Yellow		60	100	60
Achromatic colors - Black & White	5	White	0	100	0	Black		0	0	0
	6	White	0	100	0	Grey		0	60	0
	7	Black	0	0	0	White		0	100	0
	8	Black	0	0	0	Grey		0	60	0

memorization. In the first question, participants chose the correct one from sentences about two confections. A wrong answer gave zero points, a right answer was one point. Recognition scores ranged from 0 to 14. In the second question, participants could answer freely about these confections. Free recall was measured by counting the number of items that participants could recall from those used in them description. These had a 15-element description. A wrong answer gave zero points, a neutral answer was three points, while a right answer was six points. To measure moods, we used the Brief Mood Introspection Scale (BMIS). Participants rated on a five-point Likert scale ranging from "Definitely do not feel" (1) to "Definitely feel" (5). To measure emotion we used a PAD scale. It included three items: pleasure, arousal, dominance. Participants rated on a five-point Likert scale ranging from "Definitely do not feel" (1) to "Definitely feel" (5). To measure buying intention, participants were asked "Do you want to buy these confections as gifts?" They answered the five items from "Strongly disagree" to "Strongly agree".

4   Data Analysis and Results

Color1 is plan1 and plan2 in Table 1. Color2 is plan3 and plan4 in Table 1. Color3 is plan5 and plan6 in Table 1. Color4 is plan7 and plan8 in Table 1.

4.1   Direct Effects of the Colors in the Graphic Chart on Memorization

The questions measuring cued recall were scored higher for patterns with color3 and color4. The patterns with a low contrast between the background and foreground colors scored higher, except for the pattern with color2. Therefore, the patterns with achromatic colors and low contrast between dominant color and dynamic color had a more positive effect on cued recall. Participants had higher scores when the contrast between dominant color and dynamic color was higher, except for the pattern with color2.

In addition, we got interesting answers for free recall. When the dominant color or dynamic color was newsvine green, some participants answered that the color of packages or website was red. But we did not use red on them. This is attributed to complementary colors. The eyes receive a color stimulus and react to it, producing a different color from the real one. Thus, they answered that packages or website color schemes used red (Fig. 2).

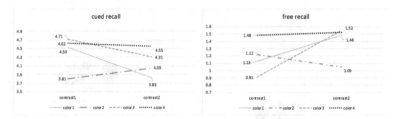

Fig. 2. Results for memorization (Color figure online)

4.2   Direct Effects of the Colors in the Graphic Chart on Moods

The hue had a positive effect on mood. Achromatic colors had more positive effects than chromatic colors. When chromatic colors were used, an increase of contrast between dominant color and dynamic color level contributed to toning down negative mood (Fig. 3).

Fig. 3. Results for mood

4.3   Direct Effects of the Colors in the Graphic Chart on Emotion

The hue contrast between dominant color and dynamic color had an interaction effects on pleasure. Achromatic colors have more positive effects on pleasure than chromatic colors. However, the brightness has no effects on pleasure.

The brightness contrast between dominant color and dynamic color had an interaction effect on domination. However, this effects difference between achromatic colors and chromatic colors. When achromatic colors were used, an increase of brightness level contributed to toning down domination. And when chromatic colors were used, a decrease of brightness level contributed to toning down domination.

The brightness contrast between dominant color and dynamic color had different effects on arousal for achromatic and chromatic colors. When chromatic colors were used, an increase of brightness level contributed to toning up arousal. On the other hand, a decrease of brightness level contributed to toning up arousal when achromatic colors were used (Fig. 4).

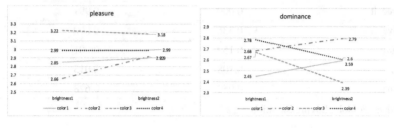

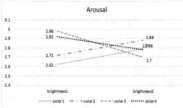

Fig. 4. Results for emotion

4.4 Direct Effects of the Colors in the Graphic Chart on Buying Intention

A higher contrast between a dominant color and dynamic color enhanced buying intention. Moreover, achromatic colors had more positive effects than chromatic colors (Fig. 5).

Fig. 5. Buying intention

4.5 Relationship Between Buying Intention and Other Items

Multiple regression analyses showed that that factor with the greatest effect on buying intention was positive mood. Among them, satisfied mood had an especially large impact on performance (Tables 2 and 3)

Table 2. Effects on buying intention

	Coefficient	P
Cued recall	−0.177	0.000
Free recall	0.000	0.991
Positive mood	0.336	0.000
Pleasure	0.159	0.001
Arousal	0.108	0.015
Dominance	0.052	0.628

Dependent variable: buying intention

Table 3. Effects of positive mood on buying intention

	Coefficient	P
Happy	0.190	0.006
Caring	−0.005	0.921
Clam	0.011	0.834
Satisfied	0.236	0.000
Active	0.080	0.025
Loving	0.188	0.000

Dependent variable: buying intention

5   Discussion

This research enabled us to bring to the fore the effects of the colors used in e-commerce websites on consumer mood, emotion, memorization and buying intention. Mood and emotion have a significant effect on buying intention on e-commerce website. Mood and emotion were affected more positively by high-brightness dominant color. According to Martinez's study [7], complementary color relation between package of product colors and dominant retail environment colors is higher effects on buying intention, in the case of food. When we used chromatic colors and high-brightness colors in the graphic charts, they have complementary color relationship.

However, memorization did not have an effect on buying intention. It is assumed that it is concerned with not needing much information on a product when we choose a gift other than CDs.

Achromatic colors are more likely to enhance four elements (cued recall, buying intention, positive mood and pleasure) than chromatic colors are. However, chromatic colors have more positive effects than achromatic colors. This is the characteristic result compared to the result of the survey conducted in France [2], It is inferred that this result is complicated as regards color preferences. Japanese people like white and black more than other countries [3, 8]. In other words, achromatic colors evoke positive effects on e-commerce websites in Japan.

6 Conclusions

This study investigated the effects of colors on e-commerce websites in Japan. Our research enabled us to bring to the fore the effects of the colors used in e-commerce websites on consumer mood, emotion, memorization and buying intention. We found that, achromatic colors in e-commerce website evoked positive effects. This result is the biggest difference between Japan and France. Our research can help realize the effective design of e-commerce websites for Japanese consumers.

References

1. WHITE PAPER Information and Communications in Japan Year2021, Ministry of Internal Affairs and Communications (MIC), Japan (2021)
2. Pelet, J-E, Papadopoulou, P.: Consumer Responses to Colors of E-Commerce Websites: An Empirical Investigation, E-Commerce, pp. 113–142. Intech, Rijeka (2010)
3. Terada, E., Takahashi, J., Aihara, K.: A proposal of web page design of Japanese enterprise for Europe and America people. Bull. Japanese Soc. Sci. Des. 55(4), 39–46 (2008). (in Japanese)
4. Yanase, T.: Quantitated study of color image. J. Vis. Soc. Jpn. **17**(64), 18–22 (1997)
5. Kondratova, I., Goldfarb, I.: Cultural interface design: global colors study. In: Meersman, R., Tari, Z., Herrero, P. (eds.) OTM 2006. LNCS, vol. 4277, pp. 926–934. Springer, Heidelberg (2006). https://doi.org/10.1007/11915034_117
6. Hsieh, Y.C., Chiu, H.C., Tang, Y.C., Lee, M.: Do colors change realities in online shopping ? J. Interact. Mark. Mark. EDGE **41**, 14–27 (2018)
7. Martinez, L.M., Rando, B., Agante, L., Abreu, A.M.: True colors: consumers' packaging choices depend on the color of retail environment. J. Retail. Consum. Serv. **59**, 1–13 (2021)
8. Saito, M.: Preference for white in Japan and its background: a comparative study in Asian areas. J. Color Sci. Assoc. Jpn. **23**(3), 158–167 (1999)

Research on Interface Design Style of Coffee Ordering Mini Programs Based on Kansei Engineering

Han Lei and Yongyan Guo[✉]

Institute of Art Design and Media, East China University of Science and Technology, 200237,
No 130 Meilong Road, Xuhui District, Shanghai, China
Harriet224@163.com

Abstract. Coffee has developed rapidly in the Chinese market in recent years with huge potential. Today, with the transformation of traditional e-commerce, the coffee industry has also begun to focus on the new sales model. It pays more attention to the personalized needs of users. In this kind of environment, how to seize the coffee market customers quickly, the interface design of the mini program is as important as the first business card on the brand line. According to the survey, there are problems such as homogenization and confusing interface design of coffee mini programs in China. There is still a lot of room for optimization in the coffee market. Therefore, it is necessary to study how to make the interface design of the new retail coffee brand more suitable for the user's perceptual needs and improve the user's experience. This paper uses the semantic difference method of Kansei Engineering to collect samples of the interface design of the coffee ordering mini program, and then collects the perceptual vocabulary of the target users and makes a Likert scale. Then, it is concluded that the user's feeling is mainly affected by two main factors named " vitality" and "comfort". Finally, these two main factors are put into the established value elements for cluster analysis, and the main types of Chinese coffee mini program interface design and the space to be explored are obtained. It provides design style reference and new ideas for the interface design.

Keywords: Kansei engineering · Mini program · Interface design · Factor analysis · Cluster analysis

1 Introduction

As the first of the three major beverages in the world today, coffee has penetrated every aspect of modern life with its refreshing effect3. With the increase of China's national income and the acceleration of the consumption process, China has become the most potential coffee consuming country in the world. The rise of various new retail coffee brands also marks that China's coffee industry has entered a period with rapid development1. In China, Coffee has gradually evolved from a functional attribute to a social

C. Stephanidis et al. (Eds.): HCII 2022, CCIS 1582, pp. 492–503, 2022.
https://doi.org/10.1007/978-3-031-06391-6_61

attribute, and now become a combination of function and social attributes5. In the current Internet era, offline stores have been unable to meet the multi-dimensional needs of coffee brands. It's normal for coffee brands to choose offline stores to develop simultaneously with online mini programs. The interface design of mini programs has also become the first face meet online and play a vital role in brand promotion. One of the characteristics of the new retail model is that it pays more attention to the individual needs of consumers, and mini programs that are recognized by users will be more willing to be shared. Therefore, how to attract more users and be more recognized by users has become topics that every coffee brand must study5. This article will be based on Kansei Engineering, make experiments around the interface design of the coffee ordering mini program.

2   State of the Coffee Industry in China

In recent years, Chinese coffee have an amazing development trend, the broad market makes it one of the new popular industries in China. Since the consumption upgrades and the help of the Internet, coffee needs are no longer single refreshing function or social attributes, but more complex product attributes. This means that users not only have higher requirements on the raw materials and taste of coffee, but also hope that coffee can have a unique brand culture2.

The characteristics of the new retail model: consumer is the center, with online and offline channel integration, will more focus on personalized consumer needs. The new retail model is generally divided into two parts: online and offline, which is the product of the booming Internet industry6. Since the new retail model swept across all walks of life from 2016, the coffee industry has also undergone corresponding reforms and upgrades, transforming from traditional offline stores to the new model.

According to data, 51% of consumers will think that coffee is a functional drink to refresh the mind and improve work efficiency; 49% of consumers regard coffee as a drink to enjoy life, and such users value enjoyment attitude to life. In addition, the main groups of coffee are office people and students. They have their own choices and preferences for beverages and pursues freshness. To meet the needs of major users, the brand's product must be diversity, fast iteration, and easy selection.

3   Mini Program Interface Design

Compared with APP, Mini Programs have obvious advantages. For example: no need to download, less difficulty, light weight, and on-the-go. Since their release in 2017, the development can be described as rapid as possible. Affected by the epidemic in recent years, more and more industries have shifted from offline to online, and mini programs have also become an important tool for online layout in all walks of life. According to statistics, the daily active users of Mini Programs have already exceeded 440 million, covering more than 200 sub-sectors. With the development of mobile Internet and new retail models, this number will increase rapidly in the future. Mini programs will still play an important role in various industries7.

Compared with APP, mini programs have obvious lightweight characteristics, and it also adheres the principle of lightweight in interface design. Compared with native APP, the interface design of mini program is usually simpler, the information is more limited, and the impact on user experience will be more direct. Different interface designs have their own characteristics in style. A good interface design style can attract the attention of users, thereby strengthening the brand image9. At present, the interface design research of mini program mainly focuses on the use of human-machine relationship and lacks the perceptual evaluation research on interface style. Moreover, the current coffee ordering mini programs have some problems such as serious homogeneity and chaotic interface design. It is necessary to research and summarize the interface design of the coffee ordering mini programs in the Chinese market.

4   Kansei Engineering and Experiment Design

4.1   Semantic Difference Method of Kansei Engineering

Kansei engineering is based on engineering, psychology, statistics, aesthetics, and other disciplines. It is a combination technology established between sensibility and engineering13. The concept of Kansei Engineering is people-oriented and design from the user's point of view. In Kansei Engineering, Semantic Difference Method is one of the most used design methods.

4.2   Experimental Design

The experimental steps of this paper are as follows: (1) Select representative product samples from a large number of coffee ordering mini-programs, extract representative and content-rich pages, and establish a sample library; (2) Confirm the perceptual vocabulary of the product. Using semantic analysis, interview respondents and design professionals to collect a many descriptions and filter perceptual vocabulary to form a perceptual vocabulary database; (3) Design a questionnaire based on the semantic difference method. Use the Likert scale to design a questionnaire that can be scored, and let the respondents rate the sample in perceptual vocabulary; (4) Data analysis. Process and analyze the data in the questionnaire through data statistics software (factor analysis, principal component analysis and cluster analysis in SPSS), Finally, visual charts is generated, and will get some reference suggestions.

4.3   Collection and Determination of Perceptual Vocabulary

First, ten coffee mini programs with a representative interface design and a large degree of difference, the number of users exceeding the average will as experimental samples. Secondly, this paper mainly collects the user's perceptual evaluation of the interface through online questionnaire and offline questionnaire. Third, extract the perceptual words in it, then delete the words that are irrelevant or far from the topic. Finally collect more than 200 main perceptual words. Then, the words with similar meanings were de-duplicated, a total of 40 representative words were obtained. Using their positive meanings to establish a perceptual vocabulary (Table 1).

Table 1. Perceptual glossary

1. Cozy	11. Lovely	21. Individuality	31. Perfect
2. Moderate	12. Cheery	22. Plain	32. Environmentally
3. Marked	13. Appetite	23. Soft	33. Convenient
4. Clear	14. Interesting	24. Professional	34. Paramount
5. Neat	15. Creative	25. Compact	35. Balanced
6. Attractive	16. Textured	26. Advanced	36. Elegant
7. Special	17. Continuous	27. Thematic	37. Young
8. Beautiful	18. Succinct	28. Suitable	38. Textured
9. Lively	19. Plentiful	29. Distinctive	39. Unique
10. Warm	20. Favorite	30. Delicate	40. Unified

Then, the words in the perceptual vocabulary database are further screened by the expert discussion method. Finally, 6 representative positive perceptual words are extracted. On this basis, 6 perceptual words with opposite meanings were selected to form 6 groups of perceptual phrases (Table 2).

Table 2. Final confirmed perceptual phrases

Number	Perceptual phrase group	Number	Perceptual phrase group
Z1	Common——Special	Z4	Cheap——Noble
Z2	Serious——Lively	Z5	Monotonous——Plentiful
Z3	Bleak——Bright	Z6	Chaotic——Neat

4.4 Questionnaire Design and Distribution Based on Semantic Difference Method

The interface design of the ten coffee ordering mini-programs screened before is used as a questionnaire sample (Table 3). Then, a 7-level Richter scale was established for these 10 samples, and the scores were from −3 to 3 to indicate the level of the respondents' emotional inclination. −3 means that the perceptual tendency is more in line with the description on the left, and 3 means that the perceptual tendency is more in line with the description on the right. The sample is comprehensively displayed. Each sample selects 4 screenshots of interface design as questionnaire materials. The perceptual questionnaire design of the final 10 samples is shown in the following. (Table 4).

Table 3. 10 representative samples used in this experiment (each one only shows two pages there)

10 samples				
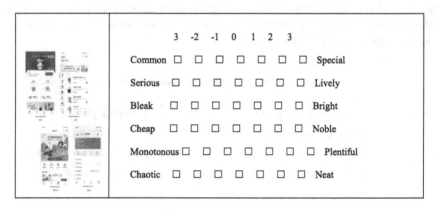				
No.1	No.2	No.3	No.4	No.5
No.6	No.7	No.8	No.9	No.10

Table 4. Questionnaire design (taking sample 1 as an example)

		3	-2	-1	0	1	2	3	
	Common	□	□	□	□	□	□	□	Special
	Serious	□	□	□	□	□	□	□	Lively
	Bleak	□	□	□	□	□	□	□	Bright
	Cheap	□	□	□	□	□	□	□	Noble
	Monotonous	□	□	□	□	□	□	□	Plentiful
	Chaotic	□	□	□	□	□	□	□	Neat

The target audience will limit the age range of the target users to 18 to 50 years old, and the occupations are mainly office workers and students. the proportion of male and female is even. Finally, there are 52 questionnaires distributed in a targeted manner, all of which have reference value after recovery.

4.5 Reliability and Validity Verification

Firstly, each group of samples of the questionnaire is preprocessed, and take the average value of each group of samples under the six groups of perceptual vocabulary (Table 5), then the processed data are tested for reliability and validity in SPSS. The reliability test value of the sample is 0.84, which is higher than 0.7, indicating that the reliability is high, and the answer is reliable and accurate. The KMO value is greater than 0.6, and the P value is 0.000, which proves significant. The questionnaire design is reasonable, and factor analysis can be carried out. Therefore, the following will use factor analysis to perform factor analysis on the average value of 10 samples under 6 groups of perceptual sample vocabulary.

Table 5. Sample mean under perceptual vocabulary

	Z1	Z2	Z3	Z4	Z5	Z6
Sample1	1.87	1.62	1.63	1.82	1.71	1.68
Sample2	1.48	1.04	1.45	1.33	1.31	1.61
Sample3	1.65	1.70	1.53	1.55	1.66	1.58
Sample4	1.56	1.62	1.76	1.56	1.77	1.31
Sample5	1.62	1.74	1.32	1.61	1.41	1.61
Sample6	1.78	1.76	1.78	1.73	1.72	1.65
Sample7	2.02	1.64	1.79	1.97	1.75	1.81
Sample8	1.73	1.23	1.31	1.61	1.52	1.86
Sample9	1.58	1.92	1.87	1.65	1.88	1.70
Sample10	1.42	1.28	1.52	1.40	1.47	1.35

5   Data Analysis

5.1   Factor Analysis to Explore the Main Design Factors

The variance of the common factor indicates the interpretation and contribution rate of the extracted common factor to the initial variable information. The higher the contribution rate, the stronger the representativeness of the extracted common factor to the initial variable.

Generally, in the research, the contribution rate of the extracted information value is more than 0.7, indicating that the information is valid. Therefore, it is verified that the six groups of perceptual vocabulary groups are all valid and representative (Table 6).

Table 6. Common factor variance

Phrase	Initial	Extract
Z1	1	0.92
Z2	1	0.717
Z3	1	0.833
Z4	1	0.941
Z5	1	0.835
Z6	1	0.917

Extraction method: principal component analysis

Import the average value into SPSS and reduce the dimensionality of the above average data through factor analysis, principal component analysis to check the importance of perceptual vocabulary, and obtain the common factor variance of typical sample perceptual vocabulary data (Table 6), the total variance explained is also as follows (Table 7), and the gravel figure are as follows (Fig. 1).

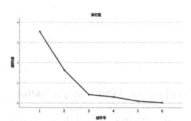

Fig. 1. Gravel figure

Table 7. Total variance explained

Element	Initial eigenvalues			Extract the load sum of squares			Rotational load sum of squares		
	Total	Percent variance	Accumulation%	Total	Percent variance	Accumulation%	Total	percent variance	accumulation%
1	3.535	58.925	58.925	3.535	58.925	58.925	2.799	46.65	46.65
2	1.627	27.12	86.044	1.627	27.12	86.044	2.364	39.394	86.044
3	0.419	6.982	93.027						
4	0.303	5.045	98.071						
5	0.096	1.599	99.67						
6	0.02	0.33	100						

The main characteristics can be judged by the slope change of the gravel figure. The change tends to be stable after the third component. Combined with the initial eigenvalues in Table 7, it is judged that the first two components are the main factors, and the cumulative proportion is 86.044%, which can cover the overall characteristics. Since the third component value is at the inflection position, component 1 and component 2 are determined as the main factors. From (Table 8), the first main factors and Z2 (lively), Z3 (bright), Z5 (plentiful) there is a clear relationship; the second main factor 2 is closely related to Z1 (special), Z4 (noble), Z6 (neat).

Table 8. Rotation composition matrix

Phrase	Main factor 1	Main factor 2
Z1	0.304	0.91
Z2	0.828	0.176
Z3	0.912	0.009
Z4	0.542	0.805
Z5	0.935	0.206
Z6	−0.144	0.902

The evaluation criteria for interface design usually include color, style, graphics, interface layout, etc10. Main factor 1 is closely related to Z2 (Lively), Z3 (bright) and Z5 (plentiful). Z2 (lively) is closely related to color matching and picture style. Usually, lively colors are expressed as exciting colors or forward colors that can create a lively visual impression. The Z2 (lively) also represent style. Most of today's interface designs are restrained. The use of elements such as illustrations with a high degree of freedom can change the seriousness of the picture. Z3 (bright) is closely related to the color matching. Among the three elements of color, about color, the most closely related to Z3 (bright) is lightness. lightness is the perception of the light and darkness of the light source and the surface of the object, which can be simply understood as the brightness of the color. It can help mini program bring a direct and relaxed feeling to the user. Z5 (plentiful) has a strong relationship with the interface color, picture style, function arrangement, etc., the overall performance is diversity, that means the visual performance should be rich enough. Finally, the performance of the main factor 1 can be summarized as: lively and progressive, high brightness color matching; plentiful element arrangement; diverse picture styles. Therefore, the main factor 1 can be summed up as "sense of vitality".

The main factor 2 is closely related to Z1 (special), Z4 (noble), Z6 (neat). Also analyzed from several main aspects of interface design, Z1 (Special) represents the degree of differentiation from other mini programs in interface design. At present, the main feature that distinguishes mini programs is the brand representative color, which make mini programs is easier to impress users. Z4 (noble) is closely related to the use of colors and layout. The colors with a sense of nobility are usually expressed in cold colors such as gold, coffee, blue, and other dark colors, giving users a sense of distance. On the page layout, the sense of nobility is expressed as appropriate blank space, not excessive performance, and precise control of details, such as the design of appropriate style icons. Z6 (neat), as the name suggests, whether it is color matching, typography, function distribution or picture style, it should be consistent and harmonious. For example, in the use of colors, try to use the same color system, and the weight, size, and proportion of the use of different color systems should be reasonably matched. Combining these, the main factor 2 can be summarized as: unique brand color system, reasonable and neat layout and function distribution, appropriate white space, proportional distribution, in line with the user's vision Habits and preferences. Combined with the above analysis, the main factor 2 is named "comfort".

5.2 Cluster Analysis Results

Substitute the two main factors analyzed above into 10 samples, analyze the relationship between the samples and them, obtain a sample clustering dendrogram (Fig. 2). The clustering of the samples is gradually stable when the distance is 4, so the 10 programs can be divided into 3 categories. Combined with the factor-sample scatter figure (Fig. 3), sample 1, sample 6, sample 7, and sample 9 are relatively close; sample 3, sample 5, and sample 4 are also relatively close. In addition, sample 2, sample 10, and sample 8 are relatively close and can be divided into a group separately. According to the clustering results of the samples, the analysis results are as follows (Table 9). The sample with the highest score is category 1, and the design style can be used as a reference for the current interface design of the coffee ordering mini programs.

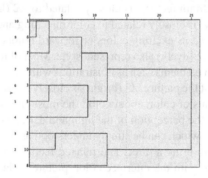

Fig. 2. Genealogy figure

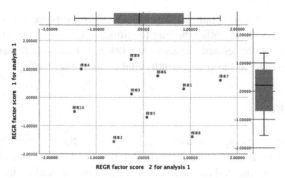

Fig. 3. Factor-sample scatter figure

Table 9. Analysis of sample taxon characteristics

Category	Sample number	Characteristics
Category 1	Sample 1, sample 6, sample 7, sample 9	Category 1 has the characteristics of bright and rich colors, lively and delicate style, full content, rich types of pictures, reasonable layout, and appropriate blank space
Category 2	Sample 3, sample 5, sample 4	Category 2 has a cute picture style, rich colors and content, and scattered layout
Category 3	Sample 2, sample 10, sample 8	Category 3 screens are mainly composed of heavy colors, the screen is simple, the content is relatively simple, and the layout distance is large, which is easy to cause a sense of alienation to users

Analyze the above three groups of samples, category 1 performs the best among the three groups. And the samples of category 1 are closer to the description of "vitality" and "comfort", For the time being, category 1 can be used as a sample that is more in line with the user's perceptual needs during design. In (Fig. 3), it shows that the first quadrant still has a lot of room, which proves that there is still a lot of design space in the market that meets the user's perceptual needs, and the interface design of the coffee ordering mini programs still has a lot of room for improvement. However, attention should be paid to the relationship between plentiful content and comfortable layout.

5.3 Reasons for the Development of Coffee to "Vitality" and "Comfort"

Combined with the changes in the target users of coffee, coffee was a symbol of enjoying life in the past, closely related to words such as elegance, slow pace, and high quality. However, with the improvement of the national economic level and consumption capacity, the target users of the coffee industry are gradually getting younger, and the living habits of users have already changed. More than half of users pay more attention to the functional requirements of coffee, hoping to stimulate vitality. And the pace of modern life has been greatly accelerated, the users at work are prone to depression, they will be more eager to be close to the sun, warmth, vitality, and other feelings.

6 Conclusion

Finally, draws the following conclusions: (1) At present, the research objects are mainly affected by the two principal components of "vitality" and "comfort". The expression of "vitality" can be summarized as bright color, rich elements, and various picture styles; "comfort" is expressed in the reasonable proportion and arrangement of unique color system. (2) At present, there is still a lot of room for development in the coffee mini-program market in terms of "Vitality" and "comfort", there is still a lot of room that can improve. (3) Combined with the main user characteristics of coffee, it is concluded that the user's preference for the interface will follow the change of the environment. The reason why "vitality" and "comfort" are favored by users may be closely related to their living habits.

Mini Programs are important for coffee industry. From the perspective of interface design, capturing users' perceptual needs can help Mini Programs improve users' experience and favor. Obviously, the design that grasp the perceptual needs of users will help the coffee industry to accelerate in China.

References

1. Li, D., Yuanyuan, H.: Situation analysis and development suggestions of China's coffee industry. Tropic. Agric. Sci. **39**(03), 105–109 (2019)
2. Zhu, Y., Wang, Z., Wang, X., Ren, X.: New brand marketing strategy in shanghai freshly ground coffee market. Cooper. Econ. Technol. **13**, 88–89 (2020). https://doi.org/10.13665/j.cnki.hzjjykj.2020.13.033
3. Wen, Z., Bi, X., Lu, W.: A brief talk on the trend of coffee consumption in China. Agric. Prod. Process. **02**, 69–70 (2018). https://doi.org/10.16693/j.cnki.1671-9646(X).2018.01.047
4. Zhang, J.: The origin, development, dissemination and beverage culture of coffee. Chin. Agric. History **02**, 22–29 (2006)
5. Wu, Z., Wu, Y.: Research on the new retail model in the internet era: taking luckin coffee as an example. Chin. Mark. **04**, 130–131 (2019)
6. Jiabao, W., Yijun, H.: The causes, characteristics, types and development trends of new retail. Bus. Econ. Res. **23**, 5–7 (2018)
7. Lin, X., Wang, J., Wang, W., Shu, Y.: Research on the user experience of Wechat mini programs. Industrial Design Industry Research Center. Industrial Design Research (Volume 5): Industrial Design Industry Research Center, p. 6 (2017)
8. Zhao, S., Xu, X.: The meaning, model and development path of "new retail." Chin. Circ. Econ. **31**(05), 12–20 (2017)
9. Wu, Y.: Research on interface problems of human-computer interaction design. Wuhan University of Technology (2004)
10. Yuan, H., Hu, S., Xu, Y., Xu, X.: Research on the design of information visualization interface for sports APP. Packag. Eng. **41**(18), 236–241 (2020)

11. Ishii, H., Ullmer, B.: Tangible Bits: Towards Seamless Interfaces between People, Bits and Atoms (1998)
12. Canqun, H., Songqin, W.: Discussion on the method and research of Kansei engineering. Decoration **10**, 16 (2006)
13. Ming, D., Jianchao, Z.: Research on gamepad experience under the theoretical system of Kansei Engineering. Design **33**(21), 20–23 (2020)

Cosmetic Products Recommendation Methods for Different Occasions Using Consumer Reviews and Geotagged Tweets

Da Li[1([✉])], Riko Yasuda[1], Tadahiko Kumamoto[2], and Yukiko Kawai[1]

[1] Kyoto Sangyo University, Kyoto, Japan
{lida,g1854616,kawai}@cc.kyoto-su.ac.jp
[2] Chiba Institute of Technology, Chiba, Japan
kumamoto@net.it-chiba.ac.jp

Abstract. With the popularity and development of online shopping, more and more people choose to buy clothes or cosmetics online. However, because online shopping users can't actually try cosmetics or directly consult the shopping guide's suggestions, it is not easy to image where to use these cosmetics when buying them. In this research, we propose a cosmetic products recommendation method that provides users with the most suitable occasions/cosmetics for each kind of cosmetics/occasions by extracting and analyzing the correlation between cosmetics and places. In particular, firstly, we utilize the public data set to obtain the word vectors. Because very few locations are mentioned in consumer review dataset, we use the geotagged tweet data which posted in different places to obtain feature vectors, and calculate the similarities between the place feature vectors and cosmetic product vectors. Then, we rank the top-n places with the high similarities. Moreover, we also asked 60 users to evaluate our recommendation system by judging the suitability of 12 cosmetic products with high relevance in five places. The results showed that our proposed method is effective.

Keywords: Recommendation system · Cosmetic products · Consumer reviews · Geotagged tweets · word2vec

1 Introduction

Since the late 1990s, with the rapid growth of many e-retailers, including Amazon (US), Taobao (China), and Rakuten (Japan), online shopping has taken off as an increasing number of consumers purchase increasingly diversified products on the Internet [4,6,10]. Using public data sets, there are a large number of studies to analyze user purchase behavior and propose products recommendation system [2,3,5]. However, there are still many problems that cannot be solved by the current online shopping or related recommendation systems, such as what cosmetics to use and what clothes to wear in different occasions—which has a significant impact on users' consumption decisions [1,8,9].

C. Stephanidis et al. (Eds.): HCII 2022, CCIS 1582, pp. 504–510, 2022.
https://doi.org/10.1007/978-3-031-06391-6_62

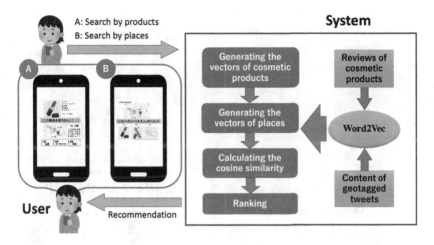

Fig. 1. Overview of the proposed cosmetic products recommendation system.

Therefore, in this article, we focus on how to recommend suitable occasions for users when they shopping online. As the first trials of cosmetic products recommendation system for different occasions, we propose a recommendation system by analyzing the product reviews and geotagged tweets. Specifically, we provide two ways of recommendation: A) when the user searches for a cosmetic product, the ranking list of the place where the product is suitable will be prompted; B) when users search for places, our recommendation system will prompt the ranking list of appropriate cosmetics. The overview of the proposed recommendation methods is shown in Fig. 1.

To implement our approach, we utilize the public data set provided by Rakuten Ichiba (containing more than 5600 cosmetics) to obtain the word vectors. Because very few locations are mentioned in the consumer review dataset, we use the geotagged tweet data which posted in different places to extract feature vectors, and calculate the similarities between the place feature vectors and cosmetic product vectors. Then, we rank the top-n places with the high similarities. Moreover, we also asked 60 users to evaluate our recommendation system by judging the suitability of 12 cosmetic products with high relevance in five places. Finally, we validate our proposed two recommendation method A and B through MSE (Mean Squared Error) and nDCG (Normalized Discounted Cumulative Gain).

2   Cosmetic Products Recommendation System

In this paper, we propose a cosmetic products recommendation system for different occasions by analyzing the product reviews and geotagged tweets. In this section, we introduce the recommendation methods of our proposed system.

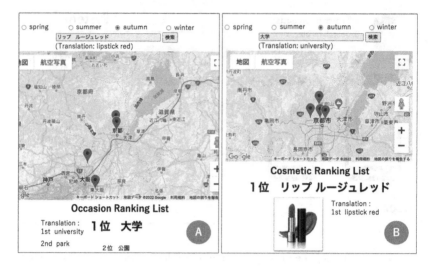

Fig. 2. User interface of the proposed system.

2.1   Dataset Description

In this research, we utilize the commodity review data of Rakuten Ichiba public dataset, and geotagged Twitter data (content and location information). For the review data, we extract 111,220 customer review data in "beauty, cosmetics and perfume" genre of Rakuten Ichiba dataset[1] from September 2016 to October 2016 (16,609 review data of the subtype of "basic makeup"). For the Twitter data, we collected 37,414 tweets on five occasions: school (4^2), hospital (4), hotel (3), park (4) and theme park (4), which are posted within a radius of 1km around of each place from October 1 to October 31, 2016.

2.2   Proposed Method

Figure 1 showed the flow of proposed cosmetic product recommendation method:

1) Training word embedding using cosmetic review data by applying Word2Vec model [7].
2) Generating the feature vectors of each place and cosmetic product using Pre-trained Word2Vec model.
3) Calculating the cosine similarity between the feature vectors and recommending the ranking list.

---

[1] https://www.nii.ac.jp/dsc/idr/rakuten/.
[2] In this paper, the numbers in brackets indicate the number of specific locations included in each occasion.

Table 1. The details of 12 cosmetic products.

ID	Cosmetic products
1003370	Mood Matcher Light Blue
1020965	Estee Lauder Pure Color
1001830	Clee de Poe Beaute Poodle Compact Esanciel
1047742	Yves Saint Laurent Rouge Pure Couture Shimmat
1135961	Maybelline Hyper Sharp Liner Midnight Black
1039429	Medica Liner Night & Hard
1005479	FASIO Mineral Foundation
1046992	Christian Dior Addict Lipstick
1033249	Estee Lauder Pure Color Crystal Lipstick
1062163	RMK Creamy Foundation N102
1080195	Astre Virgo Eye Beauty Fixer WP
1001454	Etude House Eyebrow Tint My Blow Gel

In the 1) process, we utilized MeCab[3] to segment the review data, and applied the segmentation results into the Word2Vec model for training word vectors. The vectors have dimensionality of 300, and the words which term frequency less than three are deleted. In the 2) and 3) process, cosmetic review C_i is generated into the feature vector v_{C_i}, tweet textual content T_j is generated into the feature vector v_{T_j}. Where v_{C_i} denotes the average of each 300 dimensions word vectors in the cosmetic review, v_{T_j} is the average of each 300 dimensions word vectors in the geotagged tweet. The cosine similarity between C_i and T_j is calculated as follows:

$$Eval(C_i, T_j) = \frac{v_{C_i} \cdot v_{T_j}}{|v_{C_i}| \cdot |v_{T_j}|} \tag{1}$$

Figure 2 showed the user interface of the proposed system. When users input the season and cosmetic products, our system can provide the ranking list of the most appropriate occasions (left side of Fig. 2). Similarly, when users input the season and places, our system can provide the ranking list of the most suitable cosmetic products to users.

3   Evaluations

In this section, we describe the evaluation method of the proposed recommendation system. We selected 12 cosmetic products (details are shown in Table 1) with the highest similarity among the cosmetics products extracted on five occasions through proposed method, and asked cosmetic users to evaluate these cosmetic products. The cosmetic users are 60 female Japanese native speakers (containing teens: 1.7%, 20s': 23.3%, 30s': 36.7%, 40s': 28.3%, and 50s': 10%). They were asked to select and rank the most suitable cosmetic products of the five places.

---

[3] https://taku910.github.io/mecab/.

Table 2. The MSE scores of the recommended cosmetics on each place.

ID	School	Hospital	Hotel	Park	Theme park
1003370	0.1855	0.1057	0.7318	0.1804	0.0252
1020965	0.1614	0.7425	0.0311	0.0349	0.6746
1001830	0.0004	0.0341	0.1111	$4.94e^{-5}$	0.0171
1047742	**0.7581**	0.1974	0.0562	0.1981	0.3832
1135961	0.0163	0.1616	0.0006	0.4479	0.0869
1039429	0.1078	0.0546	0.6442	0.1661	0.0009
1005479	0.0161	0.2396	0.1220	0.0429	0.2223
1046992	0.4625	0.0040	0.0004	0.3183	**$4.88e^{-5}$**
1033249	0.0446	0.2851	0.0032	0.0071	0.2768
1062163	0.3208	0.0214	0.0967	0.4907	0.0246
1080195	0.2429	0.0813	0.0080	0.4507	0.3240
1001454	0.3362	0.1395	0.3021	0.4035	0.4938
average	0.2211	**0.1722**	0.1756	**0.2284**	0.2108

The results are treated as ground truth, then we compare the ranking provided by our method and the ground truth.

3.1 Adequacy Evaluation of the Recommended Cosmetics on Each Place

Table 2 showed the MSE scores of the recommended cosmetics on each place, where the recommended cosmetics are treated as estimated values, and the cosmetic users' evaluation are treated as actual values. The smallest MSE score is "theme park" $4.88e^{-5}$ with commodity ID "10046992", and the largest MSE score is "school" 0.7581 with commodity ID "1047742". When it comes to the average MSE value of each place, the school is 0.2211, the theme park is 0.2108, and the average MSE value of all places is 0.2016. The effectiveness of the proposed method is confirmed.

3.2 Evaluation on Occasion Ranking List of Each Cosmetics

In our system, we rank the relationship between products and places by the cosine similarity. Table 3 showed the nDCG@5 scores of the occasion (place) ranking (provided by our system/user evaluation). In all cosmetic items, The smallest nDCG@5 value is 0.8282 with commodity ID "1135961". On the other hand, the largest nDCG@5 value is 0.9857 with commodity ID "1001830", "1047742" and "1046992". The average value of all commodities is 0.942, which confirms that the place ranking of commodities using proposed method is effective.

3.3 Evaluation on Cosmetic Ranking List of Each Occasions

Table 4 showed the nDCG@12 scores of the cosmetic ranking (provided by our system/user evaluation). In all five places, The smallest nDCG@12 value is

Table 3. The nDCG@5 scores of each cosmetics.

ID	1003370	1020965	1001830	1047742	1135961	1039429
nDCG@5	0.9608	0.8571	**0.9857**	0.9857	**0.8282**	0.9576
ID	1005479	1046992	1033249	1062163	1080195	1001454
nDCG@5	0.9005	0.9857	0.9647	0.9647	0.9608	0.9538

Table 4. The nDCG@12 Scores of each occasions.

School	Hospital	Totel	Park	Theme park	Average
0.7736	0.7620	0.7175	**0.6879**	**0.7770**	0.7436

0.6879 ("park") and the largest is 0.7770 ("theme park"). However, the average nDCG@12 value of all places was relatively low (0.7436). In cosmetic reviews, there are "lighter/darker" and other characteristic information in the evaluation of lipstick color. For the cosmetics evaluation that users want to use at outdoor places such as "park" and "theme park", they might consider these characteristics of cosmetics. It seems has an impact on the results. In the future, we plan to consider the various characteristics and various purposes of cosmetic products in our system, such as the brightness of color or using at indoor/outdoor places.

4 Conclusion

In this paper, we proposed a cosmetic products recommendation method that provides users with the most suitable cosmetics for each kind of occasions by extracting and analyzing the correlation between cosmetics and places. We provided two approaches of recommendation: A) when the user searches for a cosmetic product, the ranking list of the place where the product is suitable will be prompted; B) when users search for places, our recommendation system will prompt the ranking list of appropriate cosmetics. Our proposed methods are relatively simple, but they can make it easier for the users to imagine the most appropriate occasions to use the cosmetics they are browsing. In addition, we asked 60 users to evaluate 12 cosmetic products with high relevance in five places. The results showed that our proposed method is effective. In our experiment, we utilized the "autumn" data which contains the review data from September to October in 2016. We plan to collect four seasons data for considering the impact of season on the choice of cosmetics and occasions. In future work, not only the textual content of geotagged tweets and cosmetic reviews, we also plan to analyze the color, shape and other characteristics of products to improve our cosmetic products recommendation system.

Acknowledgments. This is a product of research activity of Institute of Advanced Technology, Center for Sciences towards Symbiosis among Human, Machine and Data which was financially supported by the Kyoto Sangyo University Research Grants, (M2001). This work was partially supported by JSPS KAKENHI Grant Numbers JP19H04118, JP19K12240, JP21K17862.

References

1. Hori, K., Okada, S., Nitta, K.: Fashion image classification on mobile phones using layered deep convolutional neural networks. In: Proceedings of the 15th International Conference on Mobile and Ubiquitous Multimedia, pp. 359–361 (2016)
2. Huang, Y., Liu, H., Li, W., Wang, Z., Hu, X., Wang, W.: Lifestyles in amazon: evidence from online reviews enhanced recommender system. Int. J. Mark. Res. **62**(6), 689–706 (2020)
3. Kagan, S., Bekkerman, R.: Predicting purchase behavior of website audiences. Int. J. Electron. Commer. **22**(4), 510–539 (2018)
4. Lee, S.M., Lee, D.: "untact": a new customer service strategy in the digital age. Serv. Bus. **14**(1), 1–22 (2020)
5. Li, M., Mao, H., Hu, J., Li, B.: Prediction and analysis of amazon user behavior based on long short-term memory and manual feature. In: 2021 International Conference on Artificial Intelligence, Big Data and Algorithms (CAIBDA), pp. 243–247. IEEE (2021)
6. Liu, C., Hong, J.: Strategies and service innovations of Haitao business in the Chinese market: a comparative case study of amazon. CN vs gmarket. co. kr. Asia Pacific J. Innov. Entrepr. (2016)
7. Mikolov, T., Chen, K., Corrado, G., Dean, J.: Efficient estimation of word representations in vector space. arXiv preprint arXiv:1301.3781 (2013)
8. Takaki, T., Murakami, T., Kurosawa, Y., Mera, K., Takezawa, T.: A searching support system for fashion items focusing on silhouettes (in Japanese). In: The 29th Annual Conference of the Japanese Society for Artificial Intelligence, pp. 1–4 (2015)
9. Ueda, M., Taniguchi, Y., Li, D., Siriaraya, P., Nakajima, S.: A research on constructing evaluative expression dictionaries for cosmetics based on word2vec. In: The 23rd International Conference on Information Integration and Web-based Applications & Services (iiWAS 2021), pp. 84–90. ACM (2021)
10. Willenborg, T.S.: Rakuten: a case study on entering new markets through an innovative business-to-business-to-consumer strategy. In: Segers, R.T. (ed.) Multinational Management, pp. 203–220. Springer, Cham (2016). https://doi.org/10.1007/978-3-319-23012-2_11

Village E-Commerce (Pasardesa ID) for Economic Recovery Due to the COVID-19 Pandemic

Nafrah Maudina[✉], Achmad Nurmandi, Isnaini Muallidin, Danang Kurniawan, and Mohammad Jafar Loilatu

Department of Government Affairs and Administration, Jusuf Kalla School of Government, University of Muhammadiyah Yogyakarta, Yogyakarta, Indonesia
nafrahmaudina99@gmail.com, nurmandi_achmad@umy.ac.id

Abstract. This research aims to uncover the village economic recovery strategy or BUMDes in Yogyakarta through digital or eCommerce applications. The digital or eCommerce application used in the village government sector to optimize BUMDes has declined due to the COVID-19 pandemic in Yogyakarta, digital and e-commerce applications in the village economic sector. Pasardesa.id is a digital application used to promote village products to customers through a network of resellers spread throughout Indonesia. This study used a descriptive qualitative approach, data analysis from the Pasardesa.ID website and application. The results indicated that using Pasardesa eCommerce.id as a strategic solution in village economic recovery or BUMDes is the right choice due to the large sales turnover and easy transactions. Therefore, many BUMDes partners join to use Pasardesa.id. Features on Pasardesa.id application or website also support the factor. Pasardesa.id application or website has affected the recovery of BUMDes or the village economy.

Keywords: E-commerce · Pasardesa.id · BUMDes · Economic recovery

1 Introduction

The COVID-19 pandemic since March 2020, which has hit almost all countries in the world, has had a lot of impact on the economic sector, not to mention in the villages. The impact of this pandemic in the economic sector is the decline in trade to industry both in the country and in the countryside [1]. The action taken to overcome the problem of the COVID-19 pandemic is to limit the activities of its citizens in several stages, ranging from physical distancing to lockdown measures [2]. Due to the steps and actions taken, many people cannot run their usual business interacting with face-to-face customers locally or globally [3].

The COVID-19 pandemic has influenced how businesses worldwide survive due to declining economic development [4]. Therefore, it is necessary to respond or answer these questions; of course, to answer these questions, various countries certainly carry out more innovative marketing strategies such as utilizing IT [5]. The marketing strategy

C. Stephanidis et al. (Eds.): HCII 2022, CCIS 1582, pp. 511–518, 2022.
https://doi.org/10.1007/978-3-031-06391-6_63

can utilize marketplaces or digital marketing to ease the community to make buying and selling practical, effective and efficient transactions. Of course, it does not take a long time. Digital marketing is used to increase sales figures and study branding to establish a good relationship between sellers and buyers. Digital marketing used eCommerce as a marketing tool for products or goods being traded [6].

COVID-19 cases have caused severe paralysis in the affected villages' economic sector [7]. During the pandemic, the village-owned business sector has changed a lot, such as BUMDes (Village Owned Enterprises) due to the limited interaction between buying and selling among the community to avoid the virus from spreading. The marketing strategy has also changed carried out by BUMDes is lacking. It is optimally resulting in a decline in the village economy [8]. To understand the effects of turmoil on the rural economy caused by the impact of COVID-19 on individual aspects of the world economy, focusing on the primary sector and industries involved in raw materials, the secondary sector involved in the production of finished products and the tertiary sector includes all service provision industry [9].

During the COVID-19 pandemic, villages in Yogyakarta experienced a decline, or the village market economy declined because of around 800 shops in the village whose marketing was hampered. After all, the management of village potential was temporarily halted [10]. However, problems regarding the village economy can be overcome by the Panggungharjo village apparatus collaborating with the Village Minister of PDTT by holding an e-commerce called Pasardesa.id [11]. Pasardesa.id aims to return the economy. With e-commerce, it can revive the village market economy, whose income has reached IDR 82,096,000 million since 25 days from the first day of operation. Pasardesa.id is hoped to allow the village government to restore and optimize the village economy [10]. This research is interesting because Panggungharjo Village is famous for the Panggung Lestari BUMDes, which received the best BUMDes reward in ASEAN and entered the pandemic. BUMDes could restore the village economy, which was fast due to the ideas of the Panggungharjo village officials regarding procurement eCommerce such as Pasardesa.ID in marketing and reselling products from the potential of their village.

2 Literature Review

2.1 E-Commerce

According to research [12], e-commerce is a method used as a modern business tool based on technology. Of course, e-commerce can facilitate the process of marketing products or market goods and facilitate market interaction (sellers and buyers) without having to gather at the market. The place of business or the seller. In e-commerce, various supporting frameworks such as people, public policy, market and advertising, support services, and business partnerships are described [13]. There are several models such as Business to Business, Business to Consumer, Consumer to Business, and Consumer to Consumer [14].

2.2 Economy Recovery

The pressure of the COVID-19 pandemic on the economic aspect has had a significant impact throughout the world [15], causing a surprise for every country faster than the financial crisis [16]. During this pandemic, a Lockdown policy is done temporarily, closing educational, commercial, religious, and other institutions [17].

The case of COVID-19 has indeed caused severe paralysis in the economic sector of the affected country [18]. The pandemic problem in China can be a clear example that the threat of a pandemic exerts enormous pressure on the economic aspect. Therefore, developing and developed countries feel high financial pressure due to the COVID-19 pandemic[19]. By feeling the pressure of this pandemic on the country's significant economy. Economic recovery is marked by increased marketing production or buying and selling in the village government sector as in BUMDes. It is hoped that the economic recovery of this village can have a more substantial impact on BUMDes in various towns. Thus, investment in economic-based villages is maintained. BUMDes are not included in the national economic program, so it is necessary to optimize BUMDes capital [20].

3 Research Method

This research revealed the importance of the village economic recovery strategy or BUMDes through digital applications related to buying and selling transactions and technology-based promotions in the village government, Yogyakarta. This study used a descriptive analysis method, and this method explains or describes the conditions and attitudes of the object being studied. The researchers analyzed the data using the https://pasardesa.id website and the Pasardesa.id application. This study focuses on the village economic recovery strategy or BUMDes through eCommerce or the Pasardesa.id digital application.

4 Discussion

In this era of globalization, technology is advancing. Internet is increasingly needed in community activities, education, and business. Social media is a source of information about government policies being implemented and sharing information with the public [21]. Like the policy on village economic recovery (BUMDes) during the pandemic, the policy was carried out by implementing e-commerce in the form of websites and applications or digital marketing to help restore the process of buying and selling inter-actions promoting superior village products. eCommerce replaces village markets with technology-based methods in promoting village products whose turnover will be used for village development in the future [22].

a. E-Commerce Pasardesa. ID

In the era of the COVID-19 pandemic, it has caused many economic crises, such as declining income from businesses and village markets in Indonesia [23]. By looking at the problem, e-commerce is used as a solution to overcome the crisis. During this economic crisis, citizen involvement is vital, either contributing or providing correct information to the government regarding the problems they face. That way, fear, confusion and anxiety among the citizens can be minimized during this critical time [24]. With E-commerce, buying and selling transactions are globally accessible via the internet [25]. One form of E-commerce in Indonesia that is part of the village government is Pasardesa.id is held by a collaboration between the Minister of Villages of PDTT and the Panggungharjo Village Apparatus. Pasardesa.id is a digital application that is the first to market potential village products through a network of resellers throughout Indonesia. Pasardesa.id has features for what products are available from the village likely production results as follows:

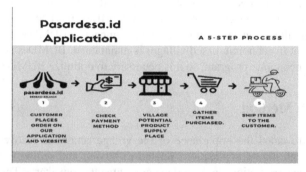

Fig. 1. Features of the Pasardesa.id application and website Source: https://pasardesa.id

Figure 1 related Pasardesa.id application or website has features explaining buying and selling transactions and procedures for promoting village products, such as supply partners registered in Pasardesa.id partners provide products to sell by posting photos of these products in the application with the "product available" feature [26]. Then, the customer only needs to check out the product, and the partner manager will carry out the packaging and delivery of the goods. Delivery of village products to customers is also carried out by couriers that have been provided. Looking at the features or methods of transactions on applications and websites that are very easy to understand and use by partners is much in demand for buying and selling transactions and promoting village products during the COVID-19 pandemic. The partners referred to here are villages with BUMDes that want to be re-managed by promoting the potential products of their village. Therefore, Pasardesa.id is in great demand to be used by various partners to carry out buying and selling transactions and promote village products.

b. **Village Economic Recovery or BUMDes in Yogyakarta, Indonesia**

Villages through BUMDes optimize village potential where the results can be an additional village budget which is stated as village income. During the pandemic, many business sectors declined, such as in the village government, called BUMDes or the village economy, which was triggered by the lack of buying and selling transactions and marketing of village products. In answering or overcoming these problems in villages in Yogyakarta. The marketing of village products through e-commerce can be carried out to reduce costs and increase efficiency, especially crises in the village economy. In the recovery of the village economy or BUMDes in Yogyakarta that uses eCommerce, called Pasardesa.id, with the website and application provided in the Playstore, can be used by the community who are already BUMDes partners in marketing their potential village products. The following is the function structure of Pasardesa.id.

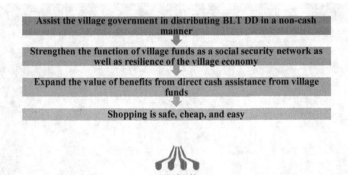

Fig. 2. Uses or Functions of Pasardesa.id Source: https://masterplandesa.id

Figure 2, regarding the use or function of Pasardesa.id itself in part 2, is explained as "Strengthening the function of village funds as a social handling network while building village economic resilience." The decline in the village economy is due to the minimal process of buying and selling interactions or promotion of village products and the absence of strengthening village funds, and weakening economic resilience. Therefore, Pasardesa.id is used as a solution in alleviating these problems. The village economy recovered and experienced an increase after the BUMDes partners used the Pasardesa.id application, which is one of the BUMDes that used this application for the first time and which held this application and website in the economic recovery of their village, Panggungharjo Village, BUMDes in 2020 until now in 2021 [27] (Fig. 3):

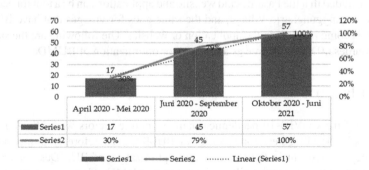

Fig. 3. Diagram 1. Data for Supply Partners Pasardesa.id Source: http://Pasardesa.id

Data for BUMDes partners who joined in April-May 2020 were only 5-17 BUMDes or as much as 30%; for June-September 2020, it was 45 BUMDes or 79% until October

2020 - June 2021 this year increased by 57 BUMDes or by 100%. By looking at the data of partners who join continues to increase, partners' trust in the success of eCommerce called Pasardesa.id application and website in the recovery of the village economy even though the partner's target to join this eCommerce is 75 BUMDes [27]. However, this issue is not an obstacle for eCommerce to keep operational (Fig. 4).

Fig. 4. Diagram 2. Marketdesa.id Turnover 2020–2021 Source: https://Pasardesa.id

The data diagram above shows that the turnover achieved from this Pasardesa.id is Rp. 82,096,000 in April-May 2020, Rp. 100,069,000 in June-September 2020, and Rp. 300,000,000 in October 2020-June 2021. It is, furthermore, related to village product data sold, 318 items in April-May 2020, 668 items in June-September 2020, and 710 items in October 2020-June 2021. For sales transaction data, 2,305 units in April-May 2020, 2,408 units in June-September 2020, and 3000 units in October 2020-June 2021. It has been counted for more than one year and every three months. There is an increase in income or turnover obtained from the existence of Pasardesa.id reaching 300 million. By looking at the data above regarding partners who joined in proportion to the turnover, products sold, and sales transactions that increased during the COVID-19 pandemic, it can be concluded that the Pasardesa.id website and application can be a tool for economic recovery in Panggungharjo Village, and the same goes for villages that have BUMDes and have become partners in the application or website. The following are the stages of using Pasardesa.ID eCommerce as a recovery or optimization of BUMDes.

5   Conclusion

In the era of the COVID-19 pandemic, many economic sectors were affected, one of which was in the village economic sector or BUMDes. Therefore, it is important that the strategy carried out in the recovery and optimization of BUMDes, recovery and optimization strategies for the village economy or BUMDes is very important so that the income of village creative businesses returns to normal or increases further. In this era of the Covid-19 pandemic, technology is being used greatly, such as in the use of social media, one of which is digital applications or e-commerce, which is one of the solutions in recovering the village economy which has declined in the era of the COVID-19 pandemic. One form of e-commerce in the recovery of the declining village economy is Pasardesa.id which is in the form of a website and application and can be accessed by all BUMDes partners in Yogyakarta. operational days has reached Rp 82,096,000 to 3 billion in June 2021.

References

1. Ayu, S., Lahmi, A.: Peran e-commerce terhadap perekonomian Indonesia selama pandemi Covid-19. J. Kaji. Manaj. Bisnis **9**(2), 114 (2020). https://doi.org/10.24036/jkmb.10994100
2. Permatasari, O.: The role of e-commerce in community economic resurgence. Int. J. Bus. Rev. (The Jobs Review) **4**(1), 63–67 (2021)
3. Patma, T.S., Wardana, L.W., Wibowo, A., Narmaditya, B.S.: The shifting of business activities during the COVID-19 pandemic: does social media marketing matter? J. Asian Financ. Econ. Bus. **7**(12), 283–292 (2020). https://doi.org/10.13106/JAFEB.2020.VOL7.NO12.283
4. Bhuiyan, M.A., Crovella, T., Paiano, A., Alves, H.: A review of research on tourism industry, economic crisis and mitigation process of the loss: analysis on pre, during and post pandemic situation. Sustainability **13**(18) (2021). https://doi.org/10.3390/su131810314
5. Laskurain-Iturbe, I., Arana-Landín, G., Landeta-Manzano, B., Uriarte-Gallastegi, N.: Exploring the influence of industry 4.0 technologies on the circular economy. J. Clean. Prod. **321** (2021). https://doi.org/10.1016/j.jclepro.2021.128944
6. Assani, S., Rosyadi, A.W., Mukhtar, A.A., Ali, A.M., Al Amin, M.: E-commerce Desa Dalam Upaya Menuju Smart Village; Studi Analisa Dan Perancangan **4**(3), 31–40 (2020). https://journals.upi-yai.ac.id/index.php/ikraith-informatika/article/download/856/645
7. Korneta, P., Rostek, K.: The impact of the sars-cov-19 pandemic on the global gross domestic product. Int. J. Environ. Res. Public Health **18**(10) (2021). https://doi.org/10.3390/ijerph18105246
8. Karim, A.: The role of BUMDes as supporting regional economy in Enrekang regency based on local wisdom. Https// Www. Acad. Edu (2020). https://www.academia.edu/download/64101046/TheRoleofBUMDesasSupportingRegionalEconomy in.pdf
9. Nicola, M., et al.: The socio-economic implications of the coronavirus pandemic (COVID-19): A review. Int. J. Surg. **78**(March), 185–193 (2020). https://doi.org/10.1016/j.ijsu.2020.04.018
10. dan H. P. Mansir, F.: Pemberdayaan Masyarakat Melalui Digital Marketing dan Media Sosial Sebagai Media Promosi Era Pandemi Covid -19 di UMKM Panggungharjo Sewon Bantul. Abdimas Singkeru **1**(1), 39–50 (2021)
11. Stiglitz, J.E.: The proper role of government in the market economy: the case of the post-COVID recovery. J. Gov. Econ. **1**, 100004 (2021). https://doi.org/10.1016/j.jge.2021.100004
12. Firmansyah, A.: Kajian Kendala Implementasi E-Commerce Di Indonesia. Masy. Telemat. Dan Inf. J. Penelit. Teknol. Inf. dan Komun. **8**(2), 127 (2018). https://doi.org/10.17933/mti.v8i2.107
13. Dinesh, S., MuniRaju, Y.: Scalability of e-commerce in the Covid-19 era. Int. J. Res. Granthaalayah **9**(1), 123–128 (2021). https://doi.org/10.29121/granthaalayah.v9.i1.2021.3032
14. Punia, R.: ISSN NO: 2347–6648 Impact of Covid-19 on E-commerce sector Page No: 8915 ISSN NO: 2347–6648 Research methodology Page No: 8916," vol. IX, no. 2347, pp. 8915–8921 (2020)
15. Fernandes, N.: Economic effects of coronavirus outbreak (COVID-19) on the world economy Nuno Fernandes Full Professor of Finance IESE Business School Spain. SSRN Electron. J., ISSN 1556–5068, Elsevier BV, pp. 0–29 (2020)

16. Prawoto, N., Purnomo, E.P., Zahra, A.A.: The impacts of Covid-19 pandemic on socio-economic mobility in Indonesia. Int. J. Econ. Bus. Adm. **8**(3), 57–71 (2020). https://doi.org/10.35808/ijeba/486

17. Guerrieri, V.: W26918.Pdf (2020). https://www.nber.org/papers/w26918

18. Yusuf, N., Shesha, L.S.: Economic role of population density during pandemics—a comparative analysis of Saudi Arabia and China. Int. J. Environ. Res. Public Health **18**(8) (2021). https://doi.org/10.3390/ijerph18084318

19. Damuri, Y.R., Fauri, A., Rafitrandi, D.: E-commerce development and regulation in Indonesia. Cent. Strateg. Int. Stud. 1–8 (2021). https://www.jstor.org/stable/resrep28866%0A

20. Setiawan, I., Krisnadi, H.: Peranan ICT Dalam Mempercepat Transformasi Digital Untuk Meningkatkan Ekonomi Pada Masa Pandemi Covid-19. J. Acad. **3**(1) (2020). https://d1wqtxts1xzle7.cloudfront.net/66769234/Peranan_ICT_Dalam_Mempercepat_Transformasi_Digital_Untuk_Meningkatkan_Ekonomi_Pada_Masa_Pandemi_Covid_19-with-cover-page-v2.pdf?Expires=1630120411&Signature=euoQ3QWPH08-GcfDz2RlIygnCGUftlTrlvh9Df9P1daoV52s8ua

21. Febty, I.M., Nurmandi, A., Muallidin, I., Kurniawan, D., Salahudin: The Effectiveness of Social Resilience in Indonesia. In: Ahram, T., Taiar, R. (eds.) IHIET 2021. LNNS, vol 319. Springer, Cham (2022). https://doi.org/10.1007/978-3-030-85540-6_22

22. Bakkar, M.: The Effect of COVID-19 spread on Egyptian consumer behavior. SSRN Electron. J. 1–14 (2020). https://doi.org/10.2139/ssrn.3673931

23. Pantelimon, F.-V., Georgescu, T.M., Posedaru, B.-S.: The impact of mobile e-commerce on GDP: a comparative analysis between Romania and Germany and how Covid-19 influences the e-commerce activity worldwide. Inform. Econ. **24**(2/2020), 27–41 (2020). https://doi.org/10.24818/issn14531305/24.2.2020.03

24. Arora, M., Raspall, F., Fearnley, L., Silva, A.: Urban mining in buildings for a circular economy: planning, process and feasibility prospects. Resour. Conserv. Recycl. **174** (2021). https://doi.org/10.1016/j.resconrec.2021.105754

25. Li, A.H.F.: E-commerce and Taobao Villages. China Perspect. **2017**(3), 57–62 (2017). https://doi.org/10.4000/chinaperspectives.7423

26. Loukis, E., Arvanitis, S., Kyriakou, N., Famelou, A., Chatzianastasiadis, M.M., Michailidou, F.: ERP, e-Commerce, social media and absorptive capacity of Greek firms - an empirical investigation. ACM Int. Conf. Proceeding Ser. (2016). https://doi.org/10.1145/3003733.3003800

27. Journal, E., Sulistiyowati, Y.: COVID-19 pandemic through establishing badan **1**(1), 68–76 (2021). https://doi.org/10.33474/PERCIPIENCE.v1i1.13516

Analysis of Customer Purchasing Behavior in an Electronics Retail Store Using Eye Tracking Data

Mei Nonaka[1](✉), Kohei Otake[2], and Takashi Namatame[3]

[1] Graduate School of Science and Engineering, Chuo University, 1-13-27, Kasuga, Bunkyo-ku, Tokyo 112-8551, Japan
nonaka.220120@gmail.com

[2] School of Information and Telecommunication Engineering, Tokai University, 2-3-23, Takanawa, Minato-ku, Tokyo 108-8619, Japan
otake@tsc.u-tokai.ac.jp

[3] Faculty of Science and Engineering, Chuo University, 1-13-27, Kasuga, Bunkyo-ku, Tokyo 112-8551, Japan
nama@kc.chuo-u.ac.jp

Abstract. In recent years, the number of customers in physical stores has been declining because of the expansion of the EC market. Therefore, in physical stores, it is necessary to investigate effective product shelves and customers' latent purchasing needs, which cannot be found only in purchase data to take advantage of the strengths of physical stores. The purpose of this study is to identify the golden zone which is attractive and easily gazed at by customers in an electronics retail store. In this study, we conducted an eye tracking observation experiment in an electronics retail store in Japan. From the experimental data, we aimed to obtain the subject's movement lanes and viewpoint information. For the analysis, we used t-test to compare the differences in gazing time at the product shelves in different areas on the same floor and network analysis to visualize the purchasing behavior in a store. Based on the results of the network analysis, The area of interest (AOI) analysis was conducted on the product shelves with high degree centrality and betweenness centrality. The AOI analysis enables us to measure the number of gazes and gazing time of the area of interest by specifying the area of interest from the recorded data.

Keywords: Consumer behavior · Eye tracking · Network analysis

1 Introduction

Recently, the frequency of customer visits to physical stores is declining. Furthermore, the spread of the new coronavirus infection has led to further expansion of the electric commerce market [1], and this trend is expected to continue into the future. Therefore, it is necessary to consider measures that take advantage of unique strengths of physical stores. One of the strengths of a physical store from the customer's point of view is the

C. Stephanidis et al. (Eds.): HCII 2022, CCIS 1582, pp. 519–526, 2022.
https://doi.org/10.1007/978-3-031-06391-6_64

ability to try out products. For physical stores, the ability to actually see and try products and to compare products side by side is a great advantage. Surveys and researches on the customer shopping path and using gaze data in physical stores have been widely conducted. In supermarkets, many studies have visualized customer behavior using flow lines, such as the patterning of customer shopping paths using RFID [2, 3] and analysis of the length of shopping routes [4]. In addition, there have been studies on in-store behavior from research on the height of gaze, which tends to attract the most shoppers [5]. However, most of these studies have been conducted in grocery stores, and there are few studies on electronics retail store.

2   The Purpose of This Study

In this study, we conducted an experiment on customer shopping path behavior in an electronics retail store which is one of the largest scale stores in Japan. We tested the following two hypotheses about the golden zone, which has been conventionally referred to, based on the flow line and viewpoint data obtained in the experiment. Based on the results of the verification, we propose a layout improvement plan of physical stores.

- Product shelves placed in the center of a store is more likely to be gazed at than product shelves placed on a wall.
- Product shelves where you can touch and try products are most likely to be gazed at products at chest height.

3   Eye Tracking Observation Experiment

We conducted an eye tracking observation experiment over two days, November 19 and 26, 2021 in an electronics retail store in Tokyo, Japan. "Tobii Pro Glasses 2" [6] and "Tobii Pro Glasses 3" [7] were used to record eye tracking during the experiment. The device is worn like a pair of glasses. This device can move freely while wearing and recording what the subjects are looking at. When we analyzed the recording data, we used the "Tobii Pro Lab" [8]. This analysis tool was used to extract the movement data of the subjects. The target floors were from the first to the sixth floor, and the condition of the experiment was to stay on not only one but several floors. In order to unify the experimental conditions of time, subjects looked around floors in the store for 20 min. The number of subjects was 26; 18 were male and 8 were female.

4   Analysis

4.1   Statistical Test

T-test is used to compare the differences in gazing time at the product shelves in different areas on the same floor. We grouped the product shelves by dividing them into two types: one on the wall side and the other on the inside. First, we performed F-test because the method of t-test changes depending on whether the variance is different or not. We set hypothesis null (H_0) and alternative one (H_1) as below.

H_0: There is no difference in variance of the gaze time of the shelves between the areas.
H_1: There is a difference in variance of the gaze time of the shelves between the areas.

We set significant level as 5%, then their p-value is less than 0.05 and the null hypothesis is rejected, we conclude that there is the difference between two areas, and we used Welch's test without assuming equal variances. On the other hand, when p-value is more than 0.05 and the null hypothesis is adopted, we conclude that there is no difference between two areas, and we used independent t-test with assuming equal variances. We hypothesized as below to perform t-test.

H_0: There is no difference in the average of the gaze time of the shelves between the areas.
H_1: There is a difference in the average of the gaze time of the shelves between the areas.

We set significance level as 5%, then p-value is less than 0.05 and the null hypothesis is rejected, we conclude that there is a difference between two areas. When p-value is more than 0.05 and the null hypothesis is adopted, we conclude that there is no difference between two areas.

4.2 Network Analysis

Network analysis is one of the powerful tools to visualize the purchasing behavior of the subjects. We used two indexes called degree centrality and betweenness centrality. The degree centrality represented the product shelves that were strongly connected to each other, while the betweenness centrality represented the product shelves that functioned well as the relay points. The adjacency matrix of a graph is $A = (a_{ij})$, and the indegree and outdegree are defined as $C_{id}(i)$ and $C_{od}(i)$ of node i. The degree centrality $C_d(i)$ is defined as the Eq. (1).

$$C_d(i) = C_{id}(i) + C_{od}(i) = \sum_{j=1}^{n} a_{ji} + \sum_{j=1}^{n} a_{ij} \tag{1}$$

For the node, we used the showcases in the store. For the size of node, we used the value obtained from the degree centrality. The dataset is an adjacency matrix of time of gazing at the showcases. For the weight of edge, the dataset is an adjacency matrix of number of moves at the showcases. Betweenness centrality [9] used two kinds of indexes. Betweenness centrality of a node v is the sum of the fraction of all-pairs shortest paths that pass through v. Betweenness centrality of an edge e is the sum of the fraction of all-pairs shortest paths that pass through e. Equation (2) shows betweenness centrality of a node v. Equation (3) shows betweenness centrality of an edge e.

$$C_B(v) = \frac{1}{(n-1)(n-2)} \sum_{s,t \in V} \frac{\sigma(s,t|v)}{\sigma(s,t)} \tag{2}$$

$$C_B(e) = \frac{1}{n(n-1)} \sum_{s,t \in V} \frac{\sigma(s,t|e)}{\sigma(s,t)} \tag{3}$$

where V is the set of nodes, $\sigma(s, t)$ is the number of shortest (s, t)-paths, and $\sigma(s, t|v)$ is the number of those paths passing through some node v other than s, t. $\sigma(s, t|e)$ is the number of those paths passing through edge e. The size of the nodes reflects the betweenness centrality of nodes, and the thickness of the edges reflects betweenness centrality of edges.

4.3 AOI Analysis

We used the AOI (area of interest) analysis to estimate the areas of the product shelves that are most likely to be gazed at. The AOI analysis is a function of the eye-tracking device software Tobii Pro Lab [8], which enables us to measure the number of gazes and gazing time of the area of interest by specifying the area of interest from the recorded data [10]. The product shelf targeted in the AOI analysis were selected under the conditions that the node size was large based on the results of the network analysis and that the products in the categories were not significantly different among the product shelves.

4.4 Analysis Result and Discussion

Table 1 shows the result of t-test for comparison of product shelves on the wall side with those on the inside.

Table 1. p-value results of t-test.

Floor	p-value
1F	0.95670
2F	0.01647
3F	0.77570
4F	0.70200
5F	0.37490
6F	0.04327

In the comparison between the product shelves located on the wall and the inside, the results showed that there was a difference between the areas, since the significance level of 5% was rejected on the second and sixth floors. Therefore, we calculated the average dwell time for the product shelves located on the wall and on the inside. The results for the second floor showed that the average time spent on product shelves placed on the wall side was 25.2 s, while the average time spent on product shelves placed on the inside was 7.4 s. On the sixth floor, the average time spent on the shelves placed on the wall was 8.0 s, while the average time spent on the shelves placed on the inside was 2.4 s. Thus, contrary to the hypothesis, the product shelves placed on the wall tend to be gazed at longer than those placed on the inside.

Figure 1 shows the layout of the second floors and Figs. 2 to 3 show the results of the network analysis in the second floors.

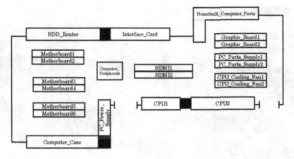

Fig. 1. The layout of the second floor.

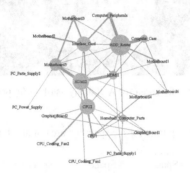

Fig. 2. Results of network analysis of degree centrality (2F)

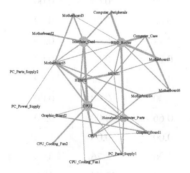

Fig. 3. Results of network analysis of betweenness centrality (2F)

From Fig. 2, we can see that the node sizes of HDD_Router, Interface_Card, HDMI2, and CPU2 are large, indicating that the gazing time at these product shelves is long. Figure 3 shows that the node sizes of HDD_Router, Interface_Card, and CPU2 are large and that the edges between adjacent product shelves tend to be thicker. In common with Fig. 2 and 3, it can be read that product shelves on the wall side are more likely to be gazed at and that product shelves are more likely to be connected to each other, thus it can be said that the product shelves on the wall side are important.

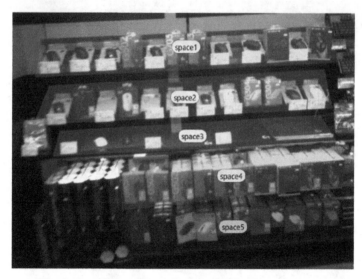

Fig. 4. Specified area for AOI analysis of an 6F product shelf

Table 2. Gazing time for the specified area of an 6F product shelf

Participant	Space1	Space2	Space3	Space4	Space5
A	0.92	2.18	0.00	0.00	0.00
B	0.00	0.64	0.00	0.00	0.00
C	0.00	0.00	0.22	0.00	0.00
D	3.44	0.34	0.00	1.16	0.26
E	0.21	0.55	0.00	0.00	0.00
F	4.30	12.11	0.69	7.28	5.22
G	0.00	0.00	0.00	0.00	0.00
H	0.66	0.00	0.00	0.00	0.00
I	0.00	0.00	1.13	0.57	0.00
Average	1.06	1.76	0.23	1.00	0.61
Share of total time (%)	22.74	37.78	4.88	21.52	13.08

Figure 4 and Table 2 showed the result of AOI analysis. Figure 4 is a product shelf on the 6th floor, where customers can touch and try products.

Table 2 shows that space1, space2, and space4 are the most likely to be gazed at. In the case of a product shelf where visitors can touch and try products, it can be said that products located below the chest, where they can easily reach out, are more likely to be gazed at. Therefore, the results were as hypothesized. Space 3 is also a space where visitors can try out products, but the duration of gazing tends to be shorter. In space1 and space2, the background color of the display is light blue, which is different from the color of the mouse, as a way of arranging the products. However, the background color of space3 is black, which is less noticeable. Therefore, it is important to use a layout with colors that make the products stand out when placing products.

4.5 Layout Improvement Suggestion

Since the target of this analysis was an electronics retail store, when proposing measures for product placement, we propose a layout from two perspectives: the location of product shelves that are easy to gaze at and easy to visit, and the areas within the product shelves that are easy to gaze at. Regarding the location of product shelves that are easy to gaze at and visit, it can be said that people are more likely to gaze at product shelves located on the wall side for a long time. Therefore, it is effective to place products that are relatively easy to purchase at the inside of the store, and to place featured product on the wall side so that the products can be easily seen. Regarding the areas of the product shelves that are most likely to be gazed at, the results showed that the areas below the chest and above the waist are most likely to be gazed at when the product shelves are arranged so that the customers can touch and try the products. In an electronics retail store, information that enables comparison of the differences between products is important. Therefore, the following product layout is ideal so that a space that enables comparison of product information can be placed at eye level.

- Video product descriptions should play in the space at the top to make them easily visible.
- Arrange product information content at eye level to facilitate intercomparison of products.
- Arrange products in the space below the chest and above the waist so that visitors can try the actual products.
- To make the products stand out, change the background color of the products when arranging them to make them stand out.
- Arrange the product inventory at the bottom.

5 Conclusion

In this study, we conducted an experiment on customer shopping path behavior in an electronics retail store an tested the two hypotheses about the golden zone, which has been conventionally referred to, based on the flow line and viewpoint data obtained in the experiment. Based on the results of the verification, we proposed two kinds of layout improvement plan of physical stores. As a future issue, we can clarify which products tend to sell well by analyzing the purchase history in physical stores in combination with product search behavior. In addition, since height difference and body size were not considered in the analysis, verification of product placement is necessary.

References

1. Impact of the coronavirus (COVID-19) pandemic on retail sales in 2020. https://www.ons.gov.uk/economy/grossdomesticproductgdp/articles/impactofthecoronaviruscovid19pandemiconretailsalesin2020/2021-01-28. 21 Jan 2022

2. Sano, N., Tsutsui, R., Yada, K., Suzuki, T.: Clustering of customer shopping paths in japanese grocery stores. Procedia Comput. Sci. **96**, 1314–1322 (2016)
3. Syaekhoni, M.A., Lee, C., Kwon, Y.S.: Analyzing customer behavior from shopping path data using operation edit distance. Appl. Intell. **48**(8), 1912–1932 (2016). https://doi.org/10.1007/s10489-016-0839-2
4. Kaewyotha, J., Songpan, W.: A study on the optimization algorithm for solving the supermarket shopping path problem. In: 2018 3rd International Conference on Computer and Communication Systems (ICCCS), pp. 11–15 (2018)
5. Chen, M., Burke, R.R., Hui, S.K., Leykin, A.: Understanding lateral and vertical biases in consumer attention: an in-store ambulatory eye-tracking study. J. Mark. Res. **58**(6), 1120–1141 (2021)
6. Tobii inc. Tobii Pro Glasses 2 wearable eye tracker. https://www.tobiipro.com/product-listing/tobii-pro-glasses-2/. Accessed 21 Jan 2022
7. Tobii inc. Tobii Pro Glasses 3 wearable eye tracker. https://www.tobiipro.com/product-listing/tobii-pro-glasses-3/. Accessed 21 Jan 2022
8. Tobii inc. Tobii Pro Lab software. https://www.tobiipro.com/product-listing/tobii-pro-lab/. Accessed 27 July 2021
9. Brandes, U.: On variants of shortest-path betweenness centrality and their generic computation. Soc. Netw. **30**(2), 136–145 (2008)
10. Saijo, N., Tosu, T., Morimura, K., Otake, K., Namatame, T.: Evaluation of store layout using eye tracking data in fashion brand store. In: Meiselwitz, G. (ed.) SCSM 2018. LNCS, vol. 10913, pp. 131–145. Springer, Cham (2018). https://doi.org/10.1007/978-3-319-91521-0_11

Mobile Augmented Reality and Consumer Experience: A Mixed-Methods Analysis on Emotional Responses and Intention to Buy Household Items

Georgios Papalazaridis, Katerina Tzafilkou[(✉)] [iD], and Anastasios A. Economides[iD]

University of Macedonia, Thessaloniki, Greece
tzafilkou@uom.edu.gr

Abstract. Mobile Augmented Reality (MAR) technology offers a new and unique way for consumers to interact with products, increasing their desire to buy. Despite the popularity of MAR apps in the retail industry, the examination of the consumers' emotional states, and the reasons evoking increased purchase intention are still under researched. To this end, this study seeks to explore the users' emotional states and the design elements that affect their intention to buy a MAR viewed product, and use the app. A prototype MAR iOS app was developed, and a user test was conducted on 21 participants. The methodology was based on a mixed design approach, combining quantitative and qualitative data emerged from scaled questionnaire items, interviews, and open-ended questions. The thematic analysis revealed eight emotional codes, and six codes of perceived usefulness. Both analyses showed that the interaction with the app triggered positive emotions of enjoyment and fascination, as well as an increased desire to use the app and buy the product. The ability to test the product in the real space and the facility to combine different objects in space before the actual purchase were the strongest indicators of purchase intention. A set of specific functionality elements caused negative emotions of confusion and disappointment. Overall, the research findings provide useful insights on the MAR elements that can positively affect the consumers' purchase intention.

Keywords: Consumer emotions · Intention to buy · Mobile Augmented Reality · MAR retail

1 Introduction

1.1 Theoretical Background

Mobile Augmented Reality (MAR) is a rapidly evolving technology and its users are increasing day by day mainly because of the MAR integration in retail (Yavuz et al. 2021; Qin et al. 2021a; Rauschnabel et al. 2019). MAR applications have emerged as one of the most important trends in the digital market and are being adopted in a variety of industries including beauty, telecommunications, tourism, manufacturing, healthcare, and education (Chen et al. 2021; Qin et al. 2021a;).

Research confirms that MAR experience brings positive effects in the consumer decision-making process, purchase intention (Kowalczuk et al. 2021; Hinsch et al. 2020; Pantano et al. 2017), actual purchase (Smink et al. 2019) and intention to recommend or reuse the app (Hilken et al. 2018; Pantano et al. 2017). MAR experience is also proved to bring positive emotional responses (Qin et al. 2021b). Emotional responses are essential in consumer research, since behavioral responses (reuse and purchase intention) are formed by affective and cognitive responses to the e-commerce (Lim and Kim 2020) or MAR characteristics (Kowalczuk et al. 2021; Qin et al. 2021a, b).

Research has also shown that more direct experiences with a product provide greater emotional engagement and allow consumers to better judge the quality of a product's features (Overmars and Poels 2015; Smink et al. 2019).

In the context of home goods retailing, MAR applications are generally preferred by consumers since they generate greater immersion, enjoyment, and perceived usefulness in the shopping process (Kowalczuk et al. 2021; Pantano et al. 2017; Qin et al. 2021a). The recently launched 'IKEA Place' allows customers to select a piece of virtual furniture through a smartphone app and view it a real physical space in real-time. Other popular retail apps like Houzz[1] and Amazon's 'View in Room'[2] share similar MAR characteristics.

Despite the ever-growing popularity of MAR, there are still important questions to be answered, like what are the MAR-triggered consumer emotions and why MAR shoppers show high purchase intention or satisfaction (Chen et al. 2021). Overall, a better understanding of the customers' emotional experience and the identification of specific MAR characteristics that trigger emotional responses, will help companies to design more effective marketing strategies for the consumer's buying journey, aiming at fulfilling the right customer need at the right time (Hilken et al. 2017).

1.2 Research Objectives

Many times, consumers face difficulties in buying online home products that fit in their personal space. In many cases, consumer dissatisfaction emerges after the online purchase as they discover for instance that a sofa that looks good on the internet, in fact does not match the decoration of their home (Hilken et al. 2017). MAR helps to overcome specific weaknesses of traditional online commerce channels, like the inability to test the product before purchase (Pantano et al. 2017; Smink et al. 2019).

The aim of this research is to examine the consumer experience in a MAR application for purchasing household goods. This research seeks to confirm that the MAR experience has positive effects on consumer emotional experience, purchase intention (Kowalczuk et al. 2021; Pantano et al. 2017; Qin et al. 2021a, b), and intention to recommend or reuse the app (Pantano et al. 2017). Therefore, this study aims to answer the following three research questions (ROs):

---

[1] https://www.houzz.com/mobileApps.

[2] https://www.amazon.com/adlp/arview.

- RO1: To investigate the consumers' emotional responses when interacting with MAR in their smartphones.
- RO2: To examine the consumers' intention to buy a household product, and reuse the MAR app.
- RO3: To identify the MAR characteristics that trigger positive or negative emotional experiences and affect purchase decision.

2 Materials and Method

2.1 Prototype MAR App

Tools and Technologies. A prototype MAR app was developed for iOs smartphones. The code was developed in Apple's Xcode 12.3 using the Swift 5.3 programming language. This version of Swift runs only on mobile devices and tablets running iOS 14 or later. A set of libraries were used to help develop the code, like SwiftUI, Reality Kit, ARKit, Combine, and FocusEntity.

The app was accessed with the help of Apple's TestFight allows the developers to invite users to test the early version of a new app before it is officially released on the market.

3D Models. Forty (40) virtual 3D models of household items were added to the products menu of the application, divided into eight (8) categories of household items, which were obtained after processing six (6) original virtual 3D models, purchased with royalties from the Sketchfab website.

The Apple Reality Converter software was used to split the models (Fig. 1) and change their texture, which concerns their appearance and shade, while the change of the color of the models was carried out in Adobe Photoshop. The scaling was implemented through Blender platform.

Kitchen #1
3D Model

Fig. 1. Splitting a virtual 3D model into smaller ones

Functionality and Interface. The functionality of the application concerned the user's access to the menu with the 3D virtual products, the possibility of selecting and placing all selected models in their real space and taking photos using the buttons of their device. Figure 3 depicts the interface menu, the AR view, and the products.

Fig. 3. Interface menu of the MAR prototype app, AR view and products

2.2 Survey Models

A 5-point Likert scale questionnaire was designed to measure the users' emotional states of i) enjoyment, ii) immersion, iii) surprise, iv) fascination, v) esthetic appeal, and vi) confusion, as well as their vii) intention to buy a product and, viii) reuse the app. Three open-ended questions were structured to ask about the MAR characteristics that caused negative and positive emotions, and the design elements that potentially affected purchase intention. An unstructured interview was also designed based on the questionnaire's open-ended items.

2.3 Participants and Procedure

Participants. A set of volunteers was invited to install the app, interact with it in their real place using their smartphone's camera, and respond to the questionnaire. Twenty-one participants (14 male/7 female; age: 30–39) successfully completed the survey, while 8 of them participated in the recorded interview as well. Several of the participants (n = 12) had no previous MAR experience, while the rest (n = 9) were familiar with only one or two AR apps.

User Scenario. The scenario assigned to the participants involved a simple AR interaction process composed of the following steps:

- To browse through the menu of products to identify one that would interest them for purchase,
- to place the selected product(s) in their space according to the user's preferences,
- to take a picture of the product or product composition in the space.

The duration of the tests ranged from 5 to 20 min and immediately after completing the user test the participants completed the online questionnaire, which was shared as a link.

2.4 Data Analysis

A mixed methodology was followed for the analysis of the collected data, as it included both qualitative and quantitative data. As regards the qualitative analysis, after the transcription of the interviews and collection of the open-ended feedback, the participants' responses were analyzed to investigate their perceptions and emotional reactions towards the MAR application. The analysis on the qualitative data was conducted by applying Thematic content analysis in which keywords were identified and matched with extracts from the qualitative data. These keywords related to emotive words mentioned by the participants; their frequency is not reported in this study due to the relatively small sample size (Dirin and Laine 2018).

As regards the quantitative analysis, the selected responses were evaluated in terms of frequencies and descriptive statistics.

3 Results

3.1 Quantitative Results

The quantitative analysis results revealed that 86% of the participants expressed a high intention to buy a product through the app, while 90% agreed that they would reuse the application in the future. Fascination and enjoyment were felt by 52%, while surprise and esthetic appeal elements were indicated by 57%. Only 5% felt confusion and immersion. Table 1 depicts the descriptive statistics results for the measured items.

Table 1. Descriptive statistics of the items

	Minimum	Maximum	Mean	Std. Deviation
intention_to_buy	3.00	5.00	4.28	.71
intention_to_use	4.00	5.00	4.90	.30
Confusion	1.00	4.00	1.66	.91
Fascination	4.00	5.00	4.52	.51
Enjoyment	3.00	5.00	4.42	.67
esthetic_appeal	4.00	5.00	4.57	.50
Surprise	2.00	5.00	4.33	.91
Immersion	1.00	5.00	4.00	1.00

3.2 Qualitative Results

The thematic analysis was focused on the identification of emotion and usefulness (including intention to use/buy) related elements.

The emotional thematic analysis identified eight codes. As depicted in Table 2, three (3) emotions were negative while the remaining five (5) were positive. The most predominant emotions seem to be of "Enjoyment", and "Surprise", followed by "Playfulness", "Satisfaction" and "Creativity". Some new emotions that emerged from the qualitative data in relation to the quantitative data were 'creativity', 'satisfaction', and 'playfulness'.

Table 2. Emotional codes

	Code	Insight	Interview (n = 8)	Questionnaire (n = 21)	Example
1	Enjoyment	Positive	5/8	1/21	"…made me feel joy"
2	Surprise/fascination	Positive	3/8	7/21	"Surprise because I could see it in life size."
3	Irritation	Negative	3/8	8/21	"A little sense of irritation, as the app does not have the ability to remove a product once you select it on the site"

(continued)

Table 2. (*continued*)

	Code	Insight	Interview (n = 8)	Questionnaire (n = 21)	Example
4	Playfulness	Positive	2/8	2/21	"It exercises creativity and allows you to play with your space and shape it using several options."
5	Disappointment	Negative	2/8	2/21	"I felt were disappointment and a decrease in enjoyment. Perhaps due to the small variety of products, interest is quickly lost."
6	Confusion	Negative	2/8	2/21	"I was confused when I had placed several products and did not have the ability to delete any without having to close the app."
7	Satisfaction	Positive	1/8	2/21	"I felt excitement and satisfaction, and this was due to the fact that the app gave me the ability to put in real space what I might want to purchase"
8	Creativity	Positive	1/8	2/21	"It exercises imagination and creativity. I was positively influenced by the combination of objects in real space"

The thematic analysis towards perceived usefulness and intention to use the app identified six (6) codes as depicted in Table 3. Perceived usefulness refers to the extent to which a user believes that using the MAR system will help them (Pantano et al., 2017) and is clearly a utilitarian benefit. The perceived 'Usefulness' theme was dominated by consumers' intention to both purchase and reuse the application. Specifically, most participants, both in questionnaire responses and interviews, indicated that they would purchase and reuse the MAR app, which is confirmed by the quantitative data as well.

Table 3. Perceived usefulness codes

	Codes	Insight	Interview (n = 8)	Questionnaire (n = 21)	Example
1	Intention to use	Positive	8/8	10/21	"I would use such an application because it would save me a lot of money."
2	Intention to buy	Positive	7/8	8/21	"I would by the product because I can see it in the real space and compare it with other products."
3	Product evaluation before purchase	Positive	5/8	12/21	"Before you even buy it, you see more or less if it fits in the space."
4	Concept	Positive	7/8	2/21	"I like the concept of being able to place and see the furniture in my space."
5	Space configuration	Positive	3/8	8/21	"I was able to understand how I can shape my space."
6	Alternative scenarios	Positive	2/8	8/21	"I would buy a product through the app because of the ease of considering various alternative scenarios."

4 Discussion and Conclusion

The findings of the study showed that consumers felt enjoyment and surprise during their interaction with the MAR prototype. The results of the research seem to be consistent with the fact that MAR interaction with realistic virtual products enhances the feeling of enjoyment (Smink et al. 2019; Pantano et al. 2017; Javornik 2016). At the same time, consumers acquired a more playful mood during their interaction, which enhanced their creativity, endowing them with satisfaction from the outcome (Jessen et al. 2020), and influencing their purchase attitude (Smink et al. 2019). Moreover, the simulated physical testing appeared to have had a strong and positive impact on the MAR experience of consumers.

This study contributes to the deeper understanding of the users' emotional states during interacting with retail MAR environments, as well as on the perceived usefulness elements that trigger positive or negative emotions and affect intention to use the app and buy a promoted product.

Although the sample size is relatively small and we cannot obtain statistically significant results, the quantitative and qualitative results together indicate useful information about the user's emotional engagement with MAR. The recommended number of participants in usability experiments ranges between three and five participants, and with five participants in a trial the maximum cost-benefit ratio is almost reached (Dirin and Laine 2018).

References

Chen, C.-A., Lai, H.-I.: Application of augmented reality in museums – factors influencing the learning motivation and effectiveness. Sci. Prog. (2021). https://doi.org/10.1177/003685042 11059045

Chen, Y., et al.: An overview of augmented reality technology. J. Phys. Confer. Ser. **1237**(2), 022082 (2019). https://doi.org/10.1088/1742-6596/1237/2/022082

Dirin, A., Laine, T.H.: User experience in mobile augmented reality: emotions, challenges, opportunities and best practices. Computers **7**(2), 33 (2018). https://doi.org/10.3390/computers702 0033

Hilken, T., de Ruyter, K., Chylinski, M., Mahr, D., Keeling, D.I.: Augmenting the eye of the beholder: exploring the strategic potential of augmented reality to enhance online service experiences. J. Acad. Mark. Sci. **45**(6), 884–905 (2017). https://doi.org/10.1007/s11747-017-0541-x

Hilken, T., Heller, J., Chylinski, M., Keeling, D.I., Mahr, D., de Ruyter, K.: Making omnichannel an augmented reality: the current and future state of the art. J. Res. Interact. Mark. **12**(4), 509–523 (2018). https://doi.org/10.1108/JRIM-01-2018-0023

Hinsch, C., Felix, R., Rauschnabel, P. A.: Nostalgia beats the wow-effect: inspiration, awe and meaningful associations in augmented reality marketing. J. Retail. Consum. Serv. **53** (2020). https://doi.org/10.1016/j.jretconser.2019.101987

Javornik, A.: AR: research agenda for studying the impact of its media characteristics on consumer behaviour. Retail. Consum. Serv. **30**, 252–261 (2016). https://doi.org/10.1016/j.jretconser.2016.02.004

Jessen, A., et al.: The playground effect: how augmented reality drives creative customer engagement. J. Bus. Res. 116, 85–98 (2020).https://doi.org/10.1016/j.jbusres.2020.05.002

Kowalczuk, P., Siepmann (née Scheiben), C., Adler, J.: Cognitive, affective, and behavioral consumer responses to augmented reality in e-commerce: a comparative study. J. Bus. Res. **124**, 357–373 (2021). https://doi.org/10.1016/j.jbusres.2020.10.050

Lim, S.H., Kim, D.J.: Does emotional intelligence of online shoppers affect their shopping behavior? From a cognitive-affective-conative framework perspective. Int. J. Hum.–Comput. Interact. **36**(14), 1304–1313 (2020). https://doi.org/10.1080/10447318.2020.1739882

Overmars, S., Poels, K.: Online product experiences: the effect of simulating stroking gestures on product understanding and the critical role of user control. Comput. Hum. Behav. **51**(PA), 272–284 (2015). https://doi.org/10.1016/j.chb.2015.04.033

Pantano, E., Rese, A., Baier, D.: Enhancing the online decision-making process by using augmented reality: a two country comparison of youth markets. J. Retail. Consum. Serv. **38**, 81–95 (2017). https://doi.org/10.1016/j.jretconser.2017.05.011

Poushneh, A., Vasquez-Parraga, A.Z.: Discernible impact of augmented reality on retail customer's experience, satisfaction and willingness to buy. J. Retail. Consum. Services, 34, 229–234 (2017) https://doi.org/10.1016/j.jretconser.2016.10.005

Qin, H., Osatuyi, B., Xu, L.: How mobile augmented reality applications affect continuous use and purchase intentions: a cognition-affect-conation perspective. J. Retail. Consum. Serv. 63(June), 102680 (2021a). https://doi.org/10.1016/j.jretconser.2021a.102680

Qin, H., Peak, D.A., Prybutok, V.: A virtual market in your pocket: How does mobile augmented reality (MAR) influence consumer decision making? J. Retail. Consum. Serv. **58**, 102337 (2021b), (August 2020). https://doi.org/10.1016/j.jretconser.2020.102337

Rauschnabel, P.A., Felix, R., Hinsch, C.: Augmented reality marketing: how mobile AR-apps can improve brands through inspiration. J. Retail. Consum. Serv. **49**, 43–53 (2019). https://doi.org/10.1016/j.jretconser.2019.03.004

Smink, A.R., Frowijn, S., van Reijmersdal, E.A., van Noort, G., Neijens, P.C.: Try online before you buy: how does shopping with augmented reality affect brand responses and personal data disclosure. Electron. Commer. Res. Appl. **35**(1), 1–10 (2019)

Yavuz, M., Çorbacıoğlu, E., Başoğlu, A.N., Daim, T.U., Shaygan, A.: Augmented reality technology adoption: case of a mobile application in Turkey. Technol. Soc. **66**, 101598 (2021). https://doi.org/10.1016/j.techsoc.2021.101598

Yim, M.Y.C., Chu, S.C., Sauer, P.L.: Is augmented reality technology an effective tool for E-commerce? an interactivity and vividness perspective. J. Interact. Mark. **39**, 89–103 (2017). https://doi.org/10.1016/j.intmar.2017.04.001

Study on the Deep Learning Product Classification Based on the Motivation of Consumers

Fei Sun[✉], Ding-Bang Luh, Yulin Zhao, and Yue Sun

School of Art and Design, Guangdong University of Technology, Guangzhou 510006, Guangdong, People's Republic of China
1111917005@mail2.gdut.edu.cn

Abstract. New Product Development (NPD) is actually a complex area involving strategy, management, research and development, production, marketing and decision-making, technology and the market need to be closely integrated. Due to the dynamic and competitive market environment, the compatibility of new products, that is, the consistency between a new product and the values of consumers, is a dynamic and complex system. Compatibility is related to the consumer's experience, lifestyle, religious beliefs, and prior knowledge of the product item. According to the process of product development, the first step is often to define the nature and function of the product, which is actually a process of new product positioning and classification in the process of product innovation. In general, the traditional process of product classification only focuses on the product and the market, and it is also the process that the designer deduces the product on the basis of successive generations. This method has become the bottleneck or restriction factor of raising productivity and standardizing production in the practical production which needs innovation constantly. We've learned that to better understand something, we need to better categorize it. In recent years, the method of artificial intelligence technology has been widely used in product classification, identification, search and other fields, which is in line with our technical requirements. And the use of machine learning to solve the classification problem in product classification has been a widespread concern of researchers, they believe that digital, intelligent and networked means to enable us to find new solutions. In this context, this paper presents a fast and effective product classification method based on deep learning technology, the deep learning-based Motivation process framework, which embeds human-based motivational thinking into machine learning. It's a new kind of experiment. This framework consists of three parts: target customer modeling method based on deep learning technology; customer feature closed loop based on Motivation process framework; Weighted fusion partially outputs an iterative classification result that combines a consumer perspective with a producer perspective. We use the consumer information reasoning method and the weighted fusion module to test the deep learning-based Motivation process framework method on Cars. The experimental data show that this method can improve the performance of new product classification. This paper introduces the consumer motivation analysis into the traditional deep learning method for the first time, and finds that it has a strong application prospect. Based on this fact, this paper proposes a framework of classification algorithm based on deep learning technology, which integrates relevant design and human psychology methods. In order to improve the traditional classification algorithm which only inputted the customer's Past purchase traces Past purchase Library-CNN, the original PPL-CNN was optimized by Motivation process framework multi-neural network fusion to improve the overall performance of the network. Firstly, the image data of the target user is preprocessed and characterized to be transformed into feature vector. For example, Pearson product-moment Correlation Coefficient was chosen to evaluate the correlation between the interests and expectations of target consumers, thus making up for the limitations of having to enter and use data from large databases. The target consumer modeling module is then used to capture consumer interest, which is then fed to subsequent Motivation process framework modules. The target consumer modeling module uses image retrieval technology to model the target consumer's past purchase behavior, explores the relationship between the consumer's purchase history information and the new product information, and consummates the target consumer's personalized modeling. In this experiment, the image data representing the user's expectation is used to extract the feature information from the user's motivation. The image is then further feature extracted from the serialized data by the convolutional neural network, so that more dimensional information can be used for classification, and finally the output is combed and converged through the fully connected layer. According to the product characteristics of the producer, the paper proposes a multi-neural network-based feature fusion method for the classification of motive requirements. Because of the bidirectional coupling of the data features, the neural network model designed based on this method can better fit the data, on the basis of the original, a two-way fit mechanism between consumer and producer is added to better deal with this kind of problems. The experimental results show that the model based on this method can effectively extract the multi-dimensional features of User requirements, compared with other comparative models, the performance of the model takes into account the optimal ranking of consumers and producers, thus producing a more comprehensive classification result. This approach and technical framework will influence the future development of NPD.

Keywords: New Product Development · Motivation process framework · Consumers · Product classification · Deep learning

1 Introduction

Due to the dynamic and competitive market environment, it is widely believed that the development of new products and processes has become a key concern of many companies. These New Product Development (NPD) areas are actually a complex area [1] that involves strategy, management, research and Development, production, marketing and decision-making, requiring the close integration of technology and the market. The timeliness of NPD is becoming more and more urgent, and if NPD fails to keep pace with business changes, companies will face the threat of a sharp decline [2].

In order to meet the NDP requirements, Luh D B. proposed The Empathetic Design Model-EDM [3], which can determine the cognitive orientation of consumers. Empathetic design is a new market research technique, which aims to satisfy consumers' needs by analyzing detailed observations. This model includes observations of related phenomena, layered cognition, and elements of a connected relevance Matrix, resulting in a design model that helps designers and consumers reach a common understanding of the cognitive structure of a product [4] and tied to the next step, which can shorten the design time, which is particularly important for NPD [5].

The EDM found that there must be a close relationship between consumer behavior and the way they define products, because both consumer behavior and the way they define products are influenced by cognitive orientation. Therefore, a better way to understand the fundamental needs of the target consumer is to interactively process the observations and data collected on site. On the basis of these studies, a Motivation process framework can be proposed [18] as shown in Fig. 1, which can help to further understand the cognitive structure of the target consumer's impression of the product, indicate more information about a consumer's area of interest, such as expectations, complaints, or appeals, and then drill down into the relationship between consumer expectations and producer interests, derive the effective incentives that the producer may provide. Therefore, it is necessary to construct A Fitted closed loop which can couple the characteristics of the new product with the characteristics of the consumer, including expectation, motivation, desire and willingness, and the output of consumer perspective accounted for a large proportion of the results of classification.

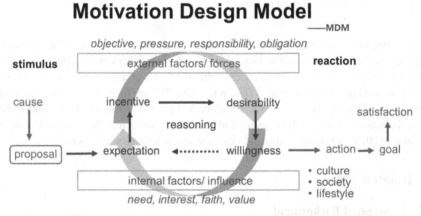

Fig. 1. Motivation process framework from Luh Ding-Bang

Because the validity and feasibility of this thinking model Motivation process framework need to be verified, a fast and effective product classification framework called The Deep Learning-based Motivation process framework (Fig. 2) is needed to meet the industry demand of intelligent and digital design of design technology, it is based on a new attempt to embed human design ideas into machine learning for verification implementation. This framework combines Motivation process framework with CNN to validate it's practical applicability through simulation algorithms. It is built on the assumption that consumer information can be expanded with some factual data and that the accuracy of product classification will improve as more information is accumulated. The framework integrates the classification results from the designer's perspective with those from the consumer's perspective to achieve more accurate classification results.

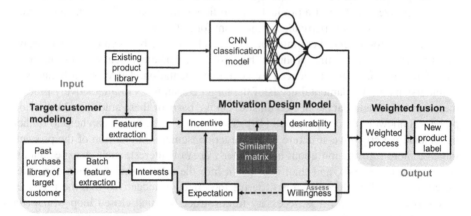

Fig. 2. Composition of the deep learning-based Motivation process framework master network: a target consumer modeling approach based on deep learning techniques and Motivation process framework based approach to consumer motivation derivation. The network sets up a closed-loop feature for the target consumer and outputs the classification results from the consumer's perspective, as well as a weighted fusion module.

The deep learning-based Motivation process framework consists of three modules: target consumer modeling method based on deep learning technology, consumer feature closed loop based on Motivation process framework and consumer perspective classification method [6], and a weighted fusion module. The performance of the proposed is demonstrated by experiments on the benchmark data set Carstanford Cars. This experimental method introduces the consumer motivation analysis into the traditional machine learning method for the first time, and has a strong application prospect.

2   Related Work

2.1   Conceptual Background

Usually the first step in the NPD process is to complete the conceptual design phase [7], that is, to define the nature and function of a new product, the underlying logic is to classify the new product. At this stage, it is usually the producer or designer who defines the product according to its appearance, function and so on. Therefore, "Product classification" plays a very important role in product design and product promotion, the concept covers the main elements of product classification according to specific characteristics in order to form structured categories. The traditional product classification process only focuses on the product and the market, which is developed by the manufacturer represented by the designer (discussed below by designer on behalf of the producer). This way of labor-intensive, inefficient, has become these enterprises to improve productivity, norms of production bottleneck or constraints. In addition, due to the designer-led design process, the limited participation of consumers often leads to a mismatch between new products and consumer needs. Specifically, it is difficult for companies that lack previous generations of product experience to find effective product classification processes and management activities [8].

2.2 Product Classification

The first step in the product development process is to define the nature and function of the product, that is, to categorize new products [9]. The concept of product classification refers to the classification of products according to their specific characteristics, forming a structured category. In order to satisfy the different purposes, many researches and organizations have put forward the methods and theories of product classification. Generally speaking, in addition to the standardized product classification system, there are many informal product classification methods designed by different industry organizations. First, product classification helps the producer to know what kind of product can be designed. Second, product classification reflects and clarifies the feasibility of design and production. Third, product classification can represent design-related methods and materials. Finally, the validity of the whole manufacturing process can be verified by product classification.

In this experiment, product classification was defined as a proof-of-concept prototype, and based on the relevant design model; its concept and elements were extended as the core thinking. The main purpose of using this prototype is to clarify the function and configuration of the product and its practical use, so as to help the product development point in the right direction. A good prototype design should have clear and well defined constraints that can help design developers understand the requirements of the product more easily, thus creating more accurate and effective discussion groups, to promote the rapid improvement of new products, shorten the market development time.

2.3 AI Application

In machine learning, computers learn how to perform tasks from exemplar data. Given the experience of defining more tasks for a machine, its performance would be improved [10]. Traditional deep learning models require high-resolution images as inputs to extract complex features, which is very energy-intensive. The high cost condition will bring many challenges to NPD's problem solving, because NPD is very strict on time and cannot tolerate the cost of long time training.

Due to the dynamic and competitive market environment, the compatibility of new products, that is, the consistency between a new product and the values of consumers is a dynamic and complex system. Compatibility is related to the consumer's experience, lifestyle, religious beliefs, and prior knowledge of the product item [11]. If the designer can predict the consumer's definition of product and improve the design method, the separation between product and market can be avoided and the economic benefit can be improved. One way to improve classification results is to integrate consumer-defined data into model training. However, because of the problem of privacy, the information of the target consumers is difficult to collect, and the way of obtaining data through questionnaire is limited by great manpower and material resources and has limitations.

To sum up, how to apply the machine learning technology to the field of NPD has been a widespread concern of researchers, but traditional market research to understand the cognitive orientation of consumers is difficult, in fact, the best way is through interaction. Therefore, effective processing of on-the-spot information is necessary to understand consumer perceptions, as they can help explain the motivations behind related phenomena.

3 Methodology

3.1 Network Structure

As mentioned above, the product classification framework based Motivation process framework is a new attempt to embed human innovation into machine learning. Unlike most product classification processes, the deep learning-based Motivation process framework can output classification results from the consumer's perspective and integrate them with the designer's perspective to achieve more comprehensive classification results. This framework consists of the target consumer modeling module, the consumer motivation derivation module and the weighted fusion module.

Application of Motivation process framework to the discovery of consumer interests and expectations. This model can construct a closed loop of consumer characteristics including expectations, incentives, expectations, and intentions. It outputs categorical results from the consumer perspective. In the deep learning-based Motivation process framework, we apply Motivation process framework to design the following experimental steps: first, we randomly select a standard image from each class of products to simulate consumer expectations. Then, as we categorize the existing product library, we evaluate the similarities between the new products we filter out and our expectations. From the consumer's perspective, similarity ranking refers to the order in which new products fall into a category. In this model, we use histograms to describe product characteristics and Pearson Correlation Coefficients to estimate similarity.

Through the first two modules, we get the classification results of consumer perspective. At the same time, by using the classification method based on Resnet, we can get the classification result from the producer's perspective. Both results are expressed in a sort sequence, meaning that the most likely category for a new product is at the top of the sequence. The lower the rating, the less likely a new product is to fall into this category. In the fusion module, we perform weighted fusion of two sequences. By adjusting the weight coefficient, we can adjust the ratio of the consumer perspective result and the producer perspective result in the final result.

3.2 Target Customer Modeling

As mentioned above, the purpose of the deep learning-based Motivation process framework is to predict the definition of a new product by the target consumer. However, it is difficult to get a consumer's opinion of the new product. Since consumer history is relatively easy to obtain, we use past purchase databases as a reference for expanding new products. This is done by looking in the historical database for products that are similar to new products. In this framework, these similar products are defined as the target consumer's interest domain. According to the EDM, we know that consumer behavior is positively correlated with their cognitive orientation. Cognition is a matter of personal experience, which does not change in the short term, nor does behavior. Thus, there is a correlation between the past and future purchases of the target consumer. We can predict their definition of a new product by analyzing their definition of the relevant product.

The goal of consumer modeling is to find the interest domain of the target consumer. In order to describe image features accurately, we need a model with high learning ability, and convolutional neural network is one such model. Their abilities can be controlled by changing depth and breadth, and they can make strong and fundamentally correct assumptions about the nature of the product. As a result, CNN may theoretically perform less well than the most accurate neural networks, but it is easier to train because of their simpler algorithms and parameters than the standard feedforward neural networks with similar size layers.

Inspired by the development of CNN, this experiment uses image retrieval technology to expand the information of target consumers. We introduce a simple and effective supervised learning framework for fast image retrieval, which takes past purchases of the target consumer as input and outputs all similar products [12]. Specifically, this module extracts functionality from products from past purchase libraries and from existing product libraries. Then, compute the distance between the new product vector and the library vector, find the similar pair, and take the corresponding similar product as the search result.

3.3 Motivation Process Framework

In the process of target consumer modeling, the method of enlarging, superimposing and multiplying by machine memory and algorithm is used to build the interest domain of target consumer with image retrieval technology, the domain of interest is then converged to the desired element in Motivation process framework, and the output continues to be classified as a consumer perspective. In the experimental comparison, the standard product image of each category is selected at random as the standard value expected by consumers, the similarity between the expectation and interest of the subsequent output of the classification result is calculated from the consumer's point of view. In Motivation process framework, a product image is described by a histogram. The experiment then assessed the similarity between the interests and expectations of the target consumer. Conclusion the correlation between Bhattacharyya Coefficient and Pearson Correlation Coefficient was used. Pearson Correlation Coefficient is a linear correlation coefficient, which reflects the degree of linear correlation between two quantities. Pearson coefficients range from −1 to 1. The closer the absolute value to 1, the stronger the correlation (negative correlation/positive correlation). Therefore, Pearson Correlation Coefficient is used to evaluate the correlation between target consumers' interest domain and expectation.

As Luh D B says (1994) [11], needs guide human behavior. Some needs are extroverted and related to the physical aspect, while others are introverted and related to the psychological aspect. In addition, these needs can be divided into individual needs, family needs and social needs. Although human beings have a variety of needs, after a lot of research, the classification of basic needs is still limited. The wealth of evidence gathered by cultural anthropology shows that, while there are huge differences in the way these needs are met across cultures, the basic needs of all people are very similar; the psychological motivation generated by demand varies with environmental parameters [13–17]. Motivation process framework is based on the concept of human-motivated requirements. In this concept, this model starts with the complaints and demands of the target consumer, and then expands the target consumer's information in terms of expectations, incentives, desires, and intentions, it will output classification results from a combination of consumer and producer perspectives.

4 Conclusion

The main work of this research is to put forward a fast and effective product classification method, which is a new attempt based on embedding human's motivation requirement thinking into machine learning technology. The deep learning-based Motivation process framework can improve the timeliness of NPD, accelerate the design process to keep up with and promote the pace of business change. It is an attempt to combine the traditional artificial design method with deep learning technology. It is composed of target consumer modeling module, Consumer Information reasoning module and weighted fusion module based on deep learning technology. Experiments on benchmark vehicle data set show that this method has good performance.

When developing large and complex new products, designers tend to collect large amounts of data about their target customers in order to understand their needs. However, this data is not readily available, can only reveal superficial information, and has various other limitations, such as privacy issues, so interacting with machine learning systems is the best way to solve these problems. When dealing with the data of the target consumers, the algorithm based on deep learning should pay more attention to the nature of their motivation demand.

While there have been many techniques for understanding consumer needs by focusing on consumer categories, most of these techniques relate only to decisions about product features and interfaces. Understanding the consumer's cognitive structure and related motivations, and deriving the concept of product classification from these motivations, has not received much attention in the field of digital computing.

Thus, the contribution of combining deep learning with other image processing techniques to capture information about consumers' motivations and to produce consumer-focused categorizations is that, demonstrating that using Motivation process framework to stimulate consumer interest and expectations can help designers better understand consumer behavior in the face of a specific product.

References

1. Mousavi, S.A., Seiti, H., Hafezalkotob, A., et al.: Application of risk-based fuzzy decision support systems in new product development: an R-VIKOR approach. Appl. Soft Comput. **109**(2), 107456 (2021)
2. Christensen, C.M., Overdorf, M.: Meeting the challenge of disruptive change. Harv. Bus. Rev. **78**, 67–76 (2000)

3. Luh, D.B., Ma, C.H., Hsieh, M.H., et al.: Applying an empathic design model to gain an understanding of consumers' cognitive orientations and develop a product prototype. J. Ind. Eng. Manage.(JIEM) **5**(1), 229–258 (2011)
4. Ferran, F.D., Grunert, K.G.: French fair trade coffee buyers' purchasing motives: an exploratory study using means-end chains analysis. Food Qual. Prefer. **18**(2), 218-229 (2007)
5. D'Antoni, A.V., Zipp, G.P.: Applications of the mind map learningtechnique in chiropractic education: a pilot study and literature review. J. Chiropractic Hum. **13**, 2–11 (2006)
6. Luh, D.B., Ko, Y.T., Ma, C.H.: A structural matrix-based modelling for designing product variety. J. Eng. Des. **22**(1), 1–29 (2011)
7. Xie, Y.J.,et al.: New Product DevelopmentNPD [EB/OL].[2017–05–10] (2017). https://max.book118.com/html/2017/0509/105611289.shtm
8. Tatikonda, M.V., Rosenthal, S.R.: Technology novelty, project complexity, and product development execution success. IEEE Trans. Eng. Manage. **47**, 74–87 (2000)
9. Piekara, A., Krzywonos, M., Kopacz, M.: Dietary supplements intended for children—proposed classification of products available on the market. J. Diet. Suppl. 1–11 (2021)
10. Krizhevsky, A., Sutskever, I., Hinton, G.E.: Imagenet classification with deep convolutional neural networks. Adv. Neural. Inf. Process. Syst. **25**, 1097–1105 (2012)
11. Luh, D.B.: The development of psychological indexes for product design and the concepts for product phases. Des. Manag. J. (Form. Ser.) **5**(1), 30–39 (1994)
12. Lin, K., Yang, H.F., Hsiao, J.H., et al.: Deep learning of binary hash codes for fast image retrieval. In: Proceedings of the IEEE Conference on Computer Vision and Pattern Recognition Workshops, pp. 27–35 (2015)
13. Lu, C.C., Luh, D.B.: A comparison of assessment methods and raters in product creativity. Creat. Res. J. **24**(4), 331–337 (2012)
14. Luh, D.B., Lu, C.C.: From cognitive style to creativity achievement: The mediating role of passion. Psychol. Aesthet. Creat. Arts **6**(3), 282 (2012)
15. Luh, D.B., Ko, Y.T., Ma, C.H.: A dynamic planning approach for new product development. Concurr. Eng. **17**(1), 43–59 (2009)
16. Tan, S.K., Kung, S.F., Luh, D.B.: A model of 'creative experience'in creative tourism. Ann. Tour. Res. **41**, 153–174 (2013)
17. Tan, S.K., Luh, D.B., Kung, S.F.: A taxonomy of creative tourists in creative tourism. Tour. Manage. **42**, 248–259 (2014)
18. Luh, D.B.: Keynote speech, design as opportunity driver. In: DSU International Conference, Dongseo University, Busan, Korea, vol. 9, no. 4, pp. 55–57 (2019)

A Study on the Interface Usability of Background Transparency Design for Shopping Websites

Weimin Zhai[(✉)] [iD] and Chien-Hsiung Chen [iD]

Department of Design, National Taiwan University of Science and Technology,
Taipei 106, Taiwan
591630470@qq.com

Abstract. The usability of the user interface for shopping websites is very important pertinent to the user experience. The purpose of this research study was to
explore the usability of different background transparency in the operation of
shopping websites, and propose design suggestions for improvement. A total of
30 participants were invited to take part in the experiment via convenience sampling methods. They were required to use a mouse to conduct 3 assigned tasks
on the hover feedback of three different of background transparency on shopping websites. A questionnaire was also created using a 7-point Likert scale to
help investigate participants' subjective evaluations. The experiment is a between-
subjects design using one-way ANOVA to examine the three different background
transparency of hover feedback designs, i.e., transparency at 0%, transparency
at 25%, transparency at 50%. The findings generated from the experiment and
post-experiment interview revealed that: (1) In the interaction with a shopping
website, there existed a significant difference in the background transparency in
terms of the task completion time. The transparency at 0% supported the best task
performance. (2) There existed no significant difference between the 25% transparency and the 0% transparency in terms of operational performance. (3) There
existed a significant difference in the degree of attractiveness. The transparency
at 25% was more likely to attract users.

Keywords: Shopping website · User experience · Background transparency ·
Hover feedback

1 Introduction

With the Internet technology leaping forward, online shopping is even more popular and
has, in a sense, become a regular shopping habit (Ma 2021). Many studies have pointed
out that the user's willingness to purchase is affected mainly by the user inter-face design
of the online shopping application (Patel et al. 2020). Detailed product information, such
as brand, price, color, stock, and user reviews, is the most critical factor influencing users'
loyalty to shopping sites (Yin and Xu 2021). Some studies have shown that transparency
will affect users' attention. Gutwin et al. (2003) believe that changing the degree of

C. Stephanidis et al. (Eds.): HCII 2022, CCIS 1582, pp. 546–550, 2022.
https://doi.org/10.1007/978-3-031-06391-6_67

transparency of the floating windows can effectively promote users' perceptions. In addition, the research on virtual environment wayfinding interfaces shows that 50% transparency performs far better than 100% transparency and 0% transparency in terms of users' perceptions of information (Chen and Chen 2020). In addition, because pop-ups as a way of highlighting, there has been little research on the background transparency of pop-ups in shopping websites. Therefore, this study aims to explore the usability of different background transparency in the operation of shopping websites.

2   Method

2.1 Participants

A total of 30 participants (18 males and 12 females) were invited to take part in the experiment via convenience sampling method. They were in the range of 18 to 30 years old and were required to experience different shopping websites. Their education level is above the bachelor's degree. They all have web-shopping experience.

2.2 Materials and Apparatus

The experimental prototypes were completed with Mockingbot. The Lenovo Ideapad Y700 notebook, with a monitor of 15.6 in. (37 cm) at a resolution of 1920 × 1080, was used as the experimental platform. In addition, the Logitech M171 wireless mouse which has an overall size of 97.7 × 61.5 × 35.2 mm with three operation keys and a two-way wheel was adopted as the input device in the experiment.

2.3 Experimental Design and Procedure

The purpose of this research study is to explore the usability of different background transparency in the operation of shopping websites. This experiment is a between-subjects single factor experimental design. The prototypes of this experiment are shown in Fig. 1. Each participant was needed to operate three tasks. The experimenter introduced the content and task of the experiment to the participants and made sure that they knew the task clearly before starting the formal experiment. The time (in seconds) of completing each task was recorded. In addition, after completing all the tasks, participants were required to fill out a questionnaire of subjective evaluations.

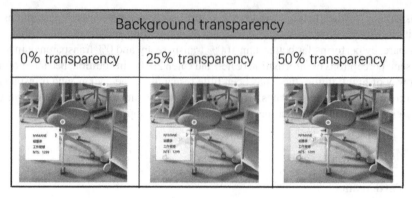

Fig. 1. The prototypes of this experiment

3 Results

The experiment results were analyzed based on a between-subjects one-way ANOVA (shown in Table 1 and Table 2). By using the SPSS software, the participant's task performance, and subjective evaluations were analyzed.

3.1 Analysis of Task Completion Time

Table 1. The one-way ANOVA results of task operation time.

	Source	SS	df	MS	F	P	η2	LSD
Task 1	Transparency	423.92	2	216.46	1.42	.260	.10	
Task 2	Transparency	1079.91	2	539.96	3.82	.035*	.22	0% transparency < 50% transparency
Task 3	Transparency	2877.31	2	1438.66	6.91	.004*	.34	0% transparency = 25% transparency < 50% transparency

* Significantly different at $\alpha = 0.05$ level (* $p < 0.05$)

Significant main effects were further analyzed by post hoc comparisons. The first task required the participants to "find out and read the prices of three tables and chairs". No significant difference (F = 1.42, P = 0.260 > 0.05) was found in the first task. The second task required the participants to "find out the data concerning the graphic sizes of different furniture". The results showed a significant difference (F = 3.82, P = 0.035 < 0.05). The post hoc comparison showed that the 0% transparency (M = 35.95, SD = 7.75) and the 50% transparency (M = 50.30, SD = 14.57) had a significant difference (P = 0.012 < 0.05). However, the 0% transparency and the 25% transparency (M = 40.39, SD = 12.31) had no significant difference (P = 0.411 > 0.05). The 25% transparency and the 50% transparency also had no significant difference (P = 0.073 > 0.05). The results indicated that the task completion time of the 0% transparency is shorter than the 50% transparency. The third task required the participants to "find out the price of two brands of products". The results showed a significant difference (F = 6.91, P = 0.004 < 0.05). The post hoc comparison showed that the 0% transparency (M = 40.13, SD = 13.63) and the 50% transparency (M = 57.86, SD = 15.38) had a significant difference (P = 0.011 < 0.05). The 25% transparency (M = 35.00, SD = 14.24) and the 50% transparency also had a significant difference (P = 0.001 < 0.05). However, the 0% transparency and the 25% transparency had no significant difference (P = 0.411 > 0.05). More specifically, the task completion time of the 0% transparency is shorter than the 50% transparency. In addition, the task completion time of the 25% transparency is the shorter than the 50% transparency. However, no difference of the task completion time was found between the 0% transparency and the 25% transparency.

3.2 Analysis of Participants' Subjective Evaluations

Table 2. The one-way ANOVA results of participants' subjective evaluations.

	Source	SS	df	MS	F	P	η2	LSD
The degree of attractiveness	Transparency	6.20	2	3.10	5.04	.014*	.27	0% transparency < 25% transparency

* Significantly different at α = 0.05 level (* p < 0.05)

The results generated from the one-way ANOVA in terms of participants' subjective evaluations are shown in Table 2. Regarding the degree of attractiveness, the results showed a significant difference (F = 5.042, P = 0.014 < 0.05). The post hoc comparison showed that the 25% transparency (M = 4.40, SD = 0.70) and the 50% transparency (M = 3.30, SD = 0.67) had a significant difference (P = 0.004 < 0.05). However, the 25% transparency and the 0% transparency (M = 3.70, SD = 0.95) had no significant difference (P = 0.056 > 0.05). The 50% transparency and the 0% transparency had also no significant difference (P = 0.264 > 0.05). The results indicated that the degree of attractiveness of the 50% transparency is lower than the 25% transparency. However, no difference of the degree of attractiveness was found between the 0% transparency and the 50% transparency. In addition, no difference of the degree of attractiveness was also found between the 0% transparency and the 25% transparency.

4   Discussions

The generated results revealed a significant difference between the transparency types regarding users' performance for Task 2 and Task 3. Specifically, it took participants longer to complete task 2 at the 50% transparency than the 0% transparency. In addition, it also took participants longer to complete task 3 at the 50% transparency than the 0%

transparency and the 25% transparency. In other words, the 50% transparency provides the worst user performance, probably because the 50% transparency affects the user's ability to distinguish between background and foreground information. However, the user's ability to distinguish between foreground and background information is not affected at the 25% transparency and the 0% transparency. In addition, the study also found that the 25% transparency had a better degree of attractiveness than the 50% transparency which is consistent with previous research that subjectively rated 25% as more harmonious by the user (Kim et al. 2015). The semi-structured interviews also revealed that participants struggled with the 50% transparency of the background when viewing the screen information.

5 Conclusion

The purpose of this research study was to explore the usability of different background transparency in the operation of shopping websites. The findings generated from the experiment revealed that: (1) In the interaction with a shopping website, there existed a significant difference in the background transparency in terms of the task completion time. Overall, the transparency at 0% supported the best task performance. (2) There was no significant difference between the 25% transparency and the 0% transparency in operational performance. (3) There existed a significant difference in the degree of attractiveness. The transparency at 25% was more likely to attract users. It is hoped that the results generated from this study can be a good design reference for future Website designers.

References

Chen, M. X., Chen, C.H.: Effects of the transparency of overview maps and gender differences on wayfinding in a virtual environment. J. Sci. Des. **4**(1), 1_9–1_18 (2020)

Gutwin, C., Dyck, J., Fedak, C.: The effects of dynamic transparency on targeting performance. In: Graphics Interface, pp. 105–112 (2003)

Kim, H., Huh, B.K., Im, S.H., Joung, H.Y., Kwon, G.H., Park, J.H.: Finding satisfactory transparency: an empirical study on public transparent displays in a shop context. In: Proceedings of the 33rd Annual ACM Conference Extended Abstracts on Human Factors in Computing Systems, pp. 1151–1156, April 2015

Ma, Y.: To shop or not: understanding Chinese consumers' live-stream shopping intentions from the perspectives of uses and gratifications, perceived network size, perceptions of digital celebrities, and shopping orientations. Telematics Inform. **59**, 101562 (2021)

Yin, W., Xu, B.: Effect of online shopping experience on customer loyalty in apparel business-to-consumer ecommerce. Text. Res. J. 00405175211016559 (2021)

Patel, V., Das, K., Chatterjee, R., Shukla, Y.: Does the interface quality of mobile shopping apps affect purchase intention? Empirical Study Australas. Mark. J. (AMJ) **28**(4), 300–309 (2020)

Social Media and the Metaverse

How Do Affordances of Gaming Technology Influence Involvement in the Digital Gaming Based Communities?

Vaibhav Jaiswal[✉][ID] and Jainendra Shukla[ID]

Indraprastha Institute of Information Technology (IIIT-Delhi), Delhi, India
{vaibhav20547,jainendra}@iiitd.ac.in

Abstract. First-person shooting games are massively popular and have prominent established digital communities. Over the years, FPSG has seen changes in game design and gaming device technologies. Previous work was primarily to understand the video-game communities' operations and identify affordances of FPS games. This paper studies how affordances of FPS gaming technology influence the social interactions in the digital gaming communities and comprehends the relation between their virtual and real communities. We explored these communities using qualitative research methods like interviews, surveys and ethnography (auto-ethnography and anthropology) and analysed the findings with the help of theories of social constructivism, technological determinism, actor-network and affordances. The results reflected that communities determine which type of games will be prevalent, which inherently decides the technology that will prevail. Technology influences the shape and structure of the community using it. The stability of communities' social networks depends on how actants are held together and whether new networks emerge through a new flow of information in the games. Different properties of affordances offered by the game, such as communication, exploration etc., influence social interactions in the community. The relationship in the virtual and real communities are not exclusive but are a continuation of each other. Members of the community with a relation beyond the game will have a stronger bond.

Keywords: First-person shooting games · Gaming communities · Affordances

1 Introduction

Since the introduction of online multiplayer games, people have resorted to games for meditated entertainment, and social interaction [9]. New digital communities popped up with gaming as the primary consumption activity to facilitate interactions between players. Shooting games are among the most-played games with

C. Stephanidis et al. (Eds.): HCII 2022, CCIS 1582, pp. 553–560, 2022.
https://doi.org/10.1007/978-3-031-06391-6_68

prominent virtual communities. The social aspect of interactions in these shooting gaming communities has been a subject of interest for many researchers in the past few decades. Shooting games have diverse sub-genres of first-person and third-person style games. First-Person Shooters are a combat-heavy genre where the player views the game from the perspective of the main character [4]. People can play on different devices like - personal computers, mobile phones and gaming consoles. The ubiquitous nature of such devices has made games to be ease-of-access. The rapid development of first-person shooting games has introduced new changes that influence the digital gaming based communities. To explore these changes, we present an investigation to understand how the affordances offered by the FPSG design and technology influence digital gaming-based communities and subsequently disambiguate the operations of digital gaming communities and the relationship between these virtual and real communities. We will analyse our findings through the lenses of theories of social constructivism, technological determinism, actor-network theory and affordances.

1.1   Previous Research

Goodman *et al.* [6] highlighted that researchers should give more attention to the unique aspects of gaming communities since it supports and encourages discussion between members. Following the paper's conclusions, this study focuses on understanding the interactions in established video-game related communities. The study accentuates social interactions because previous research indicates that discussions in video games lead to community bonding and prosocial behaviour within the members. The ties within the communities lead to building social capital in members [12,15]. Seay *et al.* [14] investigated 'guilds' in MMOGs and found similar results on the positive effect of communication towards commitment to the guild, time spent in the community and maintenance of the player organisation. Frazer [4] concluded that FPS games perform strongly in affording conversation, displaying new knowledge, encouraging exploration, immersing the player and offering rewards for success. The research study focuses on FPS games due to their support for discussion, world creation, and contextualisation of information, which would aid in understanding the influence of games on digital communities. Morris [13] provided invaluable insights and methodological considerations for conducting and analysing the ethnographic research on FPS digital gaming communities for this study. Researchers have studied the motivation and appeal behind playing FPS games. The results indicate that online FPS gaming was motivated by social reasons, and members in (semi)professional clans had more social interaction than non-clan members. The gamers used FPS to gain more experiences than real life could give them. The communication between gamers was about gaming rules, and other profound subjects such as personal problems [5,9]. The factor of communication and interactions backs the importance of focusing on FPS games.

2   Methodology and Reflections

The researcher has to identify relevant communities and conduct qualitative research (survey, interviews and ethnography) to obtain insights into social interactions between members and further use the information in the disambiguation of operations of the gaming community. The selection of research methods [3] brought a multi-directional perspective by gathering the members' views through interviews and indulging in the digital community's interactions through ethnography. Triangulation of different methodologies is essential because one method on its own is not reliable.

2.1   Identifying Digital Communities

Based on a few factors listed in Table 1, two digital FPS communities were identified. The factors were chosen based on the knowledge obtained from previous research work and the requirement of the research question:

1) A digital community based out of a tech university. It is a broad community of over 600 students, consisting majorly of undergrad students from the same university, with an average age of 18–22 years. The community comprises students from majors in Computer Science and Electrical Engineering. They are deeply involved in the gaming culture, especially FPS games, interacting virtually on a discord server called "E-Sports" and physically on the university campus. The university's student council promotes the gaming culture by organising special gaming tournaments. The bonding between the community members is low due to social interactions between smaller communities inside the larger community.

2) A small digital community of 12 students. It consists of students in different schools and colleges pursuing different education backgrounds like Engineering, Design, Commerce and Liberal Arts. The age of members is between 17–20 years. The community is actively involved in playing FPS Games. The members interact virtually through a discord server and interact physically by organising meetups and trips. The high bonding levels in the community are due to smaller size and more significant social interactions.

Table 1. Factors to identify digital communities for the study

Factor	Characteristic
Type of community	Geek and building community
Central consumption activity	FPS gaming
Social interactions	Regular interactions
Community strength	Large or small
Bonding levels	Low or high
Establishment status	Pre-established community
Researcher's involvement	Non-active/semi-active member in the community
Digital and virtual relations	Interactions should exist beyond virtual community

2.2   Surveys

An open-ended online survey, having multiple choice and one-liner questions, was conducted to get a macro-view of the E-Sports community. The flow of questions were designed to find the type of FPS games, the gamer level and the type of technology utilized for gaming in the community. In addition, the survey also collected the number of hours spent interacting while playing FPS games and the overall degree of participation in the community. Furthermore, the one-liners raised questions about the reasoning behind playing a particular game. We distributed the survey form over the esports discord server, and the groups used to manage gaming tournaments.

2.3   Interviews

From the larger community, ten interviewees were chosen based on various survey responses to get distinct viewpoints. On the other hand, active participants were selected to be interviewed from the smaller community since they had more involvement in the overall social interactions and a better discernment about the gaming culture in the community. Unstructured interviews were conducted with open-ended questions over video conference, and the conversation was transcribed to be used for analysis. The unstructured interviews gave flexibility to the participants and focused primarily on comprehending the association of the participants in different communities, with necessary attention given to the elements of FPS games and the specification of gaming technology used (Table 2).

Table 2. Insights obtained about communities from survey and interviews

Information	Large community	Small community
Prominent games	CODM, Valorant, COD Warzone	Valorant
Prominent devices	High-end mobile phones and PC	High-end mobile phones and PC
Time spent	2.5 h	4 h
Type of players	Mix (highly diverse)	Competent players
Individual involvement	Low participation	High participation

2.4   Ethnography

We conducted auto-ethnographic research to understand the social interactions by participating in a Call of Duty Mobile (CODM)[1] gaming tournament organised for the Esports Community. The student body conducted the event for two days in August 2021. Communication was done over Whatsapp[2] and discord[3] with over 100 participants registered in different teams. There were 5 participants in a single team, and the teams were divided into four factions that played

---

[1] https://callofduty.com/.
[2] https://www.whatsapp.com/.
[3] https://discord.com/.

amongst them. The winners of each faction participated in the semi-finals and finals. The researcher took on the role of 'participant as an observer' to play and research in parallel as the same engaged activity [2]. The researcher joined the team Whatsapp group. Communications between the members were using calls and texts on the Whatsapp group. The team connected as "friends" on the CODM platform to play together. Some practice matches were conducted before the actual tournament to familiarise ourselves with each other's gaming styles. While playing CODM, the team members used the in-game audio feature to interact. The team made two rounds of the tournament before being knocked out. After the completion of the tournament number of social interactions dropped, and the group was later disbanded.

We covertly conducted an anthropological observation of the social interactions in the small community in both offline and online settings to primarily understand the relationship between real and virtual communities. We conducted it on the smaller digital community since it was more efficient and less time-consuming due to the smaller group size and higher bonding level between the community members. The researcher took the "participant-observation" [1] approach to observe the interaction between members on discord while playing Valorant and other FPS games. Furthermore, the researcher observed the interaction between members in regular offline meetings and trips to understand the changes in virtual and real interactions.

3   Analysis

We will thematically analyse the reflections with a deductive approach based on social aspects of technology and science.

3.1   Social Constructivism and Technological Determinism

The digital FPSG-communities influence the individual choices of their members. Players with lower levels of bonding are more inclined to play the FPSG with a greater number of players and a significant appeal in the community to increase their social interactions with other members. The most active and socially influential members in the community play a key role in determining the FPS game that the members play. Community members prefer purchasing gaming devices that enable parallel gaming with their fellow gamers [10].

Gaming technology can be viewed as a unidirectional abstract force that influences the formation of new social relations in the digital FPSG communities. Participants who had access to similar specifications of gaming technologies and similar FPS game preferences tend to form smaller social groups together within the larger community. Members who have been playing a particular FPSG to improve their learning curve or/and have made in-game purchases such as skins, weapons, and game passes are more active in their community and have more significant social interactions. The points above imply that the technology directly impacts the community using it [8].

3.2 Actor-Network Theory

The actor-network depends on how the actants are held together and whether new networks emerge to disrupt or eclipse it [11]. The introduction of game updates and tournaments results in new networks within the community, replacing and reinforcing network actants. If a new purpose does not emerge for the community, the networks break and become disrupted, resulting in the community becoming non-active over time [7]. The network fails to hold the gaming community together if any network elements fail, like map design, weapons, or anti-cheat software. Interaction features such as in-game audio and chats play a significant role in shaping the interaction between community members during game-play.

3.3 Affordances

The affordances offered by the FPS Games and the affordances offered by the gaming devices to the user are interconnected, and interrelated [8] in influencing the community using them. The enabling functional properties of the FPSG like in-game audio and friends list allow easier interaction while constraining factors like game time limit, player limit and level restrictions bounds interactions and limits the community. The relational properties of gaming devices depend on the requirements of FPS games. The relational properties of FPSG depend on the individual players in the community. Each element of the game, such as weapons, armours, and special powers, is used uniquely by individual members to increase their performance in the game, which increases overall social interactions. The game affords unique elements for newbies and advanced players. The range of affordances offered by the FPS game gradually opens for perception. This new flow of information and purpose helps form new social networks within the community. Individual members have to learn about the social rules that delimit the affordances [8]. Breaking such social rules are frowned upon in the community. The social involvement, interaction, and position of a community member is associated with how the member interprets the affordances offered by the FPS gaming technology.

3.4 Relationship Between Virtual and Real Community

Some community members only had virtual interactions, but they have created a strong bond since they shared personal problems and ideas and asked for opinions from fellow players. The relationship in virtual and real communities are not exclusive; they are a continuation of each other. The conversations of the virtual community are picked up in real communities and vice versa. The social structures in the community can change depending on the different events taking place in online and offline modes. It was observed that when future-anticipated interactions and/or positive past relations between members are present, players are expected to be cooperative, self-disclosing, and generally engage in socially positive interaction if they interact.

4   Discussions and Future Work

The study discussed how different affordances of FPS gaming technology influences social interactions in a digital gaming-based community. The analyses showed that changes in technology and changes in the community impact each other. The study also showed the dependence on the game elements to keep the social network stable. In addition, the study concluded that the relationship between virtual and real gaming communities is not exclusive but a continuation of each other. The relationship between community members with some form of connection other than the community itself has more substantial bonding levels.

The type of FPS based communities, first-person shooting games and gaming technologies studied are not exhaustive. There is scope for studying different digital communities and FPS game variations. Plenty of room is still available for further research to improve our understanding of how FPS games influence digital communities.

Acknowledgments. This research was supported by the Center for Design and New Media (sponsored by Tata Consultancy Service, A TCS Foundation Initiative), IIIT-Delhi.

References

1. Bernard, R., Russell, H., Pedraza, J.: Research Methods in Cultural Anthropology. SAGE Publications, Thousand Oaks (1988)
2. Boellstorff, T., Nardi, B., Pearce, C., Taylor, T., Marcus, G.: Ethnography and Virtual Worlds: A Handbook of Method. Princeton University Press, Princeton (2012)
3. Churchill, E., Bly, S., Consulting, S.: Culture vultures: considering culture and communication in virtual environments. ACM SIGGROUP Bull. **21**, 6–11 (2001). https://doi.org/10.1145/377272.377279
4. Frazer, A., Argles, D., Wills, G.: The same, but different: the educational affordances of different gaming genres. In: 2008 Eighth IEEE International Conference on Advanced Learning Technologies (2008). https://doi.org/10.1109/icalt.2008.228
5. Frostling-Henningsson, M.: First-person shooter games as a way of connecting to people: "brothers in blood". CyberPsychol. Behav. **12**(5), 557–562 (2009). https://doi.org/10.1089/cpb.2008.0345
6. Goodman, W., McFerran, E., Purves, R., Redpath, I., Beeken, R.J.: The untapped potential of the gaming community: narrative review. JMIR Serious Games **6**(3), e10161 (2018). https://doi.org/10.2196/10161
7. Hung, A.C.Y.: Beyond the player: a user-centered approach to analyzing digital games and players using actor-network theory. E-Learn. Digit. Media **13**(5–6), 227–243 (2016). https://doi.org/10.1177/2042753017691655
8. Hutchby, I.: Technologies, texts and affordances. Sociology **35**(2), 441–456 (2001). https://doi.org/10.1177/s0038038501000219
9. Jansz, J., Tanis, M.: Appeal of playing online first person shooter games. CyberPsychol. Behav. **10**(1), 133–136 (2007). https://doi.org/10.1089/cpb.2006.9981
10. Kim, B.: Social constructivism. Emerg. Perspect. Learn. Teach. Technol. **1**(1), 16 (2001)

11. Latour, B.: Reassembling the Social: An Introduction to Actor-Network-Theory. OUP, Oxford (2007)
12. Molyneux, L., Vasudevan, K., Gil de Zúñiga, H.: Gaming social capital: exploring civic value in multiplayer video games. J. Comput.-Mediat. Commun. **20**(4), 381–399 (2015). https://doi.org/10.1111/jcc4.12123
13. Morris, S.: Shoot first, ask questions later: ethnographic research in an online computer gaming community. Media Int. Aust. **110**(1), 31–41 (2004). https://doi.org/10.1177/1329878x0411000106
14. Seay, A.F., Jerome, W.J., Lee, K.S., Kraut, R.E.: Project massive. In: Extended Abstracts of the 2004 Conference on Human Factors and Computing Systems - CHI 2004 (2004). https://doi.org/10.1145/985921.986080
15. Tseng, F.C., Huang, H.C., Teng, C.I.: How do online game communities retain gamers? Social presence and social capital perspectives. J. Comput.-Mediat. Commun. **20**(6), 601–614 (2015). https://doi.org/10.1111/jcc4.12141

Exploring the Impacts of COVID-19 on Digital and Metaverse Games

Chutisant Kerdvibulvech[✉]

Graduate School of Communication Arts and Management Innovation, National Institute of Development Administration, 118 SeriThai Rd., Klong-chan, Bangkapi, Bangkok 10240, Thailand
chutisant.ker@nida.ac.th

Abstract. The coronavirus (COVID-19) pandemic has markedly changed the ways we live and the ways we play games. This is because the situations disrupted by the virus have forced so many people to quarantine and self-isolate. These can lead to many serious problems such as mental and physical health. At the same time, the metaverse, particularly virtual reality and augmented reality, has been very popular in the fields of human-computer interaction and computer science in recent years. Therefore, in this paper, we propose a new research work for exploring recent digital games inspired during the virus outbreak to support people in various aspects, such as entertaining people during the pandemic period, enhancing awareness among people about the virus, suggesting preventive measures against the spread of the virus. Next, more specifically, the impacts of COVID-19 on recent games from virtual and augmented realities are examined. We investigate metaverse games to support people during COVID-19 and the post-pandemic period, including enhancing the healthcare education toolkit, simulating health protection protocols, and supporting healthcare workers.

Keywords: Digital game · Metaverse · Virtual reality game · Augmented reality game · Coronavirus · COVID-19

1 Digital Games During COVID-19

The coronavirus pandemic, a pandemic of coronavirus disease 2019 created by severe acute respiratory syndrome coronavirus 2, has posed tremendous impacts to many people around the world. Despite the negative impacts of the virus outbreak, well-designed and computer-generated games can be a great positive tool to help people to benefit human society during the pandemic in many ways. This paper explores recent computer-generated games inspired during COVID-19 to support children and adults in various aspects. After that, more specifically, we investigate the impacts of COVID-19 on recent games from virtual and augmented realities. In this section, we divide computer-generated games during COVID-19 into two main categories based on their objectives: supporting children/students and helping adults.

To begin with, there are games aimed to entertain children or help students deal with the virus during the pandemic period. For example, Satu et al. [1] implemented a mobile game for enhancing awareness among children about the virus using machine learning regression models. Their game, called COVID-Hero, allows children to grab objects from their superhero-shaped player so that it can create children's awareness and endurable behavior from COVID-19. Similarly, Ndulue and Orji [2] also implemented a mobile persuasive game to enhance the awareness to raise the attention of African people towards physical distancing and related preventive measures against the virus proliferation. Their game, called COVID Dodge, uses the story of young African children to start journeys for their grandmother. In addition, Grizioti et al. [3] designed a serious choice-driven simulation game to improve awareness of outbreak threats and outcomes for students during COVID-19 social isolation. Their game, named COVID-19 Survivor, energizes the daily routine of a user through a simulation game of available options and consequences through decision making. Therefore, the school students can understand the awareness of pandemic risks more clearly. Moreover, Naaj et al. [4] studied the possible impact of digital game addiction on the accomplishment of students in the virus outbreak period in the United Arab Emirates. According to their study, digital gaming addiction levels differ significantly based on sex, in which male students are more addicted and use more time playing digital games than female students.

Second, there are gaming works focusing on supporting people, particularly adults, to deal with the virus during the virus outbreak. For instance, Venigalla et al. [5] developed a collaborative multiplayer desktop-based game for educating people of different backgrounds with the proper rights and duties of citizens by following COVID-19 safety measures. Their game, titled SurviveCovid-19++, helps people to increase empathy and unite human society during this contagious virus outbreak. Also, Hill et al. [6] created a multiplayer serious game for exploring changes of a serious game on behavior and perception of preventive measures from the virus. They examine the implications of a serious game, such as Point of Contact, towards outbreak risk modeling. Also similarly, Zhao et al. [7] created a persuasive game for shopping to enhance people's awareness and preventive measures for COVID-19, such as keeping social distance and wearing masks. Their game, named Dino-Store, uses grocery shopping and the mechanic to suggest that each preventive measure can decrease the risk of infection effectively. Furthermore, Kleinman et al. [8] studied how people leveraged digital games to deal with the COVID-19 quarantine. By using a thematic Twitter analysis from 2000 tweets in April 2020 to derive questions, their study can explain the ways in which isolated people brought and used digital games as a tool to deal with their lockdowns.

2   Reality-Based Games for COVID-19

In this section, we examine the impacts of COVID-19 on games from metaverse or reality-based technologies. According to our research, COVID-19 has given an obvious impact on creating reality-based games. We have found that there are many reality-based games built because of the virus outbreak in different aspects. For example, Pallavicini et al. [9] gave a systematic review of metaverse games for exploring the main impact of the virus on human mental health. They suggest that reality-based games will possibly change the way to help human mental health, building methods inexpensively and comfortably accessible to many people around the world in near future. This paper will focus on two reality-based technologies: virtual reality and augmented reality.

First, there are virtual reality games for dealing with the contagious virus. For instance, Kao et al. [10] designed a virtual game, titled Fighting COVID-19 at Purdue University, for teaching hygienic best practices to prevent the virus by leveraging people from different backgrounds, such as educational technology designers, game designers, and health experts. They build the game in a virtual computer laboratory in the university based on the physical laboratory to study and compare the game to a video for rising hygienic self-efficacy and positive hygienic attitudes for the contagious virus outbreak. Furthermore, Wang and Huang [11] built an adventure console game for facilitating the conceptual learning of COVID-19 mechanisms. Their game, called Viruscape, can enhance the healthcare education toolkit using three-dimensional modeling and motion graphics. In addition, there are several recent works dealing with virtual reality serious games during the virus outbreak, such as Sipiyaruk et al.'s work for dental education [12], Ang et al.'s work for curing dementia patients [13], and Pavlou et al.'s work for simulating health protection protocols [14]. In detail, Sipiyaruk et al. gave a literature review on serious games, including virtual reality games, in dental education during the COVID-19 outbreak. They build a conceptual framework of the advantages of the use of serious games during the virus outbreak. They suggest key strengths, including positive educational outcomes, interactive asynchronous remote learning, enhanced engagement and motivation, the advantage of stealth assessment, and a safe learning environment. Moreover, Ang et al. developed a real-time virtual reality serious game for helping people with the impaired ability to think, remember, or make decisions during the virus outbreak. They use this game as a form of therapy for supporting healthcare professionals and researchers to cure dementia patients. There is also a similar work to the mentioned virtual reality serious game, focusing on simulating protection protocols and infection spread. Pavlou et al. designed a virtual reality serious game simulation from the indoor safety guidelines during COVID-19. They simulate preventive protocols to give awareness about the transmission of the virus.

Second, there are augmented reality games, particularly location-based games, to entertain people in many aspects. Our previous work [15] discussed location-based augmented reality games mainly for entertainment. However, it does not focus on supporting people disrupted by the COVID-19 pandemic. In this way, here, we focus on augmented reality gaming works for helping people during the outbreak. For example, Laato et al. [16, 17] analyzed how location-based augmented reality game players and developers reacted to the COVID-19 pandemic for Pokémon GO. By using the research method of netnography—a term integrating "ethnography" into "internet", they utilize the data of in-game changes from the virus made by game developers, social media reactions, and the Pokémon GO's raiding activity in Finland. Interestingly, their study has implications on how gamification and games can be utilized in movement of human directly in the virus pandemic. In addition, Bhattacharya et al. [18] gave a good discussion on how the next design of augmented reality location-based games should improve mental and physical health when the virus outbreak is over. A two-week diary study with augmented reality location-based games was also conducted by Bhattacharya et al. [19] dealing with challenging life situations disrupted by the virus outbreak. They attempt to reimagine proximity-based social interactions and the essential principles of location-based metaverse applications in the post-pandemic era.

Acknowledgments. This research presented herein was partially supported by a research grant from the Research Center, NIDA (National Institute of Development Administration).

References

1. Satu, M.S., et al.: COVID-hero: machine learning based COVID-19 awareness enhancement mobile game for children. In: Mahmud, M., Kaiser, M.S., Kasabov, N., Iftekharuddin, K., Zhong, N. (eds.) AII 2021. CCIS, vol. 1435, pp. 321–335. Springer, Cham (2021). https://doi.org/10.1007/978-3-030-82269-9_25
2. Ndulue, C., Rita, O.: COVID dodge: an African-centric game for promoting COVID-19 safety measures. In: AfriCHI 2021, pp. 166–169 (2021)
3. Grizioti, M., Oliveira, W., Garneli, V.: Covid-19 survivor: design and evaluation of a game to improve students' experience during social isolation. In: de Rosa, F., Marfisi Schottman, I., Baalsrud Hauge, J., Bellotti, F., Dondio, P., Romero, M. (eds.) GALA 2021. LNCS, vol. 13134, pp. 283–288. Springer, Cham (2021). https://doi.org/10.1007/978-3-030-92182-8_30
4. Abou Naaj, M., Nachouki, M., LEzzar, S.: The impact of video game addiction on students' performance during COVID-19 pandemic. In: ICCSE 2021, pp. 55–60 (2021)
5. Venigalla, A.S.M., Vagavolu, D., Chimalakonda, S.: SurviveCovid-19++: a collaborative healthcare game towards educating people about safety measures for Covid-19. In: CSCW Companion 2021, pp. 222–225 (2021)
6. Hill, J., et al.: Point of contact: investigating change in perception through a serious game for COVID-19 preventive measures. Proc. ACM Hum. Comput. Interact. 5(CHI), 1–19 (2021)
7. Zhao, Y., et al.: Shopping in a pandemic: a persuasive game for COVID-19. In: CHI PLAY 2021, pp. 371–375 (2021)
8. Kleinman, E., Chojnacki, S., Seif El-Nasr, M.: The gang's all here: how people used games to cope with COVID19 quarantine. In: CHI 2021, pp. 327:1–327:12 (2021)
9. Pallavicini, F., Chicchi Giglioli, I.A., Kim, G.J., Alcañiz, M., Rizzo, A.: Virtual reality, augmented reality and video games for addressing the impact of COVID-19 on mental health. Front. Virtual Real. 91, 719358 (2021)
10. Kao, D., et al.: Fighting COVID-19 at Purdue university: design and evaluation of a game for teaching COVID-19 hygienic best practices. In: FDG 2021, pp. 15:1–15:23 (2021)
11. Wang, T., Huang, I.Y.: Viruscape: a microscopic adventure game to guide conceptual learning of SARS-CoV-2 Mechanisms. In: CHI PLAY 2021, pp. 209–215 (2021)
12. Sipiyaruk, K., Hatzipanagos, S., Reynolds, P.A., Gallagher, J.E.: Serious games and the COVID-19 pandemic in dental education: an integrative review of the literature. Computer 10(4), 42 (2021)
13. Ang, A.J.Y., Principio, R.D., Juayong, R.A.B., Caro, J.D.L.: GunitaHu: a VR serious game with Montessori approach for dementia patients during COVID-19. In: NiDS 2021, pp. 111–116 (2021)
14. Pavlou, M., et al.: Remote adversarial VR serious game simulating COVID-19 infection spread and protection protocols. In: VR Workshops 2021, pp. 683–684 (2021)
15. Kerdvibulvech, C.: Location-based augmented reality games through immersive experiences. In: Schmorrow, D.D., Fidopiastis, C.M. (eds.) HCII 2021. LNCS (LNAI), vol. 12776, pp. 452–461. Springer, Cham (2021). https://doi.org/10.1007/978-3-030-78114-9_31
16. Laato, S., Laine, T.H., Islam, A.K.M.: Location-based games and the COVID-19 pandemic: an analysis of responses from game developers and players. Multimodal Technol. Interact. 4(2), 29 (2020)
17. Laato, S., Najmul Islam, A.K.M., Laine, T.H.: Did location-based games motivate players to socialize during COVID-19? Telemat. Inform. 54, 101458 (2020)

18. Bhattacharya, A., Lee, J.H., Yip, J.C., Kientz, J.A.: Life goes on with Pokémon: reimagining the design of location-based games during the COVID-19 pandemic. XRDS **28**(2), 70–75 (2021)
19. Bhattacharya, A., et al.: The pandemic as a catalyst for reimagining the foundations of location-based games. Proc. ACM Hum. Comput. Interact. **5**(CHI), 1–25 (2021)

Examining Bias in Sentiment Analysis Algorithms Interacting with Emojis with Skin Tone Modifiers

Isabel Laurenceau, Jean D. Louis[✉], and Juan E. Gilbert

University of Florida Computer Science, Gainesville, FL, USA
{isalau,jeandlouis1,juan}@ufl.edu

Abstract. Emojis are commonplace in text, and skin-toned emojis have gained widespread adoption. Unfortunately, the level of bias or errors in Sentiment Analysis (SA) algorithms is unknown when working with online text containing emojis with skin tone modifiers. This study investigates SA algorithms to understand potential changes in polarity when the same sentence is presented with emojis of different skin tone modifiers. We found that many of the SA algorithms ignored the skin tone of the emoji in their calculations; however, for some algorithms, the method used to translate the emoji to text affected the SA polarity score. We aim to present a methodology to compare commonly used SA algorithms and lexicons and to highlight potential bias areas. This research shows that there may be discrepancies based on the SA methods and algorithms used to process text with skin tone emojis.

Keywords: Emoji · Sentiment analysis · Bias

1 Introduction

Sentiment Analysis (SA) is used to gain insights from writers' text and SA has grown in use with the rise of online communication [9,22,23]. SA algorithms provide a polarity score that states how positive or negative a sentence is [18]. It has been shown that SA algorithms can be biased based on gender and race words [16]. Kiritchenko and Mohammad found that of 219 Natural Language Processing (NLP) systems tested, 75% contain gender or race biases [16]. These biases could lead to inequitable political and business decisions and potentially perpetuate certain inequalities by giving the wrong view of certain users [16].

Emojis and the addition of skin tone modifiers in 2015 have given people new ways to express and represent themselves online [5]. According to media richness theory, emojis should improve the richness and effectiveness of the communication format [6,8,14]. Emojis are a large part of computer-mediated communication (CMC), but present challenges to the accuracy of some SA algorithms.

The purpose of this study is to explore potential biases built into SA algorithms when interacting with emoji skin tone modifiers. The results will determine if the skin tone modifiers used with emojis influence the sentiment polarity

© The Author(s), under exclusive license to Springer Nature Switzerland AG 2022
C. Stephanidis et al. (Eds.): HCII 2022, CCIS 1582, pp. 566–573, 2022.
https://doi.org/10.1007/978-3-031-06391-6_70

returned by a SA system, examining if current sentiment analysis systems contain bias between skin tones of emoji. A non-biased system should return the same amount of information (richness) regardless of skin tone.

We aim to present a methodology to compare commonly used SA algorithms and lexicons and highlight potential areas of bias. Our goal is that by using this methodology in practice with different systems and emoji translations, others will be able to better determine what tools to use in their work.

2   Background and Relevant Research

Media richness theory comes from research in CMC and states that different means of communication (textual, vocal, visual etc.) can provide varying levels of information or richness [8]. Written communication is lower on the richness list; however, researchers have claimed that the added use of emojis and emoticons help improve written communication's media richness [6,14]. A non-biased system should return the same information, represented here by sentiment polarity score, regardless of skin tone. Therefore, if there is a difference in information due only to the skin tone, then emojis may not actually lead to increased richness but instead lead to biases and false analysis.

2.1   Emojis

Emojis were developed by Shigetaka Kurita for a Japanese mobile phone provider and later added to the Unicode system in 2009 by the Unicode consortium [17,23]. In 2015, five skin tone modifiers were added for certain emojis to better represent the diversity of users [7,21]. Each tone is based on the Fitzpatrick scale for skin color: light 👍, medium-light 👍, medium 👍, medium-dark 👍 , and dark 👍 [11].

Guibon et al. state that alot of SA work in NLP has been done on social media data [13]. Guibon et al. indicated that the emoji's name is not always sufficient to express emotional or cognitive states, but the emoji must be seen in context. The authors also point to non-sentiment reasons for using emojis such as for "convenience, to type faster, or just for fun and emphasis" [13].

Robertson, Magdy, and Goldwater note the "positive role [of] emoji skin tone modifiers" [21]. Self-representation is one of the main uses of skin tone modifiers [7,21]. Coats reports that modifiers were especially popular among dark-skin users, but the darkest skin tone modifiers were less likely to be used [7]. On a global level, Coats found the use of skin tone modifier used were 36% light, 25% medium-light, 20% medium, 16% medium-dark, and 3% dark [7].

Other researchers have explored the use of skin tone modifiers to make inferences about people. Suntwal et al. stated that "emojis can be studied to understand product consumption and learn if certain endorsements using particular skin tones are likely to affect purchase intentions for different products" [23]. Other works either do not directly focus on emoji skin tones or manually add emoji sentiment scores to lexicons for SA [10, 22, 24]. We further existing work by examining emojis with skin tone modifiers to see effects on SA algorithms without manually altering the existing SA implementation.

3 Methods

3.1 Dataset Creation

Sentence Templates. The dataset used for investigation was modeled after Kiritchenko and Mohammad's Equity Evaluation Corpus [16]. The goal of the investigation was to see effects of varying skin tones on sentiment polarity while keeping the remaining portion of the sentence constant. Sentence templates such as "The restaurant was amazing" provide a baseline sentiment score for each method used. Each template resulted in six data entries: the original template, the template with an emoji in default yellow, and a template with an emoji in four skin tones. Light, medium, dark, and one of the compound skin tones (medium-dark) were used to create the data set.

Emotional face emojis such as the smiling 😃 and sad 😦 emojis do not contain skin tone modifiers and emojis that are associated with people such as the medium skin toned woman health worker 🧑, which do allow for skin tone modification, add additional information such as gender and age which have been shown to influence SA [3, 16]. The emojis chosen represent positive and negative sentiments, can have varied skin tones, and do not include any additional demographic information. The thumbs-up 👍 and raising-hand 🙌 emojis were used for positive sentences and the thumbs-down 👎 were used for negative sentences.

Each template was created to be either strongly positive, negative or neutral and short in length. We focus on the change in sentiment not the accuracy of the baseline sentiment. Many of the templates have keywords such as great, happy, or sad to explicitly set the sentiment of a sentence. We also tested neutral sentences such as "Your appointment is at 11:00" to see how adding an emoji with an emotional context such as the thumbs-up 👍 would affect the sentiment score of the sentence.

Emoji Translation. Sentiment analysis practitioners may translate graphical emojis into text before using SA tools. Two translation methods were used and evaluated against the graphical emoji representation. The *emoji* library converts 👍 to *:thumbs_up::light_skin_tone*. The *demoji* library writes the 👍 as *:thumbs up: light skin tone*. The convention *sentence* is used to refer to the sentence template appended with a graphical emoji i.e. "The restaurant was amazing 👍". *emoji-text* is used to refer to a template with an emoji appended and translated using *emoji* i.e. "The restaurant was amazing :thumbs_up::light_skin_tone.". *demoji-text* is used to refer to a template with an emoji appended and translated using *demoji* i.e. "The restaurant was amazing :thumbs up: light skin tone".

3.2 Lexicons

Sentiment140L, SentiWordNet, VADER, AFINN, and TextBlob were tested in this evaluation [2,4,15,19,20]. These were chosen based on their usability, availability in Python, and their common use among the community. All five SA systems include their own lexicon, but VADER, AFINN, and TextBlob also include their own sentiment scorer which include added heuristics discussed below.

The Sentiment140L lexicon is mined from tweets determined to be positive or negative based on present emoticons [12]. The Natural Language Tool Kit (NLTK) library includes an interface for SentiWordNet [4]. The first word found in the lexicon is used for analysis. Each word is assigned a positive, negative, and objectivity score.

VADERs' built-in SentimentIntensityAnalyzer returns a tuple of polarity scores which includes a negative, neutral, positive, and compound score [15]. VADER's analyzer can take into account additional heuristics which are represented in the compound score. VADER's heuristics include punctuation, capitalization use, degree modifiers, contrapositive conjunction use, and tri-gram analysis to determine any polarity flips [15].

AFINN includes a lexicon of 2,477 words scored between -5 and 5 [20]. The score function returns a single result which is the sum of the valence of each word in the sentence divided by the number of words. TextBlob's default sentiment analysis uses CLiPS Pattern module, which includes a lexicon of adjectives and considers negations and modifiers [1]. The sentiment function returns a tuple of polarity and subjectivity between -1 and 1 [2].

3.3 Analysis Procedure

An aggregation algorithm was created to return a polarity score for each test sentence similar to ones found in previous literature [20]. Once each sentence and word were tokenized using the NLTK [4], the words were converted to lowercase, and their values were then queried from each lexicon. If found in the lexicon, each word's value was added to the overall sentence sentiment score.

Our aggregation method used the lexicon provided by each SA system. The dataset includes the original template and graphical emoji *sentence*, the *emoji-text* form, and the *demoji-text* form.

VADER, AFINN, TextBlob were run once with their lexicons and built in analyzers for the dataset and once using only their lexicons with the aggregation method described above. The run using only the lexicon allowed for a comparison of the lexicons themselves to the Sentiment140L and SentiWordNet lexicons. In practice, many users may utilize these systems out of the box and not create their own scoring algorithm, so both types of runs are included in the analysis.

4 Results

Aggregation Method. Sentiment140L, AFINN, and VADER returned no differences between any variables. The template sentence with the default skin tone emoji returned the same value as the template sentence with any skin tone modifier. For SentiWordNet the default and skin tone modifiers returned the same value using both the *emoji* and the *emoji-text*. The skin tones all returned the same polarity using *demoji-text* but this value was different from the defaults' polarity. MANOVAs were run for each skin tone option per lexicon on the *demoji-text* output, see Table 1. From these results, we can see that TextBlob and SentiWordNet, have statistically significant differences between the skin tones, see Table 2.

Table 1. Demoji-text aggregation method: one-way MANOVA p-values, $\alpha = 0.05$

	Sentiment-140L	SentiWordNet	VADER	AFINN	TextBlob
Pillai Trace	0.452	0	0.762	0.759	2.046E−09
Wilk's Lambda	0.448	0	0.761	0.758	9.689E−10
Hotelling Trace	0.444	0	0.790	0.757	4.598E−10

Table 2. Demoji-text aggregation method: group means of TextBlob and SentiWordNet

	None	Default	Light	Medium	Medium-Dark	Dark	Total
Polarity	0.279	0.484	0.484	0.484	0.484	0.484	0.460
SentiWordNet	0.047	−0.281	−0.953	−0.953	−0.953	−0.953	−0.716
TextBlob	−0.209	−0.234	0.281	−0.234	−0.234	−0.375	−0.165

Built-In Methods. Both VADER's and AFINN's built-in score functions returned no difference between any variable. No differences were observed between skin tones or between skin tones and the default when using the *emoji* and *emoji-text* in TextBlob. However, when using the *demoji-text*, statistically significant differences between the default and skin tones as well as differences between the skin tones themselves were observed, see Table 3 and 4.

Table 3. Demoji-text built-in methods: one-way ANOVA p-values, $\alpha = 0.05$

	Sentiment 140L	SentiWordNet	VADER	AFINN	TextBlob
Emoji-Icon	1.075E−46	1.156E−11	4.716E−17	1.080E−24	1.215E−12
Emoji-Text	1.075E−46	8.346E−10	4.716E−17	1.080E−24	2.551E−19
Demoji-Text	6.885E−18	1.941E−122	4.716E−17	1.080E−24	6.696E−27

Further evaluation of the data revealed that while the "medium" and "medium-dark" skin tones returned the same polarity as the default emoji, the

Table 4. Demoji-text built-in methods: one-way MANOVA p-values, $\alpha = 0.05$

	VADER	AFINN	TextBlob
Pillai Trace	0.762	0.759	2.046E−09
Wilk's Lambda	0.761	0.758	9.689E−10
Hotelling Trace	0.760	0.757	4.598E−10

"light" and "dark" skin tones returned different values. When the returned sentiment was negative, both the "light" and "dark" values were higher (more positive) with the "light" skin tone returning the most positive valence value. When the returned sentiment was positive, both the "light" and "dark" values were lower (more negative) with the "light" skin tone again returning the more positive value of the two.

5   Discussion

Both VADER and AFINN returned no changes in polarity score between using and not using an emoji while Sentiment140, SentiWordNet and TextBlob all reported changes in at least one run. This demonstrates that emojis may play a role in sentiment analysis whether users prefer out-of-the box functionality with an API such as TextBlobs' or prefer to create their own SA algorithm such as our aggregation method.

Some sentiment analysis systems already come with their own emoji translation lexicon, such as VADER. When comparing the built-in VADER scoring functionality and the VADER lexicon with our aggregation method, the scores between identical inputs differed. This is to be expected even without the inclusion of the emoji lexicon, as heuristics are included with the API that were not taken into account in the aggregation method. The VADER emoji lexicon utilizes the *demoji-text* translation, but the descriptors are not found within the lexicon and do not contribute to the score.

The type of translation (*emoji-text* v. *demoji-text*) used to process the emoji text influences the returned score if the descriptors are included in the lexicon. Different scores between the skin tone modifiers on the same template occurred when the additional description words were found in the lexicon. *Demoji-text* separates each word and parts of the emoji name or description are found in some of the lexicons.

TextBlobs' analyzer returned a more positive score with the light skin tone compared to the dark skin tone modifier regardless if it was a positive or negative statement when *demoji-text* was used. The inclusion of descriptors in the lexicons allow for analysis of phrases such as "You are the light of my life"; however, using lexicons with set sentiment values for words has a large limitation of context. If and when lexicons are used in methods where only scores of individual words are used and context is not taken into account, i.e., when the descriptor should not have an effect on the sentiment, unintended biases arise.

5.1   Limitations

Our study only looked at a small subset of possible emojis and their skin-tone description. Future work includes expanding the set to all skin-tone enabled emojis and using datasets that already include emojis. The number of sentiment analysis lexicons and systems was also limited due to feasibility constraints and the large number of systems that exist. Many newer sentiment analysis machine learning models try to address the context challenge. With the increased use of such models, future work should also consider those techniques when evaluating the potential introduction of bias in frequently used systems.

6   Conclusion

New features such as emojis and emoji skin tone modifiers have enabled users to be more expressive in their communication. This study aimed to understand how SA polarity scores changed relative to a sentence containing emojis with skin tone modifiers. Changes in polarity were found based on varying the skin-tones in some SA systems. This study presents a methodology to the community for sentiment analysis, which may help uncover biases in selected systems in future work. Unmitigated or unintentional bias in a system could lead to the perpetuation of disparities in other areas. Emoji's added richness can be accessed when systems truly capture the message a user would like to communicate about themselves and their ideas.

References

1. Pattern, June 2018. https://www.clips.uantwerpen.be/clips.bak/pages/pattern?https%3A%2F%2Ftextblob_readthedocs_io%2Fen%2Fdev%2Fadvanced_usage_html=#sentiment-analyzers
2. API reference, April 2020. https://textblob.readthedocs.io/en/dev/api_reference.html
3. Emojipedia (2021). https://emojipedia.org/
4. Nltk.corpus.reader package, April 2021. https://www.nltk.org/api/nltk.corpus.reader.html
5. Barbieri, F., Camacho-Collados, J.: How gender and skin tone modifiers affect emoji semantics in Twitter, pp. 101–106 (2018). https://doi.org/10.18653/v1/S18-2011
6. Chairunnisa, S., Benedictus, A.S.: Analysis of emoji and emoticon usage in interpersonal communication of blackberry messenger and Whatsapp application user. Int. J. Soc. Sci. Manag. **4**, 120–126 (2017)
7. Coats, S.: Skin tone emoji and sentiment on Twitter. CoRR abs/1805.00444 (2018). http://arxiv.org/abs/1805.00444
8. Daft, R.L., Lengel, R.H.: Organizational information requirements, media richness and structural design. Manag. Sci. **32**(5), 554–571 (1986). https://doi.org/10.1287/mnsc.32.5.554
9. Feldman, R.: Techniques and applications for sentiment analysis. Commun. ACM **56**(4), 82–89 (2013)

10. Fernández-Gavilanes, M., Juncal-Martínez, J., García-Méndez, S., Costa-Montenegro, E., González-Castaño, F.J.: Creating emoji lexica from unsupervised sentiment analysis of their descriptions. Expert Syst. Appl. **103**, 74–91 (2018)
11. Fitzpatrick, T.B.: Soleil et peau. J. Med. Esthet. **2**, 33–34 (1975)
12. Go, A., Bhayani, R., Huang, L.: Twitter sentiment classification using distant supervision. CS224N Proj. Rep. Stanford **1**(12), 2009 (2009)
13. Guibon, G., Ochs, M., Bellot, P.: From emojis to sentiment analysis. In: WACAI 2016 (2016)
14. Hsieh, S.H., Tseng, T.H.: Playfulness in mobile instant messaging: examining the influence of emoticons and text messaging on social interaction. Comput. Hum. Behav. **69**, 405–414 (2017). https://doi.org/10.1016/j.chb.2016.12.052, https://www.sciencedirect.com/science/article/pii/S0747563216308810
15. Hutto, C., Gilbert, E.: Vader: a parsimonious rule-based model for sentiment analysis of social media text. In: Proceedings of the International AAAI Conference on Web and Social Media, vol. 8, no. 1, pp. 216–225, May 2014. https://ojs.aaai.org/index.php/ICWSM/article/view/14550
16. Kiritchenko, S., Mohammad, S.M.: Examining gender and race bias in two hundred sentiment analysis systems. CoRR abs/1805.04508 (2018). http://arxiv.org/abs/1805.04508
17. Ljubešić, N., Fišer, D.: A global analysis of emoji usage. In: Proceedings of the 10th Web as Corpus Workshop, pp. 82–89. Association for Computational Linguistics, Berlin, August 2016. https://doi.org/10.18653/v1/W16-2610, https://aclanthology.org/W16-2610
18. Medhat, W., Hassan, A., Korashy, H.: Sentiment analysis algorithms and applications: a survey. Ain Shams Eng. J. **5**(4), 1093–1113 (2014). https://doi.org/10.1016/j.asej.2014.04.011, https://www.sciencedirect.com/science/article/pii/S2090447914000550
19. Mohammad, S., Kiritchenko, S., Zhu, X.: NRC-Canada: building the state-of-the-art in sentiment analysis of tweets. In: Second Joint Conference on Lexical and Computational Semantics (*SEM), Volume 2: Proceedings of the Seventh International Workshop on Semantic Evaluation (SemEval 2013), pp. 321–327. Association for Computational Linguistics, Atlanta, June 2013. https://aclanthology.org/S13-2053
20. Nielsen, F.: A new anew: evaluation of a word list for sentiment analysis in microblogs. In: Proceedings of the ESWC2011 Workshop on 'Making Sense of Microposts': Big Things Come in Small Packages, pp. 93–98. No. 718 in CEUR Workshop Proceedings, CEUR-WS (2011). 1st Workshop on Making Sense of Microposts: Big Things Come in Small Packages, MSM2011, 30 May 2011
21. Robertson, A., Magdy, W., Goldwater, S.: Emoji skin tone modifiers: analyzing variation in usage on social media. Trans. Soc. Comput. **3**(2) (2020). https://doi.org/10.1145/3377479
22. Shiha, M., Ayvaz, S.: The effects of emoji in sentiment analysis. Int. J. Comput. Electr. Eng. (IJCEE.) **9**(1), 360–369 (2017)
23. Suntwal, S., Brown, S., Brandimarte, L.: Pictographs, ideograms, and emojis (pie): a framework for empirical research using non-verbal cues (2021). https://doi.org/10.24251/HICSS.2021.771
24. Yoo, B., Rayz, J.T.: Understanding emojis for sentiment analysis. In: The International FLAIRS Conference Proceedings, vol. 34 (2021)

Understanding User Behavior in Social Media Using a Hierarchical Visualization

Erick López-Ornelas[(✉)] and Rocío Abascal-Mena

Information Technology Department, Universidad Autónoma Metropolitana – Cuajimalpa,
Mexico City, México
{elopez,mabascal}@correo.cua.uam.mx

Abstract. People use microblogging platforms like Twitter to involve with other users for a wide range of interests and practices. Twitter profiles run by different types of users such as humans, bots, spammers, businesses and professionals. This research uses a treemap visualization to identify different users profile on Twitter. For this purpose, we exploit users' profile and tweeting behavior information. We evaluate our approach by visualizing the different Twitter profiles. We focus just on user activity, ignoring the content of messages. We take into consideration both social interactions and tweeting patterns, which allow us to profile users according to their activity patterns using treemaps.

Keywords: Treemaps · Hierarchical visualization · Twitter · User profile

1 Introduction

Microblogging platforms have become an interesting and fast way to share and consume information of interest on the Web in real-time. For instance, in recent years, Twitter (http://twitter.com) has emerged as an important source of real-time information exchange platform. It has empowered citizens, companies, marketers to act as content generators, that is, people share information about what they experience, eyewitness, and observe about topics from a wide range of fields such as epidemics, disasters, elections and more. This allows users not only to be consumers of the information, but prosumers of the information, where the information is produced by themselves.

To consume information, Twitter users follow other users who they think can provide useful information of their interest. Information shared on Twitter in the form of short text messages (\tweets") immediately propagated to followers, and implicitly starts a one-way conversation, which is also known as social interaction [1].

Social interaction on social media has a resemblance to social interaction that one practices in daily routine. For instance, companies leverage insights from social media information to better market to its customers and increase sales. In this case, companies always seek to gain more in-depth information of their customers for better understanding and to improve interaction with them despite it is one-to-one, through a phone call, or on social media.

C. Stephanidis et al. (Eds.): HCII 2022, CCIS 1582, pp. 574–580, 2022.
https://doi.org/10.1007/978-3-031-06391-6_71

Moreover, understanding the types of users on social media is important for many reasons. For example, this includes detecting bots or spam users [2], recommending friends (e.g., potential users to follow on twitter) [3], finding credible information and users [4], for example, to receive trusted analysis or feedback of products or to ask questions to fulfill information needs [5], and so on.

In recent years, Twitter has been extensively used in a number of research studies that analyze and process mainly tweets content using different natural language processing (NLP) techniques to differentiate Twitter users [6]. Moreover, many studies focus on aspects like, who follows whom, who is in which list, etc. However, understanding the types of twitter users using their tweeting behavior or more importantly what their profile information reflects, is an aspect which is broadly overlooked. Twitter profiles provide useful information, furthermore determining various behavioral aspects of users on Twitter such as how often they post, re-tweet, or reply could provide significant insights about users.

2   Related Work

Analyzing users and their behavior on online social networks has been the subject of many previous works [7]. The particular domain of the Twitter microblogging service has not been an exception. By looking at the contents produced by users, or at the actions they perform, researchers have been able to derive user characterizations and other useful information, with the goal of, for example, doing sentiment analysis [8] or predicting the diffusion of information [9]. Chu et al. [10], observe the differences between human users and what they designate as bot and cyborg users. The authors characterize a bot as a user whose actions are all automatic, i.e. without any human intervention. Java et al. propose a taxonomy of user intentions on Twitter [11]. To achieve this, users were manually categorized according to their link structure and tweet contents. Based on link structure, three main categories of users where identified: (1) Information Sources, (2) and (3) Information Seekers.

Tweeting behavior, network structure, and the linguistic content were used by Pennacchiotti et al. to infer the political orientation and ethnicity of users [12]. Cha et al., for instance, define three types of influence on Twitter: Indegree, Retweet and Mention [13]. Gomez-Rodriguez et al. [14] developed a method to trace diffusion and influence paths through the network on a dataset of MemeTracker.

3   Tweeting Behavior and Hierarchical Visualization

Twitter users can be analyzed based on their profiles, posts, and tweeting behavior. Users' profiles exhibit an extensive set of informational pieces, users' posts represent rich content (i.e., tweets) often used to perform NLP based analysis, and users' tweeting behavior represents different aspects related to a user's interaction with the platform as well as with other users (e.g., followers). In Fig. 1 we show a partial view of the information that can be obtained from Twitter about a user. The figure shows a meta-data part (i.e., profile specific information, followers, and friends), and a content part

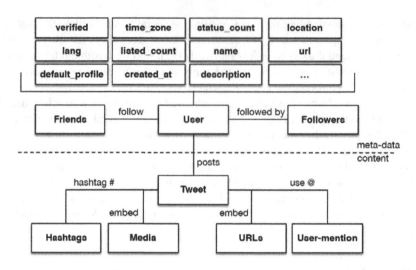

Fig. 1. Information obtained from Twitter.

(i.e., tweets). To identify Twitter users into different classes, we exploit users' profile and their tweeting behavior.

Users on Twitter can be anyone. These users can be classified into two broad categories, that are, (i) real-users, (ii) digital-actors. Real-users represent human-beings (e.g., home users, business users, or professional users), and digital-actors represent automated computer programs (e.g., bots, online services, etc.). Both types of user built their profiles on Twitter by specifying information such as name, website, description, bio, etc. Other information such as created at, status count, listed count that a twitter profile contains automatically provided or manipulated by Twitter platform and it tends to change over time (e.g., number of followers change over time, listed count change over time).

In general, tweets posted by users are publicly available and are followed by subscribers called followers. Users who share particular interests are included in one's reading list.

A profile's listed count is the number of users whose reading lists contain the profile's tweets.

In other hand, treemaps are a space-filling graph visualization technique first introduced in [15]. An important feature of treemaps is that they make very efficient use of display space. Thus it is possible to display large trees with many hierarchical levels in a minimal amount of space. In Fig. 2a shows a sample tree structure and in Fig. 2b shows the corresponding treemap.

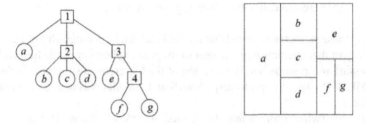

Fig. 2. A) hierarchical tree, b) treemap visualization.

The algorithm used to partition the display space is known as the "slice-and-dice algorithm" and functions like a k-d tree space partition. The positioning of tree nodes in a treemap is a recursive process.

First, the children of the root are placed across the display area horizontally, where each node's area is directly proportional to its weight. Then, for each node n already displayed, each of n's children is placed across vertically within n's display area. This process is repeated, alternating between horizontal and vertical placement until all nodes have been displayed.

Treemaps can be especially helpful when dealing with large clustered graphs. When viewing a graph at some level of abstraction, the viewer is really looking at nodes belonging to some level in the cluster tree. A treemap can display the whole structure of a cluster tree, thus allowing the user to place the current view in context.

In the standard treemap of Shneiderman [15] the nodes are represented as rectangles of various shapes. This makes a visual comparison of their importance (as determined by area) difficult, especially as the rectangles vary in orientation as well.

4   Hierarchical Structure of Users Profiles

Twitter provides us information through its official API in JSON (Java Script Object Notation) format, that in general terms we obtain is simply text, which by its nature does not allow a comparative analysis in large amount of data, on the other hand there are variables difficult to identify without any visual tool. Using the Twitter API, we have the information generated by the user when a tweet is published, this by itself provides us a lot of information. Also, we have the option to extract a dataset limited to 200 tweets that have been published or republished (retweet) by a specific user.

Then we created a web application in order to visualize using treemaps of all different users. We identify the steps that the web application will carry out:

1. Twitter Username has to be inserted on the application.
2. The application will connect to through the API and extract tweets from the Twitter account.
3. Each of the tweets will be analyzed and the important data is grouped sharing similar characteristics.
4. The system will create a hierarchical structure (tree) where they will be grouped the different data.

5. A treemap is created using these hierarchical structure.

Having these steps, the frontend and the backend can be distinguishing. The frontend will be the part that interacts with the user of the web application, while backend will be the processing information and the creation of the hierarchical structure. Technologies like HTML, CSS, Java Script, Reactjs, VueJS and Angular was used to implement the web application.

To identify Twitter profiles into the defined groups, we choose 16 features as summarized below. These features include a few trivial ones, which can be easily obtained from profiles, for example, statistical features like # of tweets, # of replies, followers, etc. However, some of the selected features are derived like Answer with hashtag and mentions or Retweets with mention, etc.

The selected features are: followers, friends, # of likes, original tweet having a hashtag, original tweet having a mention, original tweet having only text, original tweet having hashtag and mention, answer having a mention, answer having only text, answer having a hashtag and a mention, retweet having a hashtag, retweet with a mention, retweet having a hashtag and a mention, retweet having only text.

All these information is then analyzed in order to create the hierarchical structure and the treemap. In Fig. 3 a treemap with all these features is shown.

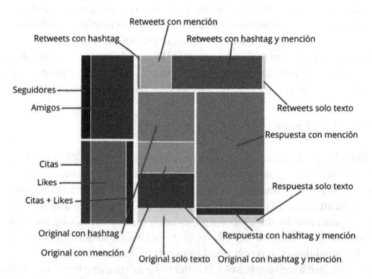

Fig. 3. User profile represented by a treemap.

5   Small Multiples Experiment

As a case os study, it was decided to use the "small multiples" technique to compare different user profiles at the same time. All users are Mexicans politicians and some recognized journalist. Figure 4 shows this Treemap.

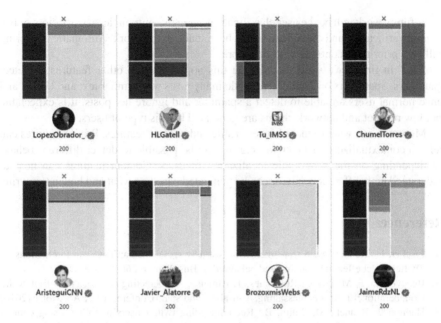

Fig. 4. Small multiples visualization and treemaps.

Comparing this small multiple visualization, some similarities can be found regarding all different users, for example the @HLGatell and @JaimeRdzNL are very similar. Both users are politicians and had a lot on interaction with other accounts (light blue) because they have a lot of answers. In the case of @AristeguiCNN and @Javier_Alatorre, (both journalist), show a similar profile with the Retweet section (light brown). In the other hand, comparing @LopezObrador_ and @BrozoxmisWebs, although they are two completely different characters (politician and journalist), their profiles are very similar, which shows that they behave very similarly in the social network.

6 Conclusions

Twitter is a famous microblogging platform used by companies, businesses, professionals, and also by home users in their daily routine to disseminate information online in real-time. Twitter users exhibit different characteristics that distinguish one user from others. Understanding Twitter users is important for many reasons such as for companies to plan their marketing campaigns differently for different types of users.

In this paper we proposed a set of features that allow us to characterize and distinguish user activity patterns on Twitter using a treemaps as a visualization tool. Through the analysis of diffusion patterns we are able to infer different kind user behavior. Our approach uses a lot of information from the user profile.

We explored the treemap visualization and demonstrate that can be very interesting tool to identify automatically some user's profiles. Also the "small multiples" technique has been used to compare different user's profile.

A future work will be the user classification using this automatic visualization, only a manual verification and classification has been made in this work. Automatic clustering will be a priority to continue with this work.

Also, in future we want to combine this approach with other features to detect spammers. Spammers on Twitter tend to do many posts with similar text and URLs, and since normal users are able to detect a spammer and ignore her posts, it is expectable that few retweet and network chains are generated by this type of users.

Moreover, we want to include user profile and content features. Profile features can help to contextualize user behavior, e.g. it may be possible to detect different behavior depending on the geographic localization of users. Content features can help to understand how different behavior can be generated based on what and how users write.

References

1. Fischer, E., Reuber, A.: Social interaction via new social media:(how) can interactions on Twitter affect effectual thinking and behavior? J. Bus. Ventur. **26**(1), 1–18 (2011)
2. Benevenuto, F, Magno, G, Rodrigues, T, Almeida, V.: Detecting spammers on Twitter. In: Collaboration, Electronic Messaging, Anti-abuse and Spam Conference (CEAS), vol. 6 (2010)
3. Hannon, J, Bennett, M, Smith, B.: Recommending twitter users to follow using content and collaborative filtering approaches. In: Proceedings of the Fourth ACM Conference on Recommender Systems, pp. 199–206. ACM (2010)
4. Castillo, C, Mendoza, M, Poblete, B.: Information credibility on Twitter. In: Proceedings of the 20th International Conference on World Wide Web, pp. 675–684. ACM (2011)
5. Paul, S, Hong, L, Chi, E.: Is Twitter a good place for asking questions? A characterization study. In: ICWSM (2011)
6. Pennacchiotti, M, Popescu, A.: A machine learning approach to Twitter user classification. In: ICWSM (2011)
7. Millen, D, Patterson, J.: Stimulating social engagement in a community network. In: Proceedings of the ACM Conference on Computer-Supported Cooperative Work, pp. 306–313 (2002)
8. Naveed, N, Gottron, T, Kunegis, J, Alhadi, A.: Bad news travel fast: a content-based analysis of interestingness on Twitter. In: Proceedings of the ACM WebSci 2011, pp. 1–7 (2011)
9. Yang, J., Counts, S.: Predicting the speed, scale, and range of information diffusion in Twitter. In: International AAAI Conference on Weblogs and Social Media (2011)
10. Chu, Z, Gianvecchio, S, Wang, H, Jajodia, S.: Who is tweeting on Twitter: human, bot, or cyborg? In: Proceedings of the 26th Annual Computer Security Applications Conference, pp. 21–30 (2010)
11. Java, A, Finin, T, Song, X, Tseng, B.: Why we Twitter: understanding microblogging usage and communities. In: Joint 9th WEBKDD and 1st SNA-KDD Workshop (2007)
12. Pennacchiotti, M, Popescu, A.: A machine learning approach to Twitter user classification. In: Fifth International AAAI Conference on Weblogs and Social Media (2011)
13. Cha, M, Haddadi, H, Benevenuto, F, Gummadi, K.: Measuring user influence in Twitter: the million follower fallacy. In: Proceedings of the 4th International AAAI Conference on Weblogs and Social Media ICWSM (2010)
14. Gomez-Rodriguez, M, Leskovec, J, Krause, A.: Inferring networks of diffusion and influence. In: DD, pp. 1019–1028 (2010)
15. Shneiderman, B.: Tree visualization with treemaps: a 2D space-filling approach. Technical report, HCI Lab University of Maryland, March 1991

Elicitation of Requirements for a NLP-Model Store for Abusive Language Detection

Kilian Müller[✉]

Department for Information Systems, University of Muenster, Leonardo-Campus 3,
48149 Münster, Germany
kilian.mueller@ercis.uni-muenster.de

Abstract. While in social media users most commonly interact with each other without a guiding entity, the discussion space of newspaper platforms is moderated by community managers, who invest considerable amounts of time and effort in keeping comment sections clean. To reduce this effort and allow community managers again to more freely interact with their users, automated comment moderation systems (ACMS) be be utilized. However, most newspapers do not have the expertise to create, update, and maintain machine learning (ML)-models. Thus, they are forced to rely on proprietary off-the-shelf solutions. However, if they want to keep their sovereignty over their data and systems, they would need access to models which could be integrated within their current moderation or content management systems. One option could be a platform for newspapers and data scientists where the data scientists could sell their pre-trained models and where newspapers could hire data scientists to create tailor-made models for them. In order to identify the requirements, community managers have for such systems, we conducted a series of semi-structured interviews with community managers of newspapers of varying size (from local to national). Furthermore, the information was enriched by the participation in multiple workshops on content moderation. We were able to elicit five major technical requirements necessary to create the described design artifact.

Keywords: Abusive language · Comment moderation · Model store

1 Introduction and Motivation

Hate and abusive comments are spreading through social media and other discussion spaces [16,18]. As this could pose a serious threat to online discussions [21] and is already being targeted by lawmakers (e.g., the Netzwerkdurchsetzungsgesetz (NetzDG) in Germany[1] [13], or other countries [6]), newspapers have

---

[1] The NetzDG forces the providers of comment spaces to remove abusive language from their sites within 24 h after being alerted.

C. Stephanidis et al. (Eds.): HCII 2022, CCIS 1582, pp. 581–588, 2022.
https://doi.org/10.1007/978-3-031-06391-6_72

to employ community managers in order to manually moderate user generated content.

These community managers used to fulfill the role of gatekeepers, interacting with their readers and fostering a healthy discussion space. However, in recent years, they are forced to act as content moderators, deleting or blocking user generated content [7]. This pushes the community managers away from their original job description [14]. Consequently, many newspapers have resorted to close their comment sections entirely (around 45% in Germany [17]), as the benefit of having a political discourse does not measure up to their necessary economic investment.

To support community managers in their work and allow newspapers to keep their comment sections, automated comment moderation systems (ACMS) utilizing different forms of machine learning (ML) are a promising option [10,20]. These ACMS utilize natural language processing (NLP) methods in order to automatically detect abusive content. Afterwards, this content can be automatically blocked from publication or be reviewed by community managers; resulting in semi-automated moderation.

In contrast to large newspapers, small- or medium-sized newspapers often times do not have the in-house competences to build such ACMS themselves [26]. Therefore, often times, they have to rely on proprietary solutions, e.g., Perspective[2] by Alphabet [25]. This, however, comes at the price of losing their sovereignty over their own and their users data, as the comments are transferred to the provider of the proprietary system. Therefore, a possible solution could be the utilization of publicly available research insights.

Favorably for newspapers, there already exist multiple, accessible research endeavors in which researchers investigate models suitable for abusive language detection (c.f. [2,4,5,8,9,16,22,24]). However, these insights are still not on a usable level for small- to medium-sized newspapers. The described approaches need to be applied to the newspaper's data and the resulting models need to be delivered in an easy to use format so that newspapers are able to seamlessly integrate them into their existing IT-architecture [26]. Thus, on the one hand, even though there exists available research in the domain, newspapers are still in need for external expertise to create proficient and usable models which can then be integrated into their ACMS. On the other hand, there exists the need for labeled training data, especially in non-English speaking communities, for the creation of refined models [3]. Therefore, apart from possible monetary benefits, data scientist could also benefit from receiving data from the different newspapers.

Apparently, both sides could benefit from either the provided data or the external expertise. Therefore, the goal of this paper is the elicitation of requirements for a NLP-model store, especially for the detection of abusive language which can be utilized to connect newspapers with data scientists/researchers. In the paper all five requirements are explained w.r.t. their implications on the community managers daily work. Additionally, the implications for the practical implementations of the desired artifact are detailed.

---

[2] https://www.perspectiveapi.com/.

The paper is structured as follows: Sect. 2 introduces the research method utilized in this paper. Afterwards, the results are presented in Sect. 3. Finally, Sect. 4 discusses the findings and concludes the paper.

2 Research Method

In order to gain insights into the daily work of community manager and their requirements towards an NLP-model store semi-structured interviews were conducted. Semi-structured interviews are a widely accepted form of building a basis for requirement elicitation [1,27]. Furthermore, this form of interview allows for deeper insights into the necessary domain knowledge of community managers [11].

Community managers from three different newspapers participated in the interviews: One national newspaper (among the three largest newspapers in Germany), one regional newspaper (with daily circulation $> 250,000$), and one local newspaper (with daily circulation $< 10,000$). During the interview the interviewees were asked questions focusing on their daily work in comment moderation, their current practices, and possible automation possibilities. Later, they were shown a comment moderation system with a functioning automated moderation support and were then asked which requirements they would have towards such a system. Following up, questions were aimed at their current moderation system and how they could envision an integration of ML-models for automated comment moderation. Afterwards, questions regarding their possible capabilities in creating their own models as well as a possible envisioned procurement process for such models were asked.

The interviews were conducted in a virtual setting via Zoom[3] and, after approval by the interviewee, recorded with both video and audio. After the finished interview each was transcribed and analyzed.

To gather additional information, we participated in three domain-specific workshops. Here, insights regarding practitioner's views and issues in their current work were gained. These insights were subsequently structured to allow for further analysis.

Combining the two sources of information, the data was analyzed to obtain the requirements. They were then evaluated by discussions with community managers.

3 Results

Utilizing the input of the interviews and the workshops, we elicit five requirements for NLP-model stores for abusive language detection. The requirements are explained in more detail in the following.

---

[3] https://zoom.us/.

3.1   Ease of Understanding

As mentioned above, community managers are rarely experts in the domain of NLP. While the community managers expressed a rather positive attitude towards ML in general they also mentioned insecurities about inner workings of ML. Furthermore, they mentioned that also the dark side of ML was not obvious to them either. However, even with these concerns, all community managers expressed the willingness to include ML in their moderation process. Thus, eliminating possible insecurities about ML and informing the community managers about the workings of the presented ML-models could pave the way for broader acceptance.

REQ_1: An NLP-model store for abusive language detection should be conceptualized in such a way, that community managers are guided towards an understanding of the necessary ML specific technical terms and workings and are thus able to make informed decisions.

3.2   Explainable Models

While transparency, regarding the moderation decision, towards the users varied between the different community managers, all community managers stated that transparency in moderation decisions is of crucial importance within their teams. Traceability between different community managers are important in order to make similar moderation decisions and present a consistent image towards their users. When confronted with model explainers[4] the community managers appreciated the quick overview provided [15,19]. However, as soon as too much text was highlighted all agreed to lose focus on the important passages. Furthermore, the community managers pointed out different aspects which they focus on during their moderation process which should be reflected in possible word highlight. Thus, highlighting the different ML outputs on the NLP-model store examples could provide the community managers with valuable feedback on model performance and fit to their specific moderation habits.

REQ_2: An NLP-model store for abusive language detection should include the option to add model-agnostic explainers in order to make the ML output understandable and transparent for community managers.

3.3   Multiple Vendors

All community managers were utilizing different moderation systems, many are tailor-made or customized for the specific newspaper. Some already had experiences with different kinds of ML input in their moderation decision. However, none expressed the desire to switch to proprietary system, sourced from one company, which would support the comment moderation with ML. Rather than

---

[4] The presented moderation system was equipped with explainers, highlighting different words or passages which were crucial to the models moderation decision.

a new solution, the community managers preferred the integration of ML into their system, either as a full integration or an interface in order to "keep control" over their own data and infrastructure. However, they expressed the desire for external support as long as they were not dependent on a single supplier.

REQ_3: An NLP-model store for abusive language detection should include the option to buy ML-models from multiple vendors in an easy to use format, preventing lock-in effects and allowing for the integration into existing moderation platforms.

3.4 Comparable Metrics

The community managers stated difficulties in evaluating ML-models. This becomes even more difficult, as researchers utilize many different metrics in evaluating different ML-models. As non data-scientists, the community managers prefer metrics which are easy to understand and also appreciate consistency when it comes to the metrics utilized when comparing different models. This is also echoed by existing literature (cf., [26]).

REQ_4: An NLP-model store for abusive language detection should offer comparable and understandable metrics for all offered models to enable community manager to find the best model suited for their specific business needs.

3.5 Customized Models

The community managers detailed significant differences between their respective moderation processes. These were also reflected in the community guidelines, the moderation process, and the harshness/lenience in moderation decision making. Thus, the community managers pointed out that a ML-model should reflect both the newspaper's community guidelines and the community managers judgment. Consequently, not every model will fit every newspaper. Therefore, the community managers expressed the desire commission tailor-made models, based on their own previous decisions, which could better gauge the desired discussion culture on their respective comment sections.

REQ_5: An NLP-model store for abusive language detection should offer the option to commission tailor-made ML-models for community managers, based on data gathered from their own newspapers.

4   Discussion and Conclusion

The goal of the research presented in this paper is the elicitation of requirements for an NLP-model store for abusive language detection to support both community managers in their daily work and provide data scientist with the necessary input to improve existing models or develop entirely new ones. By connecting these distinct stakeholder groups new collaboration possibilities should arise which could benefit both sides.

Towards this goal, three interviews with community managers were conducted and three workshops on content moderation were visited. Based on the acquired knowledge, five requirement have been elicited and presented in this paper. These requirements should guide researchers and practitioners in creating an NLP-model store for abusive language detection.

However, the presented research in progress does not come without limitations. First, we only interviewed community managers. This excludes the views from data scientists from our results and, therefore, does not include important aspects and requirements they have towards such an IT-artifact. Second, only three interviews with community managers have been conducted up-to-date. Consequently, the insights acquired from these interviews should be validated with different community managers from other newspapers. Third, the presented research is purely conceptual and should be demonstrated and evaluated by implementing a functioning model store.

Thus, our next steps in our research agenda include conducting more interviews; both with additional community managers to validate the current findings, as well as with data scientist to include their viewpoints. Next, utilizing design science research [12], the NLP-model store needs to be developed based on the generated requirements. Utilizing the developed store the requirements and further insights can be evaluated [23]. Lastly, the developed store will be integrated into the currently existing moderation system[5] to offer practitioners the ability to procure models from data scientists.

Acknowledgements. The research leading to these results received funding from the federal state of North Rhine-Westphalia and the European Regional Development Fund (EFRE.NRW 2014-2020), Project: M●DERAT! (No. CM-2-2-036a).

Furthermore, I would like to thank Marco Niemann and Holger Koelmann for their assistance in conducting the interviews used in this paper.

References

1. Agarwal, R., Tanniru, M.R.: Knowledge acquisition using structured interviewing: an empirical investigation. J. Manag. Inf. Syst. **7**(1), 123–140 (1990)
2. Agarwal, S., Sureka, A.: Using KNN and SVM based one-class classifier for detecting online radicalization on Twitter. In: Natarajan, R., Barua, G., Patra, M.R. (eds.) ICDCIT 2015. LNCS, vol. 8956, pp. 431–442. Springer, Cham (2015). https://doi.org/10.1007/978-3-319-14977-6_47
3. Assenmacher, D., Niemann, M., Müller, K., Seiler, M., Riehle, D.M., Trautmann, H.: RP-mod & RP-crowd: moderator- and crowd-annotated German news comment datasets. In: Thirty-Fifth Conference on Neural Information Processing Systems Datasets and Benchmarks Track (Round 2) (2021)
4. Badjatiya, P., Gupta, S., Gupta, M., Varma, V.: Deep learning for hate speech detection in tweets. In: Proceedings of the 26th International Conference on World Wide Web Companion, pp. 759–760 (2017)
5. Bartlett, J., Reffin, J., Rumball, N., Williamson, S.: Anti-social media. Demos **2014**, 1–51 (2014)

---

[5] moderat.nrw.

6. Bloch-Wehba, H.: Automation in moderation. Cornell Int. Law J. **53**(1), 41–96 (2020)
7. Boberg, S., Schatto-Eckrodt, T., Frischlich, L., Quandt, T.: The moral gatekeeper? Moderation and deletion of user-generated content in a leading news forum. Media Commun. **6**(4), 58–69 (2018)
8. Djuric, N., Zhou, J., Morris, R., Grbovic, M., Radosavljevic, V., Bhamidipati, N.: Hate speech detection with comment embeddings. In: Proceedings of the 24th International Conference on World Wide Web, pp. 29–30 (2015)
9. Gitari, N.D., Zuping, Z., Damien, H., Long, J.: A lexicon-based approach for hate speech detection. Int. J. Multimedia Ubiquitous Eng. **10**(4), 215–230 (2015)
10. Gorwa, R., Binns, R., Katzenbach, C.: Algorithmic content moderation: Technical and political challenges in the automation of platform governance. Big Data Soc. **7**(1), 1–15 (2020)
11. Hadar, I., Soffer, P., Kenzi, K.: The role of domain knowledge in requirements elicitation via interviews: an exploratory study. Requirements Eng. **19**(2), 143–159 (2012). https://doi.org/10.1007/s00766-012-0163-2
12. Hevner, A., Chatterjee, S.: Design science research in information systems. In: Hevner, A., Chatterjee, S. (eds.) Design Research in Information Systems, pp. 9–22. Springer, Boston (2010). https://doi.org/10.1007/978-1-4419-5653-8_2
13. der Justiz, B.: Gesetz zur verbesserung der rechtsdurchsetzung in sozialen netzwerken (netzwerkdurchsetzungsgesetz - netzdg) (2017). https://www.gesetze-im-internet.de/netzdg/BJNR335210017.html
14. Loosen, W., et al.: Making sense of user comments: identifying journalists' requirements for a comment analysis framework. Stud. Commun. Media **6**(4), 333–364 (2017)
15. Lundberg, S.M., Lee, S.I.: A unified approach to interpreting model predictions. In: Proceedings of the 31st International Conference on Neural Information Processing Systems, pp. 4768–4777 (2017)
16. Mondal, M., Silva, L.A., Benevenuto, F.: A measurement study of hate speech in social media. In: Dolong, P., Vojtas, P. (eds.) Proceedings of the 28th ACM Conference on Hypertext and Social Media. HT 2017, pp. 85–94. ACM, Prague (2017)
17. Niemann, M., Müller, K., Kelm, C., Assenmacher, D., Becker, J.: The German comment landscape. In: Bright, J., Giachanou, A., Spaiser, V., Spezzano, F., George, A., Pavliuc, A. (eds.) MISDOOM 2021. LNCS, vol. 12887, pp. 112–127. Springer, Cham (2021). https://doi.org/10.1007/978-3-030-87031-7_8
18. Nobata, C., Tetreault, J., Thomas, A., Mehdad, Y., Chang, Y.: Abusive language detection in online user content. In: Proceedings of the 25th International Conference on World Wide Web. WWW 2016, pp. 145–153. ACM Press, Montreal (2016)
19. Ribeiro, M.T., Singh, S., Guestrin, C.: "Why should i trust you?" Explaining the predictions of any classifier. In: Proceedings of the 22nd ACM SIGKDD International Conference on Knowledge Discovery and Data Mining, pp. 1135–1144 (2016)
20. Ruckenstein, M., Turunen, L.L.M.: Re-humanizing the platform: content moderators and the logic of care. New Media Soc. **22**(6), 1026–1042 (2020)
21. Salminen, J., Veronesi, F., Almerekhi, H., Jung, S.G., Jansen, B.J.: Online hate interpretation varies by country, but more by individual: a statistical analysis using crowdsourced ratings. In: Proceedings of 5th International Conference Social Networks and Analysis Management and Security. SNAMS 2018, pp. 88–94. IEEE, Valencia (2018)

22. Ting, I.H., Chi, H.M., Wu, J.S., Wang, S.L.: An approach for hate groups detection in Facebook. In: Uden, L., Wang, L., Hong, TP., Yang, HC., Ting, IH. (eds.) The 3rd International Workshop on Intelligent Data Analysis and Management, pp. 101–106. Springer, Dordrecht (2013). https://doi.org/10.1007/978-94-007-7293-9_11

23. Venable, J., Pries-Heje, J., Baskerville, R.: Feds: a framework for evaluation in design science research. Eur. J. Inf. Syst. **25**(1), 77–89 (2016)

24. Warner, W., Hirschberg, J.: Detecting hate speech on the world wide web. In: Proceedings of the Second Workshop on Language in Social Media, pp. 19–26 (2012)

25. Wulczyn, E., Thain, N., Dixon, L.: Ex machina: personal attacks seen at scale. In: Proceedings of the 26th International Conference on World Wide Web, pp. 1391–1399 (2017)

26. Xiu, M., Jiang, Z.M.J., Adams, B.: An exploratory study of machine learning model stores. IEEE Softw. **38**(1), 114–122 (2020)

27. Zowghi, D., Coulin, C.: Requirements elicitation: a survey of techniques, approaches, and tools. In: Aurum, A., Wohlin, C. (eds.) Engineering and Managing Software Requirements, pp. 19–46. Springer, Heidelberg (2005). https://doi.org/10.1007/3-540-28244-0_2

Emotions Inference Through Content and Sentimental Analysis in COVID- 19 Context

Stefanie Niklander[✉]

Universidad Autónoma de Chile, Av. Pedro de Valdivia 425, Santiago, Chile
stefanie.niklander@uautonoma.com

Abstract. Emotions are part of a person's behavior, and some feelings can affect their actions, they can even prevent a person from producing an intelligent result. Interest in researching all aspect of the relationship between humans and computers has been increasing during the last years. Emotion is a fundamental component of being human; enjoying, hating, disgusting, among a lot of other emotions, help to value the entire human experience. Nowadays, it is recognized that the emotions play a critical and important role in all relationships with the computer, from playing games, shopping online to reading some news in a digital newspaper. Human computing interaction is an area that involves elements from different disciplines of psychology, anthropology, computer science, artificial intelligence, among others, for the study of emotions. In this paper, we took different digital Chilean newspaper to analyze if the designs of the texts influence the emotions contained in the comments of the news about COVID-19. We combine content and sentiment analysis to help an effective recognition of feelings, including ironies and hybrid language. Interesting results were obtained to identify and understand the models associated with the design of texts and the reactions of readers.

Keywords: HCI · Content analysis · Sentiment analysis · COVID-19

1 Introduction

With the arrival of the first case of COVID-19 in Chile, in March 2020, the population began to follow with great interest the information about the health crisis originating in China in December 2019. Until mid-March 2022, 3,323,324 people have been infected with Covid 19 and 44,039 have died in Chile.

Since the beginning of the pandemic, the media have played an important role in informing the population about relevant issues. As announced in an article published in the MIT Technology Review on February 12, 2020, COVID-19 is the first global pandemic of social networks [1], a fact that has caused numerous challenges in relation to communication.

This pandemic has changed social structures and the way we inform ourselves is developing in a new socio-economic context. We are now facing an information pandemic of COVID-19, which is what is called an "infodemic", defining it as information

© The Author(s), under exclusive license to Springer Nature Switzerland AG 2022
C. Stephanidis et al. (Eds.): HCII 2022, CCIS 1582, pp. 589–592, 2022.
https://doi.org/10.1007/978-3-031-06391-6_73

associated with fear, speculation and rumors, amplified and rapidly transmitted by modern information technologies and negatively affecting the economy, politics and security disproportionately to reality.

The dangers of misinformation, especially caused by infoxication or infodemic, are being made visible through the role that social networks are playing during confinement. Finding truthful information that offers us a rigorous analysis of the context in which we live is sometimes a complicated task.

Considering the global and the local context, it is necessary to study the influence of text designs on the emotions contained in the comments on the news about COVID-19. The aim of perceiving emotion is to identify whether the user is feeling satisfied and from there make the adjustments required to make better developments [2].

For this purpose, news about COVID-19 in digital newspapers in January and February 2022 will be studied. Based on Content and Sentiment Analysis, this research analyzes the relationship between the journalistic design of news texts and readers' comments. The analysis will provide information about the readers' emotions in relation to the design of each of the news items. In addition, the Content Analysis will provide us with important information about who delivered the message.

"Content analysis, a method which can be used qualitatively or quantitatively for systematically analyzing written, verbal, or visual documentation, goes back to the 1950s and the study of mass communication [3]. Content analysis is a research technique used to establish the presence of certain meanings in a text. Content analysis is a research technique used to establish the presence of certain meanings in a text. This tool will help us to know how journalistic texts are constructed and sentiment analysis will help us to qualify the tone of each of the comments in those news items.

This paper is organized as follows: Sect. 2 presents the problem, results, and discussion. Conclusions and some lines of future directions are given at the end.

2 Discussion and Results

When we refer to the journalistic design of a text, we are referring to the subject and sources used, photographs, size, tables, and graphics present in the text. All this configures a form of expression.

The categories of analysis that will guide our study are denominations, stereotypes, ironies, sources, and presence of additional elements in the informative text.

The Content Analysis of the news about COVID-19 in the analyzed period allows us to observe interesting findings. The first thing to note was the absence of stereotypes and irony in the journalistic texts. Nor was there any use of qualifying adjectives.

The main source in the news items studied was the Chilean Minister of Health, Enrique Paris. On some occasions, the Assistant Secretary of Health was also used as a source. These were the two most frequently cited sources of information. Only government sources were used in the news items studied.

In relation to the topics covered in the news, the information on COVID-19 was related to two themes. The first one, was the increase of cases in Chile. These news items always also indicated the number of deaths. The second topic referred to the vaccines, focusing on the fourth booster dose currently being applied in Chile.

The typography was quite similar in all the news stories. The same font size was used, and no colors were used to highlight any concept. All news items were accompanied by a photograph. The photography did not provide additional information to the text, the images were constantly repeated.

It should be noted that 50% of the selected news items had no comments. This situation was presented in news referring to an increase of cases in regions of Chile and when the vaccination schedule for the fourth dose was reported. In the first case, it could be inferred that the audience commenting on the news is mainly from the Chilean capital and has no interest in commenting on news that is not directly related to them.

All news that had a government source was commented on. The comments were 100% negative, criticizing the government's handling of the pandemic. In the remaining cases, 93% of the comments were critical of the government or the media for their handling of the pandemic. In 7% of the comments, the government and the Minister of Health were congratulated for their work in this health crisis.

Thus, after applying Content Analysis to the news items studied, we affirm that negative comments increase when a government source is present. However, when the news item presented infographics, the comments congratulated the government of S. Piñera.

After applying the Content Analysis, a sentiment analysis was performed on the comments of the selected news items (using SentiStrength). The positive sentiment strength ranges from 1 (not positive) to 5 (extremely positive) and the negative sentiment strength from -1 (not negative) to -5 (extremely negative). By using sentiment analysis, we can recognize whether a text is positive, negative or neutral (Table 1).

Table 1. Polarity statistics in COVID-19 news

Positive	24%
Negative	40%
Neutral	36%

When we apply emotional computing to the comments, we can observe that 40% of people issue negative comments about this news. However, 36% of them were rated as neutral and the remaining 24% as positive.

3 Conclusions

We were able to verify that in the months of January and February in Chile in the news about COVID-19, the news mainly referred to the increase in cases and information about vaccination. In addition, we were able to verify through sentiment analysis that 40% of the comments had a negative connotation. However, we believe that in order to establish relationships we need to take a larger sample.

References

1. Hao, K., Basu. T.: The coronavirus is the first true social media infodemia. MIT Technology Review (2020)
2. Picard, R.W.: Affective Computing. MIT press, Cambridge (2000)
3. White, M.D., Marsh, E.E.: Content analysis: a flexible methodology. Libr. Trends **55**(1), 22–45 (2006)

The Effects of Self-representation & Immersive Experiences on Social Presence in Emerging Markets

Ketaki Shriram[1]([✉]), Hugues Vigner[1], and Imanuel Jason[2]

[1] Krikey Inc., San Francisco, CA, USA
ketaki@krikey.com
[2] Krikey Inc., Los Angeles, CA, USA

Abstract. As smartphone adoption surges in new markets, casual gaming has become a fast growing vertical. Emerging markets typically experience three challenges: network connection, network bandwidth, and device storage capacity [1]. To deploy new technologies such as augmented reality with high fidelity assets, novel approaches are needed. High fidelity assets are necessary to generate a sense of presence, or being there, in virtual environments [2]. In our paper, we explore the deployment of a mobile application to 2.5 million users across South Asia. This application allows users to build their own interactive 3D avatar. Our work discusses novel approaches to deploy high fidelity assets in emerging markets. We next explore two topics central to virtual worlds: self-representation and self-presence [3]. Key to virtual environments are the realism and connection to avatars [4]. The stronger the human-avatar connection, the more likely virtual experiences are to have an impact on physical world identity. While self-representation has long been a concept explored in research, only recently have emerging markets gained technology for culturally accurate virtual representations. As such, our work is one of the first large scale field explorations of self-avatars' impact on identity in new markets. Our paper explores the quantitative and qualitative engagement with a user's self-avatar. We find that self-representation, particularly clothing and animations can strongly influence user's connections to their virtual self. This leads to positive associations with the user's avatar. Long term implications of virtual identity via mobile experiences are discussed.

Keywords: Mixed reality and environments · User survey · Heuristics and guidelines for design · Game design and game mapping · Cultural differences and HCI

1 Introduction

Recent years have seen a rise in usage of mobile games in emerging markets. Driven by an increase in access to mobile devices, interest and engagement with mobile games has grown. Games of all genres have seen success with new access to millions of users. To produce a high-quality game, developers must consider many factors. These include (but are not limited to): high fidelity 3D assets, customization options for users, and

C. Stephanidis et al. (Eds.): HCII 2022, CCIS 1582, pp. 593–600, 2022.
https://doi.org/10.1007/978-3-031-06391-6_74

low latency experiences [5]. There is an appetite for using network-based applications in emerging markets; an eMarketer survey found that users in India spent 1h39 on the internet daily across mobile and computer devices in 2020 and that time is predicted to grow 6% compounded yearly [6]. Services like mobile payments have also seen a 23% compounded annual growth rate, largely driven by the ease of sharing money over a network [7].

3D Assets & Customization. High fidelity 3D assets are here defined as objects that are three-dimensional and look realistic to an end user. These assets can be used to build a compelling virtual world that immerses a user. These objects frequently use animations and may interact with the user. In some cases, users can also control their own 3D character in mobile games. High fidelity experiences here are defined as visual experiences that involve 3D, media rich content. These experiences—including augmented and virtual reality =—have been shown to produce a strong sense of presence, or "being there" in recipients. Media experiences that make us feel as though we are transported to another location can have many prosocial effects, ranging from environmental consciousness to increased empathy [8]. It would be beneficial for mobile applications deployed in new markets to showcase this content without technical restriction. Therefore, developing high quality assets is necessary for compelling game experiences.

Customization within games is also an important component of interactive games. This can take on many different forms. Most commonly, users can customize their appearance in virtual environments to develop a persona they will display to others. This often involves customization of face, clothing, and body details. A digital character can function as a powerful conduit to virtual interactions. High fidelity digital characters also drive virtual economies with purchases for virtual clothing accounting for 50 billion USD of all virtual game transactions by 2018 in a recent study [9]. For digital characters to have high impact, they must appear interactive and contain realistic detail. A similar pattern holds true for the customization of game worlds. Rich in detail, these often allow for users to build their own world and share it with friends. These worlds can often serve as backdrops for millions of hours of social interaction, virtual transactions, and more. More granular customization of both virtual environments and digital characters appears to result in unique game experiences and valuable social interactions.

Delivering Optimized Experiences. Low latency experiences are also important to users. Latency, or the lag in virtual environments, can reduce the overall quality of a given game as it makes real-time gameplay decisions difficult. Latency can be controlled with technical optimizations of asset size prior to cloud download and reducing concurrent scripts on the client device during a gameplay session. For games to succeed they must have fast response times to user input and be available on demand [10]. A smooth experience without delays can increase engagement with mobile games.

When considering mobile games for emerging markets, new challenges arise in distribution of high fidelity, customizable content. A key challenge we will focus on is device storage, defined as the ability of a device to store content locally. Although many manufacturers have distributed their mobile phones widely, these devices often do not have the capacity to store large volumes of data as premium phones do [11]. This means that to deliver high fidelity experiences, they must be either: highly size-optimized to produce a small local data footprint or stored in the cloud so that the content does not live directly on the phone.

Early exploration has been done with dynamic asset downloading to reduce device storage. A small subset of essential assets is pre-bundled in the client application that is distributed on ecosystem marketplaces to preserve functionality while reducing size. The remaining assets are stored on the Content Delivery Network as described above and are available from proximity servers on demand. When the client reaches a point of the experience that requires given assets they are downloaded on an as-needed basis over the network connection. This allows the initial download size of the application to be kept to an acceptable size for low-bandwidth connections. It also avoids filling up limited device non-volatile data storage capacity, another concern in emerging markets in which devices often have more limited technical specifications to make them more affordable [12].

In our exploration, we focused on two main components: the first was a dynamic asset download system build to deliver high fidelity, interactive assets to emerging markets. The second was to review the popularity of specific assets to determine which, if any, resulted in a stronger overall human-avatar connection.

2 Methods and Analysis

2.1 Data Privacy and Sample Standardization

During our research process one of the priorities was to ensure user privacy by keeping users anonymous both in our technical logs data and our user research. Regarding our logs data, we removed Personally Identifiable Information (PII) that was not essential for our work such as precise geolocation data, only retaining it at a city-level, Internet Protocol address, and any other user-provided contact information. We also looked through all the data to make sure no information could, in combination with others, identify a user personally [13].

2.2 Dynamic Asset Download

We first examined the effects of dynamically downloaded assets on game loading latency before and after a system of proximate servers was introduced. Our sample included the same 3 sets of assets groups for both proximate and non-proximate servers. The 3 asset groups ranged in size from 0.5 megabytes (MB) to 17 MB. Two of the asset groups contained 1 grouped file, while another contained 92 individual files. A mobile application was deployed to users across the South Asia region. We collected a random sample of 22,227 data points total. Our data sample included raw latency per asset group download (in seconds) and mean latency per asset group (also in seconds). We coded a categorical variable of size (small, medium and large) for the dataset to include this as an interaction effect in our analyses (Table 1).

Data Cleaning. Upon initial visualization of the data, we found that each asset group had an abnormal distribution, driven by outliers. This also increased the mean of the asset group. An outlier was classified as any value more than three standard deviations

Table 1. Asset group size in megabytes.

Asset group name	Size (MB)
Asset group Y	11.7
Asset group K	17.5
Asset group F	0.5

away from the group mean. To address this, we removed 313 outliers before proceeding with our analysis [14]. We also examined the mean latency for the three asset groups before and after adjusting for outliers (Table 2).

Table 2. Asset group summary statistics (seconds)

Asset group	Mean latency 1	Standard deviation	Mean latency 2
Group Y	21.44	49.89	13.96
Group K	0.56	8.84	0.17
Group F	7.80	33.17	4.51

Once the outliers had been removed from our dataset, we began our quantitative analyses, with a focus on linear regressions to answer specific questions [15].

2.3 Human-Avatar Connection

To quantify the human-avatar connection, we looked at forms of self representation. In our app, users can customize their 3D avatar and utilize it in augmented reality games. Customizations can be broadly broken into a few categories: body, clothing, accessories, and animations. Body customizations include hair, eyebrows, eyes, skin tone, and body shape. Clothing includes many different types of outfits, including culturally relevant ones to our market in South Asia. Accessories include jewelry, bags, and other props. Finally, animations are seasonal and culturally specific. For example, avatars can perform cricket catch and Bollywood dance animations. We chose to focus on clothing and animations, as these tend to be the best forms of self-representation in our market. For example, clothing and animation customized to regional South Asian festivals or events contains a higher likelihood of representing users than a generic outfit or animation.

Connection in our context can best be defined as the number of salient interactions a user elects to have with their avatar. Each time users open our app, they interact with their avatar. These interactions can involve customization, video creation, or gameplay. A metric called App Session captures all these interactions by counting the number of times a user returns to the application to interact with their avatar. We chose to use correlations to examine the relationship between these variables.

Data Cleaning. As this dataset was primarily dealing with categorical variables, there were no outliers to remove.

2.4 Quantitative Analysis

We wanted to answer two key questions in our work.

RQ1: Is there a significant difference in latency between asset groups, and does this vary by server proximity conditions?

To answer this question, we chose to run a linear regression with and without an additive effect of server proximity. In our regression, asset group was the independent variable, and latency was the dependent variable.

RQ3: Are there specific assets within Group K that have high popularity?

Asset Group K contained the high-fidelity assets for interactive avatars. Within this group, there were many categories of assets (example: cultural clothing, headwear, and more). To answer this question, we visualized the correlation between visits to our mobile app and the usage of specific asset categories.

2.5 Quantitative Results

Research Question 1. We found a significant effect of asset group on raw latency, meaning that the asset group category affected the amount of latency for the asset download, $R^2 = 0.31$, $F(2,21910) = 5030$, $p < 0.01$. From the graph below it appears that Asset Group Y has a significantly higher latency overall than the other two groups. We also found a significant additive effect between server proximity and asset group on raw latency, $R^2 = 0.34$, $F(3,21909) = 3782$, $p < 0.01$. This means that the relationship between raw latency and asset group improves with the addition of servers proximate to the user's location.

Research Question 2. In Figs. 1 and 2 we compare the number of app sessions on average per user to respectively the number of avatar clothing selections and avatar animations. On average per user, over the period of 30 days. Our sample size was 322,800. Users selected an average of 16 animations and 17 clothing items (outfits, tops, bottoms) for 2.5 sessions, showing high engagement with the character and the desire to fully use and customize the avatar representation of the self. Our library of avatar characteristics, supported by our low latency architecture therefore could enable better immersion in the virtual world.

2.6 Discussion

Dynamic Asset Download. Our study found that the proximity of servers and the type of assets provided can affect the download latency for mobile gaming experiences. The size of assets downloaded seems to matter less than the proximity at which they are being downloaded. This indicates that assets of any size and fidelity may be provided to users for mobile gaming, so long as they are downloaded dynamically from a relatively proximate location. Especially in emerging markets, downloading assets on-demand is a useful solution to ensure that initial app size can remain small. This helps drive user adoption.

In some cases where network connection is sparse, it is possible that high fidelity assets may not be accessible. For example, we saw some download latencies greater than 5 s in our sample, which may be longer than the acceptable period users will wait to play

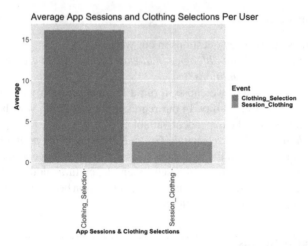

Fig. 1. Comparison of clothing selections across app sessions on average per user across 30 days

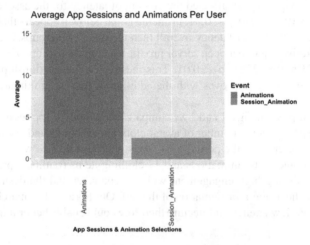

Fig. 2. Comparison of animation selections across app sessions on average per user across 30 days.

games. To combat this, we started providing an Android Lite version of our experience for low-spec devices that enables users to still access content and basic functionality even with low-bandwidth networks.

Human Avatar Connection. Our study found that the avatar customization flow, proven by the high number of interactions with the assets available to setup one's avatar could show a high desire for connection to the avatar form of the user, by spending time and effort to tailor it to their desired appearance (clothing) and behavior (animations) [16]. The multitude of assets chosen suggests variety is important. This human avatar connection is capital to social presence and engagement in virtual worlds.

3   Limitations

Running a field study produced specific limitations to our user population. First, because we used fully anonymized data to capture our logs, we could not be sure about details of the conditions under which assets were downloaded. This included: device type, network connection strength, device location & distance from nearest server, and demographic data about our users.

As such, it is possible that some anomalies existed in this dataset. For example, network connection and speed likely varied by participant. As we used data from the field, we could not effectively control the connection of each participant, which would have standardized the experience. However, we felt that the ultimate result showed a more accurate picture than a lab study, since it simulated what real-world conditions might be like for a deployed mobile application.

4   Future Work

Lab Study

This field study provided useful information on how real-world conditions might impact the download speed of assets for mobile gaming. To gain more granular insights, we recommend a lab study. Such a study could focus on isolating conditions like network speed, asset size, and more to confirm under which conditions assets will be most quickly downloaded for users. Such results could then be confirmed against additional field data.

Interactive Experiences

Additional experimentation is needed to understand what specific types of experiences with our assets could elicit the strongest social presence between humans and avatars. For example, multiplayer games or networked virtual social sessions could have higher levels of social presence than our current single player experience.

References

1. Strusani, D., Houngbonon, G.: What COVID-19 means for digital infrastructure in emerging markets. EMCompass; No. 83. International Finance Corporation, Washington, DC. © International Finance Corporation (2020). https://openknowledge.worldbank.org/handle/10986/34306License:CCBY-NC-ND3.0IGO
2. Howard, M.: Avatars: The art and science of social presence. Facebook Tech (2019). https://tech.fb.com/avatars-the-art-and-science-of-social-presence/, Accessed 19 Jan 2022
3. Seung, A.A.: The virtual malleable self and the virtual identity discrepancy model: Investigative frameworks for virtual possible selves and others in avatar-based identity construction and social interaction. Comput. Hum. Behav. **28**(6), 2160–2168 (2012). ISSN 0747–5632, https://doi.org/10.1016/j.chb.2012.06.022, https://www.sciencedirect.com/science/article/pii/S0747563212001744
4. van Gisbergen, M., Kovacs, M., Campos, F., van der Heeft, M., Vugts, V.: What we don't know. the effect of realism in virtual reality on experience and behaviour. In: tom Dieck, M.C., Jung, T. (eds.) Augmented Reality and Virtual Reality. PI, pp. 45–57. Springer, Cham (2019). https://doi.org/10.1007/978-3-030-06246-0_4

5. Chehimi, F., Coulton, P., Edwards, R.: Evolution of 3D mobile games development. Pers Ubiquit Comput **12**, 19–25 (2008). https://doi.org/10.1007/s00779-006-0129-9
6. Cramer, E.: India Time Spent with Media 2020 - Insider Intelligence Trends, Forecasts & Statistics. EMarketer (2020). https://www.emarketer.com/content/india-time-spent-with-media-2020, Accessed 6 Dec 2021
7. PwC India. The Indian payments handbook – 2020–2025. PwC India, https://www.pwc.in/assets/pdfs/consulting/financial-services/fintech/payments-transformation/the-indian-payments-handbook-2020-2025.pdf. Accessed 6 Dec 2021
8. Riva, G., et al.: CyberPsychology & Behavior, pp. 45–56 (2007). https://doi.org/10.1089/cpb.2006.9993
9. Kharif, O.: The World's Biggest Video Game Skins Site Raised $41 Million With Crypto Tokens. Bloomberg.com (2017). https://www.bloomberg.com/news/articles/2017-11-13/the-world-s-biggest-video-game-skins-site-raised-41-million-with-crypto-tokens, Accessed 9 Dec 2021
10. Shea, R., Liu, J., Ngai, E.C., Cui, Y.: Cloud gaming: architecture and performance. IEEE Netw. **27**(4), 16–21 (2013). https://doi.org/10.1109/MNET.2013.6574660
11. Kim, H., Agrawal, N., Ungureanu, C.: Revisiting storage for smartphones. ACM Trans. Storage 8(4), 25, Article 14 (2012). https://doi.org/10.1145/2385603.2385607
12. Laghari, A.A., He, H., Shafiq, M., Khan, A.: Impact of storage of mobile on quality of experience (QoE) at user level accessing cloud. In: 2017 IEEE 9th International Conference on Communication Software and Networks (ICCSN), pp. 1402–1409 (2017). https://doi.org/10.1109/ICCSN.2017.8230340
13. Marx, M., Zimmer, E., Mueller, T., Blochberger, M., Federrath, H.: Hashing of personally identifiable information is not sufficient. In: Langweg, H., Meier, M., Witt, B.C., Reinhardt, D. (eds.) SICHERHEIT 2018, pp. 55–68. Gesellschaft für Informatik e.V. Bonn (2018). https://doi.org/10.18420/sicherheit2018_04
14. Sharma, N.: Ways to Detect and Remove the Outliers | by Natasha Sharma. Towards Data Science. https://towardsdatascience.com/ways-to-detect-and-remove-the-outliers-404d16608dba, Accessed 9 Dec 2021
15. Montgomery, D.C., et al.: Introduction to Linear Regression Analysis. Wiley, Hoboken (2021). Accessed 13 Dec 2021
16. Messinger, P.R., et al.: On the relationship between my avatar and myself. J. Virtual Worlds Res **1**(2) (2008). ISSN 1941–8477. https://jvwr-ojs-utexas.tdl.org/jvwr/index.php/jvwr/article/view/352, Accessed: 17 Mar 2022, https://doi.org/10.4101/jvwr.v1i2.352

Study on the Interaction Design Concept and Strategy of "Age-Appropriateness" for Short Video Social Application

Lu Yan and Feng Liu[✉]

School of Journalism and Communication, Shanghai University, Shanghai, People's Republic of China
Panda197@163.com

Abstract. It is widely assumed that Short video are rising fast and the world enters ageing. The purpose of this paper is to improve the "ageing-appropriateness" of short video application interaction design. Based on the experience of elderly users, this paper extracts the needs of elderly people through three aspects: physical, psychological and scenario, summarizes the factors influencing the interaction design of short video social application for the elderly, and examines the shortcomings and problems in the current short video social applications from the perspective of "ageing appropriateness". Simultaneously, we summarize the concept of "ageing appropriateness" interaction design for short video applications from the framework of Norman's instinct layer, behavior layer and reflection layer. Eventually, the strategies of "aging- appropriateness" interaction design for short video social applications is proposed in three dimensions: multi-channel guidance, ease of use and socialization, scene adaptation and care. This paper aims to enrich the research on human-computer interaction, improve the experience of elderly users, and optimize the digital life of the elderly.

Keywords: Short video · Interaction design · Ageing

1 Introduction

In the context of digitalization, the world is grasped as images, more and more capital is injected into the short video field, and short video social applications are emerging, such as Tik Tok, Likee, Zynn, Triller, Dubsmash and so on. The global population is aging, UNFP points out in its annual report State of the World Population 2021 that the proportion of people aged 65 and above has increased by 0.3% to 9.6%. In China, for example, the population aged 65 and above is 176.03 million, accounting for 12.6% of the total population, and China has entered the stage of an aging society. As of June 2021, the proportion of Internet users aged 50 and above was 28.0%, an increase of 5.2 percentage points from June 2020. Older people face special physiological and psychological needs, and the interaction design of short video application needs to enhance "age-appropriateness". Particularly, in the related research on human-computer interaction,

C. Stephanidis et al. (Eds.): HCII 2022, CCIS 1582, pp. 601–608, 2022.
https://doi.org/10.1007/978-3-031-06391-6_75

short video application is relatively new and has not been given enough theoretical attention [1]. Therefore, it is urgent and necessary to improve the age-appropriate interaction design of short video application.

In the field of human-computer interaction, how to create "interaction contexts" in cold computing terminals to maximize user perception has been a hot topic of research [2]. The ideal human-computer interaction mode is "human-centered". Therefore, based on the analysis of the special needs of the elderly, this paper refines the concept of "age-appropriateness" interaction design for short video social applications and proposes specific design strategies under the perspective of humanistic care.

2   Features of Short Video Social Application Interaction Design

The process of "human-computer interaction" is to realize the dialogue between human and computer in an effective way through computer input and output devices, in which the human inputs instructions or actions to the product through the implementation of operations, eventually the instruction information outputs the results to the user. This process is bound to a level - "interface". Based on the analysis of the existing short video social applications interface on the market, it is found that they have the characteristics of personalization, simplicity and simplicity of operation.

First of all, the short video social platform has built-in algorithm technology for content pushing, and the user's action characteristics, including clicking, staying, swiping, commenting, sharing, environmental characteristics and social characteristics are transformed into data, which becomes the basis for information recommendation by the algorithm and determines the information visibility-the content of the "interface" that the user sees. This information pushing based on user habits precisely meets user needs. Therefore, the interaction design of short video application has the characteristics of personalization. Secondly, take the interaction design of Tik Tok and Kwai as examples, their designs follow the characteristics of simplicity and efficiency, for example, the main color of Tik Tok is black and white, with simple color scheme, the interface has "concern", "find", and "city". The buttons are simple and unified, while Kwai is mainly in black, white and orange. Finally, in terms of interaction, most of the short video social applications are operated by sliding and clicking gestures, which adapt to the user's common way of operation.

3   Influencing Factors of Short Video Social Application for the Aging Group

Combining Maslow's Hierarchy of Needs Theory and the Technology Acceptance Model, which is most commonly used to explain the digital engagement of older people, this paper extracts three major influencing factors: physical, psychological and scenario.

3.1   Physical

The motor function of the elderly are reduced. The joints of the hands of the elderly become less flexible and sometimes even tremble, so it is easy to make mistakes when operating some of the more delicate product interfaces. In terms of vision, in addition to not being able to see tiny objects, older people are more likely to experience "glare" than younger people, they are more likely to be afraid of light in daylight or at night, and cannot see outside objects or targets. In terms of hearing, about 30% of the elderly over 60 years of age in China have some degree of hearing impairment. In terms of cognition, the elderly are prone to cognitive decline, which affects their ability to learn and operate in a closely related way. Older adults are slower to learn a new operation and less flexible to change the mode of operation in time according to the requirements of the current task. If the operation method of the task they are facing is very different from their previous experience, it will take them a longer time to adapt.

3.2 Psychological

At the psychological level, the two most important factors influencing interaction among older adults are psychological safety and social needs, respectively. In studies of ICT use among older adults, subjective factors frequently cited by researchers include negative attitudes toward the Internet and a sense of unfamiliarity and fear [3]. Some older adults have a "technophobia" of Internet applications, and they subjectively reject new things, and some of them even suffer from high-tech anxiety. Some elderly people are easily frustrated when using the products. Based on the weakening of karma, kinship and local ties, elderly people are gradually marginalized in society, work and family, and face a huge transition in their social roles, coupled with limited physical mobility and shrinking social networks, social needs are not met, resulting in psychological loneliness, and illness is often closely related to loneliness and social isolation. Conversely, when social needs are met, older adults tend to avoid illness and depression, which in turn can increase their self-esteem and actively seek avenues for self-actualization [4].

3.3 Scenes

The scenario refers to the physical environment around when the interaction between people and products occurs, including the communication space, lighting conditions and other related facilities. Short video social applications are characterized by mobility, and their use scenarios can be switched at any time. In different usage scenarios, the elderly have different usage needs, such as walking from indoors to outdoors, the visibility of the cell phone will become poor.

4   The Shortage of Interaction Design of Short Video Social Application from the Perspective of "Age-Appropriateness"

When we look at the interaction design of current short video social applications from the perspective of "age-appropriateness", there are still many shortcomings. For example, the distance between elements on the product interface is too narrow, which makes it easy for the elderly to make mistakes in operation. The cache of short videos occupies the content of cell phones, which often leads to the problem of insufficient cell phone memory. In the era of information monopoly, media information is authoritative, which has shaped the inertia of the elderly to trust information blindly, coupled with the decline of cognitive ability, it is difficult to distinguish the authenticity of information, and in the digital environment of short video applications, there are more information such as online fraud, privacy leakage and "pseudo-health" information, which threaten the physical and mental safety of the elderly. Although the intelligent algorithm recommendation effectively solves the contradiction between attention and massive content, which is more likely to trigger the immersion experience of users, once they cannot control their over-immersion, it may lead to the so-called "addictive behavior". A part of the elderly people have nothing to do in real life and feel lonely, indulge in the virtual world of the Internet, the elderly user groups fall into "digital addiction". Therefore, for the short video social media application interaction design, the unified algorithm recommendation standard is worth reconsidering, and the technology of algorithm recommendation still has a lot of room for improvement.

5   The "Age-Appropriateness" Interaction Design Concept of Short Video Social Application

In *Design Psychology 3: Emotional Design*, Norman proposes three levels of human brain activity: instinct, behavior and reflection from the perspective of human evolution [5]. Corresponding to the above body, mind and scene, this paper proposes the following interaction design concepts.

5.1 Instinctive Layer

The instinctive layer focuses on the sensory level, which corresponds to the decline of motor and perceptual functions in the elderly population. Older people receive information through visual, auditory and tactile channels. When a product interface provides information to older people only through a single channel, there is a risk of interaction failure if this channel does not work. For the elderly with normal sensory functions, the multi-channel design principle can expand the information flow and enhance the immersive experience of elderly users. Specifically, vision is the most direct and important sensory channel for humans to relate to the external world. Visual optimization of product interface is through adjusting the text symbols, patterns and colors of the interface. The auditory channel is an important way for human beings to obtain information, and psychology believes that about 15% of the amount of information human beings obtain from the outside world comes from the auditory channel, therefore, it is necessary to optimize the auditory experience of users.

5.2 Behavioral Layer

The behavioral layer focuses on the functionality of the product and the process of realizing the functionality, addressing the "technophobia" and social needs of older people. "Ease of use" is considered to be one of the most important factors to enhance user experience, including three dimensions: easy to understand, easy to operate, and easy to remember. Rogers' theory of innovation diffusion involves the discussion of "compatibility" and "cultural perceptions", which focuses on the extent to which the innovation is consistent with "existing values, past practices, and the needs of potential adopters". The more the content of the application interface matches with the user's previous cognitive experience, the better the user experience of the mobile Internet application interface will be. Easy to operate needs to consider two directions, that is, as a communicator and as a consumer of elderly users, the corresponding functions need to make the elderly feel simple and humanized. Easy to remember means that the operation process is easy to remember, so for short video interaction design, we need to design reasonable operation navigation, and summarize and associate metaphors through good analysis ability and rich artistic imagination.

Social presence theory is the degree to which a person is perceived as a "real person" and connected to others in the process of using media to communicate [6]. Social presence is considered to play an important role in the process of human-computer interaction [7]. The interaction design of short video application needs to focus on the social needs of the elderly and improve the social connection of the elderly users through the interface design. However, some studies have pointed out that elderly people who adopt online social networks are not interested in weak relationships, except for maintaining strong relationships with family and friends [8]. Therefore, in terms of social relationships, short video application should focus more on strong relationships rather than weak ones.

5.3 Reflective Layer

The reflective layer requires consideration of multiple aspects and, as Don Norman puts it, refers to "conscious thinking, learning about new concepts, and generalizing about the world." According to philosopher Arbor Bowman, a single product cannot be separated from the context in which it is used. The use of a product is the relationship between the user and the product, and the relationship between the product and the world in which people live. The environment largely influences the usability of the interface, so in the interaction design of short video applications, the constraints of the environment need to be taken into account. "Caring" aims to create a media environment that is suitable for the use of short videos by older people. Studies have shown that the perceived quality of content and the social responsibility of the short video application platform affects the immersive experience of users [9]. Therefore, optimizing algorithm recommendation criteria, presenting high-quality content interface, injecting humanistic care and taking social responsibility become the direction of short video application interaction design.

6 Specific Strategies for "Ageing" Interaction Design of Short Video Social Application

6.1 Multi-channel Instructive

Firstly, Ensure the Autonomy of Font Size Selection. Short video application interaction design, only emphasize the large font size is completely inadequate, independent choice of font size can adapt to the needs of different older users at different times, at the same time, the choice of font needs to be clear, such as "Microsoft elegant black" is easier to recognize than "Song font". **Secondly, emphasise the balance and accentuation**

of colours, increase the contrasting colors, avoid large complementary colors and high brightness colors to avoid visual damage to the elderly, and choose low-saturation colors that can bring relaxation and comfort. Thirdly, focus on auditory and operational correspondence. In the auditory sense, voice prompts, event bells, operating feedback sounds and other bells have their necessity, creating associations through the correspondence of operating functions and sounds, helping the elderly to better remember the functions of the application.

6.2 Ease of Use and Socialization

First of all, add voice handwriting input. Increase voice input and handwriting input in the chat interface and comment interface with friends to ensure the basic interaction needs of the elderly. Next, allow withdrawal of operations. When the elderly users have operation failure, give a key to withdraw can return to their familiar interface, to avoid the unfamiliar interface to bring the elderly psychological panic. Again, following the principle of consistency. Respect the user's mental model in the interface design of short video social application mainly in two aspects: the design of new application interface and existing application interface iterative design. For example, the shooting function of short video application should be similar to the shooting function of cell phone as much as possible to reduce the learning cost of elderly users, when iterating and updating the new product, it should be gradual, with compatibility and consistency among multiple functions, respecting the inherent mental model of elderly users to avoid increasing the memory burden of elderly people. Finally, expanding social recommendations. Socially strengthen the social recommendation of strong relationship for senior users, for example, the recommendation based on address book and geographic location is the core, recommend "friends of friends" to expand the social circle and avoid loneliness. For senior users of short video content production, it is necessary to expand the recommendation range, highlight the comments of friends, and enhance the sense of social presence.

6.3 Scene Adaptation and Care

To start with, Enhance environment adaptation. The product needs to change with the environment. For example, the product interface is sometimes used in extreme brightness, darkness or natural light, and the light of the interface in different environments needs to be suitable for the physiological needs of the elderly. Simultaneously, add intelligent tips. When the elderly users fall into "digital addiction", the short video social application needs to make thoughtful and warm tips to remind the elderly to move their bodies at the right time. Moreover, avoid complicated gestures, such as turning pages, zooming in and out, two-finger tapping, or you need to guide the elderly users. In response to the situation that induced information and "pseudo-healthy" information threaten the normal life of the elderly, short video application should strengthen information audit and video tagging to remind the elderly users. Subsequently, Optimise algorithm recommendations. Social emotional selection theory suggests that the elderly pay more attention to emotion-related information due to ageing, especially favoring to pay attention to positive emotional information, so the corresponding algorithm can be moderately adjusted and optimized to avoid the recommendation of a large amount of negative information. The algorithm can increase the weight of official, disinformation, health and other high quality short videos in the recommendation criteria, or increase the corresponding content sections of interest to the elderly, for example, the Himalaya application selects history, health and other quality sections for the large-word elderly users. Last but not least, automatic cache cleaning. It is also a humanized design, solving the use of elderly people's problems.

7 Conclusion

This paper aims to improve the "Age-Appropriateness " of short video application inter-action design, based on the needs of the elderly through three aspects: physical, psycho-logical and scenario, summarizes the influencing factors affecting the interaction design of short video social application for the elderly. On the basis of this, we propose the following strategy:In the principle of multi-channel guiding, set a font size or font for users to choose, emphasise the balance and prominence of colours, focus on the corre-spondence between hearing and operation; in the principle of ease of use and sociality, simplify the interface by deleting, organize and hiding, add voice handwriting input, allow withdrawal. What is more, follow the principle of consistency and expanding social recommendations. In the principle of scene adaptation and care, enhance environ-mental adaptation, add intelligent prompts, optimise algorithmic recommendations and automatically clearing the cache. Through these specific strategies, the user experience of older users will be optimised to promote "active ageing".

Being able to access the Internet does not mean being able to use the Internet safely. The community needs to build a digital environment that is friendly to the elderly from hardware to software. The "age- appropriateness "design of the interaction of short video social application is one of the small steps, under the care of humanistic vision, the deep-seated needs of the elderly can be explored, enhancing the stickiness of the platform while helping the elderly to integrate digitally.

References

1. Dai, B., Liu, Y.: A review of research on mind-flow experiences in the Internet: concepts, antecedents and consequences. J. Inf. Syst. **1**, 15 (2015)
2. Zhao, Y.: Narrative and immersion: interaction types and user experience of Bilibili's "'interactive short videos.'" J. Southwest Univ. Natl. Human. Social Sci. Ed. **42**(2), 6 (2021)
3. Wagner, N., Hassanein, K., Head, M.: Computer use by older adults: a multi-disciplinary review. Comput. Hum. Behav. **26**(5), 870–882 (2010). https://doi.org/10.1016/j.chb.2010.03.029
4. Barnes, T., Tkatch, R., Ahuja, M., Albright, L., Schaeffer, J., Yeh, C.: Loneliness, social isola-tion and all-cause mortality in older adults. Innov. Aging **5**(Supplement_1), 925 (2021). https://doi.org/10.1093/geroni/igab046.3321
5. Norman, D.A.: Design Psychology.3, Emotional Design. CITIC Press, Beijing (2012). ISBN: 9787508650111
6. Parker, E.B., Short, J., Williams, E., et al.: The social psychology of telecommunications. Contemp. Sociol. **7**(1), 32 (1976). https://doi.org/10.2307/2065899

7. Li, J., Xue, C., Song, H.: A study of social presence in human-computer interaction - taking pop-up short videos as an example. Library Forum, 1–12 (2022)
8. Lüders, M., Gjevjon, E.R.: Being old in an always-on culture: older people's perceptions and experiences of online communication. Inf. Soc. **33**(2), 64–75 (2017)
9. Xiong, K.R., Liu, C., Gan, Z.: Is swiping ShakeYin addictive? -- factors influencing the immersive experience of short video app users and the formation mechanism. Journalist **2021**(05):83–96 (2021).https://doi.org/10.16057/j.cnki.31-1171/g2.2021.05.009

Correction to: Swedish Recreational Businesses Coping with COVID-19 Using Technologies

Ala Sarah Alaqra⑩ and Akhona C. Khumalo⑩

Correction to:
Chapter "Swedish Recreational Businesses Coping with COVID-19 Using Technologies" in: C. Stephanidis et al. (Eds.): *HCI International 2022 Posters*, CCIS 1582, https://doi.org/10.1007/978-3-031-06391-6_45

Chapter "Swedish Recreational Businesses Coping with COVID-19 Using Technologies" was previously published non-open access. It has now been changed to open access under a CC BY 4.0 license and the copyright holder updated to 'The Author(s)'. The book has also been updated with this change.

The updated original version of this chapter can be found at
https://doi.org/10.1007/978-3-031-06391-6_45

C. Stephanidis et al. (Eds.): HCII 2022, CCIS 1582, p. C1, 2022.
https://doi.org/10.1007/978-3-031-06391-6_76

Author Index

Printed in the United States
by Baker & Taylor Publisher Services